The New Testament
A STUDENT'S INTRODUCTION

Also of interest from Mayfield:

The New Testament

A STUDENT'S INTRODUCTION

Stephen L. Harris

CALIFORNIA STATE UNIVERSITY, SACRAMENTO

MAYFIELD PUBLISHING COMPANY

Mountain View, California

Copyright © 1988 by Mayfield Publishing Company

Library of Congress Cataloging-in-Publication Data
Harris, Stephen L., 1937–
    The New Testament, a student's introduction.

    Bibliography: p.
    Includes index.
    1. Bible. N.T.—Introductions.   2. Bible.   N.T.—
Text-books. I. Bible.   N.T.   II. Title.
BS2330.2.H326   1988   225.6'1   87-31283
ISBN 0-87484-746-X

Manufactured in the United States of America

10 9 8 7 6 5 4 3 2 1

Mayfield Publishing Company
1240 Villa Street
Mountain View, California 94041

Sponsoring editor, James Bull; production editor, Linda Toy; text and
cover designer, Al Burkhardt; illustrator, George Samuelson; cover
photographer, © Zev Radovan. The text was set in 10/12 Bembo by
Carlisle Communications and printed on 50# Finch Opaque by George
Banta Company.

Excerpts from *The New English Bible* © The Delegates of the Oxford
University Press and The Syndics of the Cambridge University Press,
1961, 1970. Reprinted by permission. Scripture quotations from the
Revised Standard Version Bible, copyright 1946, 1952, 1971 by the
Division of Christian Education of the National Council of the
Churches of Christ in the USA, and are used by permission. Excerpts
from *The New Testament in Context: Sources and Documents* by Howard
Clark Kee, © 1984, p. 225. Reprinted by permission of Prentice-Hall,
Inc., Englewood Cliffs, New Jersey. Excerpts from *The Peloponnesian
War* by Thucydides, translated by Rex Warner (Penguin Classics, 1954,
1972), copyright © Rex Warner, 1954, 1972, p. 48. Excerpt from *The
Other Gospels* edited by Ron Cameron, © 1982, p. 25. Reprinted by
permission of the Westminster Press, Philadelphia, Pennsylvania.

Contents

PART II *Four Portraits of Jesus*

Afterword

To Geoffrey Edwin and Jason Marc

To the Student

This book is designed for the student who is studying the New Testament for the first time. Its purpose is to acquaint the reader with the content and major themes of each book of the New Testament.

Today the most widely read book from the ancient world, the New Testament is best understood in its original historical and cultural context. We therefore begin by surveying the diverse and sophisticated world in which it took shape. Jesus and his first disciples were products of a complex Jewish society, but the Jewish-Christian New Testament writers directed their work at the larger Greek-speaking audience living in the far-flung Roman Empire. We examine both of these worlds.

After providing necessary historical and other background information for each New Testament book, we delve into the biblical text, exploring the author's ideas and purpose. This guide is not a substitute for reading the New Testament, but it closely follows the actual text so that the student can trace each individual author's train of thought.

The writers of the various New Testament books are allowed to speak for themselves. We do not attempt to make the viewpoints of one book conform to those of another, nor do we advocate any denominational or sectarian program. The contributions of leading New Testament scholars are summarized in the text where appropriate.

Special features are included to help the student analyze the New Testament text as efficiently as possible. Summaries of key topics and/or themes at the beginning of each chapter, as well as questions for discussion and review at the end, focus the information presented.

As an aid to the student in recognizing important concepts and characters, key ideas and the names of major historical figures are printed in boldface type. In addition, the principal terms involved in New Testament study are defined in a glossary at the end of the book.

Students who wish to pursue a particular subject may do so by consulting the list of recommended readings at the conclusion of each chapter. Available in most college libraries, the reference books listed represent the thinking of leading scholars engaged in New Testament research.

Although it is aimed at college undergraduates beginning their first systematic investigation of New Testament literature, this book incorporates the findings of hundreds of scholars whose labor has greatly illuminated the background, purpose, and message of early Christian writers. Our indebtedness to their research is gratefully acknowledged by their inclusion in the bibliographies.

Reading the twenty-seven New Testament books is an exciting experience—and sometimes a bewildering one as well. From the four contrasting portraits of Jesus, to Paul's complex and brilliant analyses of Jesus' significance, to Revelation's dazzling images of the world's end, the reader travels through strange and alien mindscapes. We hope that the journey through the New Testament world of some nineteen hundred years ago will be easier and more enjoyable with this student's guide.

Acknowledgments. I am particularly grateful to the colleagues who reviewed the first draft of this book: Marion L. Soards, United Theological Seminary; Philip Pharr, Pfeiffer College;

Shirley Lund, Boston University; William Countryman, Church Divinity School of the Pacific; Dale Patrick, Drake University; Kenneth Mull, Aurora College; and Susan Lau, University of Pittsburgh. I appreciate their incisive criticism and many helpful suggestions.

I am also grateful to Jim Bull, my sponsoring editor at Mayfield Publishing Company, for his good advice and support. I also thank the skilled and patient copy editors, Mary Ann Stewart and Kate Engelberg as well as my efficient production editor, Linda Toy.

The New Testament

A STUDENT'S INTRODUCTION

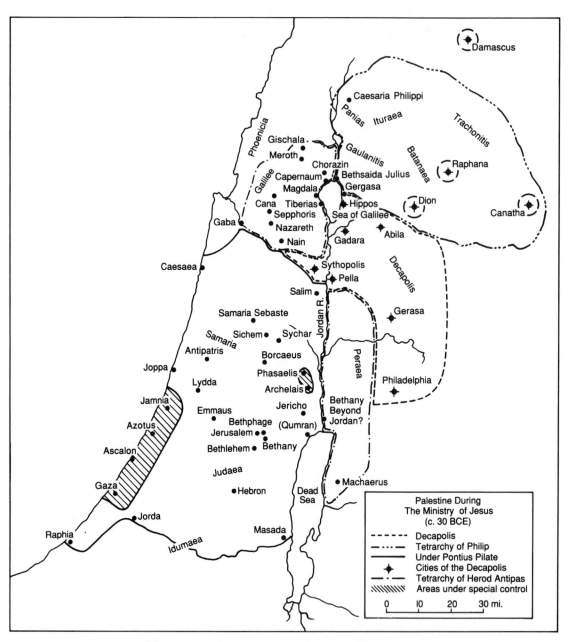

The political divisions of Palestine during the ministry of Jesus (c. 30 CE). Note that Rome directly administered Judea and Samaria through its procurator Pontius Pilate; Herod Antipas ruled Galilee (Jesus' home district) and Peraea; another son of Herod the Great, Philip, ruled an area to the northeast. The Decapolis was a league of ten Greek-speaking cities on the east side of the Jordan River.

1   *An Overview of the New Testament*

Here begins the Gospel of Jesus Christ.
(Mark 1:1)

KEY THEMES: This chapter places the New Testament in the context of its relationship to the older Hebrew Bible, describes the New Testament's literary forms, and summarizes the process by which the New Testament canon was formed.

People read the New Testament for an almost infinite variety of reasons. Some read to satisfy their curiosity about the origins of one of the great world religions. They seek to learn more about the social and historical roots of Christianity, a faith that began in the early days of the Roman Empire and that today commands the allegiance of nearly one and a half billion people, a quarter of the global population. Because Christianity bases its most characteristic beliefs on the New Testament writings, it is to this source that the historian and social scientist must turn for information about the religion's birth and early development.

Most people, however, probably read the New Testament for more personal reasons. Many readers search its pages for answers to some of life's important ethical and religious questions. For hundreds of millions of Christians, the New Testament sets the only acceptable standards of personal belief and behavior. Readers attempt to discover authoritative counsel on issues that modern science or speculative philosophy cannot resolve, such as the nature of God, the survival of the soul after death, and the ultimate destiny of humankind.

Jesus of Nazareth, the central character of the New Testament, provides many people with the most compelling reason to read the book. As presented by the Gospel writers, he is like no other figure in world history. His teachings and pronouncements have an unequaled power and authority. As an itinerant Jewish prophet, healer, and teacher in early first-century Pales-

tine, the historical Jesus—in terms of the larger Greco–Roman world around him—lived a relatively obscure life and died a criminal's death at the hands of Roman executioners. His followers' conviction that he subsequently rose from the grave and appeared to them launched a vital new faith that eventually swept the Roman Empire. In little more than three centuries after Jesus' death, Christianity became Rome's official state religion.

Clearly, the New Testament authors present Jesus as much more than an ordinary man. The Gospel of John pictures him as the human expression of divine wisdom, the **Word** of God made flesh. Jesus' teaching about the eternal world of spirit is thus definitive, for he is depicted as having descended from heaven to earth to reveal ultimate truth. About three hundred years after Jesus' crucifixion, Christian leaders assembled at the town of Nicea in Asia Minor to decree that Jesus was not only the Son of God but God himself.

Given the uniquely high status that orthodox Christianity accords the person of Jesus, the New Testament accounts of his life have extraordinarily great value. Jesus' words recorded in the Gospels are seen not merely as the utterances of a preeminently wise teacher but also as the declarations of the Being who created and sustains the universe. The hope of encountering "God's thoughts," of discovering otherwise unattainable knowledge of unseen realities, gives many believers a powerful incentive for studying the New Testament.

What Is the New Testament?

When asked to define the New Testament, many students respond with such traditional phrases as "the Word of God" or "Holy Scriptures." These responses are really confessions of faith that the Christian writings are qualitatively different from ordinary books. Some students express surprise that non-Christian religions also have "**scriptures**"—documents that these groups consider sacred and authoritative (having the power to command belief and prescribe behavior). In fact, many other world religions possess holy books that their adherents believe to represent a divine revelation to humankind. The Hindus cherish the Vedas, the Upanishads, and the Bhagavadgita; the Buddhists venerate the recorded teachings of Buddha, the "enlightened one"; and the followers of Islam (meaning submission to the will of Allah) revere the Qur'an (Koran) as transmitting the one true faith. Ideally we approach all sacred writings with a willingness to appreciate the religious insights they offer and to recognize their connection with the particular culture and historical situation out of which they grew.

Given the historical fact that the New Testament is a book written by and for believers in Jesus' divinity, in practice many readers tend to approach it as they do no other work of ancient literature. Whether or not they are practicing Christians, students commonly bring to the New Testament attitudes and assumptions very different from those they employ when reading other works of antiquity. The student usually has little trouble bringing an open or neutral mind to exploring stories about the Greek and Roman gods. One can read Homer's *Iliad*, a poem celebrating the Greek heroes of the Trojan War, without any particular emotional involvement with the Homeric gods. However, this objective attitude toward supernatural beings is rare among persons studying the New Testament.

To be fair to the New Testament, we will want to study it with the same open-mindedness we grant to the writings of any world religion. This call for objectivity is a challenge to all of us, for we live in a culture that defines its highest values largely in terms of the Judeo-Christian tradition. We can most fully appreciate the New Testament if we begin by recognizing that it developed in, and partly in reaction to, a society profoundly different from our own. It will help, too, if we remember that reading the Bible in church as part of an act of worship is necessarily a different experience from studying it analytically in a classroom. Each situation requires an appropriate mode of appreciation. By examining the New Testament in the complex social environment in which it originated and by attempting to discover the historical concerns and purposes of its authors, we can free ourselves to hear the voices of early Christianity speaking as meaningfully to us today as they did to their first audience almost nineteen hundred years ago.

The New Testament and the Hebrew Bible

If someone from another planet asked us to define the New Testament, describing it as a divine revelation would not be very enlightening to the curious visitor. An extraterrestrial might point out that the scriptures of virtually all the world's principal religions make that claim. It is more useful to begin by stating exactly what the book itself is. Although sometimes published as a separate book, the New Testament is typically printed as the second part of a larger volume containing both the Jewish and Christian Scriptures and known as the Bible. Derived from the term *biblia* (meaning "little books"), the word **Bible** is an appropriate title because this volume is really a collection of many different books. An anthology of religious documents composed over a time span exceeding one thousand years, the first section of the Christian Bible is much longer and more diverse than the New Testament. Often called the Old Testament, this part is properly known as the Hebrew or **Jewish Bible**. Written largely in the Hebrew language (some late books were composed in a related tongue called Aramaic), the **Hebrew Bible** records the history of the Jewish people's relationship with their God. Also called the Tanak, the Hebrew Bible contains many different types of literature, ranging from lyric poetry to legal material to historical narrative to prophecy.

At the time of Jesus and the first several generations of his followers, this collection was the only written authority for both Jews and Christians. When the New Testament writers refer to "Scripture" or "the Law and the Prophets" they mean the Hebrew Bible, although they commonly use a Greek translation of the Hebrew text known as the **Septuagint**.

Testament and Covenant. The term *New Testament* is intimately connected with the Hebrew Scriptures. In biblical terms, **testament** is a synonym for **covenant**, which means an agreement, contract, or bond. To appreciate the New Testament concept of the bond between God and humanity, we must review briefly the older Hebrew tradition. The Hebrew Bible is largely a meditation on the consequences of God's making a covenant with the nation of Israel, whom the Deity chose to be his representative people on earth. Exodus, the second book of the Hebrew Bible, recounts the solemn ceremony in which the Israelites conclude their central covenant with **Yahweh** (the sacred personal name of Israel's God) (Exod. 19–20; 24). Under the terms of the **Mosaic Covenant** (so called because the Israelite leader **Moses** acts as the covenant mediator between Yahweh and the people), Israel swears to uphold all the laws and

commandments that Yahweh enjoins upon them. These legal injunctions are contained in the Books of Exodus, Leviticus, Numbers, and Deuteronomy. Together with the Book of Genesis, which serves as a general introduction to the giving of the Mosaic Covenant, this section of the Hebrew Bible is known as the **Torah**. Meaning "law," "teaching," or "instruction," the Torah is also referred to as the **Pentateuch** (meaning "five scrolls" or books).

In the Torah, Yahweh's protection of Israel was made contingent upon the people's faithfulness in keeping Yahweh's Law as handed down through Moses (Deut. 28–29). Some of Israel's prophets concluded that the people had been so unfaithful to the Mosaic Covenant that eventually Yahweh regarded it as broken. Writing about six hundred years before the time of Jesus, the prophet Jeremiah promised that Yahweh would replace the old Mosaic agreement with a "new covenant [testament]" (Jer. 31:31).

The Gospel writers believed that Jesus instituted the promised "new covenant" at the **Last Supper** he held with his disciples. "And he took the cup, and gave thanks, and gave it to them, saying Drink ye all of it: For this is my blood of the new testament . . ." (Matt. 26:27–28, King James Version). The adjective *new,* not present in the earliest manuscripts, was added later to emphasize the change in God's relationship with humankind. (Most modern translations, including the Revised Standard Version, the Jerusalem Bible, and the New English Bible, omit the interpolated "new" and use "covenant" instead of "testament" in this passage.) Believing themselves to be the people of the new covenant with God, Christians eventually called their Gospels and other sacred writings the New Testament. The Hebrew Bible, which dealt with the older Mosaic Covenant, became known as the Old Testament. The Christian community, however, regarded both parts of the Bible as authoritative and suitable for religious instruction.

BOX 1-1   *Hebrew Bible Canon and Apocrypha*

TORAH

Genesis
Exodus
Leviticus
Numbers
Deuteronomy

PROPHETS

Former Prophets
  Joshua
  Judges
  Samuel (1 and 2)
  Kings (1 and 2)
Latter Prophets
  Isaiah
  Jeremiah
  Ezekiel
The Twelve (Minor Prophets)
  Hosea
  Joel
  Amos

Obadiah
Jonah
Micah
Nahum
Habakkuk
Zephaniah
Haggai
Zechariah
Malachi

WRITINGS

Psalms
Job
Proverbs
Ruth
Song of Solomon
Ecclesiastes
Lamentations
Esther
Daniel
Ezra-Nehemiah
Chronicles (1 and 2)

BOOKS OF THE APOCRYPHA
(New English Bible edition)

1 Esdras
2 Esdras
Tobit
Judith
The Rest of the Chapters of the
  Book of Esther
The Wisdom of Solomon
Ecclesiasticus, or the Wisdom of
  Jesus Son of Sirah
Baruch
A Letter of Jeremiah
The Song of the Three
Daniel and Susanna
Daniel, Bel, and the Snake
The Prayer of Manasseh
1 Maccabees
2 Maccabees

The Septuagint

Although the New Testament writers regarded the Jewish Bible as their chief written authority, they did not quote from the original Hebrew text. Instead they used a popular Greek translation of the Hebrew Bible that had been published in Alexandria, during the last two and a half centuries BCE (BCE means "before the common era," a religiously neutral calendar that can be used by Jews, Christians, Moslems, and others. As a chronological symbol it is the same as BC, "before Christ." CE, the "common era," is synonymous with AD, "*anno domini*," Latin for "in the year of the Lord.")

According to one tradition, the Septuagint translation was the work of seventy-two Hebrew scholars who labored seventy-two days to produce seventy-two identical translations.

Popularly known as the work of "the seventy" and called the Septuagint, this version became the standard biblical text for Greek-speaking Jews scattered throughout the Greco-Roman world. It was then adopted by Christians as their favored version of the Jewish Scriptures and is the version cited most often in the New Testament.

Language and Literature of the New Testament

Koinē Greek. The New Testament was written in the same kind of **koinē** (common) Greek as the Septuagint. The most widely spoken language of the early Christian era, *koinē* became the dominant tongue of the eastern Mediterranean region after the conquests of Alexander the Great (332–323 BCE). Although less polished and elegant than the classical Greek of the great Athenian poets and philosophers, *koinē* was then spoken by so large a percentage of the population that it communicated far more effectively than Hebrew or Latin.

Most of the twenty-seven books of the New Testament were composed during the half century between about 50 and 100 CE, although a few were written as late as the mid–second century CE. The oldest surviving Christian writings are the letters of **Paul**, a Greek-educated Jew from **Tarsus**, a prosperous city in an eastern province of the Roman Empire (now southeast Turkey). Paul's letters span the dozen years between about 50 and 62 CE. Most of the remaining books, including the four Gospels and the Book of Acts, were written somewhat later, between about 65 and 100 CE. A few letters ascribed to some of Jesus' most eminent disciples and known collectively as the **catholic** (general) **epistles** appeared several decades after the turn of the first century.

New Testament Literary Forms

The New Testament contains several different categories (genres) of literature, although it has considerably less variety than the Hebrew Bible. The contents are not arranged in chronological order but according to four literary classifications, beginning with the Gospels and ending with the Book of Revelation.

Gospels. The first four books are called Gospels, a term that translates the Greek word *euangelion* ("good news"). Designed to proclaim the "good news" about Jesus, the Gospels tell the story of Jesus' ministry, death, and resurrection. The term **Evangelist** refers to the writer of an *euangelion* (Gospel).

In the Greek-speaking world of New Testament times, *euangelion* commonly was used to denote public proclamations about the Roman emperor. The "good news" of the emperor's military victories, welfare policies, or his being elevated to the status of a god were typical examples of Roman political "evangelizing." Paul uses *euangelion* to describe his message about salvation through Jesus Christ. Matthew also employs it to denote Jesus' oral teaching (Matt. 4:23; 9:35; 24:14; 26:13). Mark, however, is apparently the first to use *euangelion* to describe a written work about Jesus' life. To distinguish *gospel,* an oral message, from *Gospel,* a literary work, we will capitalize the term when it refers to the written Gospel form.

The only literary genre the early Christians invented, the **Gospel** is a narrative—a story—about Jesus' deeds and teachings. Although the Gospels recount the actions and sayings of Jesus in ostensibly chronological order, they are not real biographies in the modern sense. They do not attempt to present a complete life of Jesus or to explain what forces—social, psychological, cultural, historical, or political—caused him to become the kind of man he was. Only two of the Gospels—Matthew and Luke—include information about Jesus' birth and infancy. None gives even a scrap of information about his formative years, education, associations, or any other experience that a modern historian would regard as essential. Luke records a single incident of Jesus' youth, a pilgrimage from his hometown of Nazareth to Jerusalem, Judaism's holy city (Luke 2:22–40). But the Gospels tell us nothing about what happened to Jesus between the ages of twelve and "about thirty" (Luke 3:23). All four concentrate exclusively on the last phase of Jesus' life, the period of his public ministry when his teachings both attracted devoted followers and created bitter enemies.

In all four Gospel accounts, only the final week of Jesus' human existence is related in detail—the events leading up to and including his arrest, trial, and execution by the Romans. The significance of Jesus' suffering and death (known as the **Passion**) are the central concern of each Evangelist. Even the **Fourth Gospel** (John), which includes a longer version of Jesus' public career than any other, devotes nearly half of its narrative to retelling the story of Jesus' last few days on earth. Observing this emphasis of the Evangelists, New Testament scholars have described the Gospel form as a Passion narrative with a long introduction. All incidents in Jesus' life leading up to his crucifixion are rigorously subordinated to the climactic circumstances of his death. The Gospels' form and contents are not shaped by purely historical or biographical considerations, however, but by their respective authors' theological viewpoints. **Theology**, a term that combines the Greek *theos* (God) with *logos* (word), "words about God." It is a religious discipline involving the study of God's nature, will, and activity among humankind. The theologian typically defines and interprets systems of belief that express a religion's essential world view. The Gospel writers are theologians, and, like all New Testament authors, the Evangelists write primarily to voice their individual understanding of Jesus' religious or theological significance.

A history of the early church. The second literary form in the New Testament is a historical narrative celebrating the deeds of a few early Christian leaders. Written by the author of **Luke**'s Gospel, the Book of Acts continues the story of Christianity's origins. Beginning with an account of Jesus' ascension to heaven and ending with the Apostle Paul's preaching activity in Rome, Acts narrates a series of crucial episodes in Christianity's early development, covering the thirty years from about 30 to 60 CE.

Letters or epistles. Whereas the first five books of the New Testament are all narratives that relate the activities of Jesus and his first disciples, the following section consists of another distinct literary type. After the Gospel and history forms comes a collection of twenty-one letters or **epistles**, all of which are ascribed to famous leaders of the early church. The first set of letters are by Paul, the most influential of all Christian missionaries, and by Pauline disciples who later wrote in his name and spirit. In addition, seven epistles (a more formal version of the letter) are attributed to other leaders associated with the original Jerusalem church, such as **Peter, James, Jude,** and **John.**

An apocalypse. The Book of Revelation represents the fourth and final literary category in the Christian Scriptures. The title *Revelation* translates the Greek noun *apokalypsis,* which means an "uncovering" or "unveiling." Like other **apocalyptic** works, Revelation features visions of an unseen world inhabited by spirit creatures both good and evil. It highlights the cosmic struggle between God and Satan, a conflict involving both heaven and earth that ultimately sees evil defeated, God's kingdom triumphant, and the creation of a new earth and heaven (Rev. 12; 16; 20–21). Revelation's message is urgent, demanding that believers hold firm in the faith because, like all apocalyptic writers, the authors believes that the universal war he visualizes is about to begin (Rev. 1:1, 3; 12:12; 22:7, 11, 12).

Apocalyptic ideas played an extremely important role in early Christian thought and dominate many passages in the New Testament. As we study the Gospel accounts of Jesus' preaching, we will find numerous apocalyptic concepts, commonly involving **eschatology.** Derived from combining two Greek phrases— *to eschaton* (referring to the world's end) and *ho logos* (meaning "study of"), eschatology refers to beliefs about events occurring at the end of time. On a personal level, eschatology involves momentous events at the end of an individual's life: death, posthumous judgment, heaven, hell, and **resurrection.** On a more general level, it relates to developments that culminate in the end of human society and history as we know them.

Formation of the New Testament Canon

Exactly how the New Testament writings were assembled in a single volume is a mystery. Each of the twenty-seven books originated as a

---

BOX 1-2   *New Testament Books: Approximate Order of Composition*

Approx. Date (CE)	Title of Book	Author
c. 50	1 Thessalonians 2 Thess. (if by Paul)	Paul
c. 54–55	1 & 2 Corinthians	Paul
c. 56	Galatians	Paul
c. 56–57	Romans	Paul
c. 61	Colossians (if by Paul)	Paul
c. 61	Philippians	Paul
c. 62	Philemon	Paul
c. 65–70	Gospel of Mark	Anonymous

66–73	*Jewish War Against Rome: Destruction of Jerusalem and Temple*	
c. 80–85	Gospel of Matthew	Anonymous
c. 85–90	Gospel of Luke and Acts	Anonymous
c. 85–95	Hebrews, 1 Peter, Ephesians, James	Anonymous
c. 90–95	Gospel of John	Anonymous
c. 95	Revelation (the Apocalypse)	John of Patmos
c. 95–100	Letters of John	The Elder
c. 110–30	1 & 2 Timothy, Titus	Anonymous
c. 130–50	Jude, 2 Peter	Anonymous

---

separate document and at first circulated independently of the others. Paul's letters, for example, were sent individually to different small Christian groups in Greece and Asia Minor. About 90 CE some unknown person searched the archives of the various Pauline churches for surviving copies of the Apostle's correspondence, gathering them together in a single unit. This anonymous Pauline disciple began a collection to which the Gospels, Acts, and other documents gradually were added, creating a New Testament canon.

A word derived from the Greek *kanon,* **canon** refers to a standard or measurement, the norm by which something is evaluated. In religious usage, a canon is the official list of books that a religious community judges to be its authoritative source of doctrinal and ethical belief. The four Gospels, Acts, and the letters of Paul apparently were widely known and used for teaching purposes by the early to mid–second century CE. The complete New Testament canon we know today, however, developed very slowly.

At no time did a single churchperson or group of church leaders formally decide upon the con-

tents of the Christian testament. A few leaders issued lists of writings their particular community considered authoritative, but such occasional lists reflect only the then-current usage in a given geographical area. The specific books accepted into the canon achieved that recognition through a long-term and widespread general use in the life and worship of the international Christian community. Canonization was a lengthy process of usage and habit, not the result of any act or decree of church officialdom.

The Role of Marcion and the Gnostics

Up to the second century the Bible used by Christians consisted primarily of the Septuagint version of the Hebrew Scriptures (which included the **Apocrypha,** about a dozen late books not accepted in the official Jewish canon), and—at least in some locations—one or more of the Gospels and the anthologized letters of Paul.

About 140 CE conflicts within the Christian community demonstrated the need to define a Christian Scripture comparable to the Hebrew Bible. At that time a Roman Christian named **Marcion** argued that Christians should dispense with the entire Old Testament, which, he asserted, presented an unworthy and savage image of God. Among the many Christian writings then extant, Marcion proposed that only the Gospel of Luke and the Pauline letters be recognized as accurately expressing the Christian faith.

Gnosticism. Marcion belonged to a movement then widespread within the early church called **Gnosticism.** Taking its name from the Greek word *gnosis* (knowledge), Gnosticism is a general label applied to an extremely diverse set of beliefs and practices. Because the church later declared the Gnostic view of Christianity heretical (guilty of false teaching), most of our information about the movement derives from churchly attacks against it.

In general, Gnosticism expresses a strongly mystical attitude toward human existence, emphasizing that a person achieves salvation through attaining a spiritual "knowledge" of heavenly truths. Gnosticism also teaches that reality consists of two distinct modes of being: an invisible realm of pure spirit that is good and to which the human soul belongs and an inferior physical world to which the desire-filled and corruptible body belongs. A "higher God" created the spirit realm and was responsible for the advent of Jesus Christ. Yahweh, the Old Testament Deity, was the inferior power responsible for making the world of matter. Focusing on the insights of a spiritual elite, Gnosticism became a major source of dissension within the Christian community during its first three centuries of existence. The Gnostics produced numerous writings, including several Gospels interpreting the teachings of Christ, all of which eventually were condemned by official church decrees.

The Process of Growth

After Marcion was expelled from the church at Rome in 140 CE, Christian leaders were forced to deal with his lingering influence. The church leadership responded to Marcion's claim that "true Christianity" is found only in the writings of Luke and Paul and by recognizing the authority of other Christian documents. Thus began the process of forming a Christian Scripture distinct from the Hebrew Bible.

As a reference in 2 Peter (3:15–16) indicates, by the middle of the second Christian century Paul's letters had been accorded the status of Scripture. It is more difficult to tell precisely when the four Gospels attained this classification. Numerous other Gospels or "memoirs" of Jesus were written and circulated in the early Christian community. The Gospel of **Thomas,** a collection of 114 sayings of Jesus discovered in Egypt in 1945, is only one among many early accounts of Jesus' teachings. Some of these Gospels were accepted as primary teaching documents by various churches.

The first surviving reference to our four Gospels occurs in a book called 2 Clement, a document written in the name of Clement, a famous early bishop of Rome. This work, dating from the early second century, quotes a passage from **Matthew** as "Scripture." Perhaps a few decades later, Justin Martyr, a church leader executed in Rome in the 160s CE, cited the "memoirs of the Apostles" or "Gospels" as though they had attained an authority equal to that of the Hebrew Bible. The titles by which we now know the Gospels ascribed to Matthew, Mark, Luke, and John, however, did not become part of the New Testament tradition until more than a century after they were written. Until late in the second century CE the Gospels apparently circulated anonymously among Christian congregations. Gradually, they came to be regarded as the work of **Apostles**—men whom Jesus himself had called to be his first close followers—or of later companions of the Apostles, such as Mark and Luke, who were not among the original **Twelve.**

The Muratorian Canon. Early lists of New Testament books are amazingly diverse. During the first three centuries CE the general consensus was that the four Gospels, Acts, and Pauline letters should be included. Beyond that short list, an interesting variety of texts prevailed. One New Testament catalogue, the Muratorian Canon, which appeared toward the end of the second (or perhaps as late as the third) century CE, is probably typical of the mixed bag of canonical and apocryphal works that different churches regarded as sacred. Compiled in Rome, this canon lists the four Gospels; Acts; thirteen letters of Paul (but excluding Hebrews); Jude; 1 (but not 2) Peter; 1 and 2 (but not 3) John; the Wisdom of Solomon; Revelation; and the Apocalypse of Peter.

Several of the Muratorian titles are probably unfamiliar to many Christians. The Wisdom of Solomon, a Jewish work composed in Greek between about 100 and 50 BCE, now belongs to the Old Testament Apocrypha, books included in Roman Catholic and Greek Orthodox editions of the Hebrew Scriptures but not accepted in the official Jewish Bible or in most Protestant Old Testaments. Incorporating numerous concepts of Greek philosophy, this wisdom book contains meditations on God's purpose in history and the immortality of the individual soul that made it popular with many Hellenistic Jewish and Christian groups. The Apocalypse of Peter, one of the many Christian writings ascribed to the chief Apostle, includes terrifying visions of hell and the torments of the damned. Like many books that were overspecific in their depiction of the rewards and punishments of the afterlife, this apocalypse was eventually dropped from general usage.

The diversity of "recognized" books represented by the Muratorian Canon remained the norm for the next two centuries. Other lists, such as the Codex Claromontanus, include much (ultimately) noncanonical material: the Epistle of **Barnabas,** the Shepherd of Hermas, the Acts of Paul, and the Revelation of Peter. As late as the fifth century CE, a Greek manuscript known as the Codex Alexandrinus included both 1 and 2 Clement as part of the New Testament. Whereas 1 Clement is a letter written about 96 CE by a historical bishop of Rome, 2 Clement

is pseudonymous (composed by an unknown writer in the name of a famous person). **Pseudonymity** was common among both Jewish and Christian writers in the Greco-Roman world.

While some Christian groups used books later deleted from the canon, others rejected certain works that were eventually canonized. Such well-known writings as Revelation and the Gospel of John (thought in some circles to be Gnostic compositions) fail to appear in many New Testament catalogues. The same is true of Hebrews and the "catholic epistles." Several important churches, such as those at **Alexandria** and **Antioch,** resisted including Revelation, partly because it was not believed to be the work of John the Apostle. Although eventually accepted, among eastern churches Revelation did not attain the same authority as most other New Testament books. The Syrian churches consistently denied it canonical status.

The Definitive List

The first official listing of the twenty-seven books that accords with the present New Testament contents was not issued until 367 CE, more than three centuries after the deaths of most of Jesus' original disciples. This historic list appeared in the Easter Letter of Athanasius, bishop (church supervisor) of Alexandria. Although Athanasius cited only the twenty-seven canonical books as authoritative, he suggested that Christians would also profit from reading selected noncanonical works then popular in many churches scattered throughout the Roman Empire. In certain areas some books now excluded from the canon were once regarded as almost on a par with what we think of as "genuine" New Testament works.

Even after Bishop Athanasius issued his definitive list in 367 CE, the canon varied from place to place. Perhaps most conclusive in the completion and sealing of the New Testament contents was the production of the Latin **Vulgate** Bible at the end of the fourth century CE. The Vulgate is a translation of the entire Bible into the "vulgar" (common) Latin of the western Roman Empire. Its translator, Jerome, one of the great scholars and theologians of the period, followed Athanasius's canon and included all seven "catholic epistles" as well as the disputed Hebrews and Revelation. Jerome's translation excluded other Christian writings, such as the Epistle of Barnabas and the Apocalypse of Peter; once considered inspired, these texts were thus relegated to obscurity.

In general, it seems that the New Testament canon evolved to serve two related purposes: (1) Canonization of certain texts clarified within the Christian community what beliefs were true and acceptable. Questioners like Marcion and his Gnostic followers could thus be confronted with an officially sanctioned list of books that largely defined the faith. (2) The canon provided a unifying force for churches scattered throughout the Empire, imparting a firm written authority for universal belief and practice.

As time went on and the age of Jesus and the Apostles receded ever farther into the distance, it was no longer possible to draw on the orally transmitted memories of persons who had heard the teachings of first- or second-generation Christians. Believers had to rely on written documents thought to be derived from persons who had witnessed the origins of Christianity. By the close of the second century CE, a movement within the international church authenticated certain writings by assigning their authorship to particular Apostles or their associates. This process of identifying previously anonymous Gospels and other works with specific "founding fathers" helped to ensure that Christianity's roots—and doctrines—would be firmly planted in apostolic soil.

One among many of the sacred books produced by various world religions, the New Testament is a small library of Greek documents written by (mostly) anonymous members of the early Christian community. It forms the second part of the Christian Bible, the larger first section of which is the Hebrew Bible, a diverse collection of writings produced by the Jewish community of faith. Each of the twenty-seven canonical New Testament books originated separately and at first circulated independently of the others. Only gradually were these writings gathered together into a single collection. Nearly three centuries elapsed between the time of the books' composition and the formation of the canonical list we know today.

The next chapter examines the story of the New Testament's preservation and transmission, including the process by which it came to be available in English translations.

QUESTIONS FOR DISCUSSION AND REVIEW

1. Try to define and describe the New Testament to someone who has never before heard of it. In what ways does this collection of early Christian documents resemble the scriptures of other world religions? In what ways does the New Testament differ from other sacred books?

2. Define the term *testament* and explain the relationship of the Old Testament (the Jewish Bible) to the New Testament.

3. What version of the Jewish Bible did early Christians use? In what common language are the Septuagint and New Testament written?

4. The literary form or category in which writers choose to convey their ideas always influences the way in which those ideas are expressed. Why do you suppose that early Christian writers invented the Gospel form to express their views about Jesus? Why do you think that all four Gospel authors focused on the last week of Jesus' life?

5. Only one Gospel writer also wrote a history of the early church, continuing his story of the Jesus movement with additional stories about a few of Jesus' followers. When the

New Testament contains *four* different accounts of Jesus' ministry, why do you think there is only *one* narrative about the church?

6. Of the twenty-seven New Testament books, twenty-one are letters or epistles. Why do you suppose that the letter form was so popular among early Christians? In a church scattered throughout the Roman Empire, what advantage did letter writing have over other literary forms?

7. What is an apocalypse? Define the terms *apocalyptic* (adjective) and *eschatology* (noun) and explain their application to the early Christian world view.

8. Briefly summarize the formation of the New Testament canon. Why did the early church decide that it needed a Scripture comparable to the Jewish Bible? Discuss the role of Marcion and Gnosticism in this process.

9. How do some of the early New Testament canons (lists of accepted New Testament books) differ from the present New Testament? Which books were almost always included in most lists and which books were commonly omitted? Why do you think that certain books were widely recognized as authoritative (possessing the authority to express correct teaching) while others were not?

10. In determining the books accepted as part of the New Testament canon, what forces or needs of early Christianity were at work? When did the first list of New Testament contents identical to today's canon appear?

TERMS AND CONCEPTS TO REMEMBER★

Hebrew Bible (Old Testament)
Septuagint
covenant (testament)
Torah
Gospel
apocalyptic

eschatology
canon
Marcion
Gnosticism
Muratorian Canon
Vulgate Bible

RECOMMENDED READING

Farmer, William R., and D. M. Farkasfalvy. *The Formation of the New Testament Canon: An Ecumenical Approach.* New York: Paulist Press, 1983.

Gnuse, Robert. *The Authority of the Bible: Theories of Inspiration, Revelation and the Canon of Scripture.* New York: Paulist Press, 1985. A short but thoughtful review of Biblical authority and means of divine inspiration.

Grant, Robert M. *The Formation of the New Testament.* New York: Harper & Row, 1965.

von Campenhausen, Hans. *The Formation of the Christian Bible.* Translated by J. A. Baker. Philadelphia: Fortress Press, 1972.

★Most of these terms appear in both the main text and in the glossary at the end of the book. The reader may find it helpful to define new terms introduced in each chapter and to check them in the glossary.

2 How the New Testament Was Handed Down to Us

The use of books is endless. (Eccles. 12:12)

KEY THEMES: This chapter surveys the history of the New Testament as a book, summarizing its transmission from ancient Greek manuscripts to modern English translations.

Originally composed for Greek-speaking audiences, the New Testament is now available in hundreds of different modern languages, including dozens of recent English translations. The process by which this ancient Greek work has been transmitted to us in English makes a fascinating story.

Transmitting the New Testament Texts

No original author's copies of any New Testament texts have yet come to light. Our oldest transcriptions are fragmentary copies dating from about 200 CE, about a century to a century and a half after the original texts were composed. The earliest surviving manuscript is a tiny scrap of the Gospel of John containing four verses from chapter 18. On the basis of its calligraphy (form of handwriting), historians date it at about 125 CE, a mere twenty-five to thirty years after the Gospel was written.

Most of these early manuscripts survive only in small fragments, and all were found in Egypt, where the dry climate favors preservation of the papyrus on which they were written. The oldest copies of the New Testament as a whole, the Codex Sinaiticus and Codex Vaticanus, were made in the fourth century CE. These famous texts are written on parchment, an expensive writing material made from sheepskin or goatskin and much more durable than papyrus.

The fourth-century parchment editions reflect the new-found prosperity of the Christian church. They appeared shortly after Christianity became the favored religion of the Roman emperors. The literary productivity encouraged by Constantine I, the first Christian emperor (306–337 CE), contrasts sharply with conditions a few years earlier under the Emperor Diocletian. During the "Great Persecution" (303–305 CE), Diocletian attempted to exterminate Christianity, ordering the imprisonment or execution of its adherents and the burning of their books. Diocletian's savage attacks on the church help explain why we have no complete New Testament texts older than Constantine's time.

In preserving their sacred writings, Christians pioneered the use of the **codex.** Rather than continue recording texts on scrolls—long sheets of papyrus or parchment rolled around a stick—Christian scribes assembled page-sized manuscript sheets in a booklike format. With individual pages bound together in the manner of a modern book, the codex made finding—and studying—scriptural passages much easier and more efficient.

Manuscript types. The great fourth-century codex editions of the New Testament are writ-

The oldest surviving manuscript of a New Testament book, this fragment of the Gospel of John dates from about 125 CE. Preserved for eighteen hundred years in the dry sands of an Egyptian grave, the tiny scrap of papyrus contains four verses from John 18. (Rylands Greek Papyrus 457 [also known as P 52]. Courtesy of the John Rylands University Library, Manchester, England.)

ten in uncial characters. Also called "majuscules," uncials are large or capital letters written in continuous script without spaces between words and usually without accents. Later manuscripts, called "minuscules," are written in small cursive letters, with individual letters connected to form groups and syllables.

Assembling a Reliable New Testament Text

The uncial codices are the most important basis of the text from which modern translations into English or other languages are made. The most valuable is the Codex Sinaiticus, a mid-fourth-century manuscript discovered dur-

ing the mid-1800s in the monastery of St. Catherine at the foot of Mount Sinai. Besides the entire New Testament (including the Epistle of Barnabas and the Shepherd of Hermas), the Sinaiticus also contains most of the Greek Old Testament.

Even older is the Codex Vaticanus (early fourth century), but it lacks part of Hebrews, several Pauline letters, and Revelation. Together with the slightly later uncial editions—the Codex Alexandrinus (which incorporates 1 and 2 Clement and a book of Jewish poetry called the Psalms of Solomon) and the Codex Bezae, which includes a Latin translation of the Greek text—these landmark editions provide scholars with the foundation upon which to construct a relatively authoritative New Testament text.

The fourth-century codices represent only the beginning of the laborious process of textual reconstruction. Scholars must consult many hundreds of manuscript fragments, abundant quotations from church writers of the second, third, and fourth centuries, various minuscule editions, as well as scores of translations made in Latin, Syriac, Coptic, and other languages spoken throughout the Greco-Roman world. With no fewer than five thousand ancient manuscript copies of the New Testament, most in fragmentary form, we have an abundance of texts from which to deduce a "standard text." The problem is that no two of these five thousand texts are identical. Some contain passages that other equally authoritative texts do not; some manifest remarkable differences in the wording or the arrangement of material. While some differences may result from scribal errors in copying, others stem from the copyists' theological interests. Copyists' changes or interpolations in the text may be detected by careful comparison of different manuscript traditions.

The standard Greek text. Beginning in the early sixteenth century, European scholars like Desiderius Erasmus, one of the most brilliant leaders of the northern Renaissance, attempted to establish a reliable Greek text from which translations could be made. After several centuries of labor among scholars in almost every Western nation, a seemingly definitive Greek text was established. In 1881–82, B. F. Westcott and F. J. Hort published *New Testament in the Original Greek,* an exhaustively researched critical text that is now the basis for virtually all contemporary work on the Greek Scriptures.

Thanks to Westcott and Hort and their successors, it is possible today to produce a much more accurate translation than ever before. Where modern translations differ from the long-familiar readings in the King James or "Authorized Version" of the Bible, it is commonly because contemporary translators work from a far better Greek text than was available to the King James editors when their version was first published in 1611.

Since the Westcott and Hort text appeared over a century ago, the scholarly process of refining and improving the text has continued. Although no single new edition threatens to replace Westcott and Hort, new discoveries of ancient manuscripts (an additional eight pages of the Codex Sinaiticus were found only recently) and a more expert understanding of the *koinē* Greek permit increasingly precise modifications of Westcott and Hort's basic work.

While we can never be certain that we possess the New Testament writings exactly as they were intended by their original authors, we can be thankful that only a relatively small proportion of the text is in doubt. Scholars find some passages highly questionable and debate the preferred version of others, but by far the majority of textual variations are comparatively minor. Considering the New Testament text as a whole, we can be reasonably sure we have a Greek edition that closely resembles the earliest documents.

English Translations

The New Testament continued to circulate in its original *koinē* Greek throughout the eastern half of the Roman Empire (later known as the Byzantine Empire). In the West, however, where Latin was the dominant tongue, Latin translations of the Septuagint and New Testament began to appear during the early centuries CE. This movement culminated in Jerome's masterful translation of the Vulgate, still the official Bible of the Roman Catholic Church. After barbarian invasions triggered the collapse of the western Empire in the late fifth century CE, both education and literacy declined precipitously. During the Dark Ages of the early Medieval period, new European languages gradually developed among the politically fractured regions and states of Europe. Latin remained the official language of the Roman Catholic Church, however, and for nearly a thousand years no major new translations of the Bible appeared.

Isolated scholars occasionally undertook to translate selected books of Scripture into one of the new European languages. The first man credited with doing so was the Venerable Bede, a Benedictine monk and historian of Anglo-Saxon England, who translated the Bible into his native English. In the 730s Bede rendered part of Jerome's Latin Vulgate into Old English. During the tenth and eleventh centuries a few other Bible books, including the Psalms and Gospels, also appeared in English. Not until the fourteenth century, however, did the entire Bible become available in English. This pioneering translation was the work of an English priest named John Wycliffe, who wished to make Scripture accessible to Christian lay people who did not understand Latin. Wycliffe finished his task of translating both Old and New Testaments by about 1384. The national church, however, fearing the consequences of the Bible's being read and interpreted by laypersons, condemned Wycliffe's version in 1408 and forbade any future translations.

The Protestant Reformation. Two historical events ensured that the Bible would find a larger reading public in English. The first was Johann Gutenberg's invention of movable type in 1455, a revolutionary advance that made it possible to print books relatively quickly rather than copying them laboriously by hand. The second was a strong religious movement known as the Protestant Reformation, begun in Germany in 1517. In that year a German priest named Martin Luther vigorously protested administrative corruption and other practices within the Roman Catholic church. Luther's German translation of the Bible (1522–34) was the first version in a modern European language based not on the Latin Vulgate but on the original Hebrew and Greek.

The first English translator to work directly from Hebrew and Greek manuscripts was William Tyndale; under the threat of church persecution, he fled to Germany, where his translation of the New Testament was published in 1525 (revised 1534). Official hostility to his work prevented him from completing his translation of the Old Testament, and in 1535–36 he was betrayed, tried for **heresy,** and burned alive at the stake. Tyndale's superb English phrasing of the New Testament has influenced almost every other English translation since.

Although the church forbade the reading of Wycliffe's or Tyndale's translations, it nevertheless permitted free distribution of the first printed English Bible—the Coverdale Bible (1535), which relied heavily on Tyndale's work. Matthew's Bible (1537), containing additional sections of Tyndale's Old Testament, was revised by Coverdale, and the result was called the Great Bible (1539). The Bishop's Bible (1568) was a revision of the Great Bible, and the King James Version was commissioned as a scholarly revision of the Bishop's Bible. The Geneva Bible (1560), which the English Puritans had produced in Switzerland, also significantly influenced the King James Bible.

The King James Bible (Authorized Version). By far the most popular English Bible of all time, the King James translation was authorized by James I, son of Mary, Queen of Scots, who appointed fifty-four scholars to make a new version of the Bishop's Bible for official use in the

St. Gregory and the three scribes, a book cover of the ninth century. Scholarly priests copied and transmitted the New Testament texts. (Courtesy of the Kunsthistoriches Museum, Vienna.)

English (Anglican) church. After seven years' labor, during which the oldest manuscripts then available were diligently consulted, the king's scholars produced in 1611 the Authorized or King James Version. One of the masterpieces of English literature, it was created at a time when the language was at its richest and most vivid. In the beauty of its rhythmic prose and colorful imagery, the King James Version remains unsurpassed in literary excellence. Later translations may be more accurate and have the advantage of being based on older and more authoritative Hebrew and Greek manuscripts, but none has phrased the Scriptures in so memorable or quotable a fashion.

Despite its wonderful poetic qualities, however, the King James Version has grave disadvantages as a text for studying the Bible. The very attributes that contribute to its linguistic elegance—the archaic diction, poetic rhythms, and Renaissance vocabulary—tend to obscure the explicit meaning of the text for many readers. Translated by scholars who grew up on the then-contemporary poetry of Edmund Spenser and William Shakespeare, and King James text presents real problems of comprehensibility to the average American student. Students who have difficulty undertaking *Hamlet* cannot expect to follow Paul's sometimes complex arguments when they are couched in terms that have been largely obsolete for centuries.

Modern English and American Translations

Realizing that language changes over the years, and that words lose their original meanings and take on new connotations, Bible scholars have repeatedly updated and reedited the King James text. A Revised Version of the King James was published in England between 1881 and 1885. A modification of this edition, the American Standard Revised Version, was issued in 1901. As knowledge of ancient manuscripts and linguistics advanced, the need for further revisions in the modern idiom became clear. Between 1946 and 1952 the Revised Standard Version (RSV) appeared, a translation now widely used in many American churches. Scholars plan to issue an updated edition of the RSV in the 1990s.

Although the King James Version and other older translations serve beautifully in church service and liturgy (rites performed in public worship), today's student will find that a mod-

ern English translation is much more helpful in studying the Bible. A number of superb new English editions, virtually all of which are clearer and more faithfully represent the authentic Hebrew and Greek texts than their predecessors do, are now easily available.

Two of the most important new translations are the Jerusalem Bible (1966) and the New American Bible (1970; revised 1987), both Roman Catholic editions. An international body of scholars, Protestant, Catholic, and Jewish, recently produced the New English Bible (NEB) (1970), which includes the complete Apocrypha. Outstanding for its scholarship, clarity, and general fidelity to the Greek text, the New English Bible (Oxford Study Edition) is the version cited in the present textbook. The study edition provides brief introductory essays to each biblical document as well as numerous footnotes that give valuable historical background. Unless otherwise indicated, all our biblical quotations are from the NEB.

For students seeking a modern translation with abundant scholarly commentary, the Doubleday Anchor Bible is an indispensable resource. Rather than a single-volume translation like the NEB, the Anchor Bible is a scholarly multivolume edition that began appearing in the 1960s and is not yet complete.

Two New Testament translations—the Good News Bible and the Living Bible—are popular with many students. Readers should be aware, however, that neither of these offers a close translation of the original Greek. Of the two, the Good News Bible is preferable because it offers a responsible paraphrase of the text. By contrast, the Living Bible gives a translation that is readable but unreliable and in places even misleading.

A third new translation that some students favor is the New International Version (NIV), which includes both the Old and New Testaments (omitting the Apocrypha). Designed to meet the doctrinal needs of Protestant Evangelicals, the NIV has been criticized for translating the Hebrew Bible from a strictly Christian

---

BOX *2-1 Abbreviations of New Testament Books in Alphabetical Order*

Acts	Acts of the Apostles		Philem.	Philemon
Col.	Colossians		Rev.	Revelation (the Apocalypse)
1 Cor.	1 Corinthians		Rom.	Romans
2 Cor.	2 Corinthians		1 Thess.	1 Thessalonians
Eph.	Ephesians		2 Thess.	2 Thessalonians
Gal.	Galatians		1 Tim.	1 Timothy
Heb.	Hebrews		2 Tim.	2 Timothy
James	James		Titus	Titus
John	John (Gospel)			
1 John	1 John (Epistle)		*Other Abbreviations*	
2 John	2 John (Epistle)			
3 John	3 John (Epistle)		BCE	Before the common era. Dates correspond to dates B.C.
Jude	Jude		CE	Common era. Dates correspond to dates A.D.
Luke	Luke (Gospel)			
Mark	Mark (Gospel)		KJV	The King James Version of the Bible, also called the Authorized Version (AV)
Matt.	Matthew (Gospel)		NEB	The New English Bible
1 Pet.	1 Peter		NIV	The New International Version of the Bible
2 Pet.	2 Peter		NT	The New Testament
Phil.	Philippians		OT	The Old Testament
			RSV	The Revised Standard Version of the Bible

viewpoint and praised for achieving a balance between a too-literal rendering of Hebrew and Greek and an overly free attempt to express ancient concepts in modern English. In many passages the NIV closely parallels the Revised Standard Version.

An even more doctrinally influenced version is the New World Translation of the Holy Scriptures, published by the Watchtower Bible and Tract Society, the official organization of Jehovah's Witnesses. Widely distributed by door-to-door preachers, the New World Translation is verbose and awkwardly worded; the anonymous translators' concern to rephrase doctrinally sensitive passages "correctly" makes it a provocative source of debate for most readers.

In addition to the above works, there are other translations by individual scholars or teams of translators, such as those by Richard F. Wey-mouth, James Moffat, J. B. Phillips, and Edgar J. Goodspeed and J. M. Powis Smith, each of which has its distinctive merits and drawbacks.

Written first on a highly perishable substance called papyrus, the oldest copies of the New Testament survive only as generally small fragments. Following Constantine's adoption of Christianity, however, more expensive editions written on parchment appeared, such as the Codex Sinaiticus and Codex Vaticanus.

Of the approximately five thousand surviving manuscript copies of all or part of the New Testament, no two are precisely alike. It was thus the task of scholars to compile a standard Greek text by consulting and comparing the (apparently) most reliable of extant manuscripts. In the late nineteenth century CE, Westcott and Hort produced a critically established text that is still the version that most modern translators use.

Based on the pioneering labors of Wycliffe and Tyndale, the King James Bible (Authorized Version, 1611) became the most popular translation in the English-speaking world. More modern translations, however, such as the Revised Standard Version and the New English Bible, offer closer and more careful approximations of the original Greek text.

QUESTIONS FOR DISCUSSION AND REVIEW

1. In what manuscript forms was the New Testament preserved during the first three centuries CE? What is the oldest surviving fragment of a New Testament book and where was it found? Why do we have more complete textual copies after the time of the emperor Constantine?

2. When no two copies of the New Testament texts are identical, how did biblical scholars compile a relatively reliable version of the Greek text? What is the standard Greek text today?

3. Discuss Jerome's role in providing a standard Latin edition of the Old and New Testaments. What is Jerome's translation called and when was it produced?

4. Summarize the historical events that stimulated the translation of the New Testament into modern languages like English. Discuss the roles of Wycliffe, Luther, and Tyndale.

5. Describe the strengths and weaknesses of the King James (Authorized Version) Bible for the modern reader.

6. Discuss the advantages for classroom study of modern English translations like the New American Bible, the Revised Standard Version, and the New English Bible (the version used in this textbook).

TERMS AND CONCEPTS TO REMEMBER

manuscript
codex
the Great Persecution
Constantine
Codex Sinaiticus
Codex Vaticanus
Westcott and Hort
   (the standard
   Greek text)

John Wycliffe
the Protestant
   Reformation
William Tyndale
the King James Bible
   (Authorized
   Version)

RECOMMENDED READING

Bruce, F. F. *History of the Bible in English.* 3d ed. New York: Oxford University Press, 1978. A concise history and critical evaluation of all major English translations from Anglo-Saxon times to the present.

Lewis, Jack P. *The English Bible from KJV to NIV: A History and Evaluation.* Grand Rapids, Michigan: Baker Book House, 1982. A scholarly review of major English translations from the King James to the New International Version.

3 *The World into Which Jesus Was Born*

Alexander of Macedon . . . ruled over countries,
nations, and dominions; all paid him tribute.

(1 Macc. 1:1, 4)

The devil took [Jesus] to a very high mountain, and showed him all the kingdoms
of the world in their glory. "All these," he said, "I will give you."

(Matt. 4:8–9)

KEY THEMES: Jesus lived in a world created by a series of military and political conquests that had radically affected the Jewish people. Beginning with Alexander the Great and his successors, this chapter summarizes the political events that brought Jesus' homeland under Roman domination.

Before beginning his public ministry, Jesus withdrew from all human contact and walked alone into the Judean desert. According to Matthew's Gospel, the **devil** pursued Jesus there to tempt him. The climactic temptation is the devil's offer of "all the kingdoms of the world and their splendor," a prize that Jesus vigorously rejects (Matt. 4:1–9). To Matthew's original readers, the "devilish" allure of political power would be regarded as a genuine test of any potential leader's character and motive. Jesus' world had been bitterly divided by individual rulers contesting for absolute domination. Shortly before Jesus' birth, a devastating series of power struggles had been resolved in favor of a one-man rule of the vast **Roman Empire,** which included Jesus' homeland. The possibility that another charismatic leader, such as Jesus, could reverse the status quo and seize power for himself was, in some minds at least, still conceivable (Luke 24:21; John 6:15; Acts 1:6–8).

To appreciate the devil's offering a single individual "all the kingdoms of the world," one must realize that recent history had provided people in Jesus' era with numerous examples of men who had become masters of most of the known world. The political environment was largely created and shaped by the exploits of several extraordinary conquerers, beginning with Alexander the Great and ending with Augustus Caesar, the emperor ruling when Jesus was born (Matt. 1:5; Luke 2:1).

Alexander and His Successors

The most spectacular, and in many ways the most influential, of all ancient leaders was **Alexander the Great** (ruled 336–323 BCE). The son of Philip II, king of Macedonia (a region in northern Greece), Alexander came to the throne at age sixteen. A brilliant military strategist and magnetic commander of men, Alexander embodied some of the most admired virtues of his age. By the time he was thirty he had led his Macedonian armies on an unprecedented series of military victories that created the largest empire the world had yet known. Stretching from Greece eastward through the ancient realms of Egypt, Babylonia, Persia, and Afghanistan into western India, Alexander's empire included most

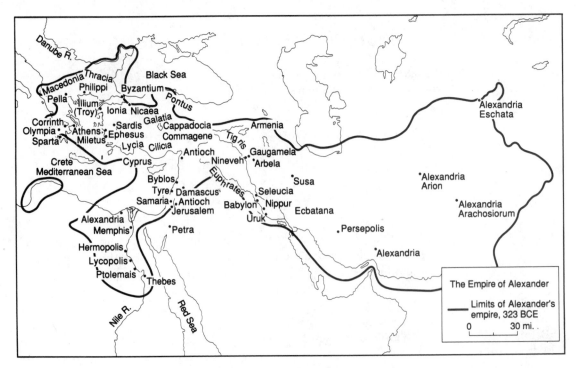

Figure 3–1. The empire of Alexander the Great (336–323 BCE).
Alexander's rapid conquest of the older Persian Empire created a new
Greek-speaking empire that included all of the ancient centers of
civilization from Greece eastward to India. Influenced by Greek
language, ideas, and customs, the resultant new international culture is
known as Hellenistic.

of the (then-recognized) civilized world (Figure
3–1). At thirty-two Alexander died in Babylon
(323 BCE). He did not live long enough to con-
solidate his far-flung conquests and achieve his
presumed goal of a single world government
united under the flag of Greek civilization.

The Hellenistic Kingdoms

After Alexander's death his empire slowly
disintegrated, but large sections remained under
the control of his successors (known collectively
as the Diadochi). By about 300 BCE three distinct powers had emerged to dominate the eastern Mediterranean world. One of Alexander's
ablest generals, **Ptolemy,** founded a dynasty
that ruled Egypt for nearly three centuries. An-

other of Alexander's successors was Seleucus,
who established the Seleucid Empire that controlled Syria, then an enormous territory that
extended from western Asia Minor to Mesopotamia (modern Iraq). Eventually the son of a
third successor, Antigonus, governed Macedonia and parts of Greece. Individual efforts to
reunite Alexander's empire failed, but the descendants of his commanders continued to rule
Greece and the Near East.

For biblical history, the two most important
nations derived from Alexander's empire are
Egypt and Syria (Figure 3–2). When Ptolemy
took control of Egypt, he also acquired Palestine, homeland of the Jewish people. We know
little of events during this period (roughly 300
to 200 BCE), but it appears that under the Ptole-

Portrait bust of Alexander the Great. Although he managed to conquer most of the known world before his death at age thirty-two, Alexander's dream of unifying east and west under a single government was never achieved. (Courtesy of the Trustees of the British Museum, London.)

maic reign the Jews enjoyed relative peace and · prosperity. Following 200 BCE, however, the Ptolemaic forces were driven out of Palestine, and the Seleucid kings of Syria assumed control. Tension between the Syrian monarchs and the Jewish people reached a climax during the reign of Antiochus IV (175–163 BCE).

Antiochus's Persecution of the Jews

Antiochus, who called himself Epiphanes ("God Manifest"), attempted to unify all the diverse religious and ethnic groups in his empire by actively promoting his subjects' adoption of Greek culture, customs, and religion. Attracted

by Greek ideas and social institutions, even many Jews voluntarily abandoned their ancestral religion to embrace the Greek way of life. Eager to become members of the gymnasium, the **Hellenistic** equivalent of a municipal athletic club, some Jewish youths underwent surgery to disguise the marks of circumcision (the ritual removal of the male's foreskin) so that they could not be identified as Jews. (All Greek athletes exercised in the nude.) Mass adoption of Hellenistic practices, particularly among the Jewish upper classes, threatened to destroy Jewish ethnic distinctiveness.

While many Jews were willingly absorbed into Hellenistic society, others firmly resisted the process. Aware that some Jews publicly opposed his policy of cultural and political assimilation, Antiochus eventually determined to outlaw the ancient rituals and practices that made the Jews so different from other peoples in his empire. Departing from the usual Greek attitude of tolerance toward non-Greek religions, Antiochus attempted to eliminate the traditional Jewish faith. He forbade reading or teaching the Mosaic Law, ordered copies of the Torah burned, executed women who had their sons circumcised, and ordered the infants' bodies tied around their mothers' necks. Keeping the Sabbath was also declared a crime punishable by death.

Besides making these Jewish religious observances a capital offense, Antiochus also directed an attack on the Jerusalem Temple, a sanctuary where Yahweh's "glory" was believed to dwell invisibly. Erecting a statue of the Olympian Zeus (king of the Greek gods) in the Temple courtyard, Antiochus deliberately polluted the sacred altar by sacrificing pigs there. Devout Jews who refused to eat swine's flesh, an act prohibited by their Law, or who refused otherwise to compromise their ancestral religion were slaughtered by royal command. These "pious ones" who preferred death to giving up cherished traditions became known as the **Hasidim,** religious loyalists from whom the Pharisees and other Jewish denominations of Jesus' day were descended.

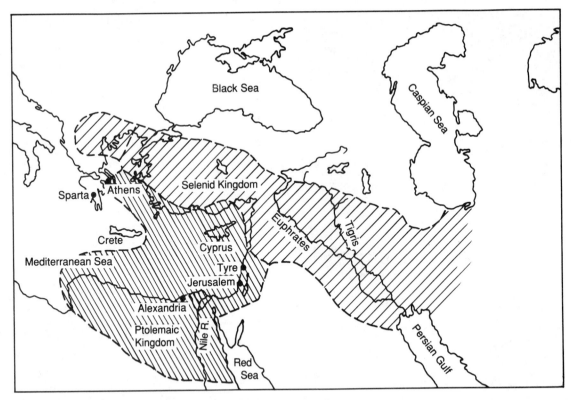

Figure 3–2. Map of the Seleucid and Ptolemaic kingdoms. After Alexander's death in 323 BCE, his vast empire was divided among his military successors. General Ptolemy assumed control of Egypt, while another general, Seleucus, ruled Syria and Mesopotamia. The Ptolemaic and Seleucid dynasties repeatedly fought each other for control of Palestine.

The Maccabean Revolt

The books of 1 and 2 Maccabees give a vivid picture of this time of great tribulation for the Jewish people, when practicing the biblical faith was to risk death by excruciating torture (see, for example, 2 Macc. 6–7). To some of the Hasidim, Antiochus's persecution seemed to herald the end of the world. The apocalyptic parts of Daniel (chs. 7–12), with their visions of God's supernatural overthrow of Antiochus's tyranny, are believed to have been written at this time.

For the Hasidim, the crisis was desperate, but help came from an unexpected quarter. When Syrian commissioners tried to force an aged village priest named Mattathias to sacrifice to the state-imposed cult, the old man killed first a fellow Jew who had sacrificed and then the king's representative (1 Macc. 2). Fleeing with his five sons to the hills, Mattathias organized a band of guerrilla fighters that proved surprisingly effective against the Syrian army. After Mattathias's death, his most capable son, **Judas Maccabeus** ("the Hammerer"), carried on the revolt. In 165 BCE, Judas's followers recaptured and purified the Jerusalem Temple, an event later commemorated annually as the "feast of dedication" (1 Macc. 4) and known today as **Hanukkah.**

Following Judas's death, leadership of the Jewish war for religious freedom passed to various Maccabean brothers, who eventually succeeded in forcing the Syrians to grant Israel national independence (142 BCE). Despite protests from other Jewish groups, including many of the Hasidim, the Maccabeans made themselves kings, establishing the Hasmonean Dynasty (named after a Maccabean ancestor, Hasmoneas).

The Maccabean political and social legacy was less effective than its military accomplishments. The Hasmonean period (142–40 BCE) is largely a record of intrigue, ambition, and treachery— a series of tragically missed opportunities for achieving Jewish unity and peace. Eventually rivalry among the Hasmonean rulers led to a decision fatal to Jewish national automony: an invitation to involve Rome militarily in Jewish affairs. In 63 BCE a claimant to the Hasmonean throne, John Hyrcanus II, asked Rome for help in ousting his younger brother, Aristobulus II, who had made himself both High Priest and king. In response, Rome dispatched General Pompey, whose troops overthrew Aristobulus and installed John Hyrcanus II as High Priest and "ethnarch" (63–40 BCE) over a Jewish state much reduced in size and prestige. The change in title from "king" to "ethnarch" (provincial governor) is significant, for after 63 BCE Jewish rulers were mere puppets of Rome, and the Holy Land merely another province in the Empire.

The Herod Family

Herod the Great, the monarch ruling Palestine for the Romans when Jesus was born (Matt. 2:1; Luke 1:5), was appointed king by the Roman Senate in 40 BCE. Although ostensibly Jewish in religion, Herod was a native of Idumea (ancient Edom, a traditional enemy of Israel) and had to overcome armed resistance to take the territory the Romans had assigned him. By 37 BCE Herod had captured Jerusalem and begun a reign marked by a strange combination of administrative skill, cruelty, and bloodshed. Politically, Herod was remarkably successful.

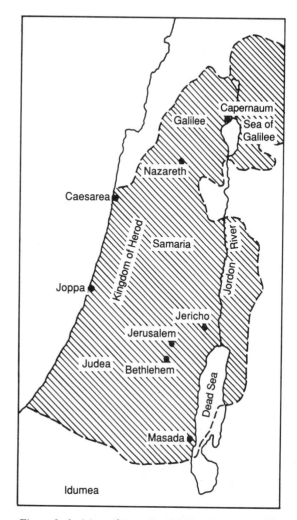

Figure 3–3. Map of Herod's kingdom. Appointed ruler by the Romans, Herod the Great (40–4 BCE) expanded the boundaries of the Jewish state to include most of the land once held by King David (1000 BCE). At his death, Herod's kingdom was divided among his three sons.

Enjoying Roman support, he extended the boundaries of his kingdom almost to the limits of David's biblical empire. Under Herod, the Jewish state expanded to include the districts of Samaria, Galilee (where Jesus grew up), and territories east of the Jordan River (Figure 3–3).

Herod's building program matched his political ambitions. He constructed monumental fortresses, the best known of which is Masada on the west shore of the Dead Sea. He also founded the port city of Caesarea, which later became the Roman administrative capital. Herod's most famous project, however, was rebuilding the Temple in Jerusalem, transforming it into one of the most magnificent sanctuaries in the ancient world. This was the Temple where Jesus and the disciples worshipped (Mark 11:27–13:2; Luke 2:22–38, 41–50; 19:47–48; 20:1–21:7; Acts 2:46; 3:1–10; 21:18–30). Begun in 20 BCE, the Temple was not completed until about 62 CE, only eight years before the Romans destroyed it.

Despite his grandiose achievements, Herod's treachery and violence made him hated by most of his Jewish subjects. He murdered his Hasmonean wife Mariamne and their two sons, Alexander and Aristobulus, as well as other family members. His fear that some conspiracy would rob him of his throne and his ruthless elimination of any potential rival provide the background for the Gospel story that Herod massacred Bethlehem's children (Matt. 2:16–17).

Herod's Successors

When Herod died in 4 BCE (according to modern calendars, Jesus was probably born a few years BCE), his kingdom was divided among his three surviving sons. Philip (4 BCE–34 CE) became tetrarch of the areas north and east of the Lake of Galilee. He seems to have been a competent ruler, and we hear little of him. His brother, **Herod Antipas** (4 BCE–39 CE), was given the territories of Galilee and Perea, a region east of the Jordan River. This is the Herod who beheaded John the Baptist (Mark 6:14–29; Matt. 14:1–12) and whom Jesus characterized as "that fox" (Luke 13:31–32). As ruler of Galilee, Jesus' homeland, Herod examined Jesus at Pilate's request (Luke 23:6–12). A third brother, Herod Archelaus, inherited the southwestern portion of Herod the Great's realm (Judea, Samaria, and Idumea) but proved a vicious and incompetent ruler. The Romans removed him

in 6 CE and in his place appointed a series of prefects (later procurators) to govern the region directly for Rome. The most celebrated of these local governors was the procurator **Pontius Pilate** (26–36 CE), the man who sentenced Jesus to death.

The Roman Emperors

Although Pilate and representatives of the Herod family are the most prominent political figures in the Gospel accounts, the real center of political power in Jesus' world lay in the person of the Roman emperor. At Jesus' birth, the emperor **Augustus** (originally named Gaius Octavius, 30 BCE–14 CE) ruled over an empire even larger and more diverse than Alexander's (Figure 3–4). Rome controlled not only the Near East, but also all of North Africa and most of Europe. Military conquests had reduced the Mediterranean Sea to the status of a Roman lake. Located at the eastern margin of the Empire, the Jewish homeland was only an insignificant, although politically troublesome, part of an international colossus. As a further insult to Jewish sensibilities, the Romans adopted the Greek name for this area, calling it **Palestine** after the Philistines, a sea people who had once been Israel's chief enemy (Judges; 1 Sam.).

The beginning of imperial rule. Rule of the Empire by a single man who could wield almost unlimited power had been instituted only a short time before Jesus' birth. The grandnephew of Julius Caesar, Gaius Octavius (the future Augustus), joined with Mark Antony to defeat Brutus and Cassius, Caesar's assassins, at the Battle of Philippi (42 BCE). With Lepidus, another of Caesar's supporters, Octavius and Mark Antony formed the Second Triumvirate (the first had been an unofficial alliance between Julius Caesar, Pompey, and Crassus) and shared the governing of Rome. The real power was divided between Mark Antony, who took control

Head of Augustus (Gaius Octavius), first emperor of Rome (30 BCE–4 CE). Defeating all rivals for control of the Roman Empire, Augustus ended centuries of civil war and introduced a new era of peace and political stability. (The Metropolitan Museum of Art, Rogers Fund, 1908.)

of the east, and Octavius, who administered Italy and the western dominions. Competition between the two men culminated in the Battle of Actium (31 BCE), a naval engagement in which Octavius's forces defeated those of Antony and his paramour, Cleopatra VII, a descendant of Alexander's general Ptolemy, who then ruled Egypt. Antony's death and Cleopatra's suicide (30 BCE) allowed Egypt to be incorporated into the Empire and left Octavius the sole ruler of the Roman state.

After decades of civil war, Rome was finally at peace. A grateful Senate voted Octavius the title of "princeps" (27 BCE), recognizing him as the undisputed head of state. The ascension of Octavius (henceforth called Augustus) to im-

perial dignity marked the end of the ancient Roman Republic and cost the citizens of Rome many of their traditional political rights. The Romans, however, seemed willing to exchange civil freedom for the restoration of public order, political stability, and economic prosperity that Augustus's reign brought.

Augustus was succeeded by his stepson Tiberius (14–37 CE), the emperor reigning during Jesus' ministry (Luke 3:1). It was Tiberius's governmental appointee Pontius Pilate who found Jesus guilty of treason against Rome (Matt. 27:11–44; Mark 15:2–32; Luke 22:66–23:38; John 18:28–19:22).

The Jewish Revolt Against Rome

About thirty years after Jesus' crucifixion, the Palestinian Jews rose in armed revolt against Rome. Led by passionate Jewish nationalists, many of whom believed it sinful even to allow idol-worshipping Gentiles to occupy the Holy Land, the Jewish War against Rome (66–73 CE) proved an overwhelming disaster for the Jewish people.

When the revolt broke out in 66 CE, the emperor **Nero** sent a veteran military commander, **Vespasian,** to crush the rebellion. Galilee fell easily to the Roman army, but before Vespasian could occupy **Judea,** the Jewish territory in southern Palestine of which Jerusalem was the capital, Nero was driven from the throne and committed suicide (June 68 CE). Following a year of political chaos, Vespasian was acclaimed emperor by the Roman legions and confirmed by the Senate. Leaving his son Titus in charge of the Jewish War, Vespasian returned to Rome. After a siege of six months, Titus captured and destroyed Jerusalem, burning Herod's splendidly rebuilt Temple in August 70 CE.

Josephus. Our main source of information about the war is **Flavius Josephus,** a first-century Jewish historian who first participated in

BOX 3-1   *Some Representative Events That Shaped the World of Jesus' Day and the Early Church*

c. 332–323 BCE. Alexander's conquests create a new international culture, the Hellenistic, bringing Greek language, literature, ideas, and customs to the entire Near Eastern world, including Palestine. This broad diffusion of Greek philosophic and religious thought plays a major role in the development of both Judaism and Christianity.

323–197 BCE. The Ptolemaic Dynasty, established by Ptolemy I, general and one of Alexander's successors, controls Palestine. Many Jews are attracted to Greek learning and the Hellenistic way of life.

200–197 BCE. The Seleucid Dynasty of Syria, descendants of Alexander's general Seleucus, drive the Ptolemys from Palestine and become the new masters of the Jews (197–142 BCE).

168–164 BCE. The Seleucid ruler, Antiochus IV, "Epiphanes," attempts to eradicate the Jewish religion. He forbids circumcision, Sabbath observance, reading of the Torah, etc. Antiochus erects a statue of the Olympian Zeus in the Temple precincts ("the abomination" of Daniel 9:27). The Hasidim ("pious ones") refuse to compromise their religion; many are tortured and murdered. Mattathias, a religious loyalist, and his five sons initiate the Maccabean Revolt.

164 BCE. Led by Judas Maccabeus, a Jewish guerrilla army recaptures, purifies, and rededicates the Temple, an event later commemorated in the festival of Hanukkah.

142–63 BCE. By 142 BCE the Jews have expelled the Syrian armies and established an independent state governed by Hasmonean (Maccabean) rulers. Internal strife and intrigue fatally weaken the Hasmonean kingdom.

63 BCE. General Pompey's legions occupy Palestine, annexing it as part of the Roman Empire.

40 BCE. The Roman Senate appoints Herod (Herod the Great), a nobleman of Idumea (the ancient Edom), king of Judea.

37–4 BCE. After laying siege to Jerusalem, Herod takes the city by force; his long reign is marked by ambitious building programs (including a massive renovation of the Jerusalem Temple) and acts of cruelty and violence.

30 BCE–14 CE. Gaius Octavius, having defeated his rival Mark Antony at the Battle of Actium (31 BCE), becomes undisputed ruler of the entire Roman Empire. Renamed Augustus by the Roman Senate, Octavius ends the civil wars that had divided Rome for generations and establishes a long period of civil order called the Pax Romana (the Roman Peace).

c. 6–4 BCE. Jesus is born to Mary and Joseph, citizens of Nazareth.

4 BCE. After Herod the Great's death, his kingdom is divided among his three sons. Herod Antipas (4 BCE–39 CE) rules Galilee and Perea; Herod Philip (4 BCE–34 CE) rules territories north and east of Galilee; Herod Archelaus (4 BCE–6 CE) rules Judea, Samaria, and Idumea but is deposed. His territories henceforth are administered directly by Roman officials.

14–37 CE. Tiberius, stepson of Augustus, rules Rome.

26–36 CE. Pontius Pilate, appointed by Rome, governs as procurator of Judea (26–36 CE). Tries and condemns Jesus of Nazareth (c. 30 or 33 CE).

c. 27–29 CE. John the Baptist conducts an apocalyptic campaign of repentance, baptizing the penitent in the Jordan River.

c. 27–30 or 29–33 CE. Jesus' public ministry: Jesus and a small band of disciples tour villages and cities in and around Galilee, including forays into Phoenicia and the Decapolis (league of Greek cities east of Galilee). A final journey to Jerusalem results in Jesus' rejection by religious authorities and his execution by Pilate on charges of treason.

c. 30 or 33 CE. A number of Jesus' followers are convinced that they have seen him risen from the dead. Gathered in Jerusalem, a commune of believers is inspired to begin carrying the oral gospel of Jesus' resurrection to Jews and (somewhat later) Gentiles. The Christian church is born.

c. 33–35 CE. Saul of Tarsus, a zealous Pharisee then persecuting Christian "heretics," experiences a vision of the risen Jesus on the road to Damascus.

50–62 CE. Paul, now the preeminent Christian missionary to the Gentiles, composes a series of letters to various Christian communities in the eastern Mediterranean region. These letters are the earliest parts of the New Testament to be written.

c. 62 CE. James, Jesus' kinsman, is killed in Jerusalem.

c. 64–65 CE. Following a major fire in Rome, the emperor Nero persecutes Christians there. According to tradition, Peter and Paul are martyred then.

c. 65–70 CE. The first account of Jesus' public ministry is written (the Gospel According to Mark).

66–73 CE. Led by the Zealot party of dedicated revolutionaries, the Palestinian Jews revolt against Roman tyranny. Titus, son of the new emperor Vespasian, captures and destroys Jerusalem and its Temple (70 CE). The Jewish loyalists holding the besieged fortress of Masada commit mass suicide (73 CE).

The Post-Apostolic Age

c. 80–85 CE. The Gospel of Matthew is written (in Antioch?).

c. 85–90 CE. Luke-Acts is published.

c. 80–100 CE. Books of James, Hebrews, and (possibly) 1 Peter are written.

c. 90 CE. Leading rabbis and Jewish scholars hold a council at Jamnia; third part of the Hebrew Bible, the Writings, is canonized. Christians are expelled from Jewish synagogues.

c. 90 CE. Letter to the Ephesians is included among Paul's correspondence.

c. 90–100 CE. Gospel of John is produced by the Johannine community. Letter of 1 Clement is written in Rome.

c. 95 CE. Persecutions of the emperor Domitian (81–96 CE) cause John of Patmos to write the Book of Revelation.

c. 100–110 CE. Letters of John are written.

c. 100–130 CE. The Didache, Shepherd of Hermas, and Epistles of Ignatius are written. Canonical New Testament books of 1 and 2 Timothy, Titus, and Jude appear.

132–135 CE. The Bar Kochba rebellion against Rome crushed by the emperor Hadrian (117–138 CE).

c. 130–50 CE. 2 Peter is written.

367 CE. Bishop Athanasius of Alexandria publishes list of twenty-seven New Testament books corresponding to present New Testament canon.

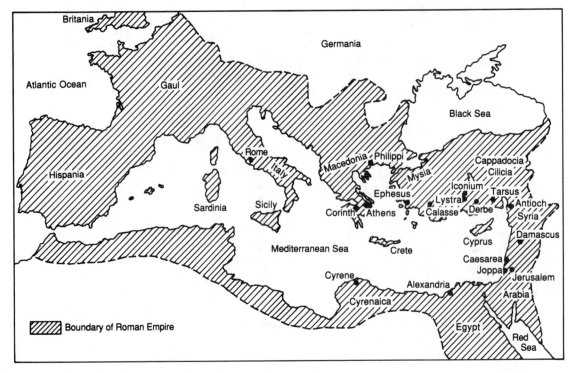

Figure 3–4. The Roman Empire. With the city of Rome as its administrative capital, the Empire governed most of the known world. Its subjects included people of virtually every race, language group, and ethnic background.

the rebellion but later became an ally of the Romans. An eyewitness of many of the events he describes, Josephus wrote to explain and defend his countrymen's action in revolting against Roman oppression. In *The Jewish War,* he vividly recounts the Roman capture of Jerusalem and the slaughter of many thousands of men, women, and children. While attempting to evoke sympathy for his people and to make their religion comprehensible to his Greek and Roman readers, Josephus also blames a small minority of political fanatics for their refusal to negotiate a compromise settlement with the Roman forces. According to Josephus, the extreme revolutionary party, the **Zealots,** virtually forced General Titus to destroy the holy city and its Temple by their obstinate refusal to accept the Roman terms of peace. Many historians doubt Jose-

phus's sometimes self-serving interpretation of events, but his surviving works, including a history of Israel called *Antiquities of the Jews,* are an invaluable record of this turbulent period.

A second Jewish revolt against Rome (132–135 CE) was led by a young man named **Bar Kochba** ("Son of the Star"), whom many Palestinian Jews believed to be the Messiah who would restore David's kingdom. Brutally suppressed by the emperor Hadrian, the Bar Kochba rebellion resulted in a second Roman destruction of Jerusalem (135 CE). A Roman shrine was then constructed on the site of Herod's Temple, and Jews were forbidden to enter their city on pain of death.

The period of Jesus' life is thus chronologically framed by two Jewish wars for religious and political independence. The first, led by the Maccabees, created an autonomous Jewish state. The second, a generation after Jesus' death, resulted in national annihilation. Bar Kochba's later attempt to restore Jewish fortunes met a similar defeat. From this time until 1948, when the modern nation of Israel was established, the Jews were to be a people without a country.

QUESTIONS FOR DISCUSSION AND REVIEW

1. Explain how Alexander the Great brought Greek language, thought, and culture to the ancient Near East, including the Jewish homeland.
2. What did the Greek-Syrian king Antiochus IV attempt to do and why did the Jewish loyalists (Hasidim) oppose him? What role did the Maccabees play?
3. After the Romans conquered Palestine, what local rulers or administrators governed the Jewish people?
4. Describe the two Jewish revolts against Rome and the disastrous results.

TERMS AND CONCEPTS TO REMEMBER

Alexander the Great
Antiochus IV
the Maccabean
    Revolt
the Hasmonean
    Dynasty
Herod the Great

Herod Antipas
the emperor
    Augustus
the Jewish revolts
    against Rome
Flavius Josephus

RECOMMENDED READING

Boardman, John, Jasper Griffin, and Oswyn Murray. *The Oxford History of the Classical World.* New York: Oxford University Press, 1986. An authoritative collection of informative essays by leading scholars.

Boren, H. C. *The Ancient World: An Historical Perspective.* 2d ed. Englewood Cliffs, N.J.: Prentice-Hall, 1986. A readable history surveying the world from ancient Sumer to the fall of Rome.

Josephus, Flavius. *The Jewish War.* Rev. ed. Translated by G. A. Williamson. Edited by E. M. Smallwood. New York: Penguin Books, 1981. The most important contemporary source for conditions in Palestine during the first century CE.

Peters, F. E. *The Harvest of Hellenism: A History of the Near East from Alexander the Great to the Triumph of Christianity.* New York: Simon & Schuster, 1970. A comprehensive presentation of Greek and Roman history affecting Palestine.

4 *The World of Hellenistic Thought and Culture*

The Greeks look for wisdom. (1 Cor. 1:23)

KEY THEMES: Early Christianity originated in a complex social and religious environment that combined Greek ideas with Jewish biblical teachings. Writing in Greek, New Testament authors reflect the rich and diverse Hellenistic culture of their day, incorporating into their works ideas that derive from or are parallel to concepts found in Greek literature, philosophy, and religion.

Alexander's conquest of the ancient world created a new international culture known as Hellenistic. A mixture of the classical Greek (Hellenic) culture with the older civilizations of the Near East, the **Hellenistic** synthesis produced a creative flowering of Greek and Oriental motifs in art, architecture, philosophy, literature, and religion. Arbitrarily dated as beginning with Alexander's death in 323 BCE, the Hellenistic period chronologically overlaps the period of Roman expansion and continues into the early Christian centuries.

Along with a new form of the Greek language, the *koinē* spoken by Alexander's soldiers, Hellenistic culture introduced new ways of thought and expression into the eastern Mediterranean region where Christianity first took root. Alexander himself was a passionate disciple of Greek literature and science. Tutored by the eminent philosopher Aristotle, Alexander is reputed to have slept with a copy of Homer's *Iliad,* a poem celebrating personal honor and heroic action, under his pillow. Under Alexander and his successors, Greek attitudes and ideas dominated the education of youths everywhere. (This process of Hellenization, however, seems to have been restricted largely to the middle and upper classes in urban centers. The inhabitants of rural areas and villages were

probably little touched by the Hellenistic innovations.) Among leading thinkers and writers, the Greek influence was all-pervasive. The Greek love of learning, intense intellectual curiosity, and confidence in the power of reason and logic to discover truth became near-universal standards in the educational process.

As a Greek book, the New Testament profoundly reflects the Hellenistic environment in which it grew. In many important ways, the New Testament writers combine their Jewish heritage of biblical traditions with Greek philosophical concepts. To understand the dual legacy that the Christian Greek Scriptures transmit to us, we must review briefly some major aspects of Hellenistic philosophy and religion.

Greek Philosophy

A term meaning "love of wisdom," *philosophy* is an attempt to understand human life and its place in the universe by applying rational analysis to a body of observable facts. At first indistinguishable from primitive science, Greek philosophy began in the late seventh century BCE in Miletus and other Greek cities along the coast of western Asia Minor. By the fifth century BCE, the center of intellectual activity had shifted to the mainland city of Athens. There it rapidly developed into numerous schools of thought that endeavored to define the nature of reality and to offer meaningful advice on ethical questions, such as how one may discover and lead the "good" or worthy life.

Socrates, Plato, and the immortal soul. The most famous philosopher was the Athenian Socrates (469–399 BCE). A brilliant and humorous "lover of wisdom," Socrates made his life an unending quest for truth. Rather than offer final answers to people's questions about life's ultimate meaning, Socrates questioned every belief that his fellow Athenians cherished as "obviously" true. Good-naturedly cross-examining tradesmen, teachers, and politicians alike—demanding to know how they could be so sure their beliefs were valid—Socrates attracted a small circle of devoted followers.

He also irritated many of Athen's influential citizens, some of whom regarded this "gadfly" with his stinging questions as dangerous to conventional morality. As a result, Socrates was eventually tried and executed for criticizing the ethical inadequacy of his opponents' beliefs and practices, the only thinker in Athens's history to be put to death for expressing his ideas.

Socrates left nothing in writing, but his disciple Plato made him the hero of a series of philosophical dialogues in which a saintly and impish Socrates always outargues and outwits his opponents. Because all of Plato's compositions feature Socrates as the chief speaker, it is difficult to separate the writer's ideas from those of his master. (Scholars face a similar problem in trying to distinguish Jesus' sayings from the Gospel writers' added commentary.)

During his eighty years, Plato developed a coherent world view that has directly or indirectly influenced all subsequent thought about ethical behavior, government, human psychology, and the nature of both physical and spiritual reality. Plato's philosophy is dualistic—it posits the coexistence of two separate worlds, one the familiar physical environment of matter

Statue of Socrates (c. 469–399 BCE). Condemned to death for challenging the religious assumptions of his fellow Athenians, Socrates lives on in the dialogues of his great disciple, the philosopher Plato. (Courtesy of the British Museum, London.)

and sense impressions, the other an invisible realm of perfect, eternal ideas. In this philosophy, our bodies belong to the material world and are chained to the physical processes of change, decay, and death. Our souls, however, originate in the unseen spirit world and after death return to it for reward or punishment.

Education involves recognizing the superiority of the soul to the body and cultivating those virtues that prepare the soul for its immortal destiny. Hence the person who truly loves wisdom, the genuine philosopher, will seek the knowledge of eternal truths that make real goodness possible, helping others along the way to realize that ambitions for worldly power or riches are unworthy goals. The wise seek the perfect justice of the unseen world and find eternal life.

Over the centuries Plato's ideas were modified and widely desseminated until, in one form or another, they became common knowledge during the Hellenistic era. Some New Testament writers, such as the author of Hebrews, use Platonic concepts to illustrate parallels and correspondences between the spiritual and physical worlds (Heb. 1:1–4; 9:1–14). Hebrews's famous definition of faith is primarily a confession of belief in the reality of the invisible realm (Heb. 11:1–2).

Stoicism. Another Greek philosophy that became extremely popular among the educated classes during Roman times was Stoicism. Founded in Athens by Zeno (c. 336–263 BCE), the Stoic school emphasizes the order and moral purpose of the universe. In the Stoic view, Reason is the divine principle that gives coherence and meaning to our universe. Identified as **Logos** (a Greek term for "word"), this cosmic intelligence unifies the world and makes it intelligible to the human intellect. Human souls are sparks from the divine Logos, which is symbolized by cosmic fire and sometimes associated with a supreme god.

Stoic endurance. Stoic teaching urges the individual to listen to the divine element within, to discipline both body and mind to attain a state of harmony with nature and the universe. Stoics must practice severe self-control, learning self-sufficiency and noble indifference to both pleasure and pain. The Stoic ideal is to endure either personal gain or loss with equal serenity, without any show of emotion.

Many celebrated Romans pursued the Stoic way, including the philosopher Seneca (Nero's tutor), the Greek slave Epictetus, and the emperor Marcus Aurelius (161–80 CE). The hero of Virgil's epic poem, *The Aeneid,* with his rigid concept of duty toward the gods and unselfish service to the state, is intended to represent the Stoic virtues. When Paul discusses self-discipline or the ability to endure want or plenty, he echoes Stoic values that were commonplace in Greco-Roman society (Phil. 4:11–14).

The Hymn to Zeus. We may easily overlook the fact that some pre-Christian philosophies manifest a deep sense of religious feeling. One often-quoted example is the Stoic poet Cleanthes' "Hymn to Zeus," which exhibits a profound reverence for the divine:

> Most glorious of immortals, O Zeus of many names, almighty and everlasting, sovereign of nature, directing all in accordance with the law, thee it is fitting that all mortals should address. . . . Thee all the universe, as it rolls circling around the earth, obeys wheresoever thou dost guide, and gladly owns thy sway. Such an agent thou holdest in thy invisible hands—the two-edged fiery, everliving thunderbolt, under whose stroke all nature shudders. No work on earth is wrought apart from thee, lord, nor through the divine ethereal sphere, nor upon the sea, except whatever deeds wicked men do in their own folly. Indeed, thou knowest how to make even the rough smooth and to bring order out of disorder: even unfriendly things are friendly in thy sight. For so thou hast fitted all things together, the good with the evil, that there might be one eternal law over all. . . .

Such prayers, with their emphasis on divine wisdom and justice, are not unlike those in the Judeo-Christian tradition.

Epicureanism. A strikingly different philosophical outlook appears in the teachings of Epicurus (c. 342–270 BCE). While the Stoics believe in the soul's immortality and a future world of rewards or penalties, Epicurus asserts that everything is completely physical or material, including the soul, which after death dissolves into nothingness along with the body. The gods may exist, but they have no contact with or interest in human beings. Without a cosmic intelligence to guide them, people must create their own individual purposes in life. A major goal is the avoidance of pain, which means that the shrewd individual will avoid public service or politics, where rivals may destroy one. Cultivating a private garden, the wise forego sensual indulgences that weaken physically and mentally. Using reason not to discover ultimate truth, but to live well, the enlightened mind seeks intellectual pleasures because mental enjoyments outlast those of the body.

Epicurus's stress on the material, perishable nature of both body and soul found support in the philosopher Democritus's atomic theory. Democritus (born about 460 BCE) taught that all things are formed of tiny invisible particles called atoms. It is the nature of atoms to move and collide, temporarily forming objects, including sentient ones like animals and human beings, and then to disintegrate and reform other objects elsewhere. Wise or foolish, all persons are merely chance collections of atoms destined to dissolve without a trace.

According to the Book of Acts, Stoic and Epicurean philosophers debated Paul in Athens when he first presented Christianity there (about 50 CE). Although Acts reports that some Athenians misunderstood Paul's preaching about Jesus and the resurrection (taking both Jesus and the resurrection as "foreign deities"), they invited Paul to address them at a public forum (Acts 17:18).

The Mystery Religions

Besides the principal philosophical schools, with their ethical stress on one's duties to the gods and state, the Greco-Roman world also fostered a number of "underground religions" that exerted a wide influence. Known as the "mysteries" (*mysterion*) because their adherents took oaths never to reveal their secret rites, some of these cults embody myths and rituals that parallel or anticipate the Christian religion. Several mystery cults honor young male gods born of a divine father and human mother, heroes who undergo death, a descent into the Underworld (**Hades**), and a rebirth to immortal life. In some of these secret religions, celebrants shared a communal meal in which they symbolically ate the flesh and drank the blood of their god. By thus absorbing the god's presence into themselves, his worshippers hoped to attain a similar immortality.

Dionysus. The most famous of the dying and resurrected gods was Dionysus, son of Zeus by Semele, a human princess of ancient Thebes. According to some version of the myth, the young Dionysus was murdered by the Titans, giant gods typically seen as evil. Zeus raised his son from the dead, granting him everlasting divinity. As god of "the vine" (representing wine, the most common beverage in the ancient world), Dionysus symbolized the cycle of vegetation, which ostensibly dies in the winter only to be reborn in the spring.

Orphism. In the Orphic Mysteries people were initiated into the secrets of Dionysus's mystic resurrection and shown visions of the future life. This cult is commonly called Orphism because Orpheus, the first poet and musician, is said to have composed poems revealing the doctrines of posthumous rewards and punishments. Those who strictly kept the Orphic code of moral and ritual purity were granted joy in the afterlife, while wrongdoers faced a painful ordeal to purge them of their sins. Orphism also taught the transmigration of souls, a belief that individual souls are eventually reborn in new bodies to work out their ultimate destinies.

Dionysus riding a panther, mosiac, House of Masks, Delos. This mosaic portrait of the young god stresses the animal power that Dionysus can liberate through his gift of wine. With a divine father and human mother, Dionysus (also called Bacchus) suffered death only to be resurrected to immortal life. (Courtesy of the École Française d'Archéologie, Athens.)

Mithraism. According to Persian myth, Mithras was the youthful god of light who killed a sacred bull, from whose blood and semen new life was generated. A cult in which secrecy was rigorously enforced, Mithraism became extremely popular among the Roman common people, soldiers, and tradesmen. Only men were initiated into the religion, after which ceremony initiates were said to have been "born again" and henceforth lived under the god's special protection.

By the end of the third century CE, Mithraism had become the official cult of the Roman Empire and Christianity's leading competitor. Mithras, who was associated with the sun, was said to have been born on December 25, then calculated as the date of winter solstice, the time when the divine sun is reborn and hours of daylight begin to lengthen. Because the solstice appropriately symbolizes the birth of God's Son, "the light of the world" (as well as the rebirth of the Mithraic sun), the Roman church eventually chose Mithras's birthday to celebrate as that of Jesus.

The Mother Goddesses

Other mystery religions stress the importance of a female figure, a mother goddess who can offer help in this life and intervene for one in the next world. Demeter ("earth mother"), goddess of the wheat harvest, and her daughter

Persephone were worshipped at Eleusis and elsewhere in the eastern Mediterranean. Originally concerned with agricultural fertility and the cycle of the seasons, the Eleusinian Mysteries developed into a mystical celebration of death and rebirth.

Isis. Even more popular in Roman times was Isis, an Egyptian mother goddess whom artists typically depicted as a madonna holding her infant son Horus. Representing motherly compassion allied with divine power, Isis was the center of a mystery cult that promised initiates personal help in resolving life's problems as well as the assurance of a happy existence after death. As a embodiment of creative intelligence and cosmic wisdom, Isis was known as the goddess of "a thousand names," a deity whom the whole world honored in one form or another. Offering the individual worshipper far more comfort than the official state religions of Greece or Rome, the Isis cult found dedicated adherents throughout the Roman Empire.

The myth of Isis involved her male consort Osiris, originally a mortal ruler of ancient Egypt. Like Dionysus, Osiris suffered death by being torn in pieces, but was resurrected to new life as a god. Through mystic rituals uniting the worshipper with Osiris, king and judge of the dead, the initiate theoretically lost the fear of death and looked forward to a posthumous union with the divine.

The world of Jesus' day offered people a wide variety of religious options. This multiplicity of philosophies and religions, both public and secret, suggests that many persons in Hellenistic society felt a need to find spiritual direction and purpose in their lives. Offering practical help in this world and immortality in the next, many mystery cults focused on the promise inherent in myths dramatizing the death of a young male figure who is reborn to eternal life. Others stressed the wisdom and compassion of a mother goddess. Virtually all such cults involved a ritual or sacred meal in which worshippers were

A priestess of Isis. Originally an Egyptian mother goddess, Isis was worshipped throughout the Roman Empire as the embodiment of wisdom who offered worldly success and protection to persons initiated into her cult. (Courtesy of the Capitoline Museum, Rome, and Art Resource, New York.)

initiated into the mysteries of spiritual regeneration.

During the century following Jesus' death, Christianity developed and spread in competition with these older philosophies and religions. Addressing persons familiar with the symbols, rites, and concepts of the Hellenistic world, New Testament writers commonly phrase their message about Jesus in terms their Greek readers will understand. In a cosmopolitan environment that offered so many different answers to important religious questions, Paul, the Gospel authors, and others strive to articulate Christianity's distinctive vision of life's purpose.

QUESTIONS FOR DISCUSSION AND REVIEW

1. Describe the developments that caused the New Testament writers to use the Greek language and employ Greek concepts.
2. Define the term *philosophy* and summarize Plato's teaching about the immortality of the soul and eternal spirit world.
3. How do the Stoics and Epicureans differ in their views of reality?
4. Describe the mystery religions involving Dionysus and Mithras. What parallels do you find between the myths of Dionysus and Osiris and the Christian story of Jesus?
5. Can you discover any parallels between the Isis cult and the later veneration of a mother figure in Christianity?

TERMS AND CONCEPTS TO REMEMBER

philosophy	mystery religion
Socrates, the "gadfly"	Dionysus and Orpheus
Platonism	Isis and Osiris
Stoicism and Epicureanism	Mithras
	December 25 and the rebirth of the sun

RECOMMENDED READING

Eusebius. *The History of the Church*. Trans. by G. A. Williamson. Baltimore: Penguin Books, 1965. A valuable early history of Christian origins.

Fox, R. L. *Pagans and Christians*. New York: Knopf, 1987. A comprehensive and insightful investigation of Greco-Roman religious life from the second to the fourth century CE.

Grant, F. C., ed. *Hellenistic Religions: The Age of Syncretism*. Indianapolis: Bobbs Merrill, 1953. Collection of Greco-Roman religious writings.

Kee, H. C. *The New Testament in Context: Sources and Documents*. Englewood Cliffs, N.J.: Prentice-Hall, 1984. An important collection of Greco-Roman documents containing parallels to New Testament ideas and teachings.

Koester, Helmut. *Introduction to the New Testament*. Vol. 1, *History, Culture, and Religion of the Hellenistic Age*. Philadelphia: Fortress Press, 1982. A scholarly study.

5 *The World of First-Century Judaism*

You yourselves [Israel] are my witnesses—it is
Yahweh who speaks—my servants whom I have
chosen, that men may know and believe me and
understand that it is I. . . . I, I am Yahweh, there is
no other savior but me.

(Isaiah 43:10–11, Jerusalem Bible)

KEY THEMES: In Jesus' day, the Jewish faith was extremely diverse, split into numerous
parties and factions, the most prominent of which included the Sadducees,
Pharisees, Essenes, Samaritans, and Zealots. While the majority of Jews did
not then belong to any particular party, most shared traditional beliefs about
the national God Yahweh, the Torah, the "promised land" (Palestine), and
the Jerusalem Temple. Many also held eschatological convictions (beliefs
about the imminent end of the world) and hoped that God's Messiah would
soon arrive to deliver them from their enemies. As Jewish writings of this
period demonstrate, even in Palestine Judaism was thoroughly saturated
with Hellenistic ideas.

Early Christianity expanded and developed
in the Hellenistic soil of the Roman Empire, but
it first took root in Palestine, the heartland of
the Jewish religion. Both Jesus and his original
disciples were children of Israel, born and raised
in the Jewish faith. Jesus' teachings are explainable only in terms of Judaism, the parent religion of Christianity.

The One God, Yahweh

Although the Judaism of Jesus' day was divided into many conflicting groups or sects, virtually all practicing Jews held certain tenets in
common that set them apart as an identifiable
religious community. Many of these shared beliefs were based on the Hebrew Bible, particularly the **Torah** and the **Prophets.** Foremost
was the **Shema,** which proclaimed the oneness
of the national God, **Yahweh:**

Listen, Israel: Yahweh your God is the one Yahweh. (Deut. 6:4, Jerusalem Bible)

Alone among the religions of the ancient world,
Judaism was absolutely monotheistic, accepting
the existence of a single Supreme Being, Creator and Judge of heaven and earth (Isa. 40–43).
According to Exodus 3:13–16, this Deity revealed himself to Moses as Yahweh, a personal
name apparently based on the Hebrew verb "to
be." Speaking in the first person, Yahweh declared that he is the eternal "I Am," the One
who brings all into existence, including his chosen nation, Israel. Because of the prohibition
against taking Yahweh's name "in vain" (Exod.
20:7), after about the fourth century BCE most
Jews began to substitute the title *Adonai* (commonly translated "Lord") when referring to
Yahweh, whose sacred name was too holy to
pronounce by unworthy persons.

Yahweh's character was qualitatively different from that of the many other gods wor-

37

shipped in the ancient world. A pure and holy Being who created and ruled the universe, he demanded absolute allegiance from his people. The many gods of Greece, Rome, and other polytheistic societies did not object to sharing with other deities the sacrifices and rituals of human worship. By contrast, Yahweh described himself as a "jealous God," demanding exclusive devotion and refusing to accept a worshipper who acknowledged any other deity (Exod. 20). This exclusivism, and a profound conviction that there is only one correct way to please the One God, Judaism passed on to Christianity (1 Cor. 8:5) and later to Islam, which is also strictly monotheistic.

The Torah

A second cohesive force in Judaism was the Torah, the five sacred books of instruction, or Law, traditionally attributed to Moses. According to Exodus and Deuteronomy, Yahweh had bound Israel to himself by a **covenant,** an arrangement by which the people vowed to obey all of their God's commandments and decrees. Nearly all Jews saw rigorous obedience to Torah regulations as one's foremost obligation. The Torah demanded an extremely high standard of personal conduct. It also included numerous ceremonial requirements, such as refraining from all work on the **Sabbath** (the seventh day of the week), **circumcising** all male children, and abstaining from certain forbidden foods, such as pork. Along with an unqualified dedication to Yahweh and good will toward one's fellow men, exact observance of the Torah regulations was the God-given way to personal righteousness and divine favor.

The Promised Land of Canaan

Another biblical concept that bound many Palestinian Jews together was the conviction that Yahweh had given them the land of Canaan

(Palestine) forever. As descendants of the patriarch (tribal father) **Abraham,** Jesus' countrymen saw themselves as Abraham's "children," permanent heirs to the "promised land" (Gen. 12:1–3; 17:1–8; John 8:33, 39). According to the Abrahamic Covenant, the Jewish people were to become a mighty and populous nation with a dynasty of kings (Gen. 17:1–9; 22:15–18).

The kingdom of David. Only briefly in their history, however, were all the Jewish tribes united under a single monarchy. During the reigns of **King David** (c. 1000–961 BCE) and his son **Solomon** (c. 961–922 BCE), the nation of Israel exercised control over the entire territory described in the Abrahamic pact. After Solomon's death, the Davidic empire was divided into the competing smaller states of Israel and Judah, which in turn were swept away by the greater Near Eastern powers of Assyria and Babylon. By Jesus' lifetime the Holy Land had been successively occupied by Persians, Greeks, Syrians, and Romans. Free control of their own land was only a memory to most Jews, many of whom lived outside Palestine in the **Diaspora** ("scattering" of Jews among foreign lands). To some patriotic Jews, however, driving foreign idolators from their native soil was a sacred duty. To such "Zealots," as they were later called, Judaism and political nationalism were inseparable.

The Jerusalem Temple

A more tangible unifying symbol for many in the Jewish faith was the great **Temple** of Yahweh in Jerusalem. According to Deuteronomy 12, Yahweh recognized only one site on earth as the place where the animal sacrifices required by the Torah were acceptable to him. King Solomon, famous for his wisdom, wealth, and building projects, had first erected a monumental sanctuary on Zion's hill in Jerusalem. Solomon's Temple had housed the **ark of the covenant,** the sacred chest containing the im-

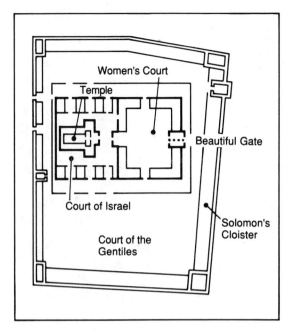

Figure 5–1. Outline of Herod's Temple, Jerusalem. With its great courtyards and porticoes, the Temple covered many acres. The main sanctuary, however, was a simple rectangular building with an outer porch, a long inner room, and an innermost chamber known as the Holy of Holies. A heavily bejeweled curtain separated the two inner chambers.

plements of the Mosaic faith. It was believed that Yahweh's *kavod* or "glory" dwelt in the innermost room, called the Holy of Holies. After the Babylonians destroyed Solomon's magnificent sanctuary in 587 BCE, a smaller building was constructed on the site and rededicated about 515 BCE. Extensively restored and enlarged by Herod the Great, this "second Temple" was commonly known in New Testament times as Herod's Temple.

Devout Jews, whenever possible, made annual pilgrimages to the Jerusalem sanctuary, for only there would Yahweh accept their obligatory offerings of grain, first fruits, and unblemished sacrificial animals. According to Luke's Gospel, Jesus' family is especially scrupulous about Temple observances. Mary journeys there

from Bethlehem to undergo the purification rites necessary after childbirth, and her infant son is presented there as required by Law (Luke 2:22–39; Exod. 13:2; Lev. 5:7). The Temple is where the twelve-year-old Jesus first manifests an awareness of his special calling (Luke 2:41–50) and where Jesus' family goes to observe the holy days of the Jewish religious calendar (John 7:2–10).

Jesus' family repeatedly traveled to Jerusalem from Galilee, but many pious Jews made arduous pilgrimages to the Temple from distant parts of the Roman Empire. Members of the large Jewish colonies established in Alexandria, Damascus, Antioch, or Rome itself journeyed to the Temple to offer sacrifices and participate in the ceremonies of such solemn occasions as the **Day of Atonement** (Yom Kippur). Held in the fall of the year, the atonement ritual required Israel's High Priest to present sin offerings for the people so that their God could absolve them both individually and collectively for their wrongdoing. On this special day alone, the High Priest entered into the Temple's Holy of Holies to present a sacrifice on the people's behalf and to utter the sacred name of Yahweh.

First-Century Jewish Diversity

Reverence for the Mosaic Torah, the land, the Jerusalem Temple, and the transcendent Being whose invisible presence sanctified it were unifying aspects of first-century Judaism. Nevertheless, the Jews of Jesus' time were so deeply divided on so many different issues, both religious and political, that it is impossible to describe the Jewish religion as a coherent whole. The more scholars learn about the period before 70 CE, the more diverse Judaism appears to have been.

The Gospels mention several distinct Jewish groups—the Sadducees, Pharisees, Herodians, Samaritans, and Zealots—but these sects or parties represent only a fraction of first-century

Portrait bust of the Emperor Vespasian (69–79 CE). Appointed by Nero to crush the Jewish Revolt (66–73 CE), Vespasian conquered Galilee but withdrew from the war after Nero's suicide. A year later he became emperor. He then appointed his son Titus to carry on the siege of Jerusalem. (Courtesy of the Trustees of the British Museum, London.)

Portrait bust of the Emperor Titus (79–81 CE). When his father, Vespasian, left him in charge of putting down the Jewish Revolt, Titus laid siege to Jerusalem, capturing the city and burning its Temple in August 70 CE. He succeeded his father as emperor in 79 CE but died after a brief reign. (Courtesy of the Trustees of the British Museum, London.)

Judaism's bewildering variety. Keeping in mind that the groups discussed here constitute a mere sample of Jewish pluralism, we will survey four of the best-known denominations (or "philosophies" as Josephus calls them).

The Sadducees

Since none of their writings survive, we know the **Sadducees** only through brief references in the New Testament and in other secondary sources, such as Josephus. Represented as among

Jesus' chief opponents, the Sadducees were typically members of the Jewish upper class, wealthy landowning aristocrats who largely controlled the priesthood and the Temple. Their name (Greek Saddoukaioi, from the Hebrew Zaddukim or tsaddiqim) means "righteous ones" and may be descriptive, or it may reflect their claim to be the spiritual heirs of Zadok, the High Priest under David and Solomon (1 Kings 1:26). Because the prophet Ezekiel had stated that only the "sons of Zadok" could "approach Yahweh" in the Temple service (Ezek. 40:46), the Sadducees, the officiating priests at the Jerusalem sanctuary,

Detail from the Arch of Titus, which the Roman Senate erected in the Forum of Rome about 100 CE. Created in honor of Titus' victories in the Jewish War, this frieze depicts Roman soldiers carrying off loot from the Jerusalem Temple, including the Menorah—the seven-branched candelabrum formerly housed in the sanctuary. (Courtesy of Art Resource, New York.)

emphasized their inherited right to this role. High Priests like **Caiaphas** (who condemned Jesus) were apparently always of their number. Along with their opponents the Pharisees, the Sadducees dominated the Great Council (Sanhedrin), Judaism's highest court of religious law.

The Sadducees and the Romans. Although the New Testament and Josephus give us an incomplete picture of the group, the Sadducees seem to have acted as the chief mediators between the Jewish people and the occupying Roman forces. As beneficiaries of the Roman-maintained political order, the Sadducees had the most to lose from civil disorder and typically opposed a Jewish nationalism that might attempt to overthrow the status quo. Their adoption of Hellenistic customs and their friendship with Rome made it possible for them to manipulate some Palestinian political affairs. The Sadducees' determination to preserve the uneasy accommodation with Rome is revealed in their eagerness to get rid of Jesus, whom they ap-

parently regarded as a potential revolutionary and a threat to Judea's political security. Their view that rebellion against Rome would lead to total annihilation of the Jewish nation was vindicated during the Jewish Revolt (66–73 CE), when Roman troops decimated Jerusalem and Judea.

As conservative religiously as they were politically, the Sadducees practiced a literal reading of the Torah, rejecting the Pharisees' "oral law" and other interpretations of the biblical text. It is uncertain how much of the Prophets or Writings they accepted, but they did not share Pharisaic beliefs about a coming judgment, resurrection, angels, or demons (Mark 12:18; Acts 23:8). As a group, the Sadducees did not survive the first Christian century. Their close association with Rome, their refusal to accept developing ideas based on the Prophets, the Writings, and the Apocrypha, and their narrow concentration on Temple ritual spelled their doom. After the Temple's destruction (70 CE), the Sadducees disappear from history. The Pharisees, emphasizing education and progressive reinterpretation of Scripture, became the founders of modern Judaism.

The Pharisees

The Gospels' bitter attacks on the **Pharisees,** who are shown as Jesus' leading opponents, have made Pharisee synonymous with hypocrisy and heartless legalism (Matt. 23). To the Gospel writers the Pharisees and their associates the **scribes** are "blind guides" who perversely reject Jesus' message and thereby doom their people to divine punishment (Matt 21:33–46; 22:1–14; 23:37–39; Luke 19:41–44). Modern historians recognize, however, that the Gospels' picture of the Pharisees is biased and unfair. According to most scholars, the Evangelists' antagonism toward the group stems not so much from the historical Jesus' debates with the Pharisees as from the historical situation at the time the Gospels were composed. Written several decades after Jesus' death, the Gospels reflect a period of intense ill feeling between the early Christian community and the Jewish leadership.

Hostility between the church and synagogue climaxed following the Roman destruction of Jerusalem in 70 CE. In the years immediately after Jerusalem's fall, the Pharisees became the dominant force within Judaism and the chief spokesmen for the position that Jesus of Nazareth was not the expected Jewish Messiah. Although Jews and Christians had previously worshipped side by side in the Temple, following the failure of the Jewish War against Rome, Jewish-Christian relations deteriorated badly. After about 90 CE Jewish Christians were expelled from the synagogues and condemned as perverters of the Jewish heritage (see John 9). The Gospels preserve the Christian response in their rancorous denunciations of the Pharisees.

Whatever their quarrel with the historical Jesus may have been, as a group the Pharisees were completely devoted to the Mosaic Torah and to applying it to all the concerns of daily life. The meaning of their name is obscure, although it seems to have been derived from the Hebrew verb "to separate." As spiritual descendants of the **Hasidim,** who separated themselves from what they saw as the corrupting influence of Hellenistic culture, the Pharisees rigorously observed a code of ritual purity. They scrupulously segregated themselves from contaminating contact with anything that the Law forbade.

Strict Torah observance. Many Pharisees were deeply learned in the Torah and skilled at its interpretation. Josephus states that the common people regarded them as the most authoritative interpreters of the Law. Unlike their rivals, the Sadducees, the Pharisees accepted not only the written Law contained in the Mosaic Torah but also a parallel oral law. This orally transmitted "tradition of the elders" (Mark 7:3), an extensive and ever-growing body of legalistic interpretation that the **rabbis** ("teachers") had compiled over many centuries, was eventually codified in the Mishnah about 200 CE. The **Mishnah,** which contains a wealth of rabbinic commentary on the Law and its application, is the first part of the **Talmud,** a vast written collection of religious material, some of which originated in oral form before the time of Jesus.

Hillel and Shammai. Two influential Pharisaic leaders whose teachings are remembered in the rabbinic commentaries were Hillel and Shammai, who lived into the first decades of the first century CE. A famous anecdote illustrates the striking differences in temperament of these two eminent Pharisees. It was said that a Gentile persistently besought Shammai, known for his aloof personality and strict interpretation of the Law, to explain the essential meaning of the Law while the Gentile stood on one foot. Appalled that anyone could be simple enough to imagine that the profundities of the Mosaic revelation could be articulated in a single phrase, Shammai sent the Gentile packing. Undaunted, the Gentile then went to Hillel with the same question. Taking the man's inquiry as sincere, Hillel is said to have replied: "Do not do to your neighbor what is hateful to yourself. That is the entire Torah. All the rest is commentary." Although expressed negatively, Hillel's concise summary of the Law's human significance anticipates Jesus' expression of the golden rule (Matt. 7:12).

Despite his remembered disagreements with Pharisees on how the Law should be practiced, Jesus is known to have been on good terms with some of their number, dining at their homes, and even benefiting from a friendly warning about a plot on his life (Luke 7:36–50; 13:31–32). Matthew's Gospel depicts Jesus as sharing the Pharisees' view that the Law is eternally binding (Matt. 5:17–19) and that they interpret it correctly (Matt. 23:2–3). On numerous matters of belief Jesus and the Pharisees see eye-to-eye (Mark 11:18–26). Unlike the Sadducees, they believe in a coming judgment day, resurrection of the dead, a future life of rewards and penalties based on deeds in this life, and the existence of angels, demons, and other inhabitants of the invisible world. By devotedly studying the Hebrew Bible and flexibly adapting its principles to the constantly changing situation in which Jews found themselves, the Pharisees depended on neither the possession of the Temple nor the promised land to perpetuate the Jewish faith. Some may have been rigid or overly ingenious in their application of the Torah's requirements, perhaps making the Law impossible for the poor or ignorant to keep (Matt. 23:6–23). As a group, however, they pursued a standard of religious commitment and personal righteousness that was virtually unique in the ancient world.

Gamaliel. It was Gamaliel, a leading first-century Pharisee reputed to be the Apostle Paul's teacher (Acts 5:34), who protected the early Christian movement from undue persecution by the Jerusalem authorities (Acts 5:34–42). Paul remained proud of his Pharisaic education even after he had been converted to Christianity (Acts 23:6–9; Phil. 3:4–7), appealing for support from his fellow Pharisees when he stood trial before the Jerusalem religious council.

The Essenes

Because their group was described in the writings of Josephus and Philo of Alexandria, historians have known of the Essenes for centuries. The **Essenes'** importance became fully evident, however, only when remnants of their library were discovered in 1947, hidden for nearly two millennia in caves along the northwest shore of the Dead Sea. Known as the **Dead Sea Scrolls,** this Essene collection was presumably stored in caves shortly before the Romans destroyed the Essene community of **Qumran** during the Jewish Revolt (68 CE).

The Dead Sea Scrolls contain not only the oldest surviving copies of the Hebrew Bible—some texts nearly a thousand years older than any previously known copies—but also a large selection of nonbiblical writings. Among the latter are several books composed by the sectarian community itself, including a detailed war plan for defeating and expelling the Roman armies from the Holy Land. Called the *War of the Sons of Light Against the Sons of Darkness,* this work reveals a characteristic Essene dualism in which the world, both material and spiritual, is divided into opposing camps of light and darkness, good and evil, God and the Devil. As God's agents, the Essenes trained for the holy war of **Armageddon,** in which God would vanquish the forces of evil, beginning with the plague of darkness represented by the occupying Roman force. Other original Essene books include a *Manual of Discipline,* containing requirements and goals for life in the Qumran community; collections of hymns and rules for liturgical worship; a list of predictions about the Messiah; and rules to direct life during the Messiah's reign. One of the most interesting of Essene writings is the commentary on the Book of Habakkuk, in which the ancient Hebrew prophet's words are applied exclusively to the history of the Qumran community. Christians later emulated this Essene practice by applying the entire Hebrew Bible to their community.

The Essenes and Christianity. After the Qumran library's discovery, scholars lost no time in finding numerous parallels between Essene beliefs and practices and those of early Christianity. Both communities regarded themselves as the "new Israel" and saw themselves as heirs to the biblical promises Yahweh had made to the Jewish people. Both parties agreed that the Jewish nation as a whole had broken Yahweh's covenant by failing to keep Torah requirements. According to this view, God had withdrawn his favor from the Jewish community and given it instead to a faithful minority, their particular group. The Essenes refused to accept the Sadducee-directed priesthood at the Jerusalem Temple, substituting their own ritual for priestly sacrifices. The Essene description of a communal meal of bread and wine seems to anticipate Christian observance of the Last Supper.

While some Essenes lived in towns and raised families, the Essene desert communities like Qumran were monastic. Their members practiced celibacy (abstinence from sexual activity), held all things in common, avoided trade and symbols of wealth, and led an austere, hardworking existence—practices not unlike those of the first Christians described in Acts and the Pauline letters.

The New Testament is silent on the Essenes, their desert monastery, and their dedicated lives of pious scholarship. The absence of references to the Essenes may reflect the fact that by the time the Gospels were written the sect had ceased to exist as an identifiable group. Some historians, however, suggest that the Gospels' silence may reflect their authors' consciousness that Jesus and his first disciples may have been influenced by Essene teachings.

Although a few scholars argue that Jesus spent the "lost years" between ages twelve and thirty as a member of the Essene community, the suggestion has not been widely accepted. By contrast, **John the Baptist**—whom the Gospels paint as a desert ascetic condemning Jewish religious and political leadership and preaching a doctrine of repentance before an impending holocaust—seems to echo some of the Essenes' characteristic views. What relationship John might have had to the Essene movement, however, remains conjectural.

The Zealots

Known for their passionate commitment to Jewish religious and political freedom, the **Zealots** formed a party dedicated to evicting the Romans from Palestine. Opposition to the Roman occupation that began in 63 BCE flared repeatedly during the first century CE, climaxing in the Jewish War against Rome (66–73 CE). In 6 CE a Jewish patriot known as **Judas the Galilean** led an armed rebellion that fueled nationalistic hopes but which the Romans crushed easily. Simon, one of Jesus' disciples, is called a "zealot" (Luke 6:15; Acts 1:13), and in Acts a parallel is drawn between Jesus' activity and that of Judas (Acts 5:37–39), causing some historians to suspect that Jesus may also have been involved in some form of rebellion against Rome. Most scholars, however, believe that Simon's designation as a "zealot" probably refers to his zeal or enthusiasm for the Law and that Jesus firmly refused to become involved in any political schemes (Mark 8:33; 10:38–39; Luke 24:21; Acts 1:6).

Although many Jews had fought against foreign oppression since the time of the Maccabees, the Zealots probably did not constitute an identifiable political party until shortly before the revolt against Rome began in 66 CE. According to Josephus, the Zealots' blind nationalism forced the Palestinian Jews on a suicidal course. In his history of the Jewish War, Josephus argues that it was the Zealots' refusal to surrender, even after Jerusalem had been captured, and their occupation of the Temple precincts that compelled the Romans to destroy the sanctuary. According to Josephus, General Titus, the Roman

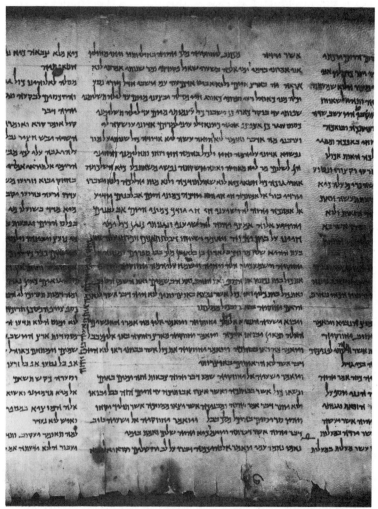

A passage from one of the Dead Sea Scrolls (1Q Isa. 49:12). Placed in clay jars and hidden in caves near the Dead Sea, the Essene library from the Qumran monastery includes the oldest surviving copies of the Hebrew Bible (Old Testament). (Courtesy of The Shrine of the Book, Israel Museum, Jerusalem.)

commander-in-chief, had not originally intended to commit this desecration. This catastrophe and the later Bar Kochba rebellion of 132–135 CE discredited both the Zealot party and its apocalyptic hope of divine intervention in achieving national liberation. Thanks to the Zealot failures, both armed revolution and end-of-the-world predictions were henceforth repudiated by mainstream Judaism.

The Messiah: First-Century Expectations

Given the vast diversity of first-century Judaism, we should not expect to find general agreement between different Jewish groups about the nature and function of the **Messiah.** It seems that the Sadducees denied that there would be one, while the Essenes anticipated two separate figures who would, respectively, fill either a priestly or a political role. The Christian view that Jesus of Nazareth was the Messiah was not accepted by mainstream Judaism for a variety of reasons that will become clearer as we study the Gospels (see Chapters 6–10). Among other things, it appears that many Jews questioned the biblical correctness of Jesus' teaching and the "shameful" manner of his death. The Hebrew prophets did not foresee that Israel's deliverer would be executed as a criminal by Gentiles (John 7:12, 27, 31, 40–44), making the crucifixion "a stumbling block" to scripturally literate Jews (1 Cor. 1:23). Mark's Gospel reflects these objections and emphasizes the unexpected or "hidden" quality of Jesus' messiahship.

The Royal Covenant of King David

Despite the heated debates between Jewish and Christian viewpoints preserved in the Gospels, it is possible to draw a general picture of Israel's concept of the Messiah by tracing its development in the Hebrew Bible. Derived from the Hebrew word *mashiah,* Messiah means "anointed one" and refers to the ceremony in which priests anointed (poured oil) on the heads of persons singled out or commissioned by God for some special undertaking. In the Hebrew Bible, *mashiah* is most frequently applied to the kings of ancient Israel, particularly those descended from King David (Ps. 18:50; 89:20, 38, 51; 132:10, 17). Because of his outstanding success in establishing a powerful Israelite state, David was regarded as the prototype of the divinely favored ruler and his kingdom a foreshadowing of the reign of God on earth. According to 2 Samuel 7, Yahweh concluded an "everlasting covenant" or treaty with David's "house" (dynasty). The covenant terms specified Yahweh's unconditional promise to maintain an unending line of Davidic kings on the throne of Israel. If certain of David's royal descendants misbehaved, Yahweh would punish

them, but he vowed never to remove them from the throne (2 Sam. 7:8–17; 23:1–5). Perhaps as a result of this "royal covenant theology" David's heirs ruled uninterrupted over the land of Judah for nearly four hundred years (961–587 BCE). (By contrast, the northern kingdom of Israel, separated from Judah in 922 BCE, saw many changes of ruling families before its destruction by the Assyrians in 721 BCE.)

Historical end of the Davidic dynasty. David's line of reigning kings came to an abrupt end in 587 BCE, when Nebuchadnezzar of Babylon destroyed Jerusalem, burned King Solomon's Temple, and removed the last Davidic monarch, Zedekiah, from the throne. Nebuchadnezzar also deported many upper-class Jews to his imperial capital. When a devoted remnant of Jews returned to Jerusalem from Babylon in 538 BCE, the Davidic monarchy was not restored. The land of Judah was placed under the administration of the Persian Empire, which installed local governors rather than kings over its Jewish subjects. The first of these Persian-appointed governors was Zerubbabel, a descendant of the Davidic family. Zerubbabel was apparently the focus of national hopes for a restoration of the Davidic kingdom and was hailed in messianic terms by the prophets Haggai and Zechariah (Hag. 2:20–23; Zech. 2:10, 6:12). Hopes for a renewed Davidic state failed to materialize, however, and the figure of Zerubbabel disappeared from history. Israel was never again to have a Davidic king, the "anointed of God."

During the long years of Persian rule, the Jewish people looked mainly to the spiritual leadership of their High Priest (who was also anointed with holy oil when installed in office [Lev. 4:3, 5]). The High Priest and his many priestly assistants administered the rebuilt Temple and provided a focus of communal religious identity. Without a king or political autonomy, Judah became increasingly a theocratic (God-ruled) community, guided by a priestly class that supervised the Temple sacrifices and interpreted the Mosaic Torah.

Israel's Hopes for a New Davidic King

Even after many centuries of foreign domination, as Judah was successively ruled by Babylonians, Persians, Greeks, Syrians, and Romans, Israel's collective memory of the Davidic Covenant did not fade. Yahweh's sworn oath that his people would have a Davidic heir to rule them forever (2 Sam. 7; 23:1–5; Ps. 89:19–31) was reinforced by Israel's prophets, who envisioned a future golden age when a man like David, "anointed of God," would rise to liberate Israel, defeat its enemies, and help bring God's kingdom to earth.

The prophet Isaiah of Jerusalem, who was a staunch supporter of the Davidic monarchy during the late eighth century BCE, had delivered unforgettable oracles (prophetic words) from Yahweh:

> For a boy has been born for us, a son given to us
> > to bear the symbol of dominion on his shoulder;
> > > and he shall be called
> > > in purpose wonderful, in battle
> > > God-like,
> > > Father for all time, Prince of peace.
>
> Great shall the dominion be and boundless the peace
> > bestowed on David's throne and on his kingdom,
> > to establish it and sustain it with justice and
> > righteousness from now and for evermore.
>
> The zeal of the LORD [Yahweh] of Hosts shall do this.
>
> (Isa. 9:6–7)

Isaiah's further allusions to a righteous king "from the stock of Jesse (David's father)" (Isa. 11:1–9) and visions of a Davidic Jerusalem to which the Gentile nations would flock (Isa. 2:1–4) not only enhanced the prestige of the Davidic royal family but associated it irrefutably with the coming earthwide reign of Yahweh.

The Messiah as a political leader. All of Israel's Davidic kings were literally "messiahs," "anointed ones." They ruled as Yahweh's "sons," adopted as such at the time of their consecration or coronation (Ps. 2:7). Because the prophets had conceived of the Messiah as a warrior-king like David, a hero whom Yahweh chose to act as his agent in establishing a dominion of universal peace, the messianic leader was typically regarded as primarily a political figure. His function was to demonstrate the omnipotence of Israel's God by setting up an earthly kingdom whose righteous government would compel the nations' respect for both Yahweh and his chosen people (Isa. 11; Dan. 2:44).

A Christian View of the Messiah

As presented in the Gospels, Jesus of Nazareth takes a view of the Messiah's role and the kingdom of God that was disappointing or perplexing to many. Despite some modern commentators' attempts to associate him with the Zealot or revolutionary party, Jesus (as portrayed by the Evangelists) does not present himself as a military or political savior of Israel. As John's Gospel concludes, his "kingdom does not belong to this world" (John 18:36).

Jesus' multiple role. Despite Jesus' reluctance to assert his right to rule Israel, the Gospel writers nonetheless are convinced that he is the same Messiah whose life Isaiah and the other Hebrew prophets foresaw. In identifying Jesus as Israel's Messiah, however, the New Testament authors broaden his role beyond that of the largely political nature of the prophesied Davidic ruler. To defend Jesus against charges that he "failed" to reestablish David's kingdom, early Christians pointed to certain passages in the Hebrew Bible that seemed to them to illustrate the nature of Jesus' unexpected messiahship. In Christian interpretations of the Messiah, he became the "prophet like Moses" described in Deuteronomy (18:15–20) and the mysterious "suffering servant" in Isaiah (52:13–53:12). In the original texts neither the Mosaic prophet nor the anonymous servant is associated with the Messiah, and we do not know whether these two unidentified figures were given a messianic emphasis before the Christian period. Isaiah's "Song of the Suffering Servant," dramatizing the unjust punishment of a righteous man who suffers for the sins of others and thereby somehow redeems them, became a crucial text for explaining the theological significance of Jesus' death (Mark 10:45). Psalms 22, which records the lament of a man tormented by Gentile enemies, was also used to reinforce the Christian view that the true Messiah was destined to suffer. The Christian concept of the Messiah is a paradox: a God-anointed king who is rejected and dies, but whose voluntary death is a triumph over forces of darkness and evil and a source of hope for mortal humanity.

After studying the New Testament documents, the student will see that their authors present Jesus as far more than a Davidic king. Taken together, the canonical writings present Jesus as a composite figure, one who represents the sum of all Israel's heritage. He is not only the anointed monarch whom David foreshadowed; he is also a lawgiver and prophet like Moses, a blameless and humble servant who suffers for others, a heavenly sacrifice and eternal priest, a teacher of supreme wisdom, and the icon or "image of the invisible God" by, through, and for whom the universe was created.

Translating the Hebrew *mashiah* as the Greek *Christos*, the New Testament writers commonly speak as if **Christ** were not a title but part of Jesus' proper name. Composed in a Hellenistic context and for a Greek-thinking audience, the New Testament books present Jesus almost exclusively in his function as Christ, a universal savior whose role goes far beyond that of the Davidic ruler. In interpreting Jesus' religious meaning, the New Testament authors apply to their hero many different concepts borrowed from the rich lore of Hellenistic Jewish ideas about the Messiah.

QUESTIONS FOR DISCUSSION AND REVIEW

1. Describe the concepts or beliefs common to most groups of first-century Judaism. How was the ideal of Jewish monotheism related to Torah practice and the Temple cult?
2. Define some essential differences between the Sadducees and Pharisees. Which party controlled the Jerusalem Temple and was apparently on better terms with the Romans?
3. Discuss some of the beliefs that Pharisees, Essenes, and Christians held in common. What connection did the Essenes have to the Dead Sea Scrolls and possibly to John the Baptist?
4. Discuss the role that the Zealots played in the Jewish Revolt against Rome. What happened to the Jewish state and religion as a result of the revolt? How does Josephus contribute to our understanding of the Jewish war for independence?
5. Summarize the concept of the Messiah found in the Hebrew Bible. To what degree is the biblical Messiah a political figure related to the restoration of King David's royal dynasty? How do New Testament writers modify the concept of the Davidic Messiah?

TERMS AND CONCEPTS

Yahweh	oral law (traditions of
Torah	the fathers)
Abrahamic Covenant	Mishnah
Yom Kippur (Day of	Essenes
Atonement)	Dead Sea Scrolls
Jews	Zealots
Sadducees	apocalyptic
Pharisees	Messiah

RECOMMENDED READING

Grant, F. C. *Roman Hellenism and the New Testament.* New York: Scribner's, 1962.

Hengel, Martin. *Jews, Greeks, and Barbarians: Aspects of the Hellenism of Judaism in the Pre-Christian Period.* Philadelphia: Fortress Press, 1980.

Jeremias, Joachim. *Jerusalem in the Time of Jesus.* Translated by F. H. Cave and C. H. Cave. London: SCM Press, 1969. Of broader scope than its title implies, discusses Palestinian economic, social, and religious conditions at the time of Jesus.

Josephus. *The Jewish War.* Rev. ed. Translated by G. A. Williamson. Edited by E. M. Smallwood. New York: Penguin Books, 1981. Our most important contemporary source for conditions in Palestine during the first century CE.

———. *Josephus: Complete Works.* Translated by W. Whiston. Grand Rapids, Mich.: Kregel Publications, 1960. A dated translation, but containing the complete texts of *The Antiquities of the Jews* and *The Jewish War,* as well as the "Discourse on Hades."

Lohse, Eduard. *The New Testament Environment.* Translated by J. E. Steely. Nashville: Abingdon Press, 1976.

Sandmel, Samuel. *Judaism and Christian Beginnings.* New York: Oxford University Press, 1978.

Stone, M. E. *Scriptures, Sects and Visions: A Profile of Judaism from Ezra to the Jewish Revolts.* Philadelphia: Fortress Press, 1980. A readable survey.

FOR MORE ADVANCED STUDY

Hengel, Martin. *Judaism and Hellenism.* 2 vols. Philadelphia: Fortress Press, 1974. A thorough and detailed analysis of Hellenistic influences on Jewish thought during the period between the Old and New Testaments.

Pharisees, Essenes, and Other Jewish Sects

Finkelstein, Louis. *The Pharisees.* 2 vols. Philadelphia: Jewish Publication Society of America, 1962. Provides reliable information.

Gaster, T. H. *The Dead Sea Scrolls in English Translation.* Rev. ed. Garden City, N.Y.: Doubleday, 1964.

Gowan, D. E. *Bridge Between the Testaments: A Reappraisal of Judaism from the Exile to the Birth of Christianity.* 2d ed. Pittsburgh: Pickwick Press, 1980.

Neusner, Jacob. *From Politics to Piety: The Emergence of Pharisaic Judaism.* Englewood Cliffs, N.J.: Prentice-Hall, 1973.

Ringgren, Helmer. *The Faith of Qumran.* Philadelphia: Fortress Press, 1981.

Rivkin, Ellis. "Defining the Pharisees." *Hebrew Union College Annual,* 1970, 205–49.

Simon, Marcel. *Jewish Sects at the Time of Jesus.* Philadelphia: Fortress Press, 1967.

Vermes, Geza. *The Dead Sea Scrolls: Qumran in Perspective.* London: Collins, 1977.

6   *The Gospels: Form and Purpose*

Many writers have undertaken to draw up an account
of the events that have happened among us [the early
Christian community] following the traditions handed
down to us by the original eyewitnesses and servants
of the Gospel.

(Luke 1:1–2)

KEY THEMES   This chapter examines the Gospel form in light of modern New Testament
scholarship. It discusses the assumptions that underlie various approaches to
studying the Gospels; it then outlines the goals and methods that scholars
use to explain the similarities and differences of the four separate portraits
of Jesus.

The first section of the New Testament contains four separate and distinct accounts of Jesus' life. The early Christian community produced many other **Gospels**—narratives about Jesus or collections of his sayings—but only these four were generally recognized among early Christian churches as authoritative and suitable for teaching.

Despite significant differences in theme and emphasis, the first three Gospels—Matthew, Mark, and Luke—bear a striking resemblance to each other. So similar are these three that one can arrange their contents in parallel columns (Box 6-1) and typically compare their three versions of the same saying or incident in Jesus' life at a single glance. In general, all three follow the same order or sequence of events. Because they present Jesus' biography from essentially the same viewpoint, they are called **Synoptic** (seeing the whole together).

In contrast to the Synoptic Gospels stands the narrative "According to John." Whereas the first three contain a large amount of material in common, the Fourth Gospel consists mostly of strikingly different accounts of Jesus' deeds and speeches. The general story is the same—a pub-

lic ministry of healing and teaching followed by rejection and death in Jerusalem—but ninety percent of John's version is unique. In John the order of events, the geographical location of Jesus' ministry, and the manner in which Jesus speaks and refers to himself reflect a portrait of Christ profoundly different from that painted in the Synoptics.

The importance of Mark. Because it contains almost nothing not found in Matthew and/or Luke, Mark is perhaps the least read of the Gospels. According to one ancient tradition, it is only a summary of Matthew, trimmed to meet the tastes of a Roman audience. Since the beginning of this century, however, scholars have accorded Mark a crucial importance. Although a few still argue that Matthew was written first, most New Testament scholars now believe that Mark is our earliest Gospel, the first attempt to record the life of Jesus. If the scholars are right, then the similarities of the three Synoptics can be explained by the assumption that Matthew and Luke both used Mark as a major source of their own Gospels.

The Gospels and Modern Scholarship

Clarifying the relationship of the three Synoptic Gospels—known as the Synoptic Problem—is one of several major goals of modern scholarship. Using the techniques of historical analysis, literary criticism, and other academic disciplines, New Testament scholars have been able to shed considerable light on the process by which the Gospels developed from the oral preaching of the early Christian community. By carefully examining both the similarities and differences between Mark, Matthew, and Luke, we can gain valuable insight into their respective authors' purposes in their diverse presentations of Jesus' words and deeds.

Assumptions and Approaches

How we undertake a study of the Gospels depends largely on our preconceptions about their nature and the kind of religious authority they represent. Approaches range from an uncritical acceptance of every Gospel statement at face value to an intense skepticism that denies the works any historical credibility. Between these two extremes lie a great variety of viewpoints, each with its characteristic assumptions—standards and attitudes that are taken for granted. These sometimes-unconscious assumptions can profoundly influence the reader's understanding of the Gospel text, predetermining its meaning.

Inerrancy. Because our conclusions are typically shaped by our presuppositions, it is helpful to clarify some common attitudes toward the Gospels. One view holds that the text is infallible and inerrant—that, when translated and interpreted "properly," all canonical books contain no historical or factual errors. This view assumes that divine inspiration—the mysterious process by which God is believed to reveal otherwise inaccessible truths to individual Bible writers—is a form of dictation in which the human being is primarily the passive recorder of the Deity's message.

Literalism. Persons advocating the absolute inerrancy of biblical texts also commonly interpret them literally, accepting each recorded incident and speech as a factually exact record of what was done and spoken. In the literalist view, Mark's accounts of Jesus' conversations with demons and evil spirits represent historical events that the author reproduces precisely as they happened (Mark 1:23–27; 3:10–12; 5:1–20).

The inerrancy approach places an extremely high value on factual accuracy. It presupposes that religious insights are somehow validated if they can be shown to have a basis in actual historical occurrences. Conversely, to cast doubt on the historicity of any element in the biblical text is to undermine its religious authority or significance. This presumed interdependence of material fact and religious value characterizes the fundamentalist position. An American Protestant movement that began in the early 1900s, fundamentalism adopts as its basic tenet the assumption that the Bible's entire content is free from error and that its text is to be interpreted strictly according to explicit statements made therein.

After reading all four Gospels attentively, however, many students may question the adequacy of the inerrancy principle. The four accounts do not agree even on such basic matters as the order of events in Jesus' ministry. The Synoptics state that Jesus drove moneychangers from the Jerusalem Temple at the close of his ministry, whereas John's Gospel places the event near the beginning. Mark and Matthew agree that Jesus' public career was well under way before his former neighbors at Nazareth rejected him (Mark 6; Matt. 13), but Luke puts the rejection at the outset of Jesus' mission, adding that his fellow townspeople tried to kill him (Luke 4:16–30). Mark declares unequivocally that John baptized Jesus, whereas Luke implies that John was already imprisoned when Jesus underwent baptism (Mark 1:9; Luke 3:19–21). Which version is inerrant?

Alert students also discover that the Gospels preserve significantly different versions of the same saying or teaching of Jesus. Did Jesus originally say "how blest are those who hunger and thirst to see right prevail" (Matt. 5:6) or the more simple "how blest are you who now go hungry" (Luke 6:21)? And did he deliver the famous sermon that contains these words on a mountain, as Matthew asserts, or on level ground as Luke maintains? Perceptive readers may suspect that the Gospel authors had goals other than merely preserving literal facts when they composed their narratives about Jesus.

Historical-analytical approach. Whereas the fundamentalist position assumes that the Gospels' inerrancy is a precondition of their religious worth, other presuppositions allow a more flexible approach. Many students perceive that the value of Jesus' teachings does not necessarily depend on their having been recorded word for word precisely as he uttered them. (The fact that Jesus spoke Aramaic whereas the Gospels are written in Greek automatically makes such precision impossible.) As a basic principle of investigation, this textbook assumes that the differences—even contradictions—among the four Gospels do not undermine their religious or historical importance. Recognizing and analyzing the Gospels' discrepancies and inconsistencies, however, can reveal much about their writers' intentions and individual perceptions of Jesus' significance.

This author believes that the Gospels are best understood when studied in the context of the Greek-speaking Jewish-Christian community that produced them. This historical-analytical approach assumes that the more we know about first-century Jewish and Hellenistic language, literary forms, ideas, and religious beliefs, the better equipped we are to appreciate the original meaning and purpose of the New Testament.

Scholarship and Criticism

An international community of scholars—Roman Catholic, Protestant, Jewish, and others—use a wide variety of methods to illuminate the nature and growth of the New Testament documents. This cosmopolitan body of scholars, historians, textual experts, literary critics, archaeologists, sociologists, and theologians includes thousands of university faculty, clergy, seminary instructors, and academic researchers from many disciplines. Collectively, their efforts have provided us with an increasingly precise and well-documented study of the New Testament literature and the environment out of which it grew.

Before briefly describing the principal fields or branches of biblical scholarship, we should clarify the term *biblical criticism*. The word *criticism* may awaken negative feelings in some people—perhaps implying fault finding or an unfavorable judgment—but in biblical study it is a positive means of understanding scriptural texts more accurately and objectively. *Criticism* derives from the Greek word *krino*, which means "to judge" or "to discern," to exercise rational analysis in evaluating something. In the fields of art and literature, it involves the ability to recognize artistic worth and to distinguish among the relative merits or defects of a given work. The major kinds or methods of critical analysis are described below.

Literary analysis. Literary criticism is particularly helpful in reading the Bible and is a skill many careful readers have acquired. Every experienced student is a literary critic to some extent. The student reads not only to acquire information but also to recognize the author's main concerns and themes and the elements of character, plot, setting, and style by which the writer's views are expressed. The reader automatically assimilates clues—characteristic words, images, and phrases—that indicate the author's intent or purpose. In reading the Gospels, the student will note that each Evangelist stresses different aspects of Jesus' life and teachings, sometimes rearranging or rephrasing material found in other Gospels so as to give it a distinctive emphasis or interpretation.

Historical analysis. Whereas literary criticism seeks to discover the meaning of a written text as we now have it, historical criticism attempts to understand the historical circumstances in which that text was first written. The historical critic investigates such matters as the time and place of a document's composition, its authorship, the author's sources, and the intended recipients or audience of the work. The historian also examines various social and cultural forces that may have influenced the writer's views of his subject.

The historical critic also tries to answer the question What really happened? Because the Gospels are as much declarations of faith in Jesus' unique revelation as they are attempts to record literal history, the historian must examine them to determine which components are based on historical fact and which are shaped by the authors' theological convictions. One major pursuit of historical criticism has become known as the "quest for the historical Jesus." This quest is the scholars' endeavor to discover the "real" Jesus of history behind the Gospels' religious interpretation of him. In their search to recover Jesus as a human being, scholars endeavor to distinguish sayings and deeds of Jesus from those later attributed to him by the Christian community and then included in the Gospels.

The problem is compounded by the fact that the Gospels were written from forty to sixty years after Jesus' death and are apparently not the work of eyewitnesses. In addition, the authors do not identify themselves in their respective texts, nor do any of them state when or where they wrote or—except for Luke—for whom they intended their work. The traditional Gospel titles—"the Gospel According to Mark," or "Matthew," or "John"—appear to be headings added late in the second century CE, long after the Gospels themselves were written. Careful study of the Gospel texts does not confirm the traditional authorship. For convenience we continue to refer to the authors by their traditional names, but it is a disappointing fact that scholarship as yet has found no way to identify the four Evangelists.

Relationship of the Synoptic Gospels

Mark's priority. Historical analysis has contributed enormously to establishing the relative age and order of composition of the four Gospels. After nearly a century of exhaustive study, the majority of scholars now agree that Mark was written first and that the other two Synoptic writers, Matthew and Luke, followed Mark's general outline, into which they incorporated material from various other sources.

The Griesbach theory. An alternative theory holds that Matthew and Luke were written before Mark. According to this view, Mark is a conflation (blending together) and abridgment of the other two Synoptics. Known as the Griesbach theory, after Johann J. Griesbach (1745–1812), who first published this solution to the Synoptic Problem, this hypothesis recently has won the allegiance of several conservative scholars, notably William R. Farmer. The new Anchor Bible translation and commentary on Mark (1986) by C. S. Mann adopts the Griesbach-Farmer hypothesis.

The two-document theory. Approximately ninety percent of scholars, however, believe that Mark is the earliest Gospel and that it forms the major source of both Matthew and Luke. According to the two-document theory, Matthew and Luke not only used Mark but also drew upon a second document, a written collection

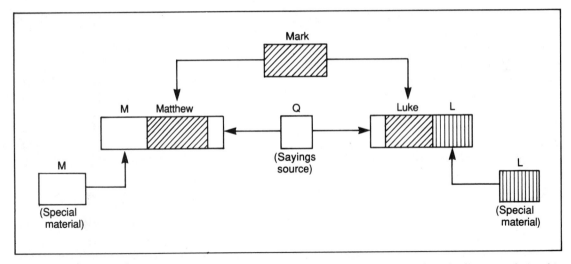

Figure 6-1. This drawing illustrates the two-document theory, an attempt to explain the literary relationship of the three Synoptic Gospels. Note that this theory takes Mark's Gospel as a major source for Matthew and Luke. In addition, both Matthew and Luke incorporate teaching material from Q (*Quelle,* a hypothetical collection of Jesus' sayings). Matthew also uses special material unique to his Gospel, here designated *M;* Luke similarly includes material found only in his account, here labeled *L.*

of Jesus' sayings. This hypothetical collection is known as **Q** (usually defined as *Quelle,* the German for "source").

Advocates of the two-document theory presume Q's former existence because there are many sayings not found in Mark that occur in both Matthew and Luke. Because many of these sayings appear in Matthew and Luke in almost identical form (or in very similar phrasing), scholars believe that they come from a written document rather than an orally transmitted memory of Jesus' words. The shared sayings (absent from Mark) include such famous passages as the "beatitudes" (blessings) (Matt. 5:1–10; Luke 6:20–23) and the "Lord's Prayer" (Matt. 6:9–13; Luke 11:1–4). Lack of proof that the Q document ever existed is a weakness in the two-source hypothesis, but thus far no scholar has advanced a more convincing explanation of why Matthew and Luke have many non-Markan sayings in common.

Special material. Whatever the origin of their shared sayings, Matthew and Luke also use ma-

terial peculiar to their individual Gospels. Although both add genealogies and birth stories to the Markan narrative, agreeing on Jesus' parentage and place of birth, each presents incidents distinctive to his version. Only Matthew has the mysterious star, the visit of the "magi" or astrologers, and King Herod's attempt to murder the infant Jesus. Luke has none of these elements but introduces an angelic song and a visit of shepherds to the birthplace. Similarly, Luke alone includes some of Jesus' most beloved parables, such as those involving the good Samaritan, the runaway son, and the unexpected fates of the beggar and the rich man. Clearly, each writer had access to information about Jesus not available to (or not used by) the other.

Methods of Critical Investigation

Form criticism. Form criticism combines the tools of literary and historical analysis. It recognizes that the Gospels are made up of many individual units—brief narrative episodes, parables, and sayings—that circulated orally and independently of one another before the Gospel writers incorporated them into their narratives. Mark's Gospel, for example, seems to consist of a string of incidents and sayings that are very loosely connected to each other. The individual units are generally self-contained, brief narrative episodes that have clear-cut beginnings and endings and can stand alone. They commonly do not depend on the larger Gospel context to convey their effect or meaning. Such brief units are called **pericopes.** Derived from the Greek *peri* ("about") and *koptein* ("to cut"), the term denotes the individual building blocks from which the longer Gospel account is constructed.

Form criticism looks behind the written form of a pericope to discover the older oral form in which it circulated before being written down. The form critic tries to discover the circumstances or "life setting" from which oral traditions about Jesus originated and were transmitted by the early church. The first Christians used oral traditions about Jesus in many ways—preaching to Jews, defending their beliefs to Greek or Roman officials, instructing new converts, settling disputes among themselves, and conducting worship services.

Form criticism has proved a great help in showing how Jesus' teachings were modified and adapted to fit the ever-changing circumstances and needs of early Christian life. By establishing the pre-written form of a particular saying or incident, the form critic also enables us to see how the Gospel writers edited these originally free-floating units to express their respective views about Jesus.

Redaction criticism. Form criticism concentrates on the stages of development particular stories about Jesus underwent before attaining their present literary form. Redaction criticism (from the German *Redaktions-geschichte*) stresses the role of the individual Gospel writer in handling these older units of oral (and written) tradition. *Redaction* refers to the authorial process of editing and shaping material. This discipline's emphasis on the author's role in assembling,

rearranging, and reinterpreting older materials has revealed an important fact: the Evangelists were not only biographers but also conscious interpreters of their subject. Each one presented Jesus' life from a distinctive theological perspective. In comparing the Synoptic Gospels, we see that Matthew and Luke did not slavishly or uncritically follow Mark. Although the two later Synoptic writers occasionally copy Mark verbatim, they more commonly modify or change the Markan version to express more closely their own understanding of Jesus' ministry and death. A careful reading of Mark himself indicates that he too compiled his materials to convey a particular theological viewpoint about Jesus. Because they are both heavily dependent on Mark and yet feel free to modify Mark's interpretation of events, Matthew and Luke are sometimes regarded as new, expanded editions of Mark's story of Jesus. No matter how similar the data used, the individual author's treatment of that data makes his Gospel theologically distinct from the others.

The Composite Portrait of Jesus

The fact that the primitive Christian community did not promote a single, uniform edition of Jesus' life or adopt one "official" version free of seeming contradictions is significant. Instead of an "authorized" biography, the church accepted the four canonical Gospels, perhaps recognizing that Jesus could not be reduced to any single viewpoint. As he elicited widely different responses during his lifetime, so he inspired the Evangelists to represent him in significantly different guises, ranging from the carpenter-prophet in Mark to the incarnate Word of God in John. This composite portrait, with all its attendant problems and unanswered questions, is the one deemed appropriate by the early community of faith.

Canonical criticism. Canonical criticism is a relatively new school of thought that stresses the importance of studying the four Gospels as

---

B O X 6–1   *Some Parallels Among the Four Gospels*

Mark (c. 65–70 CE)	Matthew (c. 80–85 CE)
• • •	• • •
• • •	• • •
• • •	1. Introduction to the Messiah: genealogy and infancy narrative (1:1–2:23).
1. Prelude to Jesus' public ministry (1:1–13).	2. The beginning of Jesus' proclamation: baptism, temptation, inauguration of Galilean ministry (3:1–4:25).
• • •	3. First major discourse: the Sermon on the Mount (5:1–7:29).
2. The Galilean ministry: inaugurating the kingdom (1:14–8:26).	4. First narrative section: ten miracles (8:1–9:28).
• • •	5. Second major discourse: instructions to the Twelve Apostles (10:1–42).
• • •	6. Second narrative section: questions and controversies (11:1–12:50).
• • •	7. Third major discourse: parables on the kingdom (13:1–52).
3. The journey to Jerusalem (8:26–10:52).	8. Third narrative section: from the rejection in Nazareth to the transfiguration (13:53–17:27).
	9. Fourth major discourse: instructions to the church (18:1–35).
	• • •
4. The Jerusalem ministry and Passion story (11:1–15:47). Postlude: the empty tomb (16:1–8).	10. Fourth narrative section: the Jerusalem ministry (19:1–22:46).
• • •	11. Fifth major discourse: warning of Final Judgment (23:1–25:46).
	12. Fifth and final narrative section: the Passion story and postresurrection appearances (26:1–28:20).
	• • •

• Indicates that the Gospel in question does not have material found in another Gospel. Note that John's Gospel contains much material not present in the three Synoptics.

---

they appear together in the New Testament canon. Instead of regarding each Gospel as an isolated unit, the canonical critic views the four works as a composite whole—four parts of a unified composition. The Gospels are to be interpreted in the context of their canonical position; standing side by side, the four narratives reflect different facets of Jesus' nature and meaning. Viewed together, the separate facets combine to create a coherent portrait of Christ that is greater than the sum of its parts. Canonical critics emphasize that the entire New Testament is a collective unity, the product of many individual voices singing essentially the same song—a celebration of God's achievement in Christ.

Although canonical criticism is useful in appreciating the New Testament as a literary whole, this book also respects the integrity of each particular document in the canonical library. This author believes that each New Testament book is best understood when studied as an independent work, reflecting the distinctive thought of its individual writer. Each book is examined on its own terms and in the context of its author's particular viewpoint without any attempt to make it conform to ideas expressed in any other book. By allowing each writer to speak for himself, we can recognize the rich diversity of New Testament Christianity as well as its thematic unity—the unparalleled significance of the Christ event. In studying the Gos-

---

BOX 6-1   *continued*

Luke (c. 85–90 CE)	John (c. 90–100 CE)

• • •

Luke (c. 85–90 CE)

1. Formal preface
2. Infancy narratives of the Baptist and Jesus (1:5–2:52).
3. Prelude to Jesus' ministry: baptism, genealogy, and temptation (3:1–4:13).

• • •

4. Jesus' Galilean ministry and Luke's "lesser interpolation" (4:14–9:50).

• • •

• • •

5. Jesus' teachings on the journey to Jerusalem, Luke's "greater interpolation" (9:51–18:14).
6. The Jerusalem ministry: Jesus' challenge to the holy city (18:31–21:38).
7. The final conflict and Passion story (22:1–23:56).
8. Epilogue: postresurrection appearances in the vicinity of Jerusalem (24:1–53).

• • •

John (c. 90–100 CE)

1. Prologue: Hymn to the Logos (Word); testimony of the Baptist (1:1–51).

• • •

• • •

2. The Book of Signs (2:1–11:57).
   a. The miracle at Cana
   b. The assault on the Temple (compare Mark II)
   c. Dialogue with Nicodemus
   d. Conversations with a Samaritan woman and a woman taken in adultery
   e. Five more miraculous signs in Jerusalem and Galilee; Jesus' discourses witnessing to his divine nature

   f. The resurrection of Lazarus (the seventh sign)
3. The book of Glory (12:1–20:31).
   a. The plot against Jesus
   b. The Last Supper and farewell discourses
   c. The Passion story
   d. The empty tomb and postresurrection appearances in Jerusalem
4. Epilogue: postresurrection appearances in Galilee; parting words to Peter and the beloved disciple (21:1–25).

---

pels, Paul's letters, and the other canonical writings, we benefit from all the scholarly tools that help illuminate the historical origins, the literary development, and the theological insights contained in the twenty-seven documents that became the standard bearers of the Christian faith.

QUESTIONS FOR DISCUSSION AND REVIEW

1. Discuss some of the factors that may have caused the early Christian community to produce several different versions of Jesus' life.

2. Define the "Synoptic Problem." Why do scholars believe that the first three canonical Gospels (Matthew, Mark, and Luke) have a literary interrelationship? In contrast to John (the Fourth Gospel), what factors indicate that the Synoptics depend upon a common tradition?

3. In what ways do our (sometimes unconscious) assumptions about the New Testament writings predetermine our understanding of the texts? How do the assumptions of the fundamentalist and historical critic differ?

4. Discuss the goals and methods of form and redaction criticism. In what ways do these schools of analysis help to illuminate the nature and meaning of traditions about Jesus?

5. The Gospel authors are not historians or biographers in the modern sense. Are the Gospel writers interested primarily in preserving historical facts about Jesus or in explaining and interpreting his life in religious terms? Cite specific characteristics of the Gospels to defend your answer.

6. The large majority of scholars believe that Mark's Gospel was the first one written and that Matthew and Luke later reedited it, inserting much additional material into the Markan framework (the two-document theory). A scholarly minority argues that Mark's Gospel is an abridgment and conflation of the two longer Synoptics (the Griesbach theory). Define and explain the two opposing theories about the literary relationship of the Synoptics.

TERMS AND CONCEPTS TO REMEMBER

the Synoptic Gospels
the Synoptic Problem
inerrancy
literalism
fundamentalism
Aramaic
the two-document
  theory

Griesbach theory
the Q (*Quelle*)
  Document
form criticism
redaction criticism
canonical criticism

RECOMMENDED READING

Bultmann, Rudolf. *The History of the Synoptic Tradition*. Translated by J. Marsh. New York: Harper & Row, 1963. A masterful, if somewhat technical, study by the great German scholar.

Farmer, W. R. *The Synoptic Problem*. New York: Macmillan, 1964. Argues for the priority of Matthew.

Gast, Frederick. "Synoptic Problem." in *The Jerome Biblical Commentary,* edited by R. E. Brown and J. A. Fitzmyer, 1–6. Englewood Cliffs, N.J.: Prentice-Hall, 1968. A brief introduction.

Grant, F. C. *The Gospels: Their Origin and Their Growth*. New York: Harper & Row, 1957. A useful introduction.

Kee, H. C. *Jesus in History: An Approach to the Study of the Gospels*. 2d ed. New York: Harcourt Brace Jovanovich, 1970. An insightful study by a leading New Testament scholar.

Koester, Helmut. *Introduction to the New Testament*. Vol. 2, *History and Literature of Early Christianity*. Philadelphia: Fortress Press, 1982. Translated from the original German, this is a major and incisive study of New Testament origins.

Kselman, J. S. "Modern New Testament Criticism." In *The Jerome Biblical Commentary,* edited by R. E. Brown and J. A. Fitzmyer. 7–20. Englewood Cliffs, N.J.: Prentice-Hall, 1968. The development of modern criticism reviewed by a Roman Catholic scholar.

Perry, A. M. "The Growth of the Gospels." In *The Interpreter's Bible*, vol. 7, 60–74. Nashville: Abingdon Press, 1951.

Streeter, B. H. *The Four Gospels*. London: Macmillan, 1924. A landmark scholarly study arguing that Mark is the earliest Gospel.

Throckmorton, B. H., ed. *Gospel Parallels: A Synopsis of the First Three Gospels*. 4th ed. New York: Thomas Nelson, 1979. A helpful tool for comparing the Synoptic Gospels side by side.

7 Mark's Story of Jesus

For even the Son of Man did not come to be served
but to serve and to give up his life as a ransom for
many.

(Mark 10:45)

KEY THEMES   Mark's Gospel is the shortest and simplest of the four, presenting Jesus as
an apocalyptic figure whose ministry heralds the end of the world.
Although Mark paints Jesus' miracles, exorcisms, and other activities with a
wealth of concrete detail, church tradition and modern scholarship agree
that the author was not an eyewitness of the events he vividly describes.
Themes peculiar to Mark include viewing Jesus as a "hidden" Messiah who
is consistently misunderstood by his disciples and the general public. Mark's
grim narrative stresses the necessity of Jesus' death and suffering and does
not include mention of his resurrection.

We begin our study of Jesus' adult life by reading Mark's Gospel. Although it appears second in the New Testament canon, Mark's narrative is probably the oldest and the basis for much that is in Matthew and Luke. It also presents a relatively direct and straightforward account. The reader must be warned, however, that despite Mark's apparent simplicity, his Gospel is artfully arranged to express his conception of Jesus' theological significance. Like his fellow Evangelists, the author is primarily concerned with advancing a religious understanding of Jesus, not with producing a complete or objective record of historical fact.

Today's reader may well wish that the Gospel writers had included more systematic information about Jesus' background and character, especially his personal view of himself and his mission. Certain elements in Jesus' story demand clarification, which neither Mark nor the later Gospel writers provide. Despite the four different versions of the event, it is still unclear exactly why Jesus was so bitterly denounced by Jewish authorities and judged a traitor by the Romans. As the reader will discover, Mark is not concerned with solving historical puzzles for us. Rather than reproducing the mass of physical detail that makes up a life, Mark is content to assemble a relatively small selection of his hero's actions and sayings to dramatize his conviction of Jesus' unique importance to all humanity.

Authorship and Date

The first reference to the authorship of Mark's Gospel is that of Papias, an early Christian writer who was bishop of Hierapolis about 130 or 140 BCE. According to the church historian Eusebius, Papias stated that Mark had been the Apostle Peter's disciple in Rome and based his Gospel account on Peter's reminiscences of Jesus. Papias notes that Mark "had not heard the Lord or been one of his followers" so that his account lacked "a systematic arrangement of the Lord's sayings" (Eusebius, *History* 3:39).

Besides Papias's intention to link the Gospel to apostolic testimony, we note two important historical observations in his remarks: (1) the author of Mark was not an eyewitness but depended on secondhand oral preaching, and (2)

Mark's version of Jesus' activities is "not in order." Careful scrutiny of Mark's Gospel has convinced most New Testament scholars that it does not derive from a single apostolic source (Peter). Rather, it is based on a multiplicity of teachings about Jesus that circulated in the author's Christian community. Some critics think that Mark's Gospel originated in Rome, but most believe that Syria or Palestine was the place of composition.

Papias's tradition asserts that Mark wrote shortly after Peter's death, which is believed to have occurred during the Emperor Nero's persecution of the Roman church in about 64–65 CE. Nothing in the Gospel gives a specific time of writing, but some of the author's major themes suggest that it was composed during a time of trouble when believers could expect to suffer for their faith as Jesus had (Mark 8:34–38; 10:38–40). This picture may reflect the period of Nero's persecution, when numerous Christians were crucified or burned alive. It may also echo the situation of Christians in Palestine or Syria during the Jewish Revolt against Rome (66–73 CE).

Another Markan theme also points to a date in the mid to late 60s CE. The longest speech that Mark attributes to Jesus is the prophesy of Jerusalem's destruction. This emphasis, along with the author's stress on wars and national uprisings, indicates that the Jewish Revolt had already begun and that Jerusalem could be expected to fall in the near future (Mark 13). These internal elements suggest that the Gospel was composed at some point between about 65 and 70 CE.

Organization of Mark's Gospel

Despite its apparent simplicity, Mark's Gospel is a subtle and complex work, its sequence of events arranged to reflect the author's views of Jesus' ministry and death (see Box 6-1). The narrative can be divided into five parts:

1. Prelude to Jesus' public ministry (1:1–13)
2. The Galilean ministry: inaugurating the kingdom (1:14–8:26)
3. The journey to Jerusalem (8:27–10:52)
4. The Jerusalem ministry (11:1–15:47)
5. Postlude: the empty tomb (16:1–8)

The prelude establishes that Jesus, from the obscure town of Nazareth, undertakes a public ministry only after associating with John the Baptist's reform movement. After his baptism, Jesus hears a voice assigning him divine sonship (1:1–13).

In narrating the Galilean ministry, Mark presents Jesus as an apocalyptic prophet, urging that people repent because God's kingdom (rule) is imminent. Beginning with a day in Capernaum (1:21–45), Jesus' Galilean campaign stresses expulsion of demons, healings, and other miraculous works (1:14–8:26). Amid growing opposition, Mark's Jesus demands that his miracles be kept secret. The disciples fail to understand Jesus' significance (4:35–8:21).

Recounting the journey to Jerusalem, Mark emphasizes the hidden or unexpected quality of Jesus' messiahship, the necessity of suffering, and the disciples' blindness. After Peter at last identifies Jesus as "the Messiah" in Caesarea Philippi, Jesus makes the first of three predictions of his coming rejection and death (8:27–33; 9:30–32; 10:32–45). The section concludes with Jesus restoring sight to the blind Bartimaeus (8:27–10:52).

The Jerusalem ministry opens on the hopeful theme of Jesus' public entry into the holy city shortly before Passover (11:1–11). Mark reports that Jesus assaults the Temple moneychangers (11:15–19), successfully debates with Jewish religious leaders (11:27–12:40), predicts the Temple's destruction (13:1–37), and holds a final Passover with his disciples (14:1–25). Mark then dramatizes the fulfillment of Jesus' earlier premonitions of death. Universally blind to his identity, the disciples betray or abandon him, while Jewish and Roman officials achieve his crucifixion.

The postlude briefly describes the first Easter. At dawn on the Sunday after Jesus' death, a few women followers discover that his tomb is

---

BOX 7-1   *Mark's Leading Characters**

John the Baptist (1:4–9); executed (6:17–29)

Jesus introduced (1:9) final words (15:34)

Simon Peter and his brother Andrew (1:16–18); Peter's imperfect discipleship (8:27–33; 9:2–6; 14:26–31, 66–72)

James and John, the fishermen sons of Zebedee (1:19–20); wish to be first in the kingdom (10:35–45)

Levi (Matthew), a tax collector (2:13–17)

The Twelve (3:13–19)

Judas Iscariot, Jesus' betrayer (3:19; 14:17–21, 43–46)

Mary, Jesus' mother, and other family members (3:20–21, 31–35; 6:3)

The Gerasene demoniac (5:1–20)

Herod Antipas, ruler of Galilee (4 BCE–39 CE) (6:17–29; 8:15)

The Syrophoenician (Canaanite) woman (7:14–30)

A rich young man (10:17–22)

The woman who anoints Jesus at Bethany (14:3–9)

The High Priest Caiaphas (14:53–64)

Pontius Pilate, Procurator of Judea (26–36 CE) (15:1–15, 43–44)

Barabbas, the terrorist released in place of Jesus (15:6–15)

Simon of Cyrene, the man impressed to carry Jesus' cross (15:21)

Joseph of Arimathaea, the Sanhedrin member who buries Jesus (15:42–46)

Mary of Magdala (in Galilee) (15:40–41, 47; 16:1)

Mary, mother of James and Joseph (15:40, 47; 16:1)

---

*Characters are listed in general order of appearance, along with the chief quality or event that distinguishes them in Mark's narrative.

empty. Because the women are afraid, they disobey a young man's instructions to inform the male disciples of Jesus' rising.

Because Mark establishes an order of events that the other two Synoptic writers generally follow, we will discuss Jesus' career in the sequence that Mark records it—a northern Galilean ministry followed by a brief southern one in Jerusalem. However, Mark arranges his material in a north-south polarity to illustrate his positive attitude toward Galilee and his negative view of Jerusalem (where his hero is rejected and killed) rather than to reproduce the exact events of Jesus' actual biography. John's Gospel, in which Jesus frequently travels back and forth between Galilee and Jerusalem, reveals that early Christians had alternative ways of organizing Jesus' story.

Prelude to Jesus' Public Ministry

Mark opens his book by announcing, "Here begins the Gospel of Jesus Christ the Son of God" (1:1). This opening phrase serves multiple purposes: it is not only a declaration of his subject—Jesus—but also a definition of a new literary form, the Gospel. The gospel (good news) about Jesus Christ had previously been proclaimed in oral form, largely without the aid of written documentation. Mark now undertakes to combine traditions from the oral preaching about Jesus with a sequential narrative of Jesus' life and death. Mark's innovation is to convey the Christian message in the form of Jesus' biography.

A New Beginning

As in John's later Gospel, the reference to a "beginning" reminds the reader of the opening line in Genesis in which God creates heaven and earth. Mark proclaims that in Jesus God has begun a new creative activity. Jesus is the **Christ** (Greek translation of the Hebrew "*mashiah*") and "the Son of God." After this initial use of Jesus' titles, Mark rarely employs them, for one of his purposes is to demonstrate that in his lifetime Jesus' divine sonship was not recognized by the large majority of his contemporaries. No person calls Jesus "a son of God" until almost the very end of Mark's account. Significantly, at that point Jesus is already dead and the speaker is neither Jewish nor a disciple, but a Roman soldier (15:39).

Instead of giving us some background about Jesus (he tells us nothing except that Jesus comes from the town of Nazareth in the district of Galilee), Mark introduces his subject with no more than a quotation from the Jewish Bible:

> In the prophet Isaiah it stands written: Here is my herald whom I send on ahead of you, and he will prepare your way. A voice crying aloud in the wilderness, Prepare a way for the Lord; clear a straight path for him. (1:2–3)

Despite Mark's allusion to the prophet Isaiah (40:3), the quoted passage is mainly a blend of lines from the Torah (Exod. 23:30) and Malachi (3:1). Mark's placing of Jesus' activities in the context of the Hebrew Bible is typical of all the Gospel writers, as is his rather free use of the text. Rather than cite the original Hebrew text precisely, the Evangelists tend to use the Greek version of the Old Testament (the Septuagint) and to quote it loosely, as if from memory.

John the Baptist and Jesus' Calling

In this case, the scriptural passage cited is applied to the work of John the Baptist, whom the Synoptic writers view as Jesus' predestined forerunner, the man who "prepares the way" for Jesus' more important ministry. Picturesquely dressed in garments of camel skin and living as a desert ascetic, John resembles an Old Testament Nazirite. A "dedicated" or "consecrated" person, the Nazirites were men or women peculiarly committed to a godly life. While under the Nazirite oath they were to abstain from wine or other forms of alcohol, never to cut their hair, and never to touch a dead body (Num. 6:1–21; Judg. 13:1–7; 1 Sam. 1:1–11). John's aloofness from social groups and his refusal of ordinary food or intoxicating drink set him apart from others, including Jesus (Matt. 11:16–19).

In recounting the circumstances of Jesus' baptism, Mark includes several elements that express his theological understanding of the event. (1) Persons whom John baptizes demonstrate "repentance for the remission of sins" (1:4). In Mark's account, Jesus is implicitly included among the repentant who undergo a spiritual renewal. (2) John predicts that one greater than he will soon arrive to baptize people with the Holy Spirit. (3) After John has immersed Jesus in the Jordan River, Jesus privately experiences a heavenly voice (a phenomenon Jews called the *bath qol*) naming him "my Son" and sees the Spirit descending upon him "like a dove" (1:4–11). To Mark, Jesus' baptism and the Spirit's descent fulfill John's prediction and signal that God adopts Jesus as his son (1:1, 4–11).

The brief reference to Jesus' successful resistance of Satan's temptations (1:12–13) introduces another of Mark's principal themes—God's son is come to break up Satan's rule over humankind. Jesus' exorcisms—the casting out of demons who have possessed human beings—are an important part of his ministry and are given proportionately greater space in Mark than in any other Gospel.

The Galilean Ministry: Inaugurating the Kingdom

Mark's chronology of Jesus' life is simple. He divides Jesus' ministry into three main parts. The first part is set principally in Jesus' native

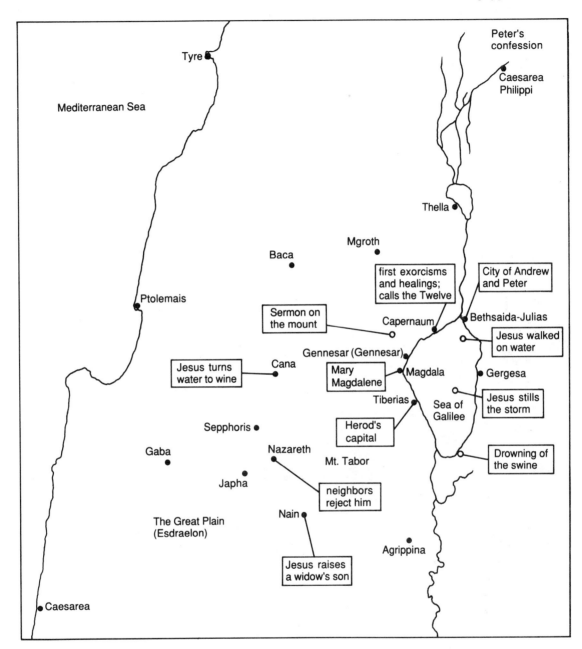

Figure 7-1 The area of Jesus' Galilean ministry. According to the Synoptic Gospels (but not John's account), Jesus spent most of his public life in and around Galilee. This map indicates the sites of some of his major activities there.

BOX 7–2   *Mark's Order of Events in Jesus' Life*

Action or Event	Approximate Date	Action or Event	Approximate Date
Jesus is baptized by John at the Jordan River (1:9–11).	27 or 29 CE	Jesus debates Torah rules with the Pharisees, who increasingly oppose his teaching (7:1–23).	30 or 33 CE
Jesus withdraws alone into the Judean desert (1:12–13).		Jesus leaves Galilee and travels through non-Jewish territories in Phoenicia and the Decapolis (7:24–37).	
Jesus begins preaching in Galilee (1:14–15).		Jesus miraculously feeds a second crowd, this time of Gentiles (8:1–10, 14–21).	
Jesus recruits Peter, Andrew, James, and John to be his first disciples (1:16–20).		Jesus cures a blind man, and, near the town of Caesarea Philippi, Peter's eyes are opened to Jesus' true identity as the Messiah; Jesus rebukes Peter for failing to understand that the Messiah must suffer and die (8:22–9:1).	
Jesus performs miraculous cures and exorcisms in Capernaum and throughout Galilee (1:21–3:12).			
Jesus appoints twelve chief disciples from among his many followers; he explains the meaning of parables to this inner circle (3:13–34).		Jesus is gloriously transfigured before Peter, James, and John (9:1–13).	
Jesus repeatedly crosses the Lake of Galilee, healing Jews on the western side and non-Jews on the eastern side (4:35–5:43).		Jesus travels with the Twelve through Galilee to Capernaum, instructing them privately (9:30–50).	
Jesus returns to Nazareth, where his neighbors reject him (6:1–6).		Jesus travels south to Judea, teaching the crowds and debating with Pharisees (10:1–33).	
Jesus sends the Twelve out on a mission to heal the sick and exorcise demons (6:7–13).		On the road to Jerusalem, Jesus for the third time predicts his imminent suffering and death (the Passion predictions) (8:31–33; 9:30–32; 10:32–34).	
Herod Antipas beheads John the Baptist (6:14–29).			
Jesus miraculously feeds a Jewish crowd of 5,000 (6:30–44).			

BOX 7–2   *continued*

Approaching Jerusalem via Jericho, Jesus performs his last public miracle, curing a blind man (10:46–52).

Events of the Last Week of Jesus' Life

Palm Sunday: Jesus arranges his public entry into Jerusalem; his followers hail him in terms of the Davidic kingdom (11:1–11).

After a night at the Jerusalem suburb of Bethany, Jesus returns to Jerusalem and drives the moneychangers out of the Temple (11:15–19).

Jesus debates the "chief priests," Sadducees, Pharisees, and other Jewish religious leaders in the Temple (11:27–12:40).

Seated on the Mount of Olives opposite Jerusalem, Jesus predicts the imminent destruction of the Temple (13:1–37).

Jesus' enemies conspire to kill him; Judas betrays Jesus (14:1–11).

Jesus hold a final Passover meal with the Twelve (14:12–31).

After the "Last Supper," Jesus is arrested at Gethsemane on the Mount of Olives outside Jerusalem (14:32–52).

Jesus is tried on charges of blasphemy before the High Priest Caiphas and the Sanhedrin (14:53–65).

After all of Jesus' followers have abandoned him, Peter denies even having known him (14:66–72).

Good Friday: Jewish leaders accuse Jesus before Pontius Pilate; Jesus is declared guilty of treason, flogged, and condemned to crucifixion (15:1–20).

A passerby, Simon of Cyrene, is impressed to carry Jesus' cross to Golgotha, where he is crucified (15:21–39).

A group of Galilean women witness the crucifixion; Joseph of Arimathaea provides a tomb for Jesus (15:40–47).

Easter Sunday: Mary of Magdala and other women discover that Jesus' tomb is empty; a young man instructs them to look for Jesus in Galilee, but the women are too frightened to tell anyone of their experience (16:1–8).

district of Galilee in the north of Palestine (1:14–8:26). The second part, the journey to Jerusalem (8:27–10:52), connects the relatively successful Galilean campaign with the third part, the disastrous southern ministry in Jerusalem (11:1–15:47). The crucial second section, containing Jesus' three Passion predictions, highlights Mark's conviction that even Jesus' divine sonship and power to work miracles will not deliver him from the world's human and supernatural evil.

Mark's Apocalyptic Urgency

Whereas in John's Gospel the ministries of Jesus and John the Baptist overlap, Mark states that Jesus began his work only after **Herod Antipas** had imprisoned John (1:14). (Herod Antipas, a son of Herod the Great, then administered Galilee and Perea for the Romans.) In Mark's report, Jesus launches his career with a startlingly apocalpytic message:

> "The time has come; the kingdom of God is upon you; repent and believe the Gospel." (1:15)

Mark's Jesus asserts that the *eschaton* (end of the world) is so near that people must immediately repent (radically change the direction of their lives). Making the right decision is critical, for in Jesus' activity, the "kingdom [or active rule] of God" has already begun.

Mark's apocalyptic urgency permeates his entire Gospel, affecting both the style and content of his writing. He uses the present tense throughout and connects the brief episodes of his narrative with the transition word "immediately." Jesus scarcely finishes conducting a healing or exorcism in one Galilean town before he "immediately" rushes off to the next village to perform another miracle. In Mark's breathless presentation, the world faces an unprecedented crisis. Jesus' intense activity announces that the world's end is near. Events associated with the End, including the fall of the holy city and the appearance of the Son of Man, are about to occur (ch. 13).

Mark represents Jesus as promising his original hearers that they will experience the *eschaton*—"the present generation will live to see it all" (13:30). The kingdom is so close that some of Jesus' contemporaries "will not taste death before they have seen the kingdom of God already come in power" (9:1). Mark believes that his own generation will witness the culmination of history. He states that the long-awaited figure of Elijah, whose reappearance is to be an infallible sign of the last days (Mal. 4:5), has already materialized in the form of John the Baptist (9:12–13; see also Matt. 11:12–14).

Jesus and the Demons

Not only does Mark's Jesus challenge the reader to prepare for the kingdom but his very existence and actions herald its arrival on the human scene. Mark emphasizes Jesus' healings and exorcisms to show that God's intervention into human society is already taking place. To allow God to rule unimpeded, Satan's control over humanity must be broken. Mark demonstrates Jesus' overthrow of Satan's power by recording numerous **exorcisms,** the ritual casting out of demons or "unclear spirits" that have possessed human minds and bodies. If we compare John's Gospel, we find that it does not mention a single exorcism, but Mark stresses the importance of this aspect of Jesus' activity, presenting Jesus' first miracle as the expelling of a demon.

The demons' witness. Reporting Jesus' activities during a single day in Capernaum (1:21–38), Mark economically combines two major themes. (1) In Jesus' presence, invisible forces operating on humanity change from demonic to divine control. (2) Even the forces of evil recognize that Jesus is God's chosen agent, the one destined ultimately to defeat them.

After Jesus' first exorcism, at the Capernaum synagogue, a demon shrieks out Jesus' identity—"the Holy One of God" (1:21–28). At a parallel exorcism in Gentile territory, "the country of the Gerasenes," the demons also identify him. After driving a whole army of devils from a Gerasene madman, Jesus casts them into a herd of pigs—the religiously unclean animals becoming a fit home for unclean spirits (5:1–20). The demons' name—"legion"—is probably an unflattering reference to the Roman legions (large military units) then occupying Palestine. (Note that in Capernaum, Jesus commands the expelled demon to remain silent, whereas in the Gerasene case he orders the dispossessed man to tell others about his cure.)

Mark arranges his material to show that Jesus does not choose to battle evil in isolation. Instead, at the outset, Jesus gathers followers who will form the nucleus of a new society, one presumably free from demonic influence. Mark reports the call of disciples even before he describes Jesus' initial miracles. The author reflects a widespread Christian tradition in making Simon Peter, a Galilean fisherman, Jesus' first choice. After Peter and his brother, Andrew, Jesus recruits two other fishermen, James and John, the sons of Zebedee (1:16–20). Mark also follows tradition in listing twelve chief disciples (3:16–19), but he rarely mentions more than three—Peter, James, and John—who make up Jesus' inner circle. Mark states that Jesus commissions the Twelve to perform exorcisms (6:7–13), although when they try to exorcise an epileptic boy, they fail miserably (9:14–18, 28–29).

Compare the disciples' failure with Jesus' approving attitude toward nonfollowers who successfully cast out evil spirits (9:38–41). According to Mark, Jesus states that anyone performing such good works is on his side. By contrast, Matthew (12:30) and Luke (11:23) report Jesus as saying the opposite: persons who do not support him are against him.

Jesus accused of sorcery. In another incident involving demonic possession (3:22–30), Mark dramatizes a head-on collision between Jesus as God's agent for overthrowing evil and persons who see Jesus himself as a tool of the devil. The

clash occurs when "doctors of the law" (teachers and interpreters of the Torah) from Jerusalem accuse Jesus of using black magic to perform miracles. Suspicious of anyone claiming supernatural powers, the Jerusalem authorities declare that Jesus is "possessed by Beelzebub" (another name for Satan).

Jesus' reply refutes the notion that evil means can be used to defeat evil and exposes the illogic of his opponents' accusation. If Jesus employs demonic forces to expel devils, then Satan's "kingdom" would be divided against itself—evil would be doing good, an effect impossible for evil to achieve. Persons who attribute good works to Satan thus "slander the Holy Spirit," the divine power made manifest in Jesus' healings of the afflicted (3:22–30).

Matthew's version of the incident (Matt. 12:22–28) presents Mark's point even more forcefully. Matthew's Jesus declares, "If it is by the Spirit of God that I drive out the devils, then be sure the kingdom of God has already come upon you" (Matt. 12:28). To both Gospel writers, Jesus' successful attack on spiritual evil is a revelation that through the person of Jesus God now rules. Willful refusal to accept Jesus' activity as evidence of divine power is to resist the Spirit, an obstinancy that prevents religious enlightenment.

The existence of demons. Mark's use of exorcisms to illustrate Jesus' war on Satan's "kingdom" provokes a real crisis of credibility for most students today. Modern readers are likely to be troubled by the writer's uncritical acceptance of devils, demons, and "unclean spirits" (invisible beings that cause their victims to break the Torah and perform ritually "unclean" actions). To many people the notion of demonic possession is a superstition unworthy of a higher religion. The concept does not fit easily into our world, which we believe to be rationally ordered and explainable by the use of scientific methodology. During the last century many scholars have attempted to rationalize or explain away the Gospel accounts of exorcisms by labeling them metaphors of mental derangement or nervous disorders, which Jesus cured. Such attempts to harmonize ancient beliefs with modern attitudes toward sickness are well intentioned but misplaced.

Mark, like other New Testament authors, reflects the common beliefs of the Hellenistic era. Throughout Greco-Roman society, people appear to have assumed the existence of unseen forces that significantly influenced human lives for good or evil. Numerous Hellenistic documents record charms to ward off malign spirits or free one from their control. In Judaism, works like the apocryphal Book of Tobit reveal a belief that demons could be exorcised by the correct use of quasimagical formulas (Tob. 6:1–8; 8:1–3).

Zoroastrianism. A belief in devils and demonic possession appears in Jewish literature primarily after the period of Persian domination (539–330 BCE) when Persian religious ideas seem to have influenced Jewish thought. According to the Persian religion, **Zoroastrianism,** the whole universe, visible and invisible, is divided into two contending powers of light and darkness, good and evil. Only after contact with Zoroastrian dualism does the figure of Satan emerge as humanity's adversary in biblical literature (Job 1–2; Zech. 3). Angels and demons thereafter populate Hellenistic Jewish writings, such as the Books of Daniel and Enoch.

Belief in supernatural evil. Although Hellenistic Greek and Jewish-Christian writers may express their beliefs about supernatural evil in terms considered naive or irrational to today's scientifically disciplined mind, they reflect a viewpoint with important implications for contemporary society. Surrounded by threats of terrorism, uncontrollable diseases, and nuclear annihilation of all life on earth, one may wonder if such pitiless violence and cruelty is not greater than the sum of its human components. Does evil exist as a force independent of human activity? Such diverse works as the Synoptic Gos-

pels, Ephesians (6:10–17), and Revelation show a keen awareness of evil so pervasive and so profound that it cannot be explained solely in terms of human acts, individual or collective. Whatever philosophical view we choose to interpret the human predicament, the Gospel portrayal of Jesus' struggle to impart wholeness and health to others expresses the Evangelists' conviction that humanity cannot save itself without divine aid.

Jesus the Healer

Physical healings, as well as exorcisms, characterize Jesus' battle against evil. Mark presents a wide range of Jesus' miraculous cures: driving a fever from Simon Peter's mother-in-law (1:29–31); cleansing a leper (1:40–42); enabling a paralyzed man to walk (2:1–12); restoring another man's withered hand (3:1–6); curing a hemorrhaging woman (5:25–34); and resuscitating the daughter of Jairus, a synagogue official (5:21–24, 35–43).

Likening Jesus' healing campaign to a triumphal procession through Galilee, Mark summarizes the effect Jesus' miracles had on the Galilean public.

> Wherever he went, to farms . . . villages, or towns, they laid out the sick in the market-places and begged to let them simply touch the edge of his cloak; and all who touched him were cured. (6:56)

Mark's eyewitness techniques. In gathering together from various oral sources short narratives picturing Jesus' phenomenal ability to cure the sick, Mark provides a miscellaneous collection of miracle stories. Although the individual anecdotes have little relationship to each other, Mark gives the healing incidents immediacy and realism by including considerable concrete detail. Notice the author's literary devices in the stories of the paralyzed man (2:1–12) and the hemorrhaging woman. Mark shows people violating ordinary norms of behavior in their eagerness to approach Jesus. The paralytic's

Christ with the Sick Around Him, Receiving Little Children by Rembrandt (1606–1669). In this painting healing light radiates from the central figure of Jesus and creates a protective circle of illumination around those whom he cures. (Courtesy of Metropolitan Museum of Art. Bequest of Mrs. H. O. Havemeyer, 1929.)

friends, for example, carry him to the top of a house where Jesus is staying, rip open the roof, and lower the man through the hole to force him on Jesus' attention.

The woman suffering an unstoppable flow of blood is equally assertive. Although her condition makes her religiously unclean by Torah standards, she pushes through a large crowd to grasp her hero's clothing. Note Mark's skillful use of specific detail to make the episode come alive. To external fact—the woman's twelve-year search for a cure, spending all her money on doctors unable to help her—Mark adds the participants' internal thoughts and unarticulated feelings. The woman's inner monologue—her silently worded conviction that if she could but touch the healer's garments she would become well—is balanced against Jesus' physical sensations. Hinting at the nature of the healer's dynamic resources, Mark reports that Jesus can feel the curative energy flow out of his body, as if the woman's touch involuntarily taps his reservoir of power. This is the only Gospel healing reported to occur without Jesus' conscious will. Mark renders the incident in such realistic detail that he gives his readers the impression of experiencing an eyewitness encounter with Jesus (5:25–34).

Mark links the two healings thematically, stressing that the man and woman gain health through their faith in Jesus' ability to cure them. Contrast these episodes with Jesus' reported inability to effect miracles when people do not trust him (6:1–6).

Miracles That Reveal Jesus' Prophetic Role

Many of Jesus' miracles—including resuscitations of the recently dead—resemble those that the prophets Elijah and Elisha performed in ancient Israel (1 Kings 17:17–24; 18:20–46; 2 Kings 2:1–25; 4:1–6:7). The story of Jesus raising the twelve-year-old daughter of Jairus, the two parts of which frame the episode of the hemorrhaging woman (5:22–24, 35–43), links Jesus to the Elijah-Elisha tradition. Again, Mark lends the miracle credibility by supplying numerous realistic details, such as the number and names of disciples accompanying Jesus to Jairus's house and the noisy wailing going on among its inhabitants. Mark also records the Aramaic phrase Jesus uses to raise the girl—"*Talitha cum,*" a command to "get up"—to which the child responds immediately.

To Mark, Jesus' healings serve a dual function: they demonstrate his hero's divine power and symbolize his messianic purpose to make Israel see and hear God's presence. Jesus unstops the ears of a deaf man, again using an Aramaic command, "*Ephphatha,*" "Be opened" (7:31–37). In two separate episodes, he restores sight to the blind (8:22–26; 10:46–52). The healing of ear and eye have a prophetic meaning above and beyond the literal physical cures. By his actions Jesus "opens" the symbolic ear of Israel, bringing a new message to those who can hear (understand). By making the blind see, he inspires a new insight into God's purpose, creating an awareness of truths hitherto unperceived. Mark locates the second healing of a blind man in Jericho, just before Jesus makes his crucial entry into Jerusalem—where his opponents refuse to "see" the value of Jesus and put him to death. The blind beggar whom Jesus heals "follows him on the road" to the cross, providing an ironic contrast to those whose spiritual blindness allows them to condemn Jesus.

Jesus' Power Over the Natural World

The Gospels contain relatively few "nature miracles," acts of Jesus that seem to defy the recognized laws or order of the material world. Two of Jesus' most famous interruptions of natural order occur on the Lake of Galilee, a normally placid body of water that can be racked by tumultuous waves when storms suddenly sweep in from the north. Such a storm occurs when Jesus and the disciples are crossing the lake in a small boat that is almost capsized by waves. In characteristic fashion, Mark offers the detail that Jesus is "in the stern asleep on a cushion" while the disciples are in terror of drowning. Awakened, Jesus orders the wind to stop

blowing, and the "sea" is reduced to "a dead calm" (4:35–41). Jesus' success in ending natural violence that threatens to claim human lives echoes ancient religious myths of creation, the bringing of order out of chaos. As Yahweh created by conquering the monstrous power of "the deep [sea]" (Pss. 74:13–14; 104; Is. 27; Job 26:12–13), so Jesus—by stilling the storm—triumphs over the forces of disorder and creates an environment safe for human life.

The ancient biblical theme of subduing the natural element of the sea is repeated in Jesus' second suspension of "natural law" on the Lake of Galilee. In this eerie late-night scene, the disciples see Jesus, like a "ghost," walking atop the lake surface beside their boat. Note that this episode focuses equally on Jesus' supernatural power and the disciples' fear and inability to understand what these powers reveal about their Master (6:45–52).

The miracle of loaves and fishes. The disciples are equally bewildered by Jesus' ability to feed multitudes of people from a tiny amount of food. Mark records two versions of this miracle, one involving Jewish followers (6:30–44) and another for a Gentile audience (8:1–9). Many scholars believe, however, that Mark's desire to show Jesus providing bread (a symbol of Jesus' body in the Christian communion ritual) for both Jews and Gentiles prompted the author to compose two accounts of what was originally a single event.

Although Mark concedes that Jesus' providing for the hungry was partly an act of compassion (6:34; 8:1–3), he uses the miracle primarily to remind his readers that the messianic age has arrived. Many Jews believed that when the Messiah came, all Israel would enjoy a rich banquet of fellowship with God (Is. 25:6–10).

Jesus as "The Son of Man"

Although Mark believes that Jesus is Israel's Messiah, he shows Jesus explicitly accepting this title only once (14:62). Instead, Mark's Jesus calls himself the **Son of Man,** a designation that appears almost exclusively in the Gospels and then always on the lips of Jesus. Although some scholars question whether Jesus really applied this term to himself, many others regard it as Jesus' preferred means of self-identification.

Origins of the term. In the Hebrew Bible, the term appears frequently in Ezekiel, where "son of man" is typically synonymous with "mortal man" or human being, commonly the prophet himself (Ezek. 2:1; 36:1; 37:3, etc.). In the Book of Daniel, however, "one like a [son of] man" appears as a heavenly figure who receives divine authority (Dan. 7:14). Most scholars believe that this manlike figure (contrasting with the "beasts" in Daniel's vision) originally symbolized a collective entity, Israel's faithful. By Jesus' time the mysterious Son of Man had assumed another identity, that of a supernatural being who judges the world.

Enoch's visions. The composite book of 1 Enoch, which belongs to the noncanonical Jewish writings known as the **Pseudepigrapha,** contains a long section (the Similitudes) that prominently features the Son of Man as the one who judges humankind at the world's end (1 Enoch 37–71). Although some scholars dispute the claim, many believe that this section of 1 Enoch was written by the first century CE. Fragments of Enoch occur among the Dead Sea Scrolls, and the canonical epistle of Jude cites the book as if it were Scripture (Jude 14–15). It seems likely that ideas about the Son of Man figure were current in Jesus' day and that he made use of them.

In Mark, the major element that Jesus adds to the Son of Man concept is that he is a servant who must suffer and die before attaining the kind of heavenly glory that Daniel 7 and 1 Enoch attribute to him (compare Mark 8:30–31; 10:45; 13:26–27; 14:62). It is as the Son of Man in his earthly role, however, that Mark's Jesus claims the authority to exercise immense religious power.

"The son of man has the right on earth . . . ." As Son of Man, the Markan Jesus assumes the right to prescribe revolutionary changes in Jewish Law and custom (2:10). Behaving as if he already reigns as world judge, Jesus forgives a paralytic's sins (2:1–12) and permits certain kinds of work on the Sabbath (3:1–5). In both instances, Jesus' pronouncements outrage Jewish leaders. Who but God can forgive sins? And who has the audacity to change Moses' inspired command to forbid all labor on God's day of rest? (Exod. 20:8–10; Deut. 5:12–15)

In the eyes of Jews scrupulously observing Torah regulations, Jesus dishonors the **Sabbath** by healing a man's withered arm on that holy day. The Pharisees interpreted the Torah to permit saving a life or to deal with other comparable emergencies on the Sabbath, but in this case (2:23–28) Jesus seems to have violated the Torah for no compelling reason.

As Mark presents the case, it is Jesus' flexible attitude toward Sabbath keeping that incites some Pharisees and supporters of Herod Antipas to hatch a murder plot against the Nazarene healer (3:5–6). To most readers, Jesus' opponents overreact inexplicably. To many law-abiding Jews, however, Jesus' Sabbath-breaking miracles and declaration that the Sabbath was made for humanity's benefit (2:27–28) seem to strike at the heart of the Jewish religion. Many pious Jews believed that the Torah is infallible and eternal. According to a principle expressed in the Book of Jubilees, the Torah existed before the world's creation and people *were* made to keep the Sabbath. Jesus' assertion that the Sabbath law is not absolute but relative to human needs appears to deny the Torah's unchanging validity and to question its status as God's final and complete revelation.

In forbidding divorce (10:1–12) and relaxing dietary restrictions (7:14–23), Jesus also interprets the Torah as provisional and open to change. Torah rules assumed the common practice of divorce and permitted men to divorce their wives for a variety of reasons (Deut. 24:1–4). (Women were not given similar legal rights.)

The Markan Jesus is revolutionary in abolishing divorce altogether and in labeling the Torah divorce laws a mere concession to male insensitivity, a position that apparently distresses his disciples (10:10). Note that Mark connects Jesus' prohibition with the Genesis account of the first human marriage. In citing the original bond between Adam and Eve, Jesus seems to demand a return to conditions that prevailed before humanity disobeyed God and became alienated from him. To come under kingdom rule, a person must live in the ideal state that existed before humankind's fall from grace. In contrast to Mark's absolute rule, note Matthew's view that marriage *can* end under certain conditions (Matt. 19:1–12).

Teaching the Mysteries of the Kingdom

Jesus' use of parables. Mark states unequivocally that Jesus never taught publicly without using parables (4:34). By parable, Mark apparently means that Jesus usually employed figurative language to convey an ethical or religious insight. The root meaning of the word *parable* is "a comparison," the discernment of similarities between one thing and another. As modern literary critics usually define the term, a parable is a brief narrative that uses familiar situations or actions to illustrate an unfamiliar or previously unrecognized truth.

Jesus' simplest parables are typically similes, comparisons using "as" or "like" and finding an unexpected resemblance between ostensibly unrelated objects, actions, or concepts. Thus, Jesus compares God's kingdom to a mustard seed: like the tiny seed, God's rule begins in an extremely small way, but eventually, like the mustard plant, it grows to an unexpectedly large dimension (4:30–32).

Although Mark's Gospel includes relatively few of Jesus' teachings, his fourth chapter contains a collection of kingdom parables. To Mark, understanding the parables correctly is vital. Grasping their correct meaning initiates one into the "secret" of God's kingdom—the mysterious

principles by which God rules. After examining Jesus' parable of a sower planting seeds on different kinds of ground (4:2–9) and its interpretation (4:13–20), the reader discovers that the sower-seed narrative is intrinsically different from the mustard seed simile. Instead of a brief comparison expressing a single perception about God's rule, as in a true parable, the sower parable is really an allegory. An **allegory** is a complex literary form in which each element of the narrative—persons, actions, even objects—has a symbolic value. Because every item in the allegory functions as a symbol of something else, the allegory's meaning can be puzzled out only by identifying what each individual component in the story represents.

According to most scholars, Mark's elaborate interpretation equating different kinds of soil with the different responses people make when they receive the "seed" (gospel message) does not represent Jesus' original meaning. By the time Mark incorporated the sower parable into his Gospel, the Christian community had already used it to explain people's differing reactions to their preaching. In this view, Jesus' simple tale has been expanded and applied to the historical experience of the early church. The interpretative reference to persecution (4:17) also appears to belong to Mark's own time rather than to Jesus' personal experience in Galilee.

In one of his Gospel's most controversial passages, Mark states that Jesus uses parables to *prevent* the public from understanding his message (4:11–12). To many readers it seems incredible that Jesus deliberately phrases his message in a way intended to confuse or alienate his audience. Mark explains the alleged obscurity of Jesus' teaching by quoting the prophet Isaiah (6:9–10). In the cited passage, Yahweh tells Isaiah that his preaching will be useless because Yahweh has already made it impossible for the Israelites to understand the prophet's meaning. Mark probably invokes Isaiah's ineffectiveness because he wants to condemn first-century Israelites who refused to accept Jesus. This rationalization tells us little about Jesus' actual motives and seems contrary to the gracious goodwill that the Gospel writers normally associate with Jesus. If we compare Luke 4:9–10, we notice that Luke also states the negative intent of Jesus' parables but does not cite Isaiah 6. Instead, he puts Isaiah's judgment in the mouth of Paul when the apostle criticizes his fellow Jews in Rome (Acts 28:25–28).

As Mark presents him, Jesus makes a great distinction between the way he lectures the curious public and the way he privately instructs a few chosen disciples. To Mark, the essence of Jesus' message is reserved for a closed inner circle. To this handful of initiates he reveals the secret of the kingdom—the mysterious principles by which God rules the universe and effects his will among humankind (4:11). Some commentators suggest that Mark employs this device to explain why the majority of people failed to appreciate Jesus during his ministry. A more likely explanation involves Mark's theology— his belief that God's plan required Jesus to suffer rejection and death. People *had* to misunderstand Jesus in order to condemn and crucify him.

Mark's Central Vision

In Mark's story of Jesus, chapter 8 forms the central pivot on which the entire Gospel turns. In this chapter Mark ties together several themes that express his essential vision of Jesus' life and what Jesus requires of those who would follow him. After reading chapter 8, review Mark's sequence of events. He begins with a joyous account of Jesus' feeding the multitudes (8:1–10), continues through the crisis of misunderstanding between Jesus, Peter, and the other disciples (8:11–21, 27–33), and ends with Jesus' warning that he will disown unfaithful followers (8:38). Note that the movement from celebration to gloom involves the disciples' failure to comprehend either the significance of Jesus' miracles or the purpose of his life and death.

Three distinctively Markan themes emerge: (1) the strange inability of Jesus' disciples to understand him, a failure that encompasses all of Jesus' associates, including his neighbors, family, and the religious leaders of his nation; (2) the hidden or unexpected quality of Jesus' messiahship, a role that brings neither earthly power nor glory, only service, self-sacrifice, and suffering; (3) the requirement that all followers must be prepared to accept potential suffering, to embrace a future as bleak as that which Jesus faced during his lifetime. Beginning with the disciples' blindness, we will explore each of these themes in turn.

The Blindness of Jesus' Associates

Jesus' disciples. Mark's negative attitude toward the disciples in chapter 8 is anticipated in earlier chapters, where virtually all of Jesus' original associates are blind to his worth. Relating the disciples' failure to understand their leader, Mark employs surprisingly negative language. When the Twelve cannot see the meaning of Jesus' feeding the multitudes or walking on water, Mark charges that "their minds were closed" (6:52, NEB). The harshness of Mark's expression is better rendered in the phrase "their hearts were hardened" (as given in the Revised Standard Version). This is the same phrase used to describe the Egyptian Pharaoh when he "hardened his heart" and refused to obey Yahweh's command (Exod. 7:13–14; 8:15).

Why does Mark attribute such "hardness of heart" to the disciples? Why does the Evangelist repeatedly insist that Jesus' closest followers— whom later generations would honor as the twelve supreme Apostles—were unwilling or unable to appreciate either his teaching or what his miracles said about his special nature? So often does Mark stress the "stupidity" of the disciples (4:13; 6:52; 8:17–21, 33; 9:10, 32; 10:35–45) and their failure to live up to Jesus' principles (9:33–35) that the reader must ask what he means by this depreciation of them. In Mark, the only follower to state that Jesus is indeed "the Messiah" (8:29), the Apostle Peter, later denies that he even knows Jesus (14:66–72). All of Jesus' male disciples abandon him after his arrest

(14:50), leaving only a few Galilean women to witness his agony on the cross (15:40–41).

Jesus' family. In Mark, none of the groups that might seem to be invaluable primary sources about Jesus' life and deeds—his family, kinsmen, neighbors, original disciples—are credited with grasping his teachings or appreciating the nature of his mission. Mark's brief references to Jesus' immediate family are no more flattering than his descriptions of Jesus' obtuse and faithless disciples. When Jesus visits his hometown, **Nazareth,** and attracts large crowds eager to see him perform miracles, his family "set out to take charge of him, convinced he was out of his mind" (3:13–19, Jerusalem Bible). If this translation of the Greek text is correct, the family's attitude toward Jesus' activities was unsympathetic and helps to explain his curt refusal to welcome the "mother and brothers" who have come for him, presumably to take him to the family home. Ignoring their pleas, Mark's Jesus declares that his true relatives are those who gather with him to do the divine will (3:31–35).

Mark divides the anecdote about Jesus' apparent alienation from his family into two parts, using it to frame the episode in which Jesus' critics accuse him of exploiting Satanic power. Observe that Mark places the family's attempt to curtail Jesus' public teaching in the context of persons who regard Jesus as an agent of evil. The effect is to associate Jesus' closest relatives with outsiders who seriously misrepresent his character and purpose. John's Gospel records a similar memory of Jesus' conflict with his "brothers" (John 7:2–10).

Jesus' neighbors. Mark reports that the inhabitants of Jesus' hometown were decidedly reluctant to accord him any special status. The Evangelist highlights the Nazareans' lack of enthusiasm for this native son by placing Jesus' return to Nazareth immediately after the story about raising Jairus's daughter from the dead. Despite this dazzling display of supernatural gifts, Jesus' former neighbors view him with open skepticism. "Where did he get his wisdom?" they ask. The Nazareans remember Jesus as "the carpenter, the son of Mary, the brother and James and Joseph and Judas and Simon." They also know his "sisters"—but they do not know of any prophetic legacy in his background that entitles him to teach others.

Note that Mark presents the Nazareans' unbelief as diminishing Jesus' power. Jesus "could work no miracle there" except for some routine healings. Mark reports that Jesus is amazed at his neighbors' lack of faith and that he cites the proverb lamenting a prophet's inability to be honored among his own people. Familiarity with Jesus' human origins prevents the townspeople from recognizing or accepting his spiritual gifts (6:1–6).

Jesus' "brothers." Because Mark's Gospel does not include a tradition of Jesus' virginal conception or birth, the references to Jesus' "brothers" (also listed by name in Matt. 13:55) may not have been an issue in the Markan community. The birth stories in Matthew and Luke, however, explicitly affirm that Jesus was virginally conceived (Matt. 1:18–25; Luke 1:26–38). Some Protestant Christians believe that following Jesus' delivery, his mother may have borne other children in the ordinary way. According to Roman Catholic belief, however, Mary remains perpetually virgin. Jesus' "brothers" (translating the Greek term *adelphoi*) are to be understood as close male relatives, perhaps cousins or stepbrothers (sons of Mary's husband Joseph by a previous marriage). (See the discussion of the Protoevangelium of James, our main apocryphal source for Jesus' family background, in Chapter 10 of this text.)

The Journey to Jerusalem

The Hidden Messiah

As Jesus approaches the close of his Galilean ministry and prepares for the fatal journey to Jerusalem (8:27–10:52), Mark explicitly links his theme of the disciples' blindness to the hidden or unexpected quality of Jesus' messiahship. The Markan Christ can be recognized only in suffering and death. In Mark's account, no one suggests that Jesus is Israel's Messiah until chapter 8, when Peter—in a flash of insight—identifies Jesus as such (8:29). Characteristically, Jesus then forbids anyone to reveal his identity—as he orders others to keep his miracles a secret (1:23–24, 34; 3:11–12; 5:7; 7:36; 8:30). Mark stresses the theme of Jesus' hidden identity so often that scholars refer to it as the "messianic secret."

Most scholars think that Mark's emphasis on Jesus' hidden identity reflects more than the mere historical fact that during Jesus' lifetime most of his contemporaries did not accept him as God's special agent and that Jesus himself made no public claims to be the Messiah or a "son of God." Rather than an attempt to reproduce historical reality, Mark's theme of the hidden Messiah probably represents the author's theological conviction that people could not know Jesus for who he is until *after* he had completed his mission. Jesus had to be undervalued and rejected, for he is God's appointed "suffering servant" (Isa. 53) who willingly sacrifices himself to benefit others:

> "For even the Son of Man did not come to be served but to serve, and to give up his life as a ransom for many." (10:45)

The concept that Jesus must suffer an unjust death—a ransom offering for others—to confirm and complete his messiahship is the heart of Mark's **Christology** (belief about the nature and function of Christ). Hence Peter's confession that Jesus is the Christ (Messiah) is immediately followed by Jesus' first prediction that he will go to Jerusalem only to die (8:29–32). When Peter objects to this notion of a rejected and defeated Messiah, Jesus calls his chief disciple a "Satan." Derived from a Hebrew term meaning "obstacle," the epithet *Satan* labels Peter as an obstacle or roadblock on Jesus' necessary path to the cross. Peter understands Jesus no better than outsiders, regarding the Messiah

as a God-empowered hero who conquers his enemies, not as a victim of their ignorant brutality.

The Suffering of Jesus' Disciples

At the end of Chapter 8, Mark introduces a third concept: true disciples must expect to suffer as Jesus does. Correcting the Twelve's false view of discipleship, Jesus states:

> "Anyone who wishes to be a follower of mine must leave self behind; he must take up his cross, and come with me." (8:34)

Two of Jesus' three Passion predictions emphasize that followers will experience disappointment, loss, and pain (8:27–34; 10:32–45). Mark thus addresses a problem that undoubtedly troubled his fellow believers in the mid-60s CE: how to explain the contrast between the high expectation of reigning with Christ in glory (10:35–37) and the believers' actual situation? Instead of being vindicated publicly as God's chosen faithful, Christians then were being treated like outcasts in the Jewish community and like criminals by the Romans. Mark offers the consolation that Christians' disappointments and hardships are foreshadowed by Jesus' experience. Servants are not greater than their Master and must submit to being treated no better than he.

The Transfiguration

Mark's stress on human failure and the inevitability of suffering gives a somewhat harsh and gloomy ambience to his Gospel, a quality seemingly at odds with his stated purpose of telling "good news" (1:1). Murder conspiracies against Jesus, even in Galilee (3:6), and Jesus' premonitions of imminent death serve to cast the shadow of the cross backward in time across the whole scene of his ministry.

Mark, however, occasionally illuminates the shadows with images of hope. The world's authorities will execute Jesus, but they cannot alter

God's plan to transform defeat into victory and death into renewed life. Mark balances prophecies of Jesus' crucifixion with promises of his resurrection from the dead (8:31; 9:31; 10:34; 14:28). The author implicitly links Jesus' assertion that some followers will live to witness the kingdom's power (9:1) with Mark's only preview of Jesus' future glory.

Some scholars believe that the event known as the **transfiguration** (9:2–8) originally represented a postresurrection appearance of the risen Jesus. According to this theory, Mark inserted the incident earlier in his narrative to give the disciples (and the reader) a glimpse of Jesus' true nature, a supernatural revelation of his divinity. Placing it between the first two Passion predictions, Mark uses the awe-inspiring transfiguration to illustrate several important ideas about Jesus' role and function.

Climbing to a solitary mountaintop, Jesus' three most intimate disciples—Peter, James, and John—behold their Master transfigured, his form changed to that of a being of light (9:2–8). When Mark shows Jesus as a luminous spirit appearing alongside Moses and Elijah, he signals the reader that Jesus is already among their immortal company. In this vision, Jesus takes his place with the two figures who, respectively, symbolize Israel's Torah and inspired prophets. Jesus represents a third component—divine wisdom— that completes God's two earlier revelations to his people. Despite opponents who condemn Jesus' interpretation of the Jewish legacy, Mark presents him as a continuation and fulfillment of Judaism. Note that for the first time since Jesus' baptism, a heavenly voice speaks, again identifying Jesus as God's beloved son.

The transfiguration confirms Peter's recognition of Jesus' identity, but Mark firmly places this revelation in the context of Jesus' earthly role. After Jesus reminds the bewildered disciples of his coming death, he orders them not to report what they have seen until after the resurrection. To Mark, the pattern of Jesus' life can be discerned only when his career is finished. Only then can the disciples perceive the kingdom's mysterious power operating in Jesus' tragic fate (9:1, 9–10).

The Jerusalem Ministry

Focus on the Temple

After reading Mark's account of the Jerusalem ministry (11:1–15:47), note how the author organizes Jesus' activities around the Temple, the center of Jewish worship. To show that the Temple is the goal of Jesus' journey from Galilee, Mark indicates that his hero's entrance into the holy city is not complete until he enters his Father's House for the first time (11:1–10).

Once in Jerusalem (where his miracles cease and where he has less than a week to live), Jesus spends most of his remaining time in the Temple. In Mark's negative presentation of the Temple and its priestly administration, Jesus comes to judge the Sanctuary rather than to worship there. His first public act is a violent assault on the moneychangers, whom he physically drives from the Temple courts (11:15–19).

During the following days, Jesus teaches in the Temple precincts, where Mark pictures him being verbally attacked and/or tested by hostile opponents who represent Judaism's major religious parties (11:27–12:44). Jesus' teaching ministry concludes with his pronouncing a negative judgment on the Temple and prophesying its imminent destruction (13:1–37). (Compare 14:56, where Jesus' attitude toward the Sanctuary is misinterpreted as a conspiracy to destroy it.)

In Mark's thematically consistent account, it is the Temple's High Priest and his associates, members of the **Sadducee** party, who are chiefly responsible for Jesus' arrest and condemnation. Mark even links the Temple to Jesus' moment of death, stating that the Messiah's last breath coincides with a miraculous tearing asunder of the Temple's curtain. (The magnificently bejeweled curtain, which could be seen through the building's open entrance, veiled the sanctuary's innermost room, the Holy of Holies, from human eyes) (15:37–38). By this last incident, the Evangelist may suggest that the Temple no longer serves its purpose as God's earthly dwelling place.

Jesus' Judgment on Jerusalem and the Temple

Besides condemning the Temple cult and the Sadducean priests who controlled it, Mark uses other devices to indicate that Jesus' Jerusalem ministry represents an adverse judgment on the city. Otherwise puzzling, Jesus' cursing the unproductive fig tree (11:12–14, 20–24) probably represents Mark's intent to condemn the Jerusalem authorities, who, in his opinion, do not bear "good fruit" and are destined to wither and die.

The parable of the wicked tenants who kill their landlord's son (12:1–11) serves the same purpose, to discredit Jesus' enemies. In Mark's view, the landlord (God) has now given his vineyard, traditionally a symbol for Israel, to "others"—the author's Christian community.

Besides creating a near-riot on the Temple, Mark shows Jesus performing other public acts that arouse the suspicions of both religious and government officials. As Mark records it, Jesus carefully arranges his entry into Jerusalem to fulfill Zechariah's prophecy about the Messiah (Zech. 9:9) and permits his Galilean followers to hail him in terms of the promised Davidic kingdom (11:1–9). Mark thus portrays Jesus suddenly making a radical change in policy. Instead of hiding his messianic identity, Jesus now seems to "go public"—challenging Jerusalem to recognize and accept him as God's agent.

Jesus' arrival as an apparent messianic claimant is also a challenge to Roman authority. Because most Jews expected the Messiah to reestablish David's kingdom, the Romans naturally regard would-be messiahs as political threats to Roman rule. When learning that crowds enthusiastically follow a charismatic prophet from Galilee, notorious for its anti-Roman rebellions,

the Roman governor, Pontius Pilate, must have marked Jesus as a potential insurrectionist.

Debates in the Temple

Despite the growing antagonism between Jesus and his Jerusalem opponents, Mark states that the authorities are afraid to interfere with the Galilean healer because of his popularity with "the people" (11:18; 12:12; 14:2). As Jesus moves through the Temple courts, thronged with Passover pilgrims, Mark depicts him scoring success after success in a series of hostile confrontations. The Pharisees and Herod's political supporters attempt to trap Jesus on the controversial issue of paying taxes to Rome. He cleverly eludes their snare, recommending that a coin bearing the emperor's (Caesar's) image be returned to its source. By analogy, the human being (formed in God's image) is the Creator's property (12:13–17).

Like the Pharisees, the Sadducees try to force Jesus into an untenable position. Attempting to demonstrate that a belief in resurrection to future life is both illogical and potentially unethical, they ask Jesus' opinion on a seemingly unsolvable moral problem involving a woman who is widowed and remarried six times. If she and all her seven husbands are resurrected, to which one is she legally bound? (The Sadducees seem to imply that raising the dead to life would make widows who remarry guilty of bigamy and adultery, automatically condemning them under the Torah.)

While avoiding the Sadducean dilemma, Mark's Jesus defines the nature of postresurrection life, which is qualitatively different from the present human condition. Transformed to a spiritual existence, risen men and women escape the differences of sexual gender (12:18–25). Because the Sadducees take only the Mosaic Torah as their doctrinal standard, Jesus cites Exodus 3:15 as proof the dead live again. If God tells Moses that he is the God of Abraham and the other Genesis patriarchs, these ancient worthies must still be alive, because the Jewish God is Lord of the living, not of the dead. Jesus' unexpected interpretation of the Exodus text must have surprised his Sadducean opponents.

The law of love. Observe that Mark ends Jesus' Temple debates with a friendly encounter in which the Galilean and a "lawyer" or Torah expert agree on the essence of the Jewish religion. Answering the man's question about the most important biblical rule, Jesus cites first the **Shema,** or Jewish declaration of monotheism: there is only one God, and Israel must love him with all its force and being (Deut. 6:4–5). To this he adds a second Torah command: to love one's neighbor as oneself (Lev. 19:18). In agreement, the lawyer and Jesus exchange compliments. Although the Jerusalem leader is not a follower, Jesus states that the man's understanding of divine principles brings him close to God's kingdom (12:28–34)—a warmer commendation than Jesus accords any of his own disciples.

Mark concludes his narration of the Temple ministry on a nonconfrontational theme. The poor widow who gives her all to a cause in which she believes provides a model of single-minded dedication for Mark's readers and also reminds them that the essence of Jewish piety is not animal sacrifice or other ritual (on which the Temple priests focus their energies) but care for widows, orphans, and other persons in need (12:41–44).

Jesus' Prophecy of the Temple's Fall

The Gospel's tone changes abruptly in chapter 13, Jesus' discourse on the imminent destruction of the Temple and the future coming of the Son of Man to judge the world. This extensive collection of Jesus' sayings appears to combine material from a variety of sources, especially Jewish apocalyptic material. How much of the discourse originated with Jesus and how much represents interpretation by visionaries and prophets in Mark's Christian community is unknown. A considerably expanded version of the speech is preserved in Matthew 24, and a sig-

nificantly modified version of the apocalyptic elements appears in Luke 21. John's Gospel contains no comparable eschatological prophecy.

After perusing Mark 13 carefully, the reader will find two somewhat contradictory views of the impending End. On the one hand, disasters, sufferings, and astronomical phenomena will provide unmistakable "signs" that the end is near. Calamities will announce the End as surely as the fig tree's budding proclaims the onset of spring (13:8, 14–20, 24–31). On the other, neither the Son nor his followers can know the time of judgment, so one must keep constant watch because the End occurs without previous warning (13:32–37).

Mark's emphasis on political and social disasters as signs of the End can be explained by the turbulent era in which he wrote. As mentioned previously, scholars believe that Mark composed his Gospel during the Jewish Revolt against Rome, when battles and violent uprisings were daily occurrences. The great war against Rome seemed to signal a turning point in history, a crisis in which the Messiah's appearance was the expected culmination. Mark is concerned that Christians are not misled by rumors of new messiahs or people claiming to be Jesus returned. Mark's anxiety about false saviors indicates that his community was familiar with predictions about Jesus' reappearance that were proven false when they failed to materialize (13:5–6, 21–23). The social or legal position of Christians living in Palestine during the Jewish Revolt is not known, but Mark suggests that many believers were persecuted. Some militant Jews may have attacked Jewish Christians for supposedly betraying their nation's interests. The Romans may have arrested or executed others for suspected disloyalty to Rome.

The "abomination." Mark adds a cryptic passage from the Book of Daniel to the prophetic discourse that he attributes to Jesus. He states that "the abomination of desolation" will appear as a decisive sign of the End. Mark reveals that he incorporates an older written source into

The Adoration of the Magi, by Fra Angelico (active
c. 1417–55). Loosely based on Matthew's nativity
story, this scene depicts the paradox of Jesus' birth.
Although humbly born in a Bethlehem stable,
the infant Jesus is a divine king destined to rule the
world. The artist pictures Jesus' future subjects as
an endless procession of worshippers—Jews and
Greeks as well as the Magi (Babylonian or Persian
astrologers). Like most Renaissance painters,
Angelico shows his characters dressed in the
fashions of his own day. (Courtesy of the Cortona
Museo, Italy, and Art Resource, New York.)

The Baptism of Christ, by Piero della Francesca
(c. 1420–92). Following Mark 1:9–10, the painter
depicts Jesus being baptized by John the Baptist as
the Holy Spirit—in the form of a dove—descends
to hover over Jesus' head. Note the figure in the
background undressing, presumably to be
immersed in the Jordan River (foreground).
(Courtesy of the National Gallery, London,
and Art Resource, New York.)

The Transfiguration, by Sanzio Raphael (1483–1520). In this brilliant recreation of Jesus' sudden transformation into a being of light, Raphael projects an overpowering sense of Jesus' divinity. Going beyond the Synoptic accounts, the artist portrays a larger audience witnessing this revelation of Jesus' supernatural character (compare Mark 9:28 and parallels). (Courtesy of the Vatican Museum, Rome, and Art Resource, New York.)

The Raising of Lazarus, by Nicolas Froment (c. 1450–90). Froment's grimly realistic depiction of Lazarus, who had been dead for four days when Jesus raised him (John 11:39), shows the resurrected figure still bearing the marks of the grave. Note Martha and an unidentified male figure to the right covering their faces to avoid the stench of decay. (Courtesy of the Uffizi Gallery, Florence, and Art Resource, New York.)

Christ Chasing the Money Changers from the Temple, by El Greco (c. 1548–1614 or 1625). The artist uses clashing colors to depict Jesus' righteous anger as he drives the moneychangers from the Jerusalem Temple. Note the contrast between the turbulence and confusion of those under Jesus' lash (on the left side of the painting) and the calm prevailing among the disciples who ponder the meaning of their leader's violent action (on the right side of the painting). (Madrid, Church of St. Gines. Courtesy of the Minneapolis Institute of Arts, Dunwoddy Fund, and Art Resource, New York.)

The Last Supper, by Tintoretto (1518–94). In this depiction of Jesus' final meal with his disciples, the Christ figure appears already to be receding into the distance. The scene is illuminated partly by the radiance surrounding Jesus' head and partly by the flames from a lamp, whose smoke twists into the outlines of angelic spiritual presences invisible to the participants. Tintoretto thus suggests that in dispensing the bread and wine that represent his flesh and blood, Jesus does more than establish the ritual of the Eucharist. He also leaves his followers the dual legacy of his personal light and the light of the lamp—the Spirit that will illuminate the way for his disciples after his departure (John 14–16). (Courtesy of the S. Giorgio Maggiore, Venice, and Art Resource, New York.)

The Sacrament of the Last Supper, by Salvador Dali (1904–86). Like that of Tintoretto, this twentieth-century version of the Last Supper (and first communion meal) interprets the supernatural significance of this event. The glowing light behind Jesus seems to emanate from him as well as shine through his body, which is already undergoing the trans–formation to a spiritual existence. The outstretched arms above Jesus suggest both the imminent crucifixion and Christ's open embrace that encompasses the meditating disciples. (Courtesy of the National Gallery, Washington, D.C.)

The Road to Calvary, by Tintoretto (1518–94). Following John's account (John 19:16–18), Tintoretto shows Jesus bearing his own cross all the way to Golgotha. Note that the two criminals to be crucified next to Jesus are rendered in the dark foreground but Jesus is shown fully illuminated. The painter visually illustrates John's theme that Jesus' crucifixion is a glorification leading to his ascension into the world of light. (Courtesy of Scoula San Rocco, Venice, and Art Resource, New York.)

The Crucifixion, from the Isenheim Altarpiece, by Matthias Grünewald (c. 1470–1528). Following John's version of Jesus' execution rather than the Synoptics, Grünewald shows Jesus' mother with the beloved disciple at the foot of the cross (John 19:25–27). Note the artist's powerful blending of realism and symbolism. Mary's intense grief and Jesus' physical torment are presented with naturalistic detail. By contrast, the presence of John the Baptist at the right and the transference of the crucifixion site from a hill outside Jerusalem to a lonely mountaintop silhouetted against a blue-black sky are symbolic. The event thus transcends ordinary history and passes into a timeless dimension. (Courtesy of the Musée Unterlinden, Colmar, France, and the Art Institute, New York.)

The Resurrection, from the Isenheim Altarpiece, by Matthias Grünewald
(c. 1470–1528). Grünewald's painting of the crucifixion depicted the
human Jesus' agony and ostensible defeat; the artist's depiction of the resurrection is a joyous burst of color celebrating Jesus' triumph over death.
Note that the Roman soldier, stunned by the force of Jesus' rising, lies in
the darkened foreground, earth-bound, while the transformed Christ is
surrounded by eternal light emanating from his own person. (Courtesy of
the Musée Unterlinden, Colmar, France, and Art Resource, New York.)

The Descent of the Spirit at Pentecost, by El Greco (c. 1548–1614 or 1625). Following the account in Acts 2, El Greco shows the Spirit's presence as tongues of flame writhing above the disciples' heads. In the vision of Luke-Acts, the church's reception of the Spirit corresponds to Jesus' experience after baptism, empowering his followers to continue the work he had begun. (Madrid, Prado. Courtesy of Art Resource, New York.)

Jesus' speech when he parenthetically warns "the reader" not to misinterpret this symbolic event (13:14). Both the mysterious "abomination" and reference to a "tribulation" so unbearable that humanity could not survive it unless God cuts it short are borrowed from the Book of Daniel (Dan. 11:32; 12:1). Like Daniel, Mark apparently wrote during a period when the faithful lived under such severe conditions that they could be saved only through divine intervention. In this case the appearance of the Son of Man would deliver those Christians who had been faithful to the end (13:13, 26).

In Daniel's apocalypse, the "abomination" was the erection of a statue (idol) of the Olympian Zeus in the Temple precincts. To what desecration of the Temple in the mid–first century Mark's Jesus refers is unknown, but for him it signals a warning to leave Jerusalem and Judea and "take to the hills." The historian Eusebius mentions an "oracle" or divine pronouncement that incited members of the early Jerusalem church to abandon the city and seek refuge in Pella, an obscure town among the Greek settlements east of the Jordan River. Mark's urgent advice to his readers not even to go back for their coats or other belongings when the apocalyptic sign appears may have been the source of the oracle Eusebius cited.

The Last Supper and Jesus' Betrayal

Following Jesus' prophecy of judgment, Mark shows him at two private gatherings where Jesus prepares for death—the ultimate sacrifice that supersedes the Temple offerings. In the first instance, Mark pictures Jesus among Israel's outcasts, at the home of a leper named Simon—a man whose disease places him outside the Jewish covenant community (Lev. 13; Deut. 24:8). There Jesus predicts that the woman who anoints him with oil, as if for burial, will be honored wherever his message is proclaimed (14:3–9).

In dramatic contrast to the woman's devotion is **Judas Iscariot's** decision to betray his Master. Mark supplies no real motive for Judas' treach-ery, simply stating that he voluntarily arranges to hand Jesus over to the Sadducean leadership, which pays him for the job (14:1–2, 10–11).

The communion bread and wine. The second gathering features the most solemn and significant event of Jesus' Jerusalem ministry, a meal known as the **Last Supper.** Pictured as a celebration of **Passover** with the Twelve, the supper concludes with Jesus instructing his disciples to partake of bread and wine as emblems of his body and blood. In equating the wine with "the blood of the covenant," Mark interprets Jesus' imminent death as a sacrifice that inaugurates a new relationship between God and believing humanity. In the Gospel writers' view, the Christian community now becomes the new covenant people, replacing Israel (14:24–25). The initiation ceremony ends with Jesus' enigmatic vow not to taste wine again until he drinks a new vintage in the kingdom—a new reality that his death brings a vital step closer.

While Mark preserves the oldest Gospel account of Jesus' instituting the **Eucharist** or **Holy Communion,** Paul's first letter to the Corinthians records an even earlier version of the ceremony (1 Cor. 11:23–26). In comparing Mark and Paul, notice that both writers associate the ritual meal with the origin of a new covenant (testament) but that Paul interprets Communion primarily as a memorial of Jesus' death—to be reenacted until the **Second Coming** (1 Cor. 11:26).

The Agony in Gethsemane

In narrating Jesus' Passion—his final suffering and death—Mark stresses Jesus' vulnerability to the world's evil. His tone stark and grim, Mark shows Jesus falling completely into the power of his enemies, who treat him with savage cruelty (14:65; 15:15–20). Emphasizing his hero's total aloneness during his last hours, the author states that all Jesus' friends abandon him (14:50)—including God (15:34).

The agony begins in Gethsemane, a grove or vineyard on the Mount of Olives to which Jesus and his disciples withdraw following the Last Supper. When reading this episode (14:28–52), notice Mark's dual emphasis on Jesus' fulfilling predictions in the Jewish Bible (14:26–31, 49) and on his personal anguish. While the disciples mindlessly sleep, Jesus faces the hard reality of his suffering, experiencing "grief" and "horror and dismay." To Mark, his hero—emotionally ravaged and physically defenseless—provides the model for all believers whose loyalty is tested. Although Jesus prays that God will spare him the humiliation and pain he dreads, he forces his own will into harmony with God's. Mark records that even during this cruel testing of the heavenly Father–Son of Man relationship, Jesus addresses the Deity as "Abba," an Aramaic term expressing a child's trusting intimacy with the parent (14:32–41).

Peter's Denial of Jesus

Mark's skill as a storyteller—and interpreter of the events he narrates—is demonstrated in the artful way he organizes his account of Jesus' Passion. Peter's testing (14:37–38) and denial that he even knows Jesus (15:65–72) provide the frame for—and ironic parallel to—Jesus' trial before the Sanhedrin (the Jewish religious council headed by Caiaphas, the High Priest). When Peter fulfills Jesus' prediction about denying him, the disciple's failure serves two purposes. It confirms Jesus' prophetic gifts and also strengthens the reader's confidence in Jesus' ability to fulfill other prophecies, including his foretold resurrection (14:28) and his reappearance as the glorified Son of Man (14:62).

Jesus Before the Sanhedrin

Mark contrasts Peter's fearful denial with Jesus' bold admission to the Sanhedrin that he is indeed the Messiah and the appointed agent of God's future judgment (14:62). The one time Jesus speaks openly to confirm that he is the Mes-

siah, the self-revelation costs him his life: the **Sanhedrin** judges his claims as worthy of death (14:63–64). The only Gospel writer to show Jesus explicitly accepting a messianic identity at his trial, Mark may do so to stress his theme that Jesus is a Messiah revealed primarily through his willing submission to a sacrificial death (10:45). Like the author of Hebrews, Mark sees Jesus' divine sonship earned and perfected through trial and suffering (Heb. 2:9–11; 5:7–10).

Mark's account of Jesus' hearing before the Sanhedrin is difficult to reconcile with what is known about that body's strict rules of evidence and legal procedure. According to judicial regulations later described in the Talmud, a vast collection of Jewish writings assembled about 200 CE, Jesus' trial was illegal. It was conducted secretly at night and did not give the accused an opportunity to present witnesses on his behalf. Many scholars question the historical reliability of the Synoptic reports because these accounts do not accurately represent the high standards of justice that the Sanhedrin traditionally maintained. Some historians argue that the Gospel trial narratives falsely implicate Jewish authorities. They argue further that there is no historical basis for believing that Jewish leaders arrested Jesus and turned one of their own people over to the Romans. Advocates of this view point out that the Roman governor convicted and executed Jesus on a charge of treason against the imperial government and that Jewish involvement was not necessary to obtain Jesus' indictment in a Roman court. In John's version of the trial Jesus is accused by a group of Sadducees, but he does not appear formally before the Sanhedrin. Instead, Jesus is given a private hearing in the house of Annas, a former High Priest and the father-in-law of Caiaphas (John 18:12–14).

The Trial Before Pilate: Charges of Treason

After arguing that the leaders of Jesus' own nation condemned him as a heretic, Mark presents a contrasting trial before the Roman governor, **Pontius Pilate.** The author does not explain why the Sanhedrin fails to execute Jesus (the Mosaic Law prescribed death for blasphemy), but John's Gospel states that the Jewish Council did not have the legal authority to inflict capital punishment (John 18:31). In fact, the extent of the Sanhedrin's legal powers during this period is not known. Mark's presentation of Jesus' two trials emphasizes the important distinction drawn between the religious and political accusations made against the prisoner. Whereas the High Priest had asked if Jesus were the Messiah (Christ), Pilate demands to know if he is (or claims to be) "the king of the Jews" (15:2)—a question loaded with political implications. If Jesus makes such a claim, his is guilty of sedition, a capital offense. Jesus' reply is ambiguous and has been variously translated " 'The words are yours' " (NEB) or " 'It is you who say it' " (15:2, Jerusalem Bible). The response may mean, among other things, that Pilate has assumed correctly that Jesus is the rightful Jewish monarch or that Pilate must draw his own conclusions. After this comment, Jesus lapses into complete silence, refusing to answer further questions (15:3–5). Like the other Gospel writers, Mark creates his record of Jesus' trials in the context of prophecies from the Hebrew Bible. This fact makes it difficult to tell if Jesus' silence represents his actual behavior or the author's reliance on Isaiah 53, where Israel's suffering servant does not respond to his accusers (Isa. 53:7).

Barabbas. At this point Mark interrupts his narrative flow to introduce the figure of **Barabbas** (whose name means "Son of the Father"), a murderer (perhaps a guerrilla fighter against Rome) whom the Romans already had condemned to death. To Mark, the Barabbas episode suggests several important concepts: the mob that prefers the guilty Barabbas to the innocent Jesus is equally blind to Jesus' identity and God's will, a condition necessary to effect Jesus' predestined death. Pilate's freeing of the unworthy prisoner also illustrates the Markan theme that Jesus dies to save others, no matter how ostensibly undeserving (10:45). From Mark's viewpoint, Barabbas is the first of many "sinners" whom Jesus' sacrifice benefits.

The Crucifixion

Mark's painfully bleak description of Jesus' trials and crucifixion contrasts with his more generalized account of the Galilean ministry. The Markan Passion story brims with concrete details, including specific geographical sites and a cast of named characters, many of whom appear for the first time. Note the specific actions Mark records, including the Roman soldiers' torment of their victim, expressing Roman contempt for a man who claims to be king but has no power to enforce respect (15:6–20).

Simon of Cyrene. Mark reports that Jesus, perhaps exhausted by the flogging that Pilate's soldiers inflict, collapses on his way to Golgotha, the hill of execution outside Jerusalem. When Jesus proves unable to bear the heavy beam that Roman custom requires a condemned man to carry to his crucifixion, soldiers impress a passerby, Simon of Cyrene, to take up the burden. (The prisoner carried only the crossbeam, which was later affixed to an upright stake that was permanently installed at Golgotha.) Specifying that Jesus is nailed to his cross at nine in the morning (15:25) and dies about three in the afternoon (15:34–37), Mark indicates that Jesus' agony lasts about six hours. Because crucifixion usually brings death by slow asphyxiation as the victim's lungs collapse, many strong prisoners suffered for days before expiring. Jesus' death occurs surprisingly quickly, as Pilate later observes (15:44).

Since the government intended public executions as a warning to potential troublemakers, Pilate orders a sign recording Jesus' crime posted on the cross: the prisoner claimed to be "The king of the Jews" (15:21–27). Reporting this touch, Mark ironically proclaims Jesus' true identity, which is also the cause of his rejection and death.

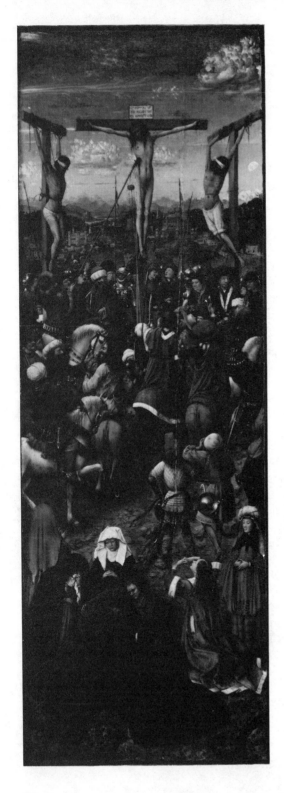

The Crucifixion by Jan Van Eyck (c. 1390–1441).
Note the unruly mob surrounding Jesus and the
Roman soldier thrusting a spear into his victim's
side (a detail found only in John 19:34). (Courtesy
of the Metropolitan Museum of Art, New York.
Fletcher Fund, 1933.)

The Paradox of Jesus' "Failure"

Mark's picture of Jesus' hanging on the cross is almost unendurably harsh. Powerless, defeated, and ridiculous in his assumed pretensions to kingly authority, Jesus endures mockery from every segment of his society—from Roman soldier to Jewish priest to his fellow victims of Roman oppression (15:29–32). As Mark so darkly paints it, the scene is a tragic paradox: Jesus is neither guilty nor defeated. The failure lies in humanity's collective inability to recognize the sufferer's inestimable value. To emphasize the spiritual blindness of Jesus' tormenters, Mark records that darkness envelops the earth (15:33).

Although a partial eclipse of the sun would have been visible in Palestine on April 13, 33 CE (one of the possible dates of the crucifixion), Mark does not state the source of the phenomenon. The Evangelist is not interested in scientific explanations but in recalling the plague of darkness that befell the Egyptians when their leaders resisted the purpose of Israel's God (Exod. 10:21–24; see also Isa. 60:2). The shutting out of light, God's first creation (Gen. 1), makes literal the symbolic state of those responsible for Jesus' death.

Emphasizing the negative relentlessly, Mark's Passion story also suggests a blackness of despair in Jesus' last words. Just before dying, Jesus cries out in Aramaic, " '*Eli, Eli, lema sabachthani?*' ": " 'My God, My God, why hast thou forsaken me?' " (15:33). In placing this question—a direct quotation of Psalms 22:1—on Jesus' lips, the author may echo a memory of Jesus' actual cry. Mark's main purpose, however, probably is to demonstrate that the manner of Jesus' death fulfills biblical prophecy. Whatever his aim, Mark's effect is to intensify the hopelessness of Jesus' death. No divine intervention rescues the Son of Man from his fate or vindicates his claim to inaugurate the kingdom.

As Mark records it, only one person sees Jesus' painful death as a divine revelation: an unnamed Roman **centurion** exclaims: " 'Truly, this man was a son of God' " (15:39). The centurion's insight, contrasting with others' blindness, probably had particular significance to Mark's original audience, many of whom were non-Jews. The only human being in the entire Gospel to perceive that Jesus is somehow divine is a Gentile!

Jesus' Burial

Mark's narative grows increasingly detailed in his description of Jesus' burial. Whereas Mark does not even mention the High Priest's name (**Caiaphas**) at the Sanhedrin trial, he precisely names the women who observe Jesus' crucifixion and entombment. As in all four Gospel accounts, **Mary of Magdala** provides the key human link connecting Jesus' crucifixion, burial, and the subsequent discovery that his tomb is empty (15:40–41, 47; 16:1).

Joseph of Arimathaea. Introduced late in Mark's narrative, **Joseph of Arimathaea** is a mysterious figure. He serves a single function: to transfer Jesus' body from Roman control to that of the dead man's disciples. Acquainted with Pilate, a member of the Sanhedrin and yet a covert supporter of Jesus' ministry, he bridges the two opposing worlds of Jesus' enemies and friends. Not only does Joseph obtain Pilate's permission to remove the body from the cross, he provides a secure place of entombment, a rock-hewn sepulcher that he seals by rolling a large stone across the entrance (15:42–47).

Postlude: The Empty Tomb

Because the Jewish Sabbath begins at sundown Friday, the day of Jesus' execution, the women disciples are unable to prepare the corpse for its permanent rest until Sunday morning. Although Mark stresses that they arrive at the tomb at an extremely early hour, the women find the entrance stone already rolled back and the sepulcher empty except for the presence of a young man dressed in white. (Is he the same unidentified youth who fled naked from Gethsemane in 14:50–51?)

Mark's empty tomb scene emphasizes themes similar to those that appear throughout the Gospel. The women are bewildered, unable to understand what has happened. Too frightened to tell what they have seen, they disobey the young man's instructions to alert Peter and the other disciples. Even the women, who have been faithful unto death, fail to muster enough faith to heed the stranger's instruction. Ending his Gospel as abruptly as he had begun it, Mark leaves the reader hanging in suspense. The youth, declaring that Jesus still lives, echoes Jesus' promise to appear posthumously "in Galilee" (14:28; 16:1–8), but Mark does not provide a confirmation of the resurrection. As it had during his hero's difficult lifetime, mystery also surrounds the risen Jesus.

Mark's strange inconclusiveness, his insistence on stressing the frustration and gloom of his vision of Jesus' mission right to the end of his narrative, must have seemed as unsatisfactory to early readers as it does to us. For perhaps that reason, Mark's Gospel has been heavily edited, with two different conclusions added at different times. All the oldest manuscripts of Mark end with the line stressing the women's terrified silence (16:8). Later editors, however, appended postresurrection appearances to their copies of Mark, apparently drawing on incidents contained in Matthew and Luke (16:9--20 and 16:20b).

To many scholars it seems likely that Mark does not include reports of Jesus' resurrection because the author expects Jesus' return in glory (the **Parousia**) to occur in the near future (9:1; 13:30). In Mark's strongly apocalyptic vision, the Messiah's reappearance would be a fitting climax to the social upheaval and persecution Christians were then experiencing during the "tribulation" of the Jewish War against Rome. If this view is correct, the young man's directive to seek Jesus "in Galilee" (16:7) is an order to await the Second Coming in the land where

Jesus first proclaimed the good news of the kingdom's arrival.

Mark's Gospel is probably early Christianity's first attempt to compile a sequential account of Jesus' public ministry, arrest, and execution. The Gospel includes relatively little of Jesus' teaching and instead stresses his actions—exorcisms, healings, and other miracles, which are presented as evidence that the kingdom of God is about to dawn. Mark paints Jesus as a strongly apocalyptic figure who appears suddenly on the earthly scene and who promises to reappear soon as the Son of Man, who judges all people at the world's End.

Mark's peculiar themes give his Gospel a somewhat austere and gloomy ambience. He depicts Jesus as an unexpected, and unwanted, kind of Messiah who is predestined to be misunderstood and rejected. Mark's Jesus is a Messiah revealed only in suffering and death. In the author's view, true followers must be prepared to suffer as their Master did. Abandoned by all his disciples except for a few Galilean women, Mark's Jesus dies alone and in apparent despair. Mark's narrative does not offer the comfort of reporting his hero's physical resurrection appearances but asks the reader to look beyond death and the world's evil to faith in Jesus' promised return.

QUESTIONS FOR DISCUSSION AND REVIEW

1. According to tradition, who wrote the Gospel of Mark? Why are modern scholars unable to verify that tradition? What themes in the Gospel suggest that it was composed after the Jewish Revolt against Rome had already begun?

2. How is Jesus' career connected to that of John the Baptist? Was Jesus originally a member of John's reform movement?

3. Describe the elements in Mark that suggest that the writer believed that the *eschaton* was near. How are Jesus' works of healing and exorcism related to the kingdom's nearness? Does the author's belief in the literal existence of demons affect the credibility of his account?

4. Discuss Mark's identification of Jesus as "the Son of Man." How is that concept related to earlier Jewish writings and how is it connected to Jesus' view of his messiahship?

5. Define *parable* and discuss Mark's statements about why Jesus "never" taught without using figurative language. Is Jesus' use of parables connected to Mark's theme of the "messianic secret"?

6. In Mark's view, why does no one really appreciate or understand Jesus? How does Mark link his related themes of the disciples' stupidity, the hidden quality of Jesus' messiahship, and the Jerusalem leadership's rejection of Jesus? Explain how these themes are interconnected.

7. Mark's Jesus predicts his coming death three times. How does Mark's story of Jesus' worldly "failure"—his public rejection and crucifixion—illustrate the age-old problem of evil, the undeserved suffering of the innocent?

8. If the author is telling "good news," why does he compose such a gloomy narrative that emphasizes death and suffering for both Jesus and his disciples? Why does he include no postresurrection appearances?

9. A careful reading of Mark's Gospel shows that the author paints a generally unfavorable picture of virtually all Jesus' earthly associates—including his family, his Nazarean neighbors, and his disciples. In ordinary circumstances a biographer relies heavily on his subject's relatives, friends, and other acquaintances for information necessary to the composition of an accurate biography. Why do you think that Mark disassociates his subject from these sources of information?

10. Mark's picture of Jesus as an apocalyptic figure announcing the imminent arrival of God's kingdom established a pattern that later Gospel writers, including Matthew and Luke, generally followed. The group that produced John's Gospel, however, did not remember Jesus as an apocalyptic preacher. Unlike the Synoptic Gospels, John's account includes no prophecies about Jerusalem's fall or other apocalyptic events. Is it possible that Mark paints the Twelve and Jesus' other associates in an unflattering light in order to downplay their original concept of Jesus and to forward the author's view that Jesus' ministry inaugurated the time of the End?

TERMS AND CONCEPTS TO REMEMBER

John the Baptist	Caiaphas
Galilee	Pontius Pilate
Mark's apocalyptic urgency	the Eucharist
the kingdom of God	the Last Supper
demons and demonic possession	the Second Coming (*Parousia*)
exorcism	the fall of Jerusalem
Zoroastrianism	the Passion
Son of Man	the Sanhedrin (Great Council)
parable	Gethsemane
simile	Golgotha
allegory	Peter
the messianic secret	Judas Iscariot
the transfiguration	Joseph of Arimathaea
the *eschaton*	

RECOMMENDED READING

Best, Ernest. *Mark, the Gospel as Story.* Edinburgh: T.&T. Clarke, 1983.

————. *The Temptation and the Passion in Mark.* Cambridge: Cambridge University Press, 1965.

Cameron, Ron. "The Secret Gospel of Mark." In *The Other Gospels: Non-Canonical Gospel Texts,* 67–71. Philadelphia: Westminster Press, 1982.

Grant, F. C. *The Gospels: Their Origins and Their Growth.* New York: Harper & Row, 1957. A useful introduction.

Grant, Michael. *Jesus: An Historian's Review of the Gospels.* New York: Scribner's, 1977. A good general introduction to the subject.

Kee, H. C. *Community of the New Age: Studies in Mark's Gospel.* Philadelphia: Westminster Press, 1976. A skilled historical-critical analysis of Mark's Gospel.

Kelber, W. H. *Mark's Story of Jesus.* Philadelphia: Fortress Press, 1979. A penetrating but succinct analysis of Mark's presentation of Jesus' life.

Rhoads, David, and Donald Michie. *Mark as Story: An Introduction to the Narrative of a Gospel.* Philadelphia: Fortress Press, 1982. An excellent literary study.

FOR MORE ADVANCED STUDY

Kelber, W. H. *The Oral and the Written Gospel: The Hermeneutics of Speaking and Writing in the Synoptic Tradition, Mark, Paul, and Q.* Philadelphia: Fortress Press, 1983. An incisive and scholarly study of Mark's place in the Jesus tradition.

Mann, C. S. *Mark: A New Translation, Interpretation and Commentary.* Vol. 27 of The Anchor Bible. Garden City, N.Y.: Doubleday, 1986.

Robinson, J. M. *The Problem of History in Mark and Other Markan Studies.* Philadelphia: Fortress Press, 1982.

Streeter, B. H. *The Four Gospels: A Study in Origins.* New York: Macmillan, 1924. A classic statement of the relationship of the Synoptic Gospels, arguing Mark's priority.

Tuckett, Christopher, ed. *The Messianic Secret.* Philadelphia: Fortress Press, 1983.

Weeden, T. J. *Traditions in Conflict.* Philadelphia: Fortress Press, 1971.

8 Matthew's Portrait of Jesus: The Great Teacher

> Do not suppose that I have come to abolish the Law
> and the prophets; I did not come to abolish, but to
> complete.
>
> (Matthew 5:17)

KEY THEMES   Matthew's Gospel presents a comprehensive collection of Jesus' ethical teachings and provides a behaviorial guide for the *ekklesia*, the early Christian community. The Gospel contains most of Mark's narrative plus much additional material that emphasizes Jesus' divine sonship and supernatural powers. An infancy narrative and a report of postresurrection appearances frame the central account of Jesus' public career, which Matthew expands by including five long discourses highlighting Jesus' kingdom teachings. In Matthew's Gospel Jesus is depicted as the supreme teacher and interpreter of the Mosaic Torah, the principles of which remain binding on the author's community. Matthew presents Jesus' life in terms of its fulfilling prophecies from the Jewish Bible and stresses Jesus' credentials as Israel's true Messiah. Like Mark's account, Matthew's Gospel represents Jesus as an apocalyptic preacher who announces that God's rule is imminent. Matthew, however, dilutes the apocalyptic content of Jesus' message by adding parables that picture the church's long-term obligation to make converts worldwide before Jesus returns.

If Mark was the first Gospel written, as most scholars believe, why does Matthew's Gospel stand first in the New Testament canon? The original compilers of the New Testament probably assigned Matthew its premier position for several reasons. It offers a more extensive coverage of Jesus' teaching than any other Gospel, making it the church's major resource in instructing its members. In addition, Matthew's Gospel was particularly important to early church leaders because it is the Gospel most explicitly concerned with the nature and function of the church (Greek, *ekklesia*). The only Gospel even to use the term *ekklesia*, Matthew devotes two full chapters (chs. 10 and 18) to providing specific guidance to the Christian community.

The placement of Matthew's Gospel at the opening of the New Testament is also thematically appropriate because it forms a strong connecting link with the Hebrew Bible (Old Testament). Matthew starts his account with a genealogy to associate Jesus with the most prominent heroes of ancient Israel. Beginning with Abraham, progenitor of the Hebrew people, Matthew lists as Jesus' ancestors celebrated kings like David, Solomon, and Josiah. From the outset, the author intends to establish Jesus' credentials as the "seed" (descendant) of Abraham through whom God will bless all nations

BOX 8-1   *Representative Examples of Matthew's Use of the Old Testament to Identify Jesus as the Promised Messiah*

Matthew: "All this happened in order to fulfil what the Lord declared through the prophet. . . ." (Matt. 1:22)	Old Testament Source
1. "The Virgin will conceive and bear a son, and he shall be called Emmanuel." (Matt. 1:22)	1. A young woman is with child, and she will bear a son and will call him Immanuel. (Isaiah 7:14)
2. "Bethlehem in the land of Judah, you are far from least in the eyes of the rulers of Judah; for out of you shall come a leader to be the shepherd of my people Israel." (Matt. 2:5–6)	2. But you, Bethlehem in Ephrathah, small as you are to be among Judah's clans, out of you shall come forth a governor for Israel, one whose roots are far back in the past, in days gone by. (Micah 5:2)
3. So Joseph . . . went away . . . to Egypt, and there he stayed till Herod's death. This was to fulfill what the Lord had declared through the prophet: "I called my son out of Egypt." (Matt. 2:15)	3. When Israel was a boy, I loved him; I called my son out of Egypt. (Hosea 11:1)
4. Herod . . . gave orders for the massacre of all children in Bethlehem and its neighborhood, of the age of two years or less. . . . So the words spoken through Jeremiah the prophet were fulfilled: "A voice was heard in Rama, wailing and loud laments; it was Rachael weeping for her children, and refusing all consolation, because they were no more." (Matt. 2:16–18)	4. Hark, lamentation is heard in Ramah, and bitter weeping, Rachel weeping for her sons. She refuses to be comforted: they are no more. (Jeremiah 31:15)
5. "He shall be called a Nazarene." (Matt. 2:23)	5. Then a shoot shall grow from the stock of Jesse, and a branch [Hebrew, *nezer*] shall spring from his roots. (Isaiah 11:1)
6. When he heard that John had been arrested, Jesus withdrew to Galilee; and leaving Nazareth he went and settled at Capernaum on the Sea of Galilee, in the district of Zebulun and Naphtali. This was to fulfil the passage in the prophet Isaiah which tells of "the land of Zebulun, the land of Naphtali, the Way of the Sea, the land beyond Jordan, heathen Galilee," and says: The people that lived in darkness saw a great light: light dawned on the dwellers in the land of death's dark shadow. (Matt. 4:12–16)	6. For, while the first invader has dealt lightly with the land of Zebulun and the land of Naphtali, the second has dealt heavily with Galilee of the Nations on the road beyond Jordan to the sea. The people who walked in darkness have seen a great light: light has dawned upon them. dwellers in a land as dark as death. (Isaiah 9:1–2)

BOX 8-1 *continued*

Matthew: "All this happened in order to fulfil what the Lord declared through the prophet. . . ." (Matt. 1:22)	Old Testament Source
7. And he drove the spirits out with a word and healed all who were sick, to fulfill the prophecy of Isaiah: "He took away our illnesses and lifted our diseases from us." (Matt. 8:16–17)	7. Yet on himself he bore our sufferings, our torments he endured, while we counted him smitten by God, struck down by disease and misery. (Isaiah 53:4)
8. Jesus . . . gave strict injunctions that they were not to make him known. This was to fulfil Isaiah's prophecy: Here is my servant, whom I have chosen, my beloved on whom my favour rests; I will put my spirit upon him, and he will proclaim judgement among the nations. He will not strive, he will not shout, nor will his voice be heard in the streets. He will not snap off the broken reed, nor snuff out the smouldering wick, until he leads justice on to victory. In him the nations shall place their hope. (Matt. 12:16–21)	8. Here is my servant, whom I uphold, my chosen one in whom I delight, I have bestowed my spirit upon him, and he will make justice shine on the nations. He will not call out or lift his voice high, Or make himself heard in the open street. He will not break a bruised reed, or snuff out a smouldering wick; he will make justice shine on every race, never faltering, never breaking down, he will plant justice on earth, while coasts and islands wait for his teaching. (Isaiah 42:1–4)
9. In all his teaching to the crowds Jesus spoke in parables; in fact he never spoke to them without a parable. This was to fulfil the prophecy of Isaiah: I will open my mouth in parables; I will utter things kept secret since the world was made. (Matt. 13:34–35)	9. Mark my teaching, O my people, listen to the words I am to speak. I will tell you a story with a meaning, I will expound the riddle of things past, things that we have heard and know, and our fathers have repeated to us. (Psalms 78:2–*not* in Isaiah)
10. Jesus instructs his disciples to bring him a donkey and her foal. "If any speaks to you, say 'Our Master needs them'; and he will let you take them at once." This was to fulfil the prophecy which says, "Tell the daughter of Zion, 'Here is your king, who comes to you riding on an ass, riding on the foal of a beast of burden.' " (Matt. 21:2–5) [Matthew shows Jesus mounted on two beasts—the donkey *and* her foal. See Luke 19:29–36, where a single mount is mentioned.]	10. Rejoice, rejoice, daughter of Zion, shout aloud, daughter of Jerusalem; for see, your king is coming to you, his cause won, his victory gained, humble and mounted on an ass, on a foal, the young of a she-ass. (Zechariah 9:9)

(Gen. 22:18) and as the heir of King David who fulfills the promise that David's line would rule "forever" (2 Sam. 7:16). Hence, he first identifies his subject as "son of David" and "son of Abraham" (Matt. 1:1)—in contrast to Mark's opening identification of Jesus as "Son of God" Mark 1:1).

Relation to the Jewish Bible. Matthew's wish to connect Jesus with the Hebrew Bible goes far beyond genealogical concerns. More than any other Gospel writer, he presents Jesus' life in the context of biblical Law and prophecy. Throughout the entire Gospel, Matthew stresses Jesus' fulfillment of ancient prophecies, repeatedly emphasizing the continuity between Jesus and the promises made to Israel, particularly to the royal dynasty of David. In order to demonstrate that Jesus' entire career, from conception to resurrection, was predicted centuries earlier by Bible writers from Moses to Malachi, Matthew quotes from, paraphrases, or alludes to the Hebrew Bible at least 60 times. (Some scholars have detected 140 or more allusions to the Hebrew Scriptures.) Nearly a dozen times Matthew employs a literary formula that drives home the connection between prophecy and specific events in Jesus' life: "All this happened in order to fulfill what the Lord declared through the prophet. . . ," Matthew writes, then citing a biblical passage to support his contention (1:22–23; 2:15; 2:23; see Box 8-1).

Matthew takes great pains to show that Jesus both taught and fulfilled the principles of the Mosaic Law (5:17–20). For these and other reasons, Matthew is usually regarded as the "most Jewish" of the Gospels. At the same time, the author violently attacks the leaders of institutional Judaism, condemning the Pharisees and scribes with extreme bitterness (ch. 23).

Authorship, Date, and Place of Composition

The author. Who was the man so deeply interested in Jesus' practice of the Jewish religion and simultaneously so fierce in his denunciation of Jewish leaders? As in Mark's case, the author does not identify himself, suggesting to most historians that the Gospel originated and circulated anonymously. The tradition that the author is the "publican" or tax collector mentioned in Matthew 9:9–13 (and called "Levi" in Mark 2:14) dates from the late second century CE and cannot be verified. The main problem with accepting the Apostle **Matthew**'s authorship is that the writer relies heavily on Mark as a source. It is extremely unlikely that one of the original Twelve would depend on the work of Mark, who was not an eyewitness to the events he describes.

The oldest apparent reference to the Gospel's authorship is that of Papias (c. 140 CE), whom Eusebius quotes:

> Matthew compiled the Sayings [Greek, *logia*] in the Aramaic language, and everyone translated them as well as he could. (*History,* 3:39:16)

As many commentators have noted, the Sayings or *logia* are not the same as the "words" [Greek, *logoi*] of Jesus, nor are they the same as the Gospel of Matthew we have today. Whereas scholars once believed that Matthew's Gospel was first written in Aramaic by the Apostle who was formerly a tax collector, modern analysts point out that there is no evidence of an earlier Aramaic version of the Gospel. Papias's use of *logia* may refer to the fact that an early Christian, perhaps one named Matthew, compiled a list of Old Testament messianic prophecies, a collection that the author of our present Gospel later may have used.

Matthew and Judaism. The author remains unknown (we call him Matthew to avoid confusion), but scholarly analysis of his work enables us to gain some insight into his theological intentions and distinctive interests. Thoroughly versed in the Hebrew Bible, the writer is remarkably skilled at its **exegesis** (the explanation and critical interpretation of a literary text). Some scholars believe that he may have received scribal training, a professional discipline he utilizes to demonstrate to his fellow Jews that Jesus of Nazareth is the predicted Messiah. The author may refer to himself or to a "school" of early Christian interpreters of the Hebrew Scriptures when he states:

> When, therefore, a teacher of the law [a scribe] has become a learner [disciple] in the kingdom of Heaven, he is like a householder who can produce from his store both the new and the old. (13:52–53)

Matthew effectively combines "the new" (Christian teaching) with "the old" (Judaism). To him Jesus' teachings are the legitimate outgrowth of Torah study.

Recent scholarly investigations have demonstrated that several varieties of Jewish Christianity existed in the first-century church. The particular type to which Matthew belongs can only be inferred from examining relevant aspects of his Gospel. Some Jewish Christians demanded that all Gentile converts to the new faith keep the entire Mosaic Law or at least undergo circumcision (Acts 15:1–6; Gal. 6:11–16). Matthew does not mention circumcision, but he insists that the Mosaic Torah is binding upon believers (5:17–20). In his view, Christians are to continue such Jewish practices as fasting (6:16–18), regular prayer (6:5–6), charitable giving (6:2), and making formal sacrifices (5:23). His account also implies that Mosaic purity laws, forbidding certain foods, apply to his community. Matthew includes Mark's report of Jesus' controversy with the Pharisees over ritual handwashing but omits Mark's conclusion that Jesus declares all foods ceremonially clean (compare 15:1–20 with Mark 7:1–23, especially 7:19).

Matthew depicts Jesus' personal religion as Torah Judaism, but he has no patience with Jewish leaders who disagree with his conclusions. He labels them "blind guides" and hypocrites (23:13–28). Despite his contempt for Jewish opponents, however, Matthew retains his respect for Pharisaic teachings and urges the church to "pay attention to their words" (23:3).

In his use of scriptural quotations and **pesher** (commentary), Matthew employs interpretative methods common to the Judaism of his day. Like the writers at Qumran, the Essene community of dedicated monklike scholars who withdrew from the world to await the final battle between good and evil, Matthew interprets the prophecies of the Hebrew Bible as applying exclusively to his group of believers, whom he regards as the true Israel. He also commonly presents Jesus' teaching as a kind of midrash on the Torah. A detailed exposition of the underlying meaning of a biblical text, a **midrash** includes interpretation of Scripture's legal rules for daily life (called **Halakah**) and explanation of nonlegal material (called **Haggadah**). At various points in his Gospel, Matthew shows Jesus providing halakic interpretations of the Torah (5:17–48), particularly on such legal matters as Sabbath observance and divorce (12:1–21; 19:3–12).

Date and place of composition. The Gospel gives few clues to its precise time of origin, but Matthew apparently refers to Jerusalem's destruction as an accomplished fact (22:7). The author's hostility to the Jewish leadership and references to "their" synagogues (9:35; 10:17; 12:9; 13:54) may suggest that he wrote after the Christians already had been expelled from Jewish meeting places, an expulsion that occurred about 85 or 90 CE.

The earliest reference to Matthew's Gospel occurs in the letters of Ignatius, who was bishop of Antioch in Syria about 110–15 CE. It appears, then, that Matthew was composed at some point between about 85 and 110 CE, perhaps in the late 80s or early 90s CE. Antioch, a major Jewish-Christian center where the Gospel was apparently first known, is the probable place of composition. The reader must remember, however, that in the case of all four Gospels we do not know for sure when, where, or by whom they were written. Modern scholarship has revealed the historical weaknesses of many old traditions about these matters but, in the absence of objective evidence, cannot provide definitive answers.

The Author's Purpose

In composing his Gospel, Matthew has several major objectives. Three of the most important are demonstrating Jesus' credentials as Israel's true Messiah; presenting Jesus as the supreme teacher and interpreter of the Mosaic Torah, the principles of which provide ethical guidance for Matthew's particular Jewish-Christian community; and instructing that community—the church—in the kind of correct belief and behavior that will ensure Jesus' approval when he returns.

Structure and Use of Sources

Matthew accomplishes his multiple purposes by assembling material from several different sources to construct his Gospel. Using Mark as his primary source, he incorporates about ninety percent of the earlier Gospel into his account. Into the Markan outline, Matthew inserts five large blocks of teaching material. Many ancient Jewish authors, consciously paralleling the Torah (the "five books of Moses"), arranged their works into fivefold divisions, as did the editors of the Psalms. The first of Matthew's five collections is the most famous as well as the most commonly quoted, the Sermon on the Mount (chs. 5–7). The other four are instructions to the Twelve Apostles (ch. 10); parables on the kingdom (ch. 13); instructions to the church (Matthew's Christian community) (ch. 18); and warnings of the Final Judgment (chs. 23–25).

The Q source. Some of the material in these five sections is peculiar to Matthew, such as the parables involving weeds in a grain field (13:24–30) and the unforgiving debtor (18:23–35). Other parts are similar or virtually identical to material found in Luke but not in Mark. Scholars believe that Matthew and Luke, independently of each other, drew much of their shared teaching from a now-lost document called **Q** (*Quelle,* the German for "source"). Containing a wide variety of sayings attributed to Jesus, including kingdom parables, instructions to the disciples, and prophecies of the Second Coming, the Q document is thought to have been compiled about 50 CE. Scholars have reconstructed the supposed contents of Q in different ways, although no single reconstruction has won universal acceptance. Nonetheless, the Q hypothesis works well in accounting for the source of Jesus' sayings absent in Mark but present in both Matthew and Luke (see Figures 6-1 and 9-3).

The M source. In addition to Mark and Q (assuming its historicity), Matthew also uses material found only in his Gospel. Scholars designate this material unique to Matthew as **M** (Matthean). M includes numerous sayings and parables, such as the stories about the vineyard laborers (20:1–16) and many of the kingdom pronouncements in chapter 13 (13:24–30; 13:44–45; 13:47–52). Finally, Matthew frames his story of Jesus with a narrative of Jesus' birth and infancy (1:18–2:23) and a concluding account of two postresurrection appearances, the first to women near Jerusalem and the second to the "eleven disciples" in Galilee (28:8–20).

Matthew's Editing of Mark

Before considering passages found only in Matthew, we can learn something of the author's intent by examining the way in which he edits and revises Markan material (see Box 8-2). Although he generally follows Mark's chronology, Matthew characteristically condenses and shortens Mark's narrative. In fact, Matthew generally summarizes and abbreviates Mark's account, rather than the other way around. In the story of the epileptic boy, Matthew severely abridges Mark's version, recounting the episode in a mere five verses (17:14–18) compared to Mark's sixteen (Mark 9:14–29). Matthew is also significantly briefer in his telling of Jesus' healing of Peter's mother-in-law (8:14–15; Mark 1:29–31); the Gerasene demoniac (8:28–34; Mark 5:1–20); and the resuscitation of Jairus's daughter and the curing of the woman with a hemorrhage (9:18–26; Mark 5:21–43). In abbreviating Mark's version of events, Matthew typically omits much physical detail as well as Jesus' emotional responses to the situation.

BOX 8-2   *Examples of Matthew's Editing of Markan Material*

MARK   MATTHEW

Jesus' Baptism

It happened at this time that Jesus came from Nazareth in Galilee

and was baptized in the Jordan by John. At the moment when he came up out of the water, he saw the heavens torn open and the Spirit, like a dove, descending upon him. And a voice spoke from heaven: "Thou art my Son, my Beloved; on thee my favour rests."

(Mark 1:9–11)

Then Jesus arrived at the Jordan from Galilee, and came to John to be baptized by him. John tried to dissuade him, "Do you come to me?" he said. "I need rather to be baptized by you." Jesus replied, "Let it be so for the present; we do well to conform in this way with all that God requires." John then allowed him to come. After baptism Jesus came up out of the water at once, and at that moment heaven opened; he saw the Spirit of God descending like a dove to alight upon him; and a voice from heaven was heard saying, "This is my Son, my Beloved, on whom my favour rests."

(Matt. 3:13–17)

In comparing the two accounts of Jesus' baptism, the reader will note that Matthew inserts a speech by John into the Markan narrative. Recognizing Jesus as "mightier" than himself, John is reluctant to baptize him. By giving John this speech, Matthew is able to stress Jesus' superiority to the Baptist. Matthew also changes the nature of Jesus' experience of the "Spirit" after his baptism. In Mark, the heavenly voice is addressed directly to Jesus and apparently represents Jesus' own private mystical experience of divine sonship at the event. Matthew changes the "thou art," intended for Jesus' ears, to "this is," making the divine voice a public declaration heard by the crowds.

Jesus' Healings

That evening after sunset they brought to him all who were ill or possessed by devils; and the whole town was there, gathered at the door. He healed many who suffered from various diseases, and drove out many devils.

He would not let the devils speak, because they knew who he was.

(Mark 1:32–34)

When evening fell, they brought to him many who were possessed by devils;

and he drove the spirits out with a word and healed all who were sick,

to fulfill the prophecy of Isaiah: "He took away our illnesses and lifted our diseases from us."

(Matt. 8:16–17)

In reproducing Mark's story, Matthew edits it in several ways that are characteristic of his particular concerns as an author: (1) He condenses Mark's narrative, omitting various details to focus on a single aspect of Jesus' miraculous power, in this case the exorcising of "devils." (2) He emphasizes the totality or comprehensiveness of Jesus' power, changing Mark's "he healed many" to "healed all." (3) Most characteristically, he adds to the account a quotation from the Hebrew Bible, citing Isaiah's poem about the suffering servant (Isa. 53:4), to demonstrate that Jesus' activities fulfilled ancient prophecy.

BOX 8–2   *continued*

Jesus' Reception by His Neighbors in His Hometown of Nazareth

He left that place and went to his home town accompanied by his disciples. When the Sabbath came he began to teach in the synagogue;

and the large congregation who heard him were amazed

and said, "Where does he get it from?", and, "What wisdom is this that has been given him?", and, "How does he work such miracles? Is not this the carpenter, the son of Mary, the brother of James and Joseph and Judas and Simon? And are not his sisters here with us?"

So they fell foul of him. Jesus said to them, "A prophet will always be held in honour except in his home town, and among his kinsmen and family." He could work no miracle there, except that he put his hands on a few sick people and healed them; and he was taken aback by their want of faith.

(Mark 6:1–6)

Jesus left that place, and came to his home town, where he taught the people in their synagogue.

In amazement they asked,

"Where does he get this wisdom from, and these miraculous powers. Is he not the carpenter's son? Is not his mother called Mary, his brothers James, Joseph, Simon, and Judas? And are not all his sisters here with us? Where then has he got all this from?" So they fell foul of him, and this led him to say, "A prophet will always be held in honour, except in his home town, and in his own family." And he did not work many miracles there: such was their want of faith.

(Matt. 13:54–58)

In editing Mark's account of Jesus' unsatisfactory reunion with his former neighbors in Nazareth, Matthew reproduces most of his source but makes some significant changes and deletions. He omits Mark's reference to the Sabbath, as well as Mark's brief list of Jesus' "few" deeds there and Jesus' apparent surprise at his fellow townsmen's refusal to respond to his healing efforts. Matthew also substitutes the phrase "the carpenter's son" for Mark's "the son of Mary," with its implication of Jesus' illegitimacy. In both accounts, the Nazareans' familiarity with Jesus' background and family (naming four "brothers" and referring to two or more "sisters") is enough to make them skeptical of Jesus' claims to special wisdom or authority.

Emphasis on the miraculous and supernatural. At the same time that he shortens Mark's description of Jesus' miracles, Matthew heightens the miraculous element, stressing that Jesus effected instant cures (9:22; 15:28; 17:18). In recounting Jesus' unfriendly reception in Nazareth, Matthew changes Mark's observation that Jesus "could work no miracle there" (Mark 6:5) to the declaration that "he did not work many miracles there," eliminating the implication that the human Jesus had any limit to his powers (13:58) (see Box 8-2). He similarly omits Mark's definition of John's baptism as a rite "in token of repentance, for the forgiveness of sins" (3:2, 6, 11; Mark 1:4). Mark's exact phrase, "for the forgiveness of sins," does appear in Matthew, but it is transferred to the Matthean Jesus' explanation of the ceremonial wine at the Last Supper (26:26–28). The author may have effected this transposition to make sure that his readers understood that divine cleansing of sin comes not from John's baptism but from Jesus' sacrificial death.

Matthew also intensifies the supernatural element in his account of Jesus' suffering and death. When a mob comes to arrest Jesus in Gethsemane, Matthew's Jesus reminds them that he has the power to call up thousands of angels to help him (26:53), a claim absent in Mark. He allows himself to be taken only to fulfill scripture (26:54).

In addition, Matthew edits Mark's crucifixion narrative, inserting several miracles to stress the event's cosmic significance. To Mark's plague of darkness and the rending of the Temple curtain, Matthew adds that a violent earthquake occurred, severe enough to open graves and permit suddenly resurrected "saints" (holy persons) to rise and walk the streets of Jerusalem (27:50–53). (This mysterious raising of saints from the dead is not mentioned elsewhere in the New Testament.) Matthew interpolates yet another miraculous earthquake into his narration of the first Easter morning. In his version, the women disciples arrive at Jesus' tomb in time to see a supernatural being descend and roll away the great stone sealing the tomb entrance. Mark's anonymous young man dressed in white linen now becomes an angel before whom the Roman guards quake in terror (28:1–4). What Mark's account implies, Matthew's makes explicit, ensuring that the reader will not miss the hand of God in these happenings. Nor are the women left wondering and frightened in Matthew's story of the empty tomb. Instead of being too terrified to report what they have seen, in Matthew's version the women joyously rush away to inform the disciples (28:8; Mark 16:8). Instead of remaining paralyzed with fright, Matthew's characters set the right example by immediately proclaiming the good news of Jesus' triumph over death (28:19).

Organization of Matthew's Gospel

Because of the complex nature of the Matthean composition and the skill with which the author has interwoven Mark's narrative with Jesus' discourses (from Q and M), it is difficult to reduce Matthew to a clear-cut outline. Separating the book into convenient divisions and subdivisions in conventional outline form tends to distort and oversimplify its interlocking themes. One can, however, identify some of the major parts that make up the Gospel whole. The following gives a rough idea of Matthew's general structure:

1. Introduction to the Messiah: genealogy and infancy narratives (1:1–2:23)
2. The beginning of Jesus' proclamation: baptism by John; the temptation by Satan; inauguration of the Galilean ministry (3:1–4:25)
3. First major discourse: the Sermon on the Mount (5–7)
4. First narrative section: ten miracles (8:1–9:38)
5. Second major discourse: instructions to the Twelve Apostles (10)
6. Second narrative section: the Baptist's questions about Jesus; controversies with Jewish authorities (11:1–12:50)
7. Third major discourse: parables on the kingdom (13:1–52)
8. Third narrative section: from the rejection in Nazareth to the transfiguration (13:53–17:27)
9. Fourth major discourse: instructions to the church (18)
10. Fourth narrative section: the Jerusalem ministry (19:1–22:46)
11. Fifth major discourse: warnings of Final Judgment (23–25)
12. Fifth and final narrative section: the Passion story and resurrection appearances (26:1–28:20)

Except for the birth narratives and final postresurrection apparitions, even a minimal outline makes clear that Matthew tells essentially the same story that we find in Mark and Luke (see Box 6-1). Only by carefully scrutinizing Matthew's handling of his sources, the Hebrew

---

BOX 8-3   *Representative Examples of Material Found Only in Matthew*

A "Table of Descent [genealogy]" listing Jesus' ancestors (1:1–17)

Matthew's distinctive version of Jesus' miraculous conception and birth at Bethlehem (1:18–2:23)

Some parables, sayings, and miracles unique to Matthew:

1. The dumb demoniac (9:32–34)
2. Wheat and darnel [weeds] (13:24–30)
3. Buried treasure (13:44)
4. The pearl of "special value" (13:45)
5. Catching fish in a net (13:47–50)
6. A learner with treasures old and new (13:51–52)
7. Earthly rulers collecting tax (17:25–26)
8. Finding a coin in a fish's mouth to pay Temple tax (17:27)

9. The unforgiving debtor (18:23–35)
10. Paying equal wages to all vineyard laborers (20:1–16)
11. The two sons and obedience (21:28–32)
12. The improperly dressed wedding guest (22:11–14)
13. The wise and foolish virgins (25:1–13)
14. The Judgment separating sheep from goats (25:31–46)
15. Judas and the chief priests (27:3–10)
16. The dream of Pilate's wife (27:19)
17. The resurrection of saints (27:52–53)
18. The Easter morning earthquake (28:2)
19. The chief priests' conspiracy to deny Jesus' resurrection (28:11–15)

---

ble, Mark, M, and (presumably) Q can we appreciate the ways in which his Gospel is distinctive (see Boxes 8-3 and 8-4).

Introduction to the Messiah: Infancy Narrative

Except for Matthew and Luke, no New Testament writers refer even briefly to the circumstances surrounding Jesus' birth. Nor do Matthew and Luke allude to Jesus' infancy in the main body of their Gospels. In both cases, the infancy narratives are self-contained units that act as detachable prefaces to the central narrative of Jesus' public ministry.

Matthew constructs his account (1:18–2:23) with phrases and incidents taken from the Hebrew Bible. To him the infant Messiah's appearance gives new meaning to ancient biblical texts, fulfilling prophecy in many unexpected ways. The child is born to a virgin, made pregnant by the Holy Spirit (1:18–19). To the author

this fulfills a passage from Isaiah 7:14, which in Hebrew states that "a young woman is with child, and she will bear a son. . . ." Matthew, however, quotes not the original Hebrew language version of the text but an Old Greek translation in which "young woman" is rendered as *parthenos,* or "virgin." Historians believe that Isaiah's words originally referred to the birth of an heir to the then-reigning Davidic king, but Matthew sees them as forecasting the Messiah's unique manner of birth. Like other New Testament writers, Matthew reads the Hebrew Bible from an explicitly Christian viewpoint, consistently giving the Jewish Scriptures a Christological interpretation. In his view, almost the entire Old Testament foreshadows the Christ event.

Matthew's concern to anchor Jesus' entrance into life firmly in the context of Scripture fulfillment is evident in his account of the mysterious "Magi" or "wise men" from the east who come to pay homage to the infant Jesus. Traditionally three in number (although Matthew does not say how many they were), the

BOX 8-4 *New Characters Introduced in Matthew*

Joseph, husband of Mary (1:16, 18–25; 2:13–14, 19–23)

Herod the Great, Roman-appointed king of Judea (40–4 BCE) (2:1–8, 16–19)

The Magi (astrologers or "wise men" from the east) (2:1–12)

Satan, the devil (as a speaking character) (4:1–11)

Two blind men (9:27–31)

A dumb demoniac (9:32–34)

Revised list of the Twelve (10:1–4)

The mother of James and John, sons of Zebedee (20:20–21)

Magi were probably Babylonian or Persian astrologers who had studied the horoscope of Judah and concluded that it was then time for "the king of the Jews" to be born. Astrology was extremely popular with all classes of society in Greco-Roman times, and it was commonly believed that the appearance of unusual celestial bodies, such as comets or "falling stars," heralded the occurrence of major events on earth (Isa. 14:12–23; Job 38:23; Judg. 5:20).

Matthew's reference to the "star" that guides the Magi to Jesus' birthplace is puzzling. Modern scientists do not know what astronomical phenomenon Matthew has in mind, but a conjunction of the planets Jupiter and Saturn in the constellation Pisces (7 BCE) may have been seen as a divine "sign" or portent. (No other New Testament writer or contemporary historian alludes to the "star of Bethlehem.")

In the Evangelist's account, the unnamed heavenly body leads the traveling astrologers to create a situation in which several biblical prophecies can be fulfilled. On reaching Jerusalem, the astrologers are brought before King Herod, who recognizes that their inquiry about

a new Jewish king refers to the Messiah's birth in Bethlehem, King David's home city, foretold in Micah 5:2.

Herod's jealous attempt to kill the child (2:1–18) fulfills prophecy (Jer. 31:15), as does the holy family's flight into Egypt (Hos. 11:1). Matthew structures the entire episode to parallel the biblical story of Moses' infancy (Exod. 1:8–2:25). As the baby Moses survived the Egyptian Pharaoh's murderous schemes, so the infant Jesus escapes another ruler's plot to kill God's chosen one. The analogy between the two figures is also intended to apply to Jesus' adult life. Like Moses, Jesus will be summoned from Egypt to deliver his people. Moses led Israel from Egyptian slavery to a covenant relationship with God; Jesus will free believers from sin and establish a new covenant (2:13–15, 19–21; 19:27–29).

The Beginning of Jesus' Proclamation

Matthew gives no information about Jesus' life from the time of his family's settling in Nazareth (2:22–23) to the appearance of John the Baptist, a gap of approximately thirty years (Luke 3:1, 23). Although he starts his account of Jesus' adult career (3:1–4:25) at exactly the same point as Mark (1:1–13), Matthew edits Mark's baptism narrative to emphasize Jesus' superiority to John and to avoid any implication that Jesus needed forgiveness of previous sins (3:1–17).

The temptation. Mark (1:12–13) briefly alludes to Satan's tempting Jesus, but Matthew expands the scene to include a dramatic dialogue between Jesus and the Evil One (4:1–11). Whether he is viewed as an objective reality or a metaphor standing for human failure to obey God, Matthew's Satan attempts to deflect Jesus from the true course of his messiahship.

As Matthew and Luke (4:1–13) present it, the confrontation with Satan serves to clarify Jesus' concept of his messianic role. Representing false notions of the Messiah, Satan prefaces his first two challenges with the phrase "If you are the Son of God," a mean-spirited attempt to capitalize on any doubts that the human Jesus may have experienced about his origins or his future authority as God's agent. The first temptation deals with Jesus' personal hunger. Satan calls for Jesus to test the extent of his miraculous power by turning stones into bread, a ploy Jesus refutes by quoting the Torah principle that one lives spiritually on the word of God (Deut. 8:3). Some modern commentators have suggested that Jesus thereby rejects the temptation to undertake a messiahship of material good works, such as feeding the hungry and destitute.

The second temptation is a profound challenge to Jesus' consciousness of his own messianic identity. "If you are the Son of God," Satan demands, show that you can fulfill the terms of Psalm 91, a poem that unconditionally asserts that God will save from all harm the man he has chosen.

> For you the LORD [Yahweh] is a safe retreat;
> you have made the Most High your refuse.
> No disaster shall befall you,
> no calamity shall come upon your home.
> For he [Yahweh] has charged his angels
>   to guard you wherever you go,
>   to lift you on their hands
> for fear you should strike your foot
> against a stone. (Ps. 91:9–12)

The poem continues to reassure God's favorite that Yahweh will "lift him beyond danger" and "rescue him and bring him to honour" (Ps. 91:14–16). In Matthew's time, many Jews must have pointed out to Christians that Jesus' death on the cross was entirely contrary to the promises of divine protection given in this well-known psalm. In Matthew 4:6 the devil quotes this scripture, and Jesus counters this "demonic" use of the Bible by citing the general Torah principle of not putting God to the test (Deut. 6:16).

In a third and final attempt to subvert Jesus' understanding of his messianic role, Satan offers him worldly power on a vastly grander scale than King David, the Messiah's prototype, had enjoyed. All Jesus must do in return is "pay homage" to Satan, a demand that Jesus recognizes as undermining the essence of Judaism's commitment to one God (Deut. 6:13). A thousand years earlier David had gained his kingdom through war and bloodshed, a procedure that Matthew recognizes as unsuitable to the Messiah, who will not impose his rule by cruelty and violence. Satan is not to be "worshipped" by imitating his methods.

First Major Discourse: The Sermon on the Mount

In the temptation scene (4:1–11), Matthew shows Jesus repudiating some of the functions then popularly associated with the Messiah. In the Sermon on the Mount (chs. 5–7), Matthew demonstrates how radically different Jesus' concept of his messiahship is from the popular expectation of a conquering warrior-king. This long discourse, in which Jesus takes his seat on a Galilean hill, reminding the reader of Moses seated on Mount Sinai, is the New Testament's most extensive collection of Jesus' teaching and admonition. Matthew's "sermon" is not the record of a single historical speech by Jesus, but a compilation of Jesus' sayings from several different sources. Some of the same teachings appear in Luke's Sermon on the Plain, the third Gospel's equivalent version of the discourse (Luke 6:17–7:1). Matthew collects the sayings in one place (5:1–8:1); Luke scatters them throughout his Gospel narrative (see Box 9-3).

Matthew opens the discourse with a collection of **beatitudes,** statements that certain kinds of people—the sorrowful, the peacemakers, the hungry, the persecuted—are particularly blessed (5:3–11). In this section, Matthew's Jesus reaffirms Judaism's principle that God takes the part of persons suffering grief or poverty. The powerless are utterly dependent on God and hence eligible for his special protection.

Matthew also represents Jesus as a staunch upholder of the Mosaic Torah. Far from ending the Torah's power, as Paul argues in his letters, Jesus confirms its unending authority (5:17–19). Matthew realizes that some fellow Christians do not have so high a regard for the Law. Such dissenters are still part of the kingdom (a term Matthew commonly uses to designate the Christian community), but they can not be recognized as leaders. The Matthean Jesus prefers Torah-observing disciples.

> If any man therefore sets aside even the least of the Law's demands, and teaches others to do the same, he will have the lowest place in the kingdom of Heaven, whereas anyone who keeps the Law, and teaches others so, will stand high in the kingdom of Heaven. (5:19)

The antitheses. In Matthew's view, Jesus gives the Torah renewed vitality by illustrating its eternal meaning. The author presents this concept in the six antitheses, a series of rhetorical statements in which Jesus formally contrasts opposing ideas in similar or parallel verbal structures. Matthew typically begins a statement with the declaration "You have learned that our forefathers were told" and balances it with Jesus' contrasting "but what I tell you is this: . . ." In this part of the discourse, Jesus contrasts commandments from the Torah, as they were then commonly taught, with new interpretations based exclusively on his own personal authority:

> You have learned that they [the biblical Israelites] were told "Eye for eye, tooth for tooth." But what I tell you is this: Do not set yourself against the man who wrongs you. If someone slaps you on the right cheek, turn and offer him your left. (5:38–39)

Ending the law of retaliation. The lex talionis or "law of retaliation" that Jesus quotes here is basic to the Mosaic concept of justice and appears in three different books of the Torah (Exod.

21:23–25; Lev. 24:19–20; Deut. 19:21). This ancient Near Eastern legal principle served to control and limit excessive punishment of an enemy: one was allowed to inflict an injury exactly equivalent to that one had suffered, but no more:

> Whenever one man injures and disfigures his fellow-countryman, it shall be done to him as he has done; fracture for fracture, eye for eye, tooth for tooth; the injury and disfigurement that he has inflicted upon another shall in turn be inflicted upon him. (Lev. 24:19–20)

Although Israelite officials responsible for enforcing the Law were instructed to "show no mercy" to criminals, requiring "life for life, . . . hand for hand, foot for foot" (Deut. 19:21), there is little evidence that such harsh legal provisions were regularly applied. By Jesus' day, most persons sought compensation for injury by less brutal means, in the public courts.

Ending the cycle of evil. As Matthew presents it, Jesus explicitly repudiates *any* attempt to seek redress for wrongs done one, whether by judicial or other procedures. Furthermore, an injured party must not only give up his or her right to legal compensation (another form of personal vengeance) but also must surrender whatever an enemy wants to take. The victim's cooperation with his or her exploiter is to be total: sued for a shirt, the victim volunteers a coat as well. If the authorities legally can force one to travel a mile, voluntarily go two!

To some readers, Jesus' demands express a highly desirable way of life; to others, they appear absurd, almost insanely impractical. On the one hand, the command to "turn the other cheek" can be seen as socially practical advice. By refusing to strike back, to repay insult with injury, a person can exercise power to end the cycle of retaliation, to replace violence with peace. On the other hand, Jesus' call for utter selflessness and quiet submission to injustice invites the strong to exploit the weak.

Some critics observe that following Jesus' advice would merely serve to perpetuate a system in which greedy and unjust persons, unresisted, would invariably control society. The German philosopher Friedrich Nietzsche labeled Jesus' ethic a "slave morality" unfit for free human beings.

Most readers may wonder if Jesus' advice applies only to life in God's future kingdom or to a posthumous existence in heaven. Matthew, however, suggests that Jesus' code of ideal behavior is a present requirement for persons already under divine rule—the Christian community. By interpreting the Torah as a call to unlimited generosity, service, and love, Matthew shows Jesus asking his followers to refashion themselves in God's image.

Entering the kingdom by imitating God. In the final antithesis and its accompanying commentary (5:43–48), Matthew's Jesus contrasts the command to love one's neighbor (Lev. 19:18) with the assumption that it is permissible to hate one's enemy. Again, he demands what some scholars refer to as a "higher righteousness," an ethic that goes beyond the Torah's specific demands in order to encompass both friend and enemy in a God-like love (5:43–45). Observing that even religiously ignorant people love their families and friends, Jesus urges his hearers to put no limit, legal or doctrinal, upon their goodwill or affection.

> There must be no limit to your goodness, as your heavenly Father's goodness knows no bounds. (5:48)

Believers must imitate the Creator, who showers nature's blessings on all kinds of people, whether deserving or not (5:45). Difficult as it is to attain, Matthew sees the pursuit of this ideal—"the narrow gate" (6:13)—as the only viable means of closing the ethical gap that now separates human beings from God. Matthew's Jesus accords the highest priority to recreating oneself in the divine image.

> Set your mind on God's kingdom and his justice [righteousness] before everything else, and all the rest will come to you as well. (6:33)

Right motives. Notice that the remaining antitheses also emphasize striving for the "higher" nature. Refraining from actions that the Torah prohibits is not enough. One must not only avoid the forbidden act, one must banish the inner feelings that motivate it (5:21–32).

Matthew's Jesus does not abolish the Torah but illuminates the principles lying behind it, in some cases intensifying its requirements. Thus, Jesus goes beyond the original Torah to forbid divorce and remarriage (5:31–32; compare Mark 10:12) and to modify the Torah decree on swearing oaths (5:33–37). In Matthew's community, Christians must observe the Jewish customs of ritual fasting (6:16–18) and giving money to the poor (6:2–4). The disciples are to practice Jewish piety, but all deeds of mercy are to be performed secretly, not in order to build a public reputation (6:5–6).

Prayer and right action. The author apparently draws his version of the Lord's Prayer (6:9–13) and the golden rule (7:12) from the same source (Q) that Luke uses (Luke 11:2–4; 6:31). In comparing their two versions of this material (see Box 9-4), however, the reader will find some significant differences. Matthew seems to have modified his source, recording an expanded edition of the prayer and adding an interpretive comment to the rule. The author interprets Jesus' command about relating to other people as if they are equivalent centers of self as fulfilling the essential purpose of "the Law and the prophets" (7:12). As noted earlier, in Chapter 4, some Jewish rabbis of the first century, such as Hillel, held similar views about the Torah's primary meaning.

Considering the extraordinarily high standards of thought and behavior that Matthew's Jesus expects of his audience, the Sermon's repeated emphasis on mercy and forgiveness of human frailty is appropriate (5:7, 44–48; 6:12, 14–15; 7:1–5). Consistently stressing right action—bearing "good fruit" (7:15–20)—Matthew places responsibility for obtaining divine

Christ Preaching by Rembrandt (1606–1669). This etching depicts Jesus conveying his message to an informal gathering of common people. While most of Jesus' audience listens in rapt attention, a child plays with a ball of string in the foreground, oblivious to the significance of what he hears. (Courtesy Trustees of the British Museum.)

mercy on the individual's willingness to show compassion to others.

Jesus' authority. At the end of the discourse, Matthew emphasizes the uniqueness of Jesus' masterful interpretation of the Torah. The crowds are amazed because, "unlike their own teachers he taught . . . with authority" (7:28–29). In contrast to rabbinic custom, Jesus does not cite traditional commentaries on the Torah, but declares its meaning solely on his own understanding. It is this unprecedented insistence upon his personal right to explain how the Law is to be interpreted and applied in daily life, in such matters as Sabbath observance and other legal obligations, that pits Jesus against the recognized Torah experts of his day. As the Synoptic authors report the issue, it is Jesus' claim of personal authority that inspires the contro-

versy that eventually causes the Jewish leadership to reject him.

First Narrative Section: Ten Miracles

In the first long narrative section of his Gospel (8:1–9:38), based largely on Mark, Matthew concentrates on depicting Jesus' miraculous healings and exorcisms. To Mark's account of the cleansing of a leper (Mark 1:40–45), Matthew adds the story of a centurion, a Roman army officer in charge of 100 infantrymen (8:5–13; also Luke 7:1–10). Notice that Matthew connects this episode with references to the practice of converting Gentiles that existed in the author's own day. After expressing Jesus' astonishment that the Gentile soldier reveals a faith stronger than that of any Israelite, the author makes his point: non-Jews like the centurion will come to feast with Abraham and the other patriarchs, and Jews, once the favored people, will be left outside. Throughout his Gospel, Matthew pictures the Christian community as the "new Israel," replacing the old, which lost its privileges because it failed to recognize Jesus as the Messiah.

Second Major Discourse: Instructions to the Twelve Apostles

In his second discourse (ch. 10), Matthew shows Jesus preparing followers for the work they are to do after their Master's death. Commissioning the Twelve (listed in 10:2–4) to continue his ministry of healing, Jesus sends them exclusively to Jews (10:5–6). (By contrast, compare this Jewish mission with the later commands to evangelize all nations [24:14; 28:28].) Notice that the Twelve are to preach the same urgent message of approaching Judgment that the author attributes to both the Baptist (3:2) and Jesus at the beginning of his career (4:17).

The extended warnings about persecution and suffering (10:16–26) seem to apply to conditions that existed in the author's generation, rather than to the time of Jesus' Galilean ministry. (Combining Jesus' remembered words with commentary relating them to later experiences of the Christian community is typical of all the Gospel writers.) In this discourse, Matthew juxtaposes threats of hell (**Gehenna,** the traditional Jewish place of posthumous punishment) with assurances that God supremely values his "little ones" (the author's favorite expression for Christians) (10:29–31). Matthew's Jesus promises that kindness shown to Christian preachers will be rewarded on the Day of Judgment (10:32–42; 25:31–46).

Although the Sermon on the Mount commended peacemakers (5:9), Matthew presents here Jesus as wielding a sword to divide families, to sever the closest relationships. By Matthew's time, the question of Jesus' identity had become a major issue that racked many Jewish households, inciting rancor between Jews who regarded Jesus as the Messiah and those who did not (10:34–39; compare Mark 13:9–13).

Perhaps Jesus' most startling declaration in this collection of sayings is his prediction that before the Twelve will have completed their missionary tour of Palestine "the Son of Man will have come" (10:23). Writing more than half a century after the events he describes, Matthew surprisingly retains a prophecy that was not fulfilled, certainly not in historical fact. The author's inclusion of what seems to be an apocalyptic foretelling of the *eschaton* (end of the world) in Jesus' day indicates that he did not understand it literally. It is likely that Matthew regards the "Son of Man" as already spiritually present in the missionary activity of the church. If so, this suggests that many of Matthew's other references to "the end of the age" and Jesus' Parousia (Second Coming) (24–25) may also be understood metaphorically.

Second Narrative Section: Questions and Controversies

Jesus and John the Baptist. Matthew opens his second extended narrative (11:1–12:50) by discussing the relationship of Jesus to **John the Baptist,** whose fate foreshadows that of Jesus. Locked in **Herod Antipas's** prison and doomed to imminent martyrdom, John writes to inquire if Jesus is really God's chosen one (11:2–3). The Baptist's question contrasts strangely with his earlier proclamation of Jesus' high status (3:11–15) and may reflect a later competition between the disciples of Jesus and John in Matthew's day.

BOX 8-5   *John the Baptist as the Apocalyptic Elijah Figure*

MATTHEW

"He is the man of whom Scripture says,

'Here is my herald, whom I send on ahead of you,

and he will prepare your way before you.'

I tell you this: never has there appeared on earth a mother's son greater than John the Baptist, and yet the least in the kingdom of Heaven is greater than he.

"Ever since the coming of John the Baptist the kingdom of Heaven has been subjected to violence and violent men are seizing it. For all the prophets and the Law foretold things to come until John appeared, and John is the destined Elijah, if you will but accept it. If you have ears, then hear."

(Matt. 11:10–14)

LUKE

"He is the man of whom Scripture says,

'Here is my herald, whom I send on ahead of you,

and he will prepare your way before you."

I tell you, there is not a mother's son greater than John, and yet the least in the kingdom of God is greater than he."

(Luke 7:27–28)

"Until John, it was the Law and the prophets; since then, there is the good news of the kingdom of God, and everyone forces his way in."

(Luke 16:16)

MARK

[Popular speculations about John's return to life after his beheading by Herod Antipas:]

Now King Herod heard of it [Jesus' miracles], for the fame of Jesus had spread; and people were saying, "John the Baptist has been raised to life, and that is why these miraculous powers are at work in him." Others said, "It is Elijah."

(Mark 6:14–15)

JOHN

This is the testimony which John gave when the Jews of Jerusalem sent a deputation of priests and Levites to ask him who he was. He confessed without reserve and avowed, "I am not the Messiah." "What then? are you Elijah?" "No," he replied. "Are you the prophet whom we await?" He answered "No."* "Then who are you?" they asked. "We must give an answer to those who sent us. What account do you give of yourself?" He answered in the words of the prophet Isaiah: "I am a voice crying aloud in the wilderness, 'Make the Lord's highway straight.' "

(John 1:19–23)

*Note that John's Gospel denies the Baptist the roles of prophet and latter-day Elijah that the Synoptics accorded him.

Matthew uses the incident to place the two prophets' roles in perspective, highlighting Jesus' superiority. Without answering John's question directly, Jesus summarizes his miracles of healing that suggest God's presence in his work (11:4–6). Matthew then contrasts the function and style of the two men, emphasizing Jesus' far greater role. Although John is the "destined Elijah" whose return to earth was to inaugurate the time of Final Judgment, he does not share in the "kingdom." Perhaps because Matthew sees John operating independently of Jesus, he does not consider him a Christian. (Box 8-5 indicates the four Gospel authors' strikingly different views of John's role.)

John is a wild and solitary figure; Jesus is gregarious, friendly with Israel's outcasts, prostitutes, and "sinners." Enjoying food and wine with socially unrespectable people, Jesus provokes critics who accuse him of gluttony and overdrinking (11:7–19). In Matthew's evaluation, neither John nor Jesus, representing two very different approaches to the religious life, can win the fickle public's approval.

Harsh sayings. At the same time that he presents Jesus performing works of mercy and forgiveness (11:28–30), Matthew also includes harsh sayings very similar to the denunciations and threats of divine judgment uttered by the Baptist. When the towns of Chorazin and Bethsaida fail to repent after witnessing Jesus' miracles there, Jesus makes a sweeping statement that Sodom, which Yahweh destroyed by fire, would fare better on Judgment day than they (11:20–24). Castigating his opponents as poisonous snakes, Jesus (12:33–37) seems to violate his own principles outlined in the Sermon on the Mount.

Third Major Discourse: Parables on the Kingdom

Matthew frames Jesus' third discourse with his version of Jesus' alienation from his family (12:46–50; Mark 3:31–35) and Jesus' rejection by the citizens of Nazareth (13:54–58; Mark 6:1–6). The author divides Jesus' parable teachings into two distinct episodes: the first public, the second private (13:10–23). Notice that although only the Twelve are initiated into the secrets of God's rule, Matthew softens Mark's explanation of Jesus' reasons for speaking in parables. Instead of using figures of speech to prevent understanding (Mark 4:11–12), Matthew states that Jesus speaks metaphorically *because* most people have the wrong attitude and unconsciously shut their mental eyes and ears (13:11–15; Isa. 6:9–10). Note also that Matthew's version of the parable lesson explicitly states that the Twelve do understand and appreciate Jesus' teaching (13:16–17, 51–52), thus

eliminating Mark's view of the disciples' chronic stupidity.

Images of the kingdom. To Mark's original collection of kingdom parables, Matthew adds several comparisons in which the kingdom is likened to a buried treasure, a priceless pearl, a harvest of fish, and a field in which both grain and "darnel [weeds]" grow (13:24–30, 36–50). The last two introduce a distinctively Matthean concept: the kingdom (church) consists of a mixture of good and bad elements that will not be separated completely until the last day. The same theme reappears in Matthew's version of the parable about ungrateful guests (22:1–13; compare Luke 14:16–23).

Third Narrative Section: From the Rejection in Nazareth to the Transfiguration

Matthew's third narrative section (13:53–17:27) slightly revises many incidents related in Mark's Gospel. Recounting Jesus' rejection by his fellow citizens of Nazareth, Matthew subtly modifies Mark's older account, calling Jesus "the carpenter's son" rather than the Markan "son of Mary" (Mark 6:3) and changing Mark's statement that Jesus "could work no miracle there" (Mark 6:5) to "did not work many miracles there" (13:54–58) (Box 8-2).

With minor changes. Matthew also follows Mark closely in his account of the Baptist's execution, the miraculous feeding of five thousand people, and the stilling of the Galilean storm (14:1–27; Mark 6:14–52). Note that Matthew's editing of this part of the Markan narrative entails a major change in Mark's order of events. The episode in which Jesus sends the Twelve on a missionary journey (Mark 6:7–13) does not appear in Matthew's third narrative section because he has already incorporated it into his version of Jesus' instructions to the Twelve (ch. 10). Matthew also revises other Markan passages dealing with the disciples. He embellishes Mark's account of Jesus' striding across the Sea of Galilee by adding that Peter also attempted to walk on water. More significantly, Matthew deletes Mark's reference to the disciples' "closed" minds, or "hard-heartedness," and replaces it with their positive recognition of Jesus as "Son of God" (14:28–33; Mark 6:52). He further modifies Mark's theme of the disciples' obtuseness by insisting that the Twelve fully comprehend the miracle of loaves and fishes (15:5–12; Mark 8:1–21). Most of these revisions to Mark's account—especially Matthew's deletion of Mark's criticisms of the Twelve—serve to enhance the disciples' role and reputation.

Describing Jesus' dispute with the Pharisees over ritual handwashing (taken from Mark 7:1–23), Matthew gives the debate a meaning significantly different from that in his Markan source. In Mark, the episode's climax is reached when the author interprets Jesus' words to mean that all foods are clean, including those the Torah forbids Jews to eat (7:19). Believing that Torah prohibitions remain in effect, Matthew drops Mark's climactic interpretation (15:1–11).

Peter and the church. One of Matthew's most celebrated additions to Mark's narrative appears in his version of Peter's recognition of Jesus' identity (16:13–29). Matthew's Peter not only confesses Jesus as the Messiah but identifies him as the Son of God (an element absent in Mark). Jesus' declaration that Peter is the rock upon which Jesus will build his church appears only in Matthew, as does the promise to award Peter spiritual powers that are honored in heaven and on earth. (The same commission is given to the church in general in 18:18.)

In spite of his singling Peter out as foremost among the **Apostles** ("ones sent out [by Jesus]"), Matthew retains Mark's tradition that Peter fundamentally misunderstands the nature of Jesus' messiahship. When Peter attempts to dissuade Jesus from a decision that will lead to his death in Jerusalem, Jesus again ironically addresses the Apostle as "Satan" (16:21–23).

Matthew repeats not only Mark's emphasis on discipleship and suffering, but also Jesus' apocalyptic pronouncement that some of his followers would not die before they saw "the Son of Man coming in his kingdom" (16:24–28). The author's reiteration of this promise is puzzling if only because he knew that it was not literally kept. Matthew may have preserved the saying because his church interpreted it metaphorically: in his miraculous service, death, and resurrection to heavenly glory, Jesus does indeed bring a "kingdom" to earth—the Christian fellowship, ruled by God.

Matthew's account of the transfiguration immediately follows (17:1–8), as if to emphasize Jesus' present fulfillment of apocalyptic hopes. Only Peter, James, and John witness this mystical event, but to Matthew these three represent the new Christian community in which God's spirit dwells. The two figures in the vision, Moses and Elijah, represent "the Law" and the prophets, traditions that Matthew's community inherits and honors (17:1–9; 18:20; 28:20). The notion that the disciples are even then experiencing a fulfillment of eschatological events is affirmed by Jesus' declaration that "Elijah," whose reappearance was to herald the world's end, has already come in the person of the Baptist (17:9–12).

Fourth Major Discourse: Instructions to the Church

In chapter 18, Matthew assembles disparate sayings of Jesus and applies them to the Christian community of the writer's generation. Taken together, chapters 10 and 18 form a rudimentary manual or book of instruction for the early church. Notice how the author combines numerous small literary units to achieve his intended effect. A brief glimpse of the disciples' squabbling for power (18:1–2) introduces opposing images of a powerless child and a drowning man (18:2–7), which are quickly followed by pictures of self-blinding and the flames of Gehenna (18:8–9). Notice the variety of different literary forms that Matthew links together to create his prescriptions for an ideal Christian community. The chapter's many diverse units include hyperbole; parable (the lost sheep and the unforgiving debtor [18:12–14, 23–35]); advice on supervising troublesome people (18:15–17); prophetic promises (18:10, 18–20); and direct commands (18:22). In Matthew's view of the church, service, humility, and endless forgiveness are the measure of leadership. Practicing the spirit of Torah mercy, the church is the earthly expression of divine rule (18:23–35), a visible manifestation of the kingdom.

Note that Matthew gives the individual "congregation" the right to exclude or ostracize a disobedient member (18:15–17). During later centuries this power of excommunication was to become a formidable weapon in controlling both belief and behavior.

Fourth Narrative Section: The Jerusalem Ministry

In this long narrative sequence (19:1–22:46), Matthew arranges several dialogues between Jesus and his opponents, interspersed with incidents on the journey south from Galilee to Jerusalem. The section opens with "some Pharisees" challenging Jesus on the matter of divorce. In Mark's version of the encounter, Jesus revokes the Torah provisions for divorce and forbids remarriage (Mark 10:1–12). Matthew modifies the prohibition, stating that "unchastity" or sexual unfaithfulness provides grounds for lawful divorce (19:3–9). He also adds a discussion with the disciples in which Jesus mentions several reasons for not marrying, including a commitment to remain single for "the kingdom" (19:10–12).

Discipleship and suffering. After the third prediction of Jesus' impending death in Jerusalem (20:17–19), Matthew again stresses that suffer-

ing must precede the disciples' heavenly reward, as it does Jesus'. In Mark, the sons of Zebedee, **James** and **John,** directly ask Jesus for positions of honor in his kingdom, presumably to satisfy personal ambition (Mark 10:35–40). In Matthew's version of the episode, it is the Apostles' mother who makes the request on their behalf (20:20–21). (Note that Jesus had already promised his followers that he would share his heavenly rule with them [19:27–29].) The prediction that the two sons of Zebedee will follow their leader to a martyr's death indicates that Matthew writes after both Apostles had died (20:23). According to Acts (12:1–2), James was beheaded by Herod Agrippa I, who reigned as king of Judea 41–44 CE. It may be that John was similarly executed at about that time.

Entrance into Jerusalem. Matthew prepares his reader for the significance of Jesus' Jerusalem experience by prefacing his account with a miracle found only in his Gospel. After Jesus restores sight to two blind men, they immediately become his followers—in contrast to the "blind" guides of Jerusalem (20:29–34). The author's determination to show that Jesus' actions match biblical prophecy in every detail causes him to create a somewhat grotesque picture of his hero's entrance into the holy city. Matthew quotes Zechariah's prophecy about the Messiah's arrival in full and inserts an additional phrase from Isaiah. However, he apparently misunderstands Zechariah's poetic use of parallelism. In Zechariah's poetic structure, "the foal of a beast of burden" on which the Messiah rides is parallel to and synonymous with the prophet's reference to "an ass" (Zech. 9:9; Isa. 62:11). To make Jesus' action precisely fit his concept of the prophecy, Matthew has Jesus mount not one but two animals simultaneously, "the donkey and her foal," for his triumphant ride into Jerusalem (21:1–11).

In his account of Jesus' Jerusalem ministry, Matthew generally adheres to Mark's narrative, although he adds some new material and edits Mark, usually to enhance his portrait of Jesus. After driving the moneychangers from the

Temple, Jesus heals some blind men and cripples (21:14), miracles absent in Mark. During this brief period, Jesus is repeatedly hailed as "Son of David," one of Matthew's chief designations for his hero (1:1; 20:30; 21:9, 16). Matthew reproduces many of the Markan debates between Jesus and Jewish Torah experts on matters of paying taxes to Rome (22:16–22), the resurrection (22:23–33), and the law of love (22:34–40). However, he significantly edits Mark's report on Jesus' encounter with a friendly Torah instructor (Mark 12:28–34). Whereas Mark states that this congenial exchange prevented further attacks on Jesus, Matthew transfers Mark's comment to the conclusion of Jesus' remarks about the Messiah as David's "son" (22:46; Mark 12:35). Matthew has only harsh words for the Jerusalem authorities and declines to show Jesus on good terms with rival Jewish teachers.

The church replaces Israel. While studying Matthew's account of Jesus' last days, the reader will discover that most of the author's changes and additions to Mark serve to express his extreme hostility toward Jewish leaders. In the author's bitter view, prostitutes and criminals stand a better chance of winning divine approval than do the Temple priests, Pharisees, or their associates (21:31).

Notice that the three parables that Matthew inserts into the Markan narrative serve to condemn the Jewish establishment. In the parable of the two sons, the disobedient youth represents Judaism (21:28–32). In a second parable, the "wicked tenants" who kill a landlord's son are the Jerusalem officials who reject Jesus (21:42–46). To Matthew, the vineyard owner's transfer of his estate to more deserving tenants means that God has abandoned Israel and adopted the church as his new chosen people.

Matthew replays the same theme in the parable featuring guests who ungratefully ignore their invitations to a wedding party (the messianic banquet). Matthew's statement that the outraged host then burns down the ingrates' city (a rather excessive reaction) probably refers to the Romans' burning Jerusalem in 70 CE. As in the wicked tenant parable, newcomers replace the formerly chosen group—the church takes Israel's place (22:1–10).

Fifth Major Discourse: Warnings of Final Judgment

In chapter 23, Matthew intensifies his attack on Jerusalem's leaders. He opens Jesus' last major discourse (chs. 23–25) with a merciless judgment on the Pharisees and their fellow Torah instructors. Matthew's Jesus denounces his opponents as religious hypocrites whose devotion to Torah traditions prevents them from perceiving that in Jesus God reveals his Messiah. As described in the Gospels, the Jewish priests, teachers of the Law, and scribal interpreters are uniformly arrogant and treacherous. None of the Evangelists credits them with humane feelings or good intentions, but Matthew judges them with passionate revulsion.

Matthew's view of Jewish guilt. According to Matthew, Jesus blames the Pharisees and their associates for every guilty act—every drop of innocent blood poured out—in Israel's entire history. He condemns the religious leaders to suffer for their generation's collective wrongdoing as well as that of their distant ancestors.

The author strongly implies that the Roman devastation executed on the Jewish nation in 70 CE, an event that occurred during Matthew's lifetime, is visible proof of God's angry judgment (23:35–36). In reporting Jesus' trial before Pilate, Matthew represents a Jerusalem crowd demanding the Messiah's crucifixion, hysterically inviting the Deity to avenge Jesus' blood upon them and their children (27:25). Pilate, symbol of the imperial Roman government, washes his hands of responsibility even while ordering Jesus' execution (27:24), thus shifting the blame for Jesus' death to the Jewish people and their as-yet-unborn descendants.

Matthew's emphasis on retribution. The Mosaic Law decreed that Yahweh would punish "the sins of the fathers to the third and fourth generations" (Exod. 20:5), a concept of retributive justice that doomed children to suffer for their grandparents' errors. Earlier in his Gospel Matthew presents Jesus as rejecting the ancient lex talionis, the embodiment of retributive justice (5:38–40), stressing instead the necessity of practicing infinite forgiveness (6:12, 14–16; 18:21–35) and exercising mercy (5:7).

In dealing with Jesus' (and his church's) opponents, however, the author judges without compassion. He apparently sees their conspiracy to eliminate the Davidic heir as falling beyond the tolerable limits of charity. In judging his enemies, Matthew in effect reintroduces the old law of retaliation that Jesus himself rejects. Historically, the consequences of the Gospel authors' placing blame for Jesus' crucifixion exclusively on the Jews helped fuel the waves of anti-Semitism that repeatedly swept through the Western world for centuries afterward. Throughout Europe Jews were indiscriminately persecuted as "Christ-killers," often with the blessing of Christian authorities. Only in 1974 did the Roman Catholic church absolve modern Jews from guilt for Jesus' death.

Unworthy religious attitudes. While Matthew's diatribe against first-century Palestinian Jewish leaders is unfair and probably applies only to a minority of extreme legalists among the Sadducees and Pharisees, it does include appropriate criticism of religious attitudes that exist in every age. Obsession with the formal details of worship and cold-blooded hairsplitting over doctrinal minutia while neglecting "the weightier demands of the Law, justice, mercy, and good faith" (23:23) have characterized some believers in many religions.

To place Matthew's negative verdict on the first-century Jewish establishment in historical perspective, we must remember that he condemns only Judaism's leadership, not the religion itself. Despite his dislike of Pharisaic custom, the author agrees with Pharisaic teaching. He reminds his readers to "pay attention to their words" and "do what they tell you," for they occupy "the seat of Moses" and their teachings are authoritative (23:1–3).

The Fall of Jerusalem and the Parousia

The second part of Jesus' long discourse on Judgment is based largely on Mark 13, the prediction of Jerusalem's fate. To Mark's report of the disciple's inquiry about when the Temple will fall (Mark 13:1–4), Matthew adds a more religiously portentous question—what apocalyptic signs will signal Jesus' Second Coming (the **Parousia**) and the "end of the age," the end of human history as we know it (24:1–3).

Signs of the end. All three Synoptic writers link the Jewish Revolt against Rome (66–73 CE) with supernatural portents of end time and Jesus' return. Mark, the first to make this association of events, seems to have written at a period when the revolt had already begun (note the "battles" and "wars" in 13:7–8) and Jerusalem was about to fall. These cataclysmic events he called "the birth pangs of the new age." Both Matthew and Luke follow Mark's lead and connect such political upheavals with persecution of believers, perhaps allusions to Nero's cruel actions against Christians in Rome (about 65 CE). The Synoptic authors agree that attacks in the church, then a tiny minority of the Greco–Roman population, are of critical importance. The sufferings the Christian community will bring God's vengeance on all humankind.

False hopes. Both Mark and Matthew are also aware that in the white heat of apocalyptic expectation there were "many" false reports of the Messiah's reappearance (Mark 13:21–23; Matt. 24:23–27). Some Christian groups must have experienced intense disappointment when their prophets' "inspired" predictions of Jesus' return failed to be confirmed in fact. Both Mark and Matthew caution that even "the Son" does not know the exact date of the Parousia (Mark 13:32; Matt. 24:36). Matthew adds further that when the Son does return, his coming will be unmistakable in its universality, "like lightning from the east, flashing as far as the west" (24:27).

The secret return. Matthew preserves the "double vision" nature of the Parousia found in Mark. Jesus' supernatural return will be preceded by unmistakable "signs" that is it near (24:21–22, 29–35); at the same time he will come without warning and when least expected (24:42–44). Although contradictory, both concepts apparently existed concurrently in the early Christian community, which was deeply influenced by apocalyptic thinking.

Although the author of Revelation links the end time with cosmic catastrophe, other New Testament writers (perhaps aware of the repeated failure of attempts to calculate the date of the Parousia) stress that the Son's reappearance is essentially unheralded (1 Thess. 5:1–5; 2 Pet. 3:10).

Matthew probably wrote about two decades after Mark's Gospel was composed, but he retains the Markan tradition that persons who knew Jesus would live to see his predictions come true (24:34; Mark 13:30). To Matthew, the Roman annihilation of the Jewish state, which coincided with the emergence of the Christian church as an entity distinct from Judaism, may essentially have fulfilled Jesus' words, or at least an important part of his prophecy. From the writer's perspective, the "new age" has already begun with God's overthrow of Israel and the church's new and decisive role in future human history.

Parables of Judgment. The author does not abandon the hope of Jesus' eventual return, but he modifies it by adding several parables that stress the duties and functions of the church while it awaits the completed *eschaton*. The first three Judgment parables dramatize the relationship between an absent authority figure (a landowner, a master, or a bridegroom) and his servants or guests, who are expected to behave properly and faithfully until his unannounced return. The first parable contrasts two servants, one of whom abuses his fellow employees until the Master suddenly reappears to execute him (24:45–51)—a clear warning to church members to treat others mercifully.

Another parable, contrasting alert and prepared believers with those who are not, similarly relates to the church membership. In this tale of wise and foolish virgins, note that the "bridegroom" is "late in coming," a hint that Christians must reconcile themselves to a delay in the Parousia (25:1–13).

The first two parables of Judgment stress good behavior and readiness to receive the Master when he reappears at a time unforeseen; the parable of the talents, in which the Master's servants invest huge sums of money for him, emphasizes the necessary growth and productivity of the church during its Lord's absence (Matt. 25:14–30). Once again, the emphasis falls on the Master's servants—his church—being unexpectedly called to account, in this case to demonstrate that it has significantly increased the value of the treasure entrusted to it.

The fourth and final parable of Judgment concerns not only the church but also "the nations." The term *nations* refers primarily to Gentile peoples living without the Mosaic Law, but it may be intended to include all humanity—Jewish, Christian, and those belonging to other world religions as well. In the parable about separating sheep and goats, the basis on which all are judged worthy "sheep" or unworthy "goats" is exclusively their behavior toward Jesus' "little ones," Matthew's favored term for Christian disciples (25:31–46).

Matthew's eschatological Judgment is notable for making charitable acts, rather than "correct" religious doctrine, the standard of distinguishing good people from bad. In such passages Matthew reflects the ancient Israelite prophetic tradition that regarded service to the poor and unfortunate as acts of worship to God. (See also the Book of James, which defines true religion as essentially humanitarian service to others [James 1:27].)

Author's purpose in the Judgment parables. By adding the four parables of Judgment to his expansion of Mark 13 and by linking them to "the kingdom" (25:1, 14), Matthew shifts the apocalyptic emphasis from expectations about the Parousia to the function and duties of the church. Note that Matthew places the parables of the alert householder, the trustworthy servant, and the talents among Jesus' predictions of the *eschaton*. By contrast, Luke, who uses the same parables, places them among the general teachings of Jesus' pre-Jerusalem ministry (compare Matt. 24:43–44 with Luke 12:39–40; Matt. 24:45–51 with Luke 12:42–46; and Matt. 25:14–30 with Luke 19:12–27).

Fifth and Final Narrative Section: The Passion Story and Resurrection

Matthew retells the story of Jesus' last two days on earth (Thursday and Friday of Holy Week) with the same grave and solemn tone we find in Mark. To the Gospel writers, Jesus of Nazareth's suffering, death, and resurrection are not only the most important events in world history but the crucial turning point in humanity's relation to God. Although Matthew's Passion narrative (26:1–28:20) closely resembles that in Mark's and Luke's Gospels, he adds a few new details, probably drawn from the oral tradition of his community. The treachery of Judas Iscariot is emphasized and linked to the fulfillment of a passage in Jeremiah, although the relevant text actually appears in Zechariah (Matt. 26:14–15, 20–25, 47–50; 27:3–10; Jer. 32:6–13; Zech. 11:12–13). The theme of a warning dream, used frequently in the birth story, is reintroduced when Pilate's wife, frightened by a dream about Jesus, urges her husband to "have nothing to do with that innocent man" (27:19).

Miraculous signs. To stress that the very foundations of the world are shaken by the supreme crime of crucifying God's son, Matthew reports that an earthquake accompanies Jesus' last moment and triggers a resurrection of the dead (27:50–53), an eschatological phenomenon usually associated with the Final Judgment. Although the author presumably includes the incident to show that Jesus' death opens the way for humanity's rebirth, neither he nor any other New Testament writer explains what eventually happens to the reanimated corpses that leave their graves and parade through Jerusalem.

The centurion's reaction. Whereas Mark reports that only one Roman soldier recognizes Jesus as God's son, Matthew states that both the centurion and his men confess Jesus' divinity (27:54). Perhaps Matthew's change of a single man's exclamation to that of a whole group indicates his belief that numerous Gentiles will acknowledge Jesus as Lord.

The empty tomb. Despite some significant differences, all three Synoptic Gospels agree fairly closely in their account of Jesus' burial and the women's discovery of the empty tomb. Matthew, however, adds details about some Pharisees persuading Pilate to dispatch Roman soldiers to guard Jesus' tomb. According to Matthew, the Pharisees are aware of Jesus' promise to rise from the grave "on the third day" and arrange for a Roman guard to prevent the disciples from stealing the body and creating the false impression that Jesus still lives. In Matthew's account, the Romans guarding the tomb on Sunday morning actually see an angel descend from heaven, a sight that paralyzes them with terror.

The plot to discredit the resurrection. After the women discover the empty gravesite and then encounter Jesus himself, some guards report what has happened to the Jerusalem priests. According to Matthew, the Sadducean priests then

The Resurrection by Matthais Grunewald (c. 1470–1528) stresses the overwhelming power revealed in Jesus' rising. (Musee d'Unterlinden, Colmar, photograph by O. Zimmerman.)

plot to undermine Christian claims that Jesus has risen by bribing the soldiers to say that the disciples secretly removed and hid Jesus' corpse (27:62–66; 28:11–15).

Matthew implies that Jews of his day used the soldiers' false testimony to refute Christian preaching about the resurrection. However, his counterargument that the Roman soldiers had admitted falling asleep while on duty is not convincing. Severe punishment, including torture and death, awaited any Roman soldier found thus derelict. In 79 CE, only a few years before Matthew wrote, soldiers guarding the gates of Pompeii preferred being buried alive during the cataclysmic eruption of Mount Vesuvius rather than face the consequences of leaving their posts without permission. A rumor about the possible theft of Jesus' body undoubtedly circulated, but probably not for the reasons that Matthew gives.

Postresurrection appearances. In Mark's Gospel Jesus promises that after his death he will reappear to the disciples in Galilee (Mark 14:28; 16:7). After recording the women's dawn encounter with the risen Lord, Matthew then reports that Jesus also appeared to the Eleven at a prearranged mountain site in Galilee. Matthew observes that some disciples had doubts about their seeing Jesus, as if mistrusting the evidence of their own senses. The author seems to imply that absolute proof of an event so contrary to ordinary human experience is impossible.

The great commission. Even though some disciples doubt, all presumably accept the final command of the One whose teachings are vindicated by his resurrection to life: they, and the community of faith they represent, are to make new disciples throughout the Gentile world (28:16–20). This commission to recruit followers from "all nations" further stresses Matthew's theme that the church has much work to do before Jesus returns. It implies that the author's tiny community had only begun what was to be a vast undertaking—a labor extending into the far-distant future.

In composing a new edition of Jesus' life, Matthew provides his community with a comprehensive survey of Jesus' teaching. The unknown author, who may have lived in Antioch or some other part of Syria in the 80s CE, was a Jewish Christian who used scribal techniques to place Jesus' life and death in the context of ancient Jewish prophecy. Writing to demonstrate that Jesus of Nazareth is the expected Messiah foretold in the Hebrew Bible, Matthew repeatedly quotes or alludes to specific biblical passages that he interprets as being fulfilled in Jesus' career.

The author's concurrent emphasis on scriptural fulfillment and on Jesus' authoritative reinterpretation of the Mosaic Torah (Matt. 5–7) suggests that his work is directed primarily to a Jewish audience. Jesus' comments on such matters as Sabbath observance (12:1–14) and divorce (19:3–12) can be seen as examples of Halakah characteristic of first-century Palestinian rabbinic teaching.

By incorporating a large body of teaching material into Mark's narrative framework, Matthew balances Mark's emphasis on Jesus' deeds—miracles of healing and exorcism—with a counterstress on the ethical content of Jesus' preaching. Instructions to the original disciples (chs. 10 and 18) are applied to conditions in the Christian community of Matthew's day.

Matthew retains the apocalyptic themes found in Mark, but he significantly modifies them. He links the apocalyptic "kingdom" to missionary activities of the early church, which is a visible manifestation of divine rule. Matthew's Gospel typically shifts the burden of meaning from speculations about the *eschaton* to necessary activities of the church during the interim between Jesus' resurrection and the Parousia. Thus, Matthew expands Mark's prediction of Jerusalem's destruction to include parables illustrating the duties and obligations of Jesus' "servant," the church (compare Mark 13 and Matt. 24–25). The shift from apocalyptic speculation to concern for the indefinitely extended work of the church will be even more evident in Luke-Acts.

By framing Mark's account of Jesus' ministry and Passion with narratives of the Savior's birth and resurrection, Matthew emphasizes the divinely directed, supernatural character of Jesus' life. In Matthew, Jesus becomes the Son of God at conception and is the inheritor of all the ancient promises to Israel. He is "son" of Abraham, heir to the Davidic throne, successor to the authoritative seat of Moses, and the embodiment of divine Wisdom. A guidebook providing instruction and discipline for the community of faith, Matthew's Gospel became the church's major source of *parenesis*—advice and instructive encouragement to the faithful.

QUESTIONS FOR DISCUSSION AND REVIEW

1. Even if Mark's Gospel is an older work, what qualities of Matthew's Gospel can account for its standing first in the New Testament canon? How does Matthew connect his account with the Hebrew Bible?

2. Why do scholars believe it unlikely that one of the Twelve wrote Matthew's Gospel? From the content of the Gospel, what can we infer about its author and the time and place of its composition?

3. In his apparent use of Mark, Q, and other sources unique to his account, how does Matthew reveal some of his special interests and purposes? To stress his individual themes, what kinds of changes does he make in editing Mark's account?

4. In adding five blocks of teaching material to Mark's framework, how does Matthew emphasize Jesus' role as an interpreter of the Mosaic Torah? How does Matthew present Jesus' teachings as the standard and guide of the Christian community?

5. What elements from the Hebrew Bible does Matthew employ to create his accounts of Jesus' infancy and his Passion? How does the author's emphasis on the supernatural affect his portrait of Jesus?

6. Stressing Jesus' kingdom message, Matthew devotes long sections to presenting a "kingdom ethic," which involves ending the cycle of retaliation and returning good for evil. If practiced fully today, would Jesus' teaching about giving up all possessions and peacefully submitting to unfair treatment successfully change modern society?

Can Jesus' policy of turning the other cheek be applied to relations among nations, or does it apply to individual relationships only? Did Jesus intend his ethic for a future ideal time, for dedicated members of the church, or for this imperfect world? Do you think that he expected everyone eventually to follow the principles in the Sermon on the Mount and thus bring about God's rule on earth?

7. Although he stresses that Jesus' personal religion is Torah Judaism, Matthew also presents his hero as founder of the church *(ekklesia)*. How "Jewish" and Torah abiding did Matthew intend the church to be?

8. In editing and expanding Mark's prophecy of Jerusalem's fall and the *eschaton*, Matthew interpolates several parables of judgment. How do these parables function to stretch the time of the end into the far-distant future?

TERMS AND CONCEPTS TO REMEMBER

ekklesia	Gehenna
Q *(Quelle)* document	Apostle
M (Matthew's special source)	Matthew's view of Peter's role in the church
halakah	Matthew's view of scribes and Pharisees
Magi	
Sermon on the Mount	
beatitudes	*Parousia*
lex talionis (the law of retaliation)	the great commission
antitheses	

RECOMMENDED READING

Beare, F. W. *The Gospel According to Matthew.* New York: Harper & Row, 1982. Standard introduction.

Brown, R. E. *The Birth of the Messiah: A Commentary on the Infancy Narratives in Matthew and Luke.* New York: Doubleday, 1977. A thorough analysis of traditions surrounding Jesus' birth.

Edwards, R. A. *Matthew's Story of Jesus.* Philadelphia: Fortress Press, 1985. A new introductory study.

Ellis, P. F. *Matthew: His Mind and His Message.* Collegeville, Minn.: Liturgical Press, 1974.

Farmer, W. B. *Jesus and the Gospel: Tradition, Scripture, and Canon.* Philadelphia: Fortress Press, 1982. Argues for the primacy of Matthew's Gospel.

Gundry, R. H. *Matthew: A Commentary on His Literary and Theological Art.* Grand Rapids, Mich.: Eerdmans, 1982. A thorough scholarly analysis and exposition.

Johnson, S. E. "The Gospel According to St. Matthew, Introduction and Exegesis." In *The Interpreter's Bible,* vol. 7, 231–625. Nashville: Abingdon Press, 1951. Covers most major issues in the study of Matthew.

Kee, H. C. *Jesus in History: An Approach to the Study of the Gospels.* 2d ed. New York: Harcourt Brace Jovanovich, 1977. A respected exploration of the Gospel texts.

Kingsbury, J. D. *Matthew as Story.* Philadelphia: Fortress Press, 1986. A more advanced analysis of the Gospel.

———. *Matthew: Structure, Christology, Kingdom.* Philadelphia: Fortress Press, 1975.

Meier, J. P. *The Vision of Matthew: Christ, Church and Morality in the First Gospel. Theological Inquiries.* New York: Paulist Press, 1979.

Senior, D. P. *What Are They Saying About Matthew?* New York: Paulist Press, 1983. A recent survey of critical approaches to interpreting Matthew.

Stendahl, Krister. *The School of St. Matthew and Its Use of the Old Testament.* Philadelphia: Fortress Press, 1968.

9

Luke's Portrait of Jesus: A Savior For "All the Nations"

Yet here I am among you like a servant.
[Jesus to the disciples

(Luke 22:27)]

Beyond all doubt, . . . this man was innocent.

[Roman soldier at Jesus' crucifixion

(Luke 24:47)]

KEY THEMES   The first part of a two-volume work (Luke-Acts), Luke's Gospel presents Jesus' career not as history's final event but as the opening stage of an indefinitely extended historical process that continues in the life of the church (Acts 1–28). Luke's account stresses the role of the Holy Spirit, which directs both Jesus and his later followers. Writing for a Greco–Roman audience, Luke emphasizes that Jesus and his disciples are innocent of any crime against Rome and that the religion they preach is a universal faith intended for all people. In general, Luke portrays his subject to highlight Jesus' gracious forgiveness of sinners, and his kindness to women, the poor, society's outcasts, and other powerless persons. The parables unique to Luke's Gospel depict the unexpected ways in which God's inbreaking kingdom overturns the normal social order and reverses conventional beliefs. Luke-Acts shows God acting through Jesus and his church to effect human salvation, a historical drama that begins in ancient Israel and continues indefinitely into the future.

Of the three Synoptic writers, **Luke** has by far the most ambitious goal. He not only creates a new life of Jesus, the third canonical Gospel, he also provides a sequel—the Book of Acts—in which Jesus' successors continue his work on an international scale.

Luke is aware that "many" others before him have produced Gospels (1:1). The author's resolve to write yet another account of Jesus' life suggests that he was not satisfied with his predecessors' efforts. From Luke's viewpoint, our understanding of Jesus' career will benefit from a fresh theological interpretation and a broader historical perspective. Thus Luke composes a two-volume work (Luke-Acts) that places Je-

sus' ministry precisely at the center of time. Jesus' life forms the connecting link between Israel's biblical past and the future age of a multinational Gentile church (16:16; Acts 1:8; 28:28).

By making the gospel story only the first act in a two-part drama, Luke offers a philosophy of history that is important to Christianity's later understanding of its mission. Instead of an apocalyptic end, Jesus' ministry is a new beginning that establishes a heightened awareness of God's intentions for humanity. Note that Luke ties Jesus' resurrection to the disciples' job of evangelizing the world (Luke 24:44–53; Acts 1:1–8). He creatively modifies early Christianity's initial emphasis on the apocalyptic end of time to focus on the continuing task of the church. Acts thus portrays the disciples entering a new historical epoch, the age of the church, and thereby extends the new faith's operations indefinitely into the future.

Luke's emphasis on seeing Jesus and his disciples in historical perspective may have helped believers deal with the long delay in the Parousia (Second Coming). By showing that the church must remain in the world until it has fully obeyed Jesus' order to carry his message to the "ends of the earth" (Acts 1:8), Luke strongly implies that much work must be done (and a long time must elapse) before the *eschaton*. The author's importance to Christian thought is fittingly represented by the relative size of his literary output. Taken together, Luke's Gospel (the longest of the four) and Acts represent the largest contribution of any single writer to the New Testament collection.

Luke's Preface and Method

Luke's methods in research and writing. Luke is the only Gospel author to introduce his work with a formal statement of purpose. In this preface (1:1–4), he briefly refers to the methods used in compiling the Gospel and addresses the gospel to **Theophilus,** the same person to whom he dedicates the book of Acts (1:1; Acts 1:1). A Greek name meaning "lover of god," Theophilus may symbolize the church for which Luke wrote. Luke, however, addresses him as "your Excellency," suggesting that Theophilus may have been a Greek or Roman official, perhaps a well-to-do patron who underwrote the expenses of publishing and distributing Luke's composition.

Theophilus already knows about Christian beliefs, but now Luke undertakes to write "a connected narrative," supplying his recipient with "authentic knowledge." Luke's use of the term translated a "connected narrative" (or "coherent account") may not refer to a chronolog-

ically accurate biography, for Luke generally follows Mark's order of events. Instead, Luke may use the phrase to indicate his intentions of arranging his subject's life in a proper literary form acceptable to educated Gentile readers.

As a Christian living two or three generations after Jesus' time, Luke must rely on other persons' information, including orally transmitted recollections about Jesus and traditional Christian preaching. Besides memories of "eyewitnesses" and later missionary accounts, the author depends on his own research skills—the labor he expends going "over the whole course of these events in detail" (1:1–4). In addition to his oral sources, Luke also uses written documents, presumably consulting the "many" Gospels then circulating among Christians.

Authorship and Date

The most important early reference to the author of Luke-Acts confirms that, like Mark, he was not an eyewitness to the events he describes. In the Muratorian list of New Testament books (compiled about 200 CE), a note identifies the author of this Gospel as Luke, "the beloved" physician who accompanied Paul on some of the Apostle's missionary journeys. It also states that he did not know Jesus. A few years earlier, Irenaeus, a bishop of Lyons in Gaul (France), also referred to the author as a companion of Paul, presumably the same Luke named in several Pauline letters (Col. 4:14; Philem. 24; 2 Tim. 4:11). If the author of Luke-Acts is Paul's friend, it helps to explain the "we" passages in Acts in which the writer changes from the third to the first person in describing certain episodes; presumably, he was a participant in these events (Acts 16:10–17; 20:5–15; 21:1–18; 27:1–28:16). Some commentators also argue for Lukan authorship on the basis of the writer's vocabulary, which includes a number of medical terms appropriate for a physician. Other scholars point out that the writer uses medical terms no more expertly than he employs legal or even maritime terminology.

The author nowhere identifies himself, either in the Gospel or Acts. His depiction of Paul's character and teaching, moreover, does not always coincide with what Paul reveals of himself in his letters. To many contemporary scholars, these facts indicate that the author could not be a person who knew the Apostle well. Perhaps the most telling argument against Luke's authorship is that the writer shows no knowledge of Paul's letters. Not only does he never refer to Paul writing, he includes none of Paul's distinctive teaching in any of the Pauline speeches contained in Acts. On the other hand, critics who uphold Lukan authorship point out that the physician associated with Paul for only brief periods and wrote long after Paul's death when the theological issues argued in Paul's letters were no longer as immediate or controversial as they had been. Luke's concern in Acts is not to re-open theological disputes but to smooth over differences that divided the early church and depict Apostles and missionaries united in spreading the faith. Although many experts regard the writer of Luke-Acts as anonymous, others retain the traditional assumption that the historical Luke is the author.

Although the author's identity is not conclusively settled, for convenience we refer to him as Luke. Because of his interest in a Gentile audience and his ease in handling the Greek language (he has the largest vocabulary and most polished style of any Evangelist), the writer may have been a Gentile.

According to most scholars, Luke-Acts was written after 70 CE, when Jerusalem was destroyed by the Roman armies under General (later, Emperor) Titus. In his version of Jesus' prediction of the holy city's fall (paralleling Mark 13 and Matthew 24), Luke reveals detailed knowledge of the Roman siege:

> But when you see Jerusalem encircled by armies, then you may be sure that her destruction is near. Then you who are in Judaea must take to the hills; those that are in the city itself must leave it . . . because this is the time of retribution. . . . For there will be great distress in the land and a terrible

judgement upon this people. They will fall at the sword's point; they will be carried captive into all countries; and Jerusalem will be trampled down by foreigners until their day has run its course.

(21:20–24)

In this quoted passage, Luke substitutes a description of Jerusalem's siege for the cryptic "sign" (the "abomination of desolation") that Mark and Matthew allude to at this point in their accounts (see Mark 13:13–19; Matt. 24:15–22). Luke also refers specifically to the Roman method of encircling a besieged town, a military technique used in the 70 CE assault on Jerusalem:

> Your enemies will set up siege-works against you; they will encircle you and hem you in at every point; they will bring you to the ground, you and your children within your walls, and not leave you one stone standing on another.

(19:43–44)

It would appear, then, that the Gospel was written at some point after the Jewish wars of 66–73 CE and before 90 CE, when publication made Paul's letters accessible to Christian readers. Many scholars place Luke-Acts in the mid to late 80s CE and favor Ephesus, a Greek-speaking city in Asia Minor with a relatively large Christian population, as the place of composition.

Luke's Use of Sources

We do not know where Luke acquired the material unique to his Gospel, including the birth stories, prayers, anecdotes about women, and parables of forgiveness that give his work such a distinctive flavor. It seems evident, however, that Luke uses Mark—one of the "many" other Gospels he consulted—as a major source, assimilating about forty-five to fifty percent of the older work into the Lukan narrative. Although generally following Mark's chronology, Luke omits several large units of Markan material (such as Mark 6:45–8:26 and 9:41–10:12), perhaps to make room for his own special additions. Adapting Mark to his creative purpose,

Luke often rearranges the sequence of individual incidents to emphasize his particular themes.

In addition, Luke frames Mark's central account of Jesus' adult career with his own unique stories of Jesus' infancy (chs. 1–2) and resurrection (ch. 24). Luke further modifies the earlier Gospel by adding two large blocks of teaching material. The first insertion—called the "lesser interpolation" (6:20–8:3)—includes Luke's version of the Sermon on the Mount, which the author transfers to level ground. Known as the Sermon on the Plain (6:20–49), this collection of Jesus' sayings is much shorter than Matthew's. Luke apparently drew on the same source as Matthew—the hypothetical Q document—for many of Jesus' statements, but instead of assembling them in long speeches as Matthew does, Luke scatters these sayings throughout his Gospel.

Luke's second major insertion into the Markan narrative, called the "greater interpolation," is nearly ten chapters long (9:51–18:14). A miscellaneous collection of Jesus' sayings and parables, this section supposedly represents Jesus' teaching on the road from Galilee to Jerusalem. It is composed almost exclusively of material from Q and from Luke's special source, which scholars call L (Lukan). After this interpolated section, during which all narrative action stops, Luke returns to Mark's account at 18:15 and then reproduces an edited version of the Passion story.

Like the other synoptic writers, Luke presents Jesus' life in terms of images and themes from the Hebrew Bible, which thus constitutes another of the author's sources. In Luke's presentation, some of Jesus' miracles, such as his resuscitating a widow's dead son, are told in such a way that they closely resemble similar miracles in the Old Testament. Jesus' deeds echo those of the prophets Elijah and Elisha (1 Kings 17–19; 2 Kings 1–6). Luke introduces the Elijah-Elisha theme early in the Gospel (4:23–28), indicating that for him these ancient men of God were prototypes of the Messiah.

Although he shares material from Mark, Q, and the Hebrew Bible with Matthew, Luke gives his "connected narrative" a special quality by including many of Jesus' words that occur only in his Gospel (the L source). Only in Luke do we find such celebrated parables as those of the prodigal son (15:11–32), the lost coin (15:8–10), the persistent widow, the good Samaritan (10:29–37), and Lazarus and the rich man (16:19–31). These and other parables embody consistent themes, typically stressing life's unexpected reversals and/or God's gracious forgiveness of wrongdoers (Box 9–1).

Despite the inclusion of some of Jesus' "hard sayings" about the rigors of discipleship, Luke's special material tends to picture a gentle and loving Jesus, a concerned shepherd who tenderly cares for his flock (the community of believers). Luke has been accused of "sentimentalizing" Jesus' message; however, the author's concern for oppressed people—the poor, the socially outcast, women—is genuine and lends his Gospel a distinctively humane and gracious ambience.

Some Typical Lukan Themes

Luke makes his Gospel a distinctive creation by sounding many themes important to the self-identity and purpose of the Christian community for which he writes. Many readers find Luke's account especially appealing because it portrays Jesus taking a personal interest in women, in the poor, in social outcasts, and in other powerless persons. In general, Luke portrays Jesus as a model of compassion who willingly forgives sinners, comforts the downtrodden, and heals the afflicted. Luke's Jesus is particularly attentive to questions of social and economic justice. In numerous parables unique to his Gospel, Luke demonstrates that Jesus' kingdom ethic demands a radical change in society's present social and religious values. Some major themes that strongly color Luke's portrait of Jesus are described below.

BOX 9-1 *Representative Examples of Material Found Only in Luke*

A formal preface and statement of purpose (1:1–4)

A narrative about the parents of John the Baptist (1:5–25, 57–80)

Luke's distinctive story of Jesus' conception and birth (1:26–56; 2:1–40)

Jesus' childhood visit to the Jerusalem Temple (2:41–52)

A distinctive Lukan genealogy (3:23–38)

The Scripture reading in the Nazareth synagogue and subsequent attempt to kill Jesus (4:16–30)

Details on the Roman siege of Jerusalem (19:43–44; 21:21–24)

Jesus' hearing before Herod Antipas (23:6–12)

The sympathetic criminal (23:39–43)

Jesus' postresurrection appearances on the road to Emmaus (24:13–35)

Some parables, sayings, and miracles unique to Luke:

1. A miraculous catch of fish (5:1–11)
2. Raising the son of a Nain widow (7:11–17)
3. Two forgiven debtors (7:41–43)

4. Satan falling like lightning from heaven (10:18)
5. The good Samaritan (10:29–37)
6. The friend asking help at night (11:5–10)
7. The rich and foolish materialist (12:13–21)
8. Remaining alert for the Master's return (12:36–38)
9. The unproductive fig tree (13:6–9)
10. Healing a crippled woman on the Sabbath (13:10–17)
11. Curing a man with dropsy (14:1–6)
12. A distinctive version of the kingdom banquet (14:12–24)
13. Counting the costs of going to war (14:31–33)
14. Parable of the lost coin (15:8–10)
15. The prodigal (spendthrift) son (15:11–32)
16. The dishonest manager (16:1–13)
17. Lazarus and the rich man (16:19–31)
18. Healing ten lepers (17:11–19)
19. The unjust judge (18:1–8)
20. The Pharisee and the tax collector (18:9–14)
21. Restoring the ear of a slave (22:47–53)

Prayer. One of Luke's principal interests is Jesus' and the disciples' use of prayer. Luke's infancy narrative is full of prayers and hymns of praise by virtually all the adult participants. In his account of John's baptizing campaign, the Spirit descends upon Jesus not at his baptism as in Mark but afterward while Jesus is at prayer (3:21). Similarly, Jesus chooses the disciples after prayer (6:12) and prays before he asks them who he is (9:18). The transfiguration occurs "while he is praying" (9:29). Jesus' instructions on prayer are also more extensive than in other Gospels (11:1–13; 18:1–14). The Lukan stress on prayer carries over into Acts, in which the heroes of the early church are frequently shown praying (Acts 1:14, 24–26; 8:15; 10:1–16).

The Holy Spirit. Luke is also convinced that Jesus' career and the growth of Christianity are not historical accidents but the direct result of God's will, which is expressed through the Holy Spirit. Luke uses this term more than Mark and Matthew together (fourteen times). It is by the Spirit that Jesus is conceived and by which he is anointed after baptism. The Holy Spirit leads him into the wilderness (4:1) and empowers his ministry in Galilee (4:14). The Spirit is conferred through prayer (11:13), and at death the Lukan Jesus commits his "spirit" to God (23:46).

The Holy spirit reappears with overwhelming power in Acts 2 when, like a "strong driving wind," it rushes upon the 120 disciples gathered in Jerusalem to observe **Pentecost**. Possession by the Holy Spirit confirms God's acceptance of Gentiles into the church (Acts 11:15–18). To Luke, it is the Spirit that is responsible for the rapid expansion of believers throughout the Roman Empire. Like Paul, Luke sees the Christian community as charismatic, Spirit led and Spirit directed.

God's plan for human salvation. Luke also stresses his view of human history as a process through which God operates to effect human salvation. In Luke's view, God's plan began with Israel, centered in the life of Jesus, and subsequently expanded to include all nations through the church. "Until John [the Baptist]," Luke writes, "it was the Law and the prophets; since then, there is the good news of the kingdom of God, and everyone forces his way in" (16:16). According to many commentators, Luke here describes three great epochs of world history: (1) the period of Israel's Law, which reached a culmination in John's work; (2) the "good news" of Jesus' kingdom proclamation, the focal turning point of history; and (3) the age of the church, indefinitely extended into the future, into which "everyone" enters.

Christianity as a universal faith. With this Lukan theory of history go several related themes. Luke presents Christianity as a religion intended for "all nations" from the outset. As **Simeon** prophesies over the infant Jesus, the child is destined to become "a revelation to the heathen [Gentiles]" (2:32). In Acts, the risen Christ's final words commission his followers to bear witness about him from Jerusalem "to the ends of the earth" (Acts 1:8).

Christianity as a lawful religion. Besides presenting Christianity as a universal faith, Luke works to show that it is a peaceful and lawful religion. In reporting Jesus' trial before the Roman magistrate and Paul's similar hearings before various other Roman officials, Luke is careful to mention that in each case the accused is innocent of any real crime. Although Pilate condemns Jesus for claiming to be "king of the Jews," an act of sedition against Rome, in Luke's Gospel Pilate also affirms Jesus' innocence, explicitly stating that he finds the prisoner "guilty of no capital offence" (23:22). In Acts, Luke creates parallels to Jesus' trial in which the Apostles and others are similarly declared innocent of subversion. Convinced that Christianity is destined to spread throughout the Empire, Luke wishes to demonstrate that is no threat to the peace or stability of the Roman government.

Jesus as Savior. Finally, Luke presents Jesus in a guise that his Greek and Roman readers will understand. Matthew had labored to prove from the Hebrew Bible that Jesus was the Davidic Messiah. In the account of Jesus' infancy, Luke also sounds the theme of prophetic fulfillment. But he is also aware that his Gentile audience is not primarily interested in a Jewish Messiah, a figure traditionally associated with Jewish nationalism. Although Mark and Matthew had declared their hero "son of God," Luke further universalizes Jesus' appeal by declaring him "Savior" (1:69; 2:11; Acts 3:13–15). He is the only Synoptic writer to do so. Luke's term (the Greek *sōter*) was used widely in the Greco-Roman world and was applied to gods, demigods, and human rulers alike. Hellenistic peoples commonly worshiped savior deities in numerous mystery cults and hailed emperors by the title "god and savior" for the material benefits, such as health, peace, or prosperity, that they conferred upon the public. For Luke, Jesus is the "Savior" of repentant humanity, one who delivers believers from the consequences of sin, as the judges of ancient Israel "saved" or delivered their people from military oppressors. (The NEB translators therefore use the English noun *deliverer* for *sōter* in Luke [1:24, 69; 2:11].)

Organization of Luke's Gospel

A simple outline of Luke's structure follows:

1. Formal preface (1:1–4)
2. Infancy narratives of the Baptist and Jesus (1:5–2:52)

3. Prelude to Jesus' ministry: baptism, genealogy, and temptation (3:1–4:13)

4. Jesus' Galilean ministry and the "lesser interpolation" (4:14–9:50)

5. Jesus' teachings on the journey to Jerusalem, the "greater interpolation" (9:51–18:14)

6. The Jerusalem ministry: Jesus' challenge to the holy city (18:31–21:38)

7. The final conflict and Passion story (22:1–23:56)

8. Epilogue: resurrection appearances in the vicinity of Jerusalem (24:1–53)

In examining Luke's work, we focus primarily on material found only in his Gospel, especially the narrative sections and parables that illustrate distinctively Lukan themes. Because we have already discussed the preface, we begin with one of the most familiar and best-loved stories in the entire Bible—the account of Jesus' conception and birth.

Infancy Narratives of the Baptist and Jesus

We do not know Luke's source for his infancy narratives (1:5–2:52), but he apparently drew on a tradition that differed in many details from Matthew's account (see Box 9-2). The two writers agree that Jesus was born in Bethlehem to **Mary**, a virgin, and **Joseph**, a descendant of David. Apart from that, however, the two Evangelists relate events in a strikingly different manner.

In composing his infancy narratives, Luke adopts a consciously biblical style, writing in the old-fashioned Greek of the Septuagint Bible. The effect is like reading the birth stories in the archaic language of the King James version and most of the rest of the Gospel in more contemporary English. Luke's purpose here, however, is more than merely stylistic: he is echoing the ancient Scriptures, both by his style and by quoting extensively from the Hebrew prophets,

---

> **BOX 9-2** *New Characters Introduced in Luke*
>
> Elizabeth and the priest Zechariah, parents of the Baptist (1:5–25, 39–79)
>
> Gabriel, the angel who announces Jesus' virginal conception (1:26–38)
>
> Augustus, emperor of Rome (2:1–2)
>
> Simeon, who foretells Jesus' messiahship (2:25–35)
>
> Anna, an aged prophetess (2:36–38)
>
> The widow of Nain (7:11–16)
>
> The unidentified sinful woman whom Jesus forgives (7:36–50)
>
> The sisters Mary and Martha (10:38–39)
>
> Zacchaeus, the wealthy tax collector (19:1–10)
>
> Herod Antipas, as one of Jesus' judges (22:7–12; also 9:7–9)
>
> Cleopas and another unidentified disciple (24:13–35)
>
> Additional minor characters include a crippled woman (13:10–17), a man with dropsy (14:1–4), and ten lepers (17:11–19).

---

because what he relates in these passages is the climactic turn of history: "Until John, it was the Law and the prophets, since then there is the good news of the kingdom" (16:16). To Luke, John the Baptist is the culmination of Israel's purpose—to prepare the way for the Christ. Jesus' birth marks the beginning of a new revelation in God's plan for human salvation.

The birth of John the Baptist. Readers should not be surprised, then, that Luke begins his account of Jesus by devoting long passages to **Zechariah**, a Temple priest, and **Elizabeth**, his wife. Not only are this aged and childless couple the future parents of John the Baptist, but their exemplary piety and devotion to the letter of Israel's religion are intended to represent the best in Judaism. Described as "upright and devout, blamelessly observing all the commandments and ordinances of the [Torah]" (1:6), Zechariah and Elizabeth are intended to remind us of Abraham and Sarah (Gen. 17:15–18:15). Like that of the Genesis couple, their only son's birth involves supernatural events, including angelic visitations.

Note that Zechariah and his wife are linked to Jesus' story in two important ways: Elizabeth is Mary's relative (1:36), a blood relationship no other Gospel writer mentions, and she is the mother of the future Baptist, the man predestined to prepare the way for Jesus. The association between John and Jesus in their adult years is thus foreshadowed by the friendship of their two mothers, as well as by the parallel circumstances of their births.

The role of Mary. Luke interweaves the two nativity accounts, juxtaposing Gabriel's visit to Mary (1:26–38) with Mary's visit to her cousin Elizabeth, a meeting that causes the unborn John to stir in his mother's womb at the approach of the newly conceived Jesus. As Mary had been made pregnant by the Holy Spirit, so Elizabeth at their encounter is empowered by the Spirit to prophesy concerning the superiority of Mary's child. This emphasis on women's role in the divine purpose (note also the prophetess Anna in 2:36–38) is a typical Lukan concern. Also significant is Luke's hint about Mary's family background. Since Elizabeth is "of priestly descent," which means that she belongs to the tribe of Levi, it seems probable that Mary also belongs to the Levitical clan rather than the Davidic tribe of Judah. Like that of Matthew, Luke's genealogy traces Jesus' Davidic ancestry through Joseph (1:5; 3:23–24).

In reading the two infancy stories, observe how subtly Luke indicates the relative importance of the two children. He dates John's birth in King Herod's reign (1:5). By contrast, when introducing Jesus' nativity, the author does not relate the event to a Judean king but to a Roman emperor, **Augustus Caesar** (2:1). Luke thus places Jesus in a worldwide (as opposed to a local Jewish) context, suggesting both the universal scope of Jesus' significance and the babe's ultimate destiny to rule all humankind.

In telling of Jesus' circumcision and Mary's ritual purification (2:21–24), Luke stresses another theme important to his picture of Jesus' Jewish background: not only relatives like Elizabeth and Zechariah observe the Mosaic law scrupulously but also Jesus' immediate family. His parents obey every Torah command (2:39), including making a yearly pilgrimage to the Jerusalem Temple for Passover (2:41–43). The author's own view is that most of the Torah's provisions no longer bind Christians (Acts 15), but he wishes to emphasize that from birth Jesus fulfilled all Torah requirements.

Luke's use of hymns. Throughout the infancy stories of Jesus and the Baptist, Luke follows the Greco-Roman biographer's practice of inserting speeches that illustrate themes vital to the writer's view of his subject. The long poem uttered by Zechariah—known by its Latin name, the Benedictus (1:67–79)—combines scriptural quotations with typically Lukan views about Jesus' significance. The same is true of the priest Simeon's prayer, the Nunc Dimittis (2:29–32) and prophecy (2:23–25). Some of the speeches ascribed to characters in the nativity accounts may be rewritten songs and prayers first used in Christian worship services. These liturgical pieces include the angel Gabriel's announcement to Mary that she will bear a son, the Ave Maria (1:28–33), and Mary's exulting prayer, the Magnificat (1:46–55). Mary's hymn closely resembles a passage from the Hebrew Bible, the prayer Hannah recites when an angel foretells the birth of her son, Samuel (1 Sam. 2:1–10). In its present form, this hymn may be as much a composition of the early church, conceived as an appropriate biblical response to the angel's visit, as a memory of Mary's literal words. Nonetheless, Luke implies that Jesus' mother may have been a source of this tradition, noting that she reflected deeply on the unusual circumstances surrounding her son's birth (2:19; see also 2:51).

The Adoration of the Shepherds, Giorgione (c. 1478–1510). This rendition of a visit by Palestinian shepherds to the humble cave in which Jesus was born well illustrates Luke's theme that Jesus is destined to be God's protector of the poor and outcast. (Courtesy of the National Gallery of Art, Washington. Samuel H. Kress Collection.)

Luke records a single incident from Jesus' childhood (the only one reported in the New Testament), probably to stress two of his characteristic interests. Jesus' visit to the Jerusalem Temple not only associates him with the center of Jewish worship but also foreshadows the twelve-year-old's future career, particularly his teaching ministry in Jerusalem (2:41–52).

Jesus' Galilean Ministry and the "Lesser Interpolation"

Jesus' rejection in Nazareth. After describing John's baptism campaign and Jesus' temptation by Satan (3:1–4:13), Luke presents an account of the Galilean ministry that significantly revises Mark's order of events. In Mark (and Matthew), the Nazareans' rejection of Jesus takes place only after the Galilean ministry is well under way (Mark 6:1–6; Matt. 13:54–58). Luke places this episode almost at the outset of Jesus' career. He also adds an incident (not found in Mark or Matthew) in which Jesus' former neighbors try to kill him (4:16–30). Luke probably makes these changes to illustrate that, from the beginning, Jesus is destined to be rejected and killed. The incident in Nazareth foreshadows the later tragic events in Jerusalem.

Luke further rewrites the Nazareth episode to illustrate other typically Lukan themes. Jesus' public reading from Isaiah (61:1–2 and 58:6) announces the kind of Messiah that the author takes him to be—a gracious healer who conveys God's goodwill toward society's "broken victims," particularly the poor, the imprisoned, and the physically afflicted. Most important to Luke, the Spirit empowers Jesus, its presence identifying him as the Lord's anointed—the Messiah. Significantly, Luke deletes Isaiah's reference to divine "vengeance" (compare 4:18–19 with Isa. 61:2).

The narrator apparently alludes to the church's future Gentile mission when Jesus angers the Nazareans by reminding them that two of Israel's leading prophets, Elijah and Elisha, performed their cures on non-Jews. Note that this reference to God's favoring Gentiles causes Jesus' former neighbors to attempt to throw him off a cliff (perhaps in the hill country outside the hollow where Nazareth is located). Although Jesus escapes, Luke has clearly indicated the tragic fate that awaits his hero.

The "Lesser Interpolation"

For the next two chapters (4:31–6:11), Luke reproduces much of the Markan narrative dealing with Jesus' miracles of healing and exorcism. Despite the violent opposition in Nazareth, Jesus draws large crowds, healing many and preaching in numerous Galilean synagogues. Luke transposes the Markan order, however, placing Jesus' calling of the Twelve after the Nazareth episode (6:12–19). This transposition serves as an introduction to Jesus' first public discourse, the Sermon on the Plain (6:20–49). The Sermon begins a long section (called the "lesser interpolation") in which the author interweaves material shared with Matthew (presumably from Q) with material that appears only in his own Gospel (6:20–8:3).

Luke's Sermon on the Plain. Resembling an abbreviated version of Matthew's Sermon on the Mount (see Box 9–3), the Lukan discourse begins with briefer forms of four beatitudes, all of which are in the second person and hence directed at "you" (the audience/reader). Matthew had phrased the beatitudes in the third person ("they") and presented them as blessings upon people who possessed the right spiritual nature, such as "those who hunger and thirst to see right prevail" (Matt. 5:6). By contrast, Luke "materializes" the beatitudes, bluntly referring to physical hunger: "how blest are you who now go hungry; your hunger shall be satisfied" (6:21). His "poor" are the financially destitute, the powerless who are to receive the "kingdom of God."

Luke follows the beatitudes with a list of "woes" ("alas for you") in which the "rich" and "well-fed" are cursed with future loss and hunger. Persons happy with the present social order are destined to regret their former complacency (6:24–26). This harsh judgment on people whom society generally considers fortunate occurs only in Luke and represents one of Luke's special convictions: the kingdom will bring a radical reversal of presently accepted values and expectations. The author does not specify his objections to the wealthy as a class, but in material exclusive to his Gospel he repeatedly attacks the rich, predicting that their present affluence and luxury will be exchanged for misery.

Reversals of status for rich and poor. In pleading the cause of the poor against the rich, Luke also includes his special rendering of Jesus' command to love one's enemies (6:32–36; compare Matt. 5:43–48). One must practice giving unselfishly because such behavior reflects the nature and purpose of God, who treats even the wicked with kindness (6:32–36). As the Lukan parables typically illustrate unexpected reversals of status between the rich and poor, so do they teach generosity and compassion—qualities that to Luke are literally divine (6:35–36).

To Luke, Jesus provides the model of compassionate behavior. When Christ raises a widow's son from the dead (7:11–17), the miracle expresses the twin Lukan themes of God's special love for the poor and unfortunate (especially women) and Jesus' role as Lord of the resurrection. (Be sure to note the awe-inspiring quality that Luke imparts to this scene, as well as Jesus' empathy for the grieving mother.) By including this episode (unique to his Gospel), the author reminds his readers of the joy they will experience when Jesus appears again to restore life to all.

Jesus' interest in women. Luke commonly uses Jesus' interaction with women to reveal his con-

BOX 9–3 *Comparison of the Beatitudes in Matthew and Luke*

MATTHEW

How blest are these who know their
    need of God [the "poor in spirit"];
  the kingdom of Heaven is theirs.
How blest are those of a gentle spirit;
    they shall have the earth for
      their possession.
How blest are those who hunger and
    thirst to see right prevail;
  they shall be satisfied.
How blest are those who show mercy;
    mercy shall be shown to them.
How blest are those whose hearts
    are pure;
  they shall see God.
How blest are the peacemakers;
    God shall call them his [children].
How blest are those who have suffered
    persecution for the cause of right;
  the kingdom of Heaven is theirs.
  "How blest you are, when you suffer insults
and persecution and every kind of calumny for
my sake. Accept it with gladness and exultation,
for you have a rich reward in heaven; in the same
way they persecuted the prophets before you.
(Matt. 5:3–12)

LUKE

How blest are you who are in need ["the poor"];
  the kingdom of God is yours.

How blest are you who now go hungry;
  your hunger shall be satisfied.

  How blest you are when men hate you, when
they outlaw you and insult you, and ban your very
name as infamous, because of the Son of Man.
On that day be glad and dance for joy; for as-
suredly you have a rich reward in heaven; in just
the same way did their fathers treat the prophets.

[The "Woes"]
  But alas for you who are rich; you have had
your time of happiness.
  Alas for you who are well-fed now; you shall
go hungry.
  Alas for you who laugh now; you shall mourn
and weep.
  Alas for you when all speak well of you; just
so did their fathers treat the false prophets. (Luke
6:20–26)

cept of Jesus' character, stressing his hero's combination of authority and tenderness. After providing ultimate comfort to the sorrowing widow
at Nain, Jesus reveals similar compassion for a
prostitute, to whom he imparts another form
of new life. All four Gospels contain an incident
in which a woman anoints Jesus with oil or
some other costly ointment (Mark 14:3–9; Matt.
26:6–13; John 12:1–8). In Luke (7:36–50), however, the anointing does not anticipate preparation for Jesus' burial, as it does in the other
Gospels, but is an act of intense love on the
unnamed woman's part. Set in the house of a
Pharisee where Jesus is dining, the Lukan ver-

BOX 9–4   *The Lord's Prayer and the Golden Rule in the Gospels of Matthew and Luke*

MATTHEW   LUKE

The Lord's Prayer

Our Father in heaven   Father, thy name be hallowed;
thy name be hallowed;   thy kingdom come.
thy kingdom come,   Give us each day our daily bread.
thy will be done,   And forgive us our sins,
on earth as in heaven.   for we too forgive all who have done
Give us today our daily bread.   us wrong.
Forgive us the wrong we have done,   And do not bring us to the test.
as we have forgiven those who have   (Luke 11:2–4)
   wronged us.
And do not bring us to the test,
but save us from the evil one.
                 (Matt. 6:9–13)

MATTHEW   LUKE

The Golden Rule

Always treat others as you would like them to   Treat others as you would like them to treat you.
treat you: that is the Law and the prophets.   (Luke 6:31)
                 (Matt. 7:12)

Note that Matthew's versions appear to include interpretative comments, a midrash on Luke's simpler tradition of Jesus' words.

---

sion focuses on the woman's overwhelming emotion as Jesus permits her to caress and fondle him, much to his host's disapproval, and on the typically Lukan theme of compassion and forgiveness. To Luke, the "immoral" woman's love proves that "her many sins have been forgiven."

In John, the woman is identified as Mary, sister of Martha and Lazarus, but there is no hint of her possessing a lurid past. It would appear that Jesus' emotional encounter with a woman who lavished expensive unguents upon him impressed onlookers enough to remember and transmit it orally to the early Christian community, but—as in the case of many other of Jesus' actions and sayings—the precise context of the event was forgotten. Each Gospel writer provides his own explanatory frame for the incident.

Fittingly, the first extensive interpolation of Lukan material concludes with a summary of the part women play in Jesus' ministry. Accompanying him are numerous female disciples, Galilean women whom he had healed and who now support him and the male disciples "out of their own resources" (8:1–3).

Jesus' Teachings on the Journey to Jerusalem: "Luke's Greater Interpolation"

Luke begins this long section (9:51–18:14) with Jesus' firm resolution to head toward Jerusalem and the final conflict that will culminate in his death and resurrection. Although ostensibly the record of a journey from Galilee to Judea, this part of the Gospel contains little action or sense of forward movement. Emphasizing Jesus' teaching, it is largely a miscellaneous collection of brief anecdotes, sayings, and parables. Here the author intermixes Q material with his individual source (L), including most of the parables unique to his Gospel.

At the beginning of this section Luke records two incidents that foreshadow later developments in Acts. On his way south to Jerusalem, Jesus passes through **Samaria,** carrying his message to several villages. In Matthew (10:5–6) Jesus expressly forbids a mission to the Samaritans, bitterly hated by Jews for their rival interpretation of the Mosaic Law. Luke, however, shows Jesus forbidding the disciples to punish an inhospitable Samaritan town and instead shows him conducting a brief ministry there (9:52–56).

Along with the celebrated story of the "good Samaritan," this episode anticipates the later Christian mission to Samaria described in Acts 8. Jesus' sending forth seventy-two disciples to evangelize the countryside (10:1–16) similarly prefigures the future recruiting of Gentiles. In Jewish terminology, the number seventy or seventy-two represented the sum total of non-Jewish nations. As the Twelve sent to proselytize Israel probably symbolize the traditional twelve Israelite tribes (9:1–6), so the activity of the seventy-two foreshadows Christian expansion among Gentiles of the Roman Empire.

Jesus' mystical insights. Note that Luke's Jesus experiences a moment of ecstatic triumph when the seventy-two return from conducting a series of successful exorcisms. Possessed by the Spirit, he perceives the reality behind his disciples' victory over evil. In a mystical vision, Jesus sees Satan, like a bolt of lightning, hurled from heaven. Through the disciples' actions, Satan's influence is in decline (although he returns to corrupt Judas in 22:23).

In this context of defeating evil through good works, Jesus thanks God that his uneducated followers understand God's purpose better than the intellectually elite. In this passage, Luke expresses ideas that are more common in John's Gospel: only Christ knows the divine nature, and only he can reveal it to those whom he chooses (10:17–24; compare Matthew's version of this prayer in Matt. 11:25–27).

Parable of the Good Samaritan

Luke is aware, however, that "the learned and wise" are not always incapable of religious insight. In 10:25–28 a Torah expert defines the essence of the Mosaic Law in the twin commands to love God (Deut. 6:5) and neighbor (Lev. 19:18). Confirming the expert's perception, Jesus replies that in loving thus, the man "will live." In this episode, Luke provides a good example of the way in which he adapts Markan material to his theological purpose. Mark places this dialogue with the Torah instructor in the Jerusalem Temple and stresses Jesus' approval of the speaker's view that the "law of love" is the epitome of Judaism (Mark 12:28–31). Luke changes the site of this encounter from the Temple to an unidentified place on the road to Jerusalem and uses it to introduce his parable of the good Samaritan. The author creates a transition to the parable by having the instructor ask Jesus to explain what the Torah means by "neighbor."

Instead of answering directly, Jesus responds in typical rabbinic fashion: he tells a story. The questioner must discover his neighbor's identity in Jesus' depiction of a specific human situation. Analyzing the tale of the good Samaritan (10:29–35), most students will find that it not only follows Luke's customary theme of the unexpected but also introduces several rather thorny problems.

Ethical complexities. Jesus' original audience would have seen enormous ethical complexities in this parable. The priest and Levite face a real dilemma: when they find the robbers' victim, they do not know whether the man is alive or dead. If they so much as touch a corpse, the Torah declares them ritually unclean and they will be unable to fulfill their Temple duties. In this case, keeping the Law means ignoring the claim of a person in need. The priest's decision to remain faithful to Torah requirements necessitates his failure to help.

By making a Samaritan the moral hero of his story, Jesus further complicates the issue. In Jewish eyes, the Samaritans, who claimed guardianship of the Mosaic Law, were corruptors of the Torah from whom nothing good could be expected. (Note that a Samaritan village had refused Jesus hospitality because he was making a pilgrimage to Jerusalem, site of the Temple cult that the Samaritans despised [10:52–56].) Finally, Jesus' tale stresses a typical Lukan reversal: the religious outsider, whom the righteous hold in contempt, is the person who obeys the Torah's essential meaning—to act as God's agent by giving help to persons in need.

When Jesus asks the Torah expert which person in the tale behaves as a neighbor, the expert apparently cannot bring himself to utter the hated term "Samaritan." Instead, he vaguely identifies the hero as "the one who showed [the victim] kindness." Jesus' directive to behave as the Samaritan does—in contrast to the priest and the Levite—contains a distinctly subversive element. When the Samaritan helps a Jew (the victim had been traveling from Jerusalem), he boldly overlooks ethnic and sectarian differences in order to aid a religious "enemy."

By constructing this particular situation, Jesus forces the Torah instructor (and Luke his reader) to recognize that a "neighbor" does not necessarily belong to one's own racial or religious group but can be any person who demonstrates generosity and human kindness. (From the orthodox view, the Samaritan belongs to a "false" religion; he is not only a foreigner, but a "heretic" as well.) An even more subversive note is sounded when the parable implies that the priest's and Levite's faithful adherence to biblical rules is the barrier that prevents them from observing religion's essential component, which the Torah expert had correctly defined as the love of God and neighbor.

Mary and Martha

Note that Luke follows the Samaritan parable with a brief anecdote about Jesus' visit at the house of two sisters, Mary and Martha (10:38–42). In its own way, this episode draws a similar distinction between strict adherence to duty and a sensitivity to "higher" opportunities. The Lukan Jesus commends Mary for abandoning her traditional woman's role and joining the men to hear his teaching. The learning experience will be hers to possess forever.

Instructions on Prayer

Luke places a greater emphasis on prayer than any other Synoptic author. Although his version of the Lord's Prayer is much shorter than Matthew's (see Box 9–4), he heightens its significance by adding several parables that extol the value of persistence. Petitioning God is implicitly compared to pestering a friend until he gives what is asked (11:5–10). The same theme reappears in the parable of the importunate or "pushy" widow (18:1–8) who seeks justice from a cynical and corrupt judge. An unworthy representative of his profession, the judge cares nothing about God or public opinion—but he finally grants the widow's petition because she refuses to give him any peace until he acts. If even an unresponsive friend and unscrupulous judge can be hounded into helping one, how much more is God likely to reward people who do not give up talking to him (18:7–8).

Luke contrasts two different kinds of prayer in his parable of the Pharisee and a "publican" (tax-gatherer) (18:9–14). In Jesus' day, the term *tax-gatherer* was then a synonym for sinner, one who betrayed his Jewish countrymen by hiring himself out to the Romans and making a living by extorting money and goods from an already-oppressed people. Notice that the parable contrasts the Pharisee's consciousness of religious worth with the tax collector's confession of his shortcomings. In Luke's reversal of ordinary expectations, it is the honest outcast who wins God's approval and not the conventionally good man. Why God does not listen to the righteous as well as the unrighteous is not explained.

Luke's Views on Riches and Poverty

More than any other Gospel writer, Luke stresses forsaking worldly ambition for the spiritual riches of the kingdom. The Lukan Jesus assures his followers that if God provides for nature's birds and flowers he will care for Christians. He urges his disciples to sell their possessions, give to the poor, and thus earn "heavenly treasures" (12:22–34).

Luke's strong antimaterialism and apparent bias against the rich is partly the result of his conviction that God's Judgment may occur at any time. The rich fool dies before he can enjoy his life's work (12:13–21), but Christians may undergo Judgment even before death. The Master may return without warning at any time (12:35–40). Rather than accumulating wealth, believers must share with the poor and the socially unwanted (14:12–14). Luke also emphasizes that the deformed and unattractive, society's rejects and have-nots, must be the Christian's primary concern in attaining Jesus' favorable verdict (14:15–24).

Lazarus and the Rich Man

Reversals in the afterlife. The Lukan Jesus makes absolute demands upon his disciples: none can belong to him without giving away everything he owns (14:33). In his parable of Lazarus and the rich man, Luke dramatizes the danger of hanging on to great wealth until death parts the owner from his possessions (16:19–31). Appearing only in Luke's Gospel, this metaphor of the afterlife embodies typically Lukan concepts. It shows a rich man experiencing all the posthumous misery that Jesus had predicted for the world's comfortable and satisfied people (6:24–26) and a poor beggar enjoying all the rewards that Jesus had promised to the hungry and outcast (6:20–21). Demonstrating Luke's usual theme of reversal, the parable shows the

two men exchanging their relative positions in the next world.

In reporting Jesus' only parable that deals with the contrasting fates of individuals after death, Luke employs ideas typical of first-century Hellenistic Judaism. The author's picture of Lazarus in paradise and the rich man in fiery torment is duplicated in Josephus's contemporary description of Hades (the Underworld).

Notice that Luke charges the rich man with no crime and assigns the beggar no virtue. To the author, it appears that present social conditions—the existence of hopeless poverty and sickness alongside the "magnificence" and luxury of the affluent—demand a radical change when God rules the world completely. The only fault of which the rich man is implicitly guilty is his toleration of the extreme contrast between his own abundance and the miserable state of the poor. For Luke, it appears to be enough. The author's ideal social order is the commune that the disciples establish following Pentecost, an economic arrangement in which the well-to-do sell their possessions, share them with the poor, and hold "everything in common" (Acts 2:42–47).

Luke modifies his severe criticism of great wealth, however, by including Mark's story of Jesus' advice to a rich man. (He returns to the Markan narrative again in 18:15.) If wealth disqualifies one for the kingdom, who can hope to please God? Note that Jesus' enigmatic reply—all things are possible (18:18–27)—leads to the concept of divine compensation. Persons who sacrifice family or home to seek the kingdom will be repaid both now (presumably referring to the spiritual riches they enjoy in church fellowship) and in the future with eternal life (18:28–30).

Jesus' Love of the Unhappy and the Outcast

All the Gospel authors agree that Jesus sought the company of "tax-gatherers and sinners," a catchall term referring to the great mass of people in ancient Palestine who were socially and religiously unacceptable because they did not or could not keep the Torah's requirements. This "unrespectable" group stood in contrast to the Sadducees, the Pharisees, the scribes, and others who conscientiously observed all Torah regulations in their daily lives. In the Synoptic Gospels, Jesus ignores the principle of contamination by association. He eats, drinks, and otherwise intimately mixes with a wide variety of persons commonly viewed as both morally and ritually "unclean." At one moment we find him dining at the homes of socially honored Pharisees (7:36–50) and the next enjoying the hospitality of social pariahs like Simon the leper (Matt. 26:6–13) and Zacchaeus the tax collector (19:1–10). Jesus' habitual associations lead some of his contemporaries to regard him as a pleasure-loving drunkard (7:34). According to Luke, Jesus answers such criticism by creating parables that illustrate God's unfailing concern for persons the "righteous" dismiss as worthless.

Parables of Joy at Finding What Was Lost

One of the ethical highlights of the entire New Testament, Luke 15 contains three parables dramatizing the joy human beings experience when they recover something precious they had thought forever lost.

The lost sheep. The parable of the lost sheep (also in Matt. 18:10–14) recounts a shepherd's delight in finding a strayed animal. In Luke's version, emphasis falls on the celebration that follows the shepherd's find: "friends and neighbors" are called together to rejoice with him (15:1–7).

A lost coin. A second parable (15:8–10) invites us to observe the behavior of a woman who loses one of her ten silver coins. She lights her lamp (an extravagant gesture for the poor) and sweeps out her entire house, looking in every corner, until she finds the coin. Then, like the shepherd, she summons "friends and neighbors" to celebrate her find. Although Luke sees these two parables as allegories symbolizing

heavenly joy over a "lost" sinner's repentance (15:7, 10), they also reveal Jesus' characteristic tendency to observe and describe unusual human behavior. Both the shepherd and woman exhibit the intense concentration on a single action—searching for lost property—that exemplifies Jesus' demand to seek God's rule first, to the exclusion of all else (6:22; Matt. 6:33).

The prodigal son. One of the most emotionally moving passages in the Bible, the parable of the prodigal son might better be called the story of the forgiving father, for the climax of the narrative focuses on the latter's attitude to his two very different sons. Besides squandering his inheritance "with his women" (15:30), the younger son violates the most basic standards of Judaism, reducing himself to the level of an animal groveling in a Gentile's pigpen. Listing the young man's progressively degrading actions, Jesus describes a person who is utterly insensitive to his religious heritage and as "undeserving" as a human being can be. Even his decision to return to his father's estate is based on an unworthy desire to eat better food.

Yet the parable's main focus is not on the youth's unworthiness but on the father's love. Notice that when the prodigal (spendthrift) is still "a long way off," his father sees him and, forgetting his dignity, rushes to meet the returning son. Note, too that the father expresses no anger at his son's shameful behavior, demands no admission of wrongdoing, and inflicts no punishment. Ignoring the youth's contrite request to be hired as a servant, the parent instead orders a lavish celebration in his honor.

The conversation between the father and his older son, who understandably complains about the partiality shown to his sibling, makes the parable's theme even clearer. Acknowledging the older child's superior claim to his favor, the father attempts to explain the unlimited quality of his affection (15:11–32). The father's nature is to love unconditionally, making no distinction between the deserving and the undeserving recipients of his care. The parable expresses the

The Return of the Prodigal Son, Bartolome Murillo (c. 1618–1682). The artist captures the father's key role in this Lukan parable, stressing the unconscious love that the parent expresses for both his worthy and unworthy children. (Courtesy of the National Gallery of Art, Washington. Gift of the Avalon Foundation 1948.)

same view of the divine Parent, who "is kind to the ungrateful and wicked," that Luke pictured in his Sermon on the Plain (6:35–36).

Parable of the Dishonest Steward

Luke's parables not only surprise us by turning accepted values upside down, consigning the fortunate rich to torment and celebrating the good fortune of the undeserving; they can also puzzle us. Luke follows the parable of the prodigal son with a mind-boggling story of a dishonest and conniving businessman who cheats his employer and is commended for it (16:1–9).

Teaching none of the conventional principles of honesty or decent behavior, this parable makes most readers distinctly uncomfortable. Like the prodigal son, the steward violates the trust placed in him and defrauds his benefactor. Yet, like the

prodigal, he is rewarded by the very person whom he has wronged. The unexpected is what happens. This upsets our basic notions of justice and fair play, as the prodigal's elder brother was upset by having no distinction drawn between his moral propriety and the younger brother's outrageous misbehavior. The meaning Luke attaches to this strange parable—worldly people like the steward are more clever than the unworldly—does not explain the moral paradox. We must ask in what context, in response to what situation, did Jesus first tell this story? Is it simply another example of the unexpected or a paradigm of the bewilderingly unacceptable that must happen when the kingdom breaks into our familiar and convention-ridden lives? Clearly, Luke's readers are asked to rethink ideas and assumptions previously taken for granted.

The Jerusalem Ministry: Jesus' Challenge to the Holy City

This segment of Luke's narrative (18:31–21:38) focuses on Jesus' teaching in or near Jerusalem. The disciples excitedly anticipate great events once Jesus arrives in the holy city (19:11). Luke, however, presents the Jerusalem ministry in a way that redefines apocalyptic hopes and interprets Jesus' kingdom teaching in the light of present realities. In Luke's version of the prophecy, foretelling the Jewish Revolt and Jerusalem's destruction, the author carefully distinguishes between historical events that have already occurred and cosmic portents that belong to the future.

Luke's Views on the End of Time

Most scholars believe that Luke writes to soften the intense apocalyptic expectations that his community inherited from very early Christianity. The fact that he follows his Gospel with an account of the church—the Book of Acts—indicates that Luke foresees a long earthly history for his religion. Luke's emphasis on the church's long-range commission to witness about Jesus "to the ends of the earth" (Acts 1:8) expresses his belief that Christians have much unfinished business to accomplish before the End arrives.

Conflicting Beliefs about the Parousia

Luke's account of Jesus' teachings about the kingdom and Jerusalem's fall seems to modify two popular ideas about the nature of end time and the Parousia. One is a belief that the Parousia has already happened, a concept also discussed in Paul's second letter to the church at Thessalonica, a town in northern Greece (2 Thess. 2:1–12). Apparently, some believed that the Second Coming was accomplished by Jesus' death, resurrection, and ascension into heaven, followed by his outpouring of the Holy Spirit

upon the church. (We find a similar concept in John's Gospel.) A more common view held that the Parousia was extremely near and would occur within the lifetimes of people then living. Luke does not reject the traditional view that Jesus' return will involve a supernatural event bringing history as we know it to a close. His Gospel retains elements of primitive Christian apocalypticism, including instructions to be constantly alert and prepared for the *eschaton,* but he also distances the End, placing it at some unknown time in the remote future.

Lukan Sayings about the Kingdom

In Luke's Gospel, we find Jesus' sayings about the imminence of the kingdom intermixed with exclusively Lukan material about the kingdom being already a reality present in Jesus' miraculous deeds and teaching. When the Pharisees accuse Jesus of exorcising demons by the power of "Beelzebub [Satan]," he answers, "If it is by the finger of God that I drive out the devils, then be sure the kingdom of God has already come upon you" (11:20). Jesus thus challenges onlookers to see in his successful fight against evil the inbreaking reign of God. A similar concept of the kingdom appears in Jesus' answer to some Pharisees who ask when God's dominion will begin:

> You cannot tell by observation when the Kingdom of God comes. There will be no saying, "Look, here it is!" or "there it is!"; for in fact the kingdom of God is among you [*or* in your midst].
> (17:20–21)

Because God rules through Jesus, the Son's work of healing and expelling devils means that the kingdom now reigns. Luke follows this saying with statements that emphasize the unexpectedness and unpredictability of the "Son of Man's" reappearance. Readers are told not to believe premature reports of Jesus' arrival, for the world will continue its normal way until the Parousia suddenly occurs. Though (in this tradition) coming without signs, it is as unmistakable as "the lightning flash that lights up the earth from end to end" (17:22–30).

In his editing of Mark's apocalyptic passages, Luke reveals his intent to modify earlier expectations. At the outset of his Gospel he omits Mark's reference to Jesus' warning about the kingdom's nearness, replacing it with Jesus' announcement of his peaceful messiahship in the Nazareth synagogue (Mark 1:14–15; Luke 4:16–22). Luke presents an edited form of the proclamation in 10:9, 11 but in the context of the disciples' healing ministry, harmonizing with the concept of the kingdom's being present in Jesus' activity. The apocalyptic declaration that some standing beside Jesus would not die before experiencing the kingdom (Mark 9:1) is preserved, but in the context of the transfiguration, which reveals Jesus' divine kingship (9:27).

The Fall of Jerusalem and the Parousia

Luke also retains Mark's apocalyptic prediction of Jerusalem's destruction (Mark 13) but edits it extensively to show that a period of indefinite length intervenes between the city's fall and the actual Parousia (ch. 21). Luke is aware that many of Jesus' followers expected his ministry to culminate in God's government being established visibly on earth. The author reports that "because he [Jesus] was now close to Jerusalem . . . they thought the reign [or kingdom] of God might dawn at any moment" (19:11), an expectation that persisted in the early church (Acts 1:6–7). Luke counters this belief with a parable explaining that their Master must go away "on a long journey" before he returns as "king" (9:12–27). (This parable of "talents," or servants investing money for their absent master, is used by Matthew [25:14–30] for the same purpose of explaining the delayed Parousia.)

Jerusalem's fall is not the End. Luke makes the point even clearer in his description of the Jerusalem siege. Christians are to flee the doomed city, knowing that "the end does not follow immediately" (21:9, 20–23). The author separates historical events preceeding Jerusalem's destruction from cosmic events that signal Jesus' return. After the Romans decimate the city and burn the Temple, an indefinitely extended period of secular history will intervene. Luke's Jesus states that

> Jerusalem will be trampled down by foreigners until their day has run its course.
>
> (21:24)

This reference to an epoch of Gentile domination occurs only in Luke and replaces the apocalyptic "sign" of the "abomination of desolation" that appears at this point in Mark's prophecy of the end (Mark 13:14; Matt. 24:15). In Luke's modified apocalypse, an age of "foreign" (Roman control) will intervene between Jerusalem's fall in 70 CE and the Parousia. In Acts, Luke shows the church's representatives exploiting the Gentiles' "day" or "time" by evangelizing the Roman Empire.

Two stages of the End. Luke's revision of Mark 13 suggests that the author divides apocalyptic time into two distinct stages. The first stage involves the Jewish Revolt and Jerusalem's fall; the second involves the Parousia. Note that Luke uses mythic and astronomical language to characterize events during the second stage. In this passage (21:25–28) he borrows terms from Jewish apocalyptic writers and follows Mark in citing cosmic phenomena—"portents in sun, moon and stars"—that herald the last day. Foreign powers (Gentile nations) will no longer dominate but become powerless with fear. The climactic event is the reappearance of the Son of Man, who then will possess a might and splendor eclipsing that of Gentile rulers. Only after the terrifying celestial display begins can the faithful regard their freedom as near.

Although he had previously included the celebrated assertion that there would be no convincing "sign" of the end (17:21), Luke now cites Mark's simile of the fig tree. When the tree buds, one knows summer is near—thus, when the believer sees the prophesied events occurring he knows that the "kingdom" (here synonymous with the Parousia) is close. Luke also reproduces Mark's confident declaration that "the present generation will live to see it all" (21:32). In its reedited context, however, the assertion that a single generation would witness the death throes of history probably applies only to the cosmic "portents" that immediately precede the Son's arrival. Luke's modified eschatology does not require that the "generation" that witnessed Jesus' ministry and/or Jerusalem's destruction be the same group living when the Parousia takes place. Even so, the believer must remain awake at all times, because the final day will dawn on all humanity with universal impact (21:34–36).

The Final Conflict and Passion Story

Luke's Interpretation of the Passion

Although Luke's account of Jesus' last days in Jerusalem roughly parallels that of Mark (14:1–16:8), it differs in enough details to suggest that Luke may have used another source as well. In this section (22:1–23:56), Luke stresses a theme that will also dominate Acts: Jesus, like his followers after him, is innocent of any sedition against Rome. Luke interprets Jesus' death as an act of legal murder brought about by the Jewish leadership. More than in any other Gospel, Pilate is represented as reluctant to condemn Jesus, repeatedly declaring that the accused is not guilty of a "capital offence." Only when pressured by a Jerusalem mob does Pilate consent to Jesus' crucifixion.

Besides insisting on Jesus' innocence, Luke also edits the Markan narrative (or another tradition parallel to that contained in Mark) to present his own theology of the cross. Mark had stated that Jesus' death was sacrificial: his life is given "as a ransom for many" (Mark

10:45). In the Lukan equivalent of this passage (placed in the setting of the Last Supper), Jesus merely says that he comes to serve (compare Mark 10:42–45 and Luke 22:24–27). Unlike some other New Testament writers, Luke does not see Jesus' Passion as a mystical atonement for human sin. Instead, Jesus appears "like a servant," providing an example for others to imitate, the first in a line of Christian models that includes Peter, Stephen, Paul, and their companions in the Book of Acts.

The Last Supper

Mark's report of the Last Supper (Mark 14:17–25) closely parallels that described in Paul's first letter to the Corinthians (1 Cor. 11:23–26). Luke's version introduces several variations: In the Lukan ceremony the wine cup is passed first and then the unleavened bread. The author may present this different order in the ritual because he wants to avoid giving Jesus' statement about drinking wine again in the kingdom the apocalyptic meaning that Mark gives it. Luke also omits the words interpreting the wine as Jesus' blood, avoiding any suggestion that Jesus sheds his blood to ransom humanity from sin or that he gives his blood to establish a new covenant. In Luke, Jesus' only interpretative comment relates the bread (**Eucharist**) to his "body" (22:17–20). The author also inverts Mark's order by having Jesus announce Judas' betrayal after the ritual meal, implying that the traitor was present and participated in the communion ceremony.

Jesus' Final Ordeal

In his report of Jesus' arrest, trials, and crucifixion, Luke makes several more inversions of the Markan order and adds new material to emphasize his characteristic themes. Softening Mark's harsh view of the disciples' collective failure, Luke states that they fell asleep in Gethsemane because they were "worn out by grief" (22:45–46). In this scene, the author contrasts

Jesus' physical anguish—he literally sweats blood—with the spiritual help Jesus receives from prayer. After asking the Father to spare him, Jesus perceives "an angel from heaven bringing him strength," after which he prays even more fervently. In extremity, Jesus demonstrates the function of prayer for those among the Lukan community who suffer similar testing and persecution (22:39–44).

In describing Jesus' hearing before the Sanhedrin, Luke makes several changes in the Markan sequence of events. In Mark the High Priest questions Jesus, Jesus is then physically abused, and Peter denies knowing him (Mark 14:55–72). Luke places Peter's denial first, the beating second, and the priest's interrogation third (22:63–71). Instead of announcing his identity as Messiah as in Mark, the Lukan Jesus makes only an ambiguous statement that may or may not be an admission. Luke also rephrases Jesus' allusion to the "Son of Man" to show that with Jesus' ministry, the Son's reign has already begun (22:67–71).

Herod Antipas. In Luke the Sanhedrin can produce no witnesses and no conviction on charges of blasphemy. Its members bring Jesus to Pilate strictly on political terms: the accused "subverts" the Jewish nation, opposes paying taxes to the Roman government, and claims to be the Messiah, a political role. When Pilate, eager to rid himself of this troublesome case, learns that Jesus is a Galilean and therefore under the jurisdiction of Herod Antipas, he sends the prisoner to be tried by Herod, who is in Jerusalem for the Passover (23:6–12). Found only in Luke, the Herod episode serves to reinforce Luke's picture of an innocent Jesus. Pilate remarks that neither he nor Herod can find anything in Jesus' case to support the Jews' charge of "subversion" (23:13–15).

In Luke's eyes, only the Jewish leaders are responsible for Jesus' condemnation. Twice Pilate declares that the prisoner "has done nothing to deserve death" (23:15) and is legally "guilty of [no] capital offence" (23:22). The Roman procurator, whom other contemporary historians depict as a ruthless tyrant contemptuous of Jewish public opinion, is here only a weak pawn manipulated by a fanatical group of his Jewish subjects.

Last words on the cross. In recounting Jesus' crucifixion, Luke provides several "last words" that illustrate important Lukan themes. Only in this Gospel do we find Jesus' prayer to forgive his executioners because they do not understand the significance of their actions (23:34). Because Luke regards both Jews and Romans as acting in "ignorance" (see Acts 2:17), this request to pardon his tormentors encompasses all parties involved in Jesus' death. Besides illustrating Jesus' heroic capacity to forgive, this prayer shows Luke's hero vindicating his teaching that a victim must love his enemy (6:27–38), and end the cycle of hatred and retaliation that perpetuates evil in the world. To Luke, Jesus' death enacts the supreme parable of reversal, forgiveness, and completion.

Even in personal suffering the Lukan Jesus thinks not of himself but of others. Carrying his cross on the road to **Calvary,** he comforts the women who weep for him (23:26–31). He similarly consoles the man crucified next to him, promising him an immediate reward in paradise (23:43). (Note that this fellow sufferer has recognized Jesus' political innocence [23:41].) The Messiah's last words are to the Father whose Spirit he had received following baptism (3:21; 4:1, 14) and to whom in death he commits his own spirit (23:46–47).

Except for the symbolic darkness accompanying the crucifixion (23:44–45), Luke mentions no natural phenomena comparable to the great earthquake that Matthew records. Consequently, the Roman centurion does not recognize in Jesus a supernatural being, "a son of God," as in Mark and Matthew (Mark 15:39; Matt. 27:54). The centurion's remark does not refer to Jesus' divinity but to the political injustice of his execution. "Beyond all doubt," he says, "this man was innocent" (23:47). This account of Jesus' death dramatizes two major Lukan themes: Jesus, rather than being a sacrifice for sin, is an example of compassion and forgiveness for all to emulate. He is also, like his followers, completely innocent of any crime against Rome.

Like Matthew, Luke generally follows Mark's order through Jesus' burial and the women's discovery of the empty tomb. Omitting any Matthean reference to supernatural phenomena such as an Easter morning earthquake or the appearance of an angel that blinds the Roman guards, Luke diverges from Mark only in that the women report they have seen to the Eleven, who do not believe them (23:49–24:11). (No Gospel writer except Mark has the women keep silent about their observation.)

Epilogue: Postresurrection Appearances in the Vicinity of Jerusalem

Because early editions of Mark contain no resurrection accounts, it is not surprising that Matthew and Luke employ distinctly different traditions when they report Jesus' postresurrection appearances. As the reader would expect from Luke's consistent focusing on Jerusalem, the Lukan appearances all occur in or near the holy city (24:1–53). (Luke omits the angelic command to seek the risen Jesus in Galilee, a tradition that Matthew preserves [Mark 16:7; Matt. 28:7, 16–20].)

In Luke Jesus' first posthumous appearance occurs on the road to Emmaus, a village "about seven miles from Jerusalem." Notice that Luke uses the episode to illustrate several important concepts. The two disciples to whom he appears, Cleopas and an unnamed companion, do not recognize that the stranger beside them is Jesus until they share a meal together. Only in breaking bread—symbolic of the Christian communion ritual—is Jesus' living presence discerned. Equally important, Luke stresses that

Jesus' career fulfills prophetic elements in the Hebrew Bible. As in Mark, Jesus' true significance can be understood only after his death and resurrection (24:13–32).

Luke's second postresurrection appearance takes place inside Jerusalem, reinforcing themes expressed in the Emmaus narrative. After having appeared to Peter—an event that Luke does not describe but that was an early church tradition (1 Cor. 15:1–5)—Jesus materializes in the midst of a large group, including the Eleven. Luke reports that the event was sudden, stunning, and terrifying. He also stresses the apparition's apparently physical qualities, perhaps to demonstrate the continuity between the human Jesus and the risen Christ. Thus, the Lukan Jesus bears the marks of crucifixion and shares ordinary food (communes) with his disciples (24:33–43).

Linking the Emmaus and Jerusalem events, Luke again emphasizes that the resurrected Jesus offers posthumous teaching that connects his ministry and death with the Jewish Bible. By showing the risen Christ intepreting biblical texts, the author expresses his belief that Jesus continues to guide the Christian church, inspiring fresh insights into the meaning of the Hebrew Scriptures. To Luke, neither the Bible nor Jesus' life can be clearly understood except in the light cast by Christ's resurrection.

Luke ends his Gospel with Jesus' promise to send the disciples his "Father's gift," the Holy Spirit, the invisible force that enables the church to appreciate Jesus' significance and hear his continuing voice. That living voice instructs them to remain in Jerusalem, awaiting "power from above" (24:44–53; fulfilled in Acts 2).

The author of the Gospel traditionally ascribed to Luke, traveling companion of the Apostle Paul, wrote primarily for a Gentile audience. His portrait of Jesus reveals a world *sōter* ("savior"or "deliverer"), conceived by the Holy Spirit, who opens a new era in God's plan for human salvation. As John the Baptist represents the culmination of Israel's role in the divine plan,

Supper at Emmaus by Rembrandt (1609–1669). The artist shows the risen Jesus dining with two disciples at the moment they recognize their companion's identity (Luke 24:28–32). (Statens Museum for Kunst.)

so Jesus—healing, teaching, and banishing evil— inaugurates the reign of God, the "kingdom," among humankind.

Emphasizing God's compassion and willingness to forgive all, the Lukan Jesus provides a powerful example for his followers to imitate in service, charity, and good works. An ethical model for Jews and Gentiles alike, Jesus establishes a Spirit-led movement that provides a religion of salvation for all people. The primitive belief that the Son of Man would return "soon" after his resurrection from the dead is replaced with Luke's concept of the disciples' role in carrying on Jesus' work "to the ends of the earth," a commission that extends the time of the End indefinitely into the future. In the meantime, a law-abiding and peaceful church will convey its message of a Savior for all nations throughout the Roman Empire—and beyond.

QUESTIONS FOR DISCUSSION AND REVIEW

1. Evaluate the evidence for and against the tradition that Luke, Paul's traveling companion, wrote the Gospel bearing his name. Since the author was aware that "many" other accounts of Jesus' life and work had already been composed, why did he—who was not an eyewitness to the events he describes— decide to write a new Gospel? Does the fact that the writer added the Book of Acts as a sequel to his Gospel narrative suggest something about his purpose?

2. In the Greco-Roman world, historians and biographers typically composed long speeches to illustrate their characters' ideas, ethical qualities, and responses to critical

events. Do you find any evidence that Luke uses this method in the Gospel and/or Acts?

3. Much of the material that appears only in Luke's Gospel highlights Jesus' concern for women, the poor, and the socially outcast. The parables unique to his account—such as the prodigal son, the good Samaritan, and Lazarus and the rich man—stress unexpected reversals of society's accepted norms. What view of Jesus' character and teaching do you think that Luke wishes to promote?

4. Compare Matthew's Sermon on the Mount (Matt. chs. 5–7) with Luke's similar Sermon on the Plain (ch. 6). When Luke's version of a saying differs from Matthew's, which of the two do you think is probably closer to Jesus' own words? Do the different versions of the same saying—such as Jesus' blessing of the poor—also illustrate the individual Gospel writer's distinctive viewpoint?

5. Luke's Gospel emphasizes such themes as prayer, the activity of the Holy Spirit, the kingdom's reversal of normal expectations, the rejection of wealth and other material ambitions, Jesus' compassion, and the divine joy in human redemption. How do these themes relate to the author's belief that Jesus' ministry completes the purpose of Israel's revelation and begins a "new age" leading to the kingdom?

6. In editing Mark's prophecy of Jerusalem's fall and Jesus' Second Coming, how does Luke modify his predecessor's emphasis on the nearness of end time? Are Luke's changes in Mark's apocalyptic viewpoint consistent with his writing a second book about the purpose and goals of the early Christian church (the Book of Acts)?

TERMS AND CONCEPTS TO REMEMBER

Luke-Acts as a two-
     volume work
Benedictus
Nunc Dimittis
the role of the Holy
     Spirit
Luke (Paul's traveling
     companion)
Theophilus
Luke's research
     methods
the L (Lukan) source
the "lesser
     interpolation"
the "greater
     interpolation"
the Sermon on the
     Plain
Savior (*sōter*)
Magnificat
Elizabeth and
     Zechariah
Simeon and Anna
Luke's interest in
     women
Luke's modification
     of Mark's
     apocalyptic
     urgency
Luke's distinctive
     themes
parables of
     forgiveness,
     reversal, and the
     unexpected
Luke's interpretation
     of Jesus' ministry
     and death

RECOMMENDED READING

Danker, F. W. *Luke*. Philadelphia: Fortress Press, 1976. Good general introduction.

Edwards, O. C., Jr. *Luke's Story of Jesus*. Philadelphia: Fortress Press, 1981.

Juel, Donald. *Luke-Acts: The Promise of History*. Atlanta: John Knox, 1984.

Robinson, W. C., Jr. "Luke, Gospel of." In *The Interpreter's Dictionary of the Bible*, supplementary vol,, 1976, 558–60. Nashville: Abingdon Press, 1976.

Stuhlmueller, Carroll. "The Gospel According to St. Luke." In *The Jerome Biblical Commentary*," edited by R. E. Brown and J. A. Fitzmeyer, vol. 2, 115–64. Englewood Cliffs, N.J.: Prentice-Hall, 1968. An older but still informative study.

Talbert, C. H. *Reading Luke: A Literary and Theological Commentary on the Third Gospel*. Los Angeles: Crossroads, 1984.

FOR MORE ADVANCED STUDY

Conzelmann, Hans. *Theology of St. Luke*. Translated by G. Buswell. New York: Harper & Row, 1960.

An influential and incisive analysis of Luke's theological purposes.

Ellis, E. E. *The Gospel of Luke*. London and Camden, N.J.: Thomas Nelso & Sons, 1966.

Fitzmyer, J. A., ed. *The Gospel According to Luke*. Vols. 1 & 2 of the Anchor Bible. Garden City, N.Y.: Doubleday, 1981, 1985.

Leaney, A. R. C. *A Commentary on the Gospel According to St. Luke*. 2d ed. Harper's New Testament Commentary. London: Black, 1966.

Talbert, C. H. *Luke-Acts: New Perspectives from the Society of Biblical Literature Seminar*. New York: Crossroads, 1984.

10 The Gospel of John: The Word of God Made Flesh

He who has faith in me will do what I am doing; and he will do greater things still. . . . Your Advocate [Paraclete], the Holy Spirit . . . will teach you everything, and will call to mind all that I have told you.

(John 14:12, 26)

KEY THEMES In John's Gospel the order of events and the portrayal of Jesus and his teaching are strikingly different from those in the Synoptic accounts. Whereas the Synoptics depict Jesus as an apocalyptic healer-exorcist whose teachings deal primarily with Torah reinterpretation, John describes Jesus as an embodiment of heavenly Wisdom who performs no exorcisms and whose teachings center on his own divine nature. In John, Jesus is the human form of God's celestial Word, the power by which God created the universe. As the Word incarnate (made flesh), Jesus reveals otherwise unknowable truths about God's being and purpose. To John, Jesus' crucifixion is not a humiliating defeat (as it is characterized in Mark) but a glorification that frees Jesus to return to heaven. John's Gospel preserves no tradition of a Second Coming (the Parousia). Instead, it argues that the risen Jesus is eternally present in the invisible form of a surrogate—the Paraclete, or Holy Spirit, that continues to inspire and direct the believing community.

From the moment we read the opening lines of John's Gospel—

When all things began, the Word already was. The Word dwelt with God, and what God was, the Word was. (1:1).

—we realize that we have entered a world of thought strikingly different from that of the Synoptic Gospels. "Word," which John uses to denote the state of Jesus' preexistence in heaven before he came to earth, translates the Greek term *Logos*. A philosophical concept with a long pre-Christian history, **Logos** can mean anything from a divine utterance to the principle of cosmic reason that orders and governs the universe. To John, it is the infinite wisdom of God personified.

Identifying his hero with the Greek Logos concept is only the first of John's many astonishing innovations in retelling Jesus' story. While the three Synoptics give remarkably similar accounts of their subject's life, John creates a portrait of Jesus that differs in both outline and content from the other Gospels. Ninety percent of John's material appears exclusively in his account and has no parallel in the Synoptics. The Fourth Gospel offers a different chronology of Jesus' ministry, a different order of events, a different teaching, and a distinctly different teacher. Instead of Mark's humble carpenter-prophet, John presents a divine hero whose supernatural glory radiates through every speech he utters and every miracle he performs. John's Jesus is a being of light even while walking the earth.

At the end of his narrative, the author clearly states his purpose: to inspire faith in Jesus' divinity. He records Jesus' miracles—which he calls "signs"—"in order that you may hold faith that Jesus is the Christ, the Son of God, and that through this faith you may possess life by his name" (20:31). This declaration of authorial intent follows the Gospel's climactic scene—a postresurrection appearance in which the reality of Jesus' living presence conquers the doubts of his most skeptical disciple, **Thomas.** Thomas states that he will not accept Jesus' return from the dead unless he can thrust his fingers into the holes that the crucifixion nails made in Jesus' flesh. A week after Thomas makes his demand for physical proof, Jesus suddenly appears among the disciples, inviting his unbelieving follower to probe his wounds. Overwhelmed at this unexpected confirmation that Jesus is not only alive but in a body that can be touched and felt, Thomas cries out: "My Lord and my God!"

Thomas' confession that Jesus (even after resurrection) somehow mysteriously combines a physical nature with true divinity occurs only in John. Jesus' reply to Thomas's reaction clearly expresses the response that John wants from his readers after they have contemplated his portrait of the divine man. Jesus remarks that while Thomas "found faith" because he physically saw and touched the risen Lord, others are "happy" because they have not seen and yet believe (20:24–29). All the Gospels were written to kindle faith, but only John presents his theological intent so explicitly.

Authorship

Since the late second century CE, the Gospel of John (commonly labeled the Fourth Gospel to distinguish it from the Synoptics) has been attributed to the Apostle **John,** son of Zebedee and brother of **James.** In the Synoptics John and James are Galilean fishermen and, along with Peter, form an inner circle of Jesus' most intimate followers. The most prominent of the Twelve, the three are present when Jesus raises Jairus's daughter (Mark 5:37), at the transfiguration (Mark 9:2), and with Jesus in the Garden of Gethsemane when he is arrested (Mark 14:33). Jesus nicknames John and his brother "Boanerges," meaning "sons of thunder," perhaps for their aggressive temperaments, as when they ask Jesus to send fire to consume a Samaritan village (Luke 9:54) or demand first place in his kingdom (Mark 10:35–40). Writing in the mid-50s CE, Paul describes John as one of the three "pillars" in the Jerusalem church (Gal. 2:6–10).

According to one church tradition, John eventually settled in Ephesus, where he lived to be an exceptionally old man, writing his Gospel, three letters, and the Book of Revelation. These five works are known collectively as the "Johannine literature."

The tradition ascribing authorship to the son of Zebedee is relatively late. Before about 180 CE church writers do not mention the Gospel's existence. After that date some leading churchmen accept it as John's composition, although others doubt its authenticity, some even suggesting that it was the work of Cerinthus, a Gnostic teacher.

One church leader, Clement of Alexandria, states what became the official view of John's origin. Clement (about 200 CE) recognized the salient differences between the Synoptics and John and noted that after the other Evangelists had preserved the "facts of history," John then wrote "a spiritual Gospel." Both traditionalists and modern critics agree with Clement on two counts: that John's Gospel was the last one written and that it profoundly "spiritualizes" its portrayal of Jesus.

Problems with the traditional theory. Most contemporary scholars doubt that the Apostle John wrote the document bearing his name. The Gospel itself does not mention the author's identity, stating instead that it is based on the testimony of an anonymous disciple "whom Jesus loved" (21:20–24). Tradition identifies this "beloved disciple" with John (whose name does not appear in the Gospel), but scholars can find no evidence to substantiate this claim. Jesus predicted that John would suffer a death similar to his (Mark 10:39), whereas the Gospel implies that its author, unlike Peter, James, and John, did not die a martyr's death (21:20–22). Many historians suggest that Herod Agrippa may have executed the Apostle John along with his brother James about 41–43 CE (Acts 12:1–3).

Some critics propose that another John, prominent in the church at Ephesus about 100 CE, is the author. Except that he was called "John the Elder" (presbyter), we know nothing that would connect him with the Johannine writings. Lacking definite confirmation of traditional authorship, scholars regard the work as anonymous. For convenience we refer to the author as John.

The author and the beloved disciple. We do not know who the author is, but editorial notes added to the Gospel's final chapter explicitly associate him with the unnamed beloved disciple, suggesting that at the very least this disciple's teachings are the Gospel's primary source (21:23–24). Although a historical character, the unidentified disciple is also an idealized figure, achieving an intimacy and emotional rapport with Jesus unmatched by Peter or the other disciples. In the Gospel he does not appear (at least as the one "Jesus loved") until the final night of Jesus' life, when we find him at the Last Supper, lying against his leader's chest (13:23). (The Twelve dined in the Greco-Roman fashion, reclining on benches set around the table.)

Portrayed to represent the Johannine community's special knowledge of Christ, the beloved disciple is invariably presented in competition with Peter, who may represent the larger apostolic church from which the disciple's group is somewhat distanced. At the Last Supper the beloved disciple is Peter's intermediary, transmitting to Jesus Peter's question about

Judas's betrayal (13:21–29). Acquainted with the High Priest, he has access to Pilate's court, thus gaining Peter's admittance to the hearing, where Peter denies knowing Jesus (18:15–18). The only male disciple at the cross, he receives Jesus' charge to care for Mary, becoming her "son" (19:26–27).

Outrunning Peter to the empty tomb on Easter morning, he arrives there first and is the first to believe that Jesus is risen (20:2–10). In a boat fishing with Peter on the Sea of Galilee, the disciple is the first to recognize the resurrected Jesus standing on the shore, identifying him to Peter (21:4–7). Peter, future "pillar" of the Jerusalem church, is commissioned to "feed" (spiritually nourish) Jesus' "sheep" (future followers), but Jesus has a special prophecy for the beloved disciple's future: he may live until the Master returns (21:20–22). (This reference to the Second Coming is virtually unique in John's Gospel.)

Editorial comments appended to the Gospel, apparently after the favored disciple's death, indicate how the Johannine church interpreted Jesus' prophecy. The editor notes that while Jesus' remark had circulated among "the brotherhood" (the community in which the Gospel originated), the saying did not mean that the "disciple would not die." It meant only that Jesus' intentions for his favorite did not involve Peter (21:21–23). The editor's comment hints at the differences between the Johannine and most apostolic Christian communities. The disciple's "brotherhood" would produce a Gospel interpreting Jesus' significance in ways that paralleled the Petrine churches' teachings but revealing, they believed, Jesus' "glory" (1:14) more meaningfully than other Gospel accounts.

Place and Time of Composition

Despite its use of Hellenistic terms and ideas, recent studies indicate that John's Gospel is deeply rooted in Palestinian tradition. It shows a greater familiarity with Palestinian geography than the Synoptics and also reveals close connections with first-century Palestinian Judaism, particularly concepts prevailing in the Essene community at Qumran. Study of the Dead Sea Scrolls from Qumran reveals many parallels between Essene ideas and those in John's Gospel and letters. Like the Essene authors, John typically contrasts pairs of abstract terms, such as *light* (symbolizing truth and goodness) and *darkness* (symbolizing deceit and evil), to distinguish between his group and the rest of the world. He sees the universe as a duality, an arena of polar opposites in which the devil (synonymous with "liar") and his "spirit of error" oppose Jesus' "spirit of truth" (8:44; 14:17; 15:26; 1 John 4:6). As "the light of the world," Jesus comes to illuminate humanity's mental and spiritual darkness. The Gospel's use of such terminology does not necessarily imply borrowing from Essene sources but suggests that the author's thought developed in a Palestinian religious environment.

Many scholars favor a Palestinian or Syrian location for the Gospel's origin, but others accept the traditional site of Ephesus. A wealthy, populous seaport and the capital of the Roman province of Asia (the western part of modern Turkey), Ephesus was a crossroads for Near Eastern religious ideas and home to many Jews and early Christians. A center for Paul's missionary work, it was also the base of a John the Baptist sect (Acts 19:1–7). If the Gospel originated in a territory where the Baptist was viewed as Jesus' superior, it would account for the writer's severe limitation of John's role in the messianic drama, reducing his function to a mere "voice" bearing witness to Jesus (1:6–9, 19–28).

Some critics once thought that John's Gospel was composed late in the second century (when Christian authors first mention it), but tiny manuscript fragments of John discovered in the Egyptian desert have been dated at about 125 and 150 CE, making them the oldest surviving copy of a New Testament book. Allowing time for the Gospel to have circulated abroad as far as Egypt, the work could not have originated much later than about 100 CE. The Gospel's references to believers' being expelled from Jewish synagogues (9:22, 34–35)—a process that began about 85 or 90 CE—suggests that the decisive break between church and synagogue was already in effect when it was written. Hence the Gospel is usually dated between about 90 and 100 CE.

Relation to the Synoptic Gospels

Although John's Gospel contains some close verbal parallels to Mark's (for example, John 6:7 and Mark 6:37; John 12:3, 5 and Mark 14:3, 5), indicating that John was familiar with the Synoptic tradition, he takes such a fresh and novel approach that most scholars conclude that the Fourth Gospel does not depend on the earlier Gospels (see Boxes 10-1 and 10-2). Concentrating on Jesus as a heavenly revealer of ultimate truth, John does not present his hero in Synoptic terms. His account avoids most of the major themes and events that the Synoptic writers employ to delineate Jesus' character and teaching.

A partial list of some principal Synoptic incidents and motifs that John regards as unnecessary to complete his picture of Jesus is given below, along with brief suggestions about the author's possible reasons for not including them.

1. John has no birth story or reference to Jesus' virginal conception, perhaps because he sees Christ as the eternal Word (Logos) who "became flesh" (1:14) as the man Jesus of Nazareth. John's doctrine of the **Incarnation** (the spiritual Logos becoming physically human) makes the manner of Jesus' human conception irrelevant.

2. John contains no record of Jesus' baptism by John, emphasizing Jesus' independence of and superiority to the Baptist.

3. John includes no period of contemplation in the Judean wilderness or temptation by Satan. His Jesus possesses a vital unity with the Father that makes worldly temptation impossible.

BOX 10–1   *Representative Examples of Material Found Only in John*

---

1. Doctrine of the Logos: before coming to earth Jesus preexisted in heaven, where he was God's mediator in creating the universe (1:1–18).

2. Miracle at Cana: Jesus changes water into wine (the first "sign") (2:1–12).

3. Doctrine of spiritual rebirth: conversation with Nicodemus (3:1–21).

4. Jesus is water of eternal life: conversation with the Samaritan woman (4:1–42).

5. Jesus heals the invalid at Jerusalem's Sheep Pool (5:1–47).

6. The "I am" sayings: Jesus speaks as divine Wisdom revealed from above, equating himself with objects or concepts of great symbolic value, such as "the bread of life" (6:22–66), "the good shepherd" (10:1–21), "the resurrection and the life" (11:25), "the way," "the truth," (14:6), and "the true vine" (15:1–17).

7. Jesus, light of the world, existed before Abraham (8:12–59).

8. Cure of the man born blind: debate between church and synagogue (9:1–41).

9. The resurrection of Lazarus (the seventh "sign") (11:1–12:11).

10. A different tradition of the Last Supper: washing the disciples' feet (13:1–20) and delivering the farewell discourses; promise of the Paraclete, the Spirit that will empower the disciples and interpret the meaning of Jesus' life (13:31–17:26).

11. Resurrection appearances in or near Jerusalem to Mary Magdalene and the disciples, including Thomas (20:1–29).

12. Resurrection appearances in Galilee to Peter and to the beloved disciple (21:1–23).

---

4. John never refers to Jesus' exorcisms, preferring to show Jesus' overcoming evil through his personal revelation of divine truth rather than through the casting out of demons (which plays so large a role in Mark's and Matthew's reports of the ministry).

5. Although he reports some friction between Jesus and his brothers (7:1–6), John does not reproduce the Markan tradition that Jesus' family thought he was unbalanced or that his neighbors at Nazareth viewed him as nothing extraordinary (Mark 3:20–21, 31–35; 6:1–6). In John, Jesus meets considerable opposition, but he is always too commanding and powerful a figure to be ignored or devalued.

6. John presents Jesus' teaching in a form radically different from that of the Synoptics. Both Mark and Matthew state that Jesus "never" taught without using parables (Mark 4:34; Matt. 13:34), but John does not record a single parable of the Synoptic type (involving homely images of agricultural or domestic life). Instead of brief anecdotes and vivid comparisons, the Johannine Jesus delivers long philosophical speeches in which Jesus' own nature is typically the subject of discussion.

7. Similarly, John reports none of Jesus' reinterpretations of the Mosaic Law, the main topic of Jesus' Synoptic discourses. Instead of the many ethical directives about divorce, Sabbath keeping, ending the law of retaliation, and forgiving enemies that we find in Matthew, Mark, and Luke, John has only one "new commandment"—to love. In both the Gospel and the letters, this is Jesus' single explicit directive; in the Johannine community, mutual love among "friends" is the sole distinguishing mark of true discipleship (13:34–35; 15:9–17).

8. Conspicuously absent from John's Gospel is any prediction of Jerusalem's fall, a concern that dominated the Synopticists' imagination (Mark 13; Matt. 24–25; Luke 21).

BOX 10-2 *Characters Introduced in John or Given New Emphasis*

Andrew, Peter's brother, as a speaking character (1:40–42, 44; 6:8–9; 12:20–22)

Philip, one of the Twelve (1:43–49; 6:5–7; 12:20–22; 14:8–11)

Nathanael, one of the Twelve (1:45–51)

Mary, as a participator in Jesus' ministry (2:1–5); at the cross (19:25–27)

Nicodemus, a leading Pharisee (3:1–12)

A Samaritan woman (4:7–42)

A paralyzed man cured in Jerusalem (5:1–15)

Jesus' unbelieving "brothers" (7:2–10)

The woman taken in adultery (8:3–11; an appendix to John in NEB)

A man born blind (9:1–38)

Lazarus, brother of Mary and Martha (11:1–44; 12:1–11)

An unidentified disciple whom "Jesus loved" (13:23–26; 18:15–16; 19:26–27; 20:2–10; 21:7, 20–24)

Annas, father-in-law of Caiaphas, the High Priest (18:12–14, 19–24)

---

9. Nor does John contain a prophecy of Jesus' Second Coming, substituting a view that Jesus is already present among believers in the form of the **Paraclete,** the Holy Spirit that serves as Christians' Helper, Comforter, or Advocate (14:25–26; 16:7–15). To John, Jesus' first coming means that believers have life now (5:21–26; 11:25–27). Presenting a realized eschatology, a belief that events usually associated with the *eschaton* (world's End) are even now realized or fulfilled by Jesus' spiritual presence among believers, John does not stress a future apocalyptic return.

10. Although he represents the sacramental bread and wine as life-giving symbols, John does not preserve a communion ritual or the institution of a new covenant between Jesus and his followers at the Last Supper. Stating that the meal took place a day before Passover, John substitutes Jesus' act of humble service—washing the disciples' feet—for the Eucharist (13:1–16).

11. As his Jesus cannot be tempted, so John's Christ undergoes no agony before his arrest in the Garden of Gethsemane. Unfailingly poised and confident, Jesus experiences his painful death

as a glorification, his raising on the cross symbolizing his imminent ascension to heaven. Instead of Mark's cry of despair, in John Jesus dies with a declaration that he has "accomplished" his life's purpose (19:30).

12. Finally, it must be stressed that John's many differences from the Synoptics are not simply the result of the author's trying to "fill in" the gaps in his predecessors' Gospels. By carefully examining John's account, we see that he does not write to supplement earlier narratives about Jesus, but that both his omissions and inclusions are determined almost exclusively by the writer's special theological convictions (20:30–31; 21:25). From his opening hymn praising the eternal Word to Jesus' promised reascension to heaven, every part of the Gospel is calculated to illustrate Jesus' glory as God's fullest revelation of his own ineffable Being.

Differences in the Chronology and Order of Events

Although John's essential story resembles the Synoptic version of Jesus' life—a public ministry featuring healings and other miracles followed by official rejection, arrest, crucifixion, and resurrection—the Fourth Gospel presents important differences in the chronology and order of events. Significant ways in which John's narrative sequence differs from the Synoptic order include the following:

1. The Synoptics show Jesus working mainly in Galilee and coming south to Judea only during his last days. By contrast, John has Jesus traveling back and forth between Galilee and Jerusalem throughout the duration of his ministry.

2. The Synoptics place Jesus' assault on the Temple at the end of his career, making it the incident that consolidates official hostility toward him; John sets it at the beginning (2:13–21).

3. The Synoptics agree that Jesus began his mission after John the Baptist's imprisonment, but John states that their missions overlapped (3:23–4:3).

4. The earlier Gospels mention only one Passover and imply that Jesus' career lasted only about a year; John refers to three Passovers (2:13; 6:4; 11:55), thus giving the ministry a duration of three to nearly four years.

5. Unlike the Synoptics, which present the Last Supper as a Passover celebration, John states that Jesus' final meal with the disciples occurred the evening before Passover and that the crucifixion took place on Nisan 14, the day of preparation when paschal lambs were being sacrificed (13:1, 29; 18:28; 19:14). Many historians believe that John's chronology is the more accurate, for it is improbable that Jesus' arrest, trial, and execution took place on Nisan 15, the most sacred time of the Passover observance.

Although most scholars consider the Synoptics more reliable sources of Jesus' actual teaching, they believe John is right about the length of Jesus' career and about the day on which he was crucified.

John's Purpose and Method

John's stated purpose is to elicit belief in his community's distinctively high **Christology,** but other purposes also can be inferred from studying the text. The author commonly refers to his fellow countrymen as "the Jews," as if they are a group from which he is entirely disassociated. His picture of an "innocent" Pontius Pilate and his placing the full responsibility for Jesus' execution on the Jerusalem leadership probably echoes the hostility existing between the author's community and Jewish leaders in the decades following 70 CE, when the church and synagogue became bitterly divided. John's claim of divinity for Jesus could only have increased the antagonism, as his subject's Jerusalem speeches suggest (chs. 7–9, 12, 16, 18).

Refutation of Gnostic ideas. Although he maintains Jesus' supernatural character, John also refutes Gnostic Christians who view Christ as pure spirit. As noted in Chapter 1, **Gnosticism** was a movement in the early church that developed into Christianity's first major heresy. Gnostic thinkers see the universe as consisting of two mutually exclusive realms. The invisible world of spirit is pure and good, and the physical world is inherently evil, the inferior creation of a lesser god (whom some Gnostics identify with Yahweh). According to Gnostic belief, human beings gain salvation only through special knowledge (*gnosis*), imparted to a chosen elite through communion with spiritual beings. A divine redeemer (presumably Christ) descends from the spirit realm to transmit saving knowledge to persons whose souls are sufficiently disciplined to escape the body's earthly desires. Transcending the material world's false reality, the soul can then perceive the eternal truths of the spirit.

A mixture of elements from marginal Judaism, Greek mystery cults, and Christianity, Gnosticism argues that Christ, being good, could not be human. Docetists (a name taken from the Greek verb "to seem") concluded that Christ only seemed to be a man; as God's true son, he was wholly spiritual, ascending to heaven while leaving another's body on the cross.

Although he uses typically Gnostic terms, John avoids Gnosticism's extremism by insisting on Jesus' physical humanity (1:14). Even after resurrection, Jesus displays fleshly wounds and consumes material food (chs. 20–21). To show that Jesus was a mortal person who truly died, John eliminates from his Passion story the tradition that Simon of Cyrene carried Jesus' cross (lest the reader think that Simon might have been substituted for Jesus at the crucifixion). John also adds a new incident in which a Roman soldier pierces Jesus' side, confirming physical death (ch. 20).

Despite the inclusion of details to confound Gnostic misinterpretations, John's Gospel was popular in many Gnostic circles (which may account for its relatively slow acceptance by the church at large). Besides the metaphysical doctrine of Christ's preexistence, John contains many statements expressing classic Gnostic ideas. Knowing the divine beings—Father and Son—is equated with "eternal life" (17:3). The assertion that "the spirit alone gives life; the flesh is of no avail" (6:63) and the emphasis on spiritual rebirth (ch. 3) strikingly parallel Gnostic notions.

John's portrayal of Jesus' teaching. The author's presentation of Jesus' teaching, both public and private, differs so completely from the Synoptic accounts that many readers may wonder how closely John reflects Jesus' actual words. If the Galilean prophet consistently spoke in parables and short, proverbial statements—as Mark, Matthew, and Luke insist that he did—why does John show him delivering only long metaphysical discourses about himself? Is John trying to reproduce Jesus' speeches as they were originally uttered, or does he have another purpose?

The role of the Paraclete. The author gives a clue to his method in the series of farewell speeches that Jesus delivers at the Last Supper (chs. 14–17). A mixture of comforting promises, prayers, and metaphors of union between God and believing humanity, these discourses present Jesus as explaining precisely why he must leave his disciples on earth while he dies and ascends to heaven. His death is not a permanent loss, for he returns to the Father only in order to empower his earthly disciples with the Paraclete, the Holy Spirit, which acts as his surrogate among them.

John believes that his community possesses that promised Spirit and that it operates upon his group exactly as Jesus had foretold. In John's view, the Spirit allows his community to perform several functions that serve the dual purpose of linking members to the human Jesus (now dead) and to the glorified Jesus, whose Spirit still lives among them. The Spirit inspires believers to continue Jesus' miraculous work of healing; it answers their prayers for power and knowledge; it provides defenses against their opponents' hostile criticism; and—most important for the presentation of Jesus' teachings—it enables the "brotherhood" to interpret Jesus' life in its full theological significance (14:12–26).

Speaking as if the Paraclete were a second self, John's Jesus refers to "the Spirit of truth" as a divine person who will witness to Christ's identity, revealing him far more fully than is possible during Jesus' human incarnation. One of the Paraclete's main purposes is to unveil Jesus' true likeness, to paint his portrait in supernal colors. Thus, John represents Jesus as saying that "he [the Paraclete] will glorify me," making Jesus' cosmic meaning known to the author's privileged group (16:12–15).

Directed by the Paraclete, the author's community not only preserves traditions about Jesus of Nazareth but experiences Spirit-directed insights into Jesus' character and nature. The author's task in this Gospel is not to record external facts about his subject's earthly biography, but to create a portrait of Jesus that duplicates what the Paraclete reveals. Since the Paraclete's function is to define Jesus' glory—both its heavenly origin and its continuing presence on earth—John's account must meet the formidable challenge of portraying the real Jesus, delineating both the man and his celestial splendor. (Compare John's method with Luke's similar implication that Jesus' real story can be told only in terms of his postresurrection divinity [Luke 24:25–27, 44–53].)

The speeches in John are thus a creative assimilation of Jesus' remembered words into highly developed confessions of faith in his divine nature and cosmic status. As they stand in the Gospel, they are probably largely the author's creation—sublime tributes to Jesus' unique role in human redemption.

Many scholars have noted that John's Gospel presents Jesus not as a figure of the recent historical past but as an immortal being who still lives within the community of faith. Promised that Jesus' followers will accomplish "greater things" than the human Jesus (14:12), the author and his church perceive Jesus' continuing presence in their own ministries. Thus, in John's Gospel Jesus' speeches and the dialogues with his opponents manifest a double vision, a two-level drama. In John's vision of events, the human Jesus of the past and the believers of the present perform the same Spirit-directed work.

Chapter 9 offers a good example of John's method. In recounting Jesus' restoration of sight to a man born blind, John skillfully combines memories of Jesus' healing ministry with the similar miraculous works his own community performs. The two elements—Jesus and his later disciples—can be equated in John's narrative because the same Paraclete operates through both parties. An awareness that John uses a double vision, combining historical past and present in telling his story, will help the reader to understand the diverse elements present in this difficult chapter. Notice that the curative miracle is followed by a series of debates and confrontations between the cured man, his parents, and officials of his synagogue. The Jewish officials' interrogation of the man reproduces circumstances prevailing not in Jesus' day but in the writer's own time, when Torah authorities cross-examined Jews suspected of regarding Jesus as

the Jewish Messiah. (Do not overlook the references to the expulsion of Jesus' followers from the synagogue [9:23, 34], a situation that did not develop until well after Jerusalem's destruction in 70 CE.)

The conversation with the Pharisee Nicodemus in chapter 3 reveals a similar conflation (blending) of Jesus' past actions with the Johannine community's ongoing ministry. Jesus' pretended astonishment that one of Israel's most famous teachers does not understand the Spirit that motivates Jesus' followers echoes the late-first-century debate between the Jewish authorities and the author's group. Using the first person plural "we" to signify the whole believing community, John affirms that his community experiences the Spirit's power, while "you" (the disbelieving opponents) refuse to credit the Johannine testimony (3:9–11). The reader will also observe that in this dialogue Jesus speaks as if he has already returned to heaven (3:13), again reflecting a conviction of the author's community.

Organization of John's Gospel

John's Gospel is framed by a prologue (1:1–51) and an epilogue (21:1–25). The main narrative (chs. 2–20) divides naturally into two long sections: an account of Jesus' miracles and public speeches (chs. 2–11) and an extended Passion story emphasizing Jesus' final prayers and speeches to the disciples (chs. 12–20). Because John regards Jesus' miracles as "signs" or public evidence of his hero's supernatural character, the first section is called the Book of Signs. (Some scholars believe that the author uses a previously compiled collection of Jesus' miraculous works as a primary source.) Because it presents Christ's death as a "glorious" fulfillment of the divine will, some commentators call the second part the Book of Glory.

The Gospel may be outlined as follows:

1. Prologue: Hymn to the Logos; testimony of the Baptist; call of the disciples (1:1–51)

2. The Book of Signs (2:1–11:57)
   a. The miracle at Cana
   b. Cleansing the Temple
   c. Dialogue with Nicodemus on spiritual rebirth
   d. Conversation with the Samaritan woman
   e. Five more miraculous signs in Jerusalem and Galilee; Jesus' discourses witnessing to his divine nature
   f. The resurrection of Lazarus (the seventh sign)
3. The Book of Glory (12:1–20:31)
   a. The plot against Jesus
   b. The Last Supper and farewell discourses
   c. The Passion story
   d. The empty tomb and resurrection appearances to Peter and the beloved disciple (21:1–25)
4. Epilogue: postresurrection appearances in Galilee; parting words to Peter and the beloved disciple (21:1–25)

Hymn to the Word (Logos)

John's opening hymn to the Word introduces several concepts vital to his portrait of Christ. The phrase "when all things began" recalls the Genesis creation account when God's word of command—"Let there be light"—illuminated a previously dark universe. In John's view, the prehuman Christ is the creative Word whom God uses to bring heaven and earth into existence. "With God at the beginning," the Word is an integral part of the Supreme Being—"what God was, the Word was" (1:1–5).

John's supreme irony is that the very world that the Word created rejects him, preferring spiritual "darkness" to the "light" he imparts. Nonetheless, the Word "became flesh"—the man Jesus—and temporarily lived among human beings, allowing them to witness his "glory, such glory as befits the Father's only Son" (1:10–14).

Greek and Jewish Background

As noted above, *Logos* (Word) is a Greek philosophical term, but John blends it with a parallel Jewish tradition about divine Wisdom that existed before the world began. According to the Book of Proverbs (8:22–31), Wisdom (depicted as a gracious young woman) was Yahweh's companion when he created the universe, transforming the original dark chaos into a design of order and light. As Yahweh's darling, she not only was his intimate helper in the creative process but also became God's channel of communication with humankind. As Israel's wisdom tradition developed in Hellenistic times, Wisdom was seen as both Yahweh's agent of creation and the being who reveals the divine mind to the faithful (Eccles. 24; Wisd. 6:12–9:18).

In the Greek philosophical tradition, Logos is also a divine concept, the principle of cosmic reason that gives order and coherence to the otherwise chaotic world, making it accessible to human intellect. The Logos concept had circulated among Greek thinkers since the time of the philosopher Heraclitus (born before 500 BCE). In John's day Logos was a popular Stoic term, commonly viewed as synonymous with the divine intelligence that created and sustains the universe.

These analogous Greek and Hebrew ideas converge in the writings of **Philo Judaeus,** a Hellenistic Jewish scholar living in Alexandria during the first century CE. A pious Jew profoundly influenced by Greek rationality, Philo attempted to reconcile Hellenic logic with the revelation contained in the Hebrew Bible. Philo used the Hebrew concept of Wisdom as the creative intermediary between the transcendent Creator and the material creation. However, he employed the Greek term *Logos* to designate Wisdom's role and function. (Philo may have preferred *Logos* because it is masculine in Greek, whereas Wisdom [*Sophia*] is feminine.) Philo's interpretation can be illustrated by an allegorical reading of Genesis 1, in which God's first act is

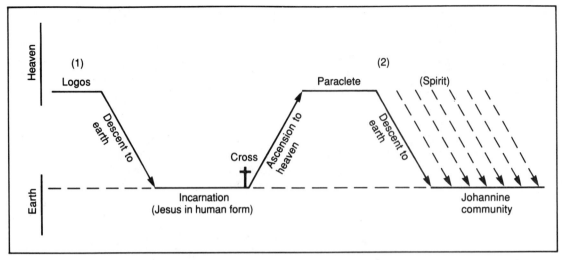

Figure 10–1. John's concept of the Incarnation (the Word made flesh). Note that Jesus' ascension to heaven (return to his place of spiritual origin) is followed by a descent of the Paraclete, Jesus' Spirit—an invisible surrogate that inspires the Johannine brotherhood. Whereas Jesus' human presence on earth was brief, John implies that the Paraclete abides permanently with the believing community.

to speak—to create the Word (Logos)—by which power the cosmos is born.

In identifying the prehuman Christ with Philo's Logos, John equates Jesus with the loftiest philosophical ideal of his age. His Christ is thus superior to every other heavenly or earthly being, all of whom owe their creation to him. John's Jesus not only speaks the word of God, he is the Word incarnate. From the author's perspective, Jesus' human career is merely a brief interlude, a temporary descent to earth preceded and followed by eternal life above (3:13). (Compare John's Logos doctrine with similar ideas discussed in Phil. 2 and Col. 1–2; see also Figure 10-1.)

Jesus and Divine Wisdom

After the prologue, John does not again refer explicitly to Jesus as the Word. He does, however, repeatedly link his hero to the concept of divine Wisdom, a personification of God's creative intelligence. In the Hebrew Bible, Wis-

dom is both the means by which God creates and the channel through whom he communicates to humankind. Old Testament writers characteristically picture Wisdom speaking in the first person, using the phrase "I am" and then defining her activities as God's agent. John casts many of Jesus' speeches in exactly the same form, beginning with a declaration "I am" and then typically equating himself with a term of great religious significance. Compare some of Wisdom's speeches with those of the Johannine Jesus:

> The Lord created me the beginning of his works,
> before all else that he made, long ago.
> Alone, I was fashioned in times long past,
> at the beginning, long before earth itself.
> (Prov. 8:22–23)

Identifying Wisdom with God's verbal command to create light (Gen. 1:3), the author of Ecclesiasticus represents her as saying:

This "Good Shepherd," is an early Christian painting of Christ on the ceiling of a crypt in the catacombs of St. Priscilla in Rome. Note that the artist pictures Jesus in a pose that would be familiar to a Greco-Roman audience: like earlier renditions of Apollo, the Greek God of intellect, music, and shepherds, the youthful Jesus carries a lamb on his shoulders to demonstrate his concern for his human flock. Compare John 10:1–18, Matt. 18:12–14, and Luke 15:4–7. (Courtesy of Benedettine Di Priscilla.)

I am the word which was spoken by the Most
   High; . . .
Before time began he created me,
and I shall remain for ever. . . .

                        (Eccles. 24:3, 9)

Sent by God to live among his people, Israel, Wisdom invites all to seek her favor:

Come to me, you who desire me,
and eat your fill of my fruit; . . .
Whoever feeds on me will be hungry for more,
and whoever drinks from me will thirst for more.
(Ecclus. 24:19, 21–22; compare to John 4:13–15)

Jesus and Yahweh

Jesus' "I am" pronouncements. Besides associating Jesus with the Hebrew principle of eternal Wisdom, John's "I am" speeches also express an important aspect of his Christology. They echo Yahweh's declaration of being to Moses at the burning bush (Exod. 3:14), in which God reveals his sacred personal name. In the Hebrew Bible, only Yahweh speaks of himself (the "I am") in this manner. Hence, Jesus' reiterated "I am . . . the bread of life" (6:35), "the good shepherd" (10:11), "the resurrection and the life" (11:25), or "the way," "the truth," and "the life" (14:6) stress his unity with God, the eternal "I am."

John attributes much of "the Jews' " hostility to Jesus to their reaction against his apparent claims to divinity. When Jesus refers publicly to his prehuman existence, declaring that "before Abraham was born, I am," his outraged audience in the Temple attempts to stone him for blasphemy (8:56–59). Many scholars doubt that Jesus really made such assertions. According to this view, the attempted stoning represents Jewish leaders' response to the preaching of John's group, which made extraordinarily high claims about Jesus' divine nature.

Role of the Baptist

Readers will notice that John repeatedly interrupts his Logos hymn to compare the Baptist unfavorably to Jesus. Insisting on the Baptist's inferiority, the author has him bear witness against himself: he is neither a prophet nor the Elijah figure, but only "a voice" whose sole function is to announce Jesus. Thus, the Baptist bears witness to seeing the Holy Spirit descend upon Jesus, a phenomenon that Mark reports as Jesus' inward or private experience of his calling (Mark 1:10–11) (see Box 8–5).

Contrary to the Markan tradition of a hidden Messiah whose identity is only gradually revealed, John has the Baptist immediately hail Jesus as the "Lamb of God . . . who takes away the sin of the world." In John, Jesus is recognized as "God's Chosen One" right from the start (1:6–9, 19–36).

The Book of Signs

John structures his account of Jesus' public ministry around seven miracles, or signs, that demonstrate Christ's divine power.

The Miracle at Cana

The first sign occurs at the Galilean town of Cana (not mentioned in the Synoptics), where Jesus, attending a wedding with his mother, changes water into wine. At first glance, this "miracle" resembles the magic tricks that priests of Dionysus (Bacchus), the Greco-Roman god of wine and inspiration, performed to impress gullible onlookers. To John, however, the act is deeply symbolic.

First, Jesus' producing a vintage wine of high quality suggests the superiority of his teaching to the "watery" doctrine of his Jewish predecessors. The fact that it occurs at a marriage festival, the joyful union of man and woman, reminds us that Jesus is the "bridegroom," whose presence brings happiness (3:29; Mark 2:19–20). Most important, the wine represents the sacramental beverage of the Christian communion, the drink symbolizing the blood Jesus sheds on the cross (2:1–11).

Assault on the Temple

Reversing the Synoptic order, John shows Jesus driving moneychangers from the Temple during a Passover at the outset of his ministry. For John, the episode's significance is Jesus' superiority to the Jerusalem sanctuary. The Temple is no longer sacred because the Holy Spirit now dwells in Jesus' person rather than the shrine King Herod constructed. Jesus' physical body may be destroyed, but unlike the Herodian edifice he will rise again as proof that God's Spirit imbues him (2:13–25).

Dialogue with Nicodemus

Jesus' conversation with **Nicodemus,** a Pharisee and member of the Jewish Council (Sanhedrin), typifies John's method of presenting Jesus' teaching (3:1–21). In most of the Johannine dialogues Jesus uses a figure of speech or metaphor that the person with whom he speaks almost comically misinterprets, usually taking Jesus' words literally. John then has Jesus explain his metaphoric meaning, commonly launching a long monologue in which Christ discourses on his metaphysical nature and unique relationship with the Father.

Thus, when Jesus remarks that unless one is "born over again" he can not "see the kingdom of God," Nicodemus mistakenly thinks he refers to reemerging from the womb. Jesus then explains that he means rebirth "from water and spirit," referring to the spiritual renewal that accompanies Christian baptism. Found only in John, this doctrine of becoming "born again" resembles beliefs characteristic of Gnosticism and Greek mystery religions. In both cults, converts undergo initiation rites, commonly involving purification by water, to achieve the soul's new birth on a higher plane of existence, leading eventually to immortality.

Perhaps aware of non-Christian parallels to this teaching, the author stresses that Jesus is uniquely qualified to reveal spiritual truths. He is intimately acquainted with the unseen world, because heaven is his natural environment, the home to which he will return when "lifted up [on the cross]" (3:12–15).

In perhaps the most famous passage of the New Testament, Jesus states his purpose in coming to earth. God so intensely loves the world that he sends his Son not to condemn but to save it, awakening in humanity a faith that gives "eternal life." Believers pass the test for eternal life through their attraction to Jesus' "light," while others judge themselves by preferring the world's "darkness" (3:16–21). Here, John's attitude toward the world is positive, although elsewhere he expresses an ambiguous attitude toward its mixed potential for good and evil. Representing Jesus' ministry and crucifixion as the world's time of Judgment (12:31), he declares that Christians are "strangers in the world" (17:16).

Despite acknowledging the world's capacity to believe (17:21, 23), the author shows Jesus telling Pontius Pilate that his "kingdom does not belong to this world"—at least not the kind of system that Pilate and the Roman Empire represent (18:36).

Conversation with the Samaritan Woman

Luke stresses Jesus' warm relationships with women, who are numbered among his most faithful disciples. John further explores Jesus' characteristic openness to women, with whom he converses freely, teaching them on the same level he instructs his male followers. As in Luke, John shows Jesus ignoring the rigid social conventions that segregate the sexes, even to the point of speaking intimately with prostitutes and others of questionable reputation.

Astonishing the disciples by his violation of the social code (4:27), Jesus publicly discusses fine points of theology with a Samaritan woman who gives him water to drink at Jacob's well. Recalling the deep hostility then existing between Jews and **Samaritans** (Chapter 5), we understand the woman's surprise at Jesus' willingness to associate with her. She assumes that he is a prophet and seizes the opportunity to learn from him. As Jesus later instructs Martha in the mysteries of the resurrection (11:17–27), so he reveals to the Samaritan woman that he is the "living water" that satisfies humanity's spiritual thirst. Disclosing that neither the Jerusalem Temple nor the Samaritans' rival shrine at Mount Gerizim is the only right place to worship, Jesus teaches her that "spirit and truth" transcend the claims of any earthly sanctuary.

John uses this episode to illustrate several provocative ideas. Although the woman is "immoral" (she has had five husbands and now lives with a man to whom she is not married), Jesus selects her to fill an important role. She is not only the first non-Jew to whom he reveals that he is the Christ (4:25–26) but also the means by which "many Samaritans" become believers (4:39). The woman's rush to inform her fellow villagers about Jesus anticipates Mary Magdalene's later role as prophet to the male disciples when she brings the news that their crucified Lord still lives (20:1–2, 10–18).

The Woman Taken in Adultery

Because it does not appear in the oldest New Testament manuscripts, editors of the New English Bible relegate the story of the adulterous woman (7:1–11) to an appendix following chapter 21. In some manuscripts the incident shows up in Luke, where it well suits the Lukan theme of forgiveness. The anecdote in which Pharisees demand that Jesus judge a woman "caught in the very act" of illicit sex was apparently a well-known tradition that had difficulty finding home in the canonical Gospels, perhaps because many early Christians found it shocking.

Asked to enforce the Torah rule that prescribed death by stoning for adulterers (Lev. 20:10; Deut. 22:20–21), Jesus turns the responsibility for deciding the woman's fate back upon her accusers. Only the person who is "faultless" (without sin) is qualified to enforce the legal penalty. Forcing those who would judge her to examine their own consciences, Jesus finds that the assembled crowd melts away, leaving him alone with the accused. He neither condemns nor imposes penance upon the woman, merely instructing her not to "sin again." Neither blamed nor lectured, she is left to ponder the meaning of her rescue. Whether this episode belongs in John or not, it is consistent with Jesus' attitude toward individual "sinners" in all four Gospels.

Further Signs and Miracles

Jesus' second sign is his curing a nobleman's dying son in Cana (4:46–54). His third is his healing a crippled man at the Sheep Pool in Jerusalem, a controversial act because it occurs on the Sabbath (5:1–15). Criticism directed at Jesus' alleged Sabbath breaking provides the opportunity for an extended discourse on his special relation to the Father. In John's view, God's work (sustaining the universe) continues unceasingly and provides a model that the Son imitates in ministering to God's human creation (5:16–17).

When accused of claiming "equality with God," Jesus clarifies the nature of his authority. The Son initiates "nothing" on his own; he can only imitate the Father. As God creates life, so the Son grants "eternal life" to those trusting him. In Jesus' ministry, the long-hoped-for resurrection to immortality is already a present reality (5:18–26). Emphasizing his dependence on the Father who sent him, Jesus states that he acts as he is told, dutifully obeying a superior intelligence (5:30). Those who reject him also misread the Hebrew Bible that anticipated God's ministry through him. If his critics really understood the Torah (including the Sabbath's true meaning), they would believe him (5:31–47).

John's presentation of the next two signs parallels the Synoptic tradition, but they are followed by a typically Johannine speech in which the author significantly reinterprets their meaning. The miraculous feeding of five thousand people (the fourth sign) is the only miracle that appears in all four Gospels (6:1–12; Mark 6:30–44; Matt. 14:13–21; Luke 9:10–17). As in Mark, the miracle is immediately followed by Jesus' walking on water (John's fifth sign) (6:16–21; Mark 6: 47–51).

The scene in which Jesus identifies himself with life-giving bread probably reflects the situation in John's day, when his community argued bitterly with other Jews about the Christian communion ritual. Jesus asserts that the only way to gain eternal life is to eat his flesh and drink his blood. Many persons, including Christians, take offense at what seems to them an absurd recommendation of cannibalism. John's church apparently taught that the sacramental bread and communion wine literally became Jesus' body and blood (6:25–65), in a process called transubstantiation. Even centuries after John's time, numerous outsiders charged that during their secret meetings Christians practiced bloodthirsty rites, including cannibalism.

Jesus' sixth sign—restoring sight to a blind man (9:1–41)—illustrates John's theme that Christ is "the light of the world" (8:12). His gift of sight dispels the darkness that afflicted the man and reflects Jesus' identity as the Word that originally brought light out of dark chaos at the world's creation (Gen. 1:1–5). As mentioned above, this lengthy episode probably mingles traditions about Jesus' healings with similar miraculous cures performed by Christian prophets in John's church. The dialogue in the synagogue that follows the miracle illustrates the tension that prevailed between church and synagogue in John's day.

The Resurrection of Lazarus

The seventh and most spectacular miracle—raising Lazarus from the dead (11:1–44)—demonstrates another Johannine conviction, that Jesus possesses irresistible power over life and death. Concluding the Book of Signs, the narrative of Lazarus' resurrection also functions to connect Jesus' good works with his arrest and crucifixion. As John relates it, Jesus' ability to raise a man who has been dead for four days is the act that consolidates Jewish opposition to him and leads directly to his death (11:45–53).

Although no other canonical Gospel mentions the Lazarus episode, John may draw upon a primitive resurrection story that was once part of Mark's narrative (see "The Secret Gospel of Mark" in Chapter 11 for an early parallel to the Lazarus miracle). Certain elements of John's account appear in Luke, who includes Mary and Martha (Lazarus's sisters) among Jesus' followers (Luke 10:38–42) but is apparently unaware that they have a brother named Lazarus. (But recall that Luke uses the name Lazarus in his parable about death and the afterlife [Luke 16:19–31].) Whatever the historical foundation of the Lazarus incident, John uses it to prove that Jesus is Lord of the resurrection. In a climactic "I am" speech, Jesus declares,

> I am the resurrection and I am life. If a man has faith in me, even though he die, he shall come to life; and no one who is alive and has faith shall ever die.   (11:25)

In dramatic fulfillment of his claims, Jesus orders Lazarus to rise from his tomb, showing all witnesses present that the eschatological hope of life comes through Jesus now (11:1–44).

In grim contrast to the joyous belief that greets Jesus' miracle, John shows the Pharisees plotting Jesus' death. Jesus' opponents fear that if the Jewish people accept his messiahship (making him "king of the Jews") their response will incite the Romans to destroy their state and place of worship. (This passage refers to the Roman destruction of Jerusalem in 70 CE.) Caiaphas, the High Priest, proposes that eliminating Jesus will spare the nation that ordeal. Caiaphas's remark—that "it is more to your interest that one man should die for the people, than that the whole nation should be destroyed"—is deeply ironic. While justifying the plot to kill Jesus, the High Priest unwittingly expresses the Christian belief that Jesus' death redeems the world (11:47–53).

The Book of Glory

John opens the second section of his Gospel (the Book of Glory), which is largely devoted to interpreting the meaning of Jesus' Passion, with a scene that connects it to the ministry of signs that Jesus has just completed. The author shows Jesus at dinner with friends, celebrating Lazarus's return to life. The festive meal unites several important themes, looking back to Jesus' feeding the multitudes and the resurrection of Lazarus and looking forward to the Last Supper and Jesus' own death. Even while rejoicing in one man's escape from the tomb, the dinner guests are forewarned of their leader's imminent death when Lazarus's sister Mary anoints Jesus' feet with expensive perfume. Christ approves her prophetic action as preparing his body for burial, for his hour of "glory" is near at hand.

Whether following different sources or reworking the older Synoptic tradition, John pictures Jesus' final days in a way that transforms the Messiah's betrayal and suffering into a glorious triumph. After his messianic entry into Jerusalem (John adds the detail of the crowds' waving palm branches that gives Palm Sunday its name) (12:12–19), Jesus foretells his death in terms resembling Mark's description of the agony in Gethsemane (14:32–36) but reinterpreted to stress the crucifixion's saving purpose:

> Now my soul is in turmoil, and what am I to say? Father, save me from this hour. No, it was for this that I came to this hour. Father, glorify thy name.
> (12:27–28)

When a celestial voice affirms that God is glorified in Christ's actions, Jesus interprets his "lifting up" (crucifixion) as God's predestined means of drawing all people to him, a process of human salvation that cannot occur without his death (12:28–33).

The Last Supper and Farewell Discourses

Perhaps because he has already presented his veiw of Jesus as the "heavenly bread" that gives life to those who partake of it (6:26–58), John's account of the Last Supper contains no reference to Jesus' distributing the ceremonial bread and wine (the Eucharist). Instead, John's narrative dramatizes a concept found also in Luke's Gospel—that Jesus comes "like a servant" (Luke 22:27). Given the author's view that Christ shares the nature of the Supreme Being (1:1), Jesus' taking the role of a domestic slave, washing his disciples' travel-stained feet, is extremely significant. The Master's humility both demonstrates God's loving care for the faithful and sets an example of humble service for the Johannine community (13:3–17).

After Judas Iscariot leaves the group to betray his Master (a treachery that John believes is predestined), Jesus delivers a series of farewell speeches intended to make clear the way in which his ministry reveals the Father and to place Jesus' inevitable death in proper perspective. Summarizing the divine purpose fulfilled in his life, Jesus gives the "new commandment" of love that distinguishes his people from the rest of the world (13:34–35). Christ's ultimate "act of love" is surrendering his life for his friends' benefit (15:11–14).

With his example of love opening the true "way" to the Father, the Johannine Jesus faces death as a transfiguring experience. In John's view, Jesus' death and return to heaven will permit believers to experience life with God (14:1–6) and simultaneously will allow God to live with them (14:23). Because the divine Parent dwells in him, Christ can reveal God fully—to see Jesus in his true meaning is to see the Father (14:7–11). John insists on Jesus' unique relationship to God—he and the Father "are one," but it is a unity of spirit and purpose that also characterizes the disciples (17:12, 20–21). Despite his close identification with the Deity, John's Jesus does not claim unequivocal equality with God. He simply states that "the Father is greater than I" (15:28).

Sending the Paraclete (Holy Spirit)

With John's emphasis on the disciples' mystic union with Christ (15:5–10; 17:12, 20–22) and the superiority of the unseen spirit to mere physical existence (6:63), it is not surprising that he presents a view of Jesus' return that differs strikingly from that in the Synoptics. Instead of an eager anticipation of the Second Coming (as in Mark 13, Matt. 24–25, or Luke 21), John teaches that Jesus is already present, inspiring the faithful. Brief allusions to Christ's reappearance after death (14:3) are fulfilled when he sends the disciples the Paraclete. The Paraclete, variously translated as "Advocate," "Helper," "Counselor," or "Comforter," is synonymous with "the Spirit of Truth" (14:17) and "the Holy Spirit" (14:26). Although unbelieving humanity will see him no more, he remains eternally present with the faithful (14:16–26). An invisible counterpart of Jesus, the Paraclete enables the disciples to understand the true significance of Jesus' teaching (16:1–15). By implication, the Paraclete also empowers the author to create a Gospel that fully portrays Jesus' glory.

By its presence in the Johannine community's preaching, the Paraclete operates to judge the world's unbelief. Affirming that Jesus is present simultaneously with the Father and with believers, the Paraclete also witnesses to the invincibility of good, resisting the spiritual darkness that claimed Jesus' physical life and now threatens his followers.

In John's view, Jesus imparts the promised Advocate (Paraclete) at his resurrection, merely by breathing on the disciples and saying, "Receive the Holy Spirit" (20:21–23). The risen Lord's action recalls the creation scene in Genesis 2 when Yahweh breathes into Adam's nostrils "the breath of life," making him an animate being or "living creature." As John's Gospel begins with the Word creating the universe (1:1–5), so it closes with the Word breathing the pure spirit of life into his renewed human creation.

John's Passion Story

After the five chapters featuring Jesus' speeches of self-interpretation—he is the "true vine" from whom all disciples are branches (15:1–17) and the "priestly" mediator between God and humankind (17:1–26)—John retells the Passion story with several significant changes. Only John relates that when the guards arrive to arrest Jesus in Gethsemane, they are thrown to the ground by Christ's statement—"I am he." The last of the "I am" declarations, its use reveals that even while human Christ has divine power and is taken by evil men only because he allows himself to be (18:1–9).

As he fixes the date of the Last Supper on the day before Passover (the slaying of Passover lambs at that time suggests the symbolization of Jesus as God's sacrificial lamb), so John presents a new version of Jesus' trial. Instead of being accused of blasphemy before the whole Sanhedrin (Mark 14), Jesus is examined at the residence of **Annas,** father-in-law of the High Priest Caiaphas. Admitted through "another disciple's" influence, Peter denies Jesus there (18:12–27). Many historians believe that John's account of a secret, informal session in Annas' private quarters is more plausible than the Syn-

optic tradition of a full-scale (but probably illegal) Sanhedrin trial.

John resembles the Synoptics, however, in presenting Jesus' execution as the result of Jewish pressure on Pontius Pilate, who implicitly witnesses to Jesus' kingship. According to John, the Jewish authorities cannot judge capital crimes (18:31) and must ask the Romans to execute their victim. Despite the writer's efforts to exonerate Pilate, he does not disguise the fact that the Roman governor frees the terrorist Barabbas and condemns Jesus (18:28–19:16).

Like the Synoptic authors, too, John stresses that Jesus' crucifixion fulfills prophecies from the Hebrew Bible, including the soldiers' casting lots for their victim's "seamless" tunic and Jesus' thirst (18:9, 32; 19:24, 29). Note that John's Jesus carries his own cross to Golgotha (19:17). In an incident unique to his Gospel, he has a Roman soldier thrust his lance into Jesus' side, initiating a flood of blood and water (emblems of redemption and truth). By including these grisly details, John affirms Christ's physical death. The only writer to show the beloved disciple present at Jesus' demise, John states that this eyewitness's testimony is the basis of his report (19:25–27).

Postresurrection Appearances in Jerusalem

Although John apparently follows the same tradition that Luke used, placing Jesus' resurrection appearances in and around Jerusalem (instead of Galilee as in Mark and Matthew), he modifies the story to illustrate his characteristic themes. On the first Easter Sunday, **Mary Magdalene** is alone when she discovers that Jesus' corpse has vanished from Joseph of Arimathaea's garden tomb where it had been placed late the previous Friday. Prophet of her Lord's resurrection, she is the first to report the empty tomb and the first to see the risen Jesus, announcing these glad tidings to the male disciples (20:1–2, 10–18).

Following Jesus' Sunday evening appearance to the disciples, infusing them with the Holy

The Crucifixion by Matthias Grunewald (c. 1470–1528). Painted on wood, this small version of Jesus' tortured death heightens the sense of the sufferer's physical pain and grief. Although his emphasis on Jesus' agony reflects Mark's account, Grunewald follows John's Gospel in showing Jesus' mother and the beloved disciple (as well as another Mary) present at the cross. (Courtesy of the National Gallery of Art, Washington. Samuel H. Kress Collection.)

Spirit, he appears again to "doubting Thomas," vanquishing his skepticism. (Note that the beloved disciple believes that Jesus lives even before physical proof is offered, illustrating the Johannine community's cultivation of faith [20:8–9, 26–29].) His "light" having "overcome" the world's spiritual darkness, Jesus also conquers death. His resurrection is the final victorious "sign" toward which all his earlier miracles pointed.

Epilogue: Postresurrection Appearances in Galilee

Most scholars believe that the Fourth Gospel originally ended at 20:31 with the author's stated purpose of inspiring faith. Chapter 21, which records traditions about Jesus' posthumous appearances in Galilee, seems to be the work of an editor, who may have prepared the Gospel manuscript for publication. This redactor also emphasizes the complementary roles of Peter, leader of the Twelve, and the unidentified "disciple whom Jesus loved."

When Jesus appears to share an early morning breakfast of bread and fish (again demonstrating that the risen Christ is not a ghost or other disembodied spirit), he questions Peter about the depth of his love. Using three different Greek verbs for "love," Jesus emphasizes that love for him means feeding his "lambs." Thus Peter and the church are to provide spiritual and other care for future believers, the "other sheep" (10:16), including Gentiles, who will soon join the apostolic fold (21:4–17). (Note the contrasting fates predicted for Peter [20:18–19] and the beloved disciple [20:20–23].)

The Gospel concludes with the editor's musing upon the vast oral tradition surrounding Jesus. If his entire career were to be recorded in detail, the "whole world" could not contain "the vast number of books that would be produced" (21:25).

In the New Testament book called 1 John, the writer successfully defends the Johannine community's Christology and behavioral ethics against (apparently) Gnostic opponents. 1 John's defense of the Fourth Gospel's protrayal of Jesus helped clear the way for the Gospel's eventual acceptance into the Christian canon. The Johannine view of a celestial preexistent Christ, who on earth was also fully human (the Word of God "made flesh"), adds a whole new dimension to Jesus' theological significance, one absent from the Synoptic tradition. By presenting Christ as God's agent of creation who, in the Incarnation, bridges the realms of spirit and matter to reveal ultimate knowledge, John imparts to Jesus a universality unmatched in earlier Gospels.

More than any single book in the New Testament, John's Gospel lays the foundations for later theological interpretations of Christ's nature and function. In post–New Testament times, theologians came to see Christ as the Second Person in the **Trinity** (a term that does not appear in canonical Scripture), coequal, cosubstantial, and coeternal with the Father. Although the Johannine writings do not articulate so formal a dogma, historically John's "high Christology" profoundly influenced Christendom's eventual understanding of its Master.

QUESTIONS FOR DISCUSSION AND REVIEW

1. The "brotherhood," or Christian community, that produced John's Gospel preserved traditions about Jesus that roughly paralleled but significantly differed from those upon which the Synoptic Gospels are based. Why do you suppose that the Johannine community so strongly identified Jesus with the divine Wisdom that God used to create the universe (Prov. 8)? How does John's introductory Hymn to the Logos (Word) express the author's view of Jesus' prehuman existence and divine nature?

2. Evaluate the arguments for and against the Apostle John's responsibility for the Gospel traditionally attributed to him. Discuss the role of the "beloved disciple" and his relationship to the Fourth Gospel.

3. List and discuss some of the major differences between the Gospel of John and the Synoptic Gospels. Compare Jesus' manner of speaking and use of parables in Mark with his long philosophical discourses in John. In composing Jesus' Johannine speeches, do you think that the author was influenced by the form of Wisdom's speeches in Proverbs, Ecclesiasticus, and the Wisdom of Solomon?

5. In presenting Jesus as a spiritual redeemer descended from heaven, John reflects or parallels some Gnostic ideas. In what specific ways does John's Gospel resemble—or differ from—Gnostic teachings?

6. Why do you suppose that John's Gospel contains almost no apocalyptic teaching and has no prediction of Jesus' Second Coming? Does

John's teaching about the Advocate or Paraclete render a belief in Jesus' eschatological return unnecessary?

7. More than any other single New Testament book, the Gospel of John has influenced subsequent Christian thought about Jesus' divine nature. What specific Johannine teachings do you think most contributed to the conception of the Trinity—the doctrine that defines the Christian God as manifesting himself in three distinct personas, Father, Son, and Holy Spirit?

In discussing the idea that the heavenly being (Logos) who became the human Jesus had no beginning but dwelt from eternity with the Father, interpret such diverse Johannine statements as "he who has seen me has seen the Father" and "the Father is greater than I am."

TERMS AND CONCEPTS TO REMEMBER

Logos (Word)
Philo Judaeus
Incarnation
Book of Signs
Book of Glory
heavenly Wisdom (Prov. 8)
Paraclete (the Advocate)

the Holy Spirit
Gnosticism
transubstantiation
Annas
Jesus' "hour"
"glory" and the crucifixion
washing the disciples' feet

RECOMMENDED READING

Brown, R. E. *The Community of the Beloved Disciple.* New York: Paulist Press, 1979. A readable and insightful study of the Christian group that produced the Gospel and the Letters of John.

———. *The Epistles of John.* Vol. 30 of the Anchor Bible. Garden City, N.Y.: Doubleday, 1982. A thoroughly annotated edition.

———. *The Gospel According to John.* Vols. 29 and 29a of the Anchor Bible. Garden City, N.Y.: Doubleday, 1966 and 1970. Provides the most complete historical and theological background and the most thorough commentary on John's Gospel.

Caird, G. B. "John, Letters of." In *The Interpreter's Dictionary of the Bible,* vol. 2, 946–52. Nashville: Abingdon Press, 1962.

Cullman, Oscar. *The Johannine Circle.* Translated by John Bowden. Philadelphia: Westminster Press, 1976. Explores the Gospel's possible source.

Dodd, C. H. *Historical Tradition in the Fourth Gospel.* Cambridge: Cambridge University Press, 1963.

———. *The Interpretation of the Fourth Gospel.* Cambridge: Cambridge University Press, 1965.

Smith, D. M., Jr. "John, Gospel of." In *The Interpreter's Dictionary of the Bible,* supplementary vol., 482–86. Nashville: Abingdon Press, 1976.

FOR MORE ADVANCED STUDY

Bultmann, Rudolf. *The Gospel of John.* Translated by G. R. Beasley-Murray. Philadelphia: Westminster Press, 1971. A somewhat dated but seminal interpretation.

Fortna, R. T. *The Gospel of Signs: A Reconstruction of the Narrative Source Underlying the Fourth Gospel.* Cambridge: Cambridge University Press, 1970.

Haenchen, Ernst. *A Commentary on the Gospel of John.* 2 vols. Hermeneia Commentary. Translated by R. W. Funk. Philadelphia: Fortress Press, 1984.

Martyn, J. L. *History and Theology in the Fourth Gospel.* 2d ed. Nashville: Abingdon Press, 1979. A brilliant interpretation of John's method of composition that focuses on John 9.

Olson, A. M., ed. *Myth, Symbol and Reality.* Notre Dame, Ind.: University of Notre Dame Press, 1981. Includes essays on the Logos.

Schnackenburg, Rudolf. *The Gospel According to John.* Vols. 1-3. Various translators. New York: Seabury Press, 1980, and Crossroads, 1982. Challenging but insightful analysis.

Smith, D. M., Jr. *Johannine Christianity: Essays on Its Setting, Sources, and Theology.* Columbia. University of South Carolina Press, 1984.

11 *Seeking to Know Jesus of Nazareth*

> There is much else that Jesus did. If it were all to be
> recorded in detail, I suppose the whole world could
> not hold the books that would be written.
>
> (John 21:25)

KEY THEMES   Besides the four canonical Gospels, the early Christian community
produced numerous other portrayals of Jesus' life and teachings, some of
which preserve authentic traditions about his ministry. Modern scholarship
has devised several critical methods to distinguish Jesus' words from those
that later writers attributed to him. Because most scholars agree that Jesus'
kingdom pronouncements are central to his message, we survey several
major ways in which Jesus uses the term *basileia tou theou* ("the kingdom of
God"). We then contrast the Synoptic Gospels' picture of the kingdom as
an apocalyptic government with the Johannine portrayal of Jesus as the
revealer of divine Wisdom, the possession of which gives one *basileia,* or
kingly status. Although modern scholarship helps us evaluate the Gospel
evidence about Jesus' teachings, the attempt to know the "real" man of
history remains an ongoing process rather than an accomplished fact.

After reading four separate accounts of Jesus' life, the student may feel a bit uncertain about who the "real" Jesus of Nazareth was in fact. Comparing Mark's account with that of John, we realize that the two Gospel writers not only emphasize different aspects of their subject's personality, actions, and teachings but also express strikingly different views about his nature and role.

Many readers find it difficult to reconcile Mark's picture of a Galilean "carpenter" (Mark 6:3) unexpectedly turned "prophet" and miracle worker with John's vision of a divine being made "flesh" who reveals otherwise unknowable truths. Both Evangelists see Jesus as God's "son," but they assign disparate meanings to that term (see Box 11-1). Mark portrays a "Son of Man" whose messianic destiny and divine sonship are fulfilled through sacrifice and suffering; he

stresses Jesus' human vulnerability and pain. By contrast, John identifies Jesus with God's eternal creative Word and characterizes Jesus as a living image of divinity, a perfect and spiritually invulnerable figure in whose unlimited wisdom and strength one may place absolute confidence. To many, the superior appeal of John's divine man is irresistible. His portrait of Christ is probably the one that most people unconsciously assume to be true when they think of Jesus.

New Testament scholars recognize that the Gospel authors do not attempt to record an objective, purely factual biography of Jesus but in their individual ways interpret him theologically. Aware of this fact, students often ask if we can find the authentic man amid the sometimes conflicting sayings and deeds that the Evangelists attribute to their hero. Are there any "unbiased" historical sources to help the reader

161

BOX 11-1   *Developing Views of Jesus as "The Son of God"*

Individual New Testament writers preserve different stages of a Christian concept that apparently developed over time—the conviction that Jesus was "the Son of God." As the passages listed below indicate, Jesus' divine sonship was interpreted in various ways. To understand the Christian authors' evolving views, we must start where they did, with the Hebrew Bible.

The Davidic kings as God's adopted sons. According to the covenant made with David's royal dynasty, the kings of Israel—Yahweh's anointed ones or "messiahs"—enjoyed a special relationship with their God, comparable to that of a son with his father. Speaking of David's heirs, Yahweh promises "I will be his father, and he shall be my son . . . My love will never be withdrawn" (2 Sam. 7:14–15). Psalms 2, sung at the enthroning of one of David's descendants, expresses a similar view of the filial bond between king and God. Yahweh tells his "anointed" ruler (messiah): "You are my son . . . this day [the date of his crowning] I become your father" (Ps. 2:7). Thus, the Davidic king's coronation was simultaneously the time of his becoming God's "son" by adoption.

Son by resurrection. The oldest recorded Christian interpretation of Jesus' sonship—Paul's letter to the Romans (mid-50s CE)—states that Jesus "was declared Son of God by a mighty act in that he rose from the dead" (Rom. 1:3). In this passage Paul follows Israel's ancient tradition that David's ultimate heir—the Messiah—would also in some sense become God's son. As Paul expresses the concept, Jesus receives sonship at his resurrection, the Deity's miraculous confirmation of his messianic worthiness. The author of Acts preserves a similar view, representing Peter shortly after the resurrection as saying that by exalting Jesus to his "right hand," "God has made this Jesus . . . both Lord and Messiah" (Acts 2:36). The oldest layer of preserved tradition suggests that the first Christians saw Jesus, like Israel's anointed kings, becoming God's son by adoption, a reward conferred at his resurrection and ascension to heaven.

Jesus' own witness. The early church's identification of Jesus as a divine son was undoubtedly stimulated by Jesus' practice of addressing God as "Abba," an Aramaic term children used to express intimacy with their male parent (Mark 14:36; Luke 11:2). Closer to "daddy" than the more formal "father," Abba suggests Jesus' sense of personal closeness to the Deity. Paul attests to his churches' continued use of the word (Rom. 8:15; Gal. 4:6).

Jesus' adoption at baptism. If Mark's Gospel (mid-60s CE) were our only Gospel, we might conclude that Jesus was designated God's son at his baptism (Mark 1:11), apparently through adoption and anointing by the Holy Spirit. In Mark, the demons recognize Jesus' relationship to God (3:11–12), but no human being acknowledges it until he has proven his faithfulness unto death (15:39). Jesus' final act of filial devotion affirms his divine sonship (an idea also expressed in Hebrews [2:20; 5:7–9]).

Sonship at conception. Adding infancy narratives to their accounts of Jesus' life, Matthew and Luke (mid-80s CE) push the beginning of Jesus' sonship back in time, to the moment of his conception (Matt. 1:10; Luke 2:26–35). Matthew and Luke interpret Yahweh's promise to become as a father to the Davidic "son" (2 Sam. 7; Ps. 2) as meaning more than mere adoption; they see the Heavenly Voice at Jesus' baptism as simply confirming the biological fact of divine parentage.

The son as creative Word. Eschewing traditions of Jesus' virginal conception, John's Gospel, the last one written (mid-90s CE), declares that Jesus existed as God's son long before he came to earth, even before the universe came into being (John 1:1–18). A variation of the concept appearing in Colossians (1:15–20; 2:9–10), John's doctrine of Jesus' eternal deity and sonship ultimately became the Christian standard of belief.

understand Jesus of Nazareth? Or have scholars discovered any analytical techniques that allow us to separate Jesus' actual words from those the early church ascribed to him? From the existing evidence, is it possible to infer what Jesus thought about himself? Did the man who walked Lake Galilee's shores see himself as a prophet, as Israel's Messiah, as an immortal spirit temporarily come to earth? as God?

Questions about Jesus' own self-identification perplexed his original audience no less than they fascinate us today. Historians, theologians, and ordinary believers have speculated about Jesus' conscious purposes for centuries. In this chapter we will survey some representative attempts that scholars and others have made to know Jesus. Without undertaking a formal quest for "the historical Jesus," we will note the scholarly criteria researchers use to recognize Jesus' authentic actions and teachings. We will also review some contrasting pictures of Jesus that such research has produced. Finally, we will reexamine the four Gospels' composite portrait, stressing those aspects of Jesus' character and message that appear with relative consistency. We begin this effort to understand Jesus better by surveying the early non-Christian testimony to his existence.

Early Historical References to Jesus

At the outset we must recognize that Christian writings (including noncanonical Gospels) are by far our most important sources for Jesus' life. Sources originating outside the church, including Jewish or Roman documents of the late first and second centuries CE, briefly mention Jesus' career but give no information not found in the Gospels. The Roman historian Tacitus, writing about 112–13 CE, states that after the great fire that ravaged Rome in 64 CE the emperor Nero found an unpopular group to blame for the disaster—Christians—many of whom he ordered burned alive. Noting that this "evil"

religion began in Judea, Tacitus says that the "sect's" "founder" was "Christus," who had been executed by Pontius Pilate (*Annals* xv.44). Another Roman historian, Suetonius (about 121 CE), recorded that the emperor Claudius had expelled the Jews from Rome because of trouble arising from "Chrestus" (probably a variant spelling of Tacitus's "Christus" (*Twelve Caesars* 25). The agitation that Suetonius alludes to may have involved Jewish Christians precipitating riots in the Roman synagogues by their preaching that the crucified Jesus was the Messiah.

Jewish sources include Flavius Josephus, historian of the Jewish Revolt against Rome (66–73 CE). Josephus twice alludes to Jesus, although his exact opinions are difficult to determine because later Christian editors apparently altered the text (*Antiquities* 18.3.3; 20.9.1). Brief references in the Talmud accuse Jesus of practicing "sorcery" (using forbidden "magic" to perform his miracles) and leading Israel "astray," for which Jewish authorities tried and condemned him on Passover eve (b Sanhedrin 43a). While tending to confirm certain events in Jesus' life, these non-Christian writers tell us nothing new.

The "Other Gospels"

With outside testimony so disappointingly uninformative, we are forced back on Christian documents. Besides the New Testament books, the early churches produced numerous other accounts of Jesus' life, some of which may be as old as our canonical Gospels. During the first Christian centuries, these noncanonical "other Gospels" circulated among many congregations and were widely read, especially in Syria and Egypt. Eventually the church officially endorsed only Matthew, Mark, Luke, and John, relegating their competitors to ultimate obscurity. Besides the representative five other Gospels we consider below, there are Gospels supposedly by or to "the Egyptians," "the Hebrews," "the Nazareans," "the Ebionites" (the

Jerusalem poor), and others. Only fragments of most of these **Apocryphal Gospels** survive, some preserved only through brief quotations in later church literature.

The Gospel of Thomas. The major exception is the Gospel of Thomas, which was found complete in 1945 at Nag Hammadi, Egypt. Although the Gospel was originally composed in Greek, the surviving version is a translation into the Coptic language. Attributed to *"Didymos* [the twin] Judas **Thomas"** (according to some traditions, Jesus' twin brother), the Gospel is a compilation of 114 sayings, proverbs, parables, and prophecies attributed to Jesus. Containing almost no narrative material, it represents the kind of sayings collection that scholars imagine the theoretical Q (Source) document to have been.

Although some of the teachings seem to have been strongly influenced by Gnostic thought and interpretation, many of the Thomas sayings parallel those in the canonical writings. According to many scholars, in some cases the Gospel of Thomas preserves an older (and perhaps closer to the original) form of Jesus' words, as well as genuine sayings not found in the canonical texts. Some historians believe that the Gospel of Thomas was compiled during the second half of the first century CE, making it roughly contemporaneous with the Synoptic narratives.

The Gospel of Thomas promises that whoever finds the right "interpretation" of Jesus' "secret sayings" (that is, understands the spiritual meaning of his metaphors) "will not experience death" (will not know what it is to die spiritually). This statement strikingly resembles the Johannine Jesus' declaration that people who believe in him will never die (John 11:25–26). Along with the "mysteries" and "secrets of the kingdom" in Mark and the concept of divine Wisdom in John, the Gospel of Thomas represents a distinctly metaphysical and otherwordly component of early Christianity, a tradition perhaps similar to but not necessarily identical to some Gnostic ideas. Because this Gospel has been available for only a relatively few years, scholars have not yet had time to evaluate fully its implications about Jesus' teaching. Future study may indicate that Thomas retains essential aspects of Jesus' world view that have long been ignored or neglected, particularly his views on the nature of reality, including the interpenetration of physical matter and spirit.

The Gospel of Peter. Although only a fragment remains, an early Gospel (incorrectly) ascribed to **Peter** preserves a version of Jesus' trial, crucifixion, and resurrection that some scholars believe is independent of the canonical tradition. The only Gospel to depict Jesus' actual rising from the tomb, Peter's Gospel has even more supernatural elements than Matthew: Late Saturday night, as Roman soldiers guarding the tomb watch, the heavens open and two celestial figures descend, rolling away the stone sealing the entrance and entering the burial chamber. Three towering figures then emerge from the sepulcher, two whose heads reach the sky and a third even taller, followed by a cross. A heavenly voice declares that Jesus has preached "to them that sleep" (the dead), after which a fourth figure descends to enter the tomb, apparently to materialize later as the "young man" Mary Magdalene finds there the next morning. The text breaks off with Peter fishing the Sea of Galilee, apparently about to witness a post-resurrection appearance.

While some commentators regard this account as a somewhat fantastic elaboration of Matthew, others judge it a more "primitive" (and thus older) "witness" to the resurrection, assigning its composition to the last third of the first century CE. Some scholars suggest that an early form of Peter's Gospel was a major source for the Passion narratives in Mark and Matthew.

The Secret Gospel of Mark. A fragment of this Gospel was discovered in 1958, preserved in a letter by Clement of Alexandria, a Christian leader of the early third century CE. The section of Secret Mark that Clement quotes narrates the resurrection of a rich young man whom Jesus subsequently initiates into "the mystery of the kingdom of God." According to Clement, the excerpt would appear in canonical Mark between verses 10:34 and 35.

A second and briefer excerpt refers to the resuscitated young man as "the youth whom Jesus loved." Although some critics dismiss Secret Mark as a second-century addition to the canonical Mark, others regard it as genuine and belonging to an early edition of the Gospel.

Besides its claim to being an original part of Mark's narrative, Secret Mark is important because it provides a link between the Synoptic Gospels and the Fourth Gospel's account of Lazarus's resurrection (John 11). It has always been a puzzle why the most spectacular of Jesus' miracles—the raising of a man dead for four days—is not described or even alluded to in the three Synoptics. John makes Lazarus's return to life the climactic event of Jesus' career and the incident that leads to his execution (John 11:45–54; 12:9–11). While the canonical Synoptics are silent about the episode, Secret Mark reveals that a version of John's resurrection story was once part of the Synoptic tradition.

The Infancy Gospel of Thomas. Early Christian curiosity about what the world Savior might have been like as a child resulted in the production of several narratives dramatizing Jesus' early youth. Most are clearly fictional, highly imaginative speculations that usually stress the boy's precocity and supernatural gifts. One such is the Infancy Gospel of Thomas, an anonymous work of the mid–second century CE and wrongly ascribed to the Apostle Thomas. The Gospel uses Luke's infancy story as a frame and fills in the gap between Jesus' birth and his visit to the Temple at age twelve (Luke 2:1–52). Possessing no connection to the Coptic Gospel of Thomas, which was written much earlier, this account seems to incorporate various legends (even superstitions) about the youthful Jesus.

The author is uncritically interested in boasting of Jesus' ability to work miracles, apparently unaware that the miracles he presents are more like magic tricks, many of which do not speak well of their perpetrator's moral character. He shows Jesus one Sabbath amusing himself by fashioning sparrows of river clay. When Joseph reproaches him for violating the day of rest, Jesus claps his hands and sends the sparrows flying off, eliminating the evidence against him. Mischievous to the point of cruelty, this Jesus hexes playmates, blinds people who criticize his behavior, and curses another youth with premature old age. Although he later cures those he had afflicted, even resurrecting a boy killed in a fall, the young Jesus seems to exploit his powers indiscriminately, frightening the neighbors into treating him with respect.

The Protoevangelium of James. Also called the Book of James, this work supplies background information on Jesus' parents and family, covering events that occurred up to and including his birth. Based partly on the infancy stories in Matthew and Luke and partly on oral tradition, this prologue to Jesus' life story may contain some historical facts among its legendary elements. The work implies that its author is **James,** Jesus' stepbrother, Joseph's son by a former marriage. The narrative focuses on the personal history of Mary, Jesus' future mother, who is born to a previously childless couple, Joachim and Anna. At age three Mary is taken to the Jerusalem Temple, where she is raised by priests who later engage her to Joseph, a widower with children, who functions strictly as her guardian and respects her virginity.

The genealogies in Matthew and Luke both trace Jesus' Davidic ancestry through his presumed father, Joseph. By contrast, James states that Mary, too, descends from David. Thus, her virgin-born son inherits his messianic heritage directly from her. The Book of James provides the names of Mary's parents, the manner of her birth and upbringing, and a doctrine of her perpetual virginity. These traditions greatly contributed toward the later veneration of Mary in the Greek Orthodox and Roman Catholic churches. The fact of its immense popularity in the church is reflected by its survival in over 130 Greek manuscripts. Although never officially listed in the New Testament canon, in some Christian groups the book has exerted as much influence as the canonical Gospels.

From the summaries given above, it is clear that some of the Apocryphal Gospels offer little that is historically reliable. With their naive emphasis on the miraculous, such accounts as the Infancy Gospel of Thomas are largely fictional attempts to fill in the parts of Jesus' life about which nothing is known. Other noncanonical Gospels, however, may well contain genuine sayings of Jesus and historical information about his ministry that are not included in the canonical New Testament. Such works as the Gospel of Thomas, the Gospel of Peter, and Secret Mark may preserve important aspects of Jesus' character and teachings. A number of scholars are increasingly aware that the "other Gospels," as well as the canonical four, must be taken into consideration in any study of the historical Jesus.

The Scholar's Jesus

In their totality, both the canonical and the Apocryphal Gospels present a theologian's Jesus, a historical figure heavily clothed in theological interpretations of his words and actions. For the last two centuries many European and American scholars have realized that even the oldest Synoptic traditions picture Jesus as he appears in the radiant light of his subsequent resurrection. Modern scholarship has thus endeavored to distinguish the preresurrection "man of history" from the glorified "Christ of faith." Perhaps naively, many scholars once assumed that if one could strip away the church's interpretative overlay, the authentic Jesus would stand revealed. Our limited space does not allow us

Head of Christ, artist unknown. This mosaic portrait of Jesus is composed of hundreds of tiny fragments of stone or tile arranged to create the lineaments of a human face. The result is not a realistic picture of an individual but a highly stylized representation of a type of humanity. The stern and grimly determined face shown here well embodies Mark's image of a Messiah predestined to endure rejection and suffering. As the artist assembled many different pieces of material to achieve this stereotype, so today's scholars work to assemble a coherent picture of the historical Jesus from thousands of literary fragments embedded in both canonical and noncanonical sources. (Courtesy of the University of Michigan Press.)

to do justice to the vast array of scholarly theories and the exhaustive research that inspired them. Without reproducing their textual analyses and arguments, we consider briefly here two of the most influential schools of thought about Jesus and his purpose.

Two Conflicting Pictures of Jesus

Just as the twentieth century dawned, the German writer Albert Schweitzer published *The Quest of the Historical Jesus,* a work that has since lent its name to the scholarly search for the man behind the Christological mask. Like a bomb exploding in a house of worship, Schweitzer's work seemed to shatter many of the traditional images people held of Jesus. Schweitzer argued that the rigorous application of scientific methodology can winnow out legendary material and uncover historical truth. To unveil the "real" man of history, he used the then relatively new techniques of **form criticism,** the research method that attempts to discover the older oral form of a tradition as it existed before becoming embedded in a written Gospel.

The apocalyptic Jesus. Schweitzer's Jesus is dominated by a conviction that he is God's chosen instrument to announce the imminent end of history. Burning with eschatological zeal, he demands that followers abandon all earthly ties and work with him to hasten the apocalyptic kingdom, which will overthrow the present Satanic world order and usher in the new age. His driving goal is to fulfill the prophetic conditions that will bring about the apocalyptic chain of events culminating in his cosmic reign as the Son of Man. When Jesus' early expectations do not materialize (Matt. 10:22–23), he marches to Jerusalem, confident that he can compel the kingdom's arrival through his voluntary death, the final "tribulation" leading to God's violent imposition of his sovereignty. The anticipated divine intervention does not occur, however, and Jesus is crushed by the system he defies.

The Jesus of realized eschatology. At the opposite end of the scholarly spectrum, another school of thought views Jesus as a highly sophisticated thinker who may have used apocalyptic imagery to express his ideas but who did not expect the world to end in his lifetime. Known as "realized eschatology"—the present or inward realization of apocalyptic hopes—this scholarly discipline regards Jesus as preaching spiritual rebirth. In this view, Jesus' kingdom message is intended to awaken his listeners to God's presence in their individual lives. Awakened and attuned to the present reality of God's life-giving power, believers learn to reject the world's false goals and allow God to rule their lives, thus beginning the process of spiritual renewal that ensures eternal life in the next world.

According to advocates of this theory, Jesus completes his revelation of God's purpose during his earthly career, making a Second Coming unnecessary. Jesus' later followers, interpreting his words in a different context, mistakenly concluded that his predictions about future spiritual growth and development applied to Jesus' literal return to earth. Some recent commentators, including J. A. T. Robinson, deny that Jesus taught anything resembling the Parousia (Second Coming) doctrine envisioned by Paul and the Synoptic writers.

Rival theories and modern readers. The theory that presents Jesus as a fanatic, deluded and doomed by his apocalyptic obsessions, does not satisfy most New Testament readers. Among many other considerations, the man embodied in the Gospels seems far too profound and insightful to try forcing an egocentric and literalist eschatology into historical fulfillment. The Jesus-as-apocalyptist view sees him as entirely the product of his own time, but the opposing theory of realized ecshatology creates a Jesus who is highly congenial to the modern temperament. To many, Jesus' challenge to realize that God's kingdom reigns now—if people can get over their spiritual blindness and recognize its transcendent existence—is intellectually attractive. Perpetuating the Johannine doctrine of cultivating eternal life in the present, this view has the advantage of presenting a Jesus who transcends his ancient Palestinian environment to speak directly to contemporary experience. Many scholars, however, doubt that this theory can be supported when all the pertinent texts about Jesus are taken into consideration.

The dangers of theories about Jesus. As many analysts observe, the picture of Jesus one attempts to paint tends to say more about the painter than it does about the subject. Almost all attempts to reconstruct Jesus' personal character and teachings tend to be projections of qualities that the individual writer consciously or unconsciously accepts as valuable. Students and scholars alike generally assume that Jesus, when found, will be relevant to contemporary needs and expectations. Most persons still reject the possibility that Jesus is too limited by his exclusively religious preoccupations to say anything truly meaningful to a largely secular and technological society.

Other Ways of Knowing the Historical Jesus

The Gospel witness. Perhaps the best way to meet the challenge of "knowing" Jesus is to examine those texts that scholars believe most plausibly represent his deeds and teachings. For this purpose we rely mainly on the Synoptic accounts, supplemented by John and the Apocryphal Gospels.

The need for critical tools. After carefully reading the Gospels, the student probably remembers finding several different versions of the same saying and wondering which one is likely to be closest to Jesus' own words. To give only one example, the reader may ask whether Matthew or Luke records the "correct" rendering of the Lord's Prayer (see Box 9-4). When the same incident or saying appears in different settings and is given a different meaning, which version should the reader accept as historical? The message Luke conveys through his "lost sheep" parable (Luke 15) differs considerably from that in Matthew (Matt. 18). As we have seen in Chapters 6 through 10, the Gospel authors apparently felt free to insert Jesus' words into dissimilar contexts, thereby giving them new meanings. We do not know whether a particular author may have been unaware of the precise circumstances under which Jesus spoke or whether he simply wished to update a saying to make it apply to the current needs of his community.

Leaving aside Jesus' ability to prophesy, how are we to view passages that depict Jesus discussing matters that reflect not his own situation but conditions in the author's later generation? Again, to cite only one instance, Jesus' instructions about dealing with problems in the church apply to Matthew's later and more organized Christian community but not to the informal group following Christ (Matt. 10:5–52; 18; 23:1–39; 24:9–27; see also Luke 19:11–27; 21:12–24).

To further complicate the situation, the Gospel writers do not necessarily distinguish between memories of Jesus' actual words and those ascribed to him by later "Spirit-led" ecstatics and prophets in the early church. Visions and pronouncements from the risen Lord abounded in many charismatic congregations, resulting in a tendency to attribute revelations about Jesus to Jesus (Matt. 28:19–20; Luke 24:44–49; John 16:12–15, 22–33; 21:14–22; Acts 1:6–8; 9:1–16; 22:1–21; 26:12; Rev. 1:9–3:22).

Criteria for investigation. The difficulties of the case have led readers to seek some method that will help them distinguish between what Jesus may plausibly have said during his lifetime and what the Gospels represent him as saying. A leading New Testament scholar, the late Norman A. Perrin, devised a set of tests or standards for evaluating the authenticity of Jesus' sayings, separating "genuine" teachings from later church additions or other modifications of the original statements. Perrin's criteria may be summarized as follows:

1. *Dissimilarity:* A saying may be authentic if it differs significantly from the tenets of both first-century Judaism and early Christianity. For example, Jesus' use of the Aramaic term "Abba" ("daddy") (Mark 14:36; Luke 11:2) differs from the church's more formal way of addressing the Deity (Matt. 6:9) and probably represents Jesus'

distinctive practice. Similarly, those sayings that differ from, or at least were not emphasized by, the early church may be genuine.

This test of dissimilarity can apply to events in Jesus' life as well. A number of Jesus' deeds and experiences are not likely to have been invented by his followers. His crucifixion was not the kind of death—public, shameful, and reserved for slaves and criminals—believers would fabricate for their leader. Paul candidly describes the awkward fact of Jesus "nailed to the cross" as a "stumbling block to Jews" and "sheer folly" to the Greeks (1 Cor. 1:23, 18). Jesus' baptism by John is another event the church would not have invented. One whom later doctrine held "sinless" would not be presented as undergoing baptism "in token of repentance, for the forgiveness of sins" (Mark 1:4) unless there existed a firm report that Jesus had indeed submitted to John's ministrations. Jesus' associations with all kinds of disreputable people—tax collectors, prostitutes, and other "sinners"—as well as the allegations that he was viewed as "a glutton and a drinker" also pass the dissimilarity test on grounds that no believer would create such tales (Matt. 10:18–19; Luke 7:33–8:3; 15:1–3).

The obvious weakness in the dissimilarity test is that Jesus' characteristic teachings, including his emphasis on love, were also shared by other Palestinian teachers of his day (Mark 12:28–34). In fact, historians find Jewish parallels to virtually all of Jesus' ethical pronouncements. Many scholars now believe that Jesus is best understood when seen operating in his first-century Palestinian Jewish environment. Recent studies have shown that Jesus has much in common with Essenes and Pharisees, in both the content and the parabolic style of his teaching.

2. *Multiple attestation:* This standard for determining reliable material considers the frequency with which a particular theme or concept is mentioned. Jesus' emphasis on the kingdom of God appears in many forms throughout virtually all the Gospel accounts. Because this term appears so often in so many different sources,

it probably reflects a genuine teaching of Jesus. (The specific form or interpretation of an individual kingdom saying, however, is open to question. Each Gospel writer tends to modify individual sayings when he incorporates them into his written text.) The criterion of multiple attestation also confirms the authenticity of several other themes, such as Jesus' interest in women, the poor, and social outcasts like prostitutes and other "sinners." Like the kingdom concept, this concern appears in a variety of forms—parables, controversy stories, and numerous sayings.

3. *Coherence:* This standard allows the scholar to regard material as authentic if it resembles material already established by the criteria of dissimilarity and multiple attestation. If a saying or action is consistent with themes and concepts generally recognized as genuine, it too may be accepted.

4. *Linguistic and environmental evidence:* This criterion uses linguistic and cultural evidence to eliminate sayings incorrectly ascribed to Jesus by later followers. If a Greek language form underlies the pre-Gospel oral version of a particular saying, it cannot be authentic. Scholars agree that Jesus spoke a Galilean dialect of Aramaic and expressed his ideas in the context of a Jewish Palestinian environment. Thus, sayings that reveal a Greco-Roman background are probably the creation of later Hellenistic disciples. The presence of a Hebrew or Aramaic form in a given saying may increase the probability of its genuineness but not prove it. The earliest Christians were Palestinian Jews who shared Jesus' linguistic and cultural environment.

Students perusing the scholarly literature evaluating the historicity of Jesus' supposed words and actions will find that not all experts agree on which ones meet the standards of acceptability. Some critics recognize no more than eight sayings and a dozen parables as representing Jesus' authentic voice; many other scholars cautiously accept a large number of teachings. Scholarly criteria are helpful in screening out words incorrectly attributed to Jesus, but the student will discover that not all sayings that fail to meet these criteria are necessarily to be dismissed.

A Summary of Events in Jesus' Life

In spite of the Gospels' theological bent, many scholars believe that they contain enough trustworthy historical information to reconstruct at least a rough outline of Jesus' life and message. In the scholarly view, the plausible elements are confined to Jesus' adult ministry. As noted in Chapters 8 and 9, the infancy narratives of Matthew and Luke do not pass the tests of historicity on two main counts: (1) they render Jesus' birth almost exclusively in terms of the Hebrew Bible, as if constructing their stories from purely literary antecedents; (2) they present events in supernatural and mythic terms, giving their accounts the kind of legendary quality found in contemporary Hellenistic fictions about the birth of mythological heroes. (We should not overlook the possibility, however, that the Evangelists may retain a core of historical memory at the heart of their highly embellished accounts.)

A scholarly consensus accepts as probable the following sequence of events in Jesus' adult life:

1. Born a few years BCE, when Herod the Great ruled Judea and Augustus was emperor of Rome, Jesus grew up in the Galilean town of Nazareth. The presumed son of Joseph, a carpenter, and his wife Mary, Jesus also had "sisters" and "brothers" (or stepsiblings), including James, who later became a leader of the Jerusalem church during the 50s and early 60s CE.

2. During a revival campaign at the Jordan River, Jesus (then "about thirty years old") (Luke 3:1) was baptized by John in token of forgiveness for sins. Depending upon how one calculates "the fifteenth year of the Emperor Tiberius," the date was about 27 or 29 CE.

3. Following his baptism and a period of isolated meditation, Jesus began preaching a distinctive variation of the Baptist's message—people must repent because the kingdom of God was about to arrive. The ministries of Jesus and the Baptist probably overlapped (John 1), and they may have competed for disciples.

4. Jesus gathered his followers from among Galilean fishermen, farmers, women, and other ordinary working people. He led his disciples in an itinerant life of deliberately chosen poverty, illustrating by his self-denial that the kingdom he preached is worth more than any earthly ties or possessions. Combining healings, exorcisms, and preaching in parables, he attracted large crowds as well as opposition.

5. Jesus' public ministry lasted about a year (the Synoptics) to perhaps three years (John). Jesus' teaching focused on his personal authority to reinterpret the Mosaic Torah, the present signs and impending reality of God's kingdom, and the necessity of making a total commitment to the divine will. The practice of an austere and self-sacrificing ethic seems to have been an important factor in Jesus' demand for submission to God's rule.

6. The ministry aroused the suspicions of King Herod Antipas, who had already beheaded John the Baptist, causing Jesus to leave Herod's territory of Galilee. Impressed by his miracles and kingdom teaching, some admirers planned to have Jesus declared "king," perhaps to lead an assault on Herod and/or the Romans (John 6:14–17). The Gospels unanimously testify that Jesus consistently rejected a political application of his "kingdom" preaching.

7. Although Jesus may have made many pilgrimages to Jerusalem and performed miracles there (John's account), his decision to abandon his Galilean ministry for a final confrontational visit to Jerusalem was decisive; it is the only trip to Judea that the Synoptic authors regard as significant. Jesus' choice to enter the holy city in a manner fulfilling messianic prophecy and his assault on the Sadducees' Temple administration

were the historical actions that sealed his fate.

8. Following a series of debates over Torah interpretation in the Temple precincts, Jesus held a farewell dinner with his most intimate disciples. That night he was arrested, interrogated by the High Priest, and turned over to the Roman authorities, charged with an illegal ambition to be king—treason against the Empire.

9. After administering the customary flogging, Roman soldiers crucified Jesus shortly before Passover (about 30 or 33 CE), posting a sign on his cross ("Jesus of Nazareth, King of the Jews") that identified the political crime for which he was executed. A few days after his entombment, his followers became convinced that he had risen from the dead.

Although this outline does not provide enough information to construct a genuine biography of Jesus, it summarizes what numerous scholars believe to have been the essential events in his life.

Jesus' Major Teachings

Although many scholars agree on the principal events of Jesus' public life, agreement on his thought and teaching is more difficult to obtain. Perhaps the majority of scholars view Jesus' proclamation of "the kingdom of God" as his central message, but commentators are deeply divided on the meaning of the term. In what sense does Jesus use it? Is the kingdom an apocalyptic concept, the sovereignty that God imposes after he has destroyed opposing human governments? The Gospels of Mark and Matthew share that view, which is the basis of Schweitzer's interpretation of Jesus as a preacher of apocalyptic doom. Early Christians had other ways of interpreting Jesus' message, however, as the traditions embodied in John's Gospel reveal. The Johannine Jesus predicts no end-of-the-world disasters to introduce the kingdom but instead stresses the present fact of divine rule through the heavenly glory and wisdom manifest in Jesus himself. Many of Jesus' sayings preserved in noncanonical Gospels, such as the Gospel of Thomas, present a similar nonapocalyptic use of the term. In these works, the revelation and discipline of divine wisdom bring Jesus' followers to the kingdom.

In the pages ahead we examine Jesus' use of the kingdom concept, first as it appears in the Synoptic Gospels and then as it appears in other traditions about Jesus' teaching. The English phrase "kingdom of God" translates the Greek expression *basileia tou theou*. *Basileia* refers primarily to the act or process of ruling, a quality or privilege that distinguishes a king or other ruler. To have *basileia* is to possess control, power, freedom and independence. The biblical God, whose infinite kingship Israel's thinkers take for granted, has these attributes in abundance. This fact must be kept in mind as we explore what Jesus may intend when he combines his kingdom teaching with assertions of his own autonomy and dominion.

Jesus' central message includes four major themes that appear in virtually all accounts of his ministry: (1) the kingdom of God (*basileia tou theou*); (2) Jesus' personal authority to represent the kingdom and interpret the divine will; (3) the related concept of Jesus' self-awareness— the views he holds about his relationship with God and the nature of his kingship; and (4) the kingdom's radical demand for total commitment. Because it forms the heart of his message, we concentrate on the first theme.

The Kingdom

In the Sermon on the Mount, Matthew presents Jesus as giving top priority to seeking the kingdom. The disciple who puts God's kingdom and his "justice" "before everything else" will also receive all that ordinary life requires (Matt. 6:33). Although the term *kingdom* dominates his parables and other teachings throughout the Synoptic Gospels, Jesus nowhere defines what he means by it. His many separate uses of the term are not easy to harmonize into a coherent statement, for at different times the Synoptic Jesus speaks as if the kingdom were a future event, a present reality, a God-ruled (theocratic) community, or even a higher plane of existence.

For a fuller understanding of Jesus' usage, let us divide his references to the kingdom into five (sometimes overlapping) categories: sayings in which the kingdom is (1) a future event; (2) a present reality; (3) an unexpected event; (4) a hidden power that grows slowly; and (5) physically present in Jesus.

The kingdom as a future event. The Synoptic writers typically stress the apocalyptic nature of the kingdom. Matthew implies that Jesus' initial kingdom proclamation is a continuation of the Baptist's eschatological message. Almost exactly reproducing Mark's summary of Jesus' first preaching, Matthew attributes the identical theme to both John (Matt. 3:2) and Jesus (Matt. 4:17): "Repent; for the kingdom of Heaven is upon you." (By using the phrase "kingdom of Heaven," Matthew follows the Jewish custom of employing a euphemism to avoid mentioning the divine name. His term is synonymous with Mark and Luke's "kingdom of God.")

Like his presumed mentor, Jesus calls for repentance, literally a reversal of a person's life direction, to prepare for the kingdom's imminent arrival. It is so close to his hearers that it is virtually "upon" them. Disciples are to pray for it to hasten so that God's will may be done "on earth as it is in heaven" (Matt. 6:10; Luke 11:2). It is so close that people who first heard it proclaimed will live to see "the kingdom of God already come in power" (Matt. 16:28; Mark 9:1; Luke 9:27). All three Synoptic writers link Jesus' death with the kingdom's nearness. At the Last Supper Jesus tells the disciples that he well never again drink "from the fruit of the

vine until that day when I drink it new in the kingdom of God" (Matt. 26:19; Mark 14:25; Luke 22:16, 18).

The kingdom is compared to a future banquet attended by people from many nations, and its opposite is an "outer darkness" of anguish and distress (Matt. 8:11–12; Luke 13:28–29). Jesus commonly associates the kingdom's arrival as a period of ethical discrimination in which good and evil deeds are made public and judged. This image of future Judgment appears in many parables, some of which represent Jesus' teaching and some of which are probably later elaborations based on that teaching. These parables and pronouncements include the two houses built respectively on sand and rock (Matt. 7:24–27); the thief in the night; and the separation of humankind into redeemed "sheep" and rejected "goats" (Matt. 24:45–51; 25:31–46).

The kingdom as a present reality. While picturing the kingdom as a future event, the Synoptic Jesus also describes it as having already begun. As noted in Chapter 9, the most celebrated depiction of the kingdom's present reality occurs in Luke (11:20; see also Matt. 12:28): "But if it is by the finger of God that I drive out the devils, then be sure that the kingdom of God has already come upon you." Jesus' response to the Baptist's disciples, who inquire if he is really the Messiah, similarly implies that Jesus' present activity is a realization of the kingdom. When John's disciples behold the blind restored to sight, the deaf restored to hearing, and the dead raised to life, we know that God now reigns (Matt. 11:2–6; Luke 7:22–23). Like his exorcisms, Jesus' healings are a defeat of Satan's misrule and a manifestation of divine sovereignty.

The kingdom as an unexpected event. In the apocalyptic predictions of Matthew 24, Mark 13, and Luke 21, Jesus' return to earth as the supernatural Son of Man is apparently equated with the kingdom's arrival. In these and comparable passages, the kingdom appears unexpectedly "like a thief in the night," its abrupt materialization a striking contrast to the parables stressing its quiet growth (Matt. 24:42; 25:13; Mark 13:33; Luke 12:40; 21:36). Texts that relate the kingdom to the Second Coming incorporate the traditional themes of Hellenistic Jewish apocalypticism, including world Judgment and resurrection. In such passages the kingdom signifies the end of history as we know it and the inception of a "new age."

The kingdom is a hidden power that grows slowly. Many of the best-known parables depict the kingdom as a hidden power that grows slowly until it achieves greatness. In the apocalyptic tradition, God's kingdom bursts suddenly and catastrophically into human affairs, destroying existing nations and expanding to fill the earth (Dan. 2:44). By contrast, Jesus' simile of the mustard plant seems to reject that concept, comparing the kingdom to a tiny seed that develops "underground," gradually maturing into a "tree" that offers shelter to wildlife (Matt. 13:31–32; Mark 4:30–32; Luke 13:18–19; Gosp. Thom. 20).

The parable of "leaven" that slowly causes bread dough to rise and expand also emphasizes the kingdom's slow and quiet maturation (Matt. 13:33; Luke 13:20–21; Gosp. Thom. 96). The parables comparing the kingdom to seeking what is lost or finding an invaluable object—a pearl, a buried treasure, or a lost coin—similarly depict a process. In all of these parables, a solitary figure—a widow, a lone merchant, a shepherd—takes time to focus on the process of discovery, a quiet and private search that ends in rejoicing (Matt. 13:44; 18:12–13; Luke 15:4–6; Gosp. Thom. 107). Employing images of life as it is daily lived, Jesus' parables of this type have little affinity with apocalyptic violence.

In shocking contrast, other kingdom statements invoke a picture of conflict and aggression. Since John's campaign, Jesus declares, "the kingdom of Heaven has been subjected to violence and violent men are seizing it" (Matt. 11:12–13). Luke records a significantly different version, using the statement to express his theory of religious history: after John comes "the kingdom of God, and everyone forces his way in" (Luke 16:16).

Some of Jesus' "hard sayings" may be related to this notion of his disciples' sometimes-violent responses to the kingdom proclamation. Rejecting the notion that he is the messianic "prince of peace" (Isa. 11), Jesus announces that his presence inspires pain, conflict, and division: "You must not think that I have come to bring peace to the earth; I have not come to bring peace, but a sword." His picture of fathers and sons, mothers and daughters bitterly fighting each other is paralleled in Luke and in the Gospel of Thomas, indicating the many family divisions that Jesus' demands occasioned (Matt. 10:34–35; Luke 12:51–53; Gosp. Thom. 16).

The equally unhappy references to "hating" one's parents or children (presumably because they reject the Christian kerygma) also demonstrate the painful consequences of the kingdom rule (Matt. 10:37; Luke 14:26; Gosp. Thom. 55; 101). As already noted, accepting Jesus' challenge to seek the kingdom requires sacrificing even the strongest ties of blood and affection.

The kingdom as physically present in Jesus. In the most explicit statement about the kingdom's presence—that "the kingdom of God is among you" (or "in your midst") (Luke 17:20)—Jesus informs the Pharisees that in his person they can witness God's ruling power. Luke immediately follows this declaration with Jesus' instructing the disciples about his imminent death. Realizing what they have lost—God's sovereignty in Jesus—they will frantically seek his return, becoming vulnerable to false apocalyptic predictions. As Jesus had repudiated supernatural "signs" as proof of the kingdom (Luke 17:20), so he teaches his followers that when the Son's "day comes," its arrival will be as immediately obvious—and universal—as sheet lightning that flashes over the entire sky (Luke 17:22–24). In such sayings the kingdom and Jesus are one.

Luke's assertion that the kingdom exists "among" or "in" Jesus' observers has an interesting parallel in the Gospel of Thomas. Here Jesus is represented as saying that

> the Kingdom is inside of you, and it is outside of you. When you come to know yourselves, then you will become known, and you will realize that it is you who are the sons of the living Father. But if you do not know yourselves, you dwell in poverty and it is you who are that poverty.
>
> (Gosp. Thom. 3:1–2)

Whereas the Lukan saying depicts the kingdom appearing through Jesus' presence, that in Thomas seems to equate it with a state of heightened spiritual awareness. Knowing the true "self" (the divine "image" within each person) means awakening to one's kinship with God. Remaining ignorant of "the god within" is "poverty." Despite alleged Gnostic elements in the Thomas saying, this concept of an indwelling divine spirit—perhaps similar to what Paul called the "mystery" of "Christ in [the believer]" (Col. 1:27)—may represent an integral part of Jesus' kingdom concept.

Jesus' Authority to Interpret the Divine Will

The Gospel writers agree that Jesus' sense of personal "authority" astonished his original audiences, for it broke decisively with the rabbinical tradition of interpreting the Torah in terms of what previous rabbis had said about it (Matt. 7:28–29). Jesus' habit of voicing God's opinion on crucial issues like Sabbath observance, divorce, forgiving others' sins, and the like offended many who assumed that no human being should speak for the Deity. This supreme self-confidence, coupled with Jesus' assertion of a unique relationship with the Father (see Box 11-1) may have seemed blasphemy to some, but to the disciples it could be seen as the self-revelation of God's chosen one.

Many scholars doubt that Jesus made the kind of claims to divine sonship or other honorific titles attributed to him by the Gospels. These scholars regard such titles as "Son of Man," "Son of God," "Savior," "Word," and even "Messiah" as tributes the early church paid to the man it honored as Christ. Other scholars acknowledge that the Gospel writers undoubtedly present Jesus as he was understood after the resurrection experience, but they nevertheless believe that the historical Jesus did see himself as Israel's Messiah, albeit one very different from that of popular expectation.

According to the latter view, Mark's theme of a "hidden" Messiah may represent Jesus' own gradually developing self-awareness. He does not announce himself as Christ because (1) he comes to a realization that God has so designated him only late in his career and (2) he realizes that public claims would lead to political expectations he does not plan to fulfill. The traditions of Satanic temptation preserved in Matthew and Luke suggest that Jesus experienced intense soul searching about the nature of his call. Jesus' rejection of the temptations implies that he regarded both political ambition and the performance of superhuman "tricks"—like leaping off the Temple towers unharmed—as essentially irrelevant to his purpose (Matt. 4:1–11; Luke 4:1–13). This view is consistent with Jesus' reiterated refusal to perform the kind of spectacular miracles or "signs" that would compel belief from those to whom his message means nothing (Matt. 12:39–40; Luke 11:29–32).

Although John presents seven miraculous "signs" as revealing Christ's divine nature, in the Synoptics Jesus seems to have a rather ambiguous attitude toward the use of ostensibly supernatural displays. Mark even shows him as unable to produce miracles when those present lacked faith that he could do so (Mark 6:6). Whatever the extent of his charismatic powers, such as his ability to accomplish "faith healings," Jesus did not regard them as more important than his proclamation of the kingdom.

The almost total absence of the kingdom message in John, replaced by the emphasis on Jesus' divine person, may represent the fourth Evangelist's assumption that the kingdom is embodied in Jesus himself.

Jesus' Self-awareness

Although Jesus' self-awareness of a special relationship to God cannot pass the test of dissimilarity, it is overwhelmingly affirmed on the grounds of multiple attestation in both canonical and noncanonical sources. To many commentators it also seems plausible that Jesus realized that most of his contemporaries would not accept the kind of divinely appointed leader that he felt himself to be. Hence, the premonitions of future public rejection and death that shadow Mark's narrative (and that are reproduced in the other Gospels) may have a basis in historical reality. Jesus' predictions that he will suffer in Jerusalem are not necessarily the Gospel authors' retrojections of later church beliefs back into the time of Jesus' ministry. The historical Jesus could reasonably anticipate an adverse reaction, even legal punishment, when he confronted the Jerusalem rulers with his kingdom message. He might well have expected the Romans to treat him no better than Herod Antipas had treated Jesus' mentor, John the Baptist. As presently worded, Mark's prophecies probably reflect the Gospel writer's postresurrection faith, but they may also testify to Jesus' own apprehension of public failure and official retaliation (Mark 8:31; 9:31–32; 10:33–34).

Jesus' Demand for Total Commitment

Jesus' determination to obey his calling even to the point of death, if need be, is consistent with his demand for total commitment to the kingdom, no matter what the cost. To the rich young man, not yet a disciple but whom Jesus "loves" on sight, he states that if one would be complete one must sell all worldly possessions, give the proceeds to the poor, and willingly follow Jesus (Mark 10:17–27). Mark's repeated emphasis on the disciples' sacrifices and potential suffering may reflect the persecutions occurring when he wrote. The admonition, however, may also echo Jesus' adamant insistence on forsaking earthly ties to achieve citizenship in the kingdom (Mark 8:34–38; 10:35–44). In all these passages, Jesus associates his own hard fate with the future lives of those who follow him.

Commitment to an undefined ideal. As the Synoptic writers present his teaching, Jesus requires his followers to give themselves, body and soul, to an ideal that is nowhere coherently explained. In the Synoptic accounts, the kingdom concept is ambiguous and its meaning elusive. Depending on which text a reader selects, the kingdom is God's direct rule violently imposed in the near future, a present reality in Jesus' healing ministry, or a mysterious power that slowly grows in the enlightened human consciousness. The Synoptic writers' lack of precision—even confusion—about the nature of Jesus' essential message may be significant. It suggests that Jesus does not view the kingdom as anything so simple and straightforward as an apocalyptic government or even a community of enlightened believers. The Gospels' ambiguous handling of the term further implies that Jesus uses *kingdom* in a highly subtle and complex way that may not be easy to grasp.

The Gospels that do not view Jesus as an apocalyptic preacher provide important insights into the possible meaning of Jesus' kingdom proclamation. John's Gospel, the Gospel of Thomas, and other early Christian documents indicate that there are ways to interpret the kingdom message not articulated in the Synoptic tradition. As we learned in Chapter 10, John interprets Jesus as a revealer of celestial wisdom. We now consider how John connects Jesus' wisdom teaching with the concept of kingdom and kingship.

Wisdom and Jesus' Kingdom

In contrast to the Synoptic Gospels, the Fourth Gospel rarely mentions the kingdom. John's account, however, makes the nature of Jesus' personal kingship the crucial issue on which Pilate's execution of Jesus hinges (John 18:33–19:22). During the confrontation with Pilate, Jesus states that his kingdom is not of this world—that it is not political—but he fails to define either his dominion or his own kingly role (John 18:36).

John nonetheless gives his readers a relatively clear idea of what Jesus' kingdom involves. From the outset of his Gospel, the author identifies Jesus with the eternal Word, the expression of immortal Wisdom by and through which God created the universe (John 1:1–18; Prov. 8:22–36). In his person Jesus reveals—and shares with others—the vital Wisdom by which God rules and communicates his will. As noted in Chapter 10, John firmly links Jesus with Israel's Wisdom tradition, the teachings of which associate the wise person with God's *basileia*—heavenly kingship.

The apocryphal Wisdom of Solomon expresses the affinity between Wisdom and divine kingship that may have influenced John's view of Jesus:

> For she [Wisdom] ranges [the earth] in search of those who are worthy of her; . . . The true beginning of wisdom is the desire to learn, and a concern for learning means the keeping of her laws; to keep her laws is a warrant of immortality; and immortality brings a man near to God. Thus the desire of wisdom leads to kingly stature [a *basileia*].
>
> (Wisdom of Solomon 6:16–20)

Notice that learning and keeping God's wise laws, the principles by which he orders the cosmos, lead to eternal life and make the obedient possessor of Wisdom a king.

Wisdom also reveals the kingdom of God:

> She [Wisdom] guided him [Jacob, the embodiment of Israel] on straight paths; she showed him the *basileia tou theou* [literally, the kingdom or sovereignty of God].
>
> (Wisdom of Solomon 10:10)

In Israel's Wisdom writings, Wisdom (Sophia, a personification of God's primary attribute) imparts knowledge, divine favor, and immortal life (Prov. 2:1–10; Job 28:12–23; Ecclus. 24; Wisd. 8:4, 13). She discloses secrets of the unseen world to those who seek her, satisfying their intellectual and spiritual thirst (Wisd. 7:17–29). The references to Jesus' unveiling the "secret" or "mystery of the kingdom of God" in Mark (4:11) and Secret Mark (2:10) may preserve a parallel to the Johannine tradition that Jesus' teaching focuses not on the apocalyptic but on Wisdom's revelation of previously hidden cosmic truths.

According to this view of Jesus' kingdom message, Jesus teaches that followers must come under God's rule by imitating and participating in the divine *basileia*. As noted above, *basileia* implies kingly autonomy, freedom, and self-determination—living one's life as the master of one's situation. The Johannine Jesus tells his followers that he had already "conquered the world" (John 16:33). The self-confidence or "authority" with which Jesus habitually teaches may derive from his profound sense of possessing the celestial Wisdom that sets people free (Matt. 7:28–29; Mark 1:22; John 8:22). At liberty to proclaim his personal views on the Torah, he inevitably antagonizes many rival teachers of the Law. As a sage through whom Wisdom speaks, he is also free to recognize his own kingship—the *basileia* that Wisdom imparts (Wisd. 6:17–20; 10:10). If Jesus publicly equated his Wisdom teaching with kingship, the connection may have inspired Pilate's suspicion. As governor for Rome, Pilate could tolerate no Jew claiming to be a king of any kind.

The Johannine Jesus informs his disciples that he fully reveals the Father, the supreme reality with whom he—and they—enjoy a life-giving unity (John 17:1–8, 20–23). Spiritual union with the Deity confers a power upon Jesus' disciples that will enable them to accomplish greater deeds than he (John 14:10–14). The arrival of the Paraclete, or Spirit of Truth, endows believers with additional heaven-sent Wisdom and allows them to continue imitating Jesus' example of kingly rulership. Indeed, the Paraclete manifests the same power of *basileia* that characterizes Jesus (John 16:7–15). Initiated into the mystery of divinity and empowered by the Spirit, the Johannine disciple possesses a kingdom authority resembling that of Jesus himself (John 14:12–21).

The kingdom teachings that the Gospels attribute to Jesus are many and diverse. They range from the kingdom as a God-ruled government to the kingdom as a revelation of divine Wisdom that gives its possessor *basileia*, kingly authority. The ambiguity and diversity of the kingdom concept make it difficult, if not impossible, to discover what the historical Jesus of Nazareth intended when he used the term.

In general, the Synoptic Gospels present Jesus as a healer, an exorcist, and a reinterpreter of the Mosaic Torah who announces that God's rule is about to dawn. By contrast, John's Gospel and the Apocryphal Gospels of Thomas and Secret Mark view Jesus as a Wisdom teacher who initiates select followers into a mystical union with the spiritual power inherent in divinely revealed Wisdom.

The wide diversity of the kingdom sayings ascribed to Jesus challenges any commentator who attempts to restrict Jesus' message to a specific doctrine or program. The very absence of scholarly agreement on what Jesus actually teaches stimulates our search to recover his essential insights. For the present, seeking to know Jesus must remain an exciting process of ongoing discovery.

QUESTIONS FOR DISCUSSION AND REVIEW

1. The four canonical Gospel writers present Jesus largely through the eyes of faith, interpreting his life and works according to their disparate religious viewpoints. In what ways do the authors' individual theological interests, and the consequent differences among their respective portraits, make it difficult to discover the "real" Jesus of Nazareth?

2. Discuss the historical sources of information about Jesus found outside the New Testament, including the works of non-Christian historians ansd noncanonical Gospels. What contributions do such works as Secret Mark and the Gospels ascribed to Peter, James, and Thomas make to our understanding of early Christian beliefs about Jesus?

3. Discuss some of the methods scholars use to evaluate sayings and actions attributed to Jesus. Define what is meant by the scholarly "quest" to recover "the historical Jesus." Can the careful reader distinguish between what Jesus actually said and did and what later believers attributed to him? (Reread the discussion of form and redaction criticism in Chapter 6.)

4. Is it possible to reconstruct a coherent picture of Jesus and his teaching using the source materials currently available? What sources do you personally regard as most trustworthy, as most likely to represent Jesus as he might have been rather than as he appeared to the believing community that worshipped him?

5. Teachings about the kingdom or rule of God are central to Jesus' message. After analyzing the different kinds of kingdom sayings found in the Gospels, do you find a consistent pattern of meaning in some or all of the sayings? Are readers likely to project their own values into the recorded sayings and accept or stress only those that accord with their own preconceptions?

6. Do we possess any sure means of finding out what Jesus actually thought about himself and his purpose? In reading the four Gospels, do you find any clues that reliably indicate the nature of Jesus' own self-awareness?

7. Contrast the Synoptic portrait of Jesus as an apocalyptic exorcist and preacher with John's portrayal of Jesus as a revealer of heavenly wisdom. How would you distinguish Mark's idea of Jesus' kingdom from John's concept of Jesus' kingship?

8. The communities that produced the Synoptic Gospels clearly had very different traditions about Jesus from those treasured in the group that created John's Gospel. How do you account for such divergent views about Jesus' nature and teaching in two roughly contemporaneous Christian communities? In what ways do these divergent traditions about Jesus' teaching make it difficult to define the term *kingdom* as Jesus uses it?

TERMS AND CONCEPTS TO REMEMBER

Apocryphal Gospels
Gospel to Thomas
    Didymos (the
    twin)
Gospel of Peter
Secret Mark
Protoevangelium of
    James (Book of
    James)
Albert Schweitzer

Jesus as apocalyptist
realized eschatology
Perrin's criteria for
    determining
    authentic material
basileia tou theou
    (kingdom of God)
the relationship of
    divine Wisdom
    and *basileia*

RECOMMENDED READING

The items listed under the first subheading below are intended to help the student begin an investigation of Jesus' life. Selected for their general approach and readability, these initial studies can be supplemented by the more scholarly works enumerated under the subheadings that follow.

General Works

Breech, James. *The Silence of Jesus: The Authentic Voice of the Historical Man.* Philadelphia: Fortress Press, 1983. Examines the "core material"—eight sayings and twelve parables—that a scholarly consensus attributes to the historical Jesus.

Carlston, Charles E. "Jesus Christ." In *Harper's Bible Dictionary*, edited by P. J. Achtemeier, 475–87. San Francisco: Harper and Row, 1985. Includes a clear survey of Jesus' principal teachings.

Carpenter, Humphrey. *Jesus.* Oxford: Oxford University Press, 1980. A short (102 pp.) paperback that uses common sense to summarize the major theories about Jesus.

Dodd, Charles H. *The Founder of Christianity.* New York: Macmillan, 1970. An influential work by the leading proponent of "realized eschatology."

———. *Historical Tradition in the Fourth Gospel.* Cambridge: Cambridge University Press, 1963.

———. "Life and Teachings of Jesus." In *A Companion to the Bible*, edited by T. W. Manson. Edinburgh: T. & T. Clark, 1956.

Kee, Howard C. *Jesus in History.* 2d ed. New York: Harcourt Brace Jovanovich, 1977.

Kingsbury, Jack D. *Jesus Christ in Matthew, Mark, and Luke.* Philadelphia: Fortress Press, 1981.

Robinson, John A. T. *Jesus and His Coming.* Philadelphia: Westminster Press, 1979. Argues that Jesus was not an apocalyptist and that beliefs about his Second Coming developed from a misunderstanding of his teachings.

Schweitzer, Albert. *The Mystery of the Kingdom of God: The Secret of Jesus' Messiahship and Passion.* Translated by W. Lowrie. New York: Macmillan, 1950.

———. *The Quest of the Historical Jesus: A Critical Study of Its Progress from Reimarus to Wrede.* Translated by W. Montgomery. New York: Macmillan, 1968.

Wilson, Ian S. *Jesus: The Evidence.* San Francisco: Harper and Row, 1984. A provocative investigation of Jesus' historical context, for the beginner.

Jesus in his Jewish Environment

Falk, Harvey. *Jesus the Pharisee: A New Look at the Jewishness of Jesus.* New York: Paulist Press, 1985. Shows the many similarities between Jesus's teachings and those of the Pharisees, including parallels in both form and content.

Sanders, E. P. *Jesus and Judaism.* Philadelphia: Fortress Press, 1985. A scholarly and highly readable evaluation of the Gospel traditions about Jesus and his teaching, particularly about the kingdom and its original meaning in the context of Palestinian Judaism.

Sandmel, Samuel. *Judaism and Christian Beginnings*. New York: Oxford University Press, 1978. Connects Jesus and early Christianity with first-century Judaism and Palestinian customs.

Sloyan, Gerard S. *Jesus in Focus: A Life in Its Setting*. Mystic, Conn.: Twenty-third Publications, 1984. Examines Jesus' career in the light of his Jewish environment.

Vermes, Geza. *Jesus the Jew: A Historian's Reading of the Gospels*. New York: Macmillan, 1973. Places Jesus in the religious and sociopolitical setting of his first-century Galilean homeland.

Introductions to Some Special Problems

Brown, Raymond E. *The Virginal Conception and Bodily Resurrection of Jesus*. New York: Paulist Press, 1973. An honest discussion of the historicity of tradition surrounding Jesus' birth and resurrection by a leading Roman Catholic thinker.

Crossan, J. D. *Four Other Gospels: Shadows on the Contours of Canon*. Minneapolis: Winston Press, 1985. A brilliant analysis of the noncanonical Gospels of Peter, Secret Mark, Thomas, and the Egerton Papyrus 2, demonstrating their contribution to an understanding of Jesus' life and work.

Mack, Burton L. "The Kingdom Sayings in Mark." *Forum*, vol. 3, no. 1, 1987, pp. 3–47. Argues that Jesus' historical teaching on the kingdom concept was not apocalyptic.

Rivkin, Ellis. *What Crucified Jesus? The Political Execution of a Charismatic*. Nashville: Abingdon Press, 1984. A short but insightful investigation into the social and political forces that led to Jesus' execution.

Aids for Comparing Gospel Texts

Aland, Kurt, ed. *Synopsis of the Four Gospels*. English ed. New York: United Bible Societies, 1985. A helpful presentation of parallels among the four canonical Gospels.

Cameron, Ron, ed. *The Other Gospels: Non-Canonical Gospel Texts*. Philadelphia: Westminster Press, 1982. A paperback collection of sixteen ancient documents containing sayings of Jesus, with introductory prefaces.

Crossan, John D., ed. *Sayings Parallels: A Workbook for the Jesus Tradition*. Philadelphia: Fortress Press, 1986. A comprehensive collection of Jesus' sayings arranged to include texts for all four canonical Gospels plus those from apocryphal sources, including the Gospel of Thomas and the Apocryphon of James.

Funk, R. W. *New Gospel Parallels*. 2 vols. Foundations & Facets. Philadelphia: Fortress Press, 1985. A major achievement in New Testament scholarship. Volume 1 provides parallels to the three Synoptic Gospels. Volume 2 assembles parallels to the Gospels of John, Thomas, and Peter, the Infancy Gospel of Thomas, the Protoevangelium of James, the Acts of Pilate, and various manuscript fragments.

12 *Acts of the Apostles*

You will bear witness for me in Jerusalem, and all over
Judaea and Samaria, and away to the ends of the earth.
[Jesus to the Jerusalem disciples] (Acts 1:8)

KEY THEMES Showing that Christianity is a Spirit-directed faith intended for people of all nations, Luke presents its early history in two parts. The first part (chs. 1–12) focuses on the original Jerusalem church; its empowerment by the Holy Spirit at Pentecost (2:1–47); its conflict with the Jewish leadership (3:1–7:60); and its expansion into the territories of Judea and Samaria (8:1–12:25).

The second part (chs. 13–28) focuses on Paul, who leads a mission to non-Jewish nations and carries the new religion into Europe, arriving in Rome about 60 CE. Arguing that the new religion offers no threat to the Roman state, Luke designs his narrative to show that the church's task is to convert Gentiles throughout the world, a work that extends indefinitely into the future   (28:28).

In the Book of Acts, the author of Luke's Gospel continues his story of Christian origins. Writing to the same Theophilus, he creates an exciting history that is also a defense of early Christianity. (For questions about the book's authorship, date, and its relationship to the Gospel, see Chapter 9.) As a history, Acts does not attempt to provide a comprehensive record of its subject. The author lists the names of the original eleven Apostles (1:13) but tells us almost nothing about most of them. Instead, he organizes his book to focus on only two representative figures from the earliest Christian period. The Apostle Peter, representing Jewish Christianity and the Jerusalem church, dominates the first half of Acts (chs. 1–12). Paul, representing the church's mission to Hellenistic Jews and Gentiles, is the major character of the second half (chs. 13–28). Whatever the author (whom we call Luke) may have known about

the activities of other Apostles and their companions, he does not include their stories in his narrative. His history is thus highly selective, giving us primarily the "acts," or deeds, of only two great leaders and their immediate associates.

As a defense of Christianity, Acts further develops the same themes we found in Luke's Gospel. Directed at a Greek-speaking audience, Acts presents the new religion as both the natural fulfillment of Judaism and a universal faith intended for all nations. Peaceful and law-abiding, Christians are commissioned by the Holy Spirit to bring "the new Way" (9:2) to both Jews and Gentiles throughout the Roman Empire. The author emphasizes that the Apostles and missionaries continue essentially the same ministry that Jesus had begun. Led by the same Spirit, members of the Christian community perform similar miraculous works—exorcisms, healings, and resuscitations of the dead—thereby demonstrating divine gifts almost identical to those of Jesus. To Luke, the church preserves and maintains the same ethical and spiritual quality that distinguished Jesus' career.

The incidents from early Christianity that Luke chooses to include in Acts are structured to express the author's major theme: the Spirit-directed growth of the church and its expansion westward from Palestine to Italy. In general, the book is arranged chronologically, showing the religion's step-by-step expansion into new geographical areas. Luke's organizing purpose is stated in Acts 1:8, in which the risen Jesus gives the disciples his final command: they are to "bear witness" to him "in Jerusalem, and all over Judaea and Samaria, and away to the ends of the earth."

Acts thus begins in Jerusalem (chs. 1–7), records a mission to Samaria (ch. 8), and then focuses on Paul's three missionary journeys throughout Asia Minor and Greece (chs. 13–28). It concludes with Paul's arrival in Rome, heart of the Empire and perhaps representative of "the ends of the earth." Besides recording the church's territorial expansion and growth in number of believers, Luke's book also stresses the historic reversal in which Israel, God's "chosen people," is replaced by the "new Israel," the Christian community. The narrative shift from Jerusalem to Rome represents the historical development in which the new faith was transmitted from its Jewish founders to Gentile communities. Acts concludes with Paul's momentous decision to turn his attention away from Jews, who largely reject his message, "to the Gentiles," because "the Gentiles will listen" (28:23–28). At the end of his history, Luke envisions a future in which Christianity, originally a Jewish phenomenon, will become a faith held by people of every nationality.

Luke's Use of Speeches

Like other historians of his day, Luke ascribes long, elaborate speeches to his leading charac-

ters, such as Peter, Stephen, James, and Paul. But whoever the speaker, most speeches sound much alike in both style and thought. This similarity among Acts' many discourses, plus the fact that they seem to reflect attitudes prevalent in the author's time rather than those of the historical figures he describes, suggests to most scholars that they are largely Luke's own compositions. In the absence of exact transcriptions of apostolic speeches, many of which were delivered amid noisy and unruly crowds, Luke apparently follows the standard practice of Greco-Roman authors by supplementing what was remembered with material of his own creation. Ancient historians and biographers like Thucydides, Livy, Tacitus, and Plutarch commonly advanced their narratives through speeches put in the mouths of historical characters. The classical writer composed such discourses based upon his conception of the speaker's character and major concerns at the time the speech was given. He was not expected to reproduce a particular speech word for word exactly as it was delivered. Thucydides explains the historian's method clearly and briefly:

> I have found it difficult to remember the precise words used in the speeches which I listened to myself and my various informants have experienced the same difficulty; so my method has been, while keeping as closely as possible to the general sense of the words that were actually used, to make the speaker say what, in my opinion, was called for by each occasion. (*The Peloponnesian War* I.22)

In short, while attempting to reproduce the "general sense" of what people said, Thucydides created their speeches according to his understanding of what "was called for by the occasion," the author's opinion of what was appropriate to a given situation. Although we cannot know the extent to which Luke's speeches reflect ideas expressed in generations before his time, they serve the important purpose of illustrating character and preserving aspects of early apostolic teaching.

Organization of the Acts

Luke arranges his narrative in ten major sections:

1. Prologue and account of the ascension (1:1–11)
2. Founding of the Jerusalem church (1:12–2:47)
3. Work of Peter and the Apostles (3:1–5:42)
4. Persecution of the "Hellenist" Jewish Christians and the first missions (6:1–8:40)
5. Preparation for the Gentile mission: the conversions of Paul and Cornelius (9:1–12:25)
6. First missionary journey of Barnabas and Paul: the Jerusalem conference (13:1–15:35)
7. Paul's second missionary journey: evangelizing Greece (16:1–18:21)
8. Paul's third missionary journey: revisiting Asia Minor and Greece (18:22–20:38)
9. Paul's arrest in Jerusalem and imprisonment in Caesarea (21:1–26:32)
10. Paul's journey to Rome and his preaching to Roman Jews (27:1–28:31)

Prologue and Account of the Ascension

In his introduction to Acts (1:1–11), Luke refers to the "first part" of his work (the Gospel) and then picks up where his earlier story of Jesus leaves off. Before ascending to heaven, the resurrected Jesus remains on earth for "forty days," a number that symbolizes the period of time required to accomplish a major religious undertaking. (Moses remained on Mount Sinai for forty days while receiving the Torah, and Jesus' wilderness temptation was of similar duration.)

Although his report of Jesus' postresurrection instruction is tantalizingly brief, Luke includes some major themes. The risen Jesus offers fresh insights into the nature of his kingdom, which is not the restoration of the Jewish state that the disciples had anticipated (Luke 19:11;

Acts 1:3, 6–7). Contrary to apocalyptic expectations, God's rule expands gradually as the Christian message slowly permeates Greco-Roman society. The historical process must begin in Jerusalem, but the Spirit will empower believers to carry their faith throughout the earth (1:1–8).

Luke is the only New Testament writer to describe Jesus' ascent to the spirit world. He presents it as a quasiphysical movement skyward, culminating in Jesus' disappearance into the clouds (symbolic of the divine presence [Exod. 40:34–35; 1 Kings 8:10; Dan. 7:13]). Note that Luke makes the peaceful ascension a prophetic model of Jesus' quiet return (the Parousia) (1:9–11).

Founding the Jerusalem Church

The Apostles. Luke is also the only New Testament author to record that the Eleven chose a replacement for Jesus' betrayer, Judas Iscariot (1:12–26). (Contrast Luke's version of Judas' suicide with Matthew's strikingly different account [Matt. 27:5]). In this episode, the author refers to two concepts important to the early church. By replacing Judas with **Matthias,** the disciples respect Jesus' example of appointing twelve followers to represent Israel's original twelve tribes. This passage also defines Luke's understanding of an Apostle, a person who had physically accompanied Jesus during his entire ministry and also witnessed his resurrection (1:21–22). Because Paul had not personally known Jesus, Luke almost never calls him an Apostle, although Paul himself passionately fought to make others acknowledge his right to that title (Gal. 1).

Notice that after Matthias's selection, the author says nothing more about him. He is equally silent about most of the other Apostles, briefly mentioning the sons of Zebedee, James and John, but offering no hint of their characters or roles in the church. As a historian, Luke describes only those persons whose activities illustrate his thesis of the church's direct expansion from its Jewish starting point to its Gentile destination.

The Holy Spirit at Pentecost. Luke presents the disciples' experience at **Pentecost** (a Jewish harvest festival held fifty days after Passover) in terms of prophetic fulfillment (2:1–47). The Holy Spirit's descent upon a tiny group of 120 disciples vindicates Jesus' promise to equip them with supernatural power (1:8; Luke 24:49), and it fulfills Joel's ancient prediction that God would someday infuse all kinds of people with his Spirit (Joel 2:28–32). Its presence symbolically rendered as wind and flame, the Spirit empowers the disciples to speak "in tongues." This phenomenon of religious ecstasy, the believer's outpouring of strange sounds (called "glossolalia"), came to characterize the early church and was generally regarded as a sign of God's presence (11:14–18; compare Paul's discussion of "ecstatic speech" in 1 Cor. 14). According to Luke, the pentecostal miracle enabled recipients of the Spirit to converse in foreign languages they had previously been unable to speak, although some onlookers accuse the inspired disciples of being "drunk," uttering unintelligible nonsense (2:1–13).

Observe that Luke has Peter, chief of the Apostles, deliver Acts' first major speech to interpret the pentecostal experience (2:14–20). Peter's discourse illustrates several Lukan themes. The pentecostal Spirit is the phenomenon that Joel had foreseen as a sign of the last days. It is bestowed upon all believers, regardless of age or sex—women prophesy equally with men.

The Lukan Peter says the the Spirit-giving event is linked to "portents in the sky" and other astronomical displays foretold in Joel's prophecy. Interestingly, Luke represents Peter as equating the disciples' religious ecstasy with Joel's vision of cosmic upheaval, such as the sun's being darkened and the moon's turning to blood. (This interpretation of the astronomical "portents" as purely metaphorical suggests that the author's references to identical phenom-

The Descent of the Holy Spirit at Pentecost by El Greco. (Courtesy of the Prado Museum, Madrid)

ena in Luke 21:25–28 may also be seen as figurative rather than as forecasts of literal events in future history.) Luke's main point, however, is that God has anointed his church, giving it the power to preach in every known tongue, the many languages of Pentecost representing the universality of the Christian mission.

Peter's long speech expresses another important Lukan theme. Jesus' death occurred "by the deliberate will and plan of God"—and was thus a theological necessity (2:23). God has vindicated his "servant" by raising him from the dead and placing him at God's "right hand" (the position of favor and power) in heaven. Linking this exaltation of Jesus with Davidic themes from the Psalms, Peter declares that by resurrecting Jesus, God has made him "both Lord and Messiah." Since Luke believes that Jesus was Messiah during his lifetime, the author may here preserve a very early Christian belief that Jesus—the "man singled out by God"—became confirmed as Messiah only on his ascension to heavenly glory (2:22, 36; see Box 11-1).

The Jerusalem commune. Stressing a theme prominent in his Gospel, the author connects the Spirit's presence with its recipients' subsequent way of life, particularly their social and economic arrangements. The overwhelming "sense of awe" that believers feel is translated into the work of creating an ideal community without rich or poor.

Luke reports that the faithful sold their possessions so that money and goods could be distributed according to individual members' needs. Holding "everything" "in common" (2:43–45; 4:32–35), the Jerusalem community meets Jesus' challenge to sacrifice material possessions to attain true discipleship (Luke 18:18–30). As a result of establishing the kingdom's economic ethic as its standard, the Jerusalem church commonly depended on finanical help from Gentile chuches to sustain its ideal (Gal. 2:10; Rom. 15:25–28).

The Work of Peter and the Apostles

In the next section (3:1–5:42), Luke reports the activities of Peter and some of his Jerusalem associates. Peter's healing a crippled man by in-

voking Jesus' authority (3:1–10) demonstrates that the disciples continue their leader's work. Reporting a second Petrine speech (3:11–26), delivered in the Temple precincts, Luke interprets the miracle's significance. God wishes to reconcile Judaism with its infant daughter, the church. Jesus' resurrection, to which Peter and his associates are living witnesses (2:32; 3:15), proves the validity of the disciples' faith and opens the way to a unity of Jew and Jewish Christian. Luke insists that the persons who condemned Jesus did so "in ignorance." The Jerusalem leaders acted blindly because God, for his own mysterious reasons, had already determined that his "servant" must die (3:13–18). Perhaps because the Deity is the ultimate cause of Jesus' death, he now offers forgiveness to those who unwittingly carried out his will (3:17–19; Luke 23:24). As Luke portrays the situation, at this critical moment in Jewish-Christian relations, union of the two parties is possible.

Part of Israel does join the Christian fold. Luke rekindles the excitement of these early days as he records large numbers of Jews flocking to the church (4:4). In contrast to the people's enthusiastic response, Luke also shows the Jerusalem leadership hardening its position and attempting to halt the new movement.

In reading this section of Acts (chs. 3–5), notice that Luke heightens the sense of dramatic tension and conflict by presenting several direct confrontations between the Apostles and the Jewish authorities. Note, too, that the author attributes much of the church's trouble to the Sadducee party, whose priests control the Temple (4:1–6; 5:17–18). By contrast, many Pharisees tend to tolerate or even champion some Christian activities (5:34–40; 23:6–9). During Peter's second hearing before the Sanhedrin, the Pharisee **Gamaliel,** a famous first-century rabbinical scholar, is represented as the protector of the infant church.

Seeing "the new Way" as divinely supported, Luke shows that its growth cannot be stopped. After the High Priest (identified as Annas in 4:6) imprisons the Apostles, celestial forces intervene to release them (5:17–26). Whether employing human agents like Gamaliel or angels from heaven, the Deity acts decisively to ensure the church's survival and expansion.

Persecution of the "Hellenist" Jewish Christians: The First Missions

While the Sadducees attack it from without, the Jerusalem community simultaneously experiences internal trouble (6:1–8:40). Strife breaks out between two different ethnic groups within the church. Although Luke only hints at the cause of this disagreement, he makes it clear that two distinct parties emerge: the **Hellenists,** who are Greek-speaking Jews of the Diaspora, and the "Hebrews," who are Aramaic-speaking Jews apparently native to Palestine. Some historians believe that this division reflects first-century Judaism's prevailing social and religious distinction between Palestinian Jews and Jews from foreign countries who have more thoroughly adopted Greek ideas and customs.

Because he wishes to picture the Jerusalem church as a model for later Christianity, Luke portrays the incipient conflict as being resolved by an orderly administrative process. Notice that the Twelve act unanimously to elect seven Greek-speaking disciples to represent the Hellenists (6:1–6).

Although he implies that the seven leaders were elected to supervise the church's communal meals, Luke soon reveals that the seven were mainly proclaimers of the gospel. Because of his public preaching, the chief Hellenist, **Stephen,** becomes the focus of Sadducean hostility. The priestly opposition accuses Stephen of attacking the Temple cult and subverting the Mosaic Torah, charges that also had been leveled against Jesus (6:8–15).

The account of Stephen's trial and public stoning effectively links the first part of Luke's history, centered in Jerusalem, with the second part, which records Christianity's outward expansion into Gentile territory. The author fashions Stephen's speech (7:2–53) as a Hellenist's severely critical indictment of Jerusalem's religious institutions. Observe that Stephen accuses the Temple leadership of "fighting against the Holy Spirit" (to Luke, the supreme offense), murdering the Messiah, and failing to keep the Torah (7:2–53). The episode concludes on typically Lukan themes: in prayer, the dying Stephen experiences a vision of heaven and, echoing Jesus' words on the cross, asks God to forgive his executioners (7:54–60).

The author contrasts Stephen's ecstatic vision with the angry presence of "a young man named **Saul,**" who guards the cloaks of those stoning the victim. Luke's contrast of the two men, each zealous for his faith, is deeply ironic. The young Saul will become **Paul** the Apostle, Christianity's most famous missionary, and eventually suffer martyrdom himself. His presence at this point in the Lukan history connects the narrative about Stephen, a Greek-educated Christian Jew, with Paul's mission to Greek-speaking Gentile nations, a development recorded in the second half of Acts.

Demonstrating that the church's enemies cannot seriously interfere with its progress, Luke states that the Sadducean priests' efforts to block "the new Way" have just the opposite effect. The persecution that follows Stephen's execution drives the Greek-speaking Jewish Christians from Jerusalem, but this event only serves to spread the faith into receptive new areas. (Note that although the Hellenists are expelled from the holy city, the Aramaic-speaking disciples are permitted to remain.) Contrary to their expectations, the priests' hostile action becomes the means by which Jesus' order to plant the faith in Judea and Samaria (1:8) is obeyed.

The Samaritan mission. In his parable of the generous Samaritan, Luke (10:29–37) indicates Jesus' goodwill toward that despised group and anticipates Christianity's later growth in Samaria. In Acts, Luke portrays the Samaritan mission mainly through the work of a single figure, **Philip,** one of Stephen's Hellenist associates. Focusing on two of Philip's new converts, the author illustrates the increasing ethnic (and ethical) diversity of the church as it takes in the mixed population living outside Judea. The first convert is **Simon Magus,** a notorious magician who later tries to buy Peter's gift of imparting the Holy Spirit, an attempt the Apostle severely rebukes (8:4–24). In legends that developed after New Testament times, Simon became a sinister figure involved in black magic and the occult. According to some historians, he is the prototype of Faust, the medieval scholar who—to gain forbidden knowledge—sells his soul to the devil.

The Simon Magus episode suggests the moral risks taken as the church absorbed potential troublemakers from the Hellenistic world; Philip's second major convert represents a significant breakthrough for the new religion. Occurring south of Jerusalem rather than in Samaria, Stephen's conversion of an Ethiopian eunuch forms the climax of his career. According to the Mosaic Torah, a eunuch (a sexually mutilated male) was excluded from full Israelite citizenship. Despite the prejudice against him, however, this eunuch is a "God-fearer," a term Luke uses to denote a class of Gentiles who have adopted the Jewish religion without undergoing circumcision or keeping all the dietary requirements.

Notice that Luke sets up the scene to illustrate several characteristic themes. The author shows Philip encountering the Ethiopian while he is reading a singularly appropriate passage from the Hebrew Bible—Isaiah 53. This poem describes an anonymous servant of God who suffers unjustly and offers Philip the perfect opportunity to identify Isaiah's mysterious servant with Jesus, who, though innocent, endured comparable suffering. Throughout this section of Acts, Luke repeatedly refers to Jesus as a "servant" (3:13, 26; 4:27, 30), the only New Testament writer to do so (compare Luke 22:26–27). Notice that Luke omits Isaiah's allusions to

the "servant" bearing punishment for others' sins, probably because the author does not interpret Jesus' death as a ransom or atonement for sinful humanity.

In depicting the primitive chuch's missionary efforts, Luke emphasizes the Spirit's directing role. Evangelists like Philip (and later Paul) go exactly where and to whom the Holy Spirit guides them, moving almost erratically from place to place. After Philip baptizes the eunuch, we are told that "the Spirit snatched Philip away, and the eunuch saw no more of him . . ." (8:39).

Preparation for the Gentile Mission: The Recruitment of Paul and Cornelius

Paul's vision of Jesus. As a literary artist, Luke skillfully prepares the reader for the historic transformation of Christianity from a movement within Judaism to an independent world religion. He does this by recording the recruitment of two different men whose acceptance of the new faith foreshadows the Gentile mission (9:1–12:25). The most dramatic event is the encounter of Saul (Paul) with the risen Lord on the road to Damascus. The author regards Paul's experience as crucially important and gives no fewer that three separate accounts of the incident (9:3–8; 22:6–11; 26:12–19). Luke clothes the event in supernatural images—a blinding light and heavenly voice—although Paul's only surviving reports of what happened are much more subdued (compare Gal. 1:12, 15–16; 1 Cor. 15:8–9).

In Luke's historical scheme, Paul becomes God's agent (9:15), explicitly chosen to bring "the Way" (as Greek-speaking Christians first called their faith) to non-Jewish nations. As a result of the mystical experience that transformed his view of Jesus, Paul now suffers the same kind of persecution he had inflicted on others. Note Luke's reference to two separate plots on Paul's life, which he foils by escaping first from Damascus and then from Caesarea (9:24–30).

Peter's call to baptize a Gentile. Luke devotes two full chapters (10–11) to narrating the conversion of **Cornelius,** a Roman military officer and the first Gentile Christian. To Luke, admitting the uncircumcised Gentile into the Christian fold represents one of the most important developments in religious history. The author's manner of telling the story reveals how crucial he believes the event to be. By this point in Luke-Acts, the reader has probably realized that whenever Luke wishes to emphasize the significance of an event, he describes it in terms of supernatural phenomena. At both Jesus' birth (Luke 1–2) and that of the church at Pentecost (Acts 2), the invisible spirit realm directly impinges upon the human world. (The resurrection and the Apostles' escape from death in prison are two other examples.) Thus, Cornelius and **Peter,** whom God calls to baptize him, experience inspired dreams and visions that symbolically convey God's intent to make Gentiles as well as Jews his own people.

Stressing his view that the Spirit's presence validates a religious decision, Luke shows Cornelius and his entire household speaking in tongues exactly as the Jewish Christians had at Pentecost. As he had at the church's spiritual baptism, Peter again interprets the incident's religious meaning—the equal worth of Jews and Gentiles in God's sight (10:35–48). Peter's statement also clarifies the meaning of his dream: God declares all animal foods "clean" and acceptable, as well as the Gentile people who eat them. Dietary restrictions are no longer a barrier between Jew and non-Jew.

Typically Lukan themes dominate the Cornelius-Peter episode. Both men receive their respective visions while at prayer. The Spirit arranges and guides the human participants in this momentous conversion, empowering Jew and Gentile alike. The reader will also note that Luke preserves words of the resurrected Jesus directing believers how to behave at moments

crucial to the evolving church. Speaking through trances or visions to Paul (9:4–6), Ananias (9:10–16), Cornelius (10:3–6), and Peter (10:10–16), the risen Lord continues to instruct his disciples (compare Luke 24:25–27, 44–50). Luke thus shows the intimate communication prevailing between the Lord and his church.

Herod Agrippa. Luke concludes this section by describing the attack on the Jerusalem church's leadership by **Herod Agrippa I.** A grandson of Herod the Great, Herod Agrippa reigned briefly (41–44 CE) over a reunited Jewish state. Although the emperor Claudius, who had appointed him king, supported Herod's rule, the puppet ruler was unpopular among his Jewish subjects. Herod apparently cultivated support from the Sadducees by persecuting their opponents, including Christians. Luke states that he beheaded James, brother of John, and also imprisoned Peter. After recording Peter's miraculous escape from prison, the author dramatizes Herod's punishment. Hailed publicly as "a god" by a fawning crowd, the king is instantly afflicted with a loathsome and fatal disease "because he had usurped the honour due to God" (12:1–24). Herod's miserable death, like that of Judas, illustrates the fate of persons who oppose the Spirit.

The First Missionary Journey of Barnabas and Paul: The Jerusalem Conference

According to Acts 11, the initial persecution and scattering of Hellenistic Jewish Christians eventually led to the formation of a mixed Jewish-Gentile church in **Antioch,** Syria. A prosperous city situated on the main trade and travel routes of the eastern Mediterranean, Antioch rapidly became the center for a hugely successful mission to the Gentiles (13:1–15:35). Paul and **Barnabas,** a Greek-speaking Jewish Christian from Cyprus, made the city their head-

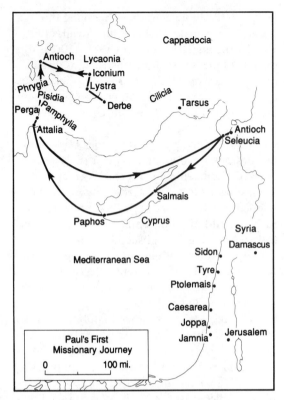

Cappadocia

Antioch Lycaonia
Phrygia •Iconium
Pisidia •Lystra
Perga Pamphylia •Derbe Cilicia •Tarsus
Attalia

Antioch
Seleucia

Salmais

Paphos   Cyprus

Syria
Damascus
Sidon•
Mediterranean Sea
Tyre•
Ptolemais•
Caesarea•
Joppa•
Jamnia Jerusalem

Paul's First
Missionary Journey
0   100 mi.

Figure 12-1. Paul's first missionary journey. According to Acts, Paul made three major tours through the northeastern Mediterranean region. Although the account in Acts may oversimplify Paul's complex travel itineraries, it correctly shows him focusing his efforts on major urban centers in Asia Minor (modern Turkey).

quarters. It was here that followers of "the Way" first received the name of Christians (11:22–26).

In Acts 13, Luke shows Barnabas and Paul leaving Antioch to begin their first missionary tour of Asia Minor. According to this account, the two made it their practice to preach first in Jewish synagogues and, when rejected there, to turn then to a Gentile audience (13:46–48; 18:6; 28:28). Luke's version of Paul's speech in Pisidian Antioch (in Asia Minor) shows little sensitivity to Paul's characteristic teaching on the saving power of Christ or his anticipation of an early Parousia. (Compare Acts' account with Paul's

letters to the Thessalonians and Corinthians.) Many scholars believe that the speeches in Acts reflect the Hellenistic preaching typical of the author's own time, late in the first century CE.

Luke announces that Barnabas and Paul opened "the gates of faith to the Gentiles" (14:27), but he is not above remarking on the religious gullibility of some pagans. When Paul and Barnabas are evangelizing Lystra, a Roman colony in Asia Minor, they are mistaken for gods in human form. After Paul miraculously heals a crippled man, the populace decides that he must be Mercury (Hermes), messenger of the Olympian gods, and that Barnabas is Jupiter (Zeus), king of the immortals. The pagan crowd's fickleness, however, matches its credulity. At one moment the Lystrans are ready to offer sacrifices to Barnabas and Paul, but at the next—persuaded by some visiting Jews— they stone Paul and leave him for dead (14:8–30). Apparently indestructible, Paul recovers quickly and completes his missionary tour, returning to Antioch.

The First Church Conference

The great success that Barnabas and Paul have in converting large numbers of Gentiles brings the church its first major crisis (15:1–25). In Antioch, many Jewish Christians insist that unless the new converts become circumcised they "[can] not be saved" (15:1). In Jerusalem, Christian Pharisees argue that Gentile converts "must be circumcised and told to keep the Law of Moses" (15:5). According to Genesis, **circumcision** is required of all Israelite males if they are to be part of the covenant community (Gen. 17:9–14). Because this ritual mark on the organ of procreation distinguishes Jews as heirs of Yahweh's promises to Abraham, Jewish Christians naturally see it as a prerequisite to entering the kingdom. In their opinion, foreigners must become Jews before they can be Christians. Paul and Barnabas oppose this notion with "fierce dissension and controversy" (15:2).

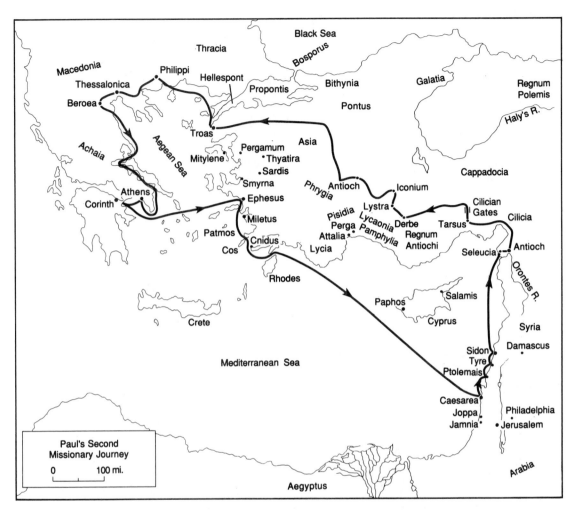

Figure 12-2. As Acts depicts it, Paul's second missionary journey brought Christianity to Europe, with new cells of Christians established in Philippi, Thessalonica, and Corinth. Note that Antioch in Syria is Paul's missionary headquarters.

The battle between advocates of the Mosaic Torah and Hellenistic Christian Jews like Barnabas and Paul gives Luke an opportunity to create a model, or paradigm, for dealing with such controversies in the church. By the time he wrote Acts, the issue had long been decided in favor of the Gentiles. Paul's advocacy of "freedom" from the "bondage" of the Mosaic Torah had triumphed over the "circumcision party." Thus, Luke presents the controversy as considerably less intense than it actually was and simplifies the historical situation by picturing a peaceful and unanimous resolution of the problem.

The first church conference, held in Jerusalem about 49 CE to decide the circumcision issue, provides Luke's model of orderly procedure. Initiating the conference, Antioch sends delegates, including Barnabas and Paul, to Jerusalem, and the Jerusalem "apostles and elders" investigate the problem, permitting an extended debate between the two sides. Peter, representing Pales-

representing Palestinian apostolic authority, delivers a speech reminding his fellow Jews that the Spirit had been given to the Gentile Cornelius the same as it had to Jewish Christians. Peter advises against laying the Torah "yoke" upon converts. The entire congregation then listens to Barnabas and Paul plead their case for the Gentiles.

According to Luke, James (Jesus' "brother" or kinsman), the person who later succeeds Peter as head of the Jerusalem church, essentially decides the issue. Although Acts pictures James as a "moderate," accepting of Gentiles who do not observe Torah rules, Paul's letters paint him as a strongly conservative Jew, advocating circumcision for all (Gal. 2). Notice that Luke presents James as using his prestige to influence the Jerusalem church to accept Gentiles without imposing Torah restrictions.

The Lukan James, however, does insist upon the observation of some Jewish dietary laws by Gentiles. The Jacobean regulations seem based largely on Torah rules from Leviticus, in which both Jews and foreigners living in Israel are forbidden to eat blood or meat that has not been drained of blood (Lev. 17–18). Recognizing that Gentiles are accustomed to a more sexually permissive culture than are Jews, James also forbids "fornication" or sexual misconduct (15:13–21). In James' speech, Luke shows a basic victory for one party (the Gentile side), accompanied by a compromise that is sensitive to the consciences of the losing sides.

The author completes his example of model church procedure by illustrating the manner in which James' recommendation is carried out. Themes of unity and cooperation dominate Luke's account: the "whole church" agrees to send "unanimously" elected delegates back to Antioch with a letter containing the Jerusalem church's directive. Characteristically, Luke notes that the decision of this precedent-setting conference is also "the decision of the Holy Spirit" (15:22–29). To the author, the church's deliberations reflect the divine will.

Although Luke shows the Jerusalem conference resolving problems peacefully and unanimously, Paul's contemporary report (Gal. 2) reveals a more sharply divided church. Rather than accepting a dietary compromise and being entrusted with a letter for Antioch, Paul asserts that he refused to make a single concession to his pro-Torah opponents (Gal. 2:4–5). In addition, Paul expresses an attitude toward eating meat sacrificed to Greco-Roman gods that differs significantly from that attributed to him in Acts (1 Cor. 8:8; 10:27).

Some historians believe that the apostolic decree involving dietary matters may have been issued at a later Jerusalem conference, one that Paul did not attend. In this view, Luke has combined the results of two separate meetings and reported them as a single event. Later in Acts, the author seems aware that Paul did not know about the Jerusalem church's decision regarding Torah-prohibited meats. During Paul's final Jerusalem visit, James is shown speaking about the dietary restrictions as if they were news to Paul (21:25).

Paul's Second Missionary Journey: Evangelizing Greece

Luke devotes the remainder of Acts to recording Paul's missionary journeys and confrontations with Jewish and Roman authorities. Stressing Christianity's acceptability to the Greco-Roman world, the author structures the book's second half to illustrate three basic themes: (1) the Spirit controls the church's growth, precisely instructing missionaries on where they may or may not travel (16:6–10); (2) when Christian preachers are not interfered with, Gentiles respond favorably to the new religion, which enjoys a huge success throughout Asia Minor and Greece; and (3) from its beginnings, Christianity is familiar to Roman officials, who invariably see it as no threat to the imperial government. As Luke tells the story, only ignorant mobs or envious Jewish leaders oppose the faith and incite Roman authorities to suppress it.

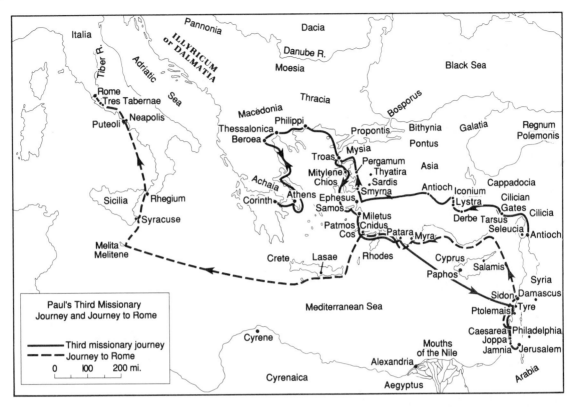

Figure 12-3. According to Acts, Paul's third missionary journey ended with his arrest in Jerusalem and two-year imprisonment in Caesarea. The dotted line shows the route of Paul's sea voyage to Rome, where he was taken to be tried in the imperial courts.

These themes dominate Luke's account of Christianity's spread from Asia into Greece (16:1–18:2). After quarreling with Barnabas (15:36–40; compare Gal. 2:13) and recruiting new companions, Silas and Timothy, Paul has a vision in which Macedonian Greeks appeal for his help (16:9–10). Accepting the vision as a divine command, Paul and his new partners cross into Macedonia, a Roman provice in northern Greece. (At this point the author begins to speak in the first person plural; his use of "we" and "us" suggests either that he was an eyewitness to this part of Paul's journey or that he incorporates another party's travel journal into his narrative.) In **Philippi,** where Paul establishes the first Christian church in Europe, an irate slaveholder accuses the missionaries of illegally

trying to convert Romans to Judaism. Wrongfully flogged and imprisoned, Paul and Silas assert their legal rights as Roman citizens, who are protected from punishment without a trial. Luke uses this incident to show that (1) only personal malice causes Paul's arrest; (2) God protects his agents, in this case sending an earthquake to open their prison doors; and (3) Philippi's legal authorities have no case against Paul or his associates.

After establishing another church at Thessalonica, Paul moves southward to **Athens,** famous for its magnificent artworks and schools of philosophy. A university city emphasizing free speech and tolerance of diverse ideas, Athens is the only place on Paul's itinerary where he is neither mobbed nor arrested. Instead, he is politely invited to speak at the Areopagus, an open-air court where speakers can express their views. In a celebrated speech, Paul identifies the Athenians' "unknown god" as the Judeo-Christian Creator. Representing Paul as quoting two ancient Greek poets on the unity of humankind, Luke incorporates their insights into the Christian message. At Paul's allusion to Jesus' physical resurrection, however, the Athenians lose interest, perhaps because their philosophers commonly taught that the body has no part in a future immortal state. Only a few among Paul's audience are converted and baptized (17:16–34).

Paul enjoys much greater success in **Corinth,** a prosperous Greek seaport notorious for its materialism and houses of prostitution. Luke enables his readers to fix the approximate time of Paul's arrival—the early 50s CE—by his reference to two secular events that coincided with the Apostle's visit. Luke notes that two Jewish Christians, Aquila and Priscilla, were in Corinth following the emperor Claudius's decree expelling all Jews from the capital. Claudius issued this edict about 49 CE. The author also mentions that **Gallio** was then proconsul (governor) of Achaia, the Greek province in which Corinth is located. Archaeologists (scientists who study the remains of ancient cultures) recently found an inscription that enables them to place Gallio's term between about 51 and 53 CE. This find is extremely important because it gives us one of the few relatively precise dates in Paul's career.

As in the episode at Philippi, Luke presents Paul's Corinthian visit as another illustration of his major themes—the new religion is both Spirit directed and lawful. In a night vision, the Lord directs Paul to remain in Corinth, despite persecution. When Paul is arrested and brought before Gallio, the governor dismisses Jewish charges against the missionary as irrelevant to Roman law. Legally exonerated, Paul and his companions continue their work unhindered (18:1–17).

Paul's Third Missionary Journey: Revisiting Asia Minor

In depicting Paul's third missionary journey (18:21–20:38), in which the Apostle revisits churches he had founded in Asia Minor and Greece, Luke concentrates on Paul's activities in **Ephesus.** A thriving port city on the west coast of Asia (modern Turkey), Ephesus had an ethnically mixed population and a great variety of religious cults. Luke demonstrates the social and religious complexity of this cosmopolitan center by having his hero encounter a wide diversity of religionists there, both Jewish and Gentile.

The author hints that even Christianity in Ephesus differs from that found elsewhere, being influenced by Jewish followers of John the Baptist. Luke records two separate incidents in which members of a Baptist-Christian group are apparently brought into line with Pauline doctrine. The first involves the eloquent **Apollos,** an educated Jew from Alexandria, who delivers persuasive sermons about Jesus—but knows "only John's baptism." Hearing him in the Ephesus synagogue, Priscilla and Aquila "take him in hand," presumably bringing his ideas into harmony with Paul's teaching. After Apollos departs for Corinth (see 1 Cor. 1), Paul finds another group of Ephesian Christians observing "John's baptism." On their being rebaptized in Jesus' name, the converts receive the Holy Spirit, confirming the superiority of Jesus to his forerunner.

Luke further illustrates Christianity's superiority by contrasting Paul's astonishing ability to heal with the inability of some Jewish competitors. The Apostle's spiritual power is so great that articles of clothing that had touched his skin are used to heal the sick and cast out "evil spirits." By contrast, seven Jewish exorcists trying to expel demons by invoking Jesus' authority fail ignominiously. Defying the exorcists, the possessed man strips all seven and hurls them naked from his house (19:11–17).

In religion, Ephesus's greatest pride was its enormous temple dedicated to **Diana** (Artemis), one of the seven wonders of the ancient world. Although bearing a Roman name, the Ephesian Diana was a mother goddess closely related to other Near Eastern fertility deities such as Cybele and Ashtoreth. Paul's success in converting Ephesians brings him into conflict with the goddesses' worshippers. Jewish-Christian monotheism, proclaiming the existence of only one God, threatens to hurt the business of Ephesian silversmiths who make their living selling replicas of Diana and her shrine.

Duplicating the trial scene in Corinth, Luke states that Ephesian officials find the missionary innocent of disturbing the city's peace. Once again, attempts to harm the disciples backfire against the persecutors (19:23–41).

Luke frames Paul's adventures in Ephesus with intimations of the Apostle's final journey—to Rome. As Luke had pictured Jesus turning his face resolutely toward Jerusalem and the servant's death that awaited him there (Luke 9:51), so the author shows Paul determined to complete his last tour and head for the imperial capital (19:21–22). After revisiting Greece (20:1–16), Paul calls the Ephesian church leaders to meet him in Miletus, an ancient Greek city on the west coast of Asia Minor. There, Paul delivers a farewell speech, predicting his imminent imprisonment and implying a coming martyrdom. In this speech, Luke stresses holding to the apostolic teaching that Paul represents and resisting heresy (20:17–38).

Paul's Arrest in Jerusalem and Imprisonment in Caesarea

In this section, Luke foreshadows Paul's death, although he never explicitly refers to it (21:1–26:32). On his way to Jerusalem, presumably to deliver the money collected from the Pauline churches for the "poor" of Jerusalem's Christian commune, Paul encounters a prophet who foretells the Apostle's fatal "binding" (arrest) there. Stressing the resemblance between Jesus and his later followers, Luke shows Paul expressing his willingness to die in Jerusalem. (Compare Paul's misgivings about the fatal return to Jerusalem in Romans 15.)

Ironically, the Apostle to the Gentiles seals his fate by cooperating with the Palestinian Jewish Christians of Jerusalem. When Paul bows to James's influence and agrees to undergo purification rites in the Temple to prove his faithfulness to Torah regulations, his presence in the sanctuary incites a riot. The Roman soldiers who intervene in the fray save Paul's life but also place him in protective custody (21:18–36). From this incident through the end of his story, Luke's hero is a prisoner of the Roman government.

Christianity and the state. Paul's arrest and his hearings before various magistrates illustrate Luke's focus on Christianity's legal relation to the Empire. The author consistently represents Roman officials as generally favoring the new religion. A Roman army officer permits Paul to explain his mission to a Jewish crowd (21:37–22:21), occasioning a speech in which Paul gives a second version of his mystical experience on the road to Damascus. When he discovers that Paul is a Roman citizen, a legal status that entitles him to protection from punishment without a proper trial, the same army commander (later identified as Lysias) personally escorts his prisoner to the Sanhedrin to answer charges the Jews had brought against him.

In reporting Paul's Sanhedrin appearance, Luke shows that the Jerusalem leaders divide along party lines as they had during Peter's two hearings. The similarity of Paul's religious doctrines and those of the Pharisees is indicated by the fact that Paul has no qualms about identifying himself with them and they take his part. As before, it is the Sadducean priests who most vehemently oppose the Christian "heresy."

In reading Luke's description of Paul's first formal hearing before a high Roman official, the governor **Antonius Felix** (24:10–21), notice the issues Luke believes to be at stake. The High Priest's emissaries charge Paul with profaning the Jerusalem sanctuary and being a "ringleader of the Nazarenes," an early Jewish designation of the Christian "sect" (24:1–9). In his defense, Paul insists that he adheres to "the written Law" (an assertion contradicted in his letters), that he has done nothing to profane the Temple, and that the "real issue" is that of Jesus' resurrection from the dead (24:10–21).

Christians' political innocence. Addressing Luke-Acts to Theophilus, who may have been an influential Greco-Roman official, the author attaches great importance to showing that from its inception Christianity is not incompatible with Roman law. Luke uses Paul's case to demonstrate his thesis and devotes approximately three chapters to Paul's two-year imprisonment in **Caesarea,** the Roman administrative capital of Palestine (chs. 23–26).

According to Luke, two Roman governors, Felix and his successor Porcius Festus, personally absolve Paul of any illegal activity (25:25; 26:30–32). In one of Hellenistic literature's most dramatic courtroom scenes, Luke shows Paul facing not only the Roman emperor's personal representative, Festus, but also rulers of Herod's line. King Julius Agrippa II, son of Herod Agrippa I, who had beheaded the Apostle James (12:1–2), appears with his sister (and mistress) Bernice. Since Festus is married to Drusilla, another of King Agrippa's sisters, the Apostle confronts a ruling family in which the power of Rome and Jewish royalty are combined. In this confrontation, Luke shows Paul fulfilling Jesus' earlier prophecy that the Apostle would testify "before kings" and the "people of Israel" (9:15).

Paul's long speech (26:1–29) is a vivid summary of his career as depicted in Acts, including a third account describing his "heavenly" vision of the risen Jesus. This discourse corresponds more closely to Paul's own account of his conversion (Gal. 1:1, 15–17) than do Acts' two earlier versions, but the author still represents Paul as operating under Jewish Law—asserting "nothing beyond what was foretold by the prophets and by Moses." In the author's view, Christianity is the logical and legitimate development of Judaism. Thus, Jews have no cause to condemn it as a perversion of their Mosaic heritage.

Luke's main emphasis, however, is that his hero is totally innocent. Echoing Pilate's opinion of Jesus, Governor Festus admits that Paul is guilty of "nothing that deserves death or imprisonment." Agrippa drives home the point: Paul could have been released a free man if "he had not appealed to the Emperor" (26:30–32). In Luke's presentation of the early church to Greco-Roman readers, the author makes clear that missionaries like Paul are prosecuted in Roman courts only through officials' misunderstanding or the malice of their false accusers.

Paul's Journey to Rome and His Preaching to Roman Jews

Luke begins his final section—Paul's sea journey to Rome—with an exciting account of a shipwreck (27:1–28:31). Told in the first person, this description of a Roman cargo ship disintegrating amid storm and pounding waves reads like an eyewitness experience. (We do not know whether the author uses the diary of a participant in this passage or simply employs the first person "we" as a literary device to heighten the immediacy of his narrative.) As always in Acts, the incident is included for its theological meaning: although Paul is a prisoner perhaps destined for conviction and death, he comforts his Roman captors during their danger at sea, assuring them that Jesus destines him (and them) to arrive safely in Rome. As Paul had prophesied, all aboard—crew, military officers, and prisoner—survive the ordeal unscathed, swimming ashore on the Island of Malta (27:6–44).

Paul's activity in Rome. Luke concludes his history of the early church with Paul's arrival in Rome, where the Apostle, kept under house arrest, enjoys considerable freedom to receive many visitors and to preach openly. The author does not reveal Paul's ultimate fate. One tradition states that after remaining in the capital for two years, Paul was released and carried out his planned missionary trip to Spain (Rom. 15:24). Many historians, however, believe that Paul's first Roman imprisonment led to his execution, perhaps about 62 CE, following the emperor **Nero's** order to impose the death penalty on any persons who spoke or behaved in a way that appeared to undermine his supreme authority. Other scholars date Paul's death at about 64 or 65 CE, when Nero first persecuted Christians as a group. According to a brief reference in 1 Clement, a letter from the church overseer in Rome (about 96 CE), both Peter and Paul were martyred during Nero's persecution.

Some critics suggest that Luke, deeply concerned with Christianity's legal status in the Roman Empire, deliberately omits mentioning that Paul and Peter, like Jesus, were tried and executed for treason against Rome. This unfortunate outcome for the religion's two leading proponents runs counter to the author's insistence that Christianity is a lawful faith innocent of any sedition against the state.

Most scholars contend that Acts ends abruptly not because Luke wants to avoid political facts that do not fit his theme but because he regards Paul's evangelizing in Rome as the fulfillment of his purpose in writing. Luke's conclusion well illustrates his principal historical-theological interest: Paul resolves to focus his message on receptive Gentiles, turning his primary attention from Jews to a Greco-Roman audience. Luke sees the church's future in the teeming millions of non-Jews throughout Rome's vast empire, a vision confirmed by later history.

As a believer who intuits religious meaning from historical events, Luke completes his picture of primitive Christianity with a sketch of Paul—representing the church's mission to all nations—vigorously proclaiming his vision of God ruling through Jesus. To Luke, Paul's activity symbolizes the divinely commanded business of the church that must continue into the remote future. Rather than end his account with a reaffirmation of Jesus' apocalyptic return (the Parousia), Luke looks to a future in which the "kingdom" can be preached "openly and without hindrance," attaining a recognized legal position in the world.

Acts' ending thus echoes Jesus' departing words to the disciples recorded at the book's beginning. Believers are not "to know about dates or times" (apocalyptic speculations about the world's end) because such knowledge belongs exclusively to "the Father" and has been "set within his own control." Instead, Christians are to carry the "good news" of Jesus "to the ends of the earth" (1:7–8). With Paul's arrival in Rome, the work is well begun. Its completion Luke entrusts to his readers.

A continuation of Luke's Gospel, Acts is a theologically oriented history of the early Christian church. Focusing principally on two representative leaders of the faith, Peter and Paul, it traces the church's growth from exclusively Jewish origins in Jerusalem to its dissemination throughout the northeastern Roman Empire. The church's rapid expansion from a Jewish nucleus to an international community composed of many different ethnic groups brings major problems of adjustment, particularly the question of requiring Gentiles to observe the Jewish Torah.

In many respects, the Book of Acts is an **apology** (*apologia,* an explanation or defense) for Christianity. Luke's history of Christian origins defends the *new* religion as the legitimate outgrowth of Judaism and a lawful faith intended for citizens of the Roman Empire. Luke stresses that there is no necessary or inherent conflict between Christianity and the Jewish religion that gave it birth or the Roman state in which it finds its natural environment. As in his Gospel, he minimizes early expectations of an imminent Parousia and emphasizes the church's objective to expand indefinitely into the distant future. Eager to find accommodation with the imperial government, the author makes no criticism of Roman officials but invariably pictures them as fair-minded and competent. He attributes Roman suspicion of the faith to the ill will of its Jewish opponents. Historically, Luke-Acts paves the way for the adoption of Christianity as the empire's official religion, a triumph foreshadowed by Paul's preaching in Rome "without [legal] hindrance."

QUESTIONS FOR DISCUSSION AND REVIEW

1. A sequel to Luke's Gospel, the Book of Acts continues the story of Christian origins. Which of the same themes that appear in the Gospel are also found in Acts? Compare the account of Jesus' trial before Pilate with that of Paul before Pilate's successors, Felix and Festus.

2. How does Luke organize his account of Christianity's birth and growth? Identify the leaders of the Jerusalem church and the missionaries who first helped carry "the new Way" into the larger world beyond the Jewish capital.

3. In recording the events of Pentecost, how does Luke emphasize his theme that Christianity is a universal religion—led by the Holy Spirit and destined for peoples of all nations? In the author's view, what ancient Hebrew prophecy is fulfilled by the Spirit's descent upon the first disciples?

4. In what ways does the Jerusalem commune put into operation the social and economic principles enunciated in Luke's Gospel? How

does the early church "equalize" wealth and poverty?

5. Summarize the events that led to the expansion of "the Way" from Jerusalem into Judea and Samaria. Describe the roles of Stephen and Philip in this process.

6. The conversions of an Ethiopian eunuch and a Roman centurion are milestones in Christianity's transformation from a Jewish sect into an international religion dominated by Gentiles. Explain how this process of ethnic change led to problems in the early church. According to Acts 15, how is the problem resolved at the first church conference in Jerusalem?

7. Describe the roles played by Barnabas and his partner, Paul (formerly Saul) of Tarsus. Summarize the results of Paul's three missionary journeys into Gentile territories. What sequence of events leads to Paul's arrest and his imprisonments in Caesarea and Rome?

8. By adding a history of primitive Christianity to his Gospel narrative, how does Luke deemphasize apocalyptic hopes of Jesus' early return? What future does Paul's arrival in Rome forecast for church-state relations?

TERMS AND CONCEPTS TO REMEMBER

ascension
Jesus' postresurrection
    commission to
    the Apostles
Matthias
Pentecost
Holy Spirit
glossolalia
Rabbi Gamaliel
Hellenists
Hebrews

Stephen
Saul of Tarsus
Philip
Barnabas
Paul
the Jerusalem
    conference
Athens
Corinth
Luke's *apologia*
    (defense)

RECOMMENDED READING

Bruce, F. F. *Commentary on the Book of Acts.* Grand Rapids, Mich.: Eerdmans, 1956.

Cadbury, H. J. "Acts of the Apostles." In *The Interpreter's Dictionary of the Bible,* vol. 1, 28–42. Nashville: Abingdon Press, 1962. A general introduction.

Fitzmyer, J. A., and R. J. Dillon. "Acts of the Apostles." In *The Jerome Bible Commentary,* edited by R. E. Brown and J. A. Fitzmyer, vol. 2, 28–42. Englewood Cliffs, N.J.: Prentice-Hall, 1968. A thorough introductory study.

Haenchen, Ernst. *The Acts of the Apostles: A Commentary.* Philadelphia: Westminster Press, 1971. An excellent study.

Hanson, R. P. C. *The Acts.* New York: Oxford University Press, 1967.

Hengel, Martin. *Acts and the History of Earliest Christianity.* Philadelphia: Fortress Press, 1980.

Juel, Donald. *Luke-Acts: The Promise of History.* Atlanta: John Knox, 1984.

Talbert, C. H. *Acts.* Atlanta: John Knox, 1984.

FOR MORE ADVANCED STUDY

Conzelmann, Hans. *The Theology of St. Luke.* Translated by G. Buswell. New York: Harper & Row, 1961. Scholarly and influential.

Dibelius, Martin. *Studies in the Acts of the Apostles.* Translated by M. Ling. Edited by H. Greeven. New York: Scribner's, 1956. A standard reference.

Dunn, J. D. G. *Unity and Diversity in the New Testament.* Philadelphia: Westminster Press, 1977. A stimulating analysis of the several different forms of early Christianity; covers the conflicts between the Palestinian Jewish Christians and the Hellenistic Gentile church.

Keck, L. E., and J. L. Martyn, eds. *Studies in Luke-Acts.* Nashville: Abingdon Press, 1966 (reprinted 1980). An important collection of scholarly essays on recent approaches to Luke's writings.

Lohse, Eduard. *The First Christians: Their Beginnings, Writings, and Beliefs.* Philadelphia: Fortress Press, 1983.

Malherbe, A. J. *Social Aspects of Early Christianity.* 2d ed. Philadelphia: Fortress Press, 1983.

Markus, R. A. *Christianity in the Roman World.* New York: Scribner's, 1974. Traces the growth of Christianity from outlawed sect to state religion of imperial Rome.

Talbert, C. H. *Luke-Acts: New Perspectives from the SBL Seminar.* Los Angeles: Crossroads, 1984.

Theissen, Gerd. *The Sociology of Early Palestinian Christianity.* Philadelphia: Fortress Press, 1978.

Tiede, D. L. *Prophecy and History in Luke-Acts.* Philadelphia: Fortress Press, 1980.

Wilken, R. L. *The Christians as the Romans Saw Them.* New Haven: Yale University Press, 1984. A careful analysis of the social, religious, and political conflicts between early Christians and their Roman critics.

Williams, C. S. C. *A Commentary on the Acts of the Apostles.* New York: Harper & Row, 1957. Another helpful study.

13 Paul: Apostle to the Nations

I am a free man . . . but I have made myself every
man's servant. . . . To the Jews I became like a Jew,
to win Jews. . . . To win Gentiles . . . I made myself
like one of them. Indeed, I have become everything in
turn to men of every sort, so that in one way or
another I may save some.

Paul to the church at Corinth (1 Cor. 9:19–22)

KEY THEMES Paul is second only to Jesus in his contribution to the development of
Christianity. Although Paul apparently never knew the living Jesus and once
persecuted his disciples, he experienced an *apokalypsis* (revelation) of the
risen Christ that transformed his life. Becoming a missionary to the
Gentiles, Paul created and disseminated a view of Jesus' cosmic significance
that profoundly shaped the future course of Christian thought. A former
Pharisee rigorously educated in Torah interpretation, Paul reinterprets parts
of the Hebrew Bible to defend his thesis that faith in Jesus' saving power
replaces Torah obedience as the means of reconciling human beings to God.

Paul's role in Acts, dominating the entire second half of the book, is historically appropriate. No other early Christian has so powerfully influenced the subsequent development of Christianity. As many scholars have observed, Paul ranks second only to Jesus as the force that determined both the content and the historical course of the new religion. The author of Acts shows Paul mainly as a worker, journeying tirelessly throughout the northeastern Mediterranean region, preaching "the new Way" to Jews and Gentiles alike. In Acts, he makes three sweeping missionary tours, evangelizing Syria, Asia Minor, and Greece, founding and revisiting new churches, and all the while enduring severe opposition, hardship, and imprisonment. To Luke, Paul is the model of hard work and endurance, the prime example for other believers to imitate.

Paul's lasting influence stems primarily not from his work, however, but from his writing.

Church tradition ascribes no fewer than thirteen canonical letters to him, in total length nearly one-third of the New Testament. Most scholars regard only seven to nine letters as genuinely Pauline, but the presence of other works attributed to Paul shows in what high esteem he was held. His ideas and personality so captured the imagination of later Christian authors that they paid tribute to the great Apostle by writing in his name and perpetuating his teaching.

In contrast to Jesus, who apparently wrote nothing, Paul speaks directly to us through his letters, permitting us to compare what he says about himself with what later writers, such as Luke, say about him. Paul's position in the canon is unique: he is the only historical personage who is both a major character in a New Testament book and the author of New Testament books himself. Paul's writings are immensely significant, not only because they are the earliest surviving Christian documents but also because

The Apostle Paul by Rembrandt (1606–1669). Rembrandt's somber portrait shows Paul in a deeply reflective mood and stresses the Apostle's consciousness of the enormous burden he bears—the task of communicating his unique vision of Christ to the Gentiles. In his letters Paul expresses a wide variety of emotions—joy, anger, bitter sarcasm— but Rembrandt captures here the sense of melancholy and isolation that typically characterize this great missionary. (Courtesy of National Gallery of Art, Washington, D.C. Widener Collection.)

they represent the first attempt to construct a theology explaining the nature and function of Christ. As the church's first major theologian, who labored selflessly to transform Christianity from a Torah-abiding Jewish sect into a cosmopolitan religion accessible to all nationalities, Paul made a contribution to religious history that is difficult to overstate.

Seeking the Historical Paul

As a Christian thinker, Paul never forgets his Jewishness. Although he fights to free Christianity from the "bondage" of Torah observance, Paul consistently stresses the unbroken continuity between Judaism and the new religion. For him, as for Matthew, Christianity is revealed through Jesus' ministry but shaped and largely defined by the Hebrew Bible. Throughout his letters Paul quotes selected parts of the Hebrew Scriptures to support the validity of his particular gospel. Despite Paul's ambivalent attitude toward the Mosaic Torah, much of the Jewish biblical tradition retains its teaching authority for him.

Our most reliable source of Paul's biography is his letters, where he repeatedly stresses his Jewish heritage. Describing himself as a circumcised "Hebrew born and bred" from the Israelite tribe of Benjamin (Phil. 3:5–6), Paul states that as a "practicing Jew" he outstripped his Jewish contemporaries in strict observance of "the traditions of [his] ancestors" (Gal. 1:13–14). A member of the **Pharisee** sect, he obeyed the Torah completely. "In legal rectitude"—keeping the Torah commandments—Paul judges himself "faultless" (Phil. 3:6).

Before his call to follow Jesus, Paul demonstrated his loyalty to Pharisaic Judaism by persecuting those who believed that Jesus was the Jewish Messiah. Whatever the nature of Paul's supernatural encounter with the risen Christ (Acts 9:1–9; 22:3–11; 16:12–19), it radically changed his attitude toward Christianity without modifying his essential personality. According to Acts and his own testimony, he displayed the same quality of religious zeal before Jesus appeared to him as he does afterward. Paul's experience seems less a conversion from one religion to another (he always stresses the connection between Judaism and the new faith) than a redirection of his abundant energies.

The Historical Reliability of Acts

Acts supplies much information about Paul not contained in his letters, but most scholars urge great caution about accepting Acts' data at face value. A great deal of the material in the letters is difficult to reconcile with Acts' narrative sequence. Where discrepancies occur, scholars prefer Paul's firsthand version of events. The author of Acts investigated various sources to compile his account of Christianity's beginnings (Luke 1:1–4), but he appears to have worked with inadequate documentation in recording Paul's career. As noted in Chapters 9 and 12, the author seems unaware of Paul's voluminous correspondence, his insistent claims to apostleship, and his distinctive teaching. Acts says virtually nothing about Paul's essential gospel—that people are saved not by obedience to Torah commands but by faith in Christ. More to the point, the writer of Acts is concerned primarily with outlining a precise scheme of history into which he fits his characters as it seems appropriate.

In some cases Acts provides biographical details that Paul never mentions, such as his birth in Tarsus, capital city of Cilicia (now included in southeastern Turkey) and the belief that Paul's family possessed Roman citizenship. These and similar traditions—such as Paul's originally being named Saul, his studying at the feet of Rabbi Gamaliel (the leading Pharisee scholar of his day), and his supporting himself by tent making—are never referred to in the Pauline letters, so we have no way of verifying their historical accuracy.

Other statements in Acts seem to contradict Paul's direct testimony (see Box 13-1), particularly the chronological order of events following his decisive confrontation with the risen Jesus. With Acts' reliability in question and Paul's biographical disclosures so few, scholars are unable to reconstruct anything resembling a satisfactory life of Christianity's Apostle to the Gentiles. We do not know when he was born, how his family gained Roman citizenship (if Acts is correct on this point), whether he was once married, where or when he wrote many of his letters, and under what precise circumstances he died. These and other missing facts are more than compensated for, however, in the brilliant revelation of thought and personality that his letters impart.

BOX 13-1   *Some Differences Between Acts and Paul's Letters*

Acts	Paul's Letters
Named Saul and raised in Tarsus	Not mentioned (but born to tribe of Benjamin, whose first king was Saul [Phil. 3:5])
Studied under Rabbi Gamaliel	Not mentioned
Belonged to the Pharisee party	Confirmed in Phil. 3:6
Persecuted Christians	Mentioned several times
Experienced a vision of Jesus on the road to Damascus	Received a "revelation" of Jesus (Gal. 1:12, 16)
Following his call, went immediately to Damascus, where he preached in synagogues	Went to "Arabia" for unspecified period (Gal. 1:17)
At first is shunned by Jerusalem disciples, is later introduced to Apostles (9:26–30)	Did not go to Jerusalem until three years after return from Arabia and met only Peter and James (Gal. 1:17–20)
Receives Holy Spirit after Ananias baptizes and lays hands upon him	Asserts he owes his apostolic gospel and commission to no one; never refers to baptism (Gal. 1:11–12, 16–17)
Attendance at apostolic conference is his third Jerusalem visit	Conference marks Paul's second Jerusalem visit (Gal. 2:1–10)
Agrees to impose Jewish dietary restrictions on Gentile converts	Refuses to accept any legal restrictions (Gal. 2:5)
Agrees to forbid eating meat sacrificed to idols	Regards eating such meat as undefiling (1 Cor. 8; 10:27; Rom. 14:13–15:6)

Paul's Experience of the Risen Jesus

In both Acts and the letters, Paul's life can be divided into two contrasting parts. During his early career he was a devout Pharisee who "savagely" persecuted the first Christians. During his later years he was a Christian missionary who successfully implanted the new religion in non-Jewish territories and established the first churches of Europe. The event that changed Paul from a persecutor of Christians into an indomitable Christian evangelist was, in his words, "a revelation [*apokalypsis*] of Jesus Christ" (Gal. 1:12). Acts depicts the "revelation" as a blinding vision of the risen Messiah on the road to Damascus. The author stresses the importance of the event by narrating it fully three times (Acts 9:1–9; 22:3–11; 26:12–19). Paul's briefer allusions to the experience speak simply of being called by God's "grace" (Gal. 1:15) to an "abnormal birth" and of witnessing a postresurrection appearance of Jesus (1 Cor. 15:8–9). Paul does not state what form the apparition took, but he does imply that he maintained an ongoing communication with divine beings, experiencing a number of mystical visions (2 Cor. 12:1–10).

Paul's physical stamina—even today duplicating his travel itinerary would exhaust most people—is matched by the strength of his feelings. Paul's letters reveal their author's emotional intensity, ranging from paternal tenderness to biting sarcasm. In one letter he insults his readers' intelligence and suggests that some of their advisers castrate themselves (Gal. 3:1; 5:12). In other letters he reacts to criticism with threats, wild boasting, and wounding anger (2 Cor. 10–13). In still others he expresses profound affection and gentle tact (1 Cor. 13; Phil. 1:3–9; 2:1–4; 4:2–3).

Paul's conviction that Jesus had privately revealed to him the one true gospel (Gal. 1–2) isolated the Apostle from many fellow believers. Acts and the letters agree that Paul quarreled with many of his intimate companions (Acts 15:37–39; Gal. 2:11–14) as well with entire groups (Gal.; 2 Cor. 10–13). This sense of a unique vision, one not shared by most other Christians, may have shaped Paul's admitted preference for preaching in territories where no Christian had preceded him. The more distant his missionary field from competing evangelizers, the better it suited him. Paul's desire to impress his individual gospel upon new converts may have influenced his ambition to work in areas as far removed from established churches as possible (Rom. 15:20–23).

Dating Paul's Career

In his letter to the Galatians, Paul briefly summarizes his career up to the time of writing, giving us a few clues on which to base a rough chronology of his life. After the decisive "revelation" of Jesus, "without going up to Jerusalem" to consult the Twelve, Paul went immediately to "Arabia" (probably an area east of the Jordan River), staying there an unspecified time before returning to Damascus. Only after "three years" had passed did he travel to Jerusalem "to get to know **Cephas**" (Peter's Aramaic name). Staying precisely two weeks with Peter (Paul evidently counted the days), he visited no other "Apostle" except "James the Lord's brother." Paul insists on this point because he wants to stress his complete independence of the Jerusalem leadership: "What I write is plain truth; before God I am not lying" (Gal. 1:16–20).

After making Peter's acquaintance, Paul went north to Syria, allowing another fourteen years to elapse before he again visited Jerusalem. The occasion for this second visit is almost certainly the church conference described in Acts 15, a meeting of delegates from Antioch with the Jerusalem congregation to discuss whether Gentile Christians must become circumcised or follow other provisions of the Mosaic Law. Paul remembers the gathering as less formal than Acts depicts it, emphasizing his private conversations with the three "pillars" of the Jerusalem leadership—Peter, John, and Jesus' kinsman James. Observing that **Titus**, a Greek youth accompanying him, was not required to become circumcised, Paul declares that the three Jerusalem "pillars" recognized the legitimacy of his peculiar "gospel" proclaiming freedom from the Torah's "bondage." The Jerusalem leaders shake hands on this agreement and endorse Paul as the recognized missionary to the Gentiles as Peter is to the Jews (Gal. 2:1–10).

Paul's account indicates that approximately seventeen years (or about fifteen, when calculated by the Hebrew method) passed between the time of his initial vision and the conference held in Jerusalem. If the Jerusalem conference took place about 49 CE, as many historians believe, then Paul must have become a Christian about 32 or (more likely) 34 CE, shortly after Jesus' crucifixion.

Two allusions to historical figures help us fix other dates in Paul's life. The first is a reference to King Aretas, whose commissioner forced Paul to escape from Damascus by being lowered down the city wall in a basket (2 Cor. 11:32–33). Aretas IV ruled the powerful Arab kingdom of Nabatea (located south and east of Palestine) between about 9 and 39 CE. Fixing the time of Aretas' reign confirms the assumption that Paul was already an active Christian missionary during the same decade that witnessed Jesus' death.

The second historical reference (Acts 18:11) notes that Gallio was the Roman governor of Greece during the period of Paul's Corinthian visit. Since Gallio's administration took place between about 51 and 53 CE and since Paul had been in Corinth for about eighteen months when he was brought before the governor, Paul probably arrived in that city about 49 or 50 CE. Additional evidence tends to confirm that date. Acts refers to the Emperor Claudius' expulsion of Jews from Rome, a decree enacted about 49 CE. Two Jewish Christians, Aquila and Priscilla, had recently moved from Rome to Corinth when Paul arrived in the city (Acts 18:1–2).

Paul's Letters

The genuine letters. New Testament historians generally agree that Paul became a Christian in the mid-30s CE and that he traveled extensively as a missionary during the 40s and 50s CE, arriving in Rome about the year 60. Scholarly agreement disappears, however, in attempting to date Paul's letters or even establish the exact order in which he wrote them.

The majority of scholars accept seven to nine letters as authentically Pauline. Virtually all scholars regard Romans, 1 and 2 Corinthians, Galatians, Philippians, 1 Thessalonians, and Philemon as Paul's own writing. Many also accept 2 Thessalonians and Colossians. By contrast, the majority doubt that Ephesians is genuine and are certain that three—Titus and 1 and 2 Timothy—were composed by a Pauline disciple after the Apostle's death. Almost no reputable scholar believes that Hebrews, which is a sermon rather than a letter, is a Pauline composition.

Order of composition. Although scholars debate the exact order in which Paul composed his letters, they generally agree that 1 Thessalonians was written first (about 50 CE) and is thus the oldest Christian writing in existence. If Paul also wrote 2 Thessalonians, it also dates from about 50 CE. 1 and 2 Corinthians are usually placed in the mid-50s, and the more theo-

logically mature letters, such as Romans and Philippians, are dated later. Four letters—Colossians, Philemon, Philippians, and possibly Ephesians—were reputedly composed while Paul was imprisoned and are known as the "captivity letters." Unfortunately, Paul does not reveal in the letters where he was jailed, so we do not know whether he wrote them from Ephesus, Caesarea, or Rome, all cities in which he presumably suffered imprisonment. The canonical letters (others have been lost) were probably all written during a relatively brief span of time, the decade between about 50 and 60 CE.

Paul's use of the letter form. Paul is aware that his letters are persuasive documents. He consciously uses letters as substitutes for his own presence, making them an effective means of influencing people and events from a distance. Although he gives directions on a wide variety of matters, his primary object is to correct his recipients' beliefs and to discipline their behavior. His letters are also potent weapons for shooting down opposition to his teaching.

Writing to the Corinthians, Paul states that his critics contrast his "weighty and powerful" letters with his unimpressive physical appearance and ineffectiveness as a speaker (2 Cor. 10:9–11). The Apostle may exaggerate his defects for rhetorical effect, but he is right about his letters. From the time they were first written until now, they have exerted enormous influence on Christian thought and conduct.

Paul writes letters so effectively that he makes this literary category the standard medium of communication for many later Christian writers. The large majority of New Testament authors imitate Paul by conveying their ideas in letter form. Twenty-one of the twenty-seven canonical books are (at least theoretically) letters. Even the writer of Revelation uses this form to transmit Jesus' message to the seven churches of Asia Minor (Rev. 2–3).

Hellenistic letters. In general, Paul follows the accepted Hellenistic literary form in his correspondence, modifying it somewhat to express his peculiarly Christian interests. Much Greco-Roman correspondence, both personal and business, has survived from early Christian times, allowing us to compare Paul's letters with those of other Hellenistic writers.

The Hellenistic letter writer typically begins with a prescript, identifying the writer and the reader, and a greeting, wishing good fortune to the reader and commonly invoking the blessing of a god. Paul varies this formula by mentioning the Christian allegiance of the writer and recipients, substituting "grace" and "peace" for the customary greetings, and frequently including an associate's name in the salutation. He also elaborates upon the Hellenistic custom by giving praise, thanks, or prayers for the welfare of his recipients. A typical example of Paul's modification of the Hellenistic greeting appears in the opening of 1 Thessalonians:

> From Paul, Silvanus, and Timothy to the congregation of Thessalonians who belong to God the Father and the Lord Jesus Christ. Grace to you and peace.
>
> (1 Thess. 1:1)

Paul also modifies his letters' prescripts according to his attitude toward the church he is addressing. Paul's letter to his trusted friends at Philippi opens with an effusive outpouring of affection and praise for the Philippians (Phil. 1:1–11). By contrast, when he writes to the churches in Galatia he is furious with the recipients and includes no warm or approving salutation (Gal. 1:1–5).

After stating the letter's principal message, the Hellenistic writer closes with additional greetings, typically including greetings from other people and sometimes adding a request that the recipient(s) convey the sender's greetings to mutual acquaintances. Paul often expands this custom to include a summary statement of faith and a benediction as well as a list of fellow Christians to be greeted (Rom. 16; 1 Cor. 16:10–21; Col. 4:7–18).

Role of dictation. As was customary in Greco-Roman correspondence, Paul apparently dictated all his letters to a secretary or scribe, occasionally adding a signature or a few other words in his own hand. In antiquity, secretaries ordinarily did not record the precise words of those dictating but paraphrased the gist of what was said (Rom. 16:21–22; Gal. 6:11; Col. 4:18; Philem. 19; 2 Thess. 3:17), a practice that helps to explain the spontaneous quality of Pauline letters.

Circumstances of writing. Most of Paul's letters are composed under the pressure of meeting an emergency in a given church. With the exception of Romans, which is addressed to a congregation that he had not yet visited, every Pauline letter is directed to a particular group, and most of the groups are personally known by the writer. In virtually every case, the recipients are experiencing some form of crisis, either of belief or behavior, which the author tries to resolve.

Paul's main concern is always pastoral; he deals with individual problems caused by church members' teaching or conduct. In counseling these small groups of infant Christians, Paul typically invokes theological arguments or examples to reinforce his advice. Because Paul's presentation of theological issues is secondary to his counseling, the letters do not represent a complete or systematic statement of Pauline belief. In addition, the reader will find Paul's thought changing and developing from one letter to another.

Paul's Major Topics and Themes

Pauline thought is commonly subtle and complex, so much so that even scholars are not able to achieve a consensus about the Apostle's views on many important topics. Among the major Pauline topics and concepts are the following:

1. *Eschatology.* In Jesus' life, death, and resurrection God has inaugurated a new age. Paul's generation lives at a crucial time of divine judgment. Recently ascended to heaven, Jesus will soon return to deliver the faithful and resurrect believers who have already died. This is the principal theme of 1 Thessalonians and 1 Corinthians 15.

2. *The centrality and preeminence of Jesus.* Absolutely central to Paul's thought is his conviction that in Jesus God accomplishes the world's salvation. Although Paul shows almost no interest in Jesus' earthly ministry or teachings (if he knew them in any detail), he sees the heavenly Christ in three roles: (1) as God's revealed wisdom (1 Cor. 1–4); (2) as the divine Lord through whom God rules (Phil. 2:11; Rom. 10:9; 1 Cor. 15:24–28); and (3) as the means by whom God's Spirit dwells in believers (Rom. 8; 14:17). The operation of the Spirit, God's active force denoting his presence and effecting his will in the world, characterizes all of Paul's churches.

3. *Christ and humanity.* In contrasting Christ with the symbol of earthly humanity, Adam (in Genesis, God's first human creation), Paul emphasizes the vast change Jesus' activity has effected for the human race. Prior to Jesus' coming, human beings existed in Adam's perishable image, victims of sin and death (Rom. 5:12–21). By contrast, believers now "in Christ" (living under his power) will also share in the glorified Christ's life-giving nature (1 Cor. 15:21–24, 45–49). "As in Adam all men die, so in Christ all will be brought to life. . . ."

4. *The faithful as Christ's body.* Using a corporate image to identify the believing community as the earthly manifestation of the exalted Christ, Paul states that the faithful collectively are Christ's "body" (1 Cor. 10:16–18; 12:12–30; Rom. 12). As a people defined and influenced by the Spirit, the church functions in union with Christ so fully that it reveals his visible form.

5. *Christ as liberator from sin, Torah, and death.* In Paul's view, all human beings are negatively influenced by sin's power and hence alienated from the perfect God (Rom. 7). Sin's invariable consequence is death, a condition of the defective humanity we share with Adam (Rom. 5:12–21). By defining the nature as well as the punishment of sin, the Torah increased its power, revealing the universality of sin and condemning all sinners—the entire human race (Rom. 1–3).

Christ's total obedience to the Father and his selfless death on the cross, taking unto himself the Torah's penalty for sin, liberates those persons accepting him (living fully under his power) from sin, death, and the Torah's curses (Gal. 3–5; Rom. 3–7). For Paul, "freedom in Christ" means deliverance from the old order of sin and punishment, including the Torah's power to condemn.

6. *Christ's universal sufficiency.* To Paul, Jesus' sacrificial death and God's act in exalting Christ as the agent by whom God rules and imparts his Spirit constitute a total change in the relationship between God and humanity. Christ is the final and complete means of canceling the powers of sin and destruction. Because Christ is now all-sufficient in reconciling human beings to God, neither "angelic powers" nor the Torah any longer play a decisive role in achieving human salvation.

7. *Justification by faith.* Since union with Christ, coming under his rule and influence, is the only way provided to share in Christ's eternal life, good deeds or works of the Torah cannot save. To Paul, one is justified or "made right" before God only through placing faith or complete trust in Jesus' power to save persons with whom he is spiritually united.

Reading Paul's letters. In the New Testament canon, Paul's letters are listed roughly according to their length. Letters to churches, such as Romans, appear first, and those to individuals, such as Philemon, appear last. In this text we discuss the letters in the general order of their composition, beginning with 1 Thessalonians and concluding with later works like Philippians and Philemon.

Paul's letters challenge the reader by combining rational analysis with mystical insight in many unexpected ways. To meet Paul on his own terms, readers should keep his major preoccupations firmly in mind. Besides the themes listed above, two basic perspectives inform all of his writings: his apocalyptic viewpoint and his personal vision of Christ.

Paul's apocalyptic viewpoint. Paul's conviction that the end of time has arrived permeates his thought and underlies much of his ethical teaching. Paul's advice on marriage, divorce, slavery, celibacy, and human behavior in general is largely shaped by his expectation of an imminent Final Judgment.

Like many of his fellow Jews, Paul sees human history as divided into two qualitatively different ages, or periods of time. The present evil age will soon be replaced by a New Age, a new creation, in which God will reign completely (Gal. 6:14; 1 Cor. 15:20–28; 2 Cor. 5:17). Because the Messiah (Christ) has already come, Paul sees his generation as the last. His letters to infant churches burn with special urgency because he believes that his day marks the crucial transition period between the two ages. This apocalyptic viewpoint strongly affects Paul's entire concept of human life and its proper goals.

Paul's vision of Christ. The second key to Paul's letters is his personal experience of Christ. Unlike the Gospel authors, Paul does not build his view of Jesus on traditions about the historical human being. It is the glorified heavenly Christ that Paul knows, not the earthly Jesus of history (1 Cor. 15:3–8).

Paul bases both his calling as an Apostle and his individual teaching on his encounter with the postresurrection Jesus (Gal. 1:11–12, 15–17). This *apokalypsis* (revelation) informs Paul that the risen Jesus exists in two separate dimensions and possesses both an objective and a subjective reality. He is at once a cosmic figure who will soon return to judge the world and a being who also mysteriously dwells within the individual believer. The tension between the transcendent and the immanent Christ, one who is simultaneously universal and yet intimately experienced by the faithful, appears in almost every letter Paul wrote.

A sensitivity to Paul's apocalyptic hope and his mystical experience of Christ may make it easier for readers to appreciate Paul's ideas. Despite the difficulty of understanding some passages (2 Pet. 3:15–16), the rewards of entering the brilliant world of Pauline thought are well worth the effort.

QUESTIONS FOR DISCUSSION AND REVIEW

1. Summarize Paul's biography, from his career as a zealous Pharisee to his work as a missionary among Gentile populations in Macedonia and Greece. In what respects does the biographical information contained in Acts differ from that found in Paul's letters?

2. How did Paul's experience of a revelation (*apokalypsis*) of the risen Jesus change his life and affect his religious outlook?

3. Discuss some of the topics and themes that dominate Paul's letters, including his apocalyptic outlook and his views on faith, righteousness, justification, and the saving power of Christ.

TERMS AND CONCEPTS TO REMEMBER

Apostle to the Gentiles

apokalypsis (the "revelation" that changed Paul's life)

Paul's use of the letter form

Torah and faith justification by faith

Christ's role in human redemption

RECOMMENDED READING

Baird, W. R. "Paul." In *Harper's Bible Dictionary,* rev. ed., 757–65. San Francisco: Harper & Row, 1985. Basic introduction to Paul's life and thought.

Beker, J. C. *Paul the Apostle: The Triumph of God in Life and Thought.* Philadelphia: Fortress Press, 1980.

Bornkamm, Gunther. *Paul.* New York: Harper & Row, 1971.

Bruce, F. F. *Paul: Apostle of the Heart Set Free.* Grand Rapids, Mich.: Eerdmans, 1978.

Fitzmyer, J. A. "A Life of Paul." In *The Jerome Biblical Commentary,* edited by R. E. Brown and J. A. Fitzmyer, vol. 2, 215–22. Englewood Cliffs, N.J.: Prentice-Hall, 1968. Analysis by a leading Roman Catholic scholar.

Jewett, Robert. *A Chronology of Paul's Life.* Philadelphia: Fortress Press, 1979. Evaluates earlier systems of dating events in Paul's career and provides a new chronology.

Keck, L. E., *Paul and His Letters.* Proclamation Commentaries. Philadelphia: Fortress Press, 1979.

Keck, L. E., and V. P. Furnish. *The Pauline Letters.* Nashville: Abingdon Press, 1984. A brief introductory survey of selected Pauline ideas.

Meeks, W. A., ed. *The Writings of St. Paul.* New York: Norton, 1972. Contains texts of Paul's letters and a collection of interpretive essays by leading scholars.

Roetzel, C. J. *The Letters of Paul.* Atlanta: John Knox, 1982.

Sanders, E. P. *Paul, the Law, and the Jewish People.* Philadelphia: Fortress Press, 1983. Explores Paul's Jewish heritage.

Sandmel, Samuel. *The Genius of Paul: A Study of History.* Philadelphia: Fortress Press, 1979. An examination of Paul's distinctive teachings by a Jewish scholar.

Soards, Marion L. *The Apostle Paul: An Introduction to His Writings and Teaching.* Mahwah, N.J.: Paulist Press, 1987. A clearly written introduction to Paul's thought that incorporates the latest in New Testament scholarship.

14 Unity, Freedom, and Christ's Return: Paul's Letters to Thessalonica and Corinth

The time we live in will not last long. . . . For the
whole frame of this world is passing away.
(1 Cor. 7:29, 31)

KEY THEMES The dominant theme of Paul's letters to Thessalonica and Corinth is that the *eschaton* is near: Paul expects to witness Jesus' return and the resurrection of the dead in his lifetime (1 Thess. 4:13–18). However, believers must not waste time speculating about the projected date of the Parousia (1 Thess. 5:1–3). The urgency of 1 Thessalonians is tempered somewhat in 2 Thessalonians by the new idea that specific events (apocalyptic signs) must occur before the Second Coming can take place (2 Thess. 2:3–12).

Paul's letters to Corinth are aimed at healing serious divisions in the newly founded church there. Paul urges members to give up their destructive competitiveness and work toward unity of belief and purpose. His most important topics include (1) differences between human and divinely revealed wisdom (1:10–3:23); (2) Christian ethics and responsibilities (5:1–11:1); (3) behavior at the Communion meal (11:17–34) and the handling of gifts of the Spirit (chs. 12–14); and (4) the resurrection of the dead (ch. 15).

A composite work composed of several letters or letter fragments, 2 Corinthians shows Paul defending his apostolic authority (2 Cor. 10–13); chapters 1–9, apparently written after chapters 10–13, describe his reconciliation with the church at Corinth.

Paul's early letters are dominated by his eschatology. Convinced that the Messiah's death and resurrection have inaugurated end time, Paul strives to achieve several related goals. Traveling from city to city, he establishes small cells of believers whom he calls to a "new life in Christ." He argues that Jesus' crucifixion has brought freedom from both Torah observance and the power of sin, and he stresses the necessity of leading an ethically pure life while awaiting Christ's return. In his letters to the young Greek churches at Thessalonica and Corinth, Paul emphasizes the nearness of the Parousia—the Second Coming—an event that he believes to be imminent. Much of Paul's advice to these congregations is based on his desire that they achieve unity and purity before Christ reappears.

While he is attempting to keep believers faithful to the high ideals of Christian practice, Paul also finds himself battling opponents who question the correctness of his teaching and/or his apostolic authority. In the first generation of Christians, an Apostle was one whom Jesus had personally called to follow him and who had witnessed the resurrection (Acts 1:21–22). Not

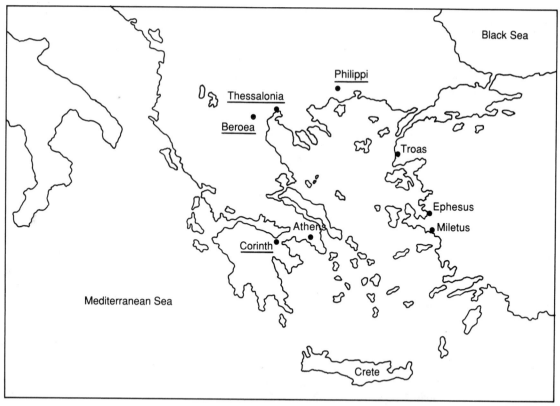

Figure 14-1. Paul established largely Gentile churches in the northeastern Mediterranean region at Philippi, Thessalonica, Beroea, and Corinth. Paul's teaching was also influential in the Asia Minor city of Ephesus, where he lived for at least two years.

only had Paul not known the earthly Jesus, he had cruelly persecuted the disciples. Paul's sole claim to apostolic status was his private revelation of the risen Lord, a claim others repeatedly challenged. To achieve the goal of guiding his flock through end time, Paul must ensure that his apostolic credentials are fully recognized (1 Cor. 15:9–10; 2 Cor. 11:1–13:10).

To appreciate the urgency of Paul's first letters, we must approach them from the writer's historical perspective: The Messiah's coming spelled an end to the old world. The new age—entailing the Final Judgment on all nations, a universal resurrection of the dead, and the ultimate fulfillment of God's purpose—was then in the process of materializing. Paul writes as a parent anxious that those in his care survive the apocalyptic ordeal just ahead and attain the saints' reward of eternal life.

First Letter to the Thessalonians

The oldest surviving Christian document, 1 Thessalonians was composed about 50 CE and sent to the newly formed Christian church at **Thessalonica** (now called Thessaloniki). Capital city of the Roman province of Macedonia, Thessalonica was located on the Via Egnatia, the major highway that linked Rome with the East. Although Acts (17:1–18:5) reports that Paul stayed only three weeks there and that he was involved mainly with Jews, the letter indicates a much longer initial visit and an association mainly with Gentiles (1 Thess. 1:9). The letter was probably written from Corinth.

Although the salutation includes Silvanus (Silas) and Timothy (1:1), Paul's missionary companions, the letter is from the Apostle himself (5:27). Paul does not mention his main purpose in writing—to correct beliefs about Jesus' Parousia and the resurrection—until the fourth chapter. The first three chapters are devoted to praising the Thessalonian Christians for their faith and generally good behavior. Gifted with the Holy Spirit, they are a shining example for believers throughout all Greece (1:7). Formerly worshipers of Greco-Roman deities, they have abandoned these "idols" to serve the Jewish God and eagerly await Jesus' imminent descent from heaven. Because they are faithful, the Parousia will rescue them from the terrors of the coming Judgment (1:9–10).

The Parousia and the Resurrection

After the long introductory section (1:1–4:12), Paul arrives at his principal reason for sending the letter—a clarification of his teaching about end time (4:13–5:11). Christians must cling firmly to their newfound faith and live ethically correct lives because Jesus will soon return to judge them. Apparently, some Thessalonians believed that the Parousia would occur so swiftly that all persons converted to Christ would live to see his Second Coming. That belief was shaken when some believers died before Jesus had reappeared. What would become of them? Had the dead missed their opportunity to join Christ in ruling over the world?

Paul explains that the recently dead are not lost but will share in the glory of Christ's return. Revealing his conviction that he would personally witness the Parousia, Paul states that "we who are left alive until the Lord comes" will have no advantage over the faithful dead. Using the traditional language of Jewish apocalyptic writing, Paul writes that when the trumpet-call of Final Judgment sounds, the Christian dead

will rise first. Simultaneously, Christians who are still alive—Paul and his fellow believers—will be lifted from earth into the air to join the resurrected saints on their journey to heaven. In both life and death, then, the believer remains with Jesus (4:13–18). (Compare 1 Thess. with Paul's more elaborate discussion of the resurrection in 1 Cor. 15.)

On Not Calculating "Dates and Times"

Although he eagerly expects Jesus' reappearance "soon," Paul has no patience with those who try to predict the exact date of the Parousia. He discourages speculation and notes that calculating "dates and times" is futile because the world's final day will come as quietly as a thief at midnight. Stressing the unexpectedness of the Parousia, Paul declares that it will occur while men proclaim "peace and security" (a common political theme in Roman times as well as the present). Disaster will strike the nations suddenly, as labor pains strike a woman without warning (5:1–3).

In the Hebrew Bible, the "Day of the Lord" was the time of Yahweh's intervention into human history, his visitation of earth to judge all nations and to impose his universal rule (Amos 5:18; Joel 2:14–15). In Paul's apocalyptic vision, Jesus serves as the divinely appointed agent of the *eschaton*. As the eschatological Judge, Jesus serves a double function: he brings punishment to the disobedient ("the terrors of judgment") but vindication and deliverance to the faithful. Paul's cosmic Jesus is paradoxical: he dies to save believers from the negative Judgment that his return imposes on unregenerate humanity. Returning to his main theme, Paul concludes that "we, awake [living] or asleep [dead]" live in permanent association with Christ (5:4–11).

Role of the Spirit. With anticipation of Jesus' speedy return a living reality, Paul reminds the Thessalonians that the Holy Spirit's visible activity among them is also evidence of the world's impending transformation. As noted in Acts, the Spirit motivating a believer to prophesy, heal, or speak in tongues was taken as evidence of the Deity's presence. Thus, Paul tells his readers not to "stifle inspiration" or otherwise discourage believers from prophesying. Christian prophets, inspired by the Spirit, play a major role in Pauline churches, but Paul is aware that enthusiastic visionaries can cause trouble. Believers are to distinguish between "good" and "bad" inspirations, avoiding the latter, but they are not to inhibit charismatic behavior. Besides providing evidence that the End is near, the Spirit's presence also validates the Christian message (Joel 2:28–32; Acts 2:1–21; 1 Cor. 2:9–16; 12–14).

Second Letter to the Thessalonians

Nearly all scholars accept 1 Thessalonians as genuine, but many question the authenticity of 2 Thessalonians. If Paul actually composed it, why does he repeat—almost verbatim—so much of what he had already just written to the same recipients? More seriously, why does the author present an eschatology so different from that presented in the first letter? In 1 Thessalonians the Parousia will occur stealthily, "like a thief in the night." In 2 Thessalonians a number of apocalyptic "signs" will first advertise its arrival. The interposing of these mysterious events between the writer's time and that of the Parousia has the effect of placing the **eschaton** further into the future—a contrast to 1 Thessalonians, in which the End is extremely close.

Scholars defending Pauline authorship advance several theories to explain the writer's apparent change of attitude toward the Parousia. In the first letter Paul stresses the tension between the shortness of time the world has left and the necessity of believers' vigilance and ethical purity as they await the Second Coming. In the second missive Paul writes to correct the Thessalonians' misconceptions or abuses of his earlier emphasis on the nearness of end time.

If Paul is in fact the author, he probably wrote 2 Thessalonians within a few months of his earlier letter. Some converts, claiming that "the Day of the Lord is already here" (2:2), were upsetting others with their otherworldly enthusiasms. In their state of apocalyptic fervor, some even scorned everyday occupations and refused to work or support themselves. It is possible that the visionary Spirit of prophecy that Paul encouraged the Thessalonians to cultivate (1 Thess. 5:19–22) had come back to haunt him. Empowered by private revelations, a few Christian prophets may have interpreted the Spirit's presence—made possible by Jesus' resurrection and ascension to heaven—as a mystical fulfillment of the Parousia. According to this belief in presently realized eschatology, the Lord's Day is now. Paul, however, consistently stresses that Jesus' resurrection and the Spirit's coming are only the first stage in God's plan of cosmic renewal. God's purpose can be completed only at the apocalyptic end of history.

Placing the Second Coming in Perspective

In 2 Thessalonians Paul (or some other writer building on his thought) takes on the difficult task of urging Christians to be ever alert and prepared for the Lord's return and at the same time to remember that certain events must take place before the Second Coming can occur. The writer achieves this delicate balance partly by insisting on a rational and practical approach to life during the unknown interim between his writing and the Parousia.

Notice that the author invokes a vivid picture of the Final Judgment to imprint its imminent reality on his readers' consciousness. He paraphrases images from the Hebrew prophets to imply that persons now persecuting Christians will soon suffer God's wrath. Christ will be revealed from heaven amid blazing fire, overthrowing those who disobey Jesus' gospel or fail to honor the one God (1:1–12).

Having assured the Thessalonians that their present opponents will be punished at Jesus' return, Paul now admonishes them not to assume that the punishment will happen immediately. Believers are not to run wild over some visionary's claim that the End is already here. Individual prophetic revelations declaring that Jesus is now invisibly present were apparently strengthened when a letter—supposedly from Paul—conveyed the same or a similar message. (This pseudo-Pauline letter indicates that the practice of composing letters in Paul's name began very early in Christian history.) Speculations founded on private revelations or forged letters, the Apostle points out, are doomed to disappointment (2:1–3).

Traditional (Non-Pauline?) Signs of the End

As mentioned above, one of the strongest arguments against Paul's authorship of 2 Thessalonians is the letter's presentation of apocalyptic events that presage the End. Although the writer maintains the Parousia's imminence (1:6–10), he also insists that the final day cannot arrive until certain developments characteristic of Jewish apocalyptic thought have taken place. At this point 2 Thessalonians reverts to the cryptic and veiled language of apocalyptic discourse, referring to mysterious personages and events that may have been understood by the letter's recipients but that are largely incomprehensible to modern readers. The End cannot come before the final rebellion against God's rule, when evil is revealed in human form as a demonic enemy who desecrates the Temple and claims divinity for himself. In this passage Paul's terminology resembles that contained in the Book of Daniel, an apocalyptic work denouncing Antiochus IV, a Greek-Syrian king who polluted the Jerusalem Temple and tried to destroy the Jewish religion.

Some commentators suggest that Paul regards the Roman emperor, whose near-absolute power gave him virtually unlimited potential for inflicting evil on humankind, as a latter-day counterpart of Antiochus. Paul's explicitly stated view of the Roman government, however, is positive (Rom. 13), so readers must look elsewhere to identify the doomed figure.

Reminding the Thessalonians that he had previously informed them orally of these apocalyptic developments, Paul states that the mysterious enemy's identity will not be disclosed until the appointed time. This is an allusion to the typically apocalyptic belief that all history is predestined: events cannot occur before their divinely predetermined hour. Evil forces are already at work, however, secretly gathering strength until the unidentified "Restrainer" disappears, allowing the evil personage to reveal himself.

Apocalyptic dualism. In this passage the writer paints a typically apocalyptic world view, a moral dualism in which the opposing powers of good and evil have their respective agents at work on earth. The enemy figure is Satan's agent; his opposite is Christ. As Jesus is God's respresentative working in human history, so the wicked rebel is the devil's tool. Operating on a cosmic scope, the conflict between good and evil culminates in Christ's victory over his enemy, who has deceived the mass of humanity into believing the "Lie." (This is, perhaps, the false belief that any being other than God is the source of humanity's ultimate welfare.) An evil parody of the Messiah, the unnamed Satanic dupe functions as an anti-Christ (2:3–12).

The writer's language is specific enough to arouse speculation about the identities of the enigmatic "wicked man" and the "Restrainer" who at the time of writing kept the anti-Christ in check. It is also vague enough to preclude connecting any known historical figures with these apocalyptic roles. In typical apocalyptic fashion, the figures are mythic archetypes that belong to a realm beyond the reach of historical investigation.

Return to Practical Advice

After his bedazzling preview of future history, the writer makes sure that the Thessalonians return to the practical affairs of this present life. Notice that this section (3:6–16) firmly reanchors the church to its earthly obligations. The author cites Paul's example of hard work and directs his readers to avoid persons too lazy to support themselves. When he asserts that people who do not work will not eat, the writer suggests that at least some Thessalonians lived in a Christian commune similar to that in Jerusalem. Thus, leaders could control the food supply.

Notice the postscript (3:17–18)—the original of which was supposedly in Paul's own hand—and the statement that the Apostle verifies all his letters by adding his personal signature. Scholars doubting Pauline authorship of this letter view the pseudonymous writer as protesting overmuch, but the Apostle appends similar comments to genuine letters (1 Cor. 16:21–24; Gal. 6:11).

First Letter to the Corinthians

According to Acts (17:1–18:17), after establishing churches at Philippi, Thessalonica, and Beroea (all in northern Greece), Paul briefly visited Athens and then journeyed to Corinth, where he remained for a year and a half (about 50–52 CE). Accompanied by Priscilla and Aquila, Jewish Christians exiled from Rome, he subsequently sailed to Ephesus, from which city he addressed several letters to the Corinthians. The first letter has been lost (1 Cor. 5:9), but the books presently numbered 1 and 2 Corinthians embody the most voluminous correspondence with any single church group in the New Testament. 1 Corinthians is a single document, but scholars believe that 2 Corinthians is a patchwork of several Pauline letters or parts of letters written at different times and later combined by an editor.

Paul's correspondence with the Corinthian church was not a one-way affair, for the Corinthians also wrote to the Apostle (1 Cor. 7:1).

Delegations from Corinth also kept Paul in touch with the group (1:11; 16:15–18; 2 Cor. 7:5–7, 13). Preserving a comprehensive picture of the diversity of ideas and behavior of a youthful Jewish and Gentile church, the Corinthian letters give us an unrivaled sociological study of primitive Christianity.

The City and Its People

The emperor Augustus made Corinth, the richest and most populous city in Greece, the Greek capital in 27 BCE. By Paul's day Corinth had long been famous for its prosperity, trade, and materialism. As a busy seaport it was also notorious for its legions of prostitutes, who entertained sailors from every part of the Greco-Roman world. With Aphrodite—supreme goddess of love and fertility—as its patron deity, Corinth enjoyed a reputation for luxury and licentiousness remarkable even in pagan society. Given this libertine environment, it is not surprising that Paul devotes more space to setting forth principles of sexual ethics to the Corinthians than he does in letters to any other churches (1 Cor. 5:1–13; 7:1–40).

Recent sociological studies of early Christianity indicate that the Corinthian group may have been typical of Gentile churches in many parts of the Roman Empire. In the past many historians thought that the first Christians largely belonged to the lower social and economic ranks of Greco-Roman society. Recent analyses of Paul's Corinthian letters, however, suggest that early Christians came from many different social classes and represented a veritable cross-section of the Hellenistic world.

Paul's statement that "few" members of the Corinthian congregation were highborn, wealthy, or politically influential (1 Cor. 1:26–28) implies that some were. This inference is borne out by that fact that some Corinthian believers apparently held important positions in the city. Acts identifies the Crispus whom Paul baptized (1 Cor. 1:14) as the leader of a local synagogue, a function ordinarily given to persons rich enough to maintain the building. Erastus, who also seems to have belonged to the Corinthian church, was the civic treasurer (Rom. 16:23).

A diverse assortment of Jews and Gentiles, slaves and landowners, rich and poor, educated and unlettered, the Corinthian group was apparently divided by class distinctions and educational differences as well as by varieties of religious belief. Even in observing the communion ritual, members' consciousness of differences in wealth and social status threatened to fragment the membership (1 Cor. 11:17–34).

From Paul's responses to their attitudes and conduct, the reader learns that the Corinthians individually promoted a wide range of ideas. Some advocated a spiritual marriage in which sexual union played no part; others visited prostitutes. Some defrauded their fellow believers, causing victims to seek restitution in the public courts. Some, believing that other gods did not exist, dined at banquets in Greco-Roman temples and attended their religious ceremonies. Still others claimed a superior understanding of spiritual matters, viewed themselves as already living in the kingdom, denied the necessity of a bodily resurrection, or questioned Paul's right to dictate their behavior.

As the Corinthian correspondence shows, Paul faced the almost impossible challenge of bringing this divisive and quarrelsome group into a working harmony of belief and purpose. In reading Paul's letters to Corinth, remember that he is struggling to communicate his vision of union with Christ to an infant church that has apparently only begun to grasp the basic principles of Christian life.

Topics of Concern

Paul's first extant letter to the group is distinguished by some of his most memorable writing. Two passages in particular, chapter 13 (on love) and chapter 15 (on the resurrection), are highlights of Pauline thought and feeling. His praise of love (ch. 13) uses the Greek term

agape, "selfless love," as opposed to *eros,* the word denoting the sexual passion associated with Aphrodite. This may be an appropriate hint to those Corinthians sexually involved with persons other than their legal mates. Paul's mystic vision of attaining immortality (ch. 15) is the most extensive commentary on life after death in the New Testament. It also contains the earliest record of Jesus' resurrection appearances.

Organization. 1 Corinthians divides into two main sections. In the first six chapters Paul directly addresses his principal objective—helping the church, split by rivalries and factions, attain the unity befitting a Christian congregation. Here, Paul shows the futility of false wisdom, human competitiveness, and attempts to demonstrate Christian freedom by violating the sexual conventions honored even by unbelievers. In the second half (chs. 7–15) he answers specific questions addressed to him by the Corinthians. These issues include marriage and divorce, eating meat previously sacrificed to Greco-Roman gods, proper conduct during the Lord's Supper, and eschatology—the Final Judgment and resurrection of the dead.

Paul's eschatological urgency. As in his letters to the Thessalonians, Paul structures his advice to the Corinthian church according to his eschatological convictions. The Parousia is imminent: the Corinthians "wait expectantly for our Lord Jesus to reveal himself," for he will keep them "firm to the end . . . on the Day of our Lord Jesus" (1:7–8). Like the Thessalonians, the recipients of Paul's Corinthian letters expect to experience the Day of Judgment soon, a belief that affects their entire way of life. Paul advises single people to remain unmarried; neither slaves nor free citizens are to change their status because "the time we live in will not last long." All emotions—sorrow and joy—are only temporary, as are ordinary human pursuits. "Buyers must not count on keeping what they buy," because "the whole frame of this world is passing away" (7:29–31). Paul speaks here not of the philosopher's conventional wisdom—that the wise person shuns life's petty goals to pursue the superior values of eternity—but of the *eschaton,* the end of all the familiar world.

In anticipating the coming resurrection, Paul echoes his words in 1 Thessalonians 4: when Judgment's trumpet sounds, "we [Christians then living] shall not all die, but we shall all be changed in a flash, in the twinkling of an eye" (15:51–55). Such passages reveal that Paul, along with his contemporaries, expects to be alive when Christ returns to raise the dead.

The Necessity of Christian Unity

Paul's first objective is to halt the rivalries that divide the Corinthians. Without imposing a dogmatic conformity, he asks his readers to work together cooperatively for their mutual benefit (1:8–10). Like all early Christian congregations, that at Corinth met in a private house large enough to accommodate the entire group. Although the membership was small, numbering perhaps fifty or one hundred persons, it was broken into several opposing cliques. Some members placed undue importance on the particular leader who had converted or baptized them and competed with each other over the prestige of their respective mentors.

A more serious cause of division may have sprung from the members' unequal social and educational backgrounds. As in any group, modern or ancient, some individuals believed they were demonstrably superior to their neighbors. Examining chapter 1 carefully, the reader will see that Paul's attack on false "wisdom" is really an attempt to discourage human competitiveness. In Paul's view, all believers are fundamentally equal:

> For through faith you are all [children] of God in union with Christ Jesus. . . . There is no such thing as Jew and Greek, slave and freeman, male and female; for you are all one person in Christ Jesus. (Gal. 3:26, 28)

This assumption underlies Paul's method of presenting the kerygma—the proclamation about Jesus. When he reminds the Corinthians that he taught them the message as simply as possible, he does so to show that the new faith is essentially incompatible with individual pride or competitiveness.

Paul's concurrent theme is that human "weakness" is the unexpected medium through which God reveals his strength. In contrast to the Roman soldiers who crucified him, Christ was weak. Paul is also weak in refusing to use the rhetorical embellishments with which Hellenistic teachers were expected to present their ideas. Thus, with almost brutal directness he proclaims "Christ nailed to the cross" (2:1; 1:23). (Paul's relative lack of success debating philosophers in Athens just before coming to Corinth [Acts 17] may have influenced his decision to preach henceforth without any intellectual pretensions [2:1; 1:23].)

Paul's weak and "foolish" proclamation of a Messiah crucified offends almost everyone. It is a major obstacle to Jews (who look for a victorious conqueror, not an executed criminal) and an absurdity to the Greeks (who seek rational explanations of the universe). To the believer, however, the paradox of a crucified Messiah represents God's omnipotent wisdom (1:22–24).

Paul's argument (1:17–2:5) is sometimes misused to justify an anti-intellectual approach to religion, in which reason and faith are treated as if they were mutually exclusive. The Apostle's attack on "worldly wisdom" is not directed against human reason, however. It is aimed at individual Corinthians who boasted of special insights that gave them a "deeper" understanding than that granted their fellow Christians. Such elitism led some persons to cultivate a false sense of superiority that devalued less educated believers, fragmenting the congregation into groups of the "wise" and the "foolish."

Paul seeks to place all believers on an equal footing and allow them no cause for intellectual competition. He reminds the Corinthians that human reason by itself did not succeed in knowing God but that God revealed his saving purpose through Christ as a free gift (1:21). No one merits or earns the Christian revelation, which comes through God's unforeseen grace, not through human effort. Because all are equally recipients of the divine benefits, no believer has the right to boast (1:21–31).

Paul does, however, teach a previously hidden wisdom to persons mature enough to appreciate it. This wisdom is God's revelation through the Spirit that now dwells in the Christian community. The hitherto unknown "mind" of God—the ultimate reality that philosophers make the object of their search—is unveiled through Christ (2:6–16). The divine mystery, although inaccessible to rational inquiry, is finally made clear in the weakness and obedient suffering of Christ, the means by which God reconciles humanity to himself.

The limits of Christian freedom. Paul's doctrine of freedom from Torah restraints is easily abused by those who interpret it as an excuse to ignore all ethical principles. As a result of the Corinthians' misuse of Christian freedom, Paul finds it necessary to impose limits on believers' individual liberty. Exercising his apostolic authority, Paul orders the Corinthians to excommunicate a Christian living openly with his stepmother. Apparently, the Corinthian church was proud of the man's bold use of freedom to live as he liked, though his incest scandalized even Greek society. Directing the congregation to evict the sinner from their midst, Paul establishes a policy that later becomes a powerful means of church control over individual members. In excommunication, the offender is denied all fellowship in the believing community and is left bereft of God as well. Although consigned "to Satan" (the devil-ruled world outside the church), the outcast remains a Christian destined for ultimate salvation on the Lord's Day (5:1–13).

Lawsuits among Christians. Claiming freedom "to do anything," some Corinthians bring lawsuits against fellow Christians in civil courts, allowing the unbelieving public to witness the internal divisions and ill will existing in the church. Paul orders that such disputes be settled within the Christian community. He also commands men who frequent prostitutes to end this practice. Answering the Corinthians' claim that physical appetites can be satisfied without damaging faith, Paul argues that Christians' bodies are temples of the Holy Spirit and must not be defiled by intercourse with prostitutes (6:1–20).

Answering Questions from the Congregation

Marriage, divorce, and celibacy. In chapters 7 through 15 Paul responds to a letter from the Corinthians, answering their questions on several crucial topics. The first item concerns human sexuality (7:1–40), a subject on which the writer takes a distant but practical interest. Paul clearly prefers a single life without any kind of sexual involvement. Notice that he begins this section by declaring that "it is a good thing for a man to have nothing to do with women," and he closes by observing that women whose husbands have died are "better off" if they do not remarry. In both these statements, Paul may be quoting some Corinthians who boasted of their superior self-control. Although he does not find marriage personally attractive, he is far from forbidding others to marry (7:2–9). He also stresses the mutual obligations of marriage, stating that husbands and wives are equally entitled to each other's sexual love. Note, however, that he pragmatically describes marriage as an inevitably painful experience that can interfere with a believer's religious commitment (7:28, 32–34).

Paul's general principle is for everyone to remain in whatever state—single or married, slave or free—that the believer was in when first converted. Although aware of Jesus' command forbidding divorce, he concedes that a legal separation is acceptable when a non-Christian wishes to leave his or her Christian mate (7:10–24).

It is important to remember that Paul's advice, particularly on celibacy, is presented in the context of an imminent Parousia. The unmarried remain free "to wait upon the Lord without distraction." Freedom from sexual ties that bind one to the world is eminently practical because "the time we live in will not last long" (7:25–35). Paul regards singleness not as the prerequisite to a higher spiritual state but as a practical response to the eschatological crisis.

A problem of conscience. In the next long section (8:1–11:1) Paul discusses a problem that ceased to be an issue over fifteen hundred years ago—eating meat that had previously been sacrificed in Greco-Roman temples. (The meat was then commonly sold in meat markets or cooked and served in public dining halls, some of which the Corinthian Christians frequented.) Although the social conditions that created the issue have long since disappeared, the principle that Paul articulates in this matter remains relevant to many believers.

Paul argues that although Christians are completely free to do as they wish when their consciences are clear, they should remember that their behavior can be misinterpreted by other believers who do not think as they do. Some may interpret such actions as eating meat that had been given to "idols" as violating religious purity. Paul rules in favor of the "weak" who have trouble distinguishing between abstract convictions and visible practice. Respecting a fellow Christian's sensitive conscience, the mature believer will forfeit his or her right to eat sacrificed meat—or, presumably, to engage in any other action that troubles the "weak" (8:1–13; 10:23–11:1).

Notice that Paul interrupts his argument to insert a vigorous defense of his apostolic authority (9:1–27) and give examples of ways in which he has sacrificed his personal freedoms to benefit others. The rights Paul has voluntarily given up suggest some significant differences between his style of life and that practiced by leaders of the Jerusalem church. Unlike Peter, Jesus' brothers, and the other Apostles, he forfeits the privilege of taking a wife or accepting money for his missionary services. He even sacrifices his own inclinations and individuality,

becoming "everything in turn to men of every sort" to save them. Paul asks the "strong" Corinthians to imitate his selfless example (9:3–23; 10:33–11:1).

Paul's demand to live largely for other people's benefit and to accommodate one's conduct to others' consciences raises important issues. Some commentators observe that although Paul's argument protects the sensibilities of believers who are less free thinking, it places the intellectually aware Christian at the mercy of the overscrupulous or the literal-minded believers. Followed explicitly, the Apostle's counsel here seriously compromises his doctrine of Christian freedom.

Regulating behavior in church. Chapters 11 through 14 contain Paul's advice regulating behavior in church. The issues he addresses include the participation of women, conduct during reenactments of the Last Supper, and the handling of charismatic "gifts," such as the Spirit-given ability to prophesy, heal, or speak in tongues. We discuss each of these areas separately below.

The importance of women in the church. In recent decades Pauline regulations about women's roles in the church have been attacked as culture-bound and chauvinistic. Because we know so little of very early Christian practice, it is difficult to establish to what degree women originally shared in church leadership. Jesus numbered many women among his most loyal disciples, and Paul refers to several women as his "fellow workers" (Phil. 4:3). In the last chapter of Romans, in which Paul lists the missionary Prisca (Priscilla) ahead of her husband Aquila, the Apostle asks the recipients to support Phoebe, a presiding officer in the Cenchreae church, in discharging her administrative duties (Rom. 16:1–6).

In Corinthians, however, Paul seems to impose certain restrictions on women's participation in church services. His insistence that women cover their heads with veils (11:3–16) is open to a variety of interpretations. Is it the writer's concession to the existing Jewish and Greco-Roman custom of secluding women, an attempt to avoid offending patriarchal prejudices? If women unveil their physical attractiveness, does this distract male onlookers or even sexually tempt angels, such as those who "lusted" for mortal women before the Flood (Gen. 6:1–4)? Conversely, is the veil a symbol of women's religious authority, to be worn when prophesying before the congregation?

Paul's argument for relegating women to a subordinate position in church strikes many readers as labored and illogical. (Some scholars think that this passage [11:2–16] is the interpolation of a later editor, added to make Corinthians agree with the non-Pauline instruction in 1 Tim. 2:8–15.) Paul grants women an active role, praying and prophesying during worship, but at the same time he argues that the female is a secondary creation, made from man, who was created directly by God. The Apostle uses the second version of human origins (Gen. 2) to support his view of a human sexual hierarchy, but he could as easily have cited the first creation account in which male and female are created simultaneously, both in the "image of God" (Gen. 1:27). Given Paul's revelation that Christian equality transcends all distinctions among believers, including those of sex, class, and nationality (Gal. 3:28), many commentators see the writer's choice in a Genesis precedent as decidedly arbitrary.

The Communion meal (the Lord's Supper, or Eucharist). Christianity's most solemn ritual, the reenactment of Jesus' last meal with his disciples, represents the mystic communion between the Lord and his followers. Meeting in a private home to commemorate the event, the Corinthians had turned the service into a riotous drinking party. Instead of a celebration of Christian unity, it had become another source of division. Wealthy participants came early and consumed all the delicacies of the Communion meal before the working poor arrived, thus rel-

egating their social inferiors to hunger and public embarrassment (11:17–22).

Paul contrasts this misbehavior with the tradition coming directly from Jesus himself. Recording Jesus' sacramental distribution of bread and wine, he stresses that the ceremony is to be decorously repeated in memory of Christ's death until he returns. This allusion to the nearness of Jesus' reappearance reminds the Corinthians of the seriousness with which they must observe the Last Supper ceremony (11:23–34).

Regulating gifts of the Spirit. Led by the Holy Spirit, the early Christian community was composed of many persons gifted with supernatural abilities. Some had the gift of prophecy; others were apostles, teachers, healers, miracle workers, or speakers in tongues. In Corinth such individual gifts and rivalries among those possessing them were yet another cause of division. Reminding them that one indivisible Spirit grants all these different abilities, Paul employs a favorite metaphor in which he compares the church to the human body, with its many differently functioning parts. Each Christian gift is to be used to benefit the whole body, the church.

The hymn to love (agape). In his most celebrated burst of inspiration, Paul interrupts his advice on the use of spiritual gifts to show the Corinthians "the best way of all" (13:1–13). Listing the most highly honored charismatic gifts—prophecy, knowledge, power, self-sacrifice—Paul states that "without love" they are meaningless. His description of love (in Greek, *agape,* meaning "selfless giving") stresses its human application: love is patient, kind, forgiving; it keeps no record of offenses. Its capacity for loyal devotion is infinite: "there is no limit to its faith, its hope, and its endurance." Love once given is never withdrawn. Whereas other spiritual gifts are only partial reflections of the divine reality and will be rendered obsolete in the perfect world to come, the supreme trio of Christian virtues—faith, hope, and love—endures forever.

Speaking in tongues (glossolalia). Although he gives love top priority, Paul also acknowledges the value of other spiritual gifts, especially prophecy, which involves rational communication. "Ecstatic utterance"—speaking in tongues—may be emotionally satisfying to the speaker, but it does not "build up" the congregation as do teaching and prophecy. Although he does not prohibit ecstatic utterance (Paul states that he is better at it than any Corinthian), the Apostle ranks it as the least useful spiritual gift (14:1–40).

The Eschatological Hope: Resurrection of the Dead

Paul's last major topic—his eschatological vision of the resurrection (15:1–57)—is theologically the most important. It appears that some Corinthians challenged Paul's teaching about the afterlife. One group may have questioned the necessity of a future bodily resurrection because they believed that at baptism (and upon receiving the Spirit) they had already achieved eternal life. Others may have denied Paul's concept of resurrection because they shared the Greek philosophical view that a future existence is purely spiritual. According to Socrates, Plato, and numerous mystery religions, death occurs when the immortal soul escapes from the perishable body. The soul does not need a body when it enters the invisible spirit realm. To believers in the soul's inherent immortality, Paul's Hebrew belief in the physical body's resurrection was grotesque and irrelevant.

The historical reality of Jesus' resurrection. To demonstrate that bodily resurrection is a reality, Paul calls on the Corinthians to remember that Jesus rose from the dead. Preserving our earliest tradition of Jesus' postresurrection appearances, Paul notes that the risen Lord appeared to as many as five hundred believers at once as well as to Paul (15:3–8). Paul uses his opponents' denial against them and argues that if there is no resurrection, then Christ was not raised and

the Christian hope is vain. He trusts not in the Greek concept of innate human immortality but in the Judeo-Christian faith in God's ability to raise the faithful dead. Without Christ's resurrection, Paul states, there is no afterlife, and of all people Christians are most pitiable (15:12–19).

Paul now invokes two archetypal figures to illustrate the means by which human death and its opposite, eternal life, entered the world. Citing the Genesis creation account, Paul declares that the "first man," Adam (God's first earthly son) brought death to the human race, but Christ (Adam's "heavenly" counterpart, a new creation) brings life. The coming resurrection (perhaps salvation as well) is universal: "as in Adam all men die, so in Christ all will be brought to life." The first product of the resurrection harvest, Christ will return to raise the obedient dead and defeat all enemies, including death itself. Christ subjects the entire universe to his rule but himself remains subordinate to God, so that God is "all in all" (15:20–28). Noting that the Corinthians practice baptism of their dead (posthumously initiating them into the church), Paul argues that this ritual presupposes the resurrection's reality (15:29).

Paul next responds to the skeptics' demand to know what possible form bodily resurrection might take. Although he admits that "flesh and blood can never possess the [immaterial] kingdom of God," Paul retains his Hebraic conviction that human beings cannot exist without some kind of body. First, he uses analogies from the natural world, demonstrating that life grows from buried seeds and that existence takes different forms. As heavenly bodies surpass earthly objects in beauty, so the resurrection body will outshine the physical body. "Sown [dead and buried] . . . as a perishable thing [it] is raised imperishable." Paul describes here a supernatural transformation of the human essence, a process that creates a paradox, a contradiction in terms—a material body that is also spirit (15:35–44).

Paul gives his exposition immediacy by unveiling a divine mystery: when the last trumpet sounds, he and other living Christians will be instantly transformed and clothed with an imperishable, immortal existence. In the universal restoration, death itself will perish, consumed in Christ's life-giving victory (15:51–57).

Closing remarks. Returning abruptly from his cosmic vision of human destiny to take up earthly affairs again, Paul reminds the Corinthians of their previous agreement to help the Jerusalem church. They are to contribute money every Sunday, an obligation Paul had assumed when visiting the Jerusalem leadership (Gal. 2). The letter ends with Paul's invocation of Jesus' speedy return—*Marana tha* ("Come, O Lord")—an Aramaic prayer dating from the first generation of Palestinian Christians.

Second Letter to the Corinthians

Whereas 1 Corinthians is a unified document, 2 Corinthians seems to be a compendium of several letters or letter fragments written at different times and reflecting radically different situations in the Corinthian church. Even casual readers will note the contrast between the harsh, sarcastic tone of chapters 10–13 and the generally friendlier, more conciliatory tone of the earlier chapters. In the opinion of many scholars, chapters 10–13 represent the "painful letter" alluded to in 2 Cor. 2:3–4, making this part necessarily older than chapters 1–9. Some authorities find as many as six or more remnants of different letters in 2 Corinthians, but for this discussion we concentrate on the work's two main divisions (chs. 10–13 and 1–9), taking them in the order in which scholars believe they were composed.

Troubles in Corinth. Behind the writing of 2 Corinthians lies a dramatic conflict between Paul and the church he had founded. After he had dispatched 1 Corinthians, several events took place that strained his relationship with the church almost to the breaking point. (1) New opponents, whom Paul satirizes as "superlative apostles" (11:5), infiltrated the congregation and rapidly gained positions of influence. Paul then made a brief, "painful" visit to Corinth, only to suffer a public humiliation there (2:1–5; 7:12). (2) His visit a failure, he returned to Ephesus, where he wrote the Corinthians a severe reprimand, part of which is preserved in chapters 10–13. (3) Having carried the severe letter to Corinth, Titus then rejoins Paul in Macedonia, bringing the good news that the Corinthians are sorry for their behavior and now support the Apostle (7:5–7). (4) Paul subsequently writes a joyful letter of reconciliation, included in chapters 1–9. Although this reconstruction of events is speculative, it accounts for the sequence of alienation, hostility, and reconciliation found in this composite document.

The Severe Letter: Paul's Defense of His Apostolic Authority

In the last three chapters of 2 Corinthians, Paul writes a passionate, almost brutal defense of his apostolic authority. A masterpiece of savage irony, chapters 10–13 show Paul boasting "as a fool," using every device of rhetoric to demolish his opponents' pretensions to superiority. We don't know the precise identity of these opponents, except that they were Jewish Christians whom Paul accuses of proclaiming "another Jesus" and imparting a "spirit" different from that introduced by his "gospel." The label "superlative apostles" suggests that these critics enjoyed considerable authority, perhaps as representatives from the Jerusalem church.

Whoever they were, the "superlative apostles" had succeeded in undermining many Corinthians' trust in Paul's individual teaching and personal integrity. Pointing to Paul's refusal to accept payment for his apostolic services (perhaps implying that he knew he was not entitled to it), his critics seriously questioned his credentials as a Christian leader. When he fights back, Paul is defending both himself (hence the many autobiographical references) and the truth of the gospel he proclaims. In some passages Paul sounds almost desperately afraid that the church for which he has labored so hard will be lost to him.

Although Paul's bitter sarcasm may offend some readers, we must realize that this unattractive quality is the reverse side of his intense emotional commitment to the Corinthians' welfare. Behind the writer's "bragging" and threats (10:2–6; 11:16–21; 13:3,10) lies the sting of unrequited affection. The nature of love that Paul had so confidently defined in his earlier letter (1 Cor. 13) is now profoundly tested.

The nature of apostleship and the Christian ministry. Whereas in 1 Corinthians Paul deals with ethical and doctrinal issues, in 2 Corinthians he struggles to define the qualities and motives that distinguish the Christian ministry. His main purpose in boasting "as a fool" (11:1–12:13) is to demonstrate that true apostleship does not depend upon external qualities like race or circumcision or having the strength to browbeat other believers. Paradoxically, it depends upon the leader's "weakness"—his complete dependence upon God, who empowers him to endure all kinds of hardship to proclaim the saving message. Outwardly "weak" but inwardly strong, Paul willingly suffers dangers, discomforts, humiliations, and unceasing toil—daily proof of selfless devotion—for the sake of a church that now openly doubts his motives (11:16–33).

It is not certain that the "superlative apostles" (11:5) are the same opponents as the "sham apostles" (11:13) whom Paul accuses of being Satan's agents (11:12–15). Whatever their identity, they apparently based their authority at least in part on supernatural visions and revelations. Paul responds by telling of a believer, caught up to "the third heaven" (in Jewish belief, the spiritual Eden), who experienced divine secrets too sacred to reveal. Disclosing that the mystic is himself, Paul states that to keep from becoming overelated by such mystical experiences, he was given a counterbalancing physical defect. This unspecified "thorn in the flesh" ties Paul firmly to his earthly frame and grounds him in the human "weakness" through which God reveals spiritual power (12:1–13; 13:3–4).

Paul implores the Corinthians to reform so that his planned third visit will be a joyous occasion rather than an exercise in harsh discipline. He closes the letter with a final appeal to the congregation to practice unity and "live in peace" (13:1–14).

The Letter of Reconciliation

Although scholars discern as many as five separate letter fragments in this section, we discuss chapters 1–9 here as a single document. The opening chapters (1:1–2:13) contrast sharply with the angry defensiveness of chapters 10–13 and show a "happy" writer reconciled to the Corinthians. The unnamed opponent who had publicly humiliated Paul on his second visit has been punished and must now be forgiven (2:5–11). Titus's welcome news that the Corinthians are now on Paul's side (7:5–16) may belong to this section of the letter, misplaced in its present position by a later copyist.

Paul's real credentials. Despite the reconciliation, the Corinthian church is still troubled by Paul's rivals, whom he denounces as mere "hawkers" (salespersons) of God's word (2:17). Although he is more controlled than in chapters 10–13, his exasperation is still evident when he asks if he must begin all over again proving his apostolic credentials (3:1). Placing the responsibility for recognizing true apostolic leadership squarely on the Corinthians, the writer reminds them that they are his living letters of recommendation. Echoing Jeremiah 31:31, Paul contrasts the Mosaic Covenant—inscribed on stone tablets—with the new covenant written on human hearts. Inhabited by the Holy Spirit, the Christian reflects God's image with a splendor exceeding that of Moses (3:2–18).

Nurturing a spiritual body. Paul pursues his theme of the indwelling Spirit and further develops ideas about the future life that he had previously outlined in discussing the resurrection (1 Cor. 15). In the earlier letter,, Paul wrote that the believer will become instantly transformed—receive an incorruptible "spiritual body"—at Christ's return. He said nothing about the Christian's state of being or consciousness during the interim period between death and the future resurrection. In the present letter (4:16–5:10), Paul seems to imply that believers are already developing a spiritual body that will clothe them at the moment of death.

Paul appears to state that God has prepared for each Christian an eternal form, a "heavenly habitation," that endows the bearer with immortality. Yearning to avoid human death, he envisions receiving that heavenly form now, putting it on like a garment over the physical body, "so that our mortal part may be absorbed into life immortal." The presence of the Spirit, he concludes, is visible evidence that God intends this process of spiritual transformation to take place during the present lifetime (5:1–5). United with Christ, the believer thus becomes a new creation (5:11–17).

The spiritual renewal is God's plan for reconciling humankind to himself. As Christ's ambassador, Paul advances the work of reconciliation; his sufferings are an act of love for them (5:18–6:13). Imploring the Corinthians to return his affection, Paul ends his defense of the apostolic purpose with a not-altogether-convincing expression of confidence in their loyalty (7:2–16). (Many scholars believe that 6:14–7:1, which interrupts Paul's flow of thought, either belongs to a separate letter or is a non-Pauline fragment that somehow was interpolated into 2 Corinthians. Because of its striking resemblance to Essene literature, some critics suggest that this passage originated in Qumran.)

Chapters 8 and 9 seem to repeat each other and may once have been separate missives before an editor combined them at the end of Paul's reconciliation letter. Both conern the collections for the Jerusalem church, a duty that had been allowed to lapse during the hostilities between the Apostle and his competitors. Highlighting Titus's key role, Paul stresses the generosity of Macedonia's churches, an example the Corinthians are expected to imitate. He reminds prospective donors that "God loves a cheerful giver" (9:7).

Paul's letters to the young Greek churches at Thessalonica and Corinth reveal that the first Christians held widely diverging opinions about the content and practice of their new religion. In 1 Thessalonians Paul battles to correct misconceptions about the fate of believers who die before the Parousia. In 1 Corinthians he urges the congregation to overcome rivalries and unite as a single body for the spiritual welfare of all believers. The passionate arguments with which Paul defends his right to lead and teach his churches (especially 2 Corinthians 10–13) are reminders that God operates through human instruments who, like Paul, are "weak" and dependent on divine power. The key to understanding the urgency of Paul's plea for unity in belief and behavior is his assumption that his generation stands at the turning point between two ages. The history of evil is nearly finished; Christ will soon return to establish the New Age, in which God rules all.

QUESTIONS FOR DISCUSSION AND REVIEW

1. Find the passages in 1 Thessalonians and 1 Corinthians indicating that Paul believed the End to be very near.
2. When Paul advises believers about choosing between marriage and a single life, to what extent does his expectation that ordinary history will soon end affect his counsel? What eschatological assumptions underlie his view of the world?

3. If Paul was wrong about the occurrence of the Parousia during his lifetime, to what extent does that mistaken view affect a reader's confidence in Paul's teachings?

4. After reading 1 Corinthians 7 and 11, discuss Paul's views on human sexuality and the relative status of men and women. On what tradition does Paul base his opinion of women's role in the church? How have Paul's attitudes influenced modern policies on the ordination of women for the ministry?

5. What kinds of wisdom does Paul discuss in 1 Corinthians 1–3?

6. Why do some Corinthians disagree with Paul's belief in the future resurrection of the body? Explain the difference between the notion of an inherently immortal soul and the concept of receiving eternal life through resurrection. How does Paul link Jesus' resurrection to the Christian hope of an afterlife?

7. After reading 2 Corinthians 10–13, describe the arguments Paul's Corinthian opponents used against him. Why does he respond by boasting "as a fool"? Why are his mystical experiences important to the Corinthians?

8. 2 Corinthians 1–9 indicates that the Corinthian majority decided to accept Paul and his individual gospel on the Apostle's own terms. Which of Paul's threats or arguments do you think most influenced the church to become reconciled with its founder?

TERMS AND CONCEPTS TO REMEMBER

eschatology
the two ages
Paul's view of the
 Parousia (1
 Thessalonians)
apocalyptic signs (2
 Thessalonians)
the "enemy" (anti-
 Christ)
causes of division in
 Corinth
the "wise" and the
 "foolish"
Aphrodite
agape (1 Corinthians
 13)
conscience
the roles of reason
 and faith
sexual ethics
the role of women
gifts of the Spirit
ecstatic speech
 (glossolalia)
the Greek doctrine of
 immortality
the Hebrew belief in
 bodily
 resurrection
the superlative
 apostles
Paul's apostolic
 credentials

RECOMMENDED READING

1 and 2 Thessalonians

Beare, F. W. "Thessalonians, Second Letter to the." In *The Interpreter's Dictionary of the Bible,* vol. 4, 625–29. Nashville: Abingdon Press, 1962.

Beker, J. C. *Paul's Apocalyptic Gospel: The Coming Triumph of God.* Philadelphia: Fortress Press, 1982.

Forestell, J. T. "The Letters to the Thessalonians." In *The Jerome Biblical Commentary,* vol. 2, 227–35. Englewood Cliffs, NJ: Prentice-Hall, 1968.

Keck, L. E., and V. P. Furnish. *The Pauline Letters.* Nashville: Abingdon Press, 1984.

Marshall, I. H. *1 and 2 Thessalonians.* Grand Rapids, Mich.: Eerdmans, 1983.

Orr, W. F., and J. A. Walther, eds. *1 and 2 Corinthians and 1 and 2 Thessalonians.* Vol. 32 of the Anchor Bible. Garden City, N.Y.: Doubleday, 1976.

Reese, J. M. *1 and 2 Thessalonians.* Wilmington: Michael Glazier, 1979.

1 and 2 Corinthians

Bruce, F. F. *1 and 2 Corinthians.* Grand Rapids, Mich.: Eerdmans, 1978.

Finegan, Jack. "Corinth." In *The Interpreter's Dictionary of the Bible,* vol. 1, 683–84.

Furnish, V. P. *Second Corinthians.* Anchor Bible Commentary, vol. 32A. Garden City, N.Y.: Doubleday, 1984.

Georgi, Dieter. "Second Letter to the Corinthians." *The Interpreter's Dictionary of the Bible,* supplementary vol. 183–86.

Gilmour, S. M. "Corinthians, First Letter to the." In *The Interpreter's Dictionary of the Bible,* vol. 1, 684–92. Nashville: Abingdon Press, 1962. A helpful introduction.

Hooker, M. D. "Authority on Her Head: An Examination of 1 Cor. 11:10." *New Testament Studies* 10 (1963): 410–16.

Hurd, J. C. *The Origin of 1 Corinthians*. Macon, Ga.: Mercer University Press, 1983.

Meeks, Wayne. *The First Urban Christians: The Social World of the Apostle Paul*. New Haven: Yale University Press, 1983. An insightful investigation into the cultural environment and socioeconomic background of the earliest Christians.

Murphy-O'Connor, Jerome. *St. Paul's Corinth: Text and Archaeology*. Wilmington: Michael Glazier, 1983. An archaeologist's illumination of the Corinthian life and customs in Paul's day.

Schmithals, Walter. *Gnosticism in Corinth: An Investigation of the Letters to the Corinthians*. Translated by J. Steely. Nashville: Abingdon Press, 1971.

Schütz, J. H., ed. *The Social Setting of Pauline Christianity*. Philadelphia: Fortress Press, 1982.

Scroggs, Robin. "Paul and the Eschatological Woman." *Journal of the American Academy of Religion* 40 (1972): 283–303; 42 (1974): 532–37.

Soards, Marian L. *The Apostle Paul: An Introduction to His Writing and Teaching*. New York: Paulist Press, 1987.

15 *Freedom from Law and Justification by Faith: Galatians and Romans*

> For through faith you are all [children] of God in
> union with Christ Jesus. . . . There is no such thing
> as Jew and Greek, slave and freeman, male and
> female; for you are all one person in Christ Jesus.
> (Gal. 3:26, 28)

KEY THEMES   In his letters to the Galatians and the Romans, Paul defines Christianity's relationship to Judaism. He uses the Jewish Bible to demonstrate that faith was always God's primary means of reconciling humanity to himself. God's revelation (*apokalypsis*) of Jesus frees believers from the "bondage" of Torah observance.

Paul argues in Romans that all humanity imitates Adam's disobedience and is therefore enslaved to sin and alienated from God. The "holy" and "just" Law of the Torah serves only to increase an awareness of human imperfection and to condemn the lawbreaker. Thus, obedience to the Torah cannot rescue people from sin's consequence, death, or unite them with the Deity. Only God's undeserved love expressed through Christ and accepted through faith can reconcile humankind with the Creator.

The Jewish lack of faith in Jesus as the divinely appointed agent of redemption is only temporary, a historical necessity that allows believing Gentiles also to become God's people.

Galatians and Romans are two of Paul's most important letters, for in these he spells out his distinctive vision of freedom from the Mosaic Torah and justification by faith in Christ. An angry declaration of Christianity's independence from Torah obligations, Galatians argues that obedience to Torah commandments cannot justify the believer before God. Only trust (faith) in God's gracious willingness to redeem humanity through Christ can now win divine approval and obtain salvation for the individual.

This uniquely Pauline gospel revolutionized the development of Christianity. By sweeping away all Torah requirements, including circum-cision and dietary restrictions, Paul opened the church wide to Gentile converts. Uncircumcised former adherents of Greco-Roman religions were now granted full equality with Jewish Christians. Although the process was only beginning in Paul's day, the influx of Gentiles would soon overwhelm the originally Jewish church, making it an international community with members belonging to every known ethnic group. This swift transformation could not have been possible without Paul's radical insistence on the abandonment of all Mosaic observances, which for centuries had separated Jew from Gentile.

An Angry Letter to the "Stupid" Galatians

Perhaps written at about the same time he was battling the "superlative apostles" of Corinth (2 Cor. 10–13), Paul's Galatian letter contains a similar impassioned defense of his apostolic authority and teaching. It seems that almost everywhere Paul founded new churches, troublemakers infiltrated the congregation, asserting that Christians must keep at least some provisions of the Mosaic Law. Influenced either by representatives from the Jerusalem church or by a wish to combine Jewish practices with elements of pre-Christian religions, the Galatians had abandoned Paul's gospel (1:6) and now required all male converts to undergo circumcision (5:2–3; 6:12–13), the physical sign of belonging to God's covenant community (Gen. 15).

The recipients. The identity of the Galatian churches Paul addresses is uncertain. In Paul's time two different geographical areas could be designated "Galatia." The first was a territory in north-central Asia Minor inhabited by descendants of Celtic tribes that had invaded the region during the third to first centuries BCE. Brief references to Galatia in Acts (16:6; 18:23) suggest that Paul traveled there, but this is not certain.

The other possibility, as some historians suggest, is that Paul was writing to Christians in the Roman province of Galatia. The southern portion of this province included the cities of Iconium, Lystra, and Derbe, places where the Apostle had established churches (Acts 14). If the "southern Galatia" theory is correct, it helps to explain the presence of "Judaizers" (those persons advocating circumcision), for the Roman province was much closer to Jewish-Christian centers at Antioch and at Jerusalem than was the northern, Celtic territory (see Figure 15-1).

The identity of Paul's opponents. Some commentators identify Paul's opponents as emissaries of the Jerusalem church, such as those apparently sent by James to inspect the congregation at Antioch (2:12). It is unlikely, however, that Jewish Christians from Jerusalem would be unaware that requiring circumcision also means keeping the entire Torah (5:2–3). Paul's opponents appear to combine aspects of Greco-Roman cult worship, such as honoring cosmic spirits and observing religious festival days (4:9–10), with selected Torah requirements (6:12–14). This **syncretism** (mixing together aspects of two or more different religions to create a new doctrine) suggests that the opponents are Galatian Gentiles. In Paul's view their attempt to infuse Jewish and pagan elements into Christianity misses the point of the Christ event.

Purpose and contents. Writing from Corinth or Ephesus about 56 CE, Paul has a twofold purpose: (1) to prove that he is a true Apostle, possessing rights equal to those of the Jerusalem "pillars" (chs. 1–2), and (2) to demonstrate the validity of his gospel that Christian faith replaces works of Law, including circumcision. The letter may be divided into five parts:

1. A biographical defense of Paul's autonomy and his relationship with the Jerusalem leadership (1:1–2:14)
2. Paul's unique gospel: justification through faith (2:15–3:29)
3. The adoption of Christians as heirs of Abraham and children of God (4:1–31)
4. The consequences and obligations of Christian freedom from the Mosaic Law (5:1–6:10)
5. Final summary of Paul's argument (6:11–18)

Paul's Defense of His Apostleship

Largely dispensing with his usual greetings and thanksgiving, Paul opens the letter with a

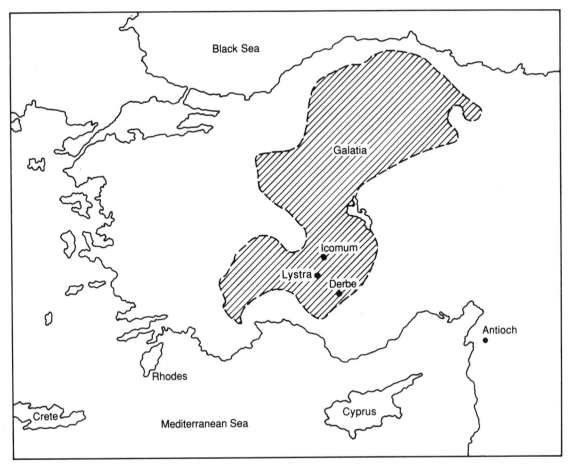

Figure 15-1. The identity of Paul's Galatians is uncertain. The letter may have been directed to churches in the north-central plateau region of Asia Minor (near present-day Ankara, Turkey) or to churches in the southern coastal area of east-central Asia Minor (also in modern Turkey). Many scholars believe that the Galatians were Christians living in Iconium, Lystra, Derbe, and other nearby cities that Paul had visited on his first missionary journey.

vigorous defense of his personal autonomy. His apostolic rank derives not from ordination or "human appointment" but directly from the Deity (1:1–5). Similarly, his message does not depend upon information learned from earlier Christians but is a direct "revelation of Jesus Christ" (1:12). Because he regards his gospel of faith as a divine communication, Paul sees no need to consult other church leaders about the correctness of his policies (1:15–17).

Although Paul presents himself as essentially independent of the mother church at Jerusalem, he apparently recognizes the desirability of having his work among the Gentiles endorsed by the Palestinian Christian leadership. His visit with the Jerusalem "pillars"—Peter, John, and James—is probably the same conference described in Acts 15. According to Paul, the pillars agree to recognize the legitimacy of his Gentile mission. Imposing no Torah restrictions on

Gentile converts, the Jerusalem trio ask only that Paul's churches contribute financially to the mother church, a charitable project Paul gladly undertakes (2:1–10; see 2 Cor. 8–9; Rom. 15).

After the Jerusalem conference, Paul meets Peter again at Antioch, a meeting that shows how far the Jewish-Gentile issue is from being resolved. Paul charges that Jesus' premier disciple is still ambivalent about associating with uncircumcised believers. When James sends emissaries to see if Antiochean Christians are properly observing Mosaic dietary laws, Peter stops sharing in communal meals with Gentiles. Apparently Peter fears James's disapproval. Although Paul denounces Peter's action as hypocrisy, claiming that Peter privately does not keep Torah regulations, we cannot be sure of Peter's motives. He may have wished not to offend more conservative Jewish believers and behaved as he did out of respect for others' consciences, a policy Paul himself advocates (1 Cor. 8:1–13).

Justification by Faith

Paul's strangely negative attitude toward the Mosaic Law has puzzled many Jewish scholars. Why does a Pharisee trained to regard the Torah as God's revelation of ultimate Wisdom so vehemently reject this divine guide to righteous living? Is it because of a personal consciousness that (for him) the Law no longer has power to justify his existence before God? In both Galatians and Romans Paul closely examines his own psychological state, attempting to show how the experience of Christ achieves for him what the Law failed to do—assure him of God's love and acceptance.

In Paul's interpretation of the crucifixion, Jesus' voluntary death pays the Torah's penalty for all lawbreakers (3:13–14). Thus, Paul can say that "through the law I died to law." He escaped the punishments of the Torah through a mystical identification with the sacrificial Messiah. Vicariously experiencing Jesus' crucifixion, Paul now shares in Christ's new life, which enables him to receive God's grace as never before (2:17–21).

Paul also appeals to the Galatians' experience of Christ, reminding them that they received the Spirit only when they believed his gospel, not when they obeyed the Law (3:1–5). If they think that they can be judged righteous by obeying the Torah, then there was no purpose or meaning to Christ's death (2:21). Paul reinforces his argument in the rabbinic tradition by finding a precedent in the Hebrew Bible that anticipates his formula of "faith equals righteousness." Paul notes that Abraham's "faith" in God's call "was counted to him as righteousness" (Gen. 15:6). Therefore, Paul reasons, persons who exercise faith today are Abraham's spiritual children, heirs to the promise that God will "bless," or justify, pagan nations through faith (3:6–10). Faith, not obedience to Law, is the key to divine approval.

In support of his appeal to biblical authority Paul finds only one additional relevant text, Habakkuk 2:4: "he shall gain life who is justified through faith." Paul interprets the Habakkuk text as prophetic of the messianic era and contrasts its emphasis on faith with the Law's stress on action (3:11–12). The faith Habakkuk promised comes to the lawless Gentiles because Christ, suffering a criminal's execution, accepted the Law's "curse" on unlawful people and allowed them to become reconciled to God (3:13–14).

Role of the Mosaic Torah in human salvation. If, as Paul repeatedly asserts, the Torah cannot really help anyone, why was it given? Paul's answer is that the Mosaic Torah is a temporary device intended to teach human beings that they are unavoidably lawbreakers, sinners whose most conscientious efforts cannot earn divine favor. Using an analogy from Roman society, Paul compares the Law to a tutor—a man appointed to guide and protect youths until they attain legal adulthood. Like a tutor imposing discipline, the Law makes its adherents aware of their moral inadequacy and their need of a power beyond themselves to achieve righteousness. That power is Christ. Having served its purpose of preparing Abraham's children for Christ, the Torah is now obsolete and irrelevant (3:19–25).

The equality of all believers. Paul abolishes the Law's power to condemn and separate Jew from Gentile and asserts the absolute equality of all believers, regardless of their nationality, social class, or sex. Among God's children "there is no such thing as Jew and Greek, slave and free-man, male and female," because all are "one person in Christ Jesus" (3:26–28).

All believers are heirs of Abraham. Because Jesus purchased Christians' freedom from slavery to the Torah's yoke, all are now God's adopted heirs. As such they are entitled to claim the Deity as "Abba" ("Father" or "Daddy") and to receive the Abrahamic promises. Paul stresses the contrast between the church and Judaism by interpreting the Genesis story of Abraham's two wives as an allegory, a narrative in which the characters symbolize some higher truth. Hagar, Abraham's Egyptian slave girl, is earthly Jerusalem, controlled by Rome. Sarah, the patriarch's free wife, symbolizes the "heavenly Jerusalem," the spiritual church whose members are also free (4:21–31).

Responsibilities of freedom. What does freedom from Torah regulations mean? Aware that some Galatians used their liberty as an excuse to indulge any desire or appetite, Paul interprets his doctrine as freedom to practice neighborly love without external restrictions. Quoting lists of vices and virtues typical of Stoic ethical teaching, the Apostle notes that the Spirit will transcend believers' natural selfishness to produce generous actions (5:13–26).

Paul's exasperation with the Galatians' failure to understand that Jesus' death and resurrection are God's complete and all-sufficient means of human salvation inspires his most brutal insult. With savage irony he suggests that persons who insist on circumcision finish the job by emasculating themselves (5:7–12). Paul's remark may refer to an infamous practice among adherents of the goddess Cybele, some of whose male adherents mutilated themselves in religious frenzy. This oblique allusion to a pagan cult also implies that Paul's opponents were Galatian syncretists.

In closing his letter Paul seizes the pen from his secretary to write a final appeal to the Galatians in his own hand. Accusing his opponents of practicing circumcision only to escape persecution, presumably from Torah-abiding Jews, Paul summarizes his position: Torah obedience is meaningless because it implies that God's revelation through Jesus is not sufficient. Contrary to his opponents' limited view, Paul asserts that Jesus alone makes possible the new creation that unites humanity with its Creator. Note that Paul's closing words are as abrupt and self-directed as his opening complaint (1:6): "In future let no one make trouble for me" (6:11–17).

Letter to the Romans

Galatians was dictated in the white heat of exasperation; Romans is a more calmly reasoned presentation of Paul's doctrine of salvation through faith. This letter is generally regarded as the Apostle's most systematic expression of his theology. In it Paul thoughtfully explores an issue central to all world religions: how to bridge the moral gap between God and humankind, to reconcile imperfect, sinful humanity to a pure and righteous Deity. As a Jew Paul is painfully aware of the immense disparity between mortals and the immaculate holiness of the Supreme Being, whose justice cannot tolerate human error or wrongdoing. Yet Paul sees these irreconcilable differences between humanity and God as overcome in Christ, the Son who closes the gulf between perfect Father and imperfect children. In Paul's vision of reconciliation, God himself takes the initiative by recreating a deeply flawed humanity in his own transcendent image.

Purpose, Place, and Time of Composition

Unlike other Pauline letters, Romans is addressed to a congregation the writer has neither founded nor previously visited. In form, the work resembles a theological essay or sermon rather than an ordinary letter, lacking the kind of specific problem-solving advice that characterizes most of Paul's correspondence. Some commentators regard Romans as a circular letter, a document intended to explain Pauline teachings to various Christian groups who may at that time have held distorted views of the Apostle's position on controversial subjects.

Most scholars view chapter 16, which contains greetings to twenty-six different persons, as a separate missive. It was probably a letter of recommendation for Phoebe, who was a deacon of the church at Cenchreae, the port of Corinth. Since Aquila and Prisca (Priscilla) are mentioned, chapter 16 may originally have been sent to Ephesus, where Paul had worked with the couple (1 Cor. 16:19; Acts 18:18, 26). According to this view, an editor later attached the Ephesian letter to Romans, making it an appendix to the longer work.

Although Paul may have intended the document we call Romans to circulate through many different churches, at the time of writing he has compelling personal reasons to open communications with Rome. As 2 Corinthians 10–13 and Galatians reveal, Paul's churches in the northeastern Mediterranean region were rife with divisions and rebellion against his authority. Perhaps in hope of leaving this strife behind, Paul intends to move westward to Spain. He frankly confesses that he prefers to work in territories where no Christian has preceded him (Rom. 15:19–24; 1 Cor. 3:10–15; 2 Cor. 10:15–16). Paul writes not only to enlist Roman support for his Spanish mission (15:24) but also to make sure that his doctrines are understood and endorsed by the prestigious church at Rome, center of the imperial government and capital of the civilized world. He assures the Romans that he intends only to pass through their city, lest they fear a long visit from so difficult and controversial a figure.

Before journeying to Rome, however, Paul plans to take the money collected from his churches in Greece to the Jerusalem headquarters. He feels some anxiety about the trip to Judea, stronghold of his Jewish and Jewish-Christian opponents, and may have composed Romans as a means of marshalling the most effective arguments for his stand on the relationship between Judaism and Christianity (15:26–32). Chapters 9 through 11 contain his most extensive analysis of the mother religion's role in the divine plan. As Acts indicates, Paul's premonition of future trouble was fully justified by his subsequent arrest in Jerusalem and imprisonment in Caesarea (Acts 21–26). The letter was probably sent from Corinth about 56–57 CE.

Organization

The longest and most complex of Paul's letters, Romans may be divided into nine thematically related parts:

1. Introduction (1:1–15)
2. Statement of theme (1:16–17) and exploration of the human predicament; God's wrath directed at all humanity because all people are guilty of deliberate error (1:18–3:31)
3. Abraham is the model of faith (4:1–25)
4. Faith in Christ ensures deliverance from sin and death (5:1–7:25)
5. Renewed life in the Spirit (8:1–39)
6. The causes and results of Israel's disbelief (9:1–11:36)
7. Behavior in the church and the world (12:1–15:13)
8. Paul's future plans and greetings (15:14–33)
9. Appendix: Letter recommending Phoebe, a woman serving as deacon of the Cenchreae church (16:1–27)

Introduction

Paul opens the letter with an affirmation of his apostleship as the result of God's direct call (again implicitly denying that he owes his authority to any human ordination). He notes that Jesus became "Son of God" upon his resurrection, an echo of the early view of divine sonship ascribed to Peter in Acts 2:36. Similarly, Paul is chosen for a special role; he is divinely commissioned to achieve both faith and obedience among all people. As Apostle to the Gentiles, he now plans to bring his gospel to Rome (1:1–15).

Wrestling with the human predicament. Paul announces his main theme in terms of Habakkuk 2:4, the same verse proclaiming salvation "through faith" that he had quoted in his earlier letter to the Galatians (Gal. 3:11). The close relationship between Galatians and Romans is suggested by this repetition. Throughout this section of Romans (1:16–3:31), Paul attempts to demonstrate that faith in Christ is humanity's only way to escape God's just anger and its own deserved punishment. Because all human beings are guilty of willful error, whether Jew or Gentile, all stand condemned by God's justice.

The Gentiles' error. Paul continues with a thorough indictment of the entire human race, using ammunition borrowed from the arsenal of Hellenistic Judaism. He echoes passages from The Wisdom of Solomon, a Greek-Jewish work included in the Old Testament Apocrypha, as well as the concepts of "natural" and "unnatural" from the philosophies of Aristotle and the Stoics to denounce everyone who fails to recognize and worship the one true God. God's qualities, he argues, can be deduced from the physical world of nature. The wisdom and power of God as well as his grand design are evident in the cosmic order, so that persons who worship idols have perverted natural law. They honor created things in human or animal form instead of the One who created them (1:18–23).

Turning their backs on the Creator, human beings fall into ethical and sexual errors as well (see Wisd. of Sol. 14:11–31). In this controversial passage, Paul attributes the homosexual love affairs that characterized Greek and Roman culture to the Gentile practice of idolatry. Notice that Paul describes homosexual acts as a deliberate or willful turning away from a person's natural state. He assumes that physical attraction to a member of the same sex is a matter of conscious moral choice (rather than culturally or genetically determined) and identifies it as a rebellion against the divine will. How this attitude relates to Paul's doctrine of human freedom and his principle of conscience he does not explain (1:24–2:16).

The Jews are equally guilty. Although God provided the Jews with the Torah to guide them in righteousness, a fact that gives them an initial advantage over the pagans, they have not, Paul asserts, lived up to the Law's high standards. As a result, Jews have not achieved justification before God any more than Gentiles have. Paul reiterates his argument to the Galatians that the Torah fails to effect a right relationship between God and the lawkeeper; it serves only to make one conscious of sin (2:17–3:20).

All humanity, then, both Jew and Gentile, is in the same sinking boat, incapable of saving itself. No one can earn through his or her own efforts the right to enjoy divine approval. Paul now goes on to show how God—whose just nature does not permit him to absolve the unjust sinner—works to rescue undeserving humankind (3:21–31).

Abraham Is the Model of One "Justified" by Faith

Paul realizes that if his doctrine is to convince Jewish Christians it must find support in the Hebrew Bible. He therefore argues that God's plan of rescuing sinners through faith began with Abraham, foremost ancestor of the Jewish people. As in Galatians, he cites Genesis 15:5: Abraham's faith in God "was counted to him as righteousness." Long before Abraham was circumcised or the Mosaic Law was given, faith was made the means by which the just God, without compromising his impartiality, succeeds in justifying or declaring "righteous" his human creation. Thus is the way opened for believers to attain union with their Creator. As the example of one possessing faith even though uncircumcised, Abraham is the progenitor not only of Jews but of believing Gentiles as well. In his person he foreshadows the equality of all who manifest a similar faith. As Abraham proved his faith by obediently responding to God's voice, so must the faithful now respond to God's new summons through Christ (4:1–25).

Faith in Christ Ensures Deliverance from Sin and Death

The roles of Adam and Christ. At the outset of his letter (1:5) Paul declared that he tries to bring the whole world to a state of obedient faith. In chapter 5 he outlines a theory of history in which God uses these two qualities—obedience and faith—to achieve human salvation. God's intervention into human affairs became necessary when the first human being, Adam (whose name means "humankind"), disobeyed the Creator. Through this act Adam alienated not only himself but all his descendants from their Maker. Like other Jewish teachers of the first century, Paul interprets the Genesis story of Adam's disobedience as a tragic fall from grace, a cosmic disaster that introduces sin and death into the world. (Paul's word for "sin"—*hamartia*—is a Greek archery term, meaning "to miss the mark," "to fall short of a desired goal." Aristotle uses the same term to denote the "fatal flaw" of the tragic hero in Greek drama. *Hamartia* commonly refers to an error of judgment rather than an act of inborn human wickedness.) In Paul's moral scheme the entire race fails to hit the target of reunion with God, thus con-

demning itself to death—permanent separation from the Source of life.

Obedience to the Torah cannot save, because the Law merely defines errors and assigns legal penalties. It is God himself who overcomes the hopelessness of the human predicament. He does this by sending his Son, whose perfect obedience and sacrificial death provide a saving counterweight to Adam's sin. As all Adam's children share his mortal punishment, so all will share the reward of Christ's resurrection to life. It is the believer's faith in the saving power of Christ that makes him or her "righteous," enabling the just Deity to accept persons trustfully responding to his call (5:12–21).

Some later theologians used Romans 5 to formulate a doctrine of **original sin,** a teaching that all human beings inherit an unavoidable tendency to do wrong and are innately corrupt. From Augustine to Calvin such theologians took a deeply pessimistic view of human nature, in some cases regarding the majority of humankind as inherently depraved and justly damned.

Paul, however, stresses the joyful aspects of God's reconciliation to humanity. It is the Deity who initiates the process, making God's "grace"—his gracious will to love and give life—far exceed the measure of human failings. So universally powerful is God's determination to redeem humanity that Paul implies he will ultimately save all people, a concept the writer also alludes to in 1 Corinthians (compare Rom. 5:18–19; 1 Cor. 15:21–23).

A distortion of Paul's teaching on freedom. In chapter 6 Paul seems to be refuting misconceptions of his doctrine on Christian freedom. As in Galatia, some persons were apparently acting as if liberty from the Law entitled them to behave irresponsibly. In some cases they concluded that "sinning" was good because it allowed God's grace more opportunity to show itself. Paul reminds such dissidents that sin is a cruel tyrant who pays wages of death. By contrast, Christ treats his servants generously, bestowing the gift of everlasting life (6:1–23).

The Law's Holiness and Human Perversity

Paul makes one final attempt to place the Torah in the context of salvation history and to account for its failure to produce human righteousness. In Galatians Paul describes the Law harshly, referring to it as slavery, bondage, and death. Writing more temperately in Romans, he judges the Law "holy and just and good" (7:12). If so, why does it not serve to justify its practitioners?

In this case Paul answers that the fault lies not in the Torah but in human nature. The Torah is "spiritual," but human beings are "unspiritual," enslaved by sin. Throughout this long passage (7:7–25) Paul uses the first person as if he were analyzing his own nature and then projecting his self-admitted defects onto the rest of humanity. His "I," however, should probably read "we"—for he means to describe human nature collectively. Laws not only define crimes, he asserts, but create an awareness of lawbreaking that does not exist in their absence. Thus, the Torah makes sin come alive in the human consciousness (7:7–11).

Speaking as if sin were an animate force inside himself, Paul articulates the classic statement of ethical frustration—the opposition between the "good" he wishes to do and the "wrong" he actually performs. As he confronts the huge gap between his conscious will and his imperfect actions, Paul can only conclude that it is not the real "he" who produces the moral failure but the "sin that lodges in me" (7:14–20).

With his reason delighting in the Torah but his lower nature fighting against it, he finds that he incurs the Law's punishment—death. He bursts with desire to attain God's approval but always "misses the mark." In agony over his fate, he seeks some power to rescue him from an unsatisfying existence that ends only in death (7:21–25). Paul may be accused of attributing his personal sense of moral imperfection to everyone else, but his despairing self-examination illustrates why he feels the Law is unable to deliver one from the lethal attributes of imperfect human nature (8:3).

Renewed Life in the Spirit

Paul then tries to show how God accomplishes his rescue mission through Christ (8:1–39). By sharing humanity's imperfect nature and dying "as a sacrifice for sin," Christ transfers the Torah's penalties to sin itself, condemning it and not the human nature in which it exists (8:3–4). Because Christ's Spirit now dwells within the believer, sin no longer exerts its former control and new life can flourish in the Christian's body. Thus, Christians escape their imperfection, having put it to death with Christ on the cross. No longer sin's slaves, they become God's children, joint heirs with Christ (8:5–17).

Universal renewal. Paul uses mystical language to describe not only human nature but the physical cosmos itself struggling to be set free from the chains of mortality. During this period of cosmic renewal, the whole universe wails as if in childbirth. Believers now hope for a saving rebirth, but the reality is still ahead. Then they will be fully reshaped in the Son's image, the pattern of a new humanity reconciled to God (8:18–30).

Doxology. Paul concludes this section of his letter with one of his most memorable doxologies. It is a moving hymn of praise to the God who has lovingly provided the means for humanity to transcend its weakness and attain "the liberty and splendour" of God's children. In this brilliant credo, Paul declares his absolute confidence that no suffering or power, human or supernatural, can separate the believer from God's love (8:31–39).

The Causes and Results of Israel's Disbelief

Now that he has explained his position on the Law and the means by which God arranges human salvation, Paul explores the difficult question of Israel's rejection of its Messiah. How does it happen that the people to whom God granted his covenants, Torah, Temple, and promises failed to recognize Jesus as the Christ? First, Paul argues that God never intended all Israelites to receive his promises; they were meant for only a faithful remnant, represented in Paul's day by Jewish Christians (9:1–9). (Note that Paul's theory of a "faithful remnant" does not fully agree with other parts of his argument.)

Secondly, Paul tries to show that Israel's present unbelief is part of God's long-range plan to redeem all of humanity. In a long discourse sprinkled with loose paraphrases of passages from the Hebrew Bible, Paul makes several important assumptions about God's nature and the manner in which the Deity controls human destiny. He first assumes that because God's will is irresistible, human beings' freedom of choice is severely limited. Citing the Exodus story, Paul reminds his readers that Yahweh manipulated the Egyptian king in order to demonstrate his divine strength (Exod. 9:15–16). He argues that God's omnipotence entitles him to show favor or cruelty to whomever he pleases. Paul compares the Deity's arbitrariness to that of a potter who can assign one clay pot an honorable use and smash another if it displeases him. Implying that might makes right, Paul declares that no human being can justly challenge the supreme Potter's authority to favor one person and not another (9:10–21; 10:7–10).

Paul's assumption is that the Creator predetermines the human ability to believe or disbelieve, thus foreordaining an individual's eternal destiny. This assumption troubles many believers for its apparent repudiation of free will, although some have embraced it. Later theologians such as Augustine and Calvin formulated a doctrine of **predestination,** in which God—before the world's creation—decreed everyone's fate, selecting a few to enjoy heavenly bliss and relegating the majority to damnation.

Paul, however, emphasizes the positive aspect of God's apparent intervention into the human decision-making process. In God's long-range plan, Jewish refusal to recognize Jesus as the Messiah allows Gentiles to receive the gospel; thus, nations previously ignorant of God can achieve redemption. In a famous analogy, Paul likens Gentile believers to branches from a wild olive tree that have been grafted onto the cultivated olive trunk, which is natural Israel. If some of the old branches from the domesticated tree had not been lopped off, there would have been no room for the new (11:16–18). For humanity's universal benefit, God has taken advantage of Israel's unresponsiveness to produce a greater good.

Paul also states that the creation of churches in which Greeks and Romans now worship Israel's God will incite a healthy envy among Jews, kindling a desire to share the churches' spiritual favor. Furthermore, Israel's disbelief is only temporary. When all Gentiles become believers, then the natural branches will be regrafted onto God's olive tree and "the whole of Israel will be saved" (11:19–27).

Paul does not explain why both Israelites and Gentiles could not have been saved simultaneously, but he remains absolutely certain that the Jews are still God's chosen people. Writing before Rome destroyed the Jewish state in 70 CE, Paul does not predict divine vengeance upon Israel. He affirms instead that God's own integrity ensures that he will honor his promises to the covenant community. Some later Christian writers argue that God disowned Israel, replacing it with the Christian church. By contrast, Paul's witness confirms Israel's continuing role in the divinely ordered drama of human salvation (11:1–36).

Behavior in the Church and the World

Paul's ethical instruction (chs. 12–15) is again closely tied to his sense of apocalyptic urgency. Because the New Age is about to dawn, believers must conduct themselves with special care. Their rescue from the present evil age is extremely near—closer now than it was when they first believed (13:11). Paul apparently believed that the Parousia lay only a few years in the future.

Cooperation with government authority. Paul's advice, written before his imprisonment and prosecution in Rome, extends to Christian behavior outside the church and includes a program of obedience and cooperation with the governmental authorities. Echoing the Stoic view that the state exists to maintain public order and punish wrongdoing, Paul argues that the Roman Empire is a "divine institution"—an opinion in contrast with his earlier view that the present world is ruled by demonic forces (2 Cor. 4:4).

Although he emphasizes the Christian's duty to pay taxes and submit to legally constituted authority, Paul does not consider the ethical problem of a citizen's duty to resist illegal or unethical acts by the state. He does not advise believers to expend energy trying to change the present social system (13:1–10), perhaps because he sees it as so near its end. (Compare his attitude toward the state-supported institution of slavery discussed in Chapter 16.)

Rome as anti-Christ. Paul implies that voluntary cooperation with Rome will benefit Christians; he could not know that he soon would be among the first victims of a state-sponsored persecution of his faith. Following the emperor Nero's legal murder of many Roman believers (about 64–65 CE) and an even more severe persecution under Domitian (81–96 CE), some New Testament authors came to regard the state as Satan's earthly instrument to destroy God's people. After the Jerusalem Temple was razed in 70 CE, Rome became the new Babylon in the eyes of many Christians. The author of Revelation pictures Rome as a beast and predicts its fall as a cause of universal rejoicing (Rev. 17–19). At the time Paul wrote, however, the adversary relationship between church and state was still in the future.

Romans is the most comprehensive statement of Paul's teaching. In it Paul wrestles with the problems of humanity's estrangement from God and God's response to human need. Arguing that Torah observance cannot justify one to the righteous God, Paul states that in Christ the Deity creates a new humanity, a new beginning. Through Christ all persons with faith are able to become God's children and benefit from the promises made to Abraham.

God's ultimate plan is to defeat sin and reconcile all humanity—ironically, first Gentiles and then Jews—to himself. Because the time remaining is so short, believers must submit to existing governments and lead blameless lives.

QUESTIONS FOR DISCUSSION AND REVIEW

1. As Paul describes it in Romans 1–3, how is all humanity trapped in a hopeless predicament? How has God acted to rescue people from the power of sin and death?

2. Define what Paul means by such terms as righteousness, justification, and faith. According to Paul's evaluation of the Torah in Galatians and Romans, why are Torah observances such as circumcision irrelevant to God's action through Christ?

3. In both Galatians and Romans Paul cites excerpts from Genesis 15 and Habakkuk 2 to prove that God always intended faith to be the means by which humanity was to be "justified." Compare Paul's interpretation of Abraham's example with that given by James (2:14–26). Does James agree with Paul's explanation of the Genesis text?

4. Some commentators have argued that Paul misunderstands the purpose of Torah obedience. They claim that most Jewish teachers of his day did not present Torah observance as a means of salvation and that Paul's contrast between "works" and "faith" misrep-

resents first-century Judaism. From your reading of Galatians and Romans, how would you explain Paul's position?

TERMS AND CONCEPTS TO REMEMBER

Galatia	original sin
Judaizers	Abraham's faith
circumcision	righteousness
Torah obedience	(justification)
Paul's apostolic	God's plan for
authority	human salvation
children of Abraham	purpose of the Torah
social and sexual	Jesus' death and the
equality in Christ	"curse" of the
Rome	Law
hamartia	universal salvation
the nature of human	the role of natural
error	Israel
Adam and Christ	the wild olive tree
the connection	governmental
between sin and	authority
death	Paul's doctrine of
	salvation by faith

RECOMMENDED READING

General

Beker, J. C. *Paul: The Triumph of God in Life and Thought*. Philadelphia: Fortress Press, 1980.

Bornkamm, Gunther. *Paul*. New York: Harper & Row, 1971. Contains an incisive summary of Paul's thought in each of the genuine letters.

Keck, Leander, and V. P. Furnish. *The Pauline Letters*. Nashville: Abingdon Press, 1984. Contains a concise survey of Paul's major ideas.

Soards, M. L. *The Apostle Paul: An Introduction to His Writings and Teaching*. Mahwah, N.J.: Paulist Press, 1987. A valuable analysis of Paul's life, letters, and theology.

Ziesler, John. *Pauline Christianity*. New York: Oxford University Press, 1983. A relatively brief but careful and systematic analysis of key Pauline concepts.

Galatians

Betz, H. D. *Galatians*. Hermeneia Commentary. Philadelphia: Fortress Press, 1979. A scholarly analysis.

Cousar, C. B. *Galatians*. Interpretation. Commentary. Atlanta: John Knox, 1982.

Ebeling, Gerhard. *The Truth of the Gospel: An Exposition of Galatians*. Philadelphia: Fortress Press, 1985.

Romans

Achtemeier, P. J. *Romans*. Interpretation. Commentary. Atlanta: John Knox, 1985.

Barrett, C. K. *A Commentary on the Epistle to the Romans*. Harper's New Testament Commentaries. New York: Harper & Row, 1957. A solid, scholarly treatment.

Cranfield, C. E. B. *A Critical and Exegetical Commentary on the Epistle to the Romans*. International Critical Commentary. 2 vols. Edinburgh: T. & T. Clark, 1975, 1979. A standard work incorporating the history of Pauline interpretation.

Kasemann, Ernst. *Commentary on Romans*. Grand Rapids, Mich.: Eerdmans, 1980. An intensely scholarly study for more serious readers.

Sanders, E. P. *Paul and Palestinian Judaism*. Philadelphia: Fortress Press, 1978. The most important recent study of Paul's relationship to rabbinic Judaism.

———. *Paul, the Law and the Jewish People*. Philadelphia: Fortress Press, 1983.

16 Letters from Prison: Philippians, Philemon, and Colossians

He [Jesus] did not think to snatch at equality with
God, but made himself nothing, assuming the nature
of a slave.

(Phil. 2:6–7)

The secret is this: Christ in you, the hope of a glory
to come.

(Col. 1:27)

KEY THEMES Although it contains some sharp criticism of his opponents, Paul's letter to
the Philippian church reveals an unusual warmth and friendliness in general.
Urging cooperation for the mutual benefit of all believers, Paul cites an
early hymn that depicts Jesus as the opposite of Adam—a humbly obedient
son whose self-emptying leads to his heavenly exaltation.

In Colossians, which may be the work of a Pauline disciple, the author
stresses Jesus' identity with the cosmic power and wisdom by and for
which the universe was created. The divine secret is revealed as Christ's
Spirit dwelling in the believer.

The Apostle's only surviving personal letter, Philemon shows Paul
accepting the Greco-Roman institution of slavery while simultaneously
stressing that Christians of all social classes are intimately related in love.

According to an early church tradition, Paul wrote four canonical letters while imprisoned in Rome—Ephesians, Philippians, Colossians, and Philemon. Known as the "captivity letters," they were long believed to represent the Apostle's most mature reflections on such topics as the divine nature of Christ (Phil. 2:5–11; Col. 1:13–20; 2:9–15) and the mystic unity of the church (Eph. 1–5).

Rigorous scholarly analysis of the four works, however, has raised serious questions about the time and place of their composition as well as the authorship of two of them. All leading scholars accept Philippians and Philemon as genuinely Pauline writings, but many (perhaps sixty percent) challenge Paul's authorship of

Colossians. Even more deny that he wrote Ephesians, a work that differs in content, tone, and style from the Apostle's accepted letters. Because so many scholars question Paul's responsibility for Colossians, we discuss it separately in the second part of this chapter. (We discuss first the undisputed letters, Philippians and Philemon.) Ephesians, which the scholarly majority think is a post-Pauline work, is included in Chapter 17. (For scholarly arguments defending or denying Pauline authorship of these works, the student may consult the recommended readings listed at the end of this chapter.)

Place of origin. Scholars pose various objections to the old belief that Paul wrote Philippians

237

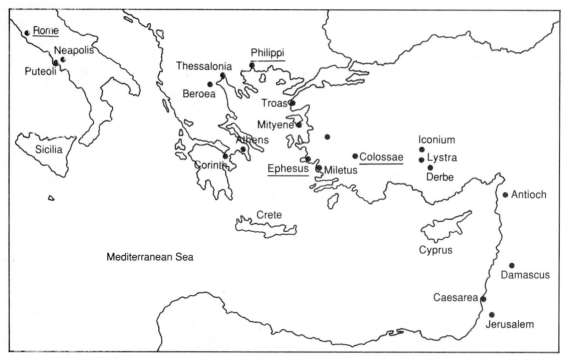

Figure 16-1. Paul may have written his "letters from prison" from Rome (in the far west on this map), from Ephesus (on the coast of present-day Turkey), or from Caesarea (in the far eastern Mediterranean). Note that Ephesus is much closer to Philippi than either of the other two cities.

and the other letters while under house arrest in Rome (Acts 28). In the Apostles' day, traveling the almost eight hundred miles between Rome and Philippi, located in northeastern Greece, took as long as ten months (see Figure 16-1). Philippians implies that Paul's friends made four journeys between Philippi and his place of imprisonment and that a fifth trip was planned (Phil. 2:25–26). Some scholars consider the distance separating these two cities too great to travel so frequently. They propose Ephesus, a city where Paul spent three years (Acts 20:31) and which is only about ten days' travel time from Philippi, as the place of origin. Philippians' references to the Praetorian Guard, the Roman emperor's personal militia (1:13), and "the imperial establishment" (4:22) do not necessar-

ily mean that the letter originated in Rome. Ancient inscriptions recently discovered in Ephesus show that members of the Praetorian Guard and other imperial officials were stationed in the Roman province of Asia, where Ephesus and Colossae are located.

Although many scholars support the "Ephesian theory," others suggest that Paul wrote from Caesarea, where he was imprisoned for two years (Acts 23–25). Still other critics point out that we lack proof that Paul was actually jailed in Ephesus; they also claim that the difficulties in traveling between Macedonia and Rome have been overstated. Where Paul was imprisoned remains an open question, although many commentators still uphold the traditional view that Paul's prison letters emanate from the Roman capital.

Letter to the Philippians

Paul enjoyed an unusually warm and affectionate relationship with Christians at Philippi. He and Timothy had established the church during their first tour of Greece (Acts 16:11–40), and he maintained an intimate communication with the Philippians, who were the only group from whom he would accept financial support (4:15–16). In welcome contrast to the "boasting" and threats that characterize the letters to Corinth and Galatia, Philippians contains no impassioned defense of his authority (his friends in Philippi did not question it). The author instead exposes a more kindly and loving aspect of his personality.

Like all genuinely Pauline letters, Philippians reveals the author's quick changes of mood, ranging from a personal meditation on the meaning of his impending death to a brief but savage attack on his opponents. The letter features so many abrupt changes of subject and shifts of emotion that many analysts believe that, like 2 Corinthians, it is a composite work, containing parts of three or four different missives.

According to this theory, the note thanking the Philippians for their financial help (4:10–20 or 23) was composed first, followed by a letter warning the church about potential troublemakers (partially preserved in 1:1–3:1a and 4:2–9). A third letter bitterly attacks advocates of circumcision (3:1b–4:1). The letter may be a unity, however, for Paul commonly leaps from topic to topic, registering different emotional responses to different problems in the course of a single letter.

Philippians is important not only for the insight it permits into Paul's volatile character but also for the clues it gives to early Christian beliefs about Jesus' nature. The key passage appears in Philippians 2:5–11, in which Paul seems to quote a primitive hymn celebrating Jesus' humble obedience and subsequent exaltation.

Organization. Philippians covers a variety of topics, but it may be divided into six relatively brief units:

1. Salutation and thanksgiving (1:1–11)
2. Paul's meditation on his imprisonment (1:12–30)
3. Exhortation to humility, in imitation of Christ's example (2:1–18)
4. Recommendation of Timothy and Epaphroditus (2:19–3:1a)
5. Attack on advocates of circumcision and exhortation to live harmoniously, in imitation of Paul (3:1b–4:9)
6. Note of thanks for financial help (4:10–23)

The significance of Paul's imprisonment. After affectionately greeting the Philippians (1:1–11), Paul explores the significance of his prison experience and courageously stresses its positive results. Apparently widely talked about, his case gives other believers the opportunity to witness publicly for Christ. On the other hand, not all of Paul's fellow Christians support him; they use his imprisonment as a means of stirring up new troubles for the prisoner. Paul does not identify those Christians whose personal jealousies complicate his already difficult situation, but they may have been connected with the "advocates of circumcision" denounced in chapter 3. In Acts' narration of Paul's arrest, imprisonment in Caesarea, and transportation to Rome under armed guard, the Jerusalem church leadership is conspicuously absent from his defense. Perhaps those who shared James's adherence to Torah obligations were in some degree pleased to see Paul and his heretical views under legal restraint.

Paul's attitude toward his troublesome rivals is far milder than it was in Galatians. Determined to find positive results even in his opponents' activities, he concludes that their motives, whether sincere or hypocritical, are finally irrelevant: they successfully proclaim the Christian message (1:12–18).

St. Paul in Prison by Rembrandt (1606–1669). In his murky cell Paul composes letters to inspire faith and hope in the membership of his tiny, scattered churches. Notice that the light from the cell's barred window seems to emanate from Paul himself, surrounding his head like a halo and glowing from the pages of the manuscript he holds. (Courtesy Staatsgalerie, Stuttgart.)

As he contemplates the possibility of his execution, Paul is torn between wishing to live for his friends' sake and wishing to "depart and be with Christ." He would thus attain a posthumous union with his Lord while awaiting resurrection (see 1 Cor. 15). Paul places himself on a par with his beloved Philippians when he states that they run the same race as he to win life's ultimate prize (1:19–30). Despite his ceaseless efforts, Paul remains aware of his imperfection and explicitly states that he is not yet certain of victory (3:10–14).

The Hymn to Christ

Chapter 2 contains the letter's most important theological concept. Urging the Philippians to place others' welfare before their own, Paul cites Jesus' behavior as the supreme example of humble services to others. To enable his readers to share the same attitude and experience as Christ, he recites a hymn that illustrates his intent. The rhythmic and poetic qualities of this work, as well as the absence of typically Pauline ideas and vocabulary, indicates that it is a pre-

Pauline composition. The first stanza reads as follows:

> Who though he was in the form of God,
> Did not count equality with God
> A thing to be grasped,
>
> But emptied himself,
> Taking the form of a servant,
> Being born in the likeness of men.
>
> And being found in human form
> He humbled himself
> And became obedient unto death
> (2:6–8, Revised Standard Version)

The hymn's second stanza (2:9–11) describes how God rewards Jesus' selfless obedience by granting him universal lordship. God elevates Jesus "to the glory of God, the Father."

In this famous passage, which has been translated in various ways to stress different theories about Christ's divinity, Jesus' relation to the Father is ambiguously stated. Since the fourth century CE, when the church adopted the doctrine of the Trinity, it has commonly been assumed that the hymn refers to Jesus' prehuman existence and affirms the son's coeternity and coequality with the Father.

Remembering Paul's explicit subordination of Jesus to God in 1 Cor. 15:24–28, many readers will be cautious about attributing post–New Testament ideas to the Apostle. A growing number of scholars believe that Paul employs the hymn in order implicitly to contrast two "sons" of God—Adam (Luke 3:38) and Jesus. (The Adam-Christ contrast figures prominently in 1 Cor. 15:21–23, 45–49, and Rom. 5:12–19.) The mention of "form" (Greek, *morphe*) refers to the divine image that both Adam and Jesus reflect (Gen. 1:26–28). But whereas Adam tried to seize God-like status (Gen. 3:5), Jesus takes the form of a slave. Instead of rebelling against the Creator, he is submissively obedient unto death.

Finally, Adam's disobedience brings shame and death, but Jesus' total obedience brings glory and exaltation. Jesus' self-emptying earns him the fullness of God's reward, the bestowal of "the name above all names," to whom all creation submits. In accordance with his usual method of using theology to drive home behavioral instruction, Paul implicitly compares the reward given Jesus' humility with that in store for humbly obedient Christians. Now shining like "stars in a dark world," they will inherit a future life similar to that now enjoyed by Jesus (2:14–18).

Recommendations of Timothy and Epaphroditus. The references to Timothy and Epaphroditus, two of his favorite companions, suggest Paul's warm capacity for friendship. Timothy, whose name appears as courtesy coauthor of this letter (1:1), is one of Paul's most reliable associates. Unlike Barnabas and John Mark, with whom Paul quarreled, Timothy (who is half-Jewish and half-Greek) shares Paul's positive attitude toward Gentile converts. In the Apostle's absence, Paul trusts him to act as he would (2:19–24).

Epaphroditus, whom the Philippians had sent to assist Paul in prison, has apparently touched Paul by the depth of his personal devotion. Epaphroditus's dangerous illness, which delayed his return to Philippi, may have resulted from having risked his life to help the prisoner. Paul implies his gratitude when urging the Philippians to give Epaphroditus an appreciative welcome home (2:25–3:1a).

Paul's concern for individual believers in Philippi is also apparent in his personal message for two estranged women, Euodia and Syntyche. Pleading with sensitivity and tact for their reconciliation, he ranks the two women as coworkers who share his efforts to promote the gospel (4:2–3).

Attacking advocates of circumcision. In Chapter 3 flashes of Paul's old fire give his words a glowing edge. This section (3:1b–20), which is thought to have originated as a separate memorandum, attacks Judaizers who insist on circumcising Gentile converts. Denouncing circumcision as "mutilation," he contemptuously dismisses his opponents as "dogs"—the common Jewish tag for the uncircumcised. Paul provides valuable autobiographical information when he cites his ethnic qualifications—superior to those of his enemies—to evaluate the advantages of being a Jew. Despite his exemplary credentials—and his perfection in keeping the Torah regulations—he discounts his Jewish heritage as "garbage." All human advantages are worthless when compared to the new life God gives in Christ (3:1–11).

Letter to Philemon

Philemon is Paul's only surviving personal letter, but it is not an entirely private communication. Besides Philemon, it is addressed to "Apphia our sister" and "Archippus our comrade in arms," perhaps the chief recipient's wife and son. The family may have been leaders in "the congregation at [their] house," before which the letter was probably intended to be read (vv. 1–2).

Although it is Paul's shortest letter, it deals with a big subject—the problem of human slavery among Christians. Paul writes to Philemon on behalf of the runaway slave Onesimus, who had apparently stolen money and illegally departed from Philemon's household. Onesimus's fate brought him from Colossae to Rome (or Ephesus, if that is where Paul's captivity letters originated), where the slave was converted to Christianity, perhaps by Paul himself.

Although Onesimus has made himself almost indispensable to the imprisoned Apostle, Paul—compelled by Roman law—has no choice but to send the slave back to his master. Maintaining a fine balance between exercising his apostolic authority and appealing to the equality existing among all Christians, Paul asks Philemon to receive Onesimus back, treating him "no longer as a slave, but . . . as a dear brother" (v. 15). We do not know if Paul is thereby requesting the master to free Onesimus, granting

him legal and social status to match his Christian freedom, but the writer clearly stresses the slave's human value. Paul writes that Onesimus is "a part of myself" and that Philemon should welcome him as he would the Apostle himself (vv. 12, 17).

Paul also gives his guarantee that he will reimburse Philemon for any debt Onesimus may have incurred (or, perhaps, money he may have stolen) (vv. 18–20). Appealing to Philemon's love (v. 7) and duty (v. 8), he anticipates the master's generosity by predicting that Philemon will "do better than [he] asks" (v. 21). Some commentators observe that Paul is asking Philemon in not too subtle a way to free Onesimus in order for him to remain in Paul's service.

In a final request, Paul asks that Philemon have a guest room prepared for him, indicating that the Apostle expects to be released from prison in the foreseeable future. The letter closes with greetings from, among others, Mark and Luke, traditional authors of the two Gospels bearing their respective names.

The Question of Slavery

Readers may be disappointed that Paul does not denounce human slavery as an intolerable evil. Instead, he merely accepts its existence as a social fact, nowhere ordering Christians to free the human beings they owned as chattel. Paul's attitude is consistent with both the biblical tradition and the practices of Greco-Roman society.

The Hebrew bible regulates slavery, distinguishing between Gentile slaves captured in battle and Hebrew slaves who sold themselves or their children to pay off financial debts. In a Torah passage known as the "Book of the Covenant," the Law decrees that after six years' servitude, a male Hebrew slave is to be set free. Any children born to him and one of his master's female slaves, however, are to remain the master's property. If at the end of six years' time the freed man wishes to remain with his wife and family, he must submit to a mutilation of the ear (the organ of obedience) and remain a slave for life (Ex. 21:2–6).

Following the Torah and the institutions of society at large, the New Testament writers neither condemn slavery nor predict its abolition. At the same time, the persistence of slavery was inconsistent with the ethical principles of Christian freedom and the human being's innate worth advocated in Paul's letters and the Gospels. In American history both pro- and antislavery parties used the New Testament to support their conflicting views. Slavery's proponents argued that Bible writers, including Paul, implicitly accepted the institution as a "natural" condition. Those against slavery extrapolated from Paul's doctrine of freedom and Christian equality a corresponding social and legal freedom for all people.

A Disputed Letter to the Colossians

If Paul is the author of Colossians, as a large minority of scholars believe, he had not yet visited the city when he wrote this theologically important letter. A small town in the Roman province of Asia, Colossae was located about one hundred miles southeast of Ephesus, the provincial capital (see Figure 16-1). Epaphras, one of Paul's missionary associates, had apparently founded the church a short time prior to Paul's writing (1:7).

If genuine, Colossians was probably composed at about the same time as Philemon, to which it is closely related. In both letters Paul writes from prison, including his friend Timothy in the salutation (1:1) and adding greetings from many of the same persons—such as Onesimus, Archippus, Aristarchus, Epaphras, Mark, and Luke—cited in the earlier missive (4:9–18). If Philemon's was the house church at Colossae, it is strange that Paul does not mention him, but his absence from the letter does not discredit Pauline authorship.

Purpose. Although it was not one of his churches, Paul (or one of his later disciples) writes to the Colossae congregation to correct some false teachings prevalent there. These beliefs apparently involved cults that gave undue honor to angels or other invisible spirits inhabiting the universe. Some Colossians may have attempted to worship beings that the angels themselves worshipped. Paul refutes these "hollow and delusive" notions by emphasizing Christ's uniqueness and supremacy. Christ alone is the channel to spiritual reality; lesser spirit beings are merely his "captives."

Organization. Paul writes to make sure that the Colossians clearly recognize who Christ really is. The author emphasizes two principal themes: (1) Christ is supreme because God's power now manifested in him was the same power that created the entire universe, including those invisible entities the false teachers mistakenly worship. (2) When they realize Christ's supremacy and experience his indwelling Spirit, the Colossians are initiated into his mystery cult, voluntarily harmonizing their lives with the cosmic unity he embodies.

Christ the Source of Cosmic Unity

In the opinion of some analysts, both the complex nature of the false teachings, which seem to blend pagan and marginally Jewish ideas into a Gnostic synthesis, and the Christology of Colossians seem too "advanced" for the letter to have originated in Paul's day. Other critics point out that if the letter was written late in Paul's career to meet a situation significantly different from others he had earlier encountered, it could well have stimulated the Apostle to produce a more fully developed expression of his views about Christ's nature and function.

Jesus as the mediator of creation. As in the second chapter of Philippians, the author seems to adapt an older Christian hymn to illustrate his vision of the exalted Jesus' cosmic role:

He is the image of the invisible god, the first-born
  of all creation;
for in him all things were created, in heaven and
  on earth, visible and invisible, whether thrones
  or dominions or principalities or authorities
all things were created through him and for him.

He is before all things,
  and in him all things hold together.
He is the head of the body, the church;

he is the beginning, the first-born from the dead,
  that in everything he might be pre-eminent.

For in him all the fullness of God was pleased to
  dwell,
and through him to reconcile to himself all things,
  whether on earth or in heaven,
  making peace by the blood of his cross.
                    (1:15–20, Revised Standard Version)

Like the prologue to John's Gospel, this
beautiful poem is modeled on biblical and Hellenistic Jewish concepts of divine Wisdom (Prov.
8:22–31; Ecclus. 24:1–22; see also the discussion
of John's use of Logos [Word] in Chapter 10).
Hellenistic Jews had created a rich lore of speculative thought in which God's chief attribute,
his infinite Wisdom, is the source of all creation
and the means by which he communicates his
purpose to humanity. Many historians believe
that early Christian thinkers adopted these ready-
made Wisdom traditions and applied them to
Jesus.

Like Philippians 2, the Colossians hymn is
traditionally seen as proclaiming Jesus' heavenly
preexistence and his personal role as mediator
in creation. More recently, many scholars—recognizing the hymn's use of Wisdom language—
view it as a declaration that the same divine
presence and power that created the cosmos now
operates in the glorified Christ. The personified
Wisdom whom God employed as his agent in
fashioning the universe is now fully revealed in
Christ, the agent through whom God redeems
his human creation.

The phrase "image [*eikon*] of the invisible
God" (1:15) may correspond to the phrase "form
[*morphes*] of God" that Paul used in Philippians
(2:6). In both cases the term echoes the words

of Genesis 1, in which God creates the first human beings in his own "image" (Gen. 1:26–
27). (Notice that the writer describes the Colossians as also bearing the divine "image"
[3:10].) Rather than asserting that the prehuman
Jesus was literally present at creation, the hymn
may affirm that he is the ultimate goal toward
which God's world trends.

Whatever Christology he advances, the writer's main purpose is to demonstrate Christ's
present superiority to all rival cosmic beings.
The "thrones, sovereignties, authorities and
powers" mentioned (1:16) probably represent
the Jewish hierarchy of angels. Christ's perfect
obedience, vindicating God's image in humanity, and his ascension to heaven have rendered
these lesser beings irrelevant and powerless. By
his triumph, Christ leads them captive as a Roman emperor leads a public procession of conquered enemies (2:9–15).

Moving from Christ's supremacy to his own
role in the divine plan, Paul states that his task
is to deliver God's message of reconciliation.
He is the agent chosen to reveal the divine "secret hidden for long ages"—the glorified Christ
dwelling in the believer, spiritually reuniting the
Christian with God. Christians thus form
Christ's visible body, here identified with the
church (1:21–2:8).

The mystical initiation into Christ. Employing
the rather obscure language of Greek mystery
religions (see Chapter 4), Paul compares the
Christian's baptism to a vicarious experience of
Christ's death and resurrection (2:12, 20; 3:1).
It is also the Christian equivalent of circumcision, the ritual sign that identifies one as belonging to God's people, and the rite of initiation into Christ's "body" (2:12–14). Raised to
new life, initiated believers are liberated from
religious obligations sponsored by those lesser
spirits who transmitted the Torah revelation to
Moses.

Empowered by Christ's Spirit, the Colossians should not be intimidated by self-styled
authorities who mortify the body and piously

forbid partaking of certain food and drink, for Christ's death ended all such legal discrimination. Although the author declares the equality of all believers, regardless of nationality or social class, notice that he omits the unity of the sexes that Paul included in Gal. 3:28 (2:20–3:11). As with many Greco-Roman mystery cults, initiation into Christ is a union of social and religious equality.

Obligations of initiation. Consistent with Paul's custom, the author concludes by stressing the ethical implications of his theology. Because Christians experience the indwelling Christ, they must live exceptionally pure and upright lives. The list of vices (3:5–9) and virtues (3:12–25) is typical of other Hellenistic teachers of ethics, but the writer adds a distinctively Christian note: believers behave well because they are being re-created in Christ's nature and "image" (3:10).

Paul's Lasting Influence

During his lifetime Paul fought constantly to win other Christians' recognition that his gospel and claim to apostleship were legitimate. Even his own churches frequently challenged his authority and doubted his view that humans receive salvation through God's free gift, accepted in faith, rather than through obedience to the biblical Torah. Ironically, in the decades following his death—as the church slowly changed from a mostly Jewish to a largely Gentile institution—Paul was recognized as chief among the missionary apostles, and his doctrine became the basis for much of the church's theology.

By the mid–second century, when the document known as 2 Peter was written, Paul's collected letters had assumed the authority of Scripture, at least in some Christian circles. At the same time, Paul's difficult ideas and sometimes obscure phrasing left his work open to a variety of interpretations. The author of 2 Peter denounces students of Paul who interpret Pau-

line thought in a way contrary to official church teaching:

> [Paul] wrote to you with his inspired wisdom. And so he does in all his other letters, . . . though they contain some obscure passages, which the ignorant and unstable misinterpret to their own ruin, as they do the other scriptures. (2 Pet. 3:16).

Then as now, not only the "ignorant and unstable" but also the well educated and relatively well balanced may disagree on Paul's intentions in many "obscure passages."

Paul's accomplishments. In a characteristic remark Paul observes that he works harder than any other Apostle to bring the Christian message to potential converts (2 Cor. 11:23) (Figure 16-2). Even today the enormous distances he traveled, by sea and on foot, would challenge the physical stamina of the most dedicated missionary. He established Christian "colonies" throughout Syria, Asia Minor, Macedonia, and Greece and left behind an impressive network of churches. These were interconnected by itinerant missionaries (many trained by Paul himself) and at least partly united by memories of Paul's preaching and the written legacy of his voluminous correspondence. As the author of Acts realized, Paul also made himself a formidable model for later believers to emulate.

Paul—Christianity's First Great Interpreter of Christ

Although not a systematic thinker, Paul was the first to create a coherent theology about Jesus and is thus counted as Christianity's first theologian. Interpreting Jesus' career theologically—showing how God (*theos*) revealed his will through Jesus' death and resurrection—Paul laid the foundations upon which later interpreters of the "Christ event" have built. We have space here to summarize only a few of Paul's main ideas. The ones we select illustrate the general trend of his views on the nature of God and his purpose in using Jesus to reconcile the

Figure 16-2. Locations of the major churches at the end of Paul's ministry (about 62 CE). Note that most of the tiny cells of Christians are at the eastern end of the Mediterranean (Palestine and Syria) or in Asia Minor (present-day Turkey). Paul established most of the churches in western Asia Minor as well as the first churches in Greece (Philippi to Corinth). We do not know who founded the Italian churches, including the one in Rome. How or when Christianity was introduced to Egypt (Alexandria and Cyrene) is also unknown.

previously alienated human and divine components of the universe.

God. As a "Hebrew born and bred" (Phil. 3:5), Paul is unquestioningly a monotheist, recognizing the Jewish God as the entire world's Supreme Power and Judge. Steeped in the Hebrew Bible's composite portrait of Yahweh, Paul regards God as embodying human traits on a superhuman scale. Both "severe" and "kind," he manifests his dual nature to human beings, alternately condemning or showing mercy according to an irresistible will. He is incomparably holy, just, and pure; his perfect justice does not allow full communion with imperfect, deliberately unjust, and otherwise sinful human-

ity. His infinite love, however, sets in motion a joyous process of reconciling an estranged human creation to himself.

The role of Jesus. Paul realized that his fellow Jews expected an undefeated Messiah and that Jesus' crucifixion was a major "stumbling block" to Jewish acceptance. He therefore formulated a theology of the cross. In Romans and Galatians he interprets the crucifixion as a redemptive act in which human "weakness"—Jesus' "shameful" death—is the means by which God bridges the great moral gulf between himself and humanity. Demonstrating absolute obedience to the divine will, Jesus sacrifices his life to satisfy God's justice and obtain forgiveness for others.

Justification. By "justification" or "righteousness" Paul means a right standing or relationship with God. Keeping the Mosaic Torah cannot justify people, because the Torah only serves to make one aware of lawbreaking, of committing "sin" (*hamartia*), of falling short of ethical perfection. When he died voluntarily, Jesus not only took on himself the Law's penalty for all sinners but transferred just punishment to sin itself. He thus rid sin of its power to operate uncontrolled in what Paul calls our "fleshly" (physical) or "lower" nature (Rom. 1–4).

Adam and Christ. In Paul's view of human history, the earthly prototype—Adam—willfully disobeyed God, thus separating himself from life's source and bringing sin (error) and death to himself and all his descendants. In Jesus God found Adam's moral opposite, a man of perfect obedience who achieved a right relationship with God and through his resurrection became God's Son (Rom. 1:4). Now the model of a renewed humanity reconciled to God, Jesus as Christ brings life to all who place their trust (faith) in him (Rom. 5; 1 Cor. 15).

Salvation through faith. The idea that human beings are saved by their faith is one of Paul's most distinctive and revolutionary ideas. By *faith* Paul does not mean belief in a creed or a set of religious doctrines. Pauline faith denotes an individual's inner awareness of and trust in God's ability—and willingness—to draw believers to him in love. To Paul, faith is a dynamic force that motivates people to accept God's free gift of salvation; it is a voluntary response to divine grace. Because God gives his rewards freely, a person can neither earn nor deserve them. Hence, works of the Torah—including circumcision and food purity laws—are irrelevant.

God and Christ. Although he calls the glorified Jesus "lord" (Greek, *kyrios*) and assigns him the highest possible status in God's plan for universal redemption, Paul remains a Jewish monotheist, always regarding the Son as sub-

ordinate to the Father (1 Cor. 15:24–28). Jesus refuses to attempt "equality with God" and is eternally the model of humble submission to the paternal will (Phil. 2:6–7). In some metaphysical sense, however, the Son is the agent by whom God created the universe, in whom "the complete being of the Godhead dwells embodied," and through whom the divine purpose is revealed (Col. 1–2). As human beings were originally created in God's "image" (Gen. 1:27), so Christ is that divine-human image perfected (Col. 1:15).

Eschatology. Since Paul believes that he is living at the very edge of the New Age introduced by Jesus' advent, Paul places much of his ethical instruction to the church in the context of end time. Jesus' resurrection and ascension to heaven now allow Christ's Spirit to dwell in each believer, giving him or her charismatic gifts of prophesying, healing, teaching, and speaking in or interpreting ecstatic language. Paul regards these spiritual gifts as further evidence of the "last days" and urges believers to produce the Spirit's good fruits—joyful virtues and a grateful awareness that in Christ they attain a new nature. Thus are they prepared for the "splendour" of the resurrection body they will receive at the Parousia.

This brief survey, concentrating on Paul's vision of the Deity's gracious plan to redeem humanity through Christ, does scant justice to the range and profundity of Pauline thought. The Apostle's views on free will and predestination, Christian ethics, the church, human sexuality, and related matters require fuller discussion than we can offer here.

Embattled in his own day, within two generations after his death Paul became a monument of oxthodoxy (correct teaching) to many church leaders. The letters to Timothy and Titus, written in Paul's name by a later disciple, show in what high regard the Apostle was held (Chapter 17). After another fourteen hundred years had passed, Paul again became a center of controversy. During the Protestant Reformation, conflicting interpretations of the Pauline belief that human beings are saved by faith and not by works (including the performance of sacramental rituals) deeply divided Roman Catholics and Protestants. Today Paul remains a stimulating, dynamic influence wherever the New Testament is read. Second only to Jesus in his lasting influence upon Christendom, he is the prism through which Jesus' image is most commonly viewed.

QUESTIONS FOR DISCUSSION AND REVIEW

1. Why is it difficult to know exactly where Paul was imprisoned when he wrote to Philemon and the church at Philippi?
2. Although the hymn Paul cites in Philippians 2 is commonly interpreted as describing Jesus' prehuman existence, many commentators believe that it contains instead an implied contrast between Adam's disobedience and Jesus' humble obedience. Discuss the arguments for and against these differing interpretations.
3. Identify Philemon and Onesimus and their connection to Paul. Why do you think that Paul does not condemn human slavery as an evil institution?
4. Summarize critical doubts about Colossians' authorship. When you read the letter, do the ideas and phrasing "sound like" Paul? Explain your answer.
5. Analyze the similarities between the two Christian hymns quoted respectively in Philippians 2 and Colossians 1. Compare the view that humanity bears God's image (Gen. 1:27) with the similar language applied to Jesus (Col. 1:15). In what ways does the Colossians hymn apply the concepts of Israel's Wisdom tradition to Jesus?
6. Summarize Paul's major contributions to Christian thought, including his beliefs about

the *eschaton,* his teachings about the nature and function of Christ (Christology), and his doctrine of justification by faith.

TERMS AND CONCEPTS TO REMEMBER

Philippi
city at which the "prison letters" originated
Jesus' submission and exaltation (Phil. 2)
Timothy
Epaphroditus
Onesimus
Paul's attitude toward slavery
biblical view of slavery

authorship of Colossians
Jesus as "image of God"
Jesus' nature and function
Jesus' cosmic role
Christology
initiation into Christ
Paul's achievements
Paul's most distinctive teachings

RECOMMENDED READING

Barth, M., ed. and trans. *Colossians and Philomen.* Vol. 34a of the Anchor Bible. Garden City, N.Y.: Doubleday, 1974. A scholarly translation and analysis.

Beare, F. W. *A Commentary on the Epistle to the Philippians.* Harper's New Testament Commentaries. New York: Harper & Row, 1959. Another new translation with solid, concise commentary.

Knox, John. *Philemon Among the Letters of Paul.* Rev. ed. New York: Abingdon Press, 1959. Develops Edgar Goodspeed's theory that about 90 CE, a Paulinist—perhaps the former slave Onesimus, who may then have been bishop of Ephesus—collected Paul's letters and circulated them among the entire church.

Lohse, Eduard. *Colossians and Philemon.* Hermeneia. Philadelphia: Fortress Press, 1971. A scholarly analysis concluding that Colossians is by a Pauline disciple.

O'Brien, P. T. *Colossians, Philemon.* Word Biblical Commentary 44. Waco, Tex.: Word Books, 1982. Defends Pauline authorship of Colossians; includes author's translation.

Schweizer, Eduard. *The Letter to the Colossians: A Commentary.* Minneapolis: Augsburg Publishing House, 1982. Less technical than works by Lohse and O'Brien, this study suggests that Timothy played a role in writing Colossians.

Stendahl, K., ed. and trans. *Romans, Galatians, and Philippians.* Vol. 33 of the Anchor Bible. Garden City, N.Y.: Doubleday, 1978. A new translation with editorial commentary.

17 Continuing the Pauline Tradition: Ephesians and the Pastoral Epistles

> Keep before you an outline of the sound teaching
> which you heard from me. . . . Guard the treasure
> put into our charge.
>
> (2 Tim. 1:13–14)

KEY THEMES Paul's continuing influence on the church was so great after his death that various Pauline disciples composed letters in his name and spirit. Scholars believe that Ephesians and the Pastoral Epistles were among these deutero-Pauline compositions. Ephesians expresses themes and ideas similar to those found in Colossians. The letter revises and updates Pauline concepts about God's universal plan of salvation for both Jews and Gentiles and about believers' spiritual warfare with supernatural evil.

Writing to Timothy and Titus as symbols of a new generation of Christians, an anonymous disciple (known as the Pastor) warns his readers against false teachings (heresy). He urges them to adhere strictly to the original apostolic teachings, supported by Jewish Scripture and the church.

A question of authorship. Both Ephesians and the letters to Timothy and Titus claim Pauline authorship. (The latter group are called the **Pastorals** because the writer—as a pastor, or shepherd—offers guidance and advice to his flock, the church.) According to tradition, Paul wrote Ephesians from his Roman prison. When he was released, he traveled to Crete, only to be imprisoned a second time (2 Tim.). During this second and final incarceration, the Apostle supposedly wrote these letters to his trusted associates, Timothy and Titus, young men who represent a new generation of Christian leadership.

Since the eighteenth century, however, scholars have increasingly doubted Paul's responsibility for either Ephesians or the Pastorals. Detailed analyses of these four documents strongly indicate that the author of Ephesians was not the author of the Pastorals and that all four were composed long after Paul's time.

The case of Ephesians. Many scholars question Paul's authorship of Colossians, but an overwhelming majority doubt that he composed the document we call Ephesians. Although it closely resembles Colossians (the style and theology of which also seem untypical of Paul), Ephesians differs from the undisputed Pauline letters in (1) vocabulary (containing over ninety words not found elsewhere in Paul's writings), (2) literary style (written in extremely long, convoluted sentences, in contrast to Paul's usually direct, forceful statements), and (3) theology (lacking typically Pauline doctrines such as justification by faith and the nearness of Christ's return).

Despite its similarity to Colossians (75 of Ephesians' 155 verses parallel phrases in Colossians), it presents a different view of the sacred "secret" or "mystery" revealed in Christ. In Colossians God's long-kept secret is Christ's mystical union with his followers (Col. 1:27),

250

but in Ephesians it is the union of Jew and Gentile in one church (Eph. 3:6).

More than any other disputed letter (except those to Timothy and Titus), Ephesians seems to reflect a time in church history significantly later than Paul's day. References to "Apostles and prophets" as the church's foundation imply that these figures belong to the past, not the author's generation (2:20; 3:5). The Gentiles' equality in Christian fellowship is no longer a controversial issue but an accomplished fact; this strongly suggests that the letter originated after the church membership had become largely non-Jewish (2:11–22). Judaizing interlopers no longer question Paul's stand on circumcision, again indicating that the work was composed after Jerusalem's destruction had largely eliminated the Jewish influence of the mother church.

When Paul uses the term *church (ekklesia),* he always refers to a single congregation (Gal. 1:2; 1 Cor. 11:16; 16:19, and so on). By contrast, Ephesians' author speaks of the "church" collectively, a universal institution encompassing all individual groups. This view of the church as a worldwide entity also points to a time after the apostolic period.

The accumulated evidence convinces most scholars that Ephesians is a deutero-Pauline document, a secondary work composed in Paul's name by an admirer thoroughly steeped in the Apostle's thought and general theology. The close parallels to Colossians, as well as phrases taken from Romans, Philemon, and other letters, indicate that unlike the author of Acts, this unknown writer was familiar with the Pauline correspondence. Some scholars propose that Ephesians was written as a kind of "cover letter," or essay to accompany an early collection of Paul's letters. Ephesians, then, can be seen as a tribute to Paul, summarizing some of his ideas and updating others to fit the changing needs of a largely Gentile and cosmopolitan church.

The phrase "in Ephesus" (1:1), identifying the recipients, does not appear in any of the oldest manuscripts. That fact, plus the absence of any specific issue or problem being addressed, reinforces the notion that Ephesians was intended to circulate among several churches in Asia Minor.

The Pastorals. In the opinion of most scholars, the case against Paul's connection with the Pastorals is even stronger. Besides the fact that they do not appear in early lists of Paul's canonical works, the Pastorals seem to reflect conditions that prevailed long after Paul's day, perhaps as late as the first half of the second century CE. Lacking Paul's characteristic ideas about faith and the Spirit, they are also unPauline in their flat style and different vocabulary (containing 306 words not found in Paul's unquestioned letters). Furthermore, the Pastorals assume a church organization far more developed than that current in the Apostle's generation.

The problem of pseudonymity. To some modern readers, the notion that unknown Christians wrote in Paul's name is ethically unacceptable on the grounds that such "forgeries" could not be part of the New Testament. To the ancient world, however, twentieth-century ideas about authorship would be irrelevant, for it was then common for disciples of great thinkers to compose works perpetuating their masters' thoughts. They wrote about contemporary issues as they believed their leader would have if he were still alive.

This practice of creating new works under the identity of a well-known but deceased personage is called **pseudonymity**. Intending to honor an esteemed figure of the past rather than to deceive the reading public, both Jews and early Christians produced a large body of pseudonymous literature. In an attempt to apply the teachings of a dead prophet or other spiritual leader to current situations, Hellenistic Jewish authors wrote books ascribed to Daniel, Enoch, Noah, Isaiah, David, and Moses. Christian writers similarly resurrected their heroes, writing Gospels, letters, apocalypses, and manuals of instruction attributed to the original Apostles and their associates, including Peter, John, James,

Barnabas, and Paul (see Chapters 18 and 20). Some of these pseudonymous writings are included in the New Testament.

Letter to the Ephesians

Date. If the letter to the Ephesians is by Paul, it probably originated from his Roman prison (60–64 CE). If it is by a later Pauline disciple, as scholars believe, Ephesians was written about the time Paul's letters first circulated as a unit, perhaps about 90 CE.

Organization. Ephesians' diverse contents can be subsumed under two major headings:

1. God's plan of salvation through the unified body of the church (1:3–3:21)
2. Instructions for living in the world while united to Christ (4:1–6:20)

Despite its long and sometimes awkward sentence structures (rephrased into shorter units in most English translations), Ephesians is a masterpiece of devotional literature. Unlike Paul's undisputed letters, it has a quiet and meditative tone with no temperamental outbursts or attacks on the writer's enemies. Although it imitates the letter form by including a brief salutation (1:1–2) and a final greeting (6:21–24), Ephesians is really a highly sophisticated tract.

God's Plan of Salvation Through the United Body of Christ

Ephesians' main theme is the union of all creation with Christ, manifested on earth by the church's international unity (1:10–14). Echoing Romans' concept of predestination, the author states that before the world's foundation, God selected Christ's future "children" (composing the church) to be redeemed by Jesus' blood, a sacrifice through which the chosen ones' sins are forgiven.

According to his preordained plan, God has placed Christ as head of the church, which is his body. The Spirit of Christ now fills the church as fully as God dwells in Christ (1:22–23). This mystical union of the human and divine is God's unforeseen gift, his grace that saves those who trust him (2:1–10).

The sacred secret—the union of Jews and Gentiles in one church. God's long-hidden secret is that Gentiles, previously under divine condemnation, can now share in the biblical promises made to Israel. This divine purpose to unite Jew and Gentile in equal grace is the special message that Paul is commissioned to preach (3:1–21). (Note that the writer assumes a general acceptance of the Gentile-dominated church, a condition that did not obtain in Paul's day.)

Instructions for Living in the World

Ephesians' last three chapters are devoted to instructions on living properly in the world while remaining united to Christ. Combining ideas from Philippians 2 and Colossians 1, the author reinterprets the concept of Jesus' descent from and reascension to the spirit realm whereby he made lesser spirits his prisoners and filled the universe with his presence. The author also alludes to Jesus' descent into the underworld, a mythical exploit that appears in 1 Peter (3:19–20).

Advancing Paul's conviction that the Christian revelation requires the highest ethical conduct, Ephesians contrasts Greco-Roman vices with Christian virtues and urges believers to transform their personalities to fit God's new creation (4:17–5:20). Home life is to be as reverent and orderly as behavior in church. Although he insists on a domestic hierarchy—"man is the head of the woman, just as Christ . . . is head of the church"—the writer reminds husbands to love their wives and thus honor them as a treasured equivalent of the self (5:21–6:9). Ephesians endorses the rigid social and domestic hierarchy of the day but makes the system more humane by insisting that Christian love apply to all public and private relationships.

Heavenly armor. In Ephesians' most famous passage, the Pauline analogy of Christians armed like Roman soldiers is vividly elaborated. In 1 Thessalonians (5:8), Paul urges believers to imitate armed sentries who stay awake on guard duty, for Christians must remain similarly alert for Christ's sudden reappearance. Ephesians discards the eschatological context of Paul's metaphor, however, and instead presents an ongoing battle between good and evil with no end in sight. In the genuine Pauline letters, the Apostle foresees evil demolished at Christ's Second Coming. The Ephesian writer, on the other hand, paints a picture of cosmic conflict reminiscent of *Zoroastrianism*—the Persian religion in which the world is viewed as a battlefield between invisible forces of light and darkness, good and evil.

In Zoroastrian terms, the Ephesian Paul describes two levels of "cosmic powers"—earthly rulers of the present dark age and the invisible forces of evil in heaven (6:10–12). Like Mark, the author apparently senses the reality of an evil so powerful that mere human wickedness cannot explain it. Instead of despairing, however, he rejoices that God provides ammunition that successfully defeats even supernatural evil. According to the author, each article of God's armor is a Christian virtue; cultivated together, qualities like truth and faith offer full protection from even the devil's worst attacks (6:13–19).

Rich in spiritual insight, Ephesians is a creative summary of some major Pauline concepts. If not by Paul, it is nevertheless a significant celebration of Christian ideals, an achievement worthy of the great Apostle himself.

Letters to Timothy and Titus

Purpose. Known for convenience as "the Pastor," the same Pauline disciple is the author of all three Pastoral letters. He views Paul's teaching as the norm or standard for all Christians and writes primarily to combat false teachings, urging the church to reject any deviations from the apostolic heritage. An examination of the Pastor's interpretation of Pauline thought shows that he does not always use terms in the same way as his master, nor is he as vigorous and creative a thinker. Writing to preserve an inherited tradition, he tends to view Christian faith as a set of static doctrines rather than as the ecstatic experience of Christ that Paul knew.

Letters to Timothy

The first two Pastorals are addressed to **Timothy,** the son of a Jewish mother and a Greek father (Acts 16:1), who served as Paul's missionary companion and trusted friend (1 Cor. 4:17; 16:10). According to Acts and Paul's authentic letters, Timothy was an important contributor to Paul's evangelism in Greece and Asia Minor, a cofounder of churches in Macedonia, and later a diplomatic emissary to Philippi, Thessalonica, and Corinth. In listing him as coauthor of as many as six different letters, Paul affirms Timothy's vital role in the Christian mission (1 Thess. 1:1; 2 Thess. 1:1; 2 Cor. 1:1; Phil. 1:1; Philem. 1:1; Col. 1:1).

In the Pastorals, however, Timothy is less a historical character than a literary symbol, representative of a new generation of believers to whom the task of preserving apostolic truths is entrusted. Youthful (postapostolic) Christians must take on the job of defending "wholesome doctrine" against devilish heresies (1 Tim. 4:2, 11–12).

1 Timothy

Organization. The first letter to Timothy does not present us with a smooth progression of thought, so it makes sense to examine it in terms of topics rather than consecutive sections:

1. Timothy's duty to repress false teachings
2. Church order: the qualifications of bishops, deacons, and elders
3. The roles of women and slaves

Attacking false teachings (heresies). As inheritor of the true faith, Timothy is to combat church members' wrong ideas (1:3). Because the Pastor, unlike Paul, does not offer a rational criticism of his opponents' errors, we do not know the exact nature of the beliefs attacked. Some commentators suggest that the false teachers practiced an early form of Gnosticism, a cult of secret "knowledge" mentioned in 6:20, but the letter reveals too little about the heresies involved to confirm this suggestion.

Because the author describes the deviants as teaching "the moral law" and wrongly preoccupied with "interminable myths and genealogies" (1:3–4, 7–9), many critics suppose that some form of Hellenistic Judaism is under attack. Practicing an extreme asceticism (severe self-discipline of the physical appetites), these persons forbid marriage and abstain from various foods (4:1–3). Gnostic practice took many diverse forms, ranging from the kind of self-denial mentioned here to the libertine behavior Paul rebuked in Corinth, Galatia, and elsewhere. Timothy (and the pastorship he represents) must correct such misguided austerity by transmitting the correct Pauline teachings (4:11), thereby saving himself as well as those who obey his orders (4:16).

Qualifications for church offices. Invoking Paul's authority, the Pastor is eager to preserve sound doctrine through a stable church organization. His list of qualifications for "bishops" (overseers), "deacons" (assistants), and "elders" (the religiously mature leadership) implies a hierarchy of church offices much more rigidly stratified than was the case in Paul's day. Paul once used the terms *bishop* and *deacon* (Phil. 1:1) but presumably as designating areas of service rather than the specific ecclesiastical offices enumerated here. Although the author says that church

officials must demonstrate all the virtues typical of Hellenistic ethical philosophy (3:2–23), he says nothing about their intellectual qualifications or possession of the Spirit. Rather than the spiritual gifts that Paul advocates, the Pastor's standards for church offices are merely hallmarks of middle-class respectability.

The Pastor regards the institution of the church—rather than the Spirit of Christ dwelling in the believer—as "the pillar and bulwark of the truth" (3:15). In the writer's time an organization administered by right-thinking leaders replaces the dynamic and charismatic fellowship of the Pauline congregations.

Ranking the church membership. In 1 Timothy the church membership reflects the social order of the larger Greco-Roman society external to it. Bishops, deacons, and elders govern a mixed group composed of different social classes, including heads of households, masters, slaves, wives, widows, and children (all of whom are commanded to submit to their respective superiors).

Women. Whereas Paul recognizes women as prophets and speakers (1 Cor. 11:5), the Pastor does not permit a woman to teach because the first woman, Eve, was weak-minded and tempted her husband to sin (2:8–15). The detailed instruction on womens' dress and conduct in 1 Timothy probably applies to public worship and parallels the restricted position assigned women in some Hellenistic societies. A reflection of then-current social customs, it is not necessarily a timeless prescription limiting women's roles in Christian life.

In his discussion of the church's treatment of widows, the Pastor distinguishes between "true" widows who demonstrate their worth by good deeds and women unqualified for that status because of their youth or inappropriate conduct. Following Jewish law (Exod. 22:22; Deut. 24:17–24), the church early assumed responsibilities for supporting destitute widows (Acts 6:1), but the author stipulates that widows must be sixty years old before they can qualify for financial assistance. Relatives must support underage widows (5:3–16).

As Christians are to pray for governmental rulers (2:1–3), so slaves are to recognize their duties to masters and obey them (6:1–2). Yet the rich and powerful are reminded to share their wealth (6:17–19). Those ambitious to acquire riches are told that a passion for money is the cause of much evil, a source of grief and lost faith (6:9–10).

The letter ends with an admonishment to Timothy to guard the apostolic legacy given him. Anyone who disagrees with the Pastor's updated interpretation of Paul's doctrine is "a pompous ignoramus" (6:3).

2 Timothy

Of the three Pastorals, 2 Timothy most closely resembles Paul's genuine letters. Although the letter is similarly concerned with refuting false teachings, its tone is more intimate and personal. Especially poignant are several passages in which the author depicts himself as abandoned by former associates and languishing alone in prison except for the companionship of Luke (1:15; 4:9–11, 16). Although these and other flashes of Paul's characteristic vigor and emotional fire (see 4:6–8, 17–18) lead some scholars to speculate that the work contains fragments of otherwise lost Pauline letters, such theories are not widely accepted.

The part of 2 Timothy with the best claim to Pauline authorship is the section ending the letter (4:6–22), in which the writer emulates the fluctuations between lofty thoughts and mundane practicalities so typical of the Apostle. In the first part, he compares himself to a runner winning the athlete's coveted prize—not the Greek competitor's laurel crown but a "garland of righteousness" justifying him on God's Judgment day (6:6–8). Switching abruptly to practical matters, the author asks the recipient to remember to bring his books when he comes. In another quick change of subject, he com-

plains that during his court hearing nobody appeared in his defense and that the testimony of one "Alexander the coppersmith" seriously damaged his case. Then, in a seemingly contradictory about-face, the writer states that he has (metaphorically) escaped the "lion's jaws" and expects to be kept safe until the Parousia (6:13–18).

Although such rapid changes of subject and shifts from gloom to optimism characterize Paul's genuine correspondence, most scholars believe that the entire document is the Pastor's work. The more vivid passages are simply the writer's most successful homage to the Apostle's memory.

In describing the false teachings within the church that he identifies as signs of the last days, the Pastor reveals that he is using Paul to predict conditions that characterize the writer's own time. During the world's last days (3:1), hypocrites insinuate their way into Christians' homes, corrupting the occupants. These pretenders typically prey upon women because, in the Pastor's insulting opinion, even when eager to learn, women lack the ability to understand true doctrine (3:6–8). Instead of the false teachers' being punished at the Second Coming, the Pastor implies that the mere passsage of time will expose their errors (3:9).

As in 1 Timothy, the Pastor does not refute the heretics with logical argument but merely calls them names and lists their vices (3:1–6, 13; 4:3–4), duplicating the catalogues of misbehavior common in Hellenistic philosophical schools. Even believers do not adhere to healthy beliefs but tolerate leaders who flatter them with what they want to hear.

Whereas the church is the stronghold of faith in 1 Timothy, in 2 Timothy the Hebrew Bible is the standard of religious orthodoxy (correct teaching), confounding error and directing the believer to salvation. Scripture also provides the mental discipline necessary to equip the believer for right action (3:15–17).

Concluding with his memorable picture of the Apostle courageously facing martyrdom, the

Pastor graciously includes all the faithful in Christ's promised deliverance. Not only Paul but all who trust in Jesus' imminent return will win victory's crown at the Parousia (6:6–8).

Letter to Titus

Although it is the shortest of the Pastorals, Titus has the longest salutation, a fulsome recapitulation of Paul's credentials and the recipient's significance (1:1–4). This highly formal introduction would be inappropriate in a personal letter from Paul to his friend, but is understandable as the Pastor's way of officially transmitting Paul's authoritative instruction to an apostolic successor.

Titus. The historical **Titus,** a Greek youth whom Paul refused to have circumcised (Gal. 2), accompanied the Apostle on his missionary tours of Greece, acting as Paul's emissary to reconcile the rebellious Corinthians (Gal. 2:1, 3, 10; 2 Cor. 8:6, 16–23). Like the "Timothy" of the other Pastorals, however, "Titus" also represents the postapostolic church leadership, the prototype of those preserving the Pauline traditions. Consequently, the commission of "Titus" is to establish an orthodox and qualified ministry. The letter's chief purpose is to outline the requirements and some of the duties of church elders and bishops.

Organization. Titus can be divided into two main sections:

1. Qualifications for the Christian ministry
2. Christian behavior in an ungodly world

Qualifications for the Christian ministry. The writer states that he left "Titus" in Crete, an ancient island center of Greek civilization, to install church assistants (elders) in every town (1:5). Such persons must be socially respectable married men who keep their children under strict parental control (1:6). In addition to possessing

these domestic credentials, bishops (church supervisors) must also have a reputation for devotion, self-control, and hospitality (1:7–8). Again, the writer says nothing about the leaders' mental or charismatic gifts so highly valued in the Pauline churches (2 Cor. 11–14).

One of the bishop's primary functions is to guard the received religion, adhering to established beliefs and correcting dissenters (1:7–9). Titus is the only book in the New Testament that uses the term *heretic* (3:10), which at the time of writing (early to mid–second century) probably meant a person who held opinions of which the elders disapproved. Such dissenters are to be warned twice and then ignored (excluded from the church?) if they fail to change their ways (3:10–11).

Christian behavior in an ungodly world. The Pastor reminds his audience that because they are Christians in a nonbelieving world, they must live exemplary lives of obedience and submission to governmental authorities (3:1). Men and women, old and young, slaves and masters, are all to behave in a way that publicly reflects well on their religion (2:1–10). Christians must preserve an ethically pure community while awaiting Christ's return (2:13–14).

In a moving passage, the author contrasts the negative personality traits that many believers had before their conversion with the grace and hope for eternal life that they now possess (3:3–8). In counsel similar to that in the letter of James, he urges believers to show their faith in admirable and useful deeds and to refrain from "foolish speculations, genealogies, quarrels, and controversies over the Law" (3:9–10).

The Pastor's Contribution

Although compared to Paul's the Pastor's style is generally weak and colorless (except for some passages in 2 Tim.), he successfully promotes

Paul's continuing authority in the church. His insistence that Paul's teaching (as he understood it) be followed and that church leaders actively employ apostolic doctrines to refute false teachers helped to ensure that the international Christian community would build its future on an apostolic foundation.

Although the Pastor values continuity, he does not seem to show an equal regard for continuing the individual revelations and ecstatic experiences of Christ's Spirit that characterized the Pauline churches. (Regarding the "laying on of hands" as the correct means of conferring authority [2 Tim. 1:6], he would probably not welcome another like Paul who insisted that his private experience of Jesus—not ordination by his predecessors—validated his calling.) Using Scripture, inherited doctrines, and the institutional church as guarantors of orthodoxy, the Pastor sees the Christian revelation as already complete, a static legacy from the past. He ignores Paul's injunction not to "stifle inspiration" or prophetic speech (1 Thess. 5:19–20); his intense conservatism allows little room for future enlightenment.

QUESTIONS FOR DISCUSSION AND REVIEW

1. Why do the majority of New Testament scholars think that Ephesians and the letters to Timothy and Titus were composed after Paul's time by later Christian writers deeply influenced by Pauline thought?
2. Discuss the practice of pseudonymity among Jewish and early Christian circles. Why are pseudonymous works to be regarded not as deceptions or forgeries but as tributes to the persons in whose name and memory they are written?
3. According to Ephesians, how are Christ and the church related? What does their union imply for believers?

4. Identify and interpret the metaphor of Christian armor. How does the attitude in Ephesians toward Christians' continuing battle against supernatural evil differ from Paul's view of the imminent end of the present evil age?
5. All three Pastorals have a similar purpose—to combat heresy and affirm the author's orthodox understanding of apostolic teachings. In what specific ways do the Pastorals reflect church conditions that are different from those obtaining in Paul's day?
6. Discuss the Pastor's views about women, children, and slaves. How does his prescription for internal church order reflect the hierarchical organization of the contemporary Greco-Roman society? What similarities and differences do you see between the character and behavior of Jesus and the Pastor's list of qualifications for church leaders? Explain your answer.

TERMS AND CONCEPTS TO REMEMBER

deutero-Pauline writings
authorship of Ephesians and the Pastorals
pseudonymity
Epehesians' "sacred secret"
cosmic conflict
Christian armor
the Pastor
Timothy and Titus as representatives of a later Christianity
heresy

heretics
bishop
deacon
elder
the Pastor's view of women
social hierarchy
role of the institutional church
the Pastor's view of qualifications for the ministry
differences between Paul and the Pastor

RECOMMENDED READING

Ephesians

Barth, Markus, ed. and trans. *Ephesians*. Vols. 34 and 34a of the Anchor Bible. Garden City, N.Y.: Doubleday, 1974. This extensive commentary defends Pauline authorship.

Goodspeed, E. J. *The Meaning of Ephesians*. Chicago: University of Chicago Press, 1933. An older but perceptive study arguing that Ephesians was written as a cover letter for the first collected edition of Paul's correspondence.

Johnston, G. "Ephesians, Letter to the." In *The Interpreter's Dictionary of the Bible,* vol. 2, 108–14. Nashville: Abingdon Press, 1962. A concise survey of issues concerning authorship and theology.

Mitton, C. L. *Ephesians*. New Century Bible. Grand Rapids, Mich.: Eerdmans, 1981. A brief study of Ephesians as a work produced by one of Paul's disciples.

The Pastorals

Dibelius, Martin, and Hans Conzelmann. *The Pastoral Epistles*. Hermeneia Commentary. Philadelphia: Fortress Press, 1972. Conzelmann's updating of Dibelius's famous commentary, first published in German in 1913.

Gealy, F. D. "Introduction and Exegesis to 1 and 2 Timothy and Titus." In *The Interpreter's Bible,* vol. 2, 342–551. Nashville: Abingdon Press, 1955. An informative introduction to the Pastoral problem.

Hanson, A. T. *The Pastoral Epistles*. New Century Bible. Grand Rapids, Mich.: Eerdmans, 1982. A brief but helpful treatment.

Quinn, J. D., ed. and trans. *1 and 2 Timothy and Titus*. Vol. 35 of the Anchor Bible. Garden City, N.Y.: Doubleday, 1976. A new translation with commentary.

18 *General Letters on Faith and Behavior: Hebrews and the Catholic Epistles*

The kind of religion which is without stain or fault
. . . is this: to go to the help of orphans and widows
in their distress and keep oneself untarnished by the
world.

(James 1:27)

The message you have heard from the beginning is
this: that we should love one another.

(1 John 3:11)

KEY THEMES Addressed to believers scattered throughout the world, Hebrews and the other general epistles make the point that God's revelation through Jesus is final and complete. The very image of God's nature, Jesus now serves in heaven as an eternal High Priest and mediator for humankind (Hebrews). Believers must therefore adhere to a high standard of conduct, maintaining a true understanding of Jesus' Incarnation (1 John), practicing charitable acts (James), setting examples of ethical behavior for the world (1 Peter), and keeping alive their hope of the Second Coming (2 Peter).

As noted in Chapter 17, Paul's extensive use of the letter form influenced many later New Testament writers. Besides authors like the Pastor, who wrote in Paul's name, other early Christians imitated the Apostle by composing "letters" to instruct and encourage the faithful. Unlike Paul's genuine correspondence, these later documents commonly are not addressed to individual congregations but directed to the Christian community as a whole. This group of eight disparate writings, headed by the Book of Hebrews, forms a discrete unit between the collection of letters traditionally ascribed to Paul and the book of Revelation.

Because of their general nature, seven of these writings are known collectively as the "**catholic epistles**" (or "universal epistles"). The seven—James, 1 and 2 Peter, 1, 2, and 3 John, and Jude—are called "epistles" because most of them are formal communications intended for

public reading in the church at large. In this respect, they differ from genuine letters like those of Paul, which were composed for specific recipients known to the author and are much less formal.

Even the term *epistle* does not adequately describe the diverse literary forms encompassed in these works. Of the three missives ascribed to John, for example, the first is actually a sermon or tract, the second is a warning letter to a specific group, and the third is a private note. In this chapter we show that although such works as James and 1 Peter superficially resemble letters, they in fact belong to different categories of religious literature.

Authors and dates. Besides their dubious categorization as epistles, another significant factor links these seven writings. All are attributed to prominent leaders of the original Jerusalem church. Six are ascribed to the three Jerusalem "pillars"—Peter, James, and John (Gal. 2)—the seventh, Jude, is purportedly by James's brother.

With the exception of 1 Peter, most of the catholic writings are also linked by the fact that, as a group, they are the last writings to be accepted into the New Testament canon. As late as the fourth century, Eusebius classified several as "doubtful" and noted that many churches did not accept them (*History* 3.39.6; 3.24.18; 3.25.4; 2.24.1; 2.3). Church writers do not even mention most of these epistles until almost 200 CE, and Jude, James, 2 Peter, and 3 John are typically absent from early lists of canonical books.

Near the close of the second century, the church began to associate many previously anonymous works with Jesus' Apostles and their companions. This seems to have been the case with the catholic epistles, which scholars believe to include the latest-written documents in the New Testament.

In our discussion of these general works on faith and behavior, we begin with two commonly associated with Jewish Christianity—Hebrews and James—followed by the epistles attributed to Peter, Jude, and John. Despite their heterogenous character, these documents are thematically united by their authors' profound commitment to prescribing an ethical way of life appropriate for believers living at the end of time. 2 Peter, which is probably the last-written book in the canon, marks a fervent reaffirmation of primitive Christianity's apocalyptic hope. However long the Parousia is delayed, Christians must live as if Jesus will return at any moment to judge the world and the conduct of the faithful (2 Pet. 3:1–15).

The Book of Hebrews

The Book of Hebrews was written by an early Christian scholar who was equally well acquainted with the Hebrew Bible and with Greek philosophical concepts. The work challenges the reader as does no other New Testa-

ment book except Revelation. With the warning that he offers "much that is difficult to explain" (5:11), the writer presents a dualistic view of the universe in which earthly events and human institutions are seen as reflections of invisible heavenly realities. Employing a popular form of Platonic thought, he assumes the existence of two parallel worlds: the eternal and perfect realm of spirit above and the inferior, constantly changing world below. Alone among New Testament authors, he attempts to show how Christ's sacrificial death links the two opposing realms of perishable matter and eternal spirit. He is the only Bible writer to present Jesus as a heavenly priest who serves as an everlasting mediator between God and humankind.

Authorship and date. Hebrews is an elaborate sermon rather than a letter, but it ends with a postscript recalling one of Paul's missives (13:17–25). Although some early Christians attributed the work to Paul, many others recognized that the theology, language, and style of Hebrews were distinctly un-Pauline. (The ending comments and reference to Timothy [13:23] do not fit the rest of the work and may have been appended by a later copyist or editor.) Various commentators have speculated that the author may have been Barnabas, Priscilla, or Paul's eloquent coworker, Apollos of Alexandria.

Such attempts to link Hebrews with some well-known figure associated with first-generation Pauline Christianity have proven futile. Most scholars agree with Origen, a church scholar prominent during the early third century, who remarked that the writer's identity is known only to God. The book's date and place of composition are also unknown. Various critics suggest Alexandria, Rome, Antioch, Corinth, or some equally cosmopolitan center as the city of origin, with the time of writing estimated as between about 80 and 100 CE.

The Writer's Methods of Interpretation

Whoever he was, the anonymous author was a master of rhetoric, the art of speaking or writing effectively. He uses excellent Greek and also shows familiarity with Hellenistic-Jewish methods of scriptural analysis and interpretation. This suggests to many scholars that the writer may have lived in Alexandria, a metropolis where Greek-educated Jews like **Philo Judaeus** developed highly sophisticated ways of making ancient biblical texts relevant to the demands of Greco-Roman culture. As expounded by Philo and other Alexandrine scholars, the Hebrew Bible became much more than a mere repository of legal commandments or a record of past events. To Philo and the author of Hebrews, it is an allegory in which earthly events symbolize heavenly realities.

Hebrews' thesis is that through Jesus God gives his ultimate revelation of spiritual reality. The author examines selected passages from the Hebrew Bible—principally Genesis 14:18–20 and Psalms 110:4—to demonstrate Christ's unique role in the universe. In his view the biblical texts can be understood only in the light of Christ's death and ascension into heaven. He thus gives the Jewish Bible a strictly Christological interpretation.

Of special importance to the author is the Genesis figure of **Melchizedek,** a mysterious king-priest of Canaanite Salem to whom the patriarch Abraham gave a tenth of the goods he had captured in war (Gen. 14:18–20). Melchizedek becomes a type or prophetic symbol of Jesus, whom the author regards as both a king (Davidic Messiah) and a priest (like Melchizedek). In the author's interpretation, Melchizedek's story serves to prefigure Jesus' priesthood.

Purpose and organization. The book's title—"to the Hebrews"—is not part of the original text; it may have been added by an editor who assumed that the writer's interest in Jewish ritual implied that he wrote for Jewish Christians. The term may apply equally well to Gentile recipients, however, and probably refers to "spiritual Israel," the Christian church at large. Whatever the intended audience, Hebrews' purpose is to urge believers to hold fast to their faith, remembering their former loyalty during

persecution (10:32–34) and avoiding the pitfalls of apathy or indifference.

After an introduction (1:1–4) Hebrews is arranged in three main sections:

1. Christ, the image of God, is superior to all other human or heavenly beings (1:5–4:16).
2. The Torah's priestly regulations foreshadowed Jesus' role as a priest like Melchizedek (5:1–10:39).
3. Believers are exhorted to emulate biblical examples and act on faith in Jesus' supremacy (11:1–13:16).

Christ's Superiority to All Other Beings

Stressing his theme of Christ's superiority to all others, the author begins Hebrews by contrasting earlier biblical revelations with that made in the last days through the person of Jesus. Whereas God formerly conveyed his message in fragmentary form through the Hebrew prophets, in Jesus he discloses a complete revelation of his essential nature and purpose. As in Colossians and John's Gospel, Jesus is the agent (or goal) of God's creative purpose and a perfect reflection of the divine being (1:1–4).

Echoing Paul's assertion that Jesus attained heavenly glory through obedient humility (Phil. 2), the author states that Jesus was perfected through suffering. As a perfectly obedient son, he is greater than Moses, leading his followers not to an earthly destination but to God's celestial throne (3:1–4:16). Through him God makes his complete and final revelation.

Christ—A Priest Like Melchizedek

Asking his hearers to move beyond basic ideas and to advance in understanding (5:11–6:3), the author introduces his unparalleled interpretation of Jesus as an eternal High Priest, one foreshadowed by Melchizedek. To show that Christ's priesthood is superior to that of **Aaron,** Israel's first High Priest, and the Levites who assisted him at the Tabernacle, Hebrews cites the narrative about Abraham paying tithes to

Melchizedek (14:18–20). Because Melchizedek blessed Abraham and accepted offerings from him, the writer argues that the king-priest of Salem was Abraham's superior. Furthermore, Abraham's descendants, the Levitical and Aaronic priests, also shared in the patriarch's homage to Melchizedek. Present in his ancestor's "loins" when Abraham honored Melchizedek, Aaron and all his priestly offspring also confessed their inferiority to Melchizedek (7:1–10). Melchizedek is thus acknowledged as the superior of Israel's founding father; he also outranks Israel's Levitical priests by virtue of his priority in time.

The author now adds Psalms 110 to his explication of Genesis 14. He notes that Yahweh swore that his king or "messiah" is both his son and an everlasting priest like Melchizedek (Ps. 110:4). Hebrews further argues that because Genesis does not mention either ancestors or descendants for Melchizedek, the absence of human roots or connections implies that the king-priest is without either beginning or end—an eternal priest. The symbolic everlastingness of Melchizedek's priesthood is thus the prototype of Christ, who similarly remains a priest for all time (7:3, 21–24).

In biblical times a priest's main function was to offer animal sacrifices to atone for the people's sins and elicit God's forgiveness. According to Hebrews, Jesus is both the priest and the sacrifice. His offering fulfills the reality of the Torah's required sacrifices, but it is superior to the old system because his life was perfected through suffering (5:8–9). Unlike the sacrifices offered at Israel's Tabernacle or Temple, which must be repeated endlessly to ensure divine approval, Jesus' sacrifice is made only once. It remains eternally effective and brings forgiveness and salvation to those accepting its efficacy (7:26–28).

Earthly Copy and Heavenly Reality

Hebrews employs the view that the universe is composed of two levels, a lower physical realm and a higher, unseen spirit world. The author envisions Israel's earthly ceremonies of sacrifice and worship as reflections, or copies, that parallel invisible realities in Heaven (8:5) (Figure 18–1). He then cites the solemn ritual of the Day of Atonement, the one time of the year that the High Priest was permitted to enter the Tabernacle's innermost room, the Holy of Holies, where God's glory was believed to dwell. Interpreting the atonement ritual allegorically, the author states that the priest's annual entry into God's presence foreshadowed Christ's ascension into heaven itself. There, his life stands as an eternally powerful sacrifice, making humankind forever "at one" with God (8:1–6; 9:1–14).

Because his sacrifice surpasses those decreed under the old Mosaic covenant, Jesus inaugurates a new covenant with his shed blood. He acts as a permanent mediator, always pleading for humanity's forgiveness (7:24–25; 9:15–22). The writer repeatedly emphasizes that neither the Mosaic Tabernacle nor Herod's Temple in Jerusalem was intended to be permanent. Both sanctuaries are only copies of heavenly realities (9:23), mere "shadows, and no true image" of Christ's supreme priestly sacrifice (10:1–25).

Exhortation to Remain Faithful

After reminding his audience that God's redemption through Christ is absolutely final, permitting no second chance at salvation (10:26–31), the writer urges Christians to imitate the many examples of faith found in the Hebrew Bible (11:4–40). The author is the only New Testament writer to define faith, and he does so in terms of his belief in two parallel worlds. Hebrews 11 expresses Plato's classic view of an eternal realm superior to the world of physical matter. This passage defines faith as primarily a hopeful confidence that the unseen universe really exists and that it is the source of the physical cosmos (11:1–3). Unlike Paul, who always associates faith with a living trust in Jesus' saving power, the author of Hebrews defines faith with no reference to Christ.

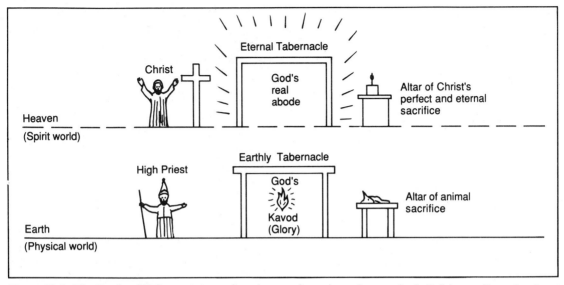

Figure 18-1. The Book of Hebrews expounds a theory of correspondences, the belief that reality exists in two separate but parallel dimensions—the spirit world (heaven) and the physical world (earth). Material objects and customs on earth are temporary replicas, or shadows, of eternal realities in heaven.

The faithful are thus armed with a conviction that invisible realities include an eternal High Priest whose perfect sacrifice provides a potentially ceaseless forgiveness and union with God. Christians must maintain their faith while awaiting the imminent Day of Judgment (10:36–39). Characters in the Hebrew Bible, such as Abel, Noah, Abraham, Moses, and Rahab (the Canaanite harlot) proved their loyalty when they had only a dim preview of heavenly realities. Believers now possess a complete vision of God's purpose and must behave accordingly. Just as God introduced the Mosaic covenant amid blazing fire, earthquake, and other frightening signs, Jesus' new covenant embodies even more awe-inspiring phenomena, not on earthly Mount Sinai but in heavenly Jerusalem. If the Israelites who disobeyed the Mosaic Law were punished by death, how much more severe will be the punishment of those who fail to keep faith in the new dispensation (12:1–29).

Urging believers to lead blameless lives of active good deeds, the author reminds them that Jesus Christ is "the same yesterday, today, and for ever." This is another powerful reason to regard this world, with its temptations and troubles, as a temporary trial resolved in the light of eternity (13:1–9). Christians have no permanent home on earth but seek the unseen and perfect city above as their life's goal (13:14).

James

Authorship. Addressing his work to "the Twelve Tribes dispersed throughout the world" (presumably "spiritual Israel," the international church), the author calls himself "James, a servant of God and the Lord Jesus Christ." He does not claim apostolic rank or mention a kinship with Jesus, but church tradition identifies him as the person whom Paul calls "James the Lord's brother" (Gal. 1:19), the principal leader of Palestinian Jewish Christianity between about 50 and 62 CE. He was a devout respecter of the

Mosaic Torah and was known to his fellow Israelites as "James the Righteous." Despite his high reputation among both Jews and Christians, however, a violent mob killed him about 62 CE.

If the author is Jesus' brother (or close relative), it is strange that he rarely mentions Christ and almost never refers to Jesus' teachings. As a man who had known Jesus all his life (Mark 6) and had seen the risen Lord (1 Cor. 15), he might be expected to use his personal acquaintance with Jesus to lend authority to his instructions. The fact that his writing contains virtually nothing about Jesus suggests the author did not personally know him and consequently could not have been a member of Jesus' family.

Two qualities of this document offer general clues to its author's background. Besides being written in excellent Greek (not something a Galilean native was likely to be capable of), it repeatedly echoes Greek editions of the Hebrew Bible, especially the book of Proverbs and later Hellenistic Wisdom books like Ecclesiasticus and The Wisdom of Solomon. Both James's subject matter and his language reflect a deep interest in Greek-Jewish Wisdom literature. This fact suggests that the author is a Hellenistic Jewish Christian concerned about applying the principles of Israel's later sages to problems in his Christian circle. The writer may have lived in any Greek-speaking Jewish community in Syria, Palestine, Egypt, or Italy.

Form and organization. Except for the brief opening salutation, the work bears no similarity to a letter. It is instead a collection of proverbs, commentaries, scriptural paraphrases, and moral advice. As a literary genre, James is the only New Testament document resembling the compilations of wise counsel found in the Hebrew Bible.

Lacking any principle of coherence, James leaps from topic to topic and then back again. The only unifying theme is the author's view of the purpose and function of religion (1:26–

27), which he defines as typically Jewish good works, charitable practices that will save the soul and cancel a multitude of sins (5:19–20). Following the author's order, we examine several of his main interests:

1. The nature of trials and temptations (1:2–27)
2. Respect for the poor (2:1–13)
3. "Works," or good deeds as the only measure of faith (2:14–26)
4. Controlling the tongue (3:1–12)
5. Warnings against violent ambition and exploitation of the poor (4:1–5:6)

The recipients and the date. From the topics covered, this book seems directed at Jewish Christian groups that had existed long enough to have developed a sense of class distinction within the church. Wealthy Christians snub poorer ones (2:1–9), fail to share their material possessions (2:14–26), engage in worldly competition (4:1–10), and exploit fellow believers of the laboring class (4:13–5:6). These socially stratified and economically divided communities suggest a time long after that of the impoverished Jerusalem commune described in Acts 2. Most scholars date the work in the late first century, considerably after the historic James's martyrdom in the early 60s.

Trials and Temptations

In this introductory section (1:2–27), James articulates a philosophy of human experience that puts his ethical advice in perspective. Dealing with the twin problems of external suffering and internal temptations to do wrong, the author offers insight into God's reasons for permitting evil to afflict even the faithful. "Trials" (presumably including persecutions) are potentially beneficial experiences because they allow the believer the opportunity to demonstrate faith and fortitude under pressure, thus strengthening character. To help Christians endure such trials, God grants insight to persons who pray for it single-mindedly and never doubt that God will provide the understanding necessary to maintain faith.

Arguing that the Creator is not responsible for tests of faith or private temptations to sin, James declares that God, "untouched by evil," does not tempt anyone. Human temptation arises from within through the secret cultivation of forbidden desire that eventually inspires the act of "sin," which in turn breeds death (1:12–15). By contrast, God is the source of perfection (1:17) and the origin of life (1:12). In this miniature **theodicy** (defense of God's goodness in spite of the world's evil), the writer insists that God is not responsible for injustice or undeserved suffering. Society's evils result from purely human selfishness. If believers resist evil, God grants them the power to drive away even the devil (4:7–8).

Religion defined. The only New Testament writer to define religion, James describes it as the active practice of good works, an imitation of the One who sets the example of generosity (1:16). The religion God approves is practical: helping "orphans and widows" and keeping "oneself untarnished by the world" (1:27). In James's two-part definition, the "orphans and widows" are Judaism's classic symbols of the defenseless who are God's special care, and "the world" represents a society that repudiates God. Thoroughly Jewish in its emphasis on merciful deeds, James's "true religion" cannot be formalized by doctrine, creed, or ritual (compare Matt. 25:31–46).

Respect for the Poor

Addressing a social problem that plagues virtually every social group, whether religious or secular, James denounces all social snobbery. Christians must make the poor feel as welcome in their midst as the rich and powerful (2:1–13). Noting that it is the wealthy who typically oppress the church, James reminds his audience that the poor will inherit "the kingdom" and that insulting them is an offence against God.

Interestingly, the author does not use Jesus' teaching to drive home God's gracious intent to reward those now poor but instead quotes from the Hebrew Bible. If believers do not love their fellow human beings (Lev. 19:18), they break all of God's laws, for to fail to keep one legal point is to disobey the entire Torah (2:10).

Faith Lives Only Through Good Works

In James's most famous passage (2:14–26), the author contrasts the futility of persons who claim they have faith but do not follow the practical religion of good works. To James, belief that fails to inspire right action is dead. Only "deeds"—serving the "orphans and widows" and others suffering comparable need—can demonstrate the reality of faith.

Many interpreters see this section as an attack on Paul's doctrine of salvation through faith (the Apostle's rejection of "works" of Torah obedience in favor of trust in God's saving purpose in Christ). Like Paul, James cites the Genesis example of Abraham to prove his point, but he gives it a strikingly different interpretation. James asserts that it was Abraham's action—his willingness to sacrifice his son Isaac—that justified him. The writer's conclusion is distinctly un-Pauline: "a man is justified by deeds and not by faith in itself" (2:24). With its implication that one earns divine approval through hard effort and service to others, this conclusion seems to contradict Paul's assertion that salvation comes only through God's grace, accepted on trust (faith) (see Gal. and Rom. 1–8).

James's conclusion that faith without actions is as dead as a corpse without breath (2:26) seems to many scholars an attack on Paul's viewpoint. Others regard it as a necessary corrective to a common misuse of Pauline doctrine. It must be remembered, however, that although Paul labored to the point of exhaustion serving others, he did not see his "works" as the means God provided for his "justification." Martin Luther doubted the validity of James's argument, describing the work as "strawlike" for its failure to recognize the primacy of divine grace.

Controlling the Tongue

Like earlier writers in the Hebrew Wisdom tradition, James stresses the importance of self-control in speech (3:1–12; compare Prov. 15:1–4, 26, 28; Ecclus. 5:11–6:1; 28:13–26). The tongue is a fire fed by the flames of hell (3:6), paradoxically both the instrument of divine praise and the organ of destructive gossip. Contrasting its abuses with spiritual wisdom, James emphasizes the constructive, peace-enhancing quality of the latter (3:13–18).

Warnings Against Ambition and Exploitation

True wisdom produces peace and harmony; James's recipients, on the other hand, are divided by envy, ambition, and conflict. Their ambitious pursuit of unworthy goals makes them God's enemy (4:3–4). Boastful of their financial successes, they forget that their continued existence depends on God's patience and mercy. Christian merchants and landowners are the author's prime target in the New Testament's most incisive attack on the rich (4:13–5:4). Those whose wealth gives them power over their economic inferiors have exploited it shamelessly. Without conscience, wealthy employers have defrauded their workers, delaying payment of wages upon which the laboring poor depend to live. Such injustice outrages the Creator, who views the luxury-loving exploiters as overfed animals ripe for slaughter.

Reminding his audience that the Lord will return (5:7), presumably to judge those who economically murder the defenseless (5:6), James ends his sermon on a positive note for any who have strayed from the right path. Sinners and others who are "sick," perhaps spiritually as well as physically, can hope for recovery. God's healing grace operates through congregational prayer for the afflicted. A good person's prayer has power to rescue a sinner from death and to erase countless sins (5:13–20).

1 Peter

Like James, 1 Peter is ascribed to one of the three Jerusalem "pillars." The two works have other points in common as well, including similar convictions about proper Christian behavior and a shared belief that spiritual gifts like love and prayer can wipe out sin (James 5:20; 1 Pet. 4:8). Both also refer to social discrimination, even persecution against believers (James 1:2–8; 5:7–11; 1 Pet. 1:6–7; 4:12–19). A philosophy of peaceful submission and patience during trials and tests of faith characterizes both documents.

Authorship and date. Scholars are divided on the authorship of 1 Peter. Many accept the tradition that the Apostle Peter composed it in Rome shortly before he was executed during Nero's persecution of Christians (about 64 or 65 CE). Other scholars point out that if the "ordeals" mentioned in the letter refer to Nero's Roman persecution, it is strange that the epistle is addressed to churches in Asia Minor (1:1). Historians find no evidence that Nero's attack on the faith extended beyond the imperial capital.

Those doubting Petrine authorship note that the fine Greek in which the epistle is written suggests that an unlettered Galilean fisherman was not the author. Advocates of Peter's responsibility for the letter retort that it was produced "through Sylvanus [Silas]" (5:12), a former companion of Paul (Acts 15:22) who acted as Peter's secretary, transforming his dictation into the epistle's smooth Greek.

Of all the catholic epistles identified with various members of the Jerusalem church, the best case for authenticity can perhaps be made for 1 Peter. Although the majority of scholars regard the work as pseudonymous, many eminent critics defend its traditional authorship and date it in the mid-60s CE. Those assigning the work a postapostolic date—between about 90 and 115 CE—note that the author does not reveal personal knowledge of Jesus, as an Apostle would be expected to do, and that the social conditions described in 1 Peter indicate a period later than Nero's reign.

According to some interpreters, the epistle's references to believers' troubles (1:6) may mean nothing more than the social discrimination and hostility Roman society accorded many early Christians. Other commentators explain the "fiery ordeals" (4:12–13) as official persecutions under the emperors Domitian (about 95 CE) or Trajan (about 112 CE). 1 Peter indicates that believers are punished merely for bearing Christ's name (4:14–16), a situation that did not obtain during Nero's era but does fit the policies of his later successors. Letters exchanged between the emperor Trajan and Pliny the Younger, his appointed governor of Bithynia, one of the provinces of Asia Minor to which 1 Peter is addressed, seem to reflect the same conditions the epistle describes (Pliny, *Letters* 97). For that reason, many scholars favor a date in the early second century for the epistle, though there is no scholarly consensus.

A date after 70 CE is indicated by the author's sending greetings from "her who dwells in Babylon" (5:13). "Her" refers to the writer's church (2 John 1), and "Babylon" became the Christian code name for Rome after Titus destroyed Jerusalem, thus duplicating the Babylonian Empire's infamous desecration of the holy city (587 BCE). As an archetype of the ungodly nation, "Babylon" is also Revelation's symbol of Rome (Rev. 14:8; 18:2). Most critics assume that 1 Peter originated in the capital, the traditional site of Peter's martyrdom.

Purpose and organization. The author's purpose is to encourage believers to hold fast to their integrity (as Christians like Peter did in Nero's time) and to promote Christian ethics. He urges the faithful to live so blamelessly that outsiders can never accuse them of anything illegal or morally reprehensible. If one endures legal prosecution, it should be only "as a Christian" (4:14–16).

1 Peter often has been described as a baptismal sermon, and indeed the author structures his work to delineate both the privileges and the dangers involved in adopting the Christian way of life. As a basic summary of Christian ideals and ethics, it may be divided into the following three sections:

1. The privileges and values of the Christian calling (1:3–2:10)
2. The obligations and responsibilities of Christian life (2:11–4:11)
3. The ethical meaning of suffering as a Christian (4:12–5:11)

The Privileges and Values of the Christian Calling

Addressing an audience who had not known Jesus, Peter stresses the rarity and inestimable value of the faith recently transmitted to them. They must regard their present trials and difficulties as opportunities to display the depth of their commitment and the quality of their love (1:3–7). By remaining faithful they will attain the salvation of which the Hebrew prophets spoke (1:9–12). Proper appreciation for Christ's sacrifice, which makes him the "living stone" of the heavenly temple, will also make the believer a living part of the eternal sanctuary (2:4–8). Christians, including Gentiles, are the new "chosen race"—"a royal priesthood, a dedicated nation, and a people claimed by God for his own" (2:9–10).

The Obligations and Responsibilities of Christian Life

Many commentators have noted that 1 Peter contains many Pauline ideas, particularly on matters of Christian behavior and obedience to the Roman state. In the second section (2:11–4:11), the author focuses on the responsibilities and moral conduct of God's people, who should act in a way that even nonbelievers admire (2:12). Echoing Romans 13, 1 Peter advises peaceful submission to governmental authorities (3:13–15). In the writer's social and political hierarchy, slaves and servants are subject to their masters (2:18) and women to their husbands (3:1–2). Those who suffer unjustly must bear it as Jesus bore his sufferings (1:19–25; 3:13–18; 4:1–5).

In alluding to Christ's crucifixion, the author includes two fascinating references about Jesus' descent into the Underworld (Hades), presumably during the interval between his death and his resurrection (3:18–20; 4:6). Suggesting the existence of a rich early Christian lore surrounding Jesus' posthumous experiences, Peter's brief allusions inspired a later tradition that after his death Jesus entered hell and rescued the souls of faithful Israelites who had been imprisoned there before the way to heaven was open.

The Ethical Meaning of Suffering as a Christian

The third part (4:12–5:11) of 1 Peter examines the ethical meaning of suffering for the faith. Believers must not be surprised to experience difficulties because as followers of Christ they must expect to share his sufferings (4:12–16). Judgment has come, and it begins with the Christian community. If the righteous are but narrowly saved, what will happen to the wicked (4:17–19)? Elders must shepherd the flock with loving care; younger people must submit humbly to their rule (5:1–7). All must remain alert, because the devil prowls the earth like a hungry lion, seeking to devour the unwary. The faithful who resist him will partake of Christ's reward (5:8–11).

Letter of Jude

Placed last among the general epistles, Jude is less a letter than a tract denouncing an unidentified group of heretics. Its primary intent is to persuade the (also unidentified) recipients to join the writer in defending orthodox Christian traditions (v.3). Rather than specify his opponents' doctrinal errors or refute their arguments, the writer instead threatens the he-

retics with apocalyptic punishment drawn from both biblical and nonbiblical sources.

Authorship and date. The author refers to himself as Jude (Judas), a servant of Jesus Christ and brother of James (v.1)—and presumably also a kinsman of Jesus (Matt. 13:55; Mark 6:3). According to Eusebius, Jude, whom he describes as "the brother, humanly speaking, of the Savior," left descendants who played an important role in the Jerusalem church, even after the Romans destroyed the city in 70 CE. Eusebius quotes an older historian, Hegesippus, who reported that during Domitian's reign the emperor ordered Jude's two grandsons to appear before him. Worried that their Davidic ancestory might make them potential leaders of another Jewish revolt, Domitian released the two when they demonstrated that they were only hard-working peasants with no pretensions to royalty (*History* 3.20).

Scholars believe that Jude is not the work of Jesus' "brother" but is rather a pseudonymous work that entered the canon because of its presumed association with the Lord's family. Like James, the author shows no personal familiarity with Jesus and cites none of his characteristic teachings. He refers to Christianity as a fixed body of beliefs that the faithful already possess (v.3) and to the Apostles as prophets of a former age (vv.17–18). This indicates that the book was composed significantly after the historical Jude's time. Most scholars suggest a date between about 100 and 125 CE.

Style and content. The letter of Jude represents a kind of rhetoric known as invective—an argument characterized by verbal abuse and insult. Without describing the heretics' teachings, Jude calls them "brute beasts" (v.10), "enemies of religion" who have wormed their way into the church to pervert it with their "licentiousness" (v.4). A "blot on [Christian] love feasts" (v.12), they are doomed to suffer divine wrath as did Cain, Balaam, Korah, and other villains of the Hebrew Bible. Because the author does not try to explain his reasons for disagreeing with his opponents but merely calls them names, accuses them of immorality, and predicts their future destruction, Jude has been called the least theologically creative book in the New Testament.

Apocalyptic Judgment

Jude views the heretics' misbehavior as fulfilling the Apostles' predictions about end time (v.18). Because their apostasy proves the nearness of the Last Judgment (an idea also expressed in 1 John 2:18), Jude reminds his audience of earlier punishments on the wicked, citing the plagues on Egypt (v.5), the fallen angels of Genesis (v.6), and the fiery punishment of Sodom and Gomorrah (vv.6–7).

Use of noncanonical writings. Jude is the only New Testament writer to go beyond the Hebrew Bible and quote directly from the **Pseudepigrapha**, Jewish religious works not included in the biblical canon. Citing the book of 1 Enoch (1:9) verbatim, Jude reproduces a passage describing the Lord's negative Judgment on "the ungodly" (v.15). From copies of Enoch preserved among the Dead Sea Scrolls, we know that the Essenes studied the work. Jude's quotation as well as several other allusions to the work (1 Enoch 18:12; 1:1–9; 5:4; 27:2; 60:8; 93:2) prove that certain early Christian groups also regarded Enoch as authoritative.

In addition, Jude's allusion to a postbiblical legend about the Archangel Michael contending with the Devil for Moses' body (v.9) may be taken from the incompletely preserved Assumption of Moses, another late noncanonical work. (When a later writer incorporated much of Jude into chapter 2 of 2 Peter, he deleted all references to the noncanonical writings.)

Exhortation to the faithful. Jude's advice to his orthodox recipients is as general as his denunciation of the false teachers. Counseling them to pray and live anticipating Jesus' return (v.20–21), he concedes that some involved with the heretics deserve pity and can be helped. Others are pitiable but corrupted by sensuality. The author's opinion that the clothing (or bodies) of such persons must be despised (v.23) suggests that Jude advocates a strict asceticism—a self-discipline that denies physical appetites and desires.

To balance its largely vindictive tone, the work closes with a particularly lyric doxology praising "the only God our Savior" (vv.24–25).

2 Peter

Like Jude, 2 Peter was written for the double purpose of condemning false teachers and warning of the imminent world Judgment. Theologically, its importance lies in the author's attempt to explain why God allows evil to continue and to reassert the primitive Christian belief that Jesus' Second Coming is near (3:1–15). Offering a theory that human history is divided into three distinct chronological epochs, or "worlds," 2 Peter is the only New Testament book to argue that the present world will be entirely consumed by fire.

Authorship and date. Whereas many scholars defend Petrine authorship of 1 Peter, virtually none believe that 2 Peter was written by Jesus' chief disciple. The unknown author, however, takes pains to claim Peter's identity (1:1), asserting that he was present at Christ's transfiguration (1:17–18) and that he wrote an earlier letter, presumably 1 Peter (3:1). Under the great fisherman's name, he writes to reaffirm his concept of the true apostolic teaching in the face of heretical misrepresentation of it. Picturing the church leader as about to face death, the writer offers this epistle as Peter's last will and testament, a final exposition of the apostolic faith (1:14–15).

The pseudonymous author's claims are not persuasive, however, because 2 Peter contains too many indications that it was written long after Peter's martyrdom in about 64 or 65 CE.

The letter's main intent—to reestablish the apostolic view of the Parousia—shows that the writer addresses a group that lived long enough after the original Apostles' day to have given up believing that Christ would return soon. The author's opponents deny the Parousia doctrine because the promised Second Coming has not materialized even though the "fathers" (first generation disciples) have long ago passed away. In addition, the writer makes use of Jude, itself an early second-century document, incorporating most of it into his work.

The work also refers to Paul's letters as Scripture (3:16), a status they did not achieve until well into the second century. A late date is also indicated by the author's insistence on divinely inspired Scripture as the principal teaching authority (1:20–21). This tendency to substitute a fixed written text for the Spirit's operation or the "living voice" of the gospel also appears in the Pastor's letters (2 Tim. 3:15–16), which are similarly products of the second century.

Finally, many leaders of the early church doubted 2 Peter's apostolic origins, resulting in the epistle's absence from numerous lists of "approved" books. Not only was 2 Peter one of the last works to gain entrance into the New Testament, scholars believe that it was also the last canonical book written. Composed at some point after 100 CE, it may not have appeared until as late as about 150 CE.

Organization and purpose. 2 Peter is a brief work and can be divided into three main sections:

1. The writer's apostolic authority and eschatological purpose (1:1–32)
2. Condemnation of false teachers (based on Jude) (2:1–22)
3. Defense of the Parousia doctrine, including a theodicy, and exhortation to behavior appropriate to end time (3:1–18)

The Delayed Parousia

Chapter 2 is devoted to invective. It is a brutal attack on false teachers whom the author describes as "slaves of corruption" and compares to dogs that eat their own vomit (2:1–22). Like the authors of Jude and 1 John, the writer seems unaware of any incongruity between the teaching of Christian love on the one hand and the savage abuse of fellow believers who disagree with him on the other. To him, dissenters have no more claim to respect than wild animals that are born only to be trapped and slaughtered (2:12).

It is not clear whether the opponents castigated in chapter 2 are the same skeptics who deny the Parousia in 3:3–4. In any case, the author's primary goal is to reinstate the early Christian apocalyptic hope. To convince his hearers, he reminds them that one world has already perished under a divine Judgment—the world destroyed in Noah's flood (3:5–6). The present "heavens and earth" are reserved for burning, a divine act that will destroy unbelieving persons, presumably including the writer's opponents.

In his prediction of this world's coming devastation, the author apparently borrows the Stoic philosophers' theory that the cosmos undergoes cycles of destruction and renewal. Employing Stoic images and vocabulary, 2 Peter foretells a cosmic conflagration in which heaven will be swept away in a roaring fire and the earth will disintegrate, exposing all its secrets (3:10).

Because the entire universe is destined to fall apart in a cosmic catastrophe, the author advises his recipients to prepare for an imminent Judgment. They should work hard to hurry it along, the implication being that correct human behavior will influence God to accelerate his schedule for the End (3:11–12).

Citing either Revelation's vision (21:1–3) or the Isaiah passages upon which it is based (Isa. 65:17; 66:22), the author states that a third world will replace the previous two destroyed respectively by water and fire. "New heavens and a new earth" will host true justice (3:13), the apocalyptic kingdom of God.

Peter's theodicy. The author is aware that some Christians who doubt the Parousia may do so because God, in spite of the arrival, death, and ascension to heaven of the Messiah, has not acted to conquer evil. God's seeming delay, however, has a saving purpose. Holding back Judgment, the Deity allows time for more people to repent and be spared the coming holocaust (3:9, 15). Although exercising his kindly patience in the realm of human time, God himself dwells in eternity where "a thousand years is like one day." From his vantage point the Parousia is not delayed; his apparent slowness to act is really a manifestation of his will to save all people (3:8–9).

Paul's letters. The author returns to criticizing his opponents in a famous reference to Paul's letters. Admitting that the Pauline correspondence contains unclear passages, he accuses immature Christians of twisting their meaning. Although he refers to Paul as a friend and brother, he clearly does not approve of the way in which some groups interpret Paul's teachings (3:15–16). Some critics suggest that if 2 Peter originated in Rome, the writer may be referring to Marcion or other Gnostic teachers who based their doctrines on a collected edition of Paul's letters. As in the case of Jude, the author does not give us enough information to identify his opponents with any certainty.

As the last-written New Testament book, 2 Peter affirms the primitive Christian hope that Jesus would soon return to establish his kingdom and eliminate evil from the universe. Although predicting that our world will disappear in a fiery holocaust, 2 Peter foresees a renewed creation in which righteousness prevails. While they await the Lord's return to bring about the promised new world, Christians must cling to the Apostles' original teachings, avoiding heretical misinterpretations and by their good works shortening the time before the final day arrives (3:10–15). Although 2 Peter adopts the Stoic view that the present universe must perish in flames (an extreme belief that even Revelation does not advocate), it also shares Revelation's ultimately optimistic vision of the final and complete triumph of absolute good.

Letters of John

Authorship, date, and relationship to John's Gospel. The three letters traditionally ascribed to the Apostle John give us some important insights into the Johannine community that produced and used the Fourth Gospel as its norm of belief. The author of 2 and 3 John identifies himself as "the Elder" (*presbyteros*) (2 John v. 1; 3 John v. 1); the writer of 1 John does not mention his office or function in the church.

Most scholars believe that the same person wrote all three documents but that he is not to be identified with either the Apostle John or the author of the Gospel. Although some analysts link him with the editor who added chapter 21 to the Gospel narrative, most commentators view the letter writer as a separate party, albeit an influential member of the Johannine "brotherhood" (John 21:23). Because the letters so closely resemble the Gospel in thought, style, vocabulary, and Christology, it seems the author was deeply imbued with the distinctive ideas contained in the Gospel, which apparently provided the theological norm for his community. The majority of scholars date the letters at about 100–110 CE, a decade or two after the Gospel's composition.

1 John

Occasion for writing. Lacking a salutation or closing greeting, 1 John is more a sermon or tract than a genuine letter. Addressed to persons who are devoted to the Son of God (5:13) (apparently the author's own group), it was written to oppose the false teaching of former members who had recently withdrawn from the Johannine community. The author calls them "anti-Christs" who have deserted his church to rejoin the outside world (2:18–19), where they spread wrong ideas about the nature of Christ and Christian behavior.

Revealing a more conventional view about end time than the Gospel writer, the Elder opines that the "anti-Christ's" activity proves that the "last hour" has arrived (2:18; see also John 21:22–

23). (In the Johannine church, the Gospel's "realized eschatology" may have existed side by side with more traditional ideas about the Parousia.) Like most early Christian churches, the Elder's community relied on prophetic inspiration, an ongoing communication with the Holy Spirit that continued the process of interpreting Jesus' message and meaning (John 15:26–27; 16:12–14). Problems arose when Christian prophets contradicted each other, as the anti-Christ secessionists were then doing. How was the believer to determine which among many opposing "inspirations" was truly from God?

Testing the spirits. Writing to a charismatic group long before a central church authority existed to enforce orthodoxy, the Elder is the first Christian writer to propose standards by which believers can distinguish "the spirit of error" from "the spirit of truth" (4:1–6). He echoes the Apostle Paul, who experienced similar difficulties (1 Thess. 5:19–21), when he asks Christians to "test the spirits" critically (4:1) to evaluate the reliability of their message.

Because the Elder sets up his particular tests to refute the secessionists' errors, we can infer something about their teaching from the nature of his proposals. Basically, he offers two areas of testing—doctrinal and behavioral. The most important doctrinal test concerns the nature of Jesus Christ. In his prologue (1:1–7), which strikingly resembles the Gospel's Hymn to the Logos, the Elder claims that his group possesses a tradition of direct, sensory experience of Jesus' humanity. The Word was visible and physical; he could be seen and touched. Yet those who abandoned the community apparently deny Christ's full humanity, causing the Elder to impose a Christological test of the true faith: Jesus (the man) and Christ (God's Messiah) were one person, "in the flesh."

Many scholars suggest that the Elder's opponents were Gnostics or Docetists, who insisted that "the Christ" was a divine Revealer from heaven who only temporarily occupied the body of Jesus, separating from the Galilean at death and reascending to the spirit realm. The Johannine community insists that Jesus and the Christ are the same being and that he truly suffered and died.

Next to the Incarnation test the Elder places a requirement expressing his community's cardinal rule. The secessionists do not behave well toward the former friends they have abandoned, thus invalidating their presumed claim to love God. In his most quoted statement, the author states that people who do not love cannot know God because God *is* love (4:8–9). The person who loves best also understands and reveals God most fully (4:17). Stressing the unity between divine and human love, the Elder reminds us that to love God is also to cherish God's human creation (4:19–21).

With the implication that the secessionists not only fail to love but also neglect Christian ethics, the author insists that loving God necessitates keeping his commandments (5:3). This means living as Jesus himself lived, serving others' welfare (2:6). The author refers to "the old command" that his group has always possessed, apparently the single commandment that John's Gospel ascribes to Jesus—the instruction to love (John 13:34–35; 15:12, 17). The Elder can cite no other ethical commandment from his group's tradition.

2 John

Containing only thirteen verses, 2 John is a true letter. It is addressed to "the Lady chosen by God" (v.1), a house church that belongs to the Johannine community. As in 1 John, the writer's purpose is to warn of "the anti-Christ," the deceiver who falsely teaches that Jesus Christ did not live as a material human being (v.7). He urges his recipients not to welcome such renegade Christians into the believers' house or otherwise encourage them (vv.10–11). As before, the author can prepare against the secessionists' attacks by citing only one cardinal rule, the love that is their community's sole guide (vv.5–6).

Disclosing that he has more to say than he cares to spell out on paper, the Elder promises to visit the recipients soon, ending with greetings from the writer's home congregation.

3 John

Equally brief, 3 John is a personal letter to "Gaius" (otherwise unknown), whom the Elder urges to show hospitality to some traveling missionaries led by the writer's friend, Demetrius. The writer asks Gaius to receive these itinerant Christians kindly, honoring their church's tradition of supporting those who labor to spread their version of "the truth" (v.8).

By contrast, one Diotrephes, a rival leader, offends the Elder not only by refusing his emissaries' hospitality but by expelling from the congregation any persons who attempt to aid them. We do not know if the spiteful charges Diotrephes brings against the Elder relate to the false teachings denounced in 1 John. Although Diotrephes may not be one of the "anti-Christ" secessionists, his malice and lack of charity suggest that he does not practice the Johannine community's essential commandment.

QUESTIONS FOR DISCUSSION AND REVIEW

1. Define the term *catholic epistle* and describe the general nature of these seven documents. According to tradition, to what specific group of authors are these works attributed? Why do many scholars believe that all seven are pseudonymous?

2. Identify and explain the major themes in Hebrews. How does the author's belief in a dualistic universe—an unseen spirit world that parallels the visible cosmos—affect his teaching about Jesus as an eternal High Priest officiating in heaven?

3. Hebrews presents certain biblical characters like Melchizedek and Israel's High Priest as foreshadowing the later role of Jesus. Explain the author's methods of biblical interpretation, including his uses of typology, allegory, and symbolism. According to his view, what is the relation of Israel's sacrificial ritual to the death and ascension of Jesus?

4. Almost every book in this unit of the New Testament—Hebrews and the catholic epistles—contains a theme or concept not found in any other canonical document. For example, only Hebrews presents Jesus as a celestial High Priest foreshadowed by Melchizedek; it is also unique in being the only New Testament work to define faith (11:1).

    Indicate which of the catholic epistles contains the following definitions or statements:

    a. A definition of religion

    b. A belief that Jesus descended into Hades (the Underworld) and preached to spirits imprisoned there

    c. A definition of God's essential nature

    d. A set of standards by which to determine the truth of a religious teaching

    e. An argument that actions are more important than faith

    f. A concept that human history is divided into three separate stages, or "worlds"

    g. A defense of the primitive apocalyptic hope involving Jesus' Second Coming (the Parousia)

    h. Citations from the noncanonical books of the Pseudepigrapha, including the book of Enoch

    i. The New Testament's most severe denunciation of the rich

TERMS AND CONCEPTS TO REMEMBER

epistle	Melchizedek
catholic epistles	Aaron
dualism	Jesus as both sacrifice
Platonism	and High Priest
corresponding worlds	definition of faith
Hebrews' major	authorship of James
theme	Wisdom literature

definition of religion
reasons for suffering
relationship of rich
and poor
salvation through
faith or through
good works
authorship of 1 Peter
privileges of
Christian belief
obligations and risks
of adopting
Christianity
Jesus' descent into
Hades
authorship of Jude
invective
Pseudepigrapha
Book of 1 Enoch
asceticism
date of 2 Peter
three "worlds"

cosmic fire
the delayed Parousia
new heavens and a
new earth
authorship of 1, 2,
and 3 John
Johannine
community
the anti-Christ
spirit of error and
spirit of truth
tests of belief and
behavior
Gnosticism
Docetism
the Incarnation
definition of God's
nature
chief rule of the
Johannine
community

RECOMMENDED READING

Hebrews

Buchanan, G. W., ed. and trans. *Hebrews*. Vol. 36 of the Anchor Bible. Garden City, N.Y.: Doubleday, 1972. Provides editor's translation and commentary.

Davies, W. D. "Ethics in the New Testament." In *The Interpreter's Dictionary of the Bible,* vol. 2, 167–76. Nashville: Abingdon Press, 1962. Includes discussion of Hebrews' ethical teachings.

Dinker, E. "Hebrews, Letter to the." In *The Interpreter's Dictionary of the Bible,* vol. 2, 571–75. Nashville: Abingdon Press, 1962. A relatively brief but useful discussion.

Fuller, R. H. "The Letter to the Hebrews, James, Jude, Revelation, 1 and 2 Peter." In *Proclamation Commentaries,* edited by G. Krodel. Philadelphia: Fortress Press, 1977.

Manson, W. *The Epistle to the Hebrews: An Historical and Theological Consideration.* London: Hodder & Stoughton, 1951. Offers some controversial views about the origin and purpose of Hebrews.

Neil, W. *The Epistle to the Hebrews.* London: SCM Press, 1955. A more popular treatment influenced by Manson's thesis.

James

Barnett, A. E. "James, Letter of." In *The Interpreter's Dictionary of the Bible,* vol. 2, 794–99. Nashville: Abingdon Press, 1962. A useful introduction.

Dibelius, Martin, and Heinrich Greeven. *A Commentary on the Epistle of James.* Hermeneia Commentary. Translated by M. A. Williams. Philadelphia: Fortress Press, 1976. An excellent study.

Laws, Sophie. *A Commentary on the Epistle of James.* Harper's New Testament Commentary. San Francisco: Harper & Row, 1980.

Milton, C. L. *The Epistle of James.* Grand Rapids, Mich.: Eerdmans, 1966. A thorough analysis.

Reicke, Bo. *The Epistles of James, Peter, and Jude.* Vol. 37 of the Anchor Bible. Garden City, N.Y.: Doubleday, 1964. Recent translations with some provocative commentary.

1 and 2 Peter and Jude

Beker, J. C. "Jude, Letter of." In *The Interpreter's Dictionary of the Bible,* vol. 2, 1009–11. Nashville: Abingdon Press, 1962. A brief but helpful introduction.

———. "Peter, Second Letter of." In *The Interpreter's Dictionary of the Bible,* vol. 3, 767–71. Nashville: Abingdon Press, 1962. An informative introduction.

Best, Ernest. *I Peter.* London: Oliphants, 1971.

Brown, R. E., K. Donfried, and J. Reumann, eds. *Peter in the New Testament; A Collaborative Assessment by Protestant and Roman Catholic Scholars.* Minneapolis: Augsburg Publishing House, 1973. A recommended study of Peter's role in the New Testament tradition and literature.

Elliott, J. H. *A Home for the Homeless: A Sociological Exegesis of I Peter, Its Situation and Strategy.* Philadelphia: Fortress Press, 1981. A sociological analysis of historical conditions underlying the message and meaning of 1 Peter.

Fitzmyer, Joseph. "The First Epistle of Peter." In *The Jerome Biblical Commentary,* edited by R. E. Brown and J. A. Fitzmyer, vol. 2, 1–27. Englewood Cliffs, N.J.: Prentice-Hall, 1968.

Kelly, J. N. D. *A Commentary on the Epistles of Peter and Jude.* New York: Harper & Row, 1969. A good introductory study.

Reicke, Bo. *The Epistles of James, Peter, and Jude.* Vol. 37 of the Anchor Bible. Garden City, N.Y.: Doubleday, 1964.

van Unnik, W. C. "Peter, First Letter of." In *The Interpreter's Dictionary of the Bible,* vol. 3, 758–66. Nashville: Abingdon Press, 1962. A helpful introduction.

1, 2, and 3 John

Brown, R. E. *The Churches the Apostles Left Behind.* New York: Paulist Press, 1984. A wonderfully concise study of several different Christian communities at the end of the first century CE.

————. *The Community of the Beloved Disciple.* New York: Paulist Press, 1979. An extraordinarily insightful analysis of the Johannine group that produced the Gospel and letters of John.

————. *The Epistles of John.* Vol. 30 of the Anchor Bible. Garden City, N.Y.: Doubleday, 1982. A scholarly translation and commentary on the letters of John.

Caird, G. B. "John, Letters of." In *The Interpreter's Dictionary of the Bible,* vol. 2, 946–52. Nashville: Abingdon Press, 1962.

Smith, D. M. "John, Letters of." In *The Interpreter's Dictionary of the Bible,* supplementary vol., 486–87. Nashville: Abingdon Press, 1976.

19 Continuing the Apocalyptic Hope: The Book of Revelation

> Then I saw a new heaven and a new earth, for the
> first heaven and the first earth had vanished. . . .
> Now at last God has his dwelling among men!
>
> (Rev. 21:1, 3)

KEY THEMES Revelation affirms Christianity's original hope for an immediate transformation of the world and assures the faithful that God's prearranged plan, including the destruction of evil and the advent of Christ's universal reign, is about to be accomplished. The book presents an *apokalypsis* ("unveiling") of unseen realities, both in heaven as it is now and on earth as it will be in the future. Placing governmental tyranny and Christian suffering in a cosmic perspective, Revelation conveys its message of hope for believers in the cryptic language of metaphor and symbol.

Although Revelation was not the last New Testament book written, its position at the end of the canon is thematically appropriate. The first Christians believed that their generation would witness the end of the present wicked age and the beginning of God's direct rule over the earth. Revelation expresses that apocalyptic hope more powerfully than any other Christian writing. Looking forward to a "new heaven and a new earth" (21:1), it envisions the glorious completion of God's creative work begun in the first book of the Bible. In this sense it provides the omega (the final letter of the Greek alphabet) to the alpha (the first letter) of Genesis.

Revelation's climactic placement is also fitting because it reintroduces Jesus as a major character. Its picture of an all-powerful heavenly Jesus provides a counterweight to the Gospels' portrait of the human Jesus' earthly career. In Revelation Jesus is no longer Mark's suffering servant or John's embodiment of divine Wisdom. Revelation's Jesus is the Messiah of popular expectation, a conquering warrior-king who slays his enemies and proves beyond all doubt

his right to universal rule. In striking contrast to the Gospel portraits, the Jesus of Revelation comes not to forgive sinners and instruct them in a higher righteousness but to inflict a wrathful punishment upon his opponents (19:11–21).

Revelation's depiction of Jesus' character and function, qualitatively different from that presented in the Gospels, derives partly from the author's apocalyptic view of human history. Like the authors of Jude and 2 Peter, the writer perceives a sharp contrast between the present world, which he regards as hopelessly corrupt, and God's planned future world, a realm of ideal purity. In the author's opinion, the righteous new order can be realized only through God's direct intervention in human affairs, an event that requires Jesus to act as God's Judge and destroyer of the world as we know it. To understand Revelation's emphasis on violence and destruction, with its correspondingly harsher picture of Jesus' cosmic role, we must remember that the author belongs to a particular branch of the Jewish and Christian apocalyptic movement.

Revelation and the Apocalyptic Tradition

The Apocalypse. "Revelation" translates the Greek term *apokalypsis,* which means an uncovering, an unveiling, a stripping naked of what was formerly covered. An apocalypse is thus a disclosure of things previously hidden, particularly unseen realities of the spirit world (Heb. 11:1) as well as future events. Apocalyptic writers typically describe visions or dreams in which they encounter supernatural beings ranging from hideous monsters to angels who communicate God's future intentions (2 Esd. 3–9; Dan. 7–12). Sometimes apocalyptists are carried out of their bodies to behold the Deity's heavenly throne or other celestial regions normally invisible to human eyes.

The apocalyptic tradition to which Revelation belongs is commonly regarded as a later outgrowth of the prophetic movement in ancient Israel. Israel's great prophets had delivered Yahweh's word to the people during the period of the Davidic monarchy (about 1000–587 BCE). Following the monarchy's end and the Babylonian captivity (587–538 BCE), however, prophecy declined rapidly. Eventually, many Jews came to believe that authentic prophecy had ceased after the time of Ezra (about 400 BCE). Priests took the place of prophets as Israel's spiritual leaders.

During the last two centuries before the Christian epoch, and for at least a century after, numerous Jewish writers attempted to fill the vacuum left by the prophets' disappearance. They composed innumerable books in the names of Israel's leaders who had lived before the time of Ezra. These pseudonymous works were attributed to figures like Enoch, Moses, Isaiah, David, Solomon, and Ezra. Many of them are apocalypses, containing visions of end time, such as Daniel (the only such work to become part of the Hebrew Bible), 1 and 2 Enoch, 4 Ezra (2 Esdras), 2 Baruch, and the Essene War Scroll from Qumran.

During the early centuries of the common era, many Christian writers contributed to the apocalyptic genre. We have already discussed the apocalyptic elements in the Gospels, especially Mark 13 and its parallels in Matthew and Luke, as well as Paul's eschatological concerns in his letters to the Thessalonians and the Corinthians. In addition to these canonical works, other Christian authors composed apocalyptic books, typically attributing them to prominent Apostles, including Peter, John, James, Thomas, and Paul. The canonical Revelation is unique in being ascribed not to a figure of the distant past but to a contemporary member of the first-century church named John. The work is also unique in being the only surviving document by a Christian prophet (1:3), which was a common function or office in the early church (Acts 2:15–17; 1 Thess. 5:19–20; 1 Cor. 12:10; 14:22, 24–25, 31–33).

Characteristics of Apocalyptic Writing

Besides the mystical, otherworldly quality of its content, apocalyptic literature is distinguished by the following characteristics:

1. Chronological dualism. The apocalyptist sees all history divided into two mutually exclusive periods of time, a current wicked era and a future age of perfection. Viewing the present world situation as too thoroughly evil to reform, the apocalyptist expects a sudden and violent change in which God or his Messiah imposes divine rule by force. In the apocalyptic vision, there is no normal historical progression from one age to the next and no real continuity between them.

2. An ethical dualism. The apocalyptist sees humanity divided into two opposing camps of intrinsically different ethical quality. The vast majority of people walk in spiritual darkness and are doomed victims of God's wrath. Only a tiny minority—the religious group to which the writer belongs and directs his message—remains faithful and receives salvation. Deeply conscious of human sinfulness and despairing

of humanity's ability to meet God's righteous standards, the apocalyptist takes a consistently pessimistic view of society's future.

3. A cosmic dualism. Besides separating history and humanity into two qualitatively exclusive components, the apocalyptic writer regards the universe as divided into opposing spiritual forces locked in constant warfare. In this view we inhabit a "two-story universe," the visible world of earthly society and an upper invisible world where superhuman agents of good or evil battle each other. Events on earth, such as persecution of the righteous, reflect the machinations of these unseen powers.

4. A conviction that history is predestined. Whereas many biblical writers stress that historical events are the consequences of our moral choices (for example, Deut. 28–29; Josh. 24; Ezek. 18), apocalyptists view history as running in a straight line toward a predetermined end. Just as the rise or fall of worldly empires occurs according to God's plan (Dan. 2, 7–8), so the End will take place at a time God has already set. Human efforts, no matter how well intended, cannot avert the coming disaster or influence God to change his mind. The vast complexity of human experience means nothing when confronted with the divinely prearranged schedule.

5. Exclusivism. Many apocalypses, including Revelation, were composed to encourage the faithful to maintain integrity and resist temptation to compromise with "worldly" values or customs. The apocalyptist typically equates religious fidelity with a total rejection of the ordinary goals, ambitions, social attachments, and other pursuits of unbelieving society. Regarding most people as doomed, the apocalyptist commonly urges his hearers to adopt a devoutly sectarian attitude, avoiding all association with unbelievers. Revelation orders Christians to "get out of" "Babylon," symbol of the society that the writer abhors.

6. Limited theology. Consistent with its strict division of history and people into divinely approved or disapproved units, the apocalyptic author usually shows little sympathy for differing viewpoints or compassion for nonbelievers. All modes of existence are either black or white, with no psychological or spiritual shades of gray in between. As a result of the author's mental set, the apocalyptic picture of God is ethically limited. The Deity is almost invariably depicted as an enthroned monarch. He is a formidably powerful authority who brings history to a violent conclusion in order to demonstrate his sovereignty, confound his enemies, and preserve his few worshippers. The notion that God might regard all people as his children or that he might establish his kingdom by less catastrophic means does not appeal to the apocalyptic temperament or satisfy the apocalyptic yearning.

7. Pictures of violence and suffering. Assuming that the Deity achieves control over heaven and earth through a cataclysmic battle with Satan, the apocalyptist dramatizes this transference of power through vivid scenes of violence and human suffering. Typically reproducing or intensifying images of the ten plagues Yahweh inflicted on Egypt (Exod. 7–12), the apocalyptist shows God angrily punishing disobedient humanity, afflicting millions with famine, starvation, and loathsome diseases. In Revelation, religious awe before God's infinite strength is combined with horror and fear at the intense misery he can create.

8. Eschatological preoccupations. Along with unveiling the mysteries of the invisible world, the apocalyptic writer reveals the fate of human beings during God's terrifying Judgment. Daniel was the first biblical writing explicitly to envision the resurrection of individuals for posthumous rewards or penalties (Dan. 12:1–3). Other Jewish and Christian authors imitated Daniel by including visions of an afterlife in which the righteous attain everlasting bliss while the wicked suffer excruciating torment. 2 Esdras, a Jewish apocalypse almost exactly contemporaneous with Revelation, provides the Bible's most detailed picture of the respective destinies of the saved and the damned; the Apoc-

alypse of Peter (a later Christian work) contains harrowing scenes of sinners' posthumous tortures. (Along with the books of Enoch, both of these apocryphal works helped to inspire Dante and Milton in their respective descriptions of the Christian hell.)

9. The use of cryptic symbols and code words. Virtually all apocalyptists use language that deliberately hides as well as expresses their meaning. Because they typically write during times of crisis and persecution, apocalyptic authors employ terms and images that their intended audience will understand but that will bewilder outsiders. In Daniel, Revelation, and other apocalypses the writers employ symbols from a wide variety of sources, both pagan and Judeo-Christian.

The importance of symbols. In its broadest sense, a symbol is a sign that represents something other than itself. It can be a person, a place, an object, or an action that suggests an association or connection with another dimension of meaning. Daniel and Revelation both depict Gentile nations as animals because, to the authors, they resemble wild beasts in their violent and irrational behavior. Kings who demand worship are symbolized as idols, and paying homage to them is called idolatry. Using code words for the writer's enemies is also common; for example, in Revelation *Babylon* stands for the hated city of Rome. (See the discussion of specific symbols below.)

Authorship and Date

Who was the writer who created the bedazzling kaleidoscope of images in Revelation? According to some late second-century traditions, he is the Apostle John and the same person who wrote the Gospel and letters of John. Other early Christian sources recognized that the immense differences in thought, language, and theology between Revelation and the Fourth Gospel indicate that they could not have originated with the same author. Eusebius suggests that another

John, known only as the "Elder," an official of the late first-century Ephesian church, may have written the apocalypse (*History* 3.39.1–11).

Virtually all modern scholars agree that the Gospel and Revelation stem from different authors. A few accept Eusebius's theory about John the Elder of Ephesus, but the scholarly majority notes that we have no evidence to link the book with that obscure figure. Most scholars prefer to accept no more than the writer's own self-identification. He simply calls himself John, a "servant" of Jesus Christ (1:2). Because he does not claim apostolic authority and never refers to having known the earthly Jesus, most analysts conclude that he is not one of the Twelve, whom he categorizes as different from himself. In the author's day, the Apostles had already become "cornerstones" of the heavenly Temple (21:14). Exiled to the island of Patmos in the eastern Aegean Sea where he received his visions (1:9), the author perhaps is best described as John of Patmos, a mystic who regarded himself as a Christian prophet and his book a preview of future events (1:1–3; 22:7–10).

John's connection with the Greco-Roman cities of Asia Minor (western Turkey) seems confirmed by his precise knowledge of conditions prevailing in the seven churches there (1:4–3:22) (see Figure 19–1). He may not have been a native of the region, however, for his use of Greek (generally judged the worst in the New Testament) and his Semitic style indicate a Palestinian background. As Acts and Paul's letters prove, early Christians traveled great distances with astonishing frequency, so John may have settled in one of the Asian cities (tradition associates the author with Ephesus) before he was deported to Patmos. It seems probable that he was a Palestinian Jew who had achieved an influential position among the Hellenistic congregations of Asia Minor.

Connection with the Johannine community. John's Gospel and Revelation share a number of concepts and terms. Both works refer to Christ as Logos, Lamb, witness, shepherd,

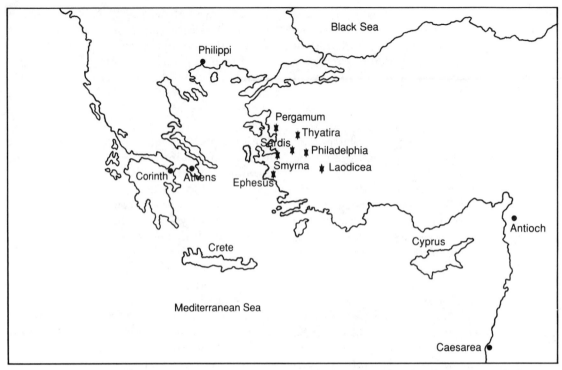

Figure 19–1. The seven churches in Asia Minor (western Turkey) addressed in Revelation 1–3 include Ephesus, one of the major seaports of the Roman Empire, and Sardis, once capital of the older Lydian Empire (sixth century BCE). John pictures the heavenly Christ dictating letters to seven angels who act as invisible guardians of the individual churches. With this image, John reminds his audience that the tiny groups of Christians scattered throughout the Roman Empire do not stand alone. Although seemingly weak and insignificant, they are part of God's mighty empire of the spirit and are destined to triumph over their earthly oppressors.

Judge, and temple. Both express a duality of spirit and matter, good and evil, God and Satan. Both regard Christ as present in the church's liturgy and view his death as a saving victory. Important differences range from the quality of the Greek—excellent in the Gospel and crude in the Apocalypse—to the writers' respective theologies. Whereas the Gospel presents God's love as his primary motive in dealing with humanity, Revelation mentions divine love only once. The Johannine Jesus' preeminent command to love is pervasively absent from Revelation.

The date. Writing about 180 CE, the churchman Irenaeus stated that Revelation was com-

posed late in the reign of Domitian, who was emperor from 81 to 96 CE. Internal references to governmental persecution of Christians (1:9; 2:10, 13; 6:9–11; 14:12; 16:6; 21:4), policies then associated with Domitian's administration, support Irenaeus's assessment. Most scholars date the work about 95 or 96 CE.

The emperor cult and persecution. Domitian was the son of Vespasian and the younger brother of Titus, the general who had successfully crushed the Jewish Revolt against Rome and destroyed the Jerusalem Temple. After Titus's brief reign (79–81 CE), Domitian inherited the imperial throne, accepting divine honors offered him and allowing himself to be wor-

Bust of Domitian, emperor of Rome from 81 to 96 CE. Many historians believe that an overzealous cult of emperor worship in Asia Minor stimulated the attacks on Christians described in Revelation. To what extent Domitian personally encouraged his subjects to honor him as a god is uncertain. Most Greco-Roman historians thoroughly disliked Domitian's policies and presented him as a tyrant. This ancient prejudice makes it difficult for modern scholars to evaluate his reign objectively. (Courtesy Alinari/Art Resource.)

shipped as a god in various parts of the empire. We have no real evidence that Domitian personally enforced a universal observance of an emperor cult, but in certain areas governors and other local officials demanded public participation in the cult as evidence of citizens' loyalty and patriotism. Perhaps to gain Domitian's favor, many cities in Asia Minor zealously promulgated the emperor's worship, punishing those who did not participate.

Because Rome had recognized their religion's monotheism, Jews were generally exempted from the emperor cult. Jewish and Gentile Christians, however, were not. To most Romans, their "stubborn" refusal to honor any of the many Greco-Roman gods or deified emperors was not only unpatriotic but also likely to bring the gods' wrath upon the whole community. Early Christians denied the existence of the Hellenistic deities and rejected offers to participate in Roman religious festivals and other communal events. They became known as unsocial "atheists" and "haters of humankind." Rumors spread that they met secretly to drink blood and perform cannibalistic rites (a distorted reference to the sacramental ingesting of Jesus' blood and body). Labeled as a seditious secret society dangerous to the general welfare, early Christian groups endured social ostracism and hostility. When they also refused their allegiance to the emperor as a symbol of the Roman state, many local governors and other magistrates had them arrested, tortured, imprisoned, or even executed.

Only a few decades after John composed Revelation, Pliny the Younger, a Roman governor of Bithynia (located in the same general region as Revelation's seven churches), wrote to the Emperor Trajan inquiring about the government's official policy toward Christians. Pliny's description of the situation as it was about 112 CE may also apply to John's slightly earlier time.

Although a humane and sophisticated thinker, Pliny reports that he did not hesitate to torture two slave women, "deacons" of a local church, and execute other believers. If Christians hold Roman citizenship, he sends them to Rome for trial. Trajan replies that although his governors are not to hunt out Christians or accept anonymous accusations, self-confessed believers are to be punished. Both the emperor and Pliny clearly regard Christians as criminals threatening the empire's security (Pliny, *Letters,* 10.96–97).

Purpose and Organization

The Christians for whom John writes were experiencing a real crisis. They were faced with Jewish hostility, public suspicion, and sporadic governmental prosecution, imprisonment, and even execution. Many believers must have been

tempted to renounce Christ, as Pliny asked his prisoners to do, and conform to the norms of Roman society. Recognizing that the costs of remaining Christian were overwhelmingly great, John recorded his visions of cosmic conflict to strengthen those whose faith wavered, assuring them that death is not defeat but victory. In the light of eternity, Rome's power was insignificant, but its victims, slaughtered for their fidelity, gained everlasting life and the power to judge the fates of their former persecutors.

Despite its vast complexities, we can outline Revelation as follows:

1. Prologue: the author's self-identification and the basis for his authority—divine revelation (1:1–20)
2. Jesus' letters to the seven churches of Asia Minor (2:1–3:22)
3. Visions from heaven: a scroll with seven seals; seven trumpets (4:1–11:19)
4. Signs in heaven: visions of the woman, the dragon, the beast, the lamb, and the seven plagues (12:1–16:21)
5. Visions of the "great whore" and the fall of Babylon (Rome) (17:1–18:24)
6. Visions of heavenly rejoicing, the warrior Messiah, the imprisonment of the beast and Satan, Judgment of the dead, and the final defeat of evil (19:1–20:15)
7. Visions of the "new heaven and new earth" and the establishment of a new Jerusalem on earth (21:1–22:5)
8. Epilogue: authenticity of the author's prophetic visions and the nearness of their fulfillment (22:6–21)

From this outline we observe that John begins his work in the real world of exile and suffering (1:1–10), then takes his readers on a visionary tour of the spirit world—including a vivid dramatization of the imminent fall of Satanic governments and the triumph of Christ. He returns at the end to earth and addresses final instructions to his contemporary audience (22:6–21). The book's structure thus resembles a vast circle starting and ending in physical reality but encompassing a panorama of the unseen regions of heaven and the future.

The author's visionary authority. Alone among New Testament writers, John claims divine inspiration for his work. He reports that on "the Lord's day"—Sunday—he "was caught up by the Spirit" to hear and see heaven's unimaginable splendors (1:9). His message derives from God's direct revelation to Jesus Christ, who in turn transmits it through an angel to him (1:1–2). John's visions generate an intense urgency, for they reveal the immediate future (1:1). Visionary previews of Jesus' impending return convince the author that what he sees is about to happen (1:3). This warning is repeated at the book's conclusion when Jesus proclaims that his arrival is imminent (22:7, 10, 12).

Revelation's Use of Symbols

John's prophetic style. Revelation's opening chapter gives a representative example of John's writing style. It shows how profoundly he was influenced by the Hebrew Bible and how he utilizes its vivid images to construct his fantastic symbols. Without ever citing specific biblical books, John typically fills his sentences with innumerable metaphors and phrases borrowed from all parts of the Old Testament. Scholars have counted approximately five hundred such verbal allusions. (The Jerusalem Bible helps the reader to recognize John's biblical paraphrases by printing them in italics.)

In his first symbolic depiction of a heavenly being (1:12–16), John paints a male figure with snow-white hair, flaming eyes, incandescent brass feet, and a sharp sword protruding from his mouth. These images derive largely from Daniel (chs. 7 and 10). To universalize this figure more completely, John adds astronomical features to his biblical symbols. Like a Greek mythological hero transformed into a stellar constellation, the figure is described as holding seven stars in his hand and shining with the brilliance of the sun.

The next verses (1:17–19) reveal the figure's identity. As the "first and the last" who has died but now lives forever, he is the crucified and risen Christ. The author's purpose in combining biblical with nonbiblical imagery is now clear: in strength and splendor the glorified Christ surpasses rival Greco-Roman deities like Mithras, Apollo, Helios, Amon-Ra, or other solar gods worshipped throughout the Roman Empire.

John further explains his symbols in 1:20. There, Christ identifies the stars as angels and the lampstands standing nearby as the seven churches of John's home territory. This identification reassures the author that his familiar earthly congregations do not exist solely on a material plane but are part of a larger visible/invisible duality in which angelic spirits protectively oversee assembled Christians. The symbols also serve John's characteristic purpose in uncovering the spiritual reality behind physical appearance. To John, the seven churches are as precious as the golden candelabrum that once stood in the Jerusalem sanctuary. Like the eternal stars above, they shed Christ's light on a benighted world.

The Lamb and the Dragon. In asking us to view the universe as God sees it, John challenges his readers to respond emotionally and intuitively as well as intellectually to his symbols. Thus, he depicts invisible forces of good or evil in images that evoke an instinctively positive or negative reaction. Using a tradition also found in the Fourth Gospel, the author pictures Christ as the Lamb of God, whose death "takes away the sin of the world" (John 1:29, 36; Rev. 4:7–14; 5:6; 7:10, 14). Harmless and vulnerable, the Lamb is appealing; his polar opposite, the Dragon, elicits feelings of fear and revulsion. A reptilian monster with seven heads and ten horns, he is equated with "that serpent of old . . . whose name is Satan, or the Devil" (12:3, 9). (In the Eden story the serpent that tempted Eve to disobey God is not described as evil. The Genesis serpent's identification with Satan is a much later development in Jewish thought [Wisd. Sol. 2:23–24].)

In his vision of the Dragon waging war and being thrown down from heaven (12:1–12), John evokes one of the world's oldest conflict myths. Dating back to ancient Sumer and Babylon, the dragon image represents the forces of chaos—darkness, disorder, and the original void—that preceded the world's creation. In the Babylonian creation story, the Enuma Elish, the young god Marduk must defeat and kill Tiamat, the dragon of chaos, before the orderly cosmos can be brought into being. Echoes of these primordial creation myths appear in the Hebrew Bible, including the symbol of the dark, watery abyss (Gen: 1:2) and passages in which Yahweh defeats the chaotic monsters Rahab, Behemoth, or Leviathan (Ps. 74:13–17; 89:9–10; Job 26:1–14; Isa. 51:9). Consistent with the ancient chaos myth, the defeat of the Dragon in Revelation returns him to the original abyss—the dark void that represents forces opposing God's light and creative purpose (20:1–3, 7).

To unspiritual eyes, the Lamb—tiny and vulnerable—might appear a ridiculously inadequate opponent of the Dragon, particularly since John views Satan as possessing immense power on earth as he wages war against the Lamb's people, the church (12:13–17). Although nations that the Dragon controls, figuratively called Sodom and Egypt (11:8), have already slain the Lamb (when Rome crucified Jesus), God uses this apparent weakness to eliminate evil in both heaven and earth. John wishes his readers to draw comfort from this paradox: Christ's sacrificial death guarantees his ultimate victory over the Dragon and all he represents.

The Lamb's death and rebirth to immortal power also. delivers his persecuted followers. The church will overcome the seemingly invincible strength of its oppressors; the blood of its faithful martyrs confirm that God will preserve it (6:9–11; 7:13–17). Although politically and socially as weak as a lamb, the Christian community embodies a potential strength that is unrecognized by its enemies. John expresses this belief in the image of an angel carrying a golden censer, an incense burner used in Jewish and Christian worship services. He interprets the censer's symbolism very simply: smoke rising upward from the burning incense represents Christians' prayers ascending to heaven, where they have an astonishing effect. In the next image the angel throws the censer to earth, causing thunder and an earthquake. The meaning is that the prayers of the faithful can figuratively shake the world (8:3–5). The author gives many of his most obscure or grotesque symbols a comparably down-to-earth meaning.

Limited space permits us to discuss here only a few of John's most significant visions. We focus on those in which he pictures the cosmic tension between good and evil, light and darkness, Christ and Satan. In commenting on the notorious beast whose "human" number is 666 (13:1–18)—a favorite topic for many of today's apocalyptists—we also briefly review the author's use of numerology, the occult art of assigning arcane meanings to specific numbers.

Jesus' Letters to the Seven Churches

Having validated his prophetic authority through the divine source of his prophecy, John now surveys the disparate churches of Asia Minor, the seven lamps that contrast with the world's darkness. Like the contemporary author of 2 Esdras (14:22–48), John presents himself as a secretary recording the dictation of a divine voice, conveying the instructions of a higher power.

Christ's letters to the seven communities all follow the same pattern. After he commands John to write, Jesus identifies himself as the sender, then employs the formula "I know," followed by a description of the church's spiritual condition. A second formula, "but I have it against you," then introduces a summary of the church's particular weaknesses. Each letter also includes a prophetic call for repentance, a promise that the Parousia will occur soon, an exhortation to maintain integrity, a directive to "hear," and then a final pledge to reward the victorious.

After reading Jesus' message to Ephesus (2:1–7), Smyrna (2:8–11), Pergamum (2:12–17), Thyatira (2:18–29), Sardis (3:1–6), Philadelphia (3:7–13), and Laodicea (3:14–22), the student will have a good idea of John's method. Church conditions in each of these cities are rendered in images that represent the spiritual reality underlying those conditions. Thus, Pergamum is labeled the site of Satan's throne (2:13), probably because it was the first center of the emperor cult. (John sees any worldly ruler who claims divine honors as an agent of Satan and hence the opposite of Jesus, an anti-Christ.) The Balaam referred to here was a Canaanite prophet hired to curse Israel (Num. 22–24) and hence a false teacher, like those who advocate eating meat previously sacrificed to Greco-Roman gods (2:14). John's strict refusal to tolerate consuming animals slaughtered in non-Christian rituals (which included virtually all meats sold in most Roman cities) is typical of his exclusivism and contrasts with Paul's freer attitude on the same issue (1 Cor. 8:1–13).

Visions in Heaven

John's initial vision made visible and audible the invisible presence of Christ; his second (4:1–11:19) opens the way to heaven. After the Spirit carries him to God's throne, John is shown pictures of events about to occur (4:1–2). It is important to remember, however, that John's purpose is not merely to predict future happenings but to remove the material veil that shrouds heavenly truths and to allow his readers to see that God retains full control of the entire universe. The visions that follow are intended to reassure Christians that their sufferings are temporary and their deliverance is certain.

Breaking the Seven Seals

John conveys this assurance in two series of seven visions involving seven seals and seven trumpets. Seen from the perspective of God's heavenly throne (depicted in terms of Isa. 6 and Ezek. 1 and 10), the opening of the seven seals reveals that the future course of events has already been determined, written down in advance on a heavenly scroll. In John's day, almost all writing was done on long narrow strips of paper that were then rolled up around a stick, forming a scroll. Important communications from kings or other officials were commonly sealed with hot wax, which was imprinted while still soft with the sender's identifying seal. Because the scroll could not be opened without breaking the seal, the wax imprint effectively prevented anyone from knowing the scroll's contents until the intended recipient opened it.

In John's vision the Lamb opens each of the seven seals in sequence, disclosing either a predestined future event or the revelation of God's viewpoint on some important matter. (Breaking the seventh seal is an exception, producing only an ominous silence in heaven—the calm preceding the Lord's Final Judgment [8:1].) Unsealing the first four seals unleashes four horses and riders—the famous Four Horsemen of the Apocalypse—representing, respectively, victory, war, food shortages (including monetary inflation), and death, the "sickly pale" rider, followed closely by Hades (the grave or Underworld) (6:1–8).

Breaking the fifth seal makes visible the souls of persons executed for their Christian faith. With their blood crying for divine vengeance, they are given white clothing and told to rest until the full number of predestined martyrs has been killed (6:9–11). In such scenes John indicates that believers' willingness to die for their religion earns them the white garment of spiritual purity—and that God soon will act to avenge their deaths.

Showing how terrifying the great day of God's vengeance will be, John pictures it in terms of astronomical catastrophes. Apparently borrowing from the same apocalyptic tradition that the Synoptic Gospel writers used to predict Jesus' Second Coming (Mark 13; Matt. 24–25; Luke 21), the author says the sun will turn black, the moon will turn a bloody red, and the stars will fall to earth as the sky vanishes into nothingness (6:12–14). As he clothes Jesus in astronomical images, so John also paints the End in livid colors of cosmic dissolution.

As the earth's population hides in fear, angels appear with God's distinctive seal to mark believers on the forehead, an apocalyptic device borrowed from Ezekiel 9. The symbolic number of those marked for salvation is 144,000 (a multiple of 12), the number representing the traditional twelve tribes of Israel. This indicates that John sees his fellow Jews redeemed at end time (compare Paul's view in Rom. 9:25–27). In chapter 14, the 144,000 are designated the first ingathering of God's harvest (14:1–5). Accompanying this Israelite group is a huge crowd from every nation on earth, probably signifying the countless multitudes of Gentile Christians. Both groups wear white robes and stand before God's throne. (By contrast, see John's description of those marked by the demonic "beast" [13:16–17].)

The seven trumpets. As if answering the churches' prayers (symbolized by the censer in 8:4–5), seven angels blow seven trumpets of doom. The first six announce catastrophes reminiscent of the ten plagues on Egypt. The initial trumpet blast triggers a hail of fire and blood, causing a third of the earth to burn (8:6–7). The second causes a fire-spewing mountain to be hurled into the sea, perhaps a reference to the volcanic island of Thera, which was visible from Patmos (8:8–9). Devastating volcanic eruptions like that of Vesuvius in 79 CE were commonly regarded as divine Judgments.

The third and fourth trumpets introduce more astronomical disasters, including a blazing comet or meteorite called Wormwood (perhaps picturing Satan's fall from heaven) and causing the sun, moon, and stars to lose a third of their light

(8:10–12). After the fifth trumpet blast, the fallen star opens the abyss, releasing columns of smoke that produce a plague of locusts, similar to those described in Exodus (10:12–15) and Joel (1:4; 2:10). Persons not angelically marked are tormented with unbearable agonies but are unable to die to end their pain (9:1–6). These disasters, in which the locusts may represent barbarian soldiers invading the Roman Empire (9:7–11), are equivalent to the first disaster predicted (8:13; 9:12).

Despite the unleashing of further hordes as the sixth trumpet sounds (9:14–19), John does not believe that such afflictions will stop the world's bad behavior. People who survive the plagues will continue committing crimes and practicing false religion (9:20–21). In fact, John presents the world's suffering as gratuitous and essentially without moral purpose. Revelation's various plagues compound human misery, but they fail to enlighten their victims about the divine nature or produce a single act of regret or repentance.

Eating the scroll. As he had taken his device of marking the saved from Ezekiel 9, John now draws upon the same prophet to describe the symbolic eating of a little scroll that tastes like honey but turns bitter in the stomach (Ezek. 2:8–3:3). The scroll represents the dual nature of John's message: sweet to the faithful but sour to the disobedient (10:8–11).

In the next section John is told to measure the Jerusalem Temple, which will continue under Gentile (pagan) domination for forty-two months. In the meantime two witnesses are appointed to prophesy for 1260 days—the traditional period of persecution or tribulation established in Daniel (7:25; 9:27; 12:7). The witnesses are killed and, after three and a half days, resurrected and taken to heaven. (The executed prophets may refer to Moses and Elijah, Peter and Paul, or, collectively, to all Christian martyrs whose testimony caused their deaths.) After the martyrs' ascension, an earthquake kills seven thousand inhabitants of the great city whose ethical reality is represented by Sodom and Egypt. Sodom, guilty of violence and inhospitality, was consumed in fire from heaven. Egypt, which enslaved God's people, was devastated by ten plagues. So Rome, the tyrannical state that executed Christ and persecutes his disciples (11:1–13), suffers deserved punishment.

The seventh trumpet does not introduce a specific calamity but proclaims God's sovereignty and the eternal reign of his Christ. With the Messiah invisibly reigning in the midst of his enemies (Ps. 2:1–12), God's heavenly sanctuary opens to view amid awesome phenomena recalling Yahweh's presence in Solomon's Temple (1 Kings 8:1–6).

Signs in Heaven: The Woman, The Dragon, The Beast, and the Seven Plagues

Chapter 12 introduces a series of unnumbered visions dramatizing the cosmic battle between the Lamb and the Dragon. In this section (12:1–16:21) John parallels unseen events in heaven with their experienced consequences on earth. The opening war in the spirit realm (12:1–12) finds its earthly counterpart in the climactic battle of **Armageddon** (16:12–16). Between these two analogous conflicts John mixes inspirational visions of the Lamb's domain with warnings about "the beast" and God's negative judgment upon disobedient humankind.

The celestial woman. This section's first astronomical sign reveals a woman dressed in the sun, moon, and stars, a figure resembling Hellenistic portraits of the Egyptian goddess Isis. Despite its nonbiblical astrological features, however, John probably means the figure to symbolize Israel, historically the parent of Christ. Arrayed in "twelve stars" suggesting the traditional twelve tribes, the woman labors painfully giving birth to the Messiah. John's fellow first-century apocalyptist, the author of 2 Es-

dras, similarly depicted Israel's holy city, Jerusalem, the mother of all believers, as a persecuted woman (2 Esd. 9:38–10:54). Like most of John's symbols, this figure is capable of multiple interpretations, including the Roman Catholic view that it represents the Virgin.

The Dragon, whom the archangel **Michael** hurls from heaven, wages war against the woman's children, identified as the faithful who witness to Jesus' sovereignty (12:13–17). Lest they despair, however, John has already informed his hearers that this Satanic attack on the church is really a sign of the Dragon's last days. His expulsion from heaven and his wrath on earth signify that Christ has already begun to rule. Satan can no longer accuse the faithful to God as he did in Job's time (Job 1–2). In John's mystic vision, the Lamb's sacrificial death and believers' testimony about it have conquered the Dragon and overthrown evil (12:10–12).

The beast from the sea. His activities now limited to human society, the Dragon lifts his ugly head in the form of a monster sprouting ten horns and seven heads. The reversed number of heads and horns shows his kinship to the Dragon, who gives the beast his power (13:1–4). Most scholars believe that at the time of writing John intended the beast as a symbol of Rome, a government he regarded as Satanic in its persecution of the church (13:3, 5–8).

The picture grows more complicated after the beast is slain, only to revive unexpectedly. A second beast emerges not from the sea but from the earth to work miracles and enforce public worship of the first beast. In a parody of the angelic sealing, the beast allows no one to conduct business unless he bears the beast's mark. John then adds a "key" to this bestial riddle: the beast's number is that of a "man's name," and the "numerical value of its letters is six hundred and sixty-six" (13:14–18).

John's Numerical Symbols

The reader is aware by this point that John's use of particular numbers is an important part of his symbolism. In this respect John is typical of the Hellenistic age in which he lived. For centuries before his time, Greco-Roman thinkers regarded certain numbers as possessing a special kind of meaning. The Greek philosopher Pythagoras speculated that the universe was structured on a harmony of numerical relationships and that certain combinations of numbers held a mystical signification.

In the Jewish tradition, seven represented the days of creation, culminating in God's Sabbath ("seventh-day") rest (Gen. 1). Hence, seven stood for earthly completion or perfection. By contrast, six may represent that which is incomplete or imperfect. When John depicts divine activities affecting earth, as in the seven seals or seven trumpets, he signifies that God's actions are perfectly completed. When he wishes to represent a personification of human inadequacy or corruption, he applies the number six, tripling it for emphasis.

The mystical number of the beast. To calculate the beast's numerical symbol, we must remember that in the author's day all numbers, whether in Hebrew, Aramaic, or Greek, were represented by letters of the alphabet. Thus, each letter in a person's name was also a number. By adding up the sum of all letters in a given name, we arrive at its "numerical value." (The awkward system of having letters double for numbers continued until the Arabs introduced their Arabic numerals to Europeans during the Middle Ages.)

John's hint that the beast's cryptic number could be identified with a specific person has inspired more irresponsible speculation than almost any other statement in his book. In virtually every generation from John's day until ours, apocalyptists have found men or institutions that they claimed fit the beast's description and thus filled the role of anti-Christ, whose appearance confirmed that the world was near its End.

By contrast, most New Testament scholars believe that John refers to a historical personage

Portrait bust of Nero (54–68 ce). According to the Roman historian Tacitus, Nero was the first emperor to persecute Christians. Nero's violence toward believers made him seem to some the image of bestial attacks on God's people. In depicting the "beast" who demands his subjects' worship, John of Patmos may have had Nero—and other worldly rulers who imitated the emperor's methods—in mind. (American Numismatic Society Photographic Services, NY.)

of his own time. Who that person might have been, however, is still hotly debated. Some historians believe the man who best fits John's description of the beast was **Nero,** the first Roman head of state to torture and execute Christians. Following Nero's suicide in 68 CE, popular rumors swept the empire that he was not dead but in hiding and planned to reappear at the head of a barbarian army to reassert his sovereignty. (This view explains the beast's recovery from its "death-blow" and his putting to death those Christians who refused to acknowledge his divinity.) Proponents of this hypothesis point to the fact that in Aramaic the "numerical value" of the name Nero Caesar is 666.

Although it is widely accepted, the theory identifying John's beast with Nero leaves much unexplained. We have no evidence that the author intended us to use Aramaic letters in computing the name's mystical significance. Other historians suggest that John intended to imply that Nero was figuratively reborn in Domitian, his vicious spirit ascending "out of the abyss" (17:8) to torment Christians in a new human form. Still others observe that we do not have "the key" (13:18) necessary to understand John's meaning.

Historians' speculations about the beast's identity have been disappointingly inconclusive. Whatever contemporary figure the author had in mind, his achievement was to create a symbol of timeless significance. Every age has its beast, a distortion of the divine image in which God created humanity (Gen. 1:27), who somehow gains the power to perpetrate evil on a large scale. In the universality of his symbols, John achieves a continuing relevance.

Methods of Interpretation

Our brief scrutiny of John's mysterious beast illustrates the more general challenge of trying to find a reliable method of interpreting Revelation's complex system of symbols. In the tentative identifications mentioned above, we have already touched on two possible methods. The first approach, favored by scholars, assumes that Revelation was composed for a first-century audience familiar with apocalyptic imagery and that its chief purpose was to give an eschatological interpretation of then-current events. Reasoning that the book could not have been written or understood well enough to have been preserved if it did not have considerable immediate significance to its original hearers, the scholar looks to contemporary Roman history to supply the primary meanings of John's symbols. According to this scholarly method, Babylon (18:2, 10) is Rome, the beast personifies the empire's blasphemous might (represented in human form by the emperors), and the various plagues described are metaphorically intensified versions of wars, invasions, famines, earthquakes, and other disasters experienced (or feared) during the late first century.

A second view, favored by apocalyptists, sees Revelation as largely predictive. The visions may

have had a contemporary application in Roman times, but John's main purpose was to prophesy about future events. Invariably, apocalyptist interpreters regard their own time as that predicted by John. During the last several centuries such interpreters, comparing Daniel's use of "times," "years," and "days" with similar terms in Revelation (12:6, 14; 13:5; and so on) have tried to calculate the exact year of the End. In the United States alone, the years 1843, 1844, 1874, 1914, 1975, 1984, and 2000 have been announced by different apocalyptic groups as the year in which Christ will return to judge the earth, slaughter the wicked, or establish a new world. Thus far, all such groups have been wrong, probably because apocalypses like John's were not intended to be blueprints of the future. To try to construct a paradigm of end time from Daniel's or Revelation's chronological or numerical symbols is to miss their purpose as well as to ignore Paul's advice about computing "dates and times" (1 Thess. 5:1). Given human nature, however, it is unlikely that their predecessors' repeated failures will deter future apocalyptists from publicizing their ingeniously revised schedules of the End.

A third method. Although the historians' attempt to correlate Revelation's images and symbols with conditions in the first-century Roman Empire is helpful, it does not exhaust the book's potential meaning. A third method recognizes that John's visions have a vitality that transcends any particular time or place. John's lasting achievement lies in the universality of his symbols and parabolic dramas. His visions continue to appeal not because they apply explicitly to his or some future era but because they reflect some of the deepest hopes and terrors of the human imagination. As long as dread of evil and longing for justice and peace motivate human beings, Revelation's promise of the ultimate triumph of good over chaos will remain pertinent. John's visions speak directly to the human condition as thousands of generations experience it.

In surveying Revelation's last chapters (17–22), we focus on those aspects of the book that dramatize the ever-repeated struggle and make John's visions relevant not merely to his or end time but to ours as well. The reader may have noted that John's method in presenting his visions is to retell the same event in different terms, using different symbols to depict the same reality. Thus, to dramatize Christ's victory over evil, he does not proceed in a straight line from the opening battle to the Devil's final defeat but turns back to narrate the conflict again and again.

After the seventh trumpet blast, we are told that Jesus is victorious and now reigns as king over the world (11:15). However, another battle ensues in chapter 12, after which John declares that Christ has now achieved total sovereignty (12:10). Yet still another conflict follows—the infamous battle of Armageddon (16:13–16), after which the angel repeats " 'It is over!' " (16:18). But it is not finished, for Satan's earthly kingdom—Babylon—is yet to fall (chs. 17–18). When she does and a fourth victory is proclaimed (19:1–3), the empowered Christ must repeat his conquest again (19:11–21). In John's cyclic visions, evil does not stay defeated but must be fought time after time. Similarly, life is a continual battleground in which the contestants must struggle to defend previous victories and combat the same opponents in new guises.

Visions of the Final Triumph

In contrast to the cyclic repetitions of earlier sections, after chapter 20 John apparently (we cannot be sure) pursues a linear narration, presenting a chronological sequence of events. In this final eschatological vision (20:1–22:5), events come thick and fast. An angel hurls the Dragon into the abyss, the primordial void that existed before God's creative light ordered the visible world (20:1–3). With the Dragon's temporary imprisonment, Christ's reign at last begins. Known as the **millennium** because it lasts one thousand years, even this triumph is imper-

manent because at its conclusion Satan is again released to wage war on the faithful. The only New Testament writer to present a thousand-year prelude to Christ's kingdom, John states that during the millennium the martyrs who resisted the beast's influence are resurrected to rule with Christ (20:4–6).

The Dragon's release and attack on the faithful (based on Ezekiel's prophetic drama involving the mythical Gog of Magog, symbols of Israel's enemies [Ezek. 38–39]) ends with fire from heaven destroying the attackers. A resurrection of all the dead ensues. Released from the control of death and Hades (the Underworld), they are judged according to their deeds (20:7–13).

The lake of fire. John's eschatology includes a place of punishment represented by a lake of fire, an image drawn from popular Jewish belief (see Josephus's *Discourse on Hades* in Whiston's edition). Defined as "the second death" (20:15), it receives a number of symbolic figures, including death, Hades, the beast, the false prophet, and persons or human qualities not listed in God's book of life (19:20; 20:14–15). Earlier, John implied that persons bearing the beast's fatal mark would be tormented permanently amid burning sulphur (14:9–11), a destiny similar to that described for the rich man in Luke (17:19–31).

John's fiery lake also parallels that depicted in 2 Esdras (written about 100 CE):

> Then the place of torment shall appear, and over against it the place of rest; the furnace of hell shall be displayed, and on the opposite side the paradise of delight . . . here are rest and delight, there fire and torments. (2 Esd. 7:36–38)

Although John uses his image of torture to encourage loyalty to Christ, his metaphor of hell incites many commentators to question the author's understanding of divine love.

The wedding of the Lamb and the holy city. John's primary purpose is to demonstrate the truth of a divine power great enough to vanquish evil for all time and create the new universe described in chapters 21–22. The author combines images from Isaiah and other Hebrew prophets to paint an oasis of peace contrasting with the violent and bloody battlefields of his previous visions. Borrowing again from ancient myth, in which epics of conflict are commonly ended with a union of supernatural entities, John features of a sacred marriage of the Lamb with the holy city that descends from heaven to earth.

The wedding of a city to the Lamb may strike the reader as a strange metaphor, but John attains great heights of poetic inspiration describing the brilliance of the heavenly Jerusalem. Rendered in terms of gold and precious stones, the jewel-like city is illuminated by the radiance of God himself. John draws again on Ezekiel's vision of a restored Jerusalem Temple to describe a crystal stream flowing from God's throne to water the tree of life. Growing in a new Eden, the tree's fruits restore humanity to full health. The renewed and purified faithful can now look directly upon God (21:1–22:5). With his dazzling view of the heavenly city, rendered in the earthy terms of the Hebrew prophets (Isa. 11, 65, 66), John completes his picture of a renewed and completed creation. God's will is finally done on earth as it is in heaven.

Warning that his visions represent the immediate future and that the scrolls on which they are written are not to be sealed (because their contents will soon be fulfilled), John adds a curse upon anyone who tampers with his manuscript (22:6, 10, 18–19). Despite his urgent affirmation of Jesus' imminent Parousia, the book's final address to the reader makes an anticlimactic conclusion to the Bible's most puzzling book.

In Revelation, John asks his readers to see the course of human history from God's viewpoint. John's series of visions unveil the spiritual realities of the universe that are ordinarily hidden from human eyes. The visions disclose that events on earth are only part of a universal drama in which invisible forces of good and evil contend for control of human society. John shows that the battle between good and evil is an ongoing process by picturing the struggle as a cycle of repeated conflicts. God's forces win, only to find their evil opponents reappearing in a new guise. In combating spiritual and social evil, the faithful must be prepared to fight again and again.

Despite the cyclic nature of the struggle against chaotic powers, John assures his audience that through Christ's death God has already determined the outcome. The last part of Revelation shows the Dragon finally defeated and creation renewed. The Lamb's marriage to heavenly Jerusalem, descended to earth, reveals that the end purpose of history is the joyous union of humanity with the presence and image of God. In John's ultimate vision, the original goal and essential goodness of creation are realized.

QUESTIONS FOR DISCUSSION AND REVIEW

1. Define the term *apocalypse* and explain how the book of Revelation unveils realities of the unseen spirit world and previews future events.
2. Identify and discuss the characteristics of apocalyptic literature. When and where did this type of visionary writing originate, and what is its main purpose?
3. Connect John's visions with conditions prevailing in his own time. What events taking place during the late first century of the common era would cause Christians to despair of the present evil world and hope for divine intervention in the near future?
4. Identify and explain some of the myths of cosmic conflict that John incorporates into his vision of the universal struggle between good and evil. In the ancient view of the world, why is disorder commonly identified

with evil and an orderly creation synonymous with good?

5. Discuss John's use of symbols and cryptic language. Do you think that the author deliberately made his mystical visions difficult to understand in order to confuse "outsiders" who might be hostile to his group?

6. Martin Luther thought that Revelation did not truly reveal the nature of God and Christ. Discuss the ethical strengths and religious limitations of John's view of the Deity and the divine purpose.

7. Revelation repeatedly shows God's kingdom triumphing only to be engaged again in further battles with evil, until the symbol and source of evil—the chaotic Dragon—is finally exterminated by fire. Do you think that Revelation's frequently repeated battles between good and evil indicate a continuing cycle in which divine rule (the kingdom) alternates with wicked influences on humanity—a cycle in which each nation and individual participates until the final Judgment? Cite specific passages to support your answer.

TERMS AND CONCEPTS TO REMEMBER

apokalypsis (Greek term)
apocalypse (literary form)
apocalyptic literature
apocalyptic dualism
ethical qualities of apocalyptic writing
cryptic language
symbol
authorship of Revelation
Roman emperor cult
Domitian
position of Christians in Roman society
Lamb
Dragon
means by which the Lamb conquers the Dragon
seven churches of Asia Minor
astrological images
seven seals
seven trumpets
four horsemen
the celestial woman
Michael
war in heaven
the beast
numerology
Nero
Armageddon
methods of interpreting apocalyptic literature
millennium
the abyss
lake of fire
descent of the heavenly city
wedding of the Lamb
a new heaven and a new earth
Revelation's abiding significance

RECOMMENDED READING

Bowman, J. W. "Revelation, Book of." In *The Interpreter's Dictionary of the Bible,* vol. 4, 58–71. Nashville: Abingdon Press, 1962. Provides a sensible beginning study.

Collins, A. Y. *The Apocalypse.* Wilmington: Michael Glazier, 1979.

Collins, J. J., ed. *Apocalypse: The Morphology of a Genre.* Semeia 14. Chico, Calif.: Scholars Press, 1979.

Fiorenza, Elizabeth Schussler. *Invitation to the Book of Revelation.* New York: Image Doubleday, 1981.

———. "Revelation, Book of." In *The Interpreter's Dictionary of the Bible,* supplementary vol., 744–46. Nashville: Abingdon Press, 1976.

Josephus, Flavius. "An Extract of Josephus' Discourse to the Greeks Concerning Hades." In *Josephus: Complete Works,* 637–638. Translated by William Whiston. Grand Rapids: Kregel Publications, 1960.

Perkins, Pheme. *The Book of Revelation.* Collegeville, Minn.: The Liturgical Press, 1983. A brief and readable introduction for Roman Catholic and other students.

Rist, Martin. "Introduction and Exegesis of the Revelation of St. John the Divine." In *The Interpreter's Bible,* vol. 12, 345–613. Nashville: Abingdon Press, 1957. A concise and informative analysis for the student.

Russell, D. S. *The Method and Message of Jewish Apocalyptic: 200 B.C.—A.D. 100.* Philadelphia: Westminster Press, 1964. A useful review of apocalyptic literature of the Greco-Roman period.

FOR MORE ADVANCED STUDY

Aune, David. *The Cultic Setting of Realized Eschatology in Early Christianity.* Leiden, Neth.: E. J. Brill, 1972.

———. *Prophecy in Early Christianity and the Ancient Mediterranean World.* Grand Rapids, Mich.: Eerdmans, 1983. Places Christian apocalyptism in historical perspective.

Charles, R. H. *The Revelation of St. John.* Vols. 1 and 2, International Critical Commentary. New York: Scribner's, 1920. A standard work providing a detailed analysis of John's apocalypse.

Collins, A. Y. *The Combat Myth in the Book of Revelation.* Chico, Calif.: Scholars Press, 1976.

———. *Crisis & Catharsis: The Power of the Apocalypse.* Philadelphia: Westminster Press, 1984. Investigates the problems of authorship, date, and social-religious background of John's apocalyptic visions.

———. *Early Christian Apocalyptism: Genre and Social Setting.* Semeia 36. Decatur, Ga.: Scholars Press, 1986.

Collins, J. J., ed. *The Apocalyptic Imagination: An Introduction to the Jewish Matrix of Christianity.* Los Angeles: Crossroads, 1984.

Efird, J. M. *Daniel and Revelation: A Study of Two Extraordinary Visions.* Valley Forge, Pa.: Judson Press, 1978.

Fiorenza, Elizabeth Schussler. *The Book of Revelation: Justice and Judgment.* Philadelphia: Fortress Press, 1985.

Hanson, P. D. *The Dawn of Apocalyptic: The Historical and Sociological Roots of Jewish Apocalyptic Eschatology.* Philadelphia: Fortress Press, 1979.

Schick, E. A. *Revelation: The Last Book of the Bible.* Philadelphia: Fortress Press, 1977.

Stone, M. E. *Scriptures, Sects, and Visions: A Profile of Judaism from Ezra to the Jewish Revolts.* Philadelphia: Fortress Press, 1980.

Sweet, J. P. M. *Revelation.* Philadelphia: Westminster Press, 1979.

20 Outside the Canon: Other Early Christian Writings

"The sovereignty of the world has passed to our Lord and his Christ, and he shall reign for ever and ever!"
(Rev. 11:15)

KEY THEMES Besides the twenty-seven books officially accepted into the New Testament canon, early Christianity produced a large number of other writings, including Gospels, letters, apocalypses, and "memoirs" of the Apostles. Some of these works appear in early lists of New Testament books but were later denied canonical status and consigned to oblivion. With the long delay in the Parousia, the apocalyptic hopes that had inspired most New Testament writers gradually faded. Even before the canon became fixed, the emperor Constantine accepted Christianity (early fourth century CE). Rome—formerly persecutor of the faithful—was transformed into the church's patron and protector.

The early Christian community produced a large number of writings in addition to the twenty-seven books comprising the New Testament, and many of them significantly influenced later Christian thought. Some of these documents, once included in church lists of "recognized books" along with familiar New Testament titles, are as old as or older than many works eventually accepted into the canon. No one knows why particular works were accepted and others were not. Paul wrote letters besides those accorded canonical status (1 Cor. 5:9–11); we cannot be sure that their exclusion was the result of their being destroyed or otherwise lost. Specific works may have been accepted or rejected primarily because of their relative usefulness in supporting the traditional church teachings.

As noted in Chapter 1, as late as the fourth century and even later, many individual churches rejected books like Hebrews, James, Jude, 2 Peter, and Revelation; others regarded them as possessing only "doubtful" authority. By contrast, 1 Clement (a letter from the Roman bishop to the Corinthian church, composed about 95–96 CE) was commonly included among the "recognized books" (Eusebius, *History,* 3.16. 24–26; 3.16.37; 6.13; and so on).

Works Included in Some Early Editions of the New Testament

The Codex Sinaiticus, an ancient Greek edition of the New Testament, contains several books that supplemented the central canon. These extracanonical works include the Shepherd of Hermas, a mystical apocalypse incorporating documents that may have been written in the late first century of the common era; the Didache (also called the Teaching of the Twelve Apostles), a two-part volume that preserves a manual of primitive church discipline perhaps dating back to apostolic times; and the Epistle of Barnabas, a moralistic commentary on the

Hebrew Bible supposedly written by Paul's mentor and traveling companion.

Although these books are contained in an appendix to the codex, they apparently achieved a quasiauthoritative position in the church's list of approved books; several prominent early churchmen attributed considerable importance to them. Clement of Alexandria, who also cites the Secret Gospel of Mark, refers to the Didache as "Scripture," and Bishop Athanasius recommends its use for teaching Christian students. The Epistle of Barnabas (about 130 CE) and 1 Clement were also held in high esteem in numerous churches. All of these works are probably older, and therefore closer to the apostolic era, than most of the canonical catholic epistles.

Another early list of New Testament books, the Muratorian *Canon,* accepts the Apocalypse of Peter, a visionary tour of hell based largely on the eschatological terrors described in Mark 13 and Matthew 24. Existing now only in an Ethiopic translation, this apocalypse—unlike the eventually canonical Revelation—paints no eschatological picture of future history or Jesus' Second Coming.

Among other writings that remained influential for centuries are the seven epistles of Ignatius, including letters to the congregations at Ephesus, Rome, Philadelphia, and Smyrna, all cities associated with Paul or the author of Revelation. The letters date from about the year 107, when Ignatius, the bishop of Antioch, was traveling under armed escort to Rome, where he was martyred. A few decades later in the second century, Polycarp, a bishop of Smyrna, wrote to Philippi, another important Pauline church. Polycarp, who was martyred about 155 CE, possessed unusual authority because he was reputed to have been a disciple of the Apostle John.

Works like the Didache, the Shepherd of Hermas, and the epistles of Clement, Ignatius, and Polycarp, as well as a few others, hovered for centuries on the fringe of the New Testament canon. Although they did not win final acceptance, they became known collectively as the "Apostolic Fathers" and continued to play a role in shaping church belief and practice.

The New Testament Apocrypha

In addition to works that for a time enjoyed near-canonical status, early Christian writers composed a large body of writings known as the New Testament Apocrypha. The term *apocrypha,* meaning "hidden" or "secret," may have been applied to these writings either because they were kept secret from the ordinary Christian or because they were believed to contain hidden meanings. Most, but not all, of the Christian Apocrypha derived from Gnostic circles, which helps to account for their ultimate exclusion from church usage.

Writers of the apocryphal books imitated the literary forms of canonical works—Gospels, apostolic histories, letters, and apocalypses. In Chapter 11 we reviewed several apocryphal Gospels, including those attributed to Apostles like Thomas and Peter or to other famous early church leaders, such as James, Jesus' "brother." Among these pseudonymous works is the Apocryphon (meaning "secret book") of James, a Coptic language edition of an originally Greek document that presents Jesus' teaching in the form of a conversation between the Apostles Peter and James. The Dialogue of the Savior, found in the Nag Hammadi Coptic library, employs a similar device, rendering Jesus' message as a three-way discussion among Christ and the disciples Judas, Matthew, and Mariam, a woman follower. Similarly, the Gnostic Gospel of the Egyptians presents a brief dialogue between Jesus and a female disciple named Salome.

Although the Apocryphon may preserve some of Jesus' authentic sayings, most apocryphal Gospels appear to contain versions of Christ's message that have been tailored to fit Gnostic preconceptions. These include the Gospel of the Hebrews, the Gospel of the

Nazaraeans, the Gospel of the Ebionites, and the Acts of Pilate, a dramatization of Jesus' confrontation with the Roman procurator. Except for the last named, most of these Gospels survive only in brief fragments. Others are known by their names alone.

The proliferation of new Gospels continued for centuries, resulting in increasingly unreliable and fanciful versions of Jesus' life and teachings. Exhausting the supply of "apostolic" writers, pseudonymous authors created Gospels attributed to the Virgin, Nicodemus, Gamaliel, and even Eve!

Noncanonical versions of the Acts also abounded. Besides Acts purportedly describing the adventures of Peter and Paul, there were fictional narratives about Andrew (Peter's brother), Thomas, and John as well. Apocryphal letters also circulated under the Apostles' names, and Christian mystics and prophets added to a collection of futuristic visions called the Sibylline Oracles. This was originally a Jewish compilation written in imitation of Greco-Roman prophecies attributed to Apollo's inspired oracle, the Sibyl.

Students interested in reading noncanonical works dating from the New Testament period can find several modern editions in most libraries. Particularly recommended are Ron Cameron's *The Other Gospels* (1982), which includes the complete text of the Gospel of Thomas as well as the surviving parts of other Gospels thought to contain authentic sayings of Jesus. For recent translations of the Didache, the Epistle of Barnabas, and the letters of Ignatius and Polycarp, see *Early Christian Writings* (1968), a Penguin paperback. The Edgar Hennecke two-volume *New Testament Apocrypha,* edited by Wilhelm Schneemelcher (1963), provides a scholarly anthology of the extracanonical texts. Marvin W. Meyer's *The Secret Teachings of Jesus* (1984) contains fresh translations of four Gnostic Gospels. (For additional references consult the bibliography at the end of this chapter.)

The New Testament: A Final Overview

Neither the Christian Scriptures nor the believing community that produced them could exist without the historical life and death of Jesus. His is the commanding figure who binds together the diverse collection of narratives, letters, sermons, and apocalyptic visions we call the New Testament. The order in which the twenty-seven canonical books are arranged reinforces his dominance: the New Testament opens with Matthew's genealogy, proclaiming "Jesus Christ, son of David, son of Abraham"; at the outset Jesus is established as the culmination and fulfillment of all Israel's prophetic hopes. Matthew and the other Gospels provide theological interpretations of Jesus' Jewish messiahship, and Acts and Paul's letters offer profound meditations on Jesus' meaning to the world at large. The pseudo-Pauline letters, Hebrews, and the general epistles further explore Jesus' continuing significance to the community developing in his name, typically distinguishing between correct and incorrect modes of belief.

The New Testament closes with John's dazzling revelation of the postresurrection Jesus as a still-living being of irresistible might, at last establishing the longed-for universal kingdom. As the First Gospel's opening verse roots Jesus in Israel's historical past, the "son" or heir of David and Abraham, so the final book concludes with a Christian seer's passionate evocation of Jesus' return to finish the task he had begun on earth. Because Christianity originated as an apocalyptic movement within first-century Judaism, it is fitting that its canonical text closes with the apocalyptic conviction that Christ is "coming soon," preserving as a final word the assurance that Jesus' activity forever changed the course of world history (Rev. 22: 17–21).

The New Testament Hope and Subsequent History

Expanding and developing in a society that commonly viewed it as a misanthropic and subversive sect, Christianity produced a literature that directly reflects the religion's original historical context, particularly its difficulties with its Jewish and Roman opponents. The Gospels agree in exonerating Roman officals for moral responsibility in Jesus' death, and the first church history—Acts—strives to demonstrate that Christians are no legal threat to the social order and that the church can coexist peacefully with the Roman state. Paul also endorses this concept of accommodation in his letter to the Romans.

By contrast, apocalyptic writers like John of Patmos and the author of 2 Peter see no redeeming value in achieving an understanding with the Roman government such as that advocated by Luke in Acts. In the apocalyptic view, nothing less than the total annihilation of the existing world order could deliver believers from the power of evil embodied in both society and the state.

Thus, John looks forward to Rome's future destruction with uncontrollable rejoicing, composing seven pictures of Rome's (Babylon's) fall and an ironic lament over the imperial government's disintegration. Echoing ancient Hebrew prophets like Isaiah and Ezekiel, who exulted over the defeat of enemy states, John writes that he heard an angel proclaim,

> "Fallen, fallen is Babylon [Rome] the great! She has become a dwelling for demons, a haunt for every unclean spirit, for every vile and loathesome bird. For all nations have drunk deep of the fierce wine of her fornication; . . . and merchants the world over have grown rich on her bloated wealth." (Rev. 18:2–3)

John goes on,

> But let heaven exult over her; exult, apostles and prophets and people of God; for in the judgment against her he has vindicated your cause! (Rev. 18:20)

To the apocalyptist, a complete and public humiliation of the empire was the means necessary to preserve and vindicate the Christian martyrs whom the state had legally murdered.

John was correct in believing that Rome, the seemingly invincible power that threatened the very existence of his faith, would follow Babylon and other ancient empires into historical oblivion. He did not foresee, however, that Rome would fall not suddenly in a blaze of divine vengeance but gradually, through the normal historical processes of war, foreign invasion, and internal social and economic weaknesses. Nor did he anticipate that a later Roman emperor, a political descendant of the "beast," would be the human means by which his church would eventually be rescued from persecution and transformed from a hated minority sect into the favored religion of the Roman Empire.

Constantine the Great

Following his victory at the Milvian Bridge over Maxentius, his rival for the imperial throne (312 CE), the emperor **Constantine** effected one of the most unexpected reversals in human history. Having experienced a vision in which Jesus was revealed as the divine power that enabled him to defeat his enemies, Constantine began a slow process of conversion to the Christian faith. The Emperor's ultimate championing of Christ as his chief god had immense repercussions throughout the empire, altering forever the relationship of church and state.

Shortly before Constantine began his long reign (306–337 CE), his predecessor Diocletian (284–305 CE) had initiated the most thorough and devastating persecution yet endured by Christians. Its worst aspects ended only with Diocletian's death. When Constantine issued his celebrated decree of religious toleration, the Edict of Milan (313 CE), and subsequently began res-

---

BOX 20–1   *Selected List of Early Christian Noncanonical Gospels, Apocalypses, and Other Writings*

Works formerly appearing in some New Testament lists

The Epistle of Barnabas (attributed to Paul's Jewish-Christian mentor)

The Didache (supposedly a summary of the twelve Apostles' teachings on the opposing ways leading to life or death)

1 Clement (letter by the third bishop of Rome to the Corinthians)

Apocalypse of Peter (visions of heaven and hell ascribed to Peter)

The Shepard of Hermas (a mystical apocalyptic work)

Gospels possibly preserving some of Jesus' teachings or other historical information about him

The Gospel of Thomas (a compilation of 114 sayings of Jesus found in the Nag Hammadi library)

The Gospel of Peter (a primitive account of Jesus' crucifixion, burial, and resurrection ascribed to Peter)

The Secret Gospel of Mark (two excerpts from an early editon of Mark preserved in a letter from Clement of Alexandria)

The Egerton Papyrus 2 (fragment of an unknown Gospel that may have provided a source for some of the Johannine discourses)

The Apocryphon of James (a private dialogue between Jesus and two disciples, Peter and James)

Other Gospels, most surviving only in fragmentary form

The Protoevangelium of James

The Dialogue of the Savior

The Gospel of the Egyptians

The Gospel of the Hebrews

The Gospel of the Nazaraeans

The Gospel of the Ebionites

The Infancy Gospel of Thomas

Papyrus Oxyrhynchus 840

Miscellaneous other works

The Acts of Pilate

The Acts of John

The Epistula Apostolorum

2 Clement

The Epistle to Diognetus

Other important early Christian writings

The Epistles of Ignatius:

To the Ephesians

To the Magnesians

To the Trallians

To the Romans

To the Philadelphians

To the Smyrnaeans

To Polycarp

The Epistle of Polycarp to the Philippians

The Martyrdom of Polycarp

---

toring confiscated church property, consulting Christian leaders about official affairs, and appointing bishops to high public office, it was as if a miraculous deliverance of the faithful had occurred. To many who benefited from Constantine's policy it seemed that Revelation's seventh angel had blown his trumpet: "the sovereignty of the world has passed to our Lord and his Christ" (Rev. 11:15).

In a more modest metaphor, Eusebius, who later became Constantine's biographer, compared the emperor's enthusiastic support of the church to the dawn of a brilliant new day, opening up hitherto-undreamt-of possibilities for the Christian faith. With the exception of Julian (361–63 CE), who was known as the Apostate for trying to revive pagan religion, all of Constantine's successors were nominally Christians.

For the last century and a half of its existence, the empire that had crucified Jesus was ruled by emperors who professed to be his followers.

Historical developments during the fourth and fifth centuries CE bore out Luke's vision of a church expanding in cooperation with the imperial power more than Revelation's picture of violent conflict. John had eagerly anticipated the "great city's" extermination, but when Rome was eventually ravaged by Alaric the Goth in 410, the event inspired horror and dismay among leading Christians. Writing of Alaric's depredations, Jerome (the monastic scholar who translated the Scriptures into Latin, creating the **Vulgate** edition that is still the official Bible of the Roman Catholic church) lamented Rome's humiliation as an irreparable loss to both civilization and Christianity.

Christianity endured the Roman Empire's slow disintegration as it had survived the destruction of the mother church in Jerusalem, the tribulations under Domitian that inspired the writing of Revelation, and far more intense attacks on the church under later emperors. The church replaced the state's crumbling authority with its own spiritual leadership. Along with the community of faith that had created it, the New Testament survived the empire's collapse, providing a continuity with the first-century church as well as a fixed standard of belief and practice in a rapidly changing world.

During the sixteenth and seventeenth centuries, fierce religious conflicts divided Western Christendom. Debates between Roman Catholic and Protestant leaders over matters of belief and ritual brought the New Testament writings into renewed prominence. Martin Luther claimed that "only Scripture"—not custom or tradition—was the correct basis of Christian teaching. As a result, many European believers studied the New Testament documents with great fervor. In most Protestant circles, the biblical texts were thought to provide the sole means of defining Christian doctrine and practice.

The New Testament message retains its vitality in the modern world. Today, literally thousands of Christian groups, each claiming the Bible as its doctrinal authority, compete for believers' allegiance. Although some persons regret Christendom's lack of unity, the student who has carefully read the New Testament books possesses an important clue to Christianity's present diversity. The observation in 2 Peter that Paul's letters contain passages that are difficult and open to more than one interpretation applies equally well to the rest of the canonical writings. The multiplicity of contemporary Christian denominations results less from the breaking up of an originally monolithic religion than from the rich variety of thought embodied in early Christian literature itself.

The New Testament Gospels, letters, apocalypses, and other documents do not conform to a single doctrinaire vision; they instead reflect their individual writers' intensely personal response to Christ's impact on human life and history. Proclaiming the good news of God's loving care for humanity, the twenty-seven different books bear a dual testimony to Christian unity and diversity: the unifying power of Christ and the multifarious ways that different canonical authors were moved to interpret Christ's meaning and message.

QUESTIONS FOR DISCUSSION AND REVIEW

1. Describe some early Christian writings that were included in several primitive editions of the New Testament but eventually excluded from the canon. Define the term *New Testament Apocrypha* and identify some of the Gospels and other works included under this heading.

2. Discuss the differences in attitude toward Rome expressed in Romans 13 (and 1 Peter) on the one hand and in Revelation on the other. What changing historical conditions can help account for the shift from the positive attitude of Paul to the negative judgment of John of Patmos?

3. After the ascension of Constantine to the imperial throne, Christianity's position in the Roman Empire changed dramatically. Describe and explain the church's role during the later empire. How did many leading Christians react to the barbarian invasions that eventually destroyed the Roman world?

4. What role did the New Testament play in formulating later church creeds and doctrines? In what ways did the Protestant Reformation during the sixteenth and seventeenth centuries increase the influence of the New Testament texts?

TERMS AND CONCEPTS TO REMEMBER

Codex Sinaiticus
Muratorian Canon
New Testament
   Apocrypha
Apocryphal Gospels
unity and diversity in
   New Testament
   thought

Apostolic Fathers
Constantine I
Edict of Milan
Diocletian
Eusebius
Rome and the church

RECOMMENDED READING

Brown, R. E. *The Churches the Apostles Left Behind*. New York: Paulist Press, 1984. A concise but extremely important analysis of the theological diversity present in early Christian communities.

Dunn, J. D. G. *Unity and Diversity in the New Testament*. Philadelphia: Westminster Press, 1977. A thoughtful study of the variety of belief found among different canonical authors. Highly recommended

Eusebius. *The History of the Church*. Translated by G. A. Williamson. Baltimore: Penguin Books, 1965. Eusebius is our principal source for the study of the growth and development of early Christianity.

Fox, R. L. *Pagans and Christians*. New York: Knopf, 1986. A comprehensive study of the historical processes that resulted in Constantine's conversion and the religious transformation of the Roman Empire.

Gonzalez, J. L. *The Story of Christianity*. Volume 1: *The Early Church to the Dawn of the Reformation*. San Francisco: Harper & Row, 1984.

MacMullen, Ramsay. *Christianizing the Roman Empire, A.D. 100–400*. New Haven: Yale University Press, 1984. A historical investigation of the social, political, and religious conditions under which the Roman people were converted.

Meeks, W. A. *The Moral World of the First Christians*. Philadelphia: Westminster Press, 1986. Explores the pagan and Jewish ethical context in which Christianity developed.

Robinson, J. M., and Helmut Koester. *Trajectories Through Early Christianity*. Philadelphia: Fortress Press, 1971.

Wilken, R. L. *The Christians as the Romans Saw Them*. New Haven: Yale University Press, 1984. A careful analysis of the social, educational, religious, and political conflicts between early Christians and their Roman critics.

Glossary of New Testament Terms and Concepts

Aaron In the Hebrew Bible, the brother of Moses and first High Priest of Israel (Exod. 4:14; 6:20, 26; Lev. 8; Num. 3:1–3). In the Book of Hebrews, the High Priest's function is said to foreshadow that of Christ (Heb. 5:1–4; 8:1–10:18).

Abba The Aramaic word for "father" or "daddy," used by Jesus and other early Christians to address God (Mark 14:36; Rom. 8:15; Gal. 4:6).

Abraham The founder of the Hebrew nation. In Genesis 12–24, Abraham (at first called Abram, meaning "exalted father") is the supreme example of obedience to Yahweh. All Jews were believed to be Abraham's descendants through his son Isaac.

Abraham's bosom In Luke's parable about Lazarus and the rich man, a term used to denote a position of divine favor (Luke 16:19–31).

Adam In Genesis 2–3, the first human being. In Paul's letters, Adam is a symbol of all humankind (1 Cor. 15:21–49; Rom. 5:12–21).

Alexander the Great Son of King Philip of Macedonia and conquerer of most of the known world. Alexander (356–323 BCE) united Greece and the vast territories of the Persian Empire as far east as India. The period of cultural assimilation and synthesis inaugurated by his conquests is called Hellenistic.

Alexandria A major port city and cultural center founded by Alexander on the Egyptian coast. The home of a large Jewish colony during the Hellenistic period, Alexandria nourished a fusion of Jewish and Greek ideas, one result of which was the Greek Septuagint translation of the Hebrew Bible (begun about 250 BCE).

allegory A literary narrative in which persons, places, and events are given a symbolic meaning. Some Hellenistic Jewish scholars like Philo of Alexandria interpreted the Hebrew Bible allegorically, as Paul does the story of Abraham, Sarah, and Hagar (Gal. 4:21–31).

Ananias (1) The High priest who presided over the full council (Sanhedrin) before which Paul was brought by Claudius Lycias for creating a "riot" in the Jerusalem Temple (Acts 22:22–23:22). (2) An early Christian who with his wife Sapphira attempted to defraud the Jerusalem church (Acts 5:1–10).

angel A spirit being commonly regarded in biblical times as serving God by communicating his will to humankind (Luke 1–2; Matt. 1); from a Greek word meaning "messenger."

Annas A former High Priest before whom Jesus was brought for trial (John 18:13). Annas was father-in-law to Caiaphas, then the currently reigning High Priest (see also Luke 3:2 and Acts 4:6).

Annunciation, the The angel Gabriel's declaration to Mary of Nazareth that she was to bear a son, Jesus, who would inherit David's throne (Luke 1:28–32).

anthropomorphism The practice of attributing human qualities to something not human; in particular, ascribing human emotions and motives to a deity.

anti-Christ The ultimate enemy of Jesus Christ who, according to Christian apocalyptic traditions, will manifest himself at the end of time to corrupt many of the faithful, only to be vanquished at Christ's Second Coming. The term appears only in 2 and 3 John but is clearly referred to in 2 Thessalonians (2:1–12) and Revelation 13.

antinomianism The belief and practice of certain early Christian groups who argued that faith in Christ absolves the believer from obeying moral laws; literally, "opponents of law." Paul attacks this libertarian attitude in Galatians (5:13–6:10; see also 1 and 2 John).

Antioch (1) In Syria, the capital of the Macedonian Seleucid kings and, under Roman rule, a province of the same name. According to Acts, the first predominantly Gentile church was founded in Antioch (Acts 11:20, 21), where followers of "the Way" were first called Christians (Acts 11:26). Paul began all three of his missionary tours from here. (2) Pisidian Antioch, a major city in Galatia (in Asia Minor), also the site of an important early church, founded by Paul and Barnabas (Acts 13:14–50).

Antiochus The name of several Syrian monarchs who inherited power from Seleucus I, a general and successor of Alexander the Great. The most famous were Antiochus III, who gained control of Palestine in 198–197 BCE, and Antiochus IV (Epiphanes, or "God Manifest") (175–163 BCE), whose persecution of the Jews led to the Maccabean revolt.

antitheses, the The section of Matthew's Sermon on the Mount (Matt. 5:21–48) in which Jesus contrasts selected provisions of the Mosaic Torah with his own ethical directives. The term refers to a rhetorical structure in which contrasting ideas are presented in parallel arrangements of words, phrases, or sentences.

apocalypse A disclosure (vision) of spiritual realities or truths that are normally hidden—in the future or in the invisible world of spirit beings; from the Greek *apokalypsis,* meaning "to uncover," "to reveal."

apocalyptic Of or pertaining to a religious world view that anticipates the imminent end of the world. Apocalyptic ideas permeate the Judaism of the first century CE, including beliefs in the impending restoration of Israel, the final conflict between God and evil, and a universal Judgment.

apocalyptic literature A branch of prophetic writing that flourished in Judaism from about 200 BCE to 140 CE and greatly influenced early Christianity. Works such as Daniel, 1 and 2 Enoch, 2 and 3 Baruch, and the book of Revelation are apocalypses. They preview the catastrophic events believed to accompany the end of time, such as Satan's final attack on the faithful, God's overthrow of evil, and the resurrection of the dead for Judgment. The Synoptic Gospel writers present Jesus as an apocalyptic preacher (Mark 13; Matt. 24–25; Luke 21).

apocalypticism The belief that God, through visions to chosen prophets, reveals future cosmic disasters heralding the end of human history and the ultimate defeat of evil. This mode of thought was common in Judaism from about 200 BCE to 140 CE and in primitive Christianity.

Apocrypha A body of Jewish religious writings dating from about 200 BCE to 100 CE that were included in Greek editions of the Jewish Bible but not in the official Hebrew Bible canon. The term *apocrypha,* meaning "hidden," was applied to these deuterocanonical works by Jerome, who included them in his famous Latin (Vulgate) translation of the Jewish and Christian Scriptures.

apology A form of literature in which the author defends and explains his particular world view and behavior.

Apollos A Hellenistic Jew of Alexandria, Egypt, noted for his eloquence. Originally a follower of John the Baptist, he later became a Christian associate of Paul (Acts 18:24–28; 1 Cor. 1:12; 3:4–6, 22–23; 4:6).

apostasy The act of abandoning or rejecting a previously held religious belief; from a Greek term meaning "to revolt." An apostate is one who has defected from or ceased to practice his or her religion.

Apostle A person sent forth or commissioned as a messenger, such as (but not restricted to) the Twelve whom Jesus selected to follow him. According to Acts 1, in the early Jerusalem church an Apostle was defined as one who had accompanied Jesus during his earthly ministry and had seen the resurrected Lord. Lists of the original Twelve differ from account to account (Matt. 10:2–5; Mark 3:16–19; Luke 6:13–16; Acts 1:13–14).

apothegm In biblical criticism, a brief saying or instructive proverb found in the Gospels. See also *pericope*.

Aquila A prominent early Christian (apparently) expelled from Rome with his wife Priscilla by Claudius's edict (about 49 CE). Aquila is often associated with Paul (Acts 18; Rom. 16:3–5; 1 Cor. 16:19).

Aramaic The language of the Arameans (ancient Syrians), a West Semitic tongue used in parts of Mesopotamia from about 1000 BCE. After the Babylonian captivity (538 BCE), it became the common language of Palestinian Jews and was probably the language spoken by Jesus.

Areopagus The civic court in Athens and the location of an important legal council of the Athenian democracy where, according to Acts 17, Paul introduced Christianity to some Athenian intellectuals.

ark of the covenant According to Israelite tradition, the portable wooden chest built in Mosaic times to contain artifacts of the Mosaic faith, such as Aaron's staff and the stone tablets of the Decalogue (Exod. 25:10–22). Sometimes carried into battle (Josh. 6:4–11; 1 Sam. 4), the ark was eventually housed in Solomon's Temple. Its fate after the Temple's destruction (587 BCE) is unknown.

Armageddon A Greek transliteration of the Hebrew place-name *Har-Megiddon,* or "Mountain of Megiddo," a famous battlefield in the Plain of Jezreel in ancient Israel (Judg. 5:19; 2 Kings 9:27;

23:29). In Revelation (16:16), it is the symbolic site of the ultimate war between good and evil.

ascension, the The resurrected Jesus' ascent to heaven (Acts 1:6–11).

Athens Greece's dominant city-state and cultural capital in the fifth century BCE. Athens remained a leading intellectual center during Hellenistic and Roman times. Acts 17 depicts Paul debating Stoic and Epicurean philosophers there.

Atonement, Day of (Yom Kippur) A solemn, annual Jewish observance in which Israel's High Priest offered blood sacrifices ("sin offerings") to effect a reconciliation between the Deity and his people (Lev. 16). The banishment of a "scapegoat" to which the priest had symbolically transferred the people's collective guilt climaxed the atonement rites. This day marked the priest's once-yearly entrance into the Temple's Holy of Holies, a ceremony that the author of Hebrews says is a foreshadowing of Jesus' sacrificial death and ascension to the heavenly Temple (Heb. 9).

Augustus (Augustus Caesar) The first emperor of Rome (27 BCE–14 CE), who brought peace to the Roman Empire after centuries of civil war. According to Luke 2, his decree ordering a census of "the whole world" was the device that brought about Jesus' birth in Bethlehem.

Babylon An ancient city on the middle Euphrates that was the

capital of both the Old Babylonian and the Neo-Babylonian empires. In 587 BCE Babylonian armies destroyed Jerusalem and its Temple. As the archetypal enemy of God's people, Babylon became the symbol of any earthly government that opposed the faithful (Rev. 14:8; 18:12).

baptism A religious ceremony first associated with John the Baptist (Mark 1:4; 11:30; Luke 7:29) and performed on converts in the infant Christian community (Acts 2:38–41; 19:3–5). Baptism may have derived from ritual cleansings with water practiced by the Essenes, from the use of it by some Pharisees as a conversion alternative to circumcision, or from initiation rites into Hellenistic mystery religions. In Christianity it is the rite of initiation into the church (1 Pet.), in which one is either totally immersed in water or water is poured on one's head.

bar Aramaic word used in names, meaning "son of."

Barabbas A condemned murderer and possibly a revolutionary whom the Roman procurator Pontius Pilate released instead of Jesus (Mark 15:6–15; Matt. 27:15–18; Luke 23:16–25; John 18:39–49).

Bar Kochba The name (meaning "son of the star") applied to the leader of the Second Jewish Revolt against Rome (132–135).

Barnabas A prominent leader of the early churches in Jerusalem and Antioch, Paul's mentor and later his traveling companion (Acts 9:26–30; 11:22–30; 13:1–3, 44–52; 14:1–15:4; 15:22–40; Col. 4:10; 1 Cor. 9:6; Gal. 2:1–13).

beatitudes The list of blessings or sources of happiness with which Jesus begins the Sermon on the Mount (Matt. 5:3–12). Luke gives a simpler version of these sayings (6:20–23).

ben Hebrew word used in names, meaning "son of."

Bethlehem A village about five miles south of Jerusalem, birthplace of David (1 Sam. 17:12) and the traditional site of the Messiah's birth (Micah 5:2; Matt. 2:5–6; Luke 2; John 7:42).

Bible A collection of Jewish and Christian sacred writings commonly divided into two main sections—the Hebrew Bible (Old Testament) and the later Christian Greek Scriptures (New Testament), from the Greek term *biblia,* meaning "little books."

bishop The supervisor or presiding officer of a church; from the Greek term *episcopos,* meaning "overseer."

Bithynia In New Testament times, a Roman province in northern Asia Minor (modern Turkey) along the Black Sea coast and the location of several Christian churches (Acts 16:7; 1 Pet. 1:1).

Boanerges "Sons of thunder," an epithet Jesus bestows upon the brothers James and John (Mark 3:17; Luke 9:52–56).

Caesar A hereditary name by which the Roman emperors commemorated Gaius Julius Caesar, great-uncle of Augustus, Rome's first emperor (Luke 2:1; 3:1; Mark 12:14; Acts 11:28; 25:11).

Caesarea An important Roman city, built by Herod the Great on the Palestinian coast about sixty-four miles northwest of Jerusalem and named in honor of Caesar Augustus. Caesarea was Pilate's administrative capital and later a Christian center (Acts 8:40; 10:1, 24; 18:22; 21:8). Paul was imprisoned there for two years (Acts 23–26).

Caesarea Philippi An inland city north of the Sea of Galilee built by Philip, son of Herod the Great, and named for the emperor Tiberius Caesar; the site of Peter's recognition that Jesus was the Messiah (Mark 8:27; Matt. 16:13).

Caiaphas Joseph Caiaphas, High Priest of Jerusalem during the reign of the emperor Tiberius (Matt. 26:3, 57–66; John 9:49; 18:13–28; Acts 4:6). Son-in-law to his immediate predecessor, Annas, he was appointed to the office by the procurator Valerius Gratus and presided over Jesus' hearing before the Sanhedrin.

Calvary The site outside Jerusalem's walls, exact location unknown, where Jesus was crucified (Luke 23:33). Calvary derives from the Latin word *calveria,* a translation of the Greek *kranion,* meaning "skull". Calvary was also called Golgotha, a name that comes from the Aramaic for "skull" (Matt. 27:33; John 19:17).

canon (1) A standard by which religious beliefs or documents are judged acceptable. (2) A list of books that a religious community finds sacred and authoritative; from the Greek *kanon.*

Capernaum A small port on the northwest shore of the Sea of Galilee that Jesus used as headquarters for his Galilean ministry (Matt. 9:1, 9–11; Mark 1:21–29; 2:3–11; Luke 7; John 4:46–54).

catholic epistles Seven short New Testament documents that were addressed to the church as a whole and thus are described as general, or "catholic" ("universal").

centurion A low-ranking officer in the Roman army in charge of a "century," or division of 100 men.

Cephas A name meaning "stone," bestowed by Jesus upon Simon Peter (John 1:42).

Chaos In ancient Greco-Roman belief, the original Void (the formless darkness) that existed before the ordered world (Cosmos) came into being.

Christ The Messiah; from the Greek *Christos,* a translation of the Hebrew *Mashiah* ("messiah") meaning "the anointed one." The term derives from Israel's practice of anointing (putting oil on the heads of) kings at their coronation.

Christology Theological interpretation of the nature and function of Jesus, including doctrines about his divinity, his prehuman existence, his role in creating the universe, and so on.

church In New Testament usage, the community of believers in Jesus Christ

(Matt. 16:18; 18:17; Eph. 5:27; 1 Tim. 3:15; 1 Cor. 12:12–27; Col. 1:18). The term translates the Greek *ekklesia,* meaning "assembly of ones called out."

circumcision An ancient Semitic operation in which the foreskin of eight-day-old males is removed as a ceremony of initiation into the religion and community of Israel. Genesis represents the practice as beginning with Abraham (Gen. 17:10–14); Exodus implies that circumcision began with Moses (Exod. 4:24–46). The question of whether to circumcise Gentile converts to the early Christian church was an important source of dissension (Acts 15; Gal. 2).

Claudius The fourth Roman emperor (41–54 CE), who expelled the Jews from Rome (Acts 11:28; 18:2).

codex A manuscript book of an ancient biblical text, a form pioneered by Christians to replace the unwieldy scrolls on which the Scriptures were originally recorded.

Colossae An ancient Phrygian city situated on the south bank of the Lycus River in central Asia Minor, important for its position on the trade route between Ephesus and Mesopotamia (Col. 1:1–2; 4:13). Paul or a Pauline disciple composed a canonical letter to Christians there.

Corinth A large and prosperous Greek city that the Romans first destroyed (146 BCE) and later rebuilt, making it the capital of the Roman province called Achaia (Greece). About 50 CE Paul and his associates founded an important church there (Acts 18:24; 19:1; 1 and 2 Cor.).

Cornelius A Roman centurion associated with the Jewish synagogue in Caesarea who became the first Gentile convert to Christianity (Acts 10–11).

Cosmos The Greek term for the ordered universe, a world system characterized by natural law.

covenant A vow, agreement, or contract between a deity and a group of people who regard themselves as the god's chosen community. In Exodus, Yahweh makes a covenant with Israel in which the people agree to obey all his laws and instruction (the Torah) and to worship him exclusively (Exod. 20–24; 34; see also Deut. 29; Josh. 24). In Christian tradition, Jesus introduced a "new covenant" with his disciples, making them the true Israel (Mark 14:22–25; Matt. 26:26–29; 1 Cor. 11:25).

cult The formalized practices of a religious group, particularly its system of worship and public (or secret) rites.

Damascus The capital of Syria and the terminus of ancient caravan routes in the Fertile Crescent. Damascus was the site of Paul's earliest experiences as a Christian (Acts 9; Gal. 1:17).

David Popular king of Israel and second king of the united twelve-tribe monarchy (about 1010–970 BCE). Son of Jesse (Ruth 4:18–22) and successor to Saul, David created an Israelite empire (1 Sam. 16; 2 Kings 2). After his short-lived kingdom disintegrated, later ages remembered his reign as a model of God's rule on earth and regarded David as a prototype of the Messiah, whom the prophets foresaw as an heir to the Davidic throne (Isa. 9:5–7; 11:1–16; Jer. 23:5; 30:9; Ezek. 34:23–31; Matt. 1–2; Rom. 1:3; and so on).

deacon A church officer in early Christianity; the term refers to one who serves or ministers.

Dead Sea Scrolls A collection of ancient documents found preserved in caves near Qumran on the northeast shore of the Dead Sea. The scrolls included copies (many in fragmental form) of all canonical books of the Hebrew Bible except Esther, works from the Apocrypha and the Pseudepigrapha, and commentaries and other writings of the Essene community.

Decalogue The Ten Commandments (Exod. 20; Deut. 5).

Dedication, Feast of An eight-day Jewish celebration (now known as Hanukkah) instituted in 165 BCE by Judas Maccabeus and held annually on the twenty-fifth day of Kislev (November-December). The holiday commemorates the cleansing and rededication of the Jerusalem Temple, which Antiochus IV had polluted. Referred to in John (10:22–38), it is also known as the Festival of Lights.

deuterocanon The fourteen books of the Old Testament

Apocrypha included in the Latin Vulgate but not in the Hebrew Bible. The Roman Catholic church regards these works as deuterocanonical, that is, belonging to a second and later canon.

devil The English word commonly used to translate two Greek words with different meanings: (1) *diabolos,* "the accuser" (John 8:44); (2) *daimonion,* one of the many evil spirits inhabiting the world, who were thought to cause disease, madness, and other afflictions (see Matt. 10:25; Mark 3:22; Luke 8; 11:14–16). In Rev. 12:9 the devil is identified with the Hebrew Satan and the serpent of Genesis 3.

Diana of the Ephesians The Near Eastern form of the Greek goddess Artemis (identified by the Romans with Diana). She was worshiped in Ephesus, which in Paul's time was the capital of the Roman province of Asia (Acts 19).

Diaspora The distribution of Jews outside their Palestinian homeland, such as the many Jewish communities established throughout the Greco-Roman world; literally, a "scattering."

disciple In the New Testament, a follower of a particular religious figure, such as Moses (John 9:28), John the Baptist (Luke 11:1; John 1:35), the Pharisees (Mark 2:18), or Jesus (Matt. 14:26; 20:17); from the Greek word meaning "learner."

Docetism The belief, commonly associated with Gnostic Christianity, that

Jesus was pure spirit and only appeared to be physically human; from the Greek verb meaning "to seem."

doxology In a religious writing or service, the formal concluding expression of praise ascribing glory to God.

Dragon The image applied in Revelation 12 to Satan, the embodiment of evil forces opposing God. Derived from ancient Near Eastern mythology, the symbol of the giant reptile represents the powers of darkness and disorder (the original Chaos) that God first conquered in creating the ordered universe (Cosmos).

Elijah The leader of Israel's prophetic movement during the ninth century BCE. Elijah fiercely championed the exclusive worship of Yahweh and opposed the Israelite cult of the Canaanite god Baal (1 Kings 17–19; 21; 2 Kings 1–2). Reportedly carried to heaven in a fiery chariot (2 Kings 2:1–13), he was expected to reappear shortly before the Day of Yahweh arrived (Mal.4:5–6). Although some Christian writers identified John the Baptist with Elijah (Luke 1:17; Mark 9:12–13), some contemporaries viewed Jesus as Elijah returned (Mark 9:28; 16:14). Along with Moses, Elijah appears in Jesus' transfiguration (Mark 9:4; Matt. 17:3; Luke 9:30).

Elizabeth The wife of the Levite priest Zechariah and mother of John the Baptist (Luke 1).

Emmaus A village (site unknown) near Jerusalem, along the road to which the resurrected Jesus appeared to two disciples (Luke 24:13–32).

Enoch A son of Cain (Gen. 4:17) or Jared (Gen. 5:18) and father of Methuselah (Gen. 5:21), taken by God (apparently to heaven). Legends surrounding Enoch's mysterious fate gave rise to a whole body of noncanonical literature in which Enoch returns to earth to describe his experiences in the spirit world and foretell events leading to the End.

Epaphras An early Christian of Colossae who reported on the Colossian church to the imprisoned Paul (Col. 1:7; 4:12; Philem. 23).

Epaphroditus A Macedonian Christian from Philippi who assisted Paul in prison (Phil. 2:25–27).

Ephesus A wealthy Hellenistic city, in New Testament times the capital of the Roman province of Asia, site of the famous temple of Artemis (Diana) (Acts 19–20). Mentioned frequently in Paul's correspondence (1 Cor. 16:19; 2 Cor. 12:14; 13:1; 1 Tim. 3:1; and so on), the Ephesian church receives the author's favorable judgment in Revelation 2:1–7.

epiphany An appearance or manifestation, particularly of a divine being.

epistle A formal communication intended to be read publicly.

eschatology Beliefs about the supernaturally directed destiny of humankind and the universe; from the Greek word meaning "study of last things." Associated with an apocalyptic world view, eschatology has both personal and general applications: (1) beliefs about the individual soul following death, including divine Judgment, heaven, hell, and resurrection; and (2) larger concerns about the fate of the cosmos, including convictions about a divinely guided renewal of the world and human society in the near future or in the present (realized eschatology).

Essenes According to Josephus, one of the three major sects of Judaism in the first century CE. Characterized by apocalyptic beliefs in the world's imminent End, some of the group founded monastic communities in the Judean desert, such as the Qumran settlement that produced the library known as the Dead Sea Scrolls.

Eucharist The Christian ceremony of consecrated bread and wine that Jesus initiated at the Last Supper (Mark 14:22–25; Matt. 26:26–29; and so on); from the Greek word meaning "gratitude" or "thanksgiving."

Evangelist One who preaches the Christian message of "good news" (*euangelion*); the writer of a Gospel.

exegesis Close analysis and interpretation of a text to discover the original author's exact intent and meaning. Once the writer's primary intent has been established, other interpretations can be considered.

exorcism The act or practice of expelling a demon or evil spirit from a person or place (Tobit 8:1–3; Mark 1:23–27, 32–34; 5:1–20; Matt. 8:25–34; Acts 19:13–19; and so on).

expiation The act of making atonement for sin, usually by offering a sacrifice to appease divine wrath (Lev. 16; Heb. 9).

Fall, the Humankind's loss of innocence and divine favor through the first human beings' sin of disobedience (Gen. 3). According to some interpretations of Pauline thought (Rom. 5:12–21; 1 Cor. 15:45–49), the Fall resulted in the transmission of death and a proclivity toward wrongdoing to the entire human race. As a medieval rhyme expressed it, "In Adam's fall, we sinned all."

Felix, Antonius The Roman procurator of Judea before whom Paul was tried at Caesarea (Acts. 23:23–24:27).

Festus, Procius The procurator of Judea whom Nero appointed to succeed Felix and through whom Paul appealed to be tried by Caesar's court in Rome (Acts 24:27–26:32).

form criticism A method of biblical analysis that attempts to isolate, classify, and analyze individual units or characteristic forms contained in a literary text and to identify the probable preliterary form of these units before their incorporation into the written text; the term is an English rendition of the German *Formsgeschichte*. Form criticism also attempts to discover the setting in life (*Sitz-im-Leben*) of each unit— that is, the historical, social, religious, and cultural environment from which it developed—and to trace or reconstruct the process by which various traditions evolved from their original oral state to their final literary form.

Gabriel In the Hebrew angelic hierarchy, one of the seven archangels whose duty it was to convey the Deity's messages. Gabriel explained Daniel's visions to him (Dan. 8:15–26; 9:20–27) and, in the New Testament, announced the birth of John the Baptist and Jesus (Luke 1:15–17, 26–38). The name may mean "person of God" or "God has shown himself mighty."

Galatia A region in the interior of Asia Minor (Turkey) settled by Gauls; in New Testament times, a Roman province visited by Paul and his associates (Acts 16:6; 18:23; 1 Cor. 16:1; Gal. 1:2; 1 Pet. 1:1).

Galilee The region of northern Palestine lying west of the Jordan River, where Jesus grew up and carried out much of his public ministry (Mark 1–9; Matt. 2:23; Luke 4); from the Hebrew term *Ghil-ha-goyim*, meaning "circle of the Gentiles." In Jesus' day, Herod Antipas administered this region for the Romans (Luke 23:5–7).

Galilee, Sea of The major body of fresh water in northern Palestine, source of livelihood to many Galilean fishermen, such as Peter, Andrew, James, and John (Matt. 4:18–22).

Gallio A proconsul of Achaia (the Roman province of

Greece) who dismissed charges brought against Paul by Corinthian Jews (Acts 18:12–17). Gallio was a brother of Seneca, the Stoic philosopher.

Gamaliel A leading Pharisee and scholar, a member of the Sanhedrin, the reputed teacher of Paul (Acts 5:34–40; 22:3), and an exponent of the liberal wing of the Pharisaic party developed by his grandfather, Hillel.

Gehenna The New Testament name for the "Valley of the Son [or Children] of Hinnom," a depression in the earth that bordered Jerusalem on the south and west and that had been the site of human sacrifices to Molech and other Canaanite gods (Jer. 7:32; Lev. 18:21; 1 Kings 11:7; 2 Chron. 28:3; 33:6). Later used as a dump in which garbage was burned, the valley became a symbol of punishment in the afterlife and is cited as such by Jesus (Matt. 5:22; 10:28–29; 18:8; 25:30, 46; and so on). *Gehenna* is commonly translated as "hell" in the Gospels.

Gemara The second part of the Talmud, an extensive commentary, in Aramaic, on the Hebrew Mishnah.

Gentile A non-Jewish person, a member of "the nations" that are not in a covenant relationship with Yahweh. Jewish writers commonly refer to Gentiles as "the uncircumcised," persons not bearing the ritual mark of the covenant people.

Gethsemane The site of a garden or orchard on the Mount of Olives where Jesus took his disciples after the Last Supper; the place where he was arrested (Matt. 26:36–56; Mark 14:32–52; Luke 22:39–53; John 18:1–14).

gnosis The Greek word for "knowledge."

Gnosticism A widespread and extremely diverse movement in early Christianity. Followers of Gnosticism believed that salvation is gained through a special knowledge (*gnosis*) revealed through a spiritual Savior (presumably Jesus) and is the property of an elite few who have been initiated into its mysteries. In its various forms, Gnosticism became a major heresy in the primitive church, though little is known about its precise tenets.

Gog In Ezekiel, a future leader of Israel's enemies (Ezek. 38) whose attack on the Jerusalem sanctuary will precipitate Yahweh's intervention and the ultimate destruction of the wicked (Rev. 20:8).

Gospel (1) The Christian message, literally meaning "good news." (2) The literary form of Christian narratives about Jesus.

Gospel, Fourth The Gospel attributed to John.

Gospels, Apocryphal Christian Gospels, such as those attributed to Peter, Thomas, James, or others, that were not admitted to the New Testament canon.

Gospels, canonical The Gospels of Matthew, Mark, Luke, and John.

Gospels, Synoptic The three canonical Gospels—Matthew, Mark, and Luke—that present Jesus' public life from a strikingly similar viewpoint, structuring their respective narratives so that the contents can be arranged in parallel columns.

Hades In Greek religion, the name of the god of the Underworld, a mythic region that also came to be known by that name. In translating the Hebrew Bible into Greek, the Septuagint translators rendered *Sheol* (the Hebrew term for the subterranean abode of all the dead) as *Hades* (Gen. 42:38; 1 Sam. 2:6; Job 7:9; Prov. 27:20; Eccles. 9:10). New Testament writers also refer to the place of the dead as Hades (Rev. 1:18; 20:14). See also *Gehenna*.

Haggadah The imaginative interpretation of the nonlegal (historical and religious) passages of the Hebrew Bible. A collection of Haggadah, dating from the first centuries CE, appears in the Palestinian Talmud. See *Halakah*.

Hagiographa The third major division of the Jewish Bible, a miscellaneous collection of poetry, Wisdom literature, history, and an apocalypse (Daniel); from the Greek term meaning "sacred writings."

Halakah The interpretation of the legal sections of the Mosaic Torah. The term derives from a Hebrew word meaning "to follow"; Halakah deals with rules that guide a person's life. Collections of halakic interpretations dating from the first centuries CE are incorporated into the Talmud. See *Haggadah*.

Hanukkah The Feast of Dedication celebrating the Maccabees' restoration of the Jerusalem Temple about 165 BCE.

Hasidim Devout Jews who refused to forsake their religion during the persecution inflicted by Antiochus IV (second century BCE). The Jewish religious parties of the New Testament period are descended from the Hasidim.

Hasmoneans The Jewish royal dynasty founded by the Maccabees and named for Hasmon, an ancestor of Mattathias.

Hebrew Bible A collection of Jewish sacred writings originally written in the Hebrew language (although some later books are in Aramaic); also known as the Old Testament. The Hebrew or Jewish Bible is traditionally divided into three main parts: the Torah or Law (Genesis through Deuteronomy); the Prophets (Joshua through the twelve minor prophets); and the Writings (Psalms through Chronicles).

Hellenism The influence and adoption of Greek thought, language, values, and customs that began with the conquest of the eastern Mediterranean world by Alexander the Great and intensified under his Hellenistic successors and various Roman emperors.

Hellenistic Greek-like; pertaining to the historical period following Alexander's death in 323 BCE during which Greek language, ideas, and customs permeated the eastern Mediterranean and Near Eastern worlds.

Hellenists Jews living outside Palestine who adopted the Greek language and, to varying degrees, Greek customs and ideas (Acts 6:1; 9:29).

heresy A religious opinion contrary to that officially endorsed by the religion to which one belongs. Applied to early Christianity by its detractors (Acts 24:14), the term was not generally used in its modern sense during New Testament times except in the Pastoral Epistles (1 Tim. 1:3; Titus 3:10).

Herod The name of seven Palestinian rulers.

1. Herod I (the Great), the Idumean Roman-appointed king of Judea (40–4 BCE), ruler when Jesus was born (Matt. 2:1). An able administrator who completely reconstructed the Jerusalem Temple, he was notorious for reputed cruelty and was almost universally hated by the Jews.

2. Herod Antipas, son of Herod I, tetrarch of Galilee (Luke 3:1) and Perea (4 BCE–39 CE), frequently mentioned in the New Testament. Jesus, who called him "that fox" (Luke 13:31–32) and regarded him as a malign influence (Mark 8:15), was tried before him (Luke 9:7, 9; 23:7–15). Antipas was also responsible for executing John the Baptist (Matt. 14:1–12).

3. Herod Archelaus, ethnarch of Judea, Samaria, who so misruled his territory that he was recalled to Rome, an event to which Jesus apparently refers in Luke 19:12–27. Archelaus's evil reputation caused Joseph and Mary to avoid Judea and settle in Nazareth (Matt. 2:22–23).

4. Herod, a son of Herod the Great and half-brother to Herod Antipas (Matt. 14:3; Mark 6:17).

5. Herod Philip II, son of Herod the Great and half-brother of Herod Antipas, who ruled portions of northeastern Palestine and rebuilt the city of Caesarea Philippi near Mount Hermon (Luke 3:1).

6. Herod Agrippa I, son of Aristobulus and grandson of Herod the Great, who ingratiated himself at the imperial court in Rome and, under Claudius, was made king over most of Palestine (41–44 CE). A persecutor of Christians, he reportedly died a horrible death immediately after accepting divine honors (Acts 12:1–23).

7. Herod Agrippa II, son of Herod Agrippa I and great-grandson of Herod the Great, first king of Chalcis (50 CE) and then of the territory formerly ruled by Philip the Tetrarch, as well as of the adjoining area east of Galilee and the Upper Jordan. This was the Herod, together with his sister Bernice, before whom Paul appeared at Caesarea (Acts 25:13–26:32).

Herodians The name applied to members of an influential political movement in first-century CE. Judaism who supported Herod's dynasty, particularly that of Herod

Antipas. Opposing messianic hopes (Mark 3:6), they conspired with some Pharisees to implicate Jesus in disloyalty to Rome (Mark 12:13; Matt. 22:16).

Herodias Granddaughter of Herod the Great, daughter of Aristobulus, and half-sister of Herod Agrippa I. Herodias was criticized by John the Baptist for having deserted her first husband for her second, Herod Antipas, who divorced his wife to marry her. In revenge, she demanded the head of John the Baptist (Mark 6:17–29; Matt. 14:1–12; Luke 2:19–20).

Hinnom, Valley of A depression in the earth lying south and west of Jerusalem; also called the "Valley of the Son (or Children) of Hinnom" (Jer. 7:32; 2 Kings 23:10). Called Gehenna in the New Testament, it is a symbol of the place of posthumous torment. See *Gehenna.*

Holy of Holies The innermost and most sacred room of the Jerusalem Temple, where Yahweh was believed to be invisibly enthroned.

Holy Spirit, the The presence of God active in human life, a concept most explicitly set forth in John 14:16–26 and in the Pentecost miracle depicted in Acts 2. In post–New Testament times, the Holy Spirit was defined as the Third Person in the Trinity (see Matt. 28:19–20).

Idumea The name (meaning "pertaining to Edom") that the Greeks and Romans applied to the country of

Edom, Judah's southern neighbor; the homeland of Herod the Great (Mark 3:8).

Immanuel The name (meaning "God is with us") that Isaiah gave to a child whose birth he predicted as a sign to King Ahaz during the late eighth century BCE. Although not originally presented as a messianic prophecy, it was later interpreted as such (Micah 5:3; Matt. 1:22–23).

Incarnation, the The Christian doctrine that the prehuman Son of God became flesh, the man Jesus of Nazareth—a concept based largely on the Logos hymn that opens John's Gospel (John 1:1–18, especially 1:14).

Isaac The son of Abraham and Sarah (Gen. 21:1–7), child of the covenant promise by which Abraham's descendants would bring a blessing to all the earth's families (Gen. 17:15–22; 18:1–15) but whom Yahweh commanded to be sacrificed to him (Gen. 18:1–18). Reprieved by an angel, Isaac marries Rebekah (Gen. 24:1–67), who bears him twin sons, Esau and Jacob (Gen. 25:19–26), the latter of whom tricks his dying father into bestowing the firstborn's birthright on him (Gen. 27:1–45). Paul interprets the near-sacrifice of Isaac as an allegory of Christ (Gal. 4:21–31).

Jairus The head of a synogogue in Galilee who asked Jesus to heal his dying child, for which act of faith he was rewarded with the girl's miraculous cure (Luke 8:41–42, 49–56; Mark 5:35–43; Matt. 9:18–20, 23–26).

James
1. Son of Zebedee, brother of John, and one of the twelve Apostles (Mark 1:19–20; 3:17; Matt. 4:21–22; 10:2; Luke 5:10; 6:14). A Galilean fisherman, he left his trade to follow Jesus and, with John and Peter, became a member of his inner circle. He was among the three disciples present at the transfiguration (Mark 9:2–10; Matt. 17:1–9; Luke 9:28–36) and was at Jesus' side during the last hours before his arrest (Mark 14:32–42, Matt. 26:36–45). James and John used their intimacy to request a favored place in the messianic kingdom, thus arousing the other Apostles' indignation (Mark 10:35–45). James was beheaded when Herod Agrippa I persecuted the Jerusalem church (41–44 CE) (Acts 12:2).
2. James, son of Alphaeus and Mary (Acts 1:13; Mark 16:1), one of the Twelve (Matt. 10:3–4), called "the less" or "the younger" (Mark 15:40).
3. James, the eldest of Jesus' three "brothers" (or close male relatives) named in the Gospels (Mark 6:3; Matt. 13:55). He first opposed Jesus' work (Matt. 12:46–50; Mark 3:31–35; Luke 8:19–21; John 7:3–5) but was apparently converted by one of Jesus' postresurrection appearances (1 Cor. 15:7) and became a leader in the Jerusalem church (Acts 15:13–34; 21:18–26). According to legend a Nazirite and upholder of the Mosaic law, he apparently clashed with Paul over the latter's policy of absolving

Gentile converts from circumcision and other legalistic requirements (Gal. 1:18–2:12). The reputed author of the New Testament Epistle of James, he was martyred at Jerusalem in the early 60s CE.

Jamnia, Academy of An assembly of eminent Palestinian rabbis and Pharisees held about 90 CE in the coastal village of Jamnia (Yabneh) to define and guide Judaism following the Roman destruction of Jerusalem and its Temple. According to tradition, a leading Pharisee named Yohanan ben Zakkai had escaped from the besieged city by simulating death and being carried out in a coffin by his disciples. Yohanan, who had argued that saving human lives was more important than success in the national rebellion against Rome, was given Roman support to set up an academy to study the Jewish Law. Under his direction, the Pharisees not only preserved the Torah traditions but apparently formulated what was to become the official biblical canon of Palestinian Judaism. Out of the deliberations at Jamnia came the authoritative list of books in the Writings, the third major division of the Hebrew Bible.

Jesus The English form of a Latin name derived from the Greek *Iesous,* which translated the Hebrew *Jeshua,* a later version of *Jehoshua* or *Joshua,* meaning "Yahweh is salvation." The name was borne by several biblical

figures, including Joshua, leader of the conquest of Canaan; an ancestor of Jesus (Luke 3:29); and a Jewish Christian also called Justus (Col. 4:11). It was also the name of the author of Ecclesiasticus, Jesus Ben Sirach.

Jesus Christ The name and title given the firstborn of Mary and Joseph (the child's legal father), the one whom Christians regard as the Spirit-begotten Son of God and Savior of the world (Matt. 1:21; Luke 1:31). The term *Christ* is not a proper name but the English version of the Greek *Christos,* a translation of the Aramaic *meshiha* and the Hebrew *mashiah* ("messiah," meaning "the anointed one").

Jew Originally, a member of the tribe or kingdom of Judah (2 Kings 16:6; 25:25). The term later included any Hebrew who returned from the Babylonian captivity (538 BCE), and it finally encompassed Hebrews scattered throughout the world (Matt. 2:2).

Jewish Bible See *Hebrew Bible.*

Joanna Wife of Chuza, an administrator in Herod Antipas's Jerusalem household, who became a disciple of Jesus (Luke 8:3) and was among the women who discovered his empty tomb (Luke 23:55–24:11).

John the Apostle A Galilean fisherman, son of Zebedee and brother of the Apostle James, called by Jesus to be among his twelve most intimate followers (Mark 1:19–20; Matt. 4:21–22). Jesus

called James and John Boanerges ("sons of thunder"), possibly because of their impetuous temperaments (Mark 3:17; 9:38; Luke 9:52–56). Always among the first four in the Gospel lists of the Twelve (Mark 3:14–17; Matt. 10:2; Luke 6:3–14), John was present at the transfiguration (Matt. 17:1; Mark 9:2; Luke 9:28) and at Gethsemane (Matt. 26:37; Mark 14:33). Tradition identifies him with the "beloved disciple" (John 13:23; 21:20) and as the author of the Gospel of John, a premise that most scholars believe is impossible to prove. Along with Peter and James, he was one of the triple "pillars" of the Jerusalem church (Acts 1:13; 3:1–4:22; 8:14–17; Gal. 2:9). He may have been martyred under Herod Agrippa, although a late second-century tradition states that he lived to old age in Ephesus.

John the Baptist The son of Zechariah, a priest, and Elizabeth (Luke 1:5–24, 56–80), John was an ascetic who preached the imminence of judgment and baptized converts in the Jordan River as a symbol of their repentance from sin (Matt. 3:1–12; Mark 1:2–8; Luke 3:1–18). The Gospel writers viewed him as an Elijah figure and forerunner of the Messiah (Luke 1:17; Matt. 11:12–14; John 1:15, 9–34; 3:22–36) who baptized Jesus but also recognized his superiority (Matt. 3:13–17; Mark 1:9–11; Luke 3:21–22). When imprisoned by Herod Antipas, he inquired whether

Jesus were the expected "one who is to come." Jesus' answer was equivocal but he praised John's work as fulfilling prophecy (Matt. 11:2–19; Luke 7:24–35). At his stepdaughter Salome's request, Herod had John beheaded (Matt. 14:6–12; Mark 6:17–29). Some of John's disciples later became Christians (John 1:37; Acts 18:25).

Joseph
1. The husband of Mary and legal father of Jesus, a descendant of the Bethlehemite David (Matt. 1:20) but resident of Nazareth (Luke 2:4) where he was a carpenter (Matt. 13:55). Little is known of him except for his piety (Luke 2:21–24, 41–42) and his wish to protect his betrothed wife from scandal (Luke 2:1–5). Since he does not appear among Jesus' family members during his (supposed) son's public ministry, it is assumed that he died before Jesus began his preaching career (Matt. 1:18–2:23; 13:55–56).
2. Joseph of Arimathea, a wealthy member of the Sanhedrin and, according to John 19:38, a secret follower of Jesus who claimed Jesus' crucified body from Pilate for burial in his private garden tomb (Matt. 27:57–60; Mark 15:42–46; Luke 23:50–53; John 19:38–42).

Josephus, Flavius An important Jewish historian (about 37–100 CE) whose two major works—*Antiquities of the Jews* and *The Jewish War* (covering the revolt against Rome, 66–70 CE)—provide valuable background material for first-century Judaism and the early Christian period.

Judaism The name applied to the religion of the people of Judah ("the Jews") after the northern kingdom of Israel fell (721 BCE) and particularly after the Babylonian exile (587–538 BCE).

Judas A late form of the name Judah, popular after the time of Judas ("the Jew") Maccabeus and borne by several New Testament figures:
1. The brother (or son) of James, one of the twelve Apostles (Luke 6:16), who is sometimes identified with the Thaddeus of Matthew 10:3 or the Judas of John 14:22.
2. The "brother" or kinsman of Jesus (Mark 6:3; Matt. 13:55).
3. Judas Iscariot ("Judas the man of Kerioth"), son of Simon Iscariot (John 6:71; 13:26), the Apostle who betrayed Jesus to the priests and Romans for thirty pieces of silver (Mark 3:19; 14:10; Luke 6:16; Matt. 26:14–16, 47; John 18:3) but later returned the blood money and committed suicide (Matt. 27:3–5; Acts 1:18–20). The Gospel writers little understood Judas's motives, attributing them to simple greed or to the influence of Satan (Luke 22:3; John 6:71; 12:1–8; 13:11, 27–29).

Judas the Galilean A Jewish patriot from Galilee who led an unsuccessful insurrection against Rome in 6 CE (Acts 5:37).

Judas Maccabeus The third of five sons of the Jewish priest Mattathias, leader of the successful Jewish uprising (c. 167–160) against the Syrian king Antiochus IV. The epithet *Maccabeus* is believed to mean "the hammerer," referring to Judas's effectiveness in striking blows for Jewish freedom. His story is told in 1 Maccabees.

Jude An Anglicized form of the name Judah or Judas; one of Jesus' "brothers" (or a close male relative) (Mark 6:3; Matt. 13:55), perhaps a son born to Joseph before his marriage to Mary. Jude is less prominent in the early Christian community than his brother James (Jude 1:1) and is the traditional author of the Epistle of Jude, though most scholars doubt this claim.

Judea The Greco-Roman designation for territory comprising the old kingdom of Judah. The name first occurs in Ezra 5:8, a reference to the "province of Judea." In the time of Jesus, Judea was the southernmost of the three divisions of the Roman province of Western Palestine, the other two of which were Samaria and Galilee (Neh. 2:7; Luke 1:39; John 3:22; 11:7; Acts 1:1; Gal. 1:22).

Judgment, Day of A theological concept deriving from the ancient Hebrew belief that the Day of Yahweh would see Israel's triumph and the destruction of its enemies, a confidence the prophet Amos shattered by proclaiming that it would mean calamity for Israel as for all who broke Yahweh's laws (Amos 5:18–20). This view prevails in Zephaniah 1:1–2; 3

and Malachi 3:1–6; 4:1–6. Isaiah also refers to "that day" of coming retribution (Isa. 11:10–16; 13:9, 13), and it is given an apocalyptic setting in Daniel 7:9–14, an idea developed in several apocryphal and pseudepigraphal books as well as in the New Testament (Matt. 25; Rev. 20).

Jupiter Latin name of the chief Roman deity, counterpart of the Greek Zeus, king of the Olympian gods for whom some ignorant men of Lycaonia mistook Paul's companion Barnabas (Acts 14:12–18).

kavod Yahweh's presence in the Jerusalem Temple; a Hebrew term commonly translated as "glory" or "splendor."

kerygma The act of publicly preaching the Christian message; a Greek term meaning "proclamation."

kingdom of God The rule or dominion of God in human affairs; the translation of the Greek *basileia tou theou*.

koinē The common Greek in which the New Testament is written. *Koinē* Greek was a later form of classical Greek and was the everyday language of the Hellenistic world.

Laodicea A commercial city on the Lycus River in Asia Minor and one of the seven churches of Asia (Col. 4:15–16; Rev. 3:14–22).

Last Supper Jesus' final meal with his disciples. Depicted as a Passover observance in the Synoptic Gospels, it was the occasion at which Jesus instituted a "new covenant" with his followers and inaugurated the ceremony of bread and wine (Holy Communion, or the Eucharist) (Mark 14:12–26; Matt. 26:20–29; Luke 22:14–23; 1 Cor. 11:23–26).

latter prophets The books of Isaiah, Jeremiah, Ezekiel, and the twelve minor prophets; also known as the "writing prophets."

Law The Torah ("teaching," "instruction"), or Pentateuch, the first five books of the Bible containing the legal material traditionally ascribed to Moses.

Lazarus (1) The brother of Mary and Martha, a resident of Bethany whom Jesus resurrected (John 11:1–12:10). (2) The beggar in Jesus' parable of rewards and punishments in the afterlife (Luke 16:20–25).

legend An unverifiable story or narrative cycle about a celebrated person or place of the past. Legends grow as the popular oral literature of a people. Their purpose is to provide not historical accuracy but entertainment; they illustrate cherished beliefs, expectations, and moral principles. Scholars consider much of the material associated with the stories of the patriarchs, Moses, and prophets as legendary.

Levites The Israelite tribe descended from Levi, son of Jacob (Num. 3; 1 Chron. 5:27–6:81) that was given priestly duties in lieu of land holdings when Israel conquered Canaan (Deut. 18:1–8). According to a priestly writer, only descendants of Aaron were to be priests (Exod. 28:1; Num. 18:7); the Levites were regarded as their assistants and servants (Num. 18:2–7; 20–32). They served as priests of secondary rank and as temple functionaries during the postexilic period, which was dominated by a priestly hierarchy (1 Chron. 24–26). Other stories involving Levites appear in Judges 19–21 and Luke 10:32.

literary criticism A form of literary analysis that attempts to isolate and define literary types, the sources behind them, the stages of composition from oral to written form with their characteristic rhetorical features, and the stages and degree of redaction (editing) of a text.

Logos A Greek term meaning both "word" and "reason," used by Greek philosophers to denote the rational principle that creates and informs the universe. Amplified by Philo Judaeus of Alexandria, Egypt, to represent the mediator between God and his material creation, as Wisdom had been in Proverbs 8:22–31, the term found its most famous expression in the prologue to the Fourth Gospel to denote the prehuman Jesus—"the Word became flesh and dwelt among us" (John 1:14).

Lord's Supper, the The ritual meal that Jesus held with his closest disciples the night before his death. Here he introduced the new covenant and shared the bread and wine that symbolized his body and blood about to be sacrificed on behalf of humankind (Mark 14:22–25; Matt. 26:26–29; Luke 22:14–20). Paul first calls the Christian "love feast" (*agape*) or Communion by this name in 1 Corinthians 11:20, in which he describes the ceremony of the Eucharist (1 Cor. 11:23–26). John's version of the event (John 13:1–35) differs strikingly from that in the Synoptics.

Lucifer An epithet applied to the king of Babylon and later mistakenly taken as a name for Satan before his expulsion from heaven. The term means "light bearer" and refers to the planet Venus when it is the morning star; the English name *Lucifer* translates the Hebrew word for "shining one" (Isaiah 14:12).

Luke A physician and traveling companion of Paul (Col. 4:14; Philem. 24; 2 Tim. 4:11) to whom a late second-century tradition ascribes the Gospel of Luke and the Book of Acts.

LXX A common abbreviation for the Septuagint, the Greek translation of the Hebrew Bible made in Alexandria, Egypt, during the last three centuries BCE.

Lycaonia A district in Asia Minor added to the Roman Empire around 25 BCE, where Paul endured persecution (Acts 13:50; 14:6–19).

Lycia A small province in southwestern Asia Minor, bordering the Mediterranean, which Paul visited on his missionary travels (Acts 21:1; 27:5–7).

Lystra A city in the Roman province of Galatia where Paul and Barnabas performed such successful healings that they were identified as Hermes and Zeus (Mercury and Jupiter) (Acts 14:6–19; 16:1; 18:23).

Maccabees A name bestowed upon the family that won religious and political independence for the Jews from their Greek-Syrian oppressors. Judas, called Maccabeus ("the hammerer"), son of the aged priest Mattathias, led his brothers and other faithful Jews against the armies of Antiochus IV (Epiphanes) (175–163 BCE). The dynasty his brothers established was called Hasmonean (after an ancestor named Hasmon) and ruled Judea until 63 BCE, when the Romans occupied Palestine.

Macedonia The large mountainous district in northern Greece ruled by Philip of Macedon (359–336 BCE). Philip's son Alexander the Great (356–323 BCE) extended the Macedonian Empire over the entire ancient Near East as far as western India, incorporating all of the earlier Persian Empire. Conquered by Rome (168 BCE) and annexed as a province (146 BCE), Macedonia was the first part of Europe to be Christianized (Acts 16:10–17:9; 18:5; 19:29; 20:1–3).

Magdala A town on the northwest shore of the Sea of Galilee, home of Mary Magdalene ("of Magdala") (Matt. 15:39).

Magnificat Mary's beautiful hymn of praise, recorded in Luke 1:46–55.

Marcion An early Gnostic Christian who attempted to establish a Christian Scripture distinct from the Jewish Bible, which he rejected. Marcion's canon included only Luke's Gospel and the Pauline letters, the only documents he believed to reflect true belief. The church at Rome expelled him as a heretic about 140 CE.

Mark (John Mark) Son of Mary, a Jerusalem Jew who accompanied Barnabas (his cousin) and Paul on an early missionary journey (Acts 12:12–25; 13:5, 13; 15:37). For reasons unstated, he left them at Perga (Acts 13:13), which so angered Paul that he refused to allow Mark to join a later preaching campaign (Acts 15:38), though he and the Apostle were later reconciled (Col. 4:10; Philem. 24). Some identify Mark with the youth who ran away naked at the time of Jesus' arrest (Mark 14:51–52). An early tradition ascribes authorship of the Gospel of Mark to him, as Papias and Eusebius (*History* 3.39.15) testify.

Martha The sister of Mary and Lazarus of Bethany (Luke 10:38–42; John 11:1–12:2), whose home Jesus frequently visited.

martyr A "witness" for Christ who prefers to die rather than relinquish his faith. Stephen, at whose stoning Saul of Tarsus assisted, is known as the first Christian martyr (Acts 22:20; Rev. 2:13; 17:6).

Mary From the Latin and Greek *Maria,* from the Hebrew *Miryam* (Miriam), a name borne by six women in the New Testament:

1. Mary the Virgin, wife of Joseph and mother of Jesus, who, the angel Gabriel informed her, was conceived by the Holy Spirit (Matt. 1:18–25; Luke 1:26–56; 2:21). From her home in Nazareth, Mary traveled to Bethlehem, where her first son was born (Luke 2:1–18), and thence into Egypt to escape Herod's persecution (Matt. 2:1–18), returning to Nazareth in Galilee after Herod's death (4 BCE) (Matt. 2:19–23). She had one sister (John 18:25), probably Salome, wife of Zebedee, mother of James and John (Matt. 27:56), and was also related to Elizabeth, mother of John the Baptist (Luke 1:36). Gabriel's Annunciation of the Messiah's birth occurs in Luke 1:26–36; the Magnificat, in Luke 1:46–55.

Mary visited Jerusalem annually for the Passover (Luke 2:41) and reprimanded the twelve-year-old Jesus for lingering behind at the temple (Luke 2: 46–50). She may have been among family members convinced that Jesus' early preaching showed mental instability (Mark 3:21) and apparently humored his requests during the wedding celebration at Cana (John 2:1–12). Although Jesus showed his mother little deference during his ministry (Mark 3:31–35; Luke 11:27–28; John 2:4), on the cross he entrusted her care to his "beloved disciple" (John 19:25–27). Mary last appears in the upper room praying with the disciples just before Pentecost (Acts 1:13–14).

2. Mary Magdalene, a woman from Magdala, from whom Jesus cast out seven demons (Luke 8:1–2) and who became his follower. A common tradition asserts that she had been a prostitute whom Jesus had rescued from her former life (Mark 16:9; Luke 7:37–50), but this is by no means certain. She was present at the crucifixion (Mark 15:40; Matt. 15:47), visited Jesus' tomb early Sunday morning (Matt 28:1; Mark 16:1; Luke 24:10; John 20:1), and was one of the first to see the risen Jesus (Matt. 28:9; Mark 16:9; John 20:11–18), although the male disciples refused to believe her (Luke 24:9–11).

3. Mary, sister of Lazarus and Martha, whose home at Bethany Jesus frequented (Luke 10:38–42; John 11:1–12:8).

4. Mary, wife of Cleophas, mother of James the Less and Joseph (Joses), was a witness of Jesus' crucifixion, burial, and resurrection (Matt. 27:56–61; 28:1; Mark 15:40, 47; 16:1; Luke 24:10; John 19:25).

5. Mary, sixter of Barnabas and mother of John Mark, provided her Jerusalem home as a meeting place for the disciples (Acts 12:12; Col. 4:10).

6. An otherwise anonymous Mary mentioned in Romans 16:6.

Masada A stronghold built by Herod the Great on a fortified plateau eight hundred feet above the Dead Sea, Masada was captured by Zealots during the revolt against Rome (66 CE). When the attacking Romans finally entered Masada (73 CE), they found only 7 women and children alive, 953 others having died in a suicide pact.

Masoretes Medieval Jewish scholars who copied, annotated, and added vowels to the text of the Hebrew Bible; from a Hebrew term meaning "tradition."

Masoretic Text (MT) The standard text of the Hebrew Bible as given final form by the Masoretes in the seventh through the ninth centuries CE.

Mattathias A Jewish priest who, with his sons John, Simon, Judas, Eleazar, and Jonathan, led a revolt against the oppressions of Antiochus IV (about 168–167 BCE) (1 Macc. 2:1–70).

Matthew A Jewish tax collector working for Rome whom Jesus called to be one of the twelve Apostles (Matt. 9:9; 10:3; Mark 2:13–17; 3:18; Luke 5:27–32; 6:15; Acts 1:13). Matthew (also called Levi) is the traditional author of the Gospel of Matthew, an attribution contested by most scholars.

Matthias The early Christian elected to replace Judas among the Twelve (Acts 1:23–26). The name means "gift of Yahweh."

Megiddo An old Palestinian city overlooking the Valley of Jezreel (Plain of Esdraelon), the site of numerous decisive battles in biblical history

(Josh. 12:21; 2 Kings 9:27; 23:29–30; 2 Chron. 35:20–24; Zech. 12:11) and symbolic location of the climactic War of Armageddon (Rev. 16:16).

Melchizedek The king-priest of Canaanite Salem (probably the site of Jerusalem) to whom Abraham paid a tenth of his spoils of war (Gen. 14:17–20); cited by the author of Hebrews as foreshadowing Jesus Christ (Ps. 110:4; Heb. 5:6–10; 7:1–25).

Mercury Roman name for Hermes, Greek god of persuasion, business, and trade and messenger of Zeus, for whom Paul was mistaken in Lystra (Acts 14:12).

Mesopotamia The territory between the Euphrates and Tigris rivers at the head of the Persian Gulf (modern Iraq); cradle of the Sumerian, Akkadian, Assyrian, and Neo-Babylonian civilizations (Gen. 24:10; Judg. 3:8–10; 1 Chron. 19:6; Acts 2:9; 7:2).

messiah A Hebrew term meaning "anointed one," designating a king or priest of ancient Israel who had been consecrated by having his head smeared with holy oil, marking him as set apart for a special role. King David is the model of Yahweh's anointed ruler; all his descendants who ruled over Judah were Yahweh's messiahs (2 Sam. 7:1–29; Ps. 89:3–45). After the end of the Davidic monarchy (587 BCE), various Hebrew prophets applied the promises made to the Davidic dynasty to a future heir who would eventually restore the kingdom of David (Pss. 2; 110; Dan. 9:25–26).

Christians believe that Jesus of Nazareth was the promised Messiah (Christ) as expressed in Peter's "confession" (Matt. 16:13–20; Mark 8:27–30; Luke 9:18–22; and so on).

Michael The angel whom the Book of Daniel represents as being the spirit prince, guardian, and protector of Israel (Dan. 10:13, 21; 12:1). Jude 9 depicts him as an archangel fighting with Satan for Moses' body. In Revelation 12:7 he leads the war against the Dragon (Satan) and casts him from heaven. His name means "Who is like God?"

midrash A commentary on or interpretation of Hebrew Scripture. Collections of such haggadic or halakic expositions of the significance of the biblical text are called midrashim; from a Hebrew word meaning "to search out."

millennium A thousand-year epoch, particularly the period of Christ's universal reign (Rev. 20:1–8) during which Satan will be chained and the dead resurrected.

Mishnah A collection of Pharisaic oral interpretations (Halakah) of the Torah compiled and edited by Rabbi Judah ha-Nasi about 200 CE; from the Hebrew verb "to repeat."

money An imprinted metal generally accepted as a medium of exchange. In early biblical times, before coins were first minted, value in business transactions was determined by weighing quantities of precious metals. In the early period, the term

shekel does not refer to a coin but a certain weight of silver. The use of coinage was first introduced into Palestine during the Persian era when the daric or dram, named for Darius I (521–486 BCE), appeared. After Alexander's conquest of Persia, Greek coinage became the standard. The silver drachma (Luke 15:8), a coin of small value, was equivalent to the Roman denarius. The lepton was a small copper coin (Luke 12:59; 21:2), the least valuable in circulation, and one of the denominations coined by the Jews for use in the temple. This was the "widow's mite" (Mark 12:42). The talent (Matt. 18:24) was not a coin but money of account; it was divided into smaller units—60 minas or 6,000 drachmas— and was worth at least $2,000. The denarius (Matt. 18:28), the basic unit in the New Testament, was a silver coin, the day's wage of a rural laborer (Matt. 20:2).

monotheism Belief in the existence of one God, a major theme of Second Isaiah (Isa. 40–46).

Mosaic Covenant In the Hebrew Bible, the pact between Yahweh and Israel mediated by Moses (Exod. 19–24). According to the terms of the Mosaic concept, Yahweh's support of Israel was dependent upon the people's obedience to his will, expressed in the laws and principles of the Torah (Deut. 28–29).

Moses The great Hebrew Lawgiver, religious reformer, founder of the Israelite nation, and central figure of the Pentateuch. Moses was the son of Amram (a Levite) and Jochebed and brother to Aaron and Miriam (Exod. 2:1–4). Adopted by pharaoh's daughter and raised at the Egyptian royal court (Exod. 2:5–10; Acts 7:22), he fled Egypt after killing an Egyptian bully and settled in Midian among the Kenites, where he married Jethro's daughter Zipporah (Exod. 2:11–22).

After an encounter with Yahweh at the burning bush (Exod. 3:1–4:17), he returned to Egypt (Exod. 4:18–31), interceded with pharaoh during the ten plagues (Exod. 5–11), and led the Israelites across the Red Sea (Exod. 14–15) to Sinai. There, he mediated the Law covenant between Yahweh and Israel (Exod. 19–31), pled for his people (Exod. 33–34; Num. 14), directed their migration through the Sinai wilderness (Num. 11–14; 20–25). He appointed Joshua as his successor (Num. 27:18–23) and died in Moab (Deut. 34:1–7; Acts 7:20–44). He is also credited with building the tabernacle (Exod. 35–40), organizing Israel (Exod. 18:13–26), restating Israel's Law code shortly before his death (Deut. 1–31), and composing several hymns (Deut. 32–33; Ps. 90). Although Moses' name became synonymous with the covenant concept and Israel's traditions (Pss. 77:20; 103:7; 105:26; 106:23; Isa. 63:12; Mic. 6:4; Matt. 17:3; Luke 16:29; John 1:17; 3:14; 5:46;

7:19; 9:29; Acts 3:22; 21:21), modern scholars have concluded that much of the material in the Pentateuch dates from post-Mosaic times. Moses also figured prominently in Paul's theology (Rom. 5:14; 10:5; 1 Cor. 10:2; 2 Cor. 3:7; 3:15) and that of the author of Hebrews (Heb. 3:2; 7:14; 9:19; 11:23). Jude preserves an old tradition, probably derived from the pseudepigraphal Assumption of Moses, that Satan disputed the angel Michael for Moses' body (Jude 9; Rev. 15:3).

mystery Derived from a Greek word meaning "to initiate" or "to shut the eyes or mouth," probably referring to the secrets of Hellenistic "mystery religions," and used variously in the New Testament. Jesus speaks at least once of the "mystery" of the kingdom (Matt. 13:11; Mark 4:11; Luke 8:10), but Paul employs the term frequently as if the profounder aspects of Christianity were a religious secret into which the Spirit-directed believer becomes initiated (Rom. 11:5; 16:25; 1 Cor. 2:7; 4:1; 13:2; 14:2; 15:51; Col. 1:26; 2:2; 4:3; 2 Thess. 2:7; 1 Tim. 3:9; 3:16. See also Rev. 1:20; 10:7; 17:5–7).

myth A narrative expressing a profound psychological or religious truth that cannot be verified by historical inquiry or other scientific means; from the Greek *mythos,* meaning a "story." When scholars speak of the "myth of Eden," for example, it is

not to denigrate the tale's historicity but to emphasize the Eden story's archetypal expression of humankind's sense of alienation from the spirit world. Myths typically feature stories about gods and goddesses who represent natural or psychological forces that deeply influence humans but that they cannot control. The psychologist Carl Jung interpreted myth as humankind's inherited concept of a primeval event that persists in the unconscious mind and finds expression through repeated reenactments in ritual worship and other cultic practices. Israel's covenant-renewal ceremonies and retellings of Yahweh's saving acts during the Exodus are examples of such cultic myths.

mythology A system or cycle of myths, such as those featuring the deities of ancient Greece or Rome. Once the embodiment of living religious beliefs, Greco-Roman and other mythologies are now seen as archetypal symbols that give philosophic meaning to universal human experiences. Mythologies are thus "falsehoods" only in the narrowest literal sense. They are probably akin to dreams in revealing persistent images and attitudes hidden in the human subconscious.

Nazarenes A name applied to early Christians (Acts 24:5).
Nazareth A town in Lower Galilee above the Plain of Esdraelon (Megiddo) where Jesus spent his youth and

began his ministry (Matt. 2:23; Luke 1:26; 4:16; John 1:46).

Nero (Nero Claudius Caesar Augustus Germanicus) Emperor of Rome (54–68 CE), the Caesar by whom Paul wished to be tried in Acts 25:11 and under whose persecution Paul was probably beheaded (64–65 CE). A first-century superstition held that Nero, slain during a palace revolt, would return at the head of an army. Regarded by some Christians as the anti-Christ, Nero's reappearance is apparently suggested in Revelation 13:4–18.

Nicodemus A leading Pharisee and member of the Sanhedrin (John 3:1; 7:50; 19:39) who discussed spiritual rebirth with Jesus (John 3:1–21), visited him by night and defended him against other Pharisees (John 7:45–52), and with Joseph of Arimathea helped entomb his body (John 19:38–42).

Olives, Mount of (Olivet) A mile-long limestone ridge with several distinct summits paralleling the eastern section of Jerusalem, from which it is separated by the narrow Kidron Valley. Here David fled during Absalom's rebellion (2 Sam. 15:30–32), and according to Zechariah 14:3–5, here Yahweh will stand at the final eschatological battle, when the mountain will be torn asunder from east to west. From its summit, with its panoramic view of Jerusalem, Jesus delivered his apocalyptic

Judgment on the city that had rejected him (Matt. 24–25). He often retreated to its shady groves in the evening (John 7:53; 8:1), including the night before his death (Matt. 26:30–56; Mark 14:26; Luke 22:39; see also Matt. 21:1; Mark 11:1; Luke 19:29; Acts 1:12).

omega The last letter in the Greek alphabet, used with alpha (the first letter) as a symbol of the eternity of God (Rev. 1:8; 21:6) and Jesus (Rev. 1:17; 22:13), probably echoing Isaiah's description of Yahweh as "the first and the last" (Isa. 44:6; 48:12).

Onesimus The runaway slave of Philemon of Colossae whom Paul converted to Christianity and reconciled to his master (Philem. 8–21; Col. 4:7–9).

oracle (1) A divine message or utterance (Rom. 3:2; Heb. 5:12; 1 Pet. 4:11) or the person through whom it is conveyed (Acts 7:38). (2) An authoritative communication, such as that from a wise person (Prov. 31:1; 2 Sam. 16:23). (3) The inner sanctum of the Jerusalem temple (1 Kings 6:5–6; 7:49; 8:6–8; Ps. 28:2). (4) The supposedly inspired words of a priest or priestess at such shrines as Delphi in ancient Greece and Cumae in Italy.

oral tradition Material passed from generation to generation by word of mouth before finding written form. Scholars believe that much of Israel's early history, customs, and beliefs about its origins, such as the stories about the patriarchs and Moses in the Pentateuch, were so transmitted before an

anonymous writer first committed them to writing about 950 BCE.

original sin The doctrine that the entire human race has inherited from the first man (Adam) a proclivity to sin. Some theologians, such as Augustine and Calvin, argued that humanity is born totally corrupt. The doctrine is based partly on an extremist interpretation of Romans 5:12.

Palestine A strip of land bordering the eastern Mediterranean Sea, lying south of Syria, north of the Sinai Peninsula, and west of the Arabian Desert. During the patriarchal period, it was known as Canaan (Gen. 12:6–7; 15:18–21). Named for the Philistines, it was first called Palestine by the Greek historian Herodotus about 450 BCE.

parable A short fictional narrative that compares something familiar to an unexpected spiritual value; from the Greek *parabole,* meaning "a placing beside," "a comparison." In the Synoptic Gospels, Jesus typically uses a commonplace object or action to illustrate a religious principle. (Matt. 13:3–53; 22:1; 24:32; Mark 4:2–3; 13:28; Luke 8:4–18; 13:18–21; 21:29). A recurrent tradition held that Jesus used parables to prevent most of his hearers from understanding his message (Matt. 13:10–15; Mark 4:10–12; Luke 8:9–10). Famous Old Testament parables or fables include Nathan's (2 Sam. 12:1–14), Isaiah's (Isa. 5:1–7), Jotham's (Judg. 9:7–21), Jehoash's (2 Kings 14:8–10), and Ezekiel's (Ezek. 17:22–24; 24:1–14), the last two of which are allegories.

Paraclete A Greek term meaning "an advocate" or "intercessor summoned to aid" used to denote the Holy Spirit in the Gospel of John. *Paraclete* is variously translated as "Comforter," "Helper," "Advocate," or "Spirit of Truth" (John 7:39; 14:12, 16–18; 15:26; 16:7; see also 1 John 2:1).

paradise Literally, a "park" or walled garden, the named applied to Eden (Gen. 2:8–17) and in post-Old Testament times to the abode of the righteous dead, of which the lower part housed souls awaiting the resurrection and the higher was the permanent home of the just. It is possible that Jesus referred to the lower paradise in his words to the thief on the cross (Luke 23:43). Paul's reference to being "caught up" into paradise may refer to the third of the seven heavens postulated in later Jewish eschatology (as in the books of Enoch) (2 Cor. 12:2–5). John's vision of the tree of life in "the garden of God" (Rev. 2:7; 22:1–3) depicts an earthlike heaven.

Parousia The Second Coming or appearance of Christ, commonly regarded as his return to judge the world, punish the wicked, and redeem the saved. The term is Greek and means "being by" or "being near." The Parousia

is a major concept in apocalyptic Christianity (Matt. 24–25; Mark 13; Luke 22; 1 and 2 Thess.; 2 Pet. 2–3; Rev.); but see also John 14:25–29, which emphasizes Jesus' continued spiritual presence rather than an eschatological apparition.

Passion, the The term commonly used to denote Jesus' suffering and death (Acts 1:3).

Passover, the An annual Jewish observance commemorating Israel's last night of bondage in Egypt when the Angel of Death "passed over" Israelite homes marked with the blood of a sacrificial lamb to destroy the firstborn of every Egyptian household (Exod. 12:1–51). Beginning the seven-day Feast of Unleavened Bread, it is a ritual meal eaten on Nisan 14 (March–April) and includes roast lamb, unleavened bread, and bitter herbs (Exod. 12:15–20; 13:3–10; Lev. 23:5; Num. 9:5; 28:16; Deut. 16:1). The Passover was scrupulously observed by Israel's great leaders, including Joshua (Josh. 5:10), Hezekiah (2 Chron. 30:1), Josiah (2 Kings 23:21–23, 2 Chron. 35:1–18), and the returned exiles (Ezra 6:19), as well as by Jesus and his disciples (Matt. 26:2, 17–29: Mark 14:1–16; Luke 22:1–13; John 13:1; 18:39). According to the Synoptics, Jesus' Last Supper with the Twelve was a Passover celebration (Matt. 26; Mark 14; Luke 22) and the model for Christian Communion (the Eucharist) (1 Cor. 11:17–27).

Pastoral Epistles The New Testament books of 1 and 2 Timothy and Titus, presumably written by the Apostle Paul to two of his fellow ministers (pastors) but believed by modern scholars to have been composed by an anonymous disciple of Pauline thought living in the mid-second century CE.

Patmos A small Agean island off the coast of western Asia Minor (Turkey) where John, author of Revelation, was exiled by the Emperor Domitian about 95 CE (Rev. 1:9).

Paul The most influential Apostle and missionary of the mid-first-century Church and author of seven or nine New Testament letters. Saul of Tarsus was born in the capital of the Asia Minor province of Cilicia (Acts 9:11; 21:39; 22:3) into a family of Pharisees (Acts 23:6) of the tribe of Benjamin (Phil. 3:5) and had both Roman and Taurean citizenship (Acts 22:28). Suddenly converted to Christianity after persecuting early Christians (Acts 7.55–8.3; 9:1–30; 22:1–21; 26:1–23; 1 Cor. 9: 1; 15:8; Gal. 1:11–24; Eph. 3:3; Phil. 3:12), he undertook at least three international missionary tours, presenting defenses of the new faith before Jewish and Gentile authorities (Acts 13:1–28:31). His emphasis on the insufficiency of the Mosaic law for salvation (Gal. 3–5; Rom. 4–11) and the superiority of faith to law (Rom. 4–11) and his insistence that Gentiles be admitted to the church without observing Jewish legal restrictions (Gal. 2; 5; Rom. 7–8) were decisive in determining the future development of the new religion. He was probably martyred in Rome about 64–65 CE.

Pella A Gentile city in Palestine east of the Jordan River, to which tradition says that Jesus' family and other Jewish Christians fled during the Jewish revolt against Rome (66–70 CE). Before this time Jerusalem had been the center of the Palestinian Jewish Christian church. References in Acts and Paul's letters indicate that Palestinian Christian teachings differed significantly from those Paul stressed in the churches of Gentile Christianity. No writings from the Palestinian Christians survive, so the fate of the Pella community is not known.

Pentateuch The first five books of the Hebrew Bible, the Torah; from a Greek word meaning "five scrolls."

Pentecost (1) Also known as the Feast of Weeks (Exod. 34:22; Deut. 16:10), the Feast of Harvest (Exod. 23:16), and the Day of the First Fruits (Num. 28:26), a one-day celebration held fifty days after Passover at the juncture of May and June. (2) The occasion of the outpouring of the Holy Spirit on early Christians assembled in Jerusalem (Acts 2:1–41), regarded as the spiritual baptism of the church.

Pergamum A major Hellenistic city in western Asia Minor (modern Bergama in west Anatolian Turkey), site of a magnificent temple of Zeus, which some commentators believe is referred to as "Satan's Throne" in Revelation 2:13. Pergamum is one of the seven churches addressed by the Revelator (Rev. 1:11; 2:12–17).

pericope In form criticism, a literary unit (a saying, an anecdote, a parable, or a brief narrative) that forms a complete entity in itself and is attached to its context by later editorial commentary. Many of Jesus' pronouncements probably circulated independently as pericopes before they were incorporated into the written Gospel records.

pesher In Hebrew, an analysis or interpretation of Scripture. The term is applied to the commentaries (*persherim*) found among the Dead Sea Scrolls.

peshitta A version of the Old Testament translated for Christian churches in Syria during the fifth century CE.

Peter The most prominent of Jesus' twelve chief disciples, also known as Simon (probably his surname), Simeon (Symeon), and Cephas (the Aramaic equivalent of *petros*, meaning "rock" or "stone") (John 1:40–42). The son of Jonas or John (Matt. 16:17; John 1:42; 21:15–17), brother of the Apostle Andrew, and a native of Bethsaida, a fishing village on the Sea of Galilee (John 1:44), he was called by Jesus to be "a fisher of men" (Matt. 4:18–20; Mark 1:16–18; Luke 5:1–11). The first to recognize Jesus as the Messiah (Matt. 16:13–20; Mark 8:27–30; Luke 9:18–22), Peter later denied him three times (Matt. 26:69–75; Mark 14:66–72; Luke 22:54–62; John 18:15–18).

Commanded to "feed [the resurrected Jesus'] sheep" (John 21:15–19), Peter became a leader of the Jerusalem church (Acts 1:15–26; 2:14–42; 15:6–12) and miracle worker (Acts 3:1–10). He was instrumental in bringing the first Gentiles into the Church (Acts 10–11), although Paul regarded him as a conservative obstacle to this movement (Gal. 2:11–14). He appeared before the Sanhedrin (Acts 4:1–12) and was miraculously rescued from at least one imprisonment (Acts 5:17–42; 12:1–19). A married man (Matt. 8:14; Mark 1:30; Luke 4:8; 1 Cor. 9:5), Peter was to be the "rock" on which Jesus' church was built (Matt. 16:16–20). Although some scholars regard him as the source of 1 Peter, virtually all experts deny Petrine authorship to the second epistle bearing his name. He was martyred under Nero about 64–65 CE.

Pharisees A leading religious movement or sect in Judaism during the last two centuries BCE and the first two centuries CE. The Pharisees were probably descendants of the Hasidim who opposed Antiochus IV's attempts to destroy the Mosaic faith. Their name may derive from the Hebrew *perisha* ("separated") because their rigorous observance of the

Law bred a separatist view toward common life. Although the New Testament typically presents them as Jesus' opponents, their views on resurrection and the afterlife anticipated Christian teachings. The "seven woes" against the Pharisees appear in Matthew 23:13–32. Paul was a Pharisee (Acts 23:6; 26:5; Phil. 3:5).

Philadelphia A city in Lydia (modern Turkey) about twenty-eight miles from Sardis, one of the seven churches addressed in Revelation 3:7–13.

Philemon A citizen of Colossae whose runaway slave, Onesimus, Paul converted to Christianity (Philem. 5, 10, 16, 19).

Philip

1. King of Macedonia (359–336 BCE), father of Alexander the Great (1 Macc. 1:1; 6:2).
2. One of the Twelve, a man of Bethsaida in Galilee (Matt. 10:3; Mark 3:18; Luke 6:14; John 1:43–49; 12:21–22; 14:8–9; Acts 1:12–14).
3. An evangelist of the Jerusalem church who was an administrator (Acts 6:1–6) and preacher (Acts 8:4–8), the convertor of Simon the sorcerer (Acts 8:9–13) and of an Ethiopian eunuch (Acts 8:26–39). Paul visited him at Caesarea (Acts 21:8–15).
4. A son of Herod the Great and Palestinian tetrarch (4 BCE–34 CE) (Luke 3:1).

Philippi A city of eastern Macedonia, the first European center to receive the Christian message (Acts 16:10–40). Philippi became the Apostle Paul's favorite church (Acts 20:6; Phil. 4:16; 2 Cor. 11:9); it is the one to which his letter to the Philippians is addressed.

Philo Judaeus The most influential philosopher of Hellenistic Judaism. Philo was a Greek-educated Jew living in Alexandria, Egypt (about 20 BCE–50 CE), who promoted a method of interpreting the Hebrew Bible allegorically (which may have influenced Paul in such passages as 1 Corinthians 10:4 and Galatians 4:24 as well as the authors of the Fourth Gospel and Hebrews). His doctrine of the Logos (the divine creative Word) shaped the prologue to the Gospel of John.

Phoebe A servant or deaconess of the church at Cenchrae, a port of Corinth, whose good works Paul commends in Romans 16:1–2.

phylacteries One of two small leather pouches containing copies of four scriptural passages (Exod. 13:1–10, 11–16; Deut. 6:4–9; 11:13–21), worn on the left arm and forehead by Jewish men during weekday prayers (Exod. 13:9, 16; Deut. 6:8; 11:18; Matt. 23:5).

Pilate, Pontius The Roman prefect (also called a procurator) of Judea (26–36 CE) who presided at Jesus' trial for sedition against Rome and sentenced him to be crucified (Matt. 27:1–26; Mark 15:1–15; Luke 3:1; 13:1; 23:1–25 John 18:28–19:22; Acts 3:13; 13:28; 1 Tim. 6:13).

polytheism Belief in more than one god, the most common form of religion in the ancient world.

Prisca (Priscilla) The wife of Aquila and a leading member of the early church (Acts 18:18; Rom. 16:3; 2 Tim. 4:19).

proconsul A Roman governor or administrator of a province or territory, such as Gallio, proconsul of Achaia, before whom Paul appeared (Acts 18:12).

procurator The Roman title of the governor of a region before it became an administrative province. During the reigns of Augustus and Tiberius, Judea was governed by a prefect, the most famous of whom was Pontius Pilate. The office was upgraded to the level of procurator under Claudius.

prophet One who preaches or proclaims the word or will of his or her deity (Amos 3:7–8; Deut. 18:9–22). A true prophet in Israel was regarded as divinely inspired.

Prophets, the The second major division of the Hebrew Bible, from Joshua through the twelve minor prophets and including the books of Samuel and Kings, Isaiah, Jeremiah, and Ezekiel.

proverb A brief saying that memorably expresses a familiar or useful bit of folk wisdom, usually of a practical or prudential nature.

providence The quasireligious concept of God as a force sustaining and guiding human destiny. It assumes that events occur as part of a divine plan or purpose working for the ultimate triumph of good.

psalm A sacred song or poem used in praise or worship of the deity, particularly those in the Book of Psalms.

Pseudepigrapha (1) Literally, books falsely ascribed to eminent biblical figures of the past, such as Enoch, Noah, Moses, and Isaiah. (2) A collection of religious books outside the Hebrew Bible canon or Apocrypha that were composed in Hebrew, Aramaic, and Greek from about 200 BCE to 200 CE.

pseudonymity A literary practice, common among Jewish writers of the last two centuries BCE and the first two centuries CE, of writing or publishing a book in the name of a famous religious figure of the past. Thus, an anonymous author of about 168 BCE ascribed his work to Daniel, who supposedly lived during the 500s BCE. The Pastoral Epistles, 2 Peter, James, and Jude are thought to be pseudonymous books written in the mid-second century CE but attributed to eminent disciples connected with the first-century Jerusalem church.

Ptolemaic Dynasty The royal dynasty that was established by Alexander's general Ptolemy I and that ruled Egypt from about 323 to 30 BCE. Ptolemaic Egypt controlled Palestine until about 200 BCE.

Ptolemy

1. Ptolemy I (323–285 BCE), a Macedonian general who assumed rulership of Egypt after the death of Alexander the Great. The Ptolemaic dynasty controlled Egypt and its dominions until 31 BCE when the Romans came to power.

2. Ptolemy II (285–246 BCE), who supposedly authorized the translation of the Hebrew Bible into Greek (the Septuagint).

publican In the New Testament, petty tax collectors for Rome, despised by the Jews from whom they typically extorted money (Matt. 9:10–13; 18:17; 21:31). Jesus dined with these "sinners" (Matt. 9:9–13) and called one, Levi (Matthew), to apostleship (Matt. 9:9–13; Luke 5:27–31). He also painted a publican as more virtuous than a Pharisee (Luke 18:9–14).

Q An abbreviation for *Quelle*, the German term for "source," a hypothetical document that many scholars believe contained a collection of Jesus' sayings (*logia*). The theory of its existence was formed to explain material common to both Matthew and Luke but absent from Mark's Gospel. It is assumed that Matthew and Luke drew on a single source (Q), assembled about 50 CE, for this shared material.

Qumran, Khirbet Ruins of a community (probably of Essenes) near the northwest corner of the Dead Sea, where the Dead Sea Scrolls were produced.

rabbi A Jewish title (meaning "master" or "teacher") given to scholars learned in the Torah. Jesus was frequently addressed by this title (Matt. 23:8; 26:25, 49; Mark 8:5; 10:51; 11:21; 14:45; John 1:38, 49; 3.2; 4:31; 6:25; 9:2; 11:8; 20:16), as was John the Baptist (John 3:26), although Jesus supposedly forbade his followers to be so called (Matt. 23:7–8).

redaction criticism A method of analyzing written texts to define the purpose and literary procedures of editors (redactors) who compile and edit older documents, transforming shorter works into longer ones, as did the redactors who collected and ordered independent traditions about Jesus to compare the present Gospels.

resurrection The returning of the dead to life, a late Old Testament belief (Isa. 26:19; Dan. 12:2–3, 13) that first became prevalent in Judaism during the time of the Maccabees (after 168 BCE) and became a part of the Pharisees' doctrine. Like the prophets Elijah and Elisha (1 Kings 17:17–24; 2 Kings 4:18–37), Jesus performed several temporal resurrections: of the widow of Nain's son (Luke 7:11–17), the daughter of Jairus (Mark 5:21–43), and Lazarus (John 11:1–44). Unlike these personages, however, Jesus ascended to heaven after his own resurrection (Acts 1:7–8). Paul gives the fullest discussion of the resurrection in the New Testament (1 Thess. 4; 1 Cor. 15), although he leaves many questions unanswered (see also Rev. 20:11–15).

Roman Empire The international, interracial government centered in Rome, Italy, that conquered and administered the entire Mediterranean region from Gaul (France and southern Germany) in the northwest to Egypt in the southeast. The empire ruled the Jewish state in Palestine from 63 BCE until Hadrian's destruction of Jerusalem during the second Roman War (132–135 CE).

Sabbath The seventh day of the Jewish week, sacred to Yahweh and dedicated to rest and worship. Enjoined upon Israel as a sign of Yahweh's covenant (Exod. 20:8–11; 23:12; 31:12–17; Lev. 23:3; 24:1–9; Deut. 5:12–15) and a memorial of Yahweh's repose after six days of creation, the Sabbath was strictly observed by leaders of the returned exiles (Neh. 13:15–22; Isa. 56:2–6; Ezek. 46:1–7). Jesus was frequently criticized for his liberal attitude toward the Sabbath, which he contended was made for humankind's benefit (Matt. 12:1–12; Mark 2:23–28; Luke 6:1–9; John 5:18).

sacrifice In ancient religion, something precious—usually an umblemished animal, fruit, or grain—offered to a god and thereby made sacred. The Mosaic law required the regular ritual slaughter of sacrificial animals and birds (Lev. 1:1–7:38; 16:1–17:14; Deut. 15:19–23; and so on).

Sadducees An ultraconservative Jewish sect of the first century BCE and first century CE composed largely of wealthy and politically influential landowners. Unlike the Pharisees, the Sadducees recognized only the Torah as binding and rejected the Prophets and the Writings, denying both resurrection and a judgment in the afterlife. An aristocracy controlling the priesthood and temple, they cooperated with Roman rule of Palestine, a collusion that made them unpopular with the common people (Matt. 3:7; 16:1; 22:23; Mark 12:18; Luke 20:27; Acts 4:1; 5:17; 23:6).

saints Holy ones, persons of exceptional virtue and sanctity, believers outstandingly faithful despite persecution (Dan. 7:18–21; 8:13; Matt. 27:52; Acts 9:13; 26:10; Rom. 8:27; 1 Cor. 6:2; 1 Thess. 3:13; 2 Thess. 1:10; Heb. 13:24; Rev. 5:8; 13:7–10; 17:6; 20:9).

Salome

1. Daughter of Herodias and Herod (son of Herod the Great) and niece of Herod Antipas, before whom she danced to secure the head of John the Baptist (Matt. 14:3–11; Mark 6:17–28). Anonymous in the New Testament, her name is given by Josephus (*Antiquities* 18.5.4).
2. A woman present at Jesus crucifixion (Matt. 27:56; Mark 15:40) and at the empty tomb (Mark 16:1).

Samaria Capital of the northern kingdom (Israel), Samaria was founded by Omri (c. 876–869 BCE) (1 Kings 16:24–25) and included a temple and altar of Baal (1 Kings 16:32). The Assyrians destroyed it in 721 BCE (2 Kings 17), a fate the prophets warned awaited Jerusalem (Isa. 8:4; 10:9–11; Mic. 1:1–7).

Samaritans Inhabitants of the city or territory of Samaria, the central region of Palestine lying west of the Jordan River. According to a probably biased southern account in 2 Kings 17, the Samaritans were regarded by orthodox Jews as descendants of foreigners who had intermarried with survivors of the northern kingdom's fall to Assyria (721 BCE). Separated from the rest of Judaism after about 400 BCE, they had a Bible consisting of their own edition of the Pentateuch (Torah) and a temple on Mount Gerizim, which was later destroyed by John Hyrcanus (128 BCE) (Matt. 10:5; Luke 9:52; John 4:20–21). Jesus discussed correct worship with a woman at Jacob's well in Samaria (John 4:5–42) and made a "good Samaritan" the hero of a famous parable (Luke 10:29–37).

sanctuary A holy place dedicated to the worship of a god and believed to confer personal security to those who took refuge in it. Solomon's temple on Mount Zion in Jerusalem was such a sacred edifice, although Jeremiah denounced those who trusted in its power to save a disobedient people from punishment (Jer. 7; 26).

Sanhedrin The supreme judicial council of the Jews from about the third century BCE until the Romans destroyed Jerusalem in 70 CE. Its deliberations were led by the High Priest (2 Chron. 19:5–11). Jesus was tried before the Sanhedrin and condemned on charges of blasphemy (Matt. 26:59; Mark 14:55; 15:1; Luke 22:66; John 11:47). Stephen was stoned as a result of its verdict (Acts 6:12–15). Peter, John, and other disciples were hailed before its court (Acts 4:5–21; 5:17–41), and Paul was charged there with violating the Mosaic Torah (Acts 22).

Sarah The wife and half-sister of Abraham (Gen. 11:29; 16:1; 20:12). Sarah traveled with Abraham from Ur to Haran and ultimately to Canaan and after a long period of barrenness bore him a single son, Isaac (Gen. 18:9–15; 21:1–21). She died in Hebron (Gen. 23:2) and was buried at Machpelah in Canaan (Gen. 23:19; see also Rom. 4:9; Heb. 11:11; 1 Pet. 3:6).

Sardis Capital of the kingdom of Lydia (modern Turkey), captured by Cyrus the Great (546 BCE); later part of the Roman province of Asia and the site of a cult of Cybele, a pagan fertility goddess (Rev. 3:1–6).

Satan In the Old Testament, "the satan" appears as a prosecutor in the heavenly court among "the sons of God" (Job 1–2; Zech. 3:1–3) and only later as a tempter (1 Chron. 21:1; cf. 2 Sam. 24:1). Although the Hebrew Bible says virtually nothing about Satan's origin, the pseudepigraphal writings contain much legendary material about his fall from heaven and the establishment

of a hierarchy of demons and devils. By the time the New Testament was written, he was believed to head a kingdom of evil and to seek the corruption of all people, including the Messiah (Matt. 4:1–11; Luke 4:1–13). Satan ("the opposer" or "the adversary") is also "the evil one" (Matt. 6:13; 13:19; Eph. 6:16; 1 John 2:13; 5:18–19), "the devil" (Matt. 4:1; 13:39; 25:41; John 8:44; Eph. 4:27), and the primordial serpent who tempted Adam (Rev. 12:9).

Saul Son of Kish, a Benjaminite, and the first king of Israel (about 1020–1000 BCE). Saul was anointed by Samuel to meet the Philistine crisis, which demanded a strong centralized leadership (1 Sam. 9:1–10:27). He defeated the Ammonites (1 Sam. 11:1–11) and Philistines at Geba and Michmash but rapidly lost support after antagonizing Samuel (1 Sam. 13:8–15) and refusing to kill the Amalekite king (1 Sam. 15:7–35). He was also upstaged by David, of whom he became intensely jealous (1 Sam. 18:6–24:23). Saul and his son Jonathan were killed by the Philistines at the Battle of Gilboa (1 Sam. 31) and commemorated by one of David's most beautiful psalms (2 Sam 1:17–27).

Savior One who saves from danger or destruction, a term applied to Yahweh in the Old Testament (Ps. 106:21; Isa. 43:1–13; 63:7–9; Hos. 13:4) and to Jesus in the New Testament (Luke 2:11; John

4:42; Acts 5:31; 13:23; Phil. 3:20; 1 Tim. 4:10; 2 Tim. 1:10; 1 John 4:14).

scapegoat According to Leviticus 16, a sacrificial goat upon whose head Israel's high priest placed the people's collective sins on the Day of Antonement, after which the goat was sent out into the desert to Azazel (possibly a demon). The term has come to signify anyone who bears the blame for others (see Isa. 53).

scribes Professional copyists who recorded commercial, royal, and religious texts and served as clerks, secretaries and archivists at Israel's royal court and temple (2 Kings 12:10; 19:2; Ezra 4:8; 2 Chron. 34:8; Jer. 36:18). After the Jews' return from exile, professional teachers or "wise men" preserved and interpreted the Mosaic Torah (Ezra 7:6; Neh. 7:73–8:18). In the New Testament, scribes are often linked with Pharisees as Jesus' opponents (Matt. 7:29; 23:2, 13; Luke 11:44) who conspired to kill him (Mark 14:43; 15:1; Luke 22:2; 23:10), although some became his followers (Matt. 8:19; see also Acts 6:12; 23:9; 1 Cor. 1:20).

scripture A writing or collection of documents that a religion holds to be sacred and binding upon its adherents. The Jewish Bible (Old Testament) is Scripture to both Jews and Christians; only Christians accord the status of Scripture to the New Testament.

scroll A roll of papyrus, leather, or parchment such as those upon which the Hebrew Bible and New Testament were written. The rolls were made of sheets about nine to eleven inches high and five or six inches wide, sewed together to make a strip up to twenty-five or thirty feet long, which was wound around a stick and unrolled when read (Isa. 34:4; Rev. 6:14; Jer. 36).

Scythians A fierce nomadic people from north and east of the Black Sea who swept southward toward Egypt and Judah about 626 BCE. Jeremiah prophesied that Judah would be devastated (Jer. 4:5–31; 5:15–17; 6:1–8, 22–26), and Zephaniah saw the invasion as a sign that the Day of Yahweh had arrived (Zeph. 1:7–8, 14–18); but the Scythians were bribed by Pharaoh Psammetichus I (664–610 BCE) and returned north by the coastal route without attacking Palestine.

Second Coming The return of the risen Jesus to earth; also called the Parousia, from the Greek *Parousia* (a standing by). The Synoptic authors use this term to denote Jesus' supernatural reappearance to establish the kingdom of God (Matt. 24; Mark 13; Luke 21).

Seleucids The Macedonian Greek dynasty founded by Alexander's general Seleucus (ruled 312–280 BCE), centered in Syria with Antioch as its capital. After defeating the Ptolemies of Egypt, it controlled Palestine from 198 to 165 BCE, after which the Maccabean revolt defeated the forces of Antiochus IV and eventually drove the Syrians from Judea (142 BCE) (1 and 2 Macc.).

Semites According to Genesis 10:21–31, peoples descended from Noah's son Shem, whose progeny included Elam, Asshur, Arpacshad (Hebrews and Arabs), Lud (Lydians), and Aram (Syrians) (Gen. 10:22). In modern usage, the term applies to linguistic rather than to racial groups, such as those who employ one of a common family of inflectional languages, including Akkadian, Aramaic, Hebrew, and Arabic.

Septuagint (LXX) A Greek translation of the Old Testament traditionally attributed to seventy or seventy-two Palestinian scholars during the reign of Ptolemy II (285–246 BCE), but actually the work of several generations of Alexandrine translators, begun about 250 BCE and not complete until the first century CE. The later additions to the Septuagint were deleted from the standard Hebrew Bible (Masoretic Text) but included in the Christian Scriptures as the Apocrypha.

serpent A common symbol in Near Eastern fertility cults, the original tempter of humankind (Gen. 3–4), and a symbol of Assyria, Babylon (Isa. 27:1), and the Israelite tribe of Dan (Gen. 49:17). A bronze image of a snake that was used to heal the Israelites during a plague of snakes in the wilderness (Num. 21:4–9) was later destroyed by King Hezekiah (2 Kings 18:4). Revelation 12:9 identifies the serpent with the devil and

Satan (the primordial dragon).

Shema Judaism's supreme declaration of monotheistic faith, expressed in the words of Deutoronomy 6:4–9 beginning "Listen (Hebrew *shema*, "hear"), Israel, Yahweh our God is the one Yahweh." The complete shema also includes Deuteronomy 11:13–21 and Numbers 14:37–41 (cf. Mark 12:29–34).

Sheol According to the Old Testament, the subterranean region to which the "shades" of all the dead descended, a place of intense gloom, hopelessness, and virtual unconsciousness for its inhabitants. The term was translated *Hades* in the Greek Septuagint. In later Hellenistic times it was regarded as an abode of the dead awaiting resurrection (Gen. 42:38; 1 Sam. 2:6; Job 7:9; 14:13–14; 26:6; Pss. 6:5; 16:10; 55:15; 139:8; Prov. 27:20; Eccles. 9:10; Isa. 14:15; 28:15; 38:10, 18; Hos. 13:14; Jon. 2:2; cf. references to Hades in Matt. 16:18; Luke 10:15; Acts 2:31; Rev. 1:18; 20:15). It is not the same theological concept as hell or Gehenna (Matt. 10:28; 23:33; Mark 9:43; Luke 12:5).

Silas The Semitic, perhaps Aramean, name of an early Christian prophet (Acts 15:32), otherwise called Silvanus, who accompanied Barnabas and Paul to Antioch with decrees from the Jerusalem council (Acts 15:1–35) and who joined Paul on his second missionary journey (Acts 16–18; 1 Thess. 1:1; 2 Thess. 1:1). He may have been the author of 1 Peter (1 Pet. 5:12).

Simeon (1) Another name for Simon Peter (Acts 15:14; 2 Pet. 1:1). (2) The devout old man who recognized the infant Jesus as the promised Messiah (Luke 2:22–34).

simile A comparison using "like" or "as," usually to illustrate an unexpected resemblance between a familiar object and novel idea. Jesus' parables about the Kingdom of God are typically cast as similes (Matt. 13:31–35, 44–50; Mark 4:26–32; Luke 13:18–19).

Simon The name of several New Testament figures: (1) Simon Peter (Matt. 4:18; 10:2). (2) One of the twelve Apostles, Simon the Canaanite (Matt. 10:4; Mark 3:18), a nationalist Zealot (Luke 6:15; Acts 1:13). (3) One of Jesus' "brothers" (Matt. 13:55; Mark 6.3). (4) A leper whom Jesus cured (Mark 14:3–9). (5) The man from Cyrene in North Africa who was forced to carry Jesus' cross (Mark 15:21). (6) A Pharisee who entertained Jesus in his home (Luke 7:36–50). (7) Simon Iscariot, father of Judas the traitor (John 6:71; 13:26). (8) A leather tanner of Joppa with whom Peter stayed (Acts 9:43; 10).

Simon Magus A Samaritan sorcerer ("magus") who tried to buy the power of the Holy Spirit from Peter (Acts 8:9–24); thought by some to be the forerunner of the Faust figure. The sale of church offices is known as *simony*, after Simon Magus.

Sitz-im-Leben In form criticism, the social and cultural environment out of which a particular biblical unit grew and developed; German, "setting in life."

Smyrna An Aegean port city of western Asia Minor (Turkey), site of an early Christian church that the author of Revelation praises for its poverty and faithfulness (Rev. 1:11; 2:8–10).

Sodom Along with Gomorrah, Admah, Zebolim, and Zoar (Gen. 13:10–12; 14:2; Deut. 29:23), one of the "five cities of the plain" (near the south shore of the Dead Sea) destroyed by a great cataclysm attributed to Yahweh (Gen. 19:1–29). Abraham, who had been royally welcomed by Sodom's king (Gen. 14:13–24), pleaded for it to be spared (Gen. 18:16–32). Contrary to legend, its sins were regarded as violence and inhospitality to strangers rather than homosexuality. Later Bible writers cite it as a symbol of divine Judgment upon wickedness (Isa. 3:9; Lam. 4:6; Matt. 10:15; 2 Pet. 2:6; Jude 7; Rev. 11:8).

Solomon Son of David and Bathsheba and Israel's third king (c. 961–922 BCE) (2 Sam. 12:24–25), who inherited the throne through David's fondness and the intrigues of his mother and the prophet Nathan (1 Kings 1:9–2:25). He became famous for his wisdom (1 Kings 3:5–28) but left his people financially exhausted and politically discontented (1 Kings 11:41–12:25). An idealized account of his reign is given in 2 Chronicles 1–9.

Solomon's porch A magnificent covered colonnade built along the east side of Herod's temple in Jerusalem in which Jesus walked (John 10:23); the site of several apostolic miracles (Acts 3:11; 5:12).

Son of Man
1. An Old Testament phrase used to denote a human being (Pss. 8:4; 80:17; 144:3; 146:3; Isa. 56:2; Jer. 51:43), including a plural usage (Pss. 31:19; 33:13; Prov. 8:4; Eccles. 3:18–19; 8:11; 9:12). The phrase is characteristic of the Book of Ezekiel, where it is commonly used to indicate the prophet himself (Ezek. 2:1).
2. In Daniel 7:12–14, a reference—"one like a [son of] man"—to Israel itself or to a divinely appointed future ruler of Israel, although this figure is not given specific messianic significance.
3. In certain pseudepigraphal writings, particularly the Similitudes of the Book of Enoch, he who serves as Yahweh's agent in the coming Day of Judgment, variously called "the Elect One," "the Anointed One," and "the Son of Man."
4. In the Gospels, a phrase always spoken by Jesus and in most cases applied to himself (Matt. 8:20; 9:6; 11:19; 12:8; 16:27–28; 19:28; 24:30; 28:31; Mark

2:28; 8:38; 9:31; 10:45; 13:26; Luke 12:8–10; 18:8; 21:27; 22:22; John 3:14). Outside the Gospels, it is used only once (Acts 7:56), although the author of Revelation echoes Daniel 7:13 (Rev. 14:14).

soul In Hebrew, *nephesh* ("breath"), meaning the quality of being a living creature, applied to both humans and animals (Gen. 1:20; 2:7; 2:19; 9:4; Exod. 1:5; 1 Chron. 5:21). Nephesh was translated *psyche* in the Greek Septuagint, the same term used (commonly for "life" rather than the immortal personality) in the New Testament (Matt. 10:28; 16:26; Acts 2:27; 3:23; Phil. 1:27; Rev. 20:4).

Stephen A Hellenistic Jew of Jerusalem who was stoned for his Christian heresy (Acts 6:8–60), thus becoming the first martyr of the early church. The name means "royal" or "crown."

Stoicism A Greek philosophy that became popular among the upper classes in Roman times. Stoicism emphasized duty, endurance, self-control, and service to the gods, the family, and the state. Its adherents believed in the soul's immortality, rewards and punishments after death, and a divine force (providence) that directs human destiny. Paul encountered Stoics when preaching in Athens (Acts 17:18–34), and Stoic ideas appear in Ecclesiastes, The Wisdom of Solomon, Proverbs, John 4:23 and

5:30, James 1:10, and 1 Peter 2:17.

symbol In its broadest usage, anything that stands for something else; from the Greek *symbolon*, a "token" or "sign," and *symballein*, to "throw together" or "compare." For example, the star of David is a symbol of Judaism, and the cross is a symbol of Christianity. The use of symbols characterizes prophetic and apocalyptic writing. In Daniel, for example, wild beasts symbolize pagan nations; in Ezekiel, Yahweh's presence is symbolized by his radiant "glory."

synagogue In Judaism, a gathering of no fewer than ten adult males assembled for worship, scriptural instruction, and administration of local Jewish affairs. Synagogues probably began forming during the Babylonian exile when the Jerusalem Temple no longer existed. Organization of such religious centers throughout the diaspora played an important role in the faith's transmission and survival. The synagogue liturgy included lessons from the Torah, the Prophets, the Shema, Psalms, and eighteen prayers.

syncretism The blending of different religions, a term Bible scholars typically apply to the mingling of Canaanite rites and customs (Baalism) with the Israelites' Mosaic faith. Although the practice was repeatedly denounced by the prophets (Judg. 2:13; 3:7;

6:31; 8:33; 1 Kings 16:31; 18:26; 2 Kings 10:18; Jer. 2:8; 7:9; 19:5; 23:13; Hos. 2:8), Judaism borrowed many of its characteristic forms, psalms, concepts, and religious rituals from earlier Canaanite models.

Synoptics The first three Gospels, so named because they share a large quantity of material in common, allowing their texts to be viewed together "with one eye."

Syro-Phoenician A woman living near the Phoenician cities of Tyre and Sidon whose daughter Jesus healed (Matt. 15:21–28; Mark 7:24–30).

Tabernacle The portable tent-shrine, elaborately decorated, that housed the Ark of the Covenant (Exod. 25–31; 35–40; Num. 7–9) from the Exodus to the building of Solomon's Temple (1 Kings 6–8); used in both Old and New Testaments as a symbol of God's presence with humankind (Num. 9:5; Deut. 31:15; Pss. 15:1; 43:3; 61:4; 132:7; Isa. 4:6; 33:20; Hos. 12:9; Acts 7:46; Heb. 8:2; 9:11; 2 Pet. 1:14; Rev. 21:3).

Talmud A huge collection of Jewish religious traditions consisting of two parts: (1) the Mishnah (written editions of ancient oral interpretations of the Torah), published in Palestine by Judah ha-Nasi (died about 220 CE) and his disciples; (2) the Gemara, extensive commentaries on the Mishnah. The Palestinian version of the Talmud, which is incomplete, was produced about 450 CE; the Babylonian Talmud, nearly four times as long, was finished about 500 CE. Both Talmuds contain Mishnah and Gemara.

Targum Interpretative translations of the Hebrew Bible into Aramaic, such as that made by Ezra after the Jews' return from the Babylonian exile (Neh. 8:1–18). The practice may have begun in the postexilic synagogues, where Hebrew passages were read aloud then translated into Aramaic with interpretative comments added.

Tarsus Capital of the Roman province of Cilicia (southeastern Turkey) and birthplace of Paul (Saul) (Acts 9:11; 11:25; 21:39; 22:3); a thriving commercial center in New Testament times.

Temple, the
1. The imposing structure built by King Solomon (using Phoenician architects and craftsmen) on Mount Zion in Jerusalem to house the Ark of the Covenant in its innermost room (the Holy of Holies) (1 Kings 5:15–9:25). Later recognized as the only authorized center for sacrifice and worship of Yahweh, it was destroyed by Nebuchadnezzar's troops in 587 BCE (2 Kings 25:8–17; 2 Chron. 36:18–19).
2. The second Temple, rebuilt by Jews returned from the Babylonian exile under Governor Zerubbabel, dedicated about 515 BCE (Ezra 1:1–11; 3:1–13; 4:24–6:22; Hag. 1–2; Zech. 1:1–8:13).
3. Herod's splendid Temple replaced the inferior edifice of Zerubbabel's time and took nearly a half-century to complete (John 2:20). Jesus, who visited the Temple as a child (Luke 2:22–38, 41–50) and often taught there (Matt. 21:23–24:1; Luke 20:1; John 7:14–52; 10:22–39), cleansed it of its money changers (Matt. 21:12–17; Mark 11:15–19; Luke 19:45–46; John 2:13–22) and prophesied its destruction (Matt. 24:1–2; Mark 13:1–4; Luke 21:5–7), which was fulfilled when the Romans sacked Jerusalem in 70 CE. Until that event, the Apostles continued to preach and worship there (Acts 3:1–26; 5:42; 21:26–22:29).

testament Either of the two main divisions of the Bible—the Old Testament (canonical Hebrew Scriptures) and the New Testament (Christian Greek Scriptures); from the Latin for "covenant."

tetragrammaton The four consonants (YHWH) comprising the sacred name Yahweh, the god of Israel. Although the name appears nearly seven thousand times in the canonical Old Testament, some modern Bible translations continue the Jewish practice of inaccurately rendering it as "the Lord."

textual criticism Comparison and analysis of ancient manuscripts to discover copyists' errors and, if possible, to reconstruct the true or original form of the document; also known as "lower criticism."

Thaddeus One of the most obscure of Jesus' Apostles, listed among the Twelve in Matthew 10:3 and Mark 3:18 but not in Luke 7:16 or Acts 1:13.

theodicy A rational attempt to understand how an all-good, all-powerful god can permit the existence of evil and undeserved suffering; from a Greek term combining "god" and "justice." Job, Habakkuk, and 2 Esdras contain notable theodicies.

theology The study and interpretation of concepts about God's nature, will, and intentions toward humankind; from the Greek *theos*, meaning "god," and *logos*, reason.

theophany An appearance of a god to a person, as when El wrestled with Jacob (Gen. 32:26–32), Yahweh appeared to Moses (Exod. 3:1–4:17; 6:2–13) and the elders of Israel (Exod. 24:9–11), or the resurrected Jesus revealed himself to Thomas (John 20:24–29) and Paul (Acts 9:3–9).

Theophilus The otherwise unknown man to whom the Gospel of Luke and the Book of Acts are addressed. He may have been a Roman official who became a Christian.

Thessalonica A major Macedonian city (modern Thessaloniki) where Paul and Silas converted "some" Jews, "many" Greeks and "Godfearers," as well as numerous "rich women" to Christianity (Acts 17:1–9).

Paul later revisited it (1 Cor. 16:5) and wrote two of his earliest surviving letters to its congregation (1 and 2 Thess.).

Thomas One of the twelve Apostles (Matt. 10:3; Mark 3:18; Luke 6:15; Acts 1:13) seldom mentioned in the Synoptics but relatively prominent in the Fourth Gospel, where he is called Didymus ("twin") (John 11:16; 20:24; 21:2). Thomas doubted the other disciples' report of Jesus' resurrection, but when suddenly confronted with the risen Jesus, he pronounces the strongest confession of faith in the Gospel (John 20:24–29). He is the reputed author of the apocryphal Gospel of Thomas.

thunder, sons of An epithet (Boanerges) applied to the apostles James and John (Mark 3:17), possibly because of their impulsive temperaments (Luke 9:52–56).

Thyatira A city of ancient Lydia in Asia Minor (modern Turkey), original home of Lydia, Paul's first European convert (Acts 16:14) and one of the seven churches of Asia in Revelation 2:18–29.

Tiberias A city on the western shore of the Sea of Galilee founded by Herod Antipas and named after the Emperor Tiberius; a well-known spa in Jesus' day.

Tiberius (Tiberius Claudius Nero) Stepson of Augustus and second emperor of Rome (14–37 CE). According to Luke 3:1, Jesus came to John for baptism in the fifteenth year of Tiberius's reign. Except for Luke 2:1, he is the Caesar referred to in the Gospels (Matt. 22:17; Mark 12:14; Luke 20:22; John 19:12).

Timothy Younger friend and fellow missionary of Paul, who called him "beloved son" (1 Cor. 4:17; 1 Tim. 1:2–28; 2 Tim. 1:2), Timothy was the son of a Greek father and a devout Jewish mother (Acts 16:1; 2 Tim. 1:5). To please the Jews, Paul circumcised Timothy before taking him on his second evangelical tour (Acts 16:1–4; 20:1–4). Paul later sent him to Macedonia (1 Thess. 3:6) and thence to Corinth to quiet the dissension there (Acts 19:22; 1 Cor. 4:17; 16:11), which he failed to do (2 Cor. 7:6, 13–14; 8:6; 16, 23; 12:18). The picture of Timothy in the Pastoral Epistles seems irreconcilable with what is known of him from Acts and Paul's genuine letters.

tithe A tenth of one's income paid in money, crops, or animals to support a government (1 Sam. 8:15–17) or religion (Lev. 27:30–33; Num. 18:24–28; Deut. 12:17–19; 14:22–29; Neh. 10:36–38); also, to pay such a part. In Israel, the High Priest, the Levites, and Temple upkeep were supported by required levies. Abraham is reported to have paid Melchizedek tithes (Gen. 14:20; see also Heb. 7:2–6). Jesus regarded tithing as an obligation of his people (Luke 11:42; 12:13–21; 18:12).

Titus A Greek whom Paul converted and who became a companion on his missionary journeys (2 Cor. 8:23; Gal. 2:1–3; Titus 1:4). Titus effected a reconciliation between Paul and the Corinthians (2 Cor. 7:5–7; 8:16–24; 12:18). A post-Pauline writer makes him the type of the Christian pastor (Titus 1–3).

Titus, Flavius Sabinius Vespasianus Son and successor of Vespasian and emperor of Rome (79–81 CE); he directed the siege of Jerusalem, which culminated in the destruction of the city and Herodian Temple in 70 CE. His carrying of the Temple treasures to Rome is commemorated in the triumphal Arch of Titus that still stands in the Roman Forum.

tongues, speaking in An ecstatic phenomenon of the early church (Acts 2:1–45), presented at first as a miraculous and intelligible speaking and understanding of foreign languages by those who did not know these tongues (Acts 2:5–12) but later criticized by Paul as an inferior spiritual gift (1 Cor. 12–14); also called glossolalia.

Torah The Pentateuch (the first five books of the Hebrew Bible) and in a general sense all the Hebrew canonical writings, which are traditionally regarded as a direct oracle, or revelation, from Yahweh. *Torah* is a Hebrew term usually translated "law," "instruction," or "teaching."

tradition (1) Collections of stories and interpretations transmitted orally from generation to generation and embodying the religious history and beliefs of a people or community. Traditions of the patriarchs were eventually compiled in narratives by Israel's earliest historians and finally incorporated into the first book of the Torah. (2) Oral explanations, interpretations, and applications of the written Torah (1 Chron. 4:22; Mark 7:5, 9; Matt. 15:2; Gal. 1:15), many of which were eventually compiled in the Mishnah. (3) Recollections and interpretations concerning Jesus that circulated orally through various early Christian churches and some of which were included in the Gospel narratives (1 Cor. 15:1–8; 2 Thess. 2:15).

tradition criticism Analysis of the origin and development of specific biblical themes—such as the Exodus motif in the Old Testament and the eschatology of the kingdom of God in the New—as presented by different Bible writers. In some cases, tradition criticism emphasizes the early and oral stages of development.

Trajan (Marcus Ulpius Nerva Trajanus) Emperor of Rome (98–117 CE) who was born in Spain about 53 CE, became a successful military leader, and brought the Roman Empire to its greatest extent, annexing Dacia, Armenia, Mesopotamia, Assyria, and Arabia. Probably following the policies of Vespasian (69–79 CE), he conducted a persecution of Christians, although he wrote to Pliny the Younger, governor of

Bithynia, that Christians were not to be sought out or denounced anonymously.

transfiguration, the According to the Synoptic Gospels, a supernatural transformation of Jesus into a being of light, witnessed by Jesus' three closest disciples—Peter, James, and John—on an isolated mountaintop. In this awesome revelation of Jesus' divinity, the Old Testament figures Elijah and Moses also appear (Matt. 17:1–13; Mark 9:2–13; Luke 9:28–36).

Trinity, the The post-New Testament doctrine that God exists as three divine Persons in One, although he manifests himself on different occasions as Father, Son, or Holy Spirit. After generations of ecclesiastical debate on the subject had seriously divided the church, Constantine, the first Christian emperor of Rome but then unbaptized, called a council of church leaders in Nicea to settle the issue (325 CE). The council decreed the orthodoxy of the trinitarian formula, so that the mystery of trinity in unity henceforth became central to the Christian faith (Matt. 28:19–20; 2 Cor. 13:14; Gal. 1:1–5).

Twelve, the The twelve Apostles whom Jesus specifically chose to follow him. Different names appear on different New Testament lists of the Twelve (Matt. 10:1–5; Mark 3:16–19; Luke 6:12–16; Acts 1:13–14).

Tychicus A loyal helper and companion of Paul who accompanied him through the Roman province of Asia on

his third missionary journey (Acts 20:4). Tychicus delivered Paul's letters to the Colossians (Col. 4:7–9) and Ephesians (Eph. 6:21).

typology A form of biblical interpretation in which the narratives and teachings of the Hebrew Bible (Old Testament) are viewed as prophetic types or patterns for what Jesus was later to say and do.

Tyre An ancient Phoenician seaport famous for its commerce and wealth, originally built on a small offshore island about twenty-five miles south of Sidon. King Solomon made an alliance with its ruler, Hiram, the skills of whose architects and craftsmen he utilized in constructing the Jerusalem Temple (1 Kings 5:15–32; 7:13–51). Its power and luxury were later denounced by the prophets (Isa. 23; Ezek. 26–28; Amos 1:19–10; Zech. 9:3–4). Alexander the Great sacked the city in 332 BCE, although it had been rebuilt by Jesus' day (Mark 7:24–31; Luke 3:8).

veil, the The elaborately decorated curtain separating the Holy Place from the Most Holy Place in the Tabernacle and Jerusalem Temple (Exod. 26:31–37), which was reputedly rent in two at Jesus' crucifixion (Matt. 27:51; Heb. 6:19; 9–10).

Vespasian Emperor of Rome 69–79 CE who led Roman legions into Judea during the Jewish Revolt (66–73 CE), the siege of Jerusalem passing to his son Titus when Vespasian became emperor.

Vulgate Jerome's Latin translation of the Bible (late fourth century CE), including the Apocrypha, which became the official version of Roman Catholicism.

Weeks, Feast of See *Pentecost*.

wisdom literature Biblical works dealing primarily with practical and ethical behavior and ultimate religious questions, such as the problem of evil. The books include Proverbs, Job, Ecclesiastes, Ecclesiasticus, and The Wisdom of Solomon. Habakkuk, 2 Esdras, and the New Testament Book of James also have characteristics of Wisdom writing.

woes, the seven messianic The series of seven condemnations of scribes and Pharisees attributed to Jesus when he was rejected by official Judaism (Matt. 23:13–32).

Word, the (1) The "word" or "oracle" of Yahweh, a phrase characteristic of the Hebrew prophets, typically referring to a divine pronouncement, judgment, or statement of purpose that the prophet delivers in his god's name. (2) The preincarnate Jesus (John 1:1–3). See *Logos*.

Yahweh A translation of the sacred name of Israel's god, represented almost seven thousand times in the canonical Old Testament by the four consonants of the tetragrammaton (YHWH). According to Exodus 6:2–4, it was revealed for the first

time to Moses at the burning bush; according to another account, it was used from the time of Enosh before the flood (Gen. 4:26). Scholars have offered various interpretations of the origin and meaning of the divine name. According to a widely accepted theory, it is derived from the Hebrew verb "to be" and means "He is" or "He causes to be," implying that Yahweh is the maker of events and shaper of history.

Yom Kippur See *Atonement, Day of.*

Zealots An extremely nationalistic party in first-century Judaism dedicated to freeing Judea from foreign domination by armed revolt if necessary. Their militarism and fanatical patriotism generated several uprisings, culminating in the great rebellion against Rome (66–73 CE). According to Josephus's possibly biased account, their intransigence led to the destruction of Jerusalem and the Temple. The Simon of Luke 6:15 and Acts 1:13 is called a "Zealot."

Zebedee A Galilean fisherman, husband of Salome, father of the Apostles James and John (Matt. 27:56; Mark 1:19–20; 3:17; 14:33; 15:40).

Zechariah
1. A Judean priest married to Elizabeth, a descendant of Aaron, whose long childless marriage was blessed in old age by the birth of the future John the Baptist (Luke 1:5–25, 57–80; 3:2). A vision foretelling the birth

rendered Zechariah temporarily paralyzed, but he recovered his speech in time to name the child and to utter a prayer of thanksgiving—the Benedictus (Luke 1:67–79).
2. A Jewish martyr mentioned in Jesus' phrase "from Abel to Zecharias" (Matt. 23:35; Luke 11:51), usually identified with Zechariah, son of Jehoiada in 2 Chronicles 24:20–24.

Zeus In Greek mythology, the son of Cronus and Rhea, king of the Olympian gods, and patron of civic order. A personification of storm and other heavenly powers, he ruled by wielding the lightning bolt. The Romans identified him with Jupiter (Jove). Some people of Lystra compared Barnabas to Zeus and Paul to Hermes (Acts 14:12). The erection of a statue of Zeus in the Jerusalem Temple courts helped spark the Maccabean revolt (about 168 BCE).

Zion The name, probably meaning "citadel," for a rocky hill in old Jerusalem, originally a Jebusite acropolis that David captured and upon which he built his palace and housed the ark of the covenant (Judg. 19:11–12; 2 Sam. 5:6–12; 6:12–17; 1 Chron. 11:5–8).

Zoroastrianism A dualistic religion established by the east Iranian prophet Zoroaster in about the late sixth century BCE. Zoroaster saw the universe as a duality of spirit and matter, light and darkness, good and evil. The present age witnesses the conflict between Ahura-Mazda, a deity of light, and his evil spirit opponents. This conflict eventually will culminate in a cosmic battle in which good finally triumphs. Zoroastrian ideas about angels, demons, and the end of the present world appear to have influenced both Jewish and Christian writers, particularly in the realm of apocalyptic thought.

General Bibliography

Bibliographic references for specific topics covered in this text are listed at the end of individual chapters. The list below includes readily accessible reference works that will help students continue their research on the New Testament.

Dictionaries and Commentaries

Achtemeier, Paul J., ed. *Harper's Bible Dictionary*. San Francisco: Harper & Row, 1985. One of the best and most accessible of recently published Bible dictionaries.

Ackroyd, P. R., et al., eds. *The Cambridge Bible Commentary*. Cambridge: Cambridge University Press, 1972. A series of brief commentaries by British scholars.

Albright, W. F., and D. N. Freedman, eds. The Anchor Bible. New York: Doubleday, 1964–. This multivolume series contains new translations of individual books of the Bible with extensive commentary by Jewish, Roman Catholic, Protestant, and other scholars.

Brown, R. E., J. A. Fitzmyer, and R. E. Murphy. *The Jerome Biblical Commentary*. Englewood Cliffs, N.J.: Prentice-Hall, 1968. Provides theological discussions of all books in the biblical canon by leading Roman Catholic scholars.

Buttrick, George A., ed. *The Interpreter's Dictionary of the Bible*. 4 vols. and supplementary vol., Nashville: Abingdon Press, 1962, 1976. Both scholarly and readable, this is the standard work for general readers.

Harvey, A. E. *The New English Bible: Companion to the New Testament*. Oxford and Cambridge: Oxford University Press and Cambridge University Press, 1979. A line-by-line commentary on the NEB translation of the New Testament.

Atlases

Aharoni, Y., and M. Avi-Yonah. *The Macmillan Bible Atlas*. New York: Macmillan, 1977. Uses numerous maps to illustrate major events in biblical history.

Rogerson, John. *Atlas of the Bible*. New York: Facts on File Publications, 1985. A well-illustrated source of geographical and historical background on both the Hebrew Bible and the New Testament.

Wright, G. E. and F. V. Filson, eds. *The Westminster Historical Atlas to the Bible*. Philadelphia: Westminster Press, 1956.

General Introductions

Kee, Howard C. *Understanding the New Testament*. 4th ed. Englewood Cliffs, N.J.: Prentice-Hall, 1983. A scholarly, analytical approach to New Testament study.

Koester, Helmut. *Introduction to the New Testament*. Vol. 1, *History, Culture and Religion of the Hellenistic Age*. Vol. 2, *History and Literature of Early Christianity*. Philadelphia: Fortress Press, 1982. An English translation of an authoritative German study. Provides superb historical and cultural background to the New Testament books.

Kummel, W. G. *Introduction to the New Testament*. Translated by H. C. Kee. Nashville: Abingdon Press, 1975. An English translation of a major study by a noted German scholar.

Perrin, Norman, and Dennis C. Duling. *The New Testament: An Introduction*. 2d ed. New York: Harcourt Brace Jovanovich, 1982. A standard scholarly introduction.

Tyson, Joseph B. *The New Testament and Early Christianity*. New York: Macmillan, 1984. An introduction that places early Christian literature, including noncanonical Gospels, in its historical Jewish-Hellenistic matrix.

Parallel Gospels and Concordances

Crossan, John D. *Sayings Parallels: A Workbook for the Jesus Tradition*. Foundations & Facets. Philadelphia: Fortress Press, 1986. Presents parallel versions of Jesus' sayings from both the canonical and the Apocryphal Gospels.

Funk, Robert W. *New Gospel Parallels*. Vol. 1, *The Synoptic Gospels*. Vol. 2, *John and the Other Gospels*. Foundations & Facets. Philadelphia: Fortress Press, 1985. The best and most comprehensive new study of its kind.

Morrison, C. *An Analytical Concordance to the Revised Standard Version of the New Testament*. Philadelphia: Westminster Press, 1979. Lists English terms and Greek original with a transliteration; gives biblical book, chapter, and verse in which the terms are found.

Index

DATE DUE

APR 5 1997			
OCT 1 2001			

HIGHSMITH   # 45220